ALSO BY GREGORY CROUCH

Enduring Patagonia

CHINA'S WINGS

CNAC FOREVER!

CHINA'S
WINGS

GREGORY CROUCH

WAR, INTRIGUE,

ROMANCE, AND ADVENTURE

IN THE MIDDLE KINGDOM

DURING THE GOLDEN AGE

OF FLIGHT

BANTAM BOOKS
NEW YORK

Published in the United States by Bantam Books, an imprint of The Random House Publishing Group, a division of Random House, Inc., New York.

BANTAM BOOKS and the rooster colophon are registered trademarks of Random House, Inc.

Excerpts from the writings of William Langhorne Bond and quotes from his book *Wings for an Embattled China* (Lehigh University Press) used courtesy of Thomas and Langhorne Bond and the Association of American University Presses.

Excerpts from the writings of Harold M. Bixby and quotes from his book *Top Side Ricksha* used courtesy of the Bixby family.

Frontispiece illustration : Edward P. Howard

Maps copyright © 2012 by David Lindroth, Inc.

Library of Congress Cataloging-in-Publication Data
Crouch, Gregory.
China's wings : War, Intrigue, Romance, and Adventure in the Middle Kingdom
During the Golden Age of Flight/
Gregory Crouch.
p. cm.
Includes bibliographical references and index.
ISBN 978-0-553-80427-0
eBook ISBN 978-0-345-53235-0
1. China National Aviation Corporation. 2. Airlines—China. I. Title.
HE9878.C47C76 2012
387.70951—dc23   2011020558

Printed in the United States of America on acid-free paper

www.bantamdell.com

2 4 6 8 9 7 5 3 1

First Edition

Book design by Liz Cosgrove

For my son,
Ryan Crouch,

and

for the men and women of
the China National Aviation Corporation

C.N.A.C. is the China National Aviation Corporation. It is one of those peculiar enterprises whose capital value in dollars and cents might barely equal that of a large American department store, but whose actual value in the war for the control of Asia can only be weighed by history.

—Theodore "Teddy" White, "China's Last Lifeline," *Fortune,* May 1943

CONTENTS

AUTHOR'S NOTE

A Bit About Names . . .

This is a period piece. The English-speaking characters in this book visited Peking—or Peiping—not Beijing, opened an airline to Chungking, not Chongqing, sailed on the Whangpoo, not the Huangpu, traveled to Hankow, not Wuhan, and they discussed Canton, not Guangzhou. The first examples are all names in the Wade-Giles system, most commonly used to transliterate the Chinese language into English prior to the Chinese government's 1958 introduction of the Pinyin system, which provides the more modern transliterations in the second examples. After much deliberation, and at risk of some confusion, I've elected to use the Wade-Giles names, as the characters in this story did while they were living it. To aid those more comfortable with the modern transliterations, I've added a glossary equating the place-names in the Wade-Giles and Pinyin systems.

A Bit About Sources . . .

This is a work of nonfiction. When I first discovered this story, I expected to focus on the airline flying the Hump from 1942 to 1945. I was aware of its adventures before Pearl Harbor, but I didn't think I could write about them vividly due to what I expected would be a dearth of colorful sources. The books in existence that treated with the airline during that period, albeit fascinating for enthusiasts, weren't the sort to engage a general readership, and only a tiny handful of people were still alive who'd worked for the company during those years. Happily, I was wrong: The more I investigated, the more, and better, 1930s material I discovered—significant CNAC-related holdings had found their way into various university archives; other important primary material remained in private hands. I gathered everything I could—reading, thinking, taking notes, and burning up photocopy machines—and I'm now confident that the world's most comprehensive CNAC archive currently resides in my file cabinet. Those original sources, coupled with material gleaned from a mélange of newspapers, magazines, and books, and from extensive interviews conducted with those few who lived the tale, constitute the material from which I've reconstructed the airline's dramatic story before the United States entered the Second World War.

Fortunately, business in the 1930s and '40s was conducted via written letters similar to the manner in which email transacts so much modern commerce, and William Langhorne Bond, this story's protagonist, wrote letters with clarity and élan, often in exquisite detail, recounting important conversations, events, and decisions and relating stories, jokes, and pithy asides. Many of those letters survived, as have many of those written to him. (Harold Bixby of Pan Am and Bond's wife, Kitsi, seem to have been his most diligent correspondents.) Knowing he'd lived an incredible story, in his twilight years, Bond began writing a memoir of his China experiences. Sadly, he died before finishing the job, having written his chronological story only through the middle of 1942, but he left notes and a manuscript totaling more than six hundred handwritten pages, an impressive accomplishment for any octogenarian, let alone one who'd never written a book—evidence of the discipline and tenacity that had served Bond so well in Asia. Many years later, James E. Ellis edited that raw material into a book, which the Lehigh University Press published as *Wings for an Embattled China* in 2001.

In my estimation, *Wings* is an important but flawed source. It incorrectly situates the time frame of many events, for which Bond can be excused because he died before he had the opportunity to check his written-from-memory rough draft against his own letters. However, within the individual anecdotes, Bond's recollections are generally very accurate—as his contemporary records confirm. Also, the characters in *Wings* banter thick, unlikely paragraphs of expository dialogue. In the interest of clarity, brevity, and plausibility, I've compressed many conversations while simultaneously attempting to preserve each speaker's voice, style, and substance. Convincingly, when treating the same conversations, Bond's contemporary letters often allude to or record the same content.

Most of the pre-1942 conversations in *China's Wings* are distilled from a combination of those Bond recorded in *Wings,* his contemporary correspondence, the transcripts of interviews he granted other historians, primary sources created by this story's other players, and my many interviews with Moon Fun Chin, a remarkable man—with awe-inspiringly accurate recall—who flew for the airline from 1933 to 1945. Dialogue after Pearl Harbor comes from a similar mix of sources, but spiced with a much more generous dose of personal interviews because I was able to meet so many more company veterans from that period.

My most fervent hope is that I've been able to do their story justice. It's a good one.

And a Bit About History . . .

The people in this story knew as much about tomorrow as we do today. Which is to say, very little. The future revealed itself to them the same way it reveals itself to us, minute by minute. They faced it with human tools: courage, imagination, intelligence, humor, fear, and anxiety; and they lived, ate, drank, fought, slept, made love, and worked just the way we do today, in near utter ignorance of what tomorrow might bring. The lucky ones were able to laugh about it. A man can only know what he knows when he knows it. There are no predetermined outcomes. There is no fate. Much could have occurred. Only one thing did. That is history; that does not make it inevitable. Only hindsight makes it seem so. Otherwise, history is like life, a chaotic matrix of alternate possible outcomes, of choices people make, actions they take, distilling into the moment we inherit. This is a story, a flying story, a story about an airline and the people who built it during the crux years of the twentieth century. It also happens to be true.

GLOSSARY OF CHINESE PLACE-NAMES

Wade-Giles	Pinyin
Amur River	Heilong River
Bias Bay	Daya Bay
Bubbling Wells Road	West Nanjing Road
Canton	Guangzhou
Changch'un	Changchun
Changsha	Changsha
Chapei	Zhabei
Chengchow	Zhengzhou
Chengtu	Chengdu
Chiating	Chiating
Chienkiang	Zhenjiang
Chungking	Chongqing
Chungshan	Zhongshan
Fongpang Road	Fangbang Zhonglu
Formosa	Taiwan
Fukien Province	Fujian Province
Gulf of Chihli	Bohai Sea
Hainan Island	Hainan Island
Han River	Han River
Hangchow	Hangzhou
Hankow	Wuhan
Hanyang	Hanyang (Wuhan)

Hengyang	Hengyang
Honan Province	Honan Province
Hongkew	Hongkou
Hong Kong	Hong Kong
Hsuchow	Xuzhou
Hunan Province	Hunan Province
Hungjao	Hongqiao
Hupeh Province	Hubei Province
Ichang	Yichang
Jehol Province	Rehe Province (no longer a province in the PRC)
Jessfield Park	Zhongshan Park
Jiangsi Province	Jiangxi Province
Kaifeng	Kaifeng
Kansu Province	Gansu Province
Kialing River	Jialing River
Kiangsu Province	Jiangsu Province
Kiangwan	Jiangwan
Kiating	Leshan
Kirin	Jilin
Kowloon	Kowloon
Kunming	Kunming
Kwangsi Province	Guangxi Province
Kwangtung Province	Guangdong Province
Kweilin	Guilin
Lanchow	Lanzhou
Luchow	Luzhou
Lukouchiao	Lugouqiao
Lunghwa	Longhua
Macau	Macao
Machuria	Manchuria
Min River	Min Jiang
Minghong	Minzong
Minya Konka	Gongga Shan
Mount Omei	Emei Shan (Mount Emei)
Mukden	Shengyang
Namyung	Nanxiong

Nanchang	Nanchang
Nanking	Nanjing
Nantao	Nanshi
Nantung	Nantong
Peiping	Beijing
Peking	Beijing
Pootung	Pudong
Shanghai	Shanghai
Shansi Province	Shanxi Province
Shantung Peninsula	Shandong
Shasi	Jingzhou/Shashi
Shensi Province	Shaanxi Province
Sian	Xi'an
Siccawei Creek	Zikawei Creek
Sikang	Xikang
Soochow Creek	Suzhou Creek
Suifu	Yibin
Sungari River	Songhua River
Szechwan Province	Sichuan Province
Tahu Lake	Taihu Lake
Taierhchuang	Taierzhuang
Tali Mountain	Dali Mountain
Tathong Channel	Nam Tong Hui Hap
Tientsin	Tianjin
Tri-cities	Wuhan (Hankow, Hanyang, Wuchang)
Tsingtao	Qingdao
Wangping Road	Shandong Road between Fuzhou and Nanjing roads
Whangpoo River	Huangpu River
Woosung	Wusong
Wuchang	Wuhan
Wuchow	Wuzhou
Wushan Mountains	Wushan Mountains
Yangtzepoo	Yangpu
Yellow River	Huang He
Yenan	Yan'an

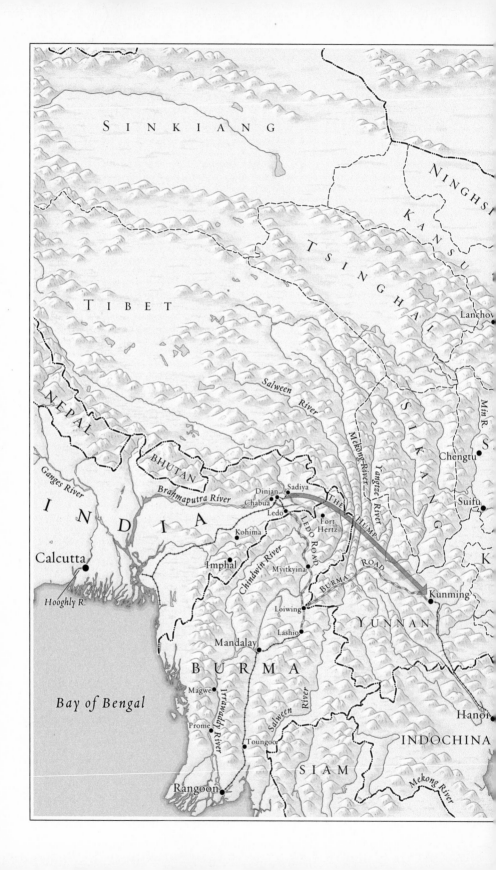

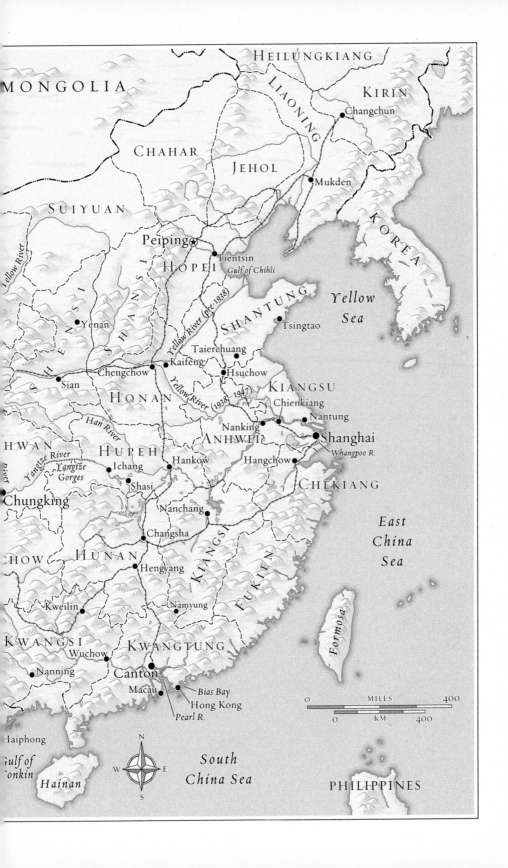

CHINA'S WINGS

WINTER 1931

It was an uncertain time. The future that just a few years before had seemed so prosperous and secure had dissolved like a morning fog. Following on the heels of the cataclysm that had been the Great War, those good years had been the best times anyone in the United States could remember. "The Jazz Age," a writer had coined it. Of course, in retrospect, people should have known it was too good to last, a painful truth that had only revealed itself slowly, in the year after the stock market crash, when a dizzying round of bank failures swept the country and struck fear into the hearts of the American people.

Europe had contracted an economic malaise, too, and it was particularly acute in Germany, where mass unemployment and astronomical inflation undermined the stability of the fledgling republic established in the aftermath of the war. The preceding summer, nearly 6.5 million Germans had cast votes for the Nazi Party and the jackbooted discipline of its brownshirt adherents, swayed by promises of work and bread for the nation and of an end to toothless democracy. The election hadn't won the Nazis a parliamentary majority, but it made Adolf Hitler a dominant force in German politics as he vowed to unify, purify, and strengthen a fragmented people, making them masters of Europe, and the world.

A similar vision was rising in Asia, in the islands of Japan, among the militaristic adherents of "the Imperial Way," who dreamed of undermining their nascent democracy and bringing the East to heel beneath the unified, harmonious power of the Japanese nation. Inevitably, dreams of empire drew their eyes toward the Asian mainland, where China lay prostrate, the nation's traditional power eviscerated by a century of foreign colonial incursions and the collapse of the Chin dynasty.

For the would-be hegemons, it was a world ripe with opportunity. To them, the Western democracies seemed weak, racked by economic difficulties and paralyzed by the horrors they'd endured in the trenches of Flanders and northern France, without the mettle for war. Many foresaw the end of capitalism and democracy, even in such stalwart societies as Britain and the United States. Worldwide, forces anathema to the ideals of individual liberty, political freedom, and unfettered expression waxed strong. It would take men and women of imagination, integrity, and extraordinary fortitude to see those values through to safer ground.

Through it all, there was aviation. It was the most exciting technology of the age; in many ways, it represented hope and the path to a better tomorrow. Realizing the dream of countless generations, mankind had at last broken free of the earth, powered by internal combustion engines and flying on wings of wood, dope, and canvas—or of age-hardened aluminum alloy. The Great War had proved the airplane's military utility; the 1920s had provided glimpses of its civil potential. As barnstormers, entrepreneurs, and corporate entities rushed to capitalize, airlines sprang up all over the world. There seemed no limit to what might be accomplished. Aloft, soaring among clouds, over roads, rivers, and railways, one felt on a direct course to the future. Aviation seemed sure to change *everything*. Its allure could spur a man to the far side of the world. . . .

PART ONE

THE MIDDLE KINGDOM

March 17, 1931, to July 6, 1937

"China is one of the largest countries in the world,
but owing in no small degree to the lack of
communications facilities, she is not yet thoroughly unified."

—Chiang Kai-shek, 1931

1

SAINT PATRICK'S DAY, 1931

A ragged wind gusted among the deep-draft vessels anchored a few miles northeast of Woosung, near the eastern edge of China, where Shanghai's river, the Whangpoo, emptied into the mighty Yangtze. The transpacific liner *Empress of Japan* drew too much water to cross the submerged mud bar the larger stream had built across the Whangpoo's mouth, so a lighter eased alongside to take her passengers the last dozen miles upriver to Shanghai. Choppy swells whumped between the hulls and pitched up fat drops of spray. As he trotted down a gangway onto the smaller craft, William Langhorne Bond turned up his coat collar and clasped his fedora tighter to his head. Close-cropped strands of reddish hair showed beneath his hatband. A toothbrush mustache edged past the corners of his mouth, dominating his thin face and drawing attention from his piercing gray-blue eyes and the bent nose that looked like it might once have been broken. It was March 17, 1931, Saint Patrick's Day, and the thirty-seven-year-old former heavy-construction foreman had come halfway around the world from his home in Petersburg, Virginia, to take a job he knew next to nothing about.

Bond found a seat inside the lighter, but he couldn't keep still. Soon back on deck, he cupped his hands, lit a cigarette, and rested his forearms on the starboard rail. The Yangtze's far northern shore was ten miles distant, a reach so wide Bond couldn't escape the sense he was still at sea. Nobody knew where the river began (he loved that); probably at some anonymous trickle on the Tibetan fringe, thousands of miles away. But by the time the Yangtze had convulsed and roared and soughed from its mountainous headwaters and undulated across the lowlands of eastern China, collecting tribute from an uncounted multitude of creeks, springs, and lesser rivers, it had grown into a truly enormous aquatic beast that spewed water into the East China Sea through a fifty-mile-wide estuary. The Sinologists whose books he'd read during the Pacific crossing identified the Yangtze as the single most powerful force governing the evolution of Chinese culture. Indeed, in many ways, the Yangtze *was* China, a unifying artery running through the heart of a nation that might not have existed without it. No other earthly waters mattered so much, to so many people. Fully one-tenth of mankind depended on the waters of the Yangtze Basin, an intersection of demographics and hydrology that any businessman could see made the Yangtze River a gateway to the largest potential marketplace on earth, and from its position near the mouth of the great stream, Shanghai was the key controlling the gate. For the last ninety years, ever since British gunboats blasted open the trade of central China in the 1840s, fortune seekers from around the world had flocked to do business in the city. William Bond stood on the cusp of joining them at a time when China was reeling from nearly a century of domestic upheaval and foreign-visited disaster, struggling to unify, modernize, unlock its long-suppressed potential, and take its place among the world's great nations. With his new job, Bond expected to participate in what would surely be one of the twentieth century's great dramas.

The deckhands cast off, the engines growled, and the lighter made way for the Whangpoo. China beyond the riverbanks was greenish and gray and surprisingly flat. A low, rounded hill that lay like a rice sack above the joining of the two rivers provided the only contour of relief. Across the bar, the Whangpoo took on an unguinous yellow tint, and the lighter pushed into the upstream traffic. Tugs plowed forward at the head of barge strings laden with sand, gravel, and coal. Laundry flapped from the lee rails of sailing junks whose brown, patch-bespeckled sails, stayed by lengths of split bamboo, held the breeze like the wings of tattered dragons. Small wooden sampans coasted in the shallows, their decks choked with agricultural produce. The people aboard—whole families, it seemed—screamed curses as they shipped wakes trailing from the larger vessels. Bond cringed as the lighter steamed past an anchored "honey barge" awaiting the tide's ebb, heaped to its putrid gunwales with Shanghai "night soil."

Evidence of unruly commerce quickened as they churned upstream. Within a few miles, warehouses, known as "godowns" in the commercial parlance of the Far East, appeared, lining both sides of the river, windowless, four-story brick structures streaked with dirt and grime. Giraffe-necked cranes nodded over the godown docks, heaving cargoes into rust-streaked steamers. Work gangs loaded smaller items at the tie-ups of junks and sampans. All along both waterfronts, cars, trucks, carts, and wheelbarrows battled through lines of blue-dungareed coolies staggering beneath preposterous burdens. Rooftops bristled with billboards touting products in English and Chinese. On the west shore, smoke plumes trailed from the trio of smokestacks above the Shanghai Power Company's new Yangtzepoo generating station, paralleling similar cloud ribbons pouring from dozens of factory chimneys. It was a chaotic scene, industrial and gritty. There was nothing quaint or picturesque about it.

Ahead, the Whangpoo curled southeastward, and Bond caught sight of the massive buildings of the Shanghai Bund as they hove into view around the Pootung bend, one by one. It was the most famous cityscape east of Suez, a half-mile run of gray buildings along the downtown riverbank, and it was the core of Western imperial power in China. Architecturally, Bond couldn't detect a shred of Chinese inspiration. He recognized the straight, art-deco lines of the Cathay Hotel, topped by a green pyramid; "Big Ching," the clock tower rising from the center of the Maritime Customs Building; and the dome over the Hong Kong Shanghai Bank. The buildings were impressive rather than artistic, breathtaking before beautiful, and shot through with more than a trace of military gothic intimidation, but it was the nautical chaos of the river that commanded the most attention. Bond had never seen such a busy stretch of water. Merchants counted Shanghai as the world's fifth-busiest port, but surely that ranking was based only on tonnage figures? In terms of sheer frenetic bustle, it was hard to imagine a greater profusion of vessels anywhere else in the world. Scores of craft plied the waterway: junks, sampans, barges, tugs, coastal steamers, freighters, lighters, men-of-war, and jaywalking ferries darting across the river perpendicular to the main flow of traffic. Bond's lighter thrummed past Garden Bridge, the trestle spanning the mouth of Soochow Creek, and approached the Bund beneath flags flapping from the taffrails of the warships anchored in center stream. There were blue-water cruisers, destroyers, and corvettes, and shallow-draft gunboats down from their up-river patrol stations, and Bond recognized Britain's Union Jack, the American Stars and Stripes, France's Tricolor, the Japanese Rising Sun, and one that must have been the standard of Mussolini's Italy. Decrepit sampans sculled in the waters alongside, poised to scuffle over galley orts ejected through the warships' slop holes.

The lighter docked at a pontoon in front of Big Ching. Bond nervously plodded down the planks and into a shoving throng. Rickshaw men and cabbies pressed into his face demanding hire; hawkers cried their wares under greasy canvas awnings. A tram clattered past on rails laid in the street, cars fought traffic with blaring horns, and swarms of two-wheeled, man-pulled rickshaws wove through the commotion. Collapsed beggars thrust misshapen arms at passersby. Marine engines growled in the river. Bond looked around with no idea what to do.

A waving figure caught his eye. George Conrad Westervelt broke through the riverfront melee, and Bond shook his hand with visible relief. A car horn screamed, and a new-model Packard shoved past. Four enormous, stone-faced Caucasians stood on the running boards, their elbows crooked through holds mounted to the car top. The pair in front held pistols; the two beside the passenger windows had shoulder-slung tommy guns. Bond glimpsed a dark-suited Chinese in the rear seat. Cossacks, explained Westervelt, bodyguards for that rich Chinese. Thousands of White Russian refugees had flooded into Frenchtown since Lenin's Bolsheviks seized power.

A short, pugnacious retired U.S. Navy captain nicknamed "Scrappy" by his Naval Academy classmates, George Conrad Westervelt was married to Bond's first cousin, Rita Langhorne, and he'd brought Bond into the Curtiss Aeroplane and Motor Company two years before, in 1929. Bond had been hankering to get into aviation ever since Charles Lindbergh flew the Atlantic in the spring of 1927. At the time of Lindbergh's flight, Bond was a job boss on a construction site in Ohio, the latest of scores of projects he'd overseen since returning home to Virginia from France at the end of the

Great War. He'd built a lot of roads, railroad beds, and bridges, and earned himself an equity position in the company. Unfortunately, the work had lost its challenge. The projects would get bigger; they wouldn't get any less routine. Lindbergh was different. Lindbergh demanded action. Lindbergh was nine years *younger* than William Bond, and he'd gone and done this great thing. Bond wasn't a man who spent money on frivolities, but in the wake of Lindbergh, he paid cash money to a barnstorming pilot giving airplane rides from an Ohio cow pasture.

The pilot flew over Bond's job site. Bond hadn't expected the roadbed he was building to look so unimpressive. Aviation was changing the world every day, and he was laboring hidebound in Ohio, sweating or freezing or soaking with the seasons on dirty construction sites. Maybe it was time for a new direction. If he didn't switch soon, he'd be stuck building roads and railroad beds for the rest of his life.

Bond wasn't alone in perceiving aviation's potential. The entire nation went airplane crazy after Lindbergh's flight. It was as if everybody, all at once, realized aviation could reshape the world—and that fortunes would be made while it did. Wall Street big wheels claimed new technologies like radio and aviation altered the rules of commerce: Business would be done faster and better, new markets would open, old ones would expand, and profits would grow exponentially. Aviation companies helped lead the most glorious stock market gains in history. Speculators considered the Curtiss Aeroplane and Motor Company to have particularly fine prospects. With United Aircraft and Transport Company, the Aviation Corporation, and the Wright Aeronautical Corporation, Curtiss was one of four conglomerates fighting to dominate the new industry. Via its twenty affiliated companies, Curtiss had fingers in every aspect of the aviation pie. Not every division turned a profit. Indeed, most of them didn't, but the industry *was* booming, and its future seemed limitless. Five times more civil airplanes were built in 1928 than in 1926. In 1928, Curtiss stock doubled. And then doubled again. Near the end of the year, Curtiss Company stock hit $192 per share, a spectacular gain from its 1924 price of $4.50. Airline operations expanded apace. From 1926 to 1928, domestic carriers like Western Air Express, Transcontinental Air Transport, National Air Transport, Eastern Air Lines, and Northwest Airways increased the nation's route miles fivefold. Internationally, the recently founded Pan American

Airways was growing from its humble Florida-to-Havana origins and beginning to cast airlines across the Caribbean into Central and South America. Aviation made headlines nearly every day.

William Bond spent 1928 mulling a career change. Once he'd examined the angles, it wasn't a difficult decision to make. Bond saw his current project through to completion, resigned his position, sold his stake in the construction company, and began looking around for an opening. George Westervelt provided the entrée.

Westervelt had joined the Curtiss Company to supervise its aircraft factories, and in June of 1929, he was looking for a good man to investigate a troubled property, a million-dollar factory that one of Curtiss's many subentities, Curtiss-Caproni, was building on the shores of the Chesapeake Bay, a few miles south of Baltimore, near Logan Field. The project had fallen far behind schedule. When Westervelt's wife told him that her cousin wanted an aviation position, Westervelt asked Bond to take a look.

The factory was intended to build seaplanes for the Navy, and an admiral in starched summer whites toured Bond through the construction site. Bond could see right away that the job foreman couldn't lead sailors to a brothel. After they completed their rounds, the admiral squared up to him and asked, "Could you finish this plant?"

"I've been an in-the-dirt guy all my life. Railroads, tunnels, roads. I've never built a factory."

"I didn't ask that. I asked if you could complete *this* job."

"Yes, sir, I can add and subtract and read a schedule, and I guarantee I can do it better than this."

Bond accepted the job without asking what he would be paid. First things first, he told himself: Get the job; get into aviation.

A few weeks after Bond started, Curtiss merged with Wright Aeronautic and Keystone Aircraft to form the Curtiss-Wright Corporation, and Bond had a job in America's biggest aviation company. Unfortunately, the gilded expectations fueling the speculative ball didn't jibe with data reporting back from the actual economy. Steel and iron production sagged; freight-car loadings drooped; home building fell; industrial production sank. The stock market wobbled in September and the first three weeks of October. Then, on Tuesday, October 29, 1929, prices collapsed, the most massive single-day meltdown in Wall Street history. Aviation stocks were among the hardest hit, and values continued to sink in subsequent trading sessions. Curtiss-Wright's stock plummeted 70 percent.

The crash didn't affect most Americans, since only one in forty owned stock. The bank failures that would turn a painful recession into the country's worst depression remained two years into the future. Few people in 1929 saw the Wall Street fiasco and the economic slowdown as anything other than a normal downturn in the boom-and-bust cycle of American business. The year 1930 was bad, but not earth-shatteringly so. Unemployment ran at a little less than 9 percent. Gross national product slumped 12.7 percent, but it had dropped a whopping 24 percent in the 1921 recession and the nation had recovered quickly. For Curtiss-Wright, however, 1930 was an unmitigated disaster. It had yoked its fortunes to projections of massive expansion in all aspects of aviation, and the dip caught the company grossly overextended. Bond finished the Chesapeake Bay factory in the last half of 1930, but the plant sat idle, and he hung on there as a glorified caretaker. In his spare time, and he had lots, he took flying lessons. Curtiss-Caproni's contract with the City of Baltimore mandated guaranteed utilities payments once the factory was complete. Bond took it upon himself to persuade the mayor to defer charges until the plant went into operation, an initiative that saved the company $30,000 (about $380,000 in modern dollars) and earmarked Bond as a man suited to greater responsibilities.

One of Curtiss-Wright's cash wounds was in China, where it had sunk half a million dollars into a 45 percent stake in the China National Aviation Corporation (CNAC), an airline it held in partnership with Chiang Kai-shek's three-and-a-half-year-old Nationalist government, part of Curtiss-Wright's grandiose plan to circle the globe with its aviation network. The company owed another $585,000 toward the full capitalization of the airline, and the corporate leadership sent George Westervelt to the Orient to decide if they should continue to support it. (In aggregate, the company's commitment would represent a modern investment of nearly $14 million.)

In China, Westervelt discovered a full manifest of operational and technical problems and a subtle force in the foreign community arrayed against the airline. Many expatriate businessmen actually *wanted* CNAC to fail. It was the first major partnership between Chinese and foreign interests in which the majority ownership was Chinese, and as such, it represented an implicit challenge to the comfortable status quo, in which such joint ventures were either fifty-fifty or had the foreigners in the driver's seat. Westervelt decreed those obstacles surmountable. The most critical problem ran deeper: Infected by the outrageous disrespect most foreigners living in Shanghai manifested toward the Chinese, many of the Americans Curtiss-Wright shipped to China treated the airline's Chinese employees with arrogance and overt prejudice, utterly disregarding the fact that the company was a partnership in which the Americans held the minority interest. In Westervelt's estimation, the company's long-term success would depend on its American personnel learning to treat the Chinese as equals. Curtiss-Wright needed a new man in China, someone who could lead by example and work with the Chinese as *partners,* treating them fairly and judging them on individual faults and merits rather than on the basis of racist stereotypes. Considering how much stock the Chinese culture placed on courtesy, the airline needed not only a man possessing common sense and business acumen, it needed one with good manners. Westervelt cabled New York and asked them to send William Bond.

To Bond, the offer came as a complete surprise. He didn't know much about China except where to find it on a map. Nor, for that matter, did he know much of anything about airline operations. He also knew he couldn't afford to stand pat in Baltimore. No job was more insecure than that of a man in charge of an idle factory. If he didn't get himself into a more productive role, he'd soon find himself among America's growing legion of unemployed. Besides, China might provide the adventure he'd been craving.

William Bond accepted the summons without hesitation.

2

"YOU WON'T BE ABLE TO HANDLE THE PILOTS"

The Bonds were Virginians. William Langhorne Bond's grandfather didn't believe in slavery, and he didn't believe in secession. He did, however, believe in Virginia, and he fought in the Confederate army during the Civil War. Although he returned to the ruins of Petersburg in the spring of 1865 with his limbs intact, the battlefields had gouged his soul. Grandfather Bond kept a bottle handy in the years after Appomattox, and his slide into an alcoholic abyss forced his eldest son—Thomas Baker Bond, William Bond's father—to quit school at age fifteen to support his mother and seven younger siblings.

Some years later, the young man landed steady, if unspectacular, work with the British American Tobacco Company and married into the Langhorne clan, a well-bred but equally unmoneyed Virginia family.* Thomas Bond and Mary Langhorne had two sons, Alan, the older, and William

---

* Two Langhorne womenfolk were destined for wide fame. Irene Langhorne married American artist Charles Dana Gibson and helped breathe life into his wildly popular "Gibson Girl" drawings and paintings celebrating a healthy, outdoorsy, broad-shouldered, narrow-waisted, luscious, busty, active brand of American beauty that flew in the face of wan European conceptions—conceptions that Irene's

Langhorne, born on November 12, 1893, whom they raised in a working-class Petersburg neighborhood a few hundred yards south of the Appomattox River, near the intersection of Adams and Washington streets. The young family attended Tabb Street Presbyterian Church. Thomas Bond had a hard life, but his two boys never heard him complain on any subject, not once, a rigid stoicism the old man expected of his sons. The Bonds never went hungry, but there wasn't any privilege. They were Virginians, however, members of Thomas Jefferson's natural aristocracy, and the Bond parents drilled their boys in good manners to ensure they'd grow up knowing how to behave in the company of kings.

Away from parental supervision, William Langhorne Bond led a much more sharp-elbowed existence. He was a red-haired, ruddy-faced, thickset boy who smiled with pursed lips, ashamed of his crooked teeth. The local boys called him "Chunky," a nickname he despised. He and his brother shared a paper route, a prize much coveted by other neighborhood toughs, and the Bond brothers regularly had to fight to protect their rights to it, set-piece duels conducted with fisticuffs in empty lots. By the time he was twelve, William Bond knew how to throw and take a punch, and no number of bruises or bloody noses proved sufficient to oust the Bond brothers from their fief. They kept their paper route until the day they decided they'd outgrown it, but their roughness survived. An avid baseball player, William Bond could always be counted on to stick up for his teammates in a sandlot dustup.

"Chunky" didn't survive childhood. Adolescence leaned him out, and it was a gamy, blue-eyed eighteen-year-old who graduated from public high school in 1911. Wearing his best Sunday shoes, William Bond stood about five feet ten inches tall. The family didn't have money for college, and he wasn't enough of a student to merit a scholarship, so like his brother before him, he entered the workforce in lieu of higher education, starting at Langhorne & Langhorne Construction, a heavy construction outfit on his mother's side of the family that built tunnels, highways, railroads, and bridges. For the next six years, he slept in a lot of hotels, month-to-month

---

sister Nancy assaulted directly by marrying Britain's Lord Astor, and, as Lady Nancy Astor, becoming the first woman elected to Parliament to take her seat in the House of Commons.

apartments, and tent camps near job sites in the hills and coalfields of Appalachia, learning the trade from the bottom up.

Bond volunteered when the United States entered the Great European War in 1917. He joined Battery B of the 111th Field Artillery, the "Norfolk Light Artillery Blues," in the Virginia National Guard, part of a Virginia contingent the Army banded together with troops from New Jersey, Maryland, and the District of Columbia to form the half-Northern, half-Southern "Blue and Gray" Twenty-ninth Division, a unit that paid a bloody toll for its piece of the Meuse-Argonne Offensive. The Army recognized young Bond's leadership potential: his bone-deep honesty, his loathing of excuses, his admiration of elbow grease far more than casual genius, and how naturally he put the needs of his unit before his own. He was sent to an officer's candidate course at a French military academy, and it was Lieutenant William Bond who debarked from the SS *Orizaba* at Newport News, Virginia, in April 1919. War hadn't done to him what it did to his grandfather. Bond demobilized and went back to work.

In the ensuing eight years, the United States amended its constitution for the eighteenth time to prohibit the production, sale, or consumption of alcohol, and for the nineteenth time to give women the right to vote, and it weathered a sharp postwar recession. Labor unrest rattled the coal and railroad industries. Lenin's Communists won the Russian Civil War. The Boston Red Sox sold Babe Ruth to the New York Yankees for $125,000, and he hit 54 home runs for the Yankees, shattering the record of 29 he'd set with Boston. James Joyce published *Ulysses,* and the U.S. Post Office burned five hundred copies of the "obscene" novel. The United States refused to join the League of Nations. Rudolph Valentino starred in wildly successful silent movies, and transcontinental airmail service began—planes flew the mail in daylight, trains carried it after dark, and it crossed the country in seventy-two hours. Incarcerated after his failed "Beer Hall Putsch," Adolf Hitler wrote his autobiography, *Mein Kampf.* Al Capone battled the O'Banion gang for control of the Chicago underworld, and Gene Tunney beat Jack Dempsey for the heavyweight boxing championship. Henry Luce published the first issue of *Time* magazine, F. Scott Fitzgerald penned *The Great Gatsby,* and Ernest Hemingway championed the World War's "Lost Generation" in his novel *The Sun Also Rises.*

William Bond worked construction through all of it, six days a week, like most employed Americans. At night, after work, he listened to music, comedy, news, and drama on the radio. Saturday nights, he attended the moving pictures, and on Sundays baseball doubleheaders if he had a job site near major or minor league cities. Bond wasn't a moralist, he was a "wet," and after work he felt free to raise an illegal tipple. And he stayed single. He made a decent living, but his work bounced him around between job sites. Perhaps he was too busy to woo the right sort of girl; perhaps he didn't think he could provide the stability a good woman deserved; perhaps he just hadn't met the right one. Whatever the case, Bond was a bachelor when the Captain, as Westervelt was known, called him to Asia in 1931.

The first company employee Bond met in Shanghai was Operations Manager Harry Smith, who took Bond aside for a private warning. "Don't take a lease on a house or buy any furniture. We'll be out of here inside six months," he cautioned.

Bond smothered his anger. He didn't appreciate the defeatism. Bond's capacity to forgive was infinite if he felt a man was giving maximum effort. He had little sympathy for those who weren't doing their best, and he sincerely doubted Smith had any visceral understanding of economic conditions back home, or he'd have been a whole lot less sanguine about the prospect of unemployment. Bond had already made up his mind that the China National Aviation Corporation wouldn't fail, not on his watch.

While Westervelt remained in China, Bond kept himself in the Captain's shadow, trying to learn as much as he could about air operations, China, and Shanghai, which surely had the strangest municipal arrangement the world had ever known.

Perched near China's eastern edge, looming over the mouth of the Yangtze, Shanghai had been the vanguard of change in China ever since its founding, but in its stunning contrasts of wealth and poverty, freebooting capitalism and calcified classism, and state-of-the-art industry and Jazz Age glitter that played against the canvas of four thousand years of Chinese tradition and values, the city reflected the tensions that would torture China throughout its struggle to modernize. It was the newest place in China, only ninety years old. Before that, the area that had grown into modern Shanghai was a swamp lying beyond the walls of the obscure Chinese city of Nantao. Western merchants had been trading with China since the 1550s, but for the first three of those four centuries most of the trade was conducted through the tiny Portuguese colony of Macau and the port of Canton on China's south coast. "Trade" was perhaps the wrong word, however; initially, China wouldn't accept anything except silver for the teas, silks, and porcelains the foreigners coveted, one-sided commerce that steadily leeched bullion from European treasuries. Near the beginning of the nineteenth century, British traders reversed the flow of silver when they discovered China's extraordinary appetite for opium. They made phenomenal profits selling opium illegally in China—for cash silver—but the drug trade caused a host of ills within the Middle Kingdom. In the late 1830s, the Manchu court acted to eradicate the commerce, hitting hard at English balance sheets. In what became known as "the First Opium War," England sent a fleet to the Far East in 1839 and abused Chinese positions until the Chinese sued for peace in 1842.

The peace settlement forced the Chinese to cede the uninhabited island of Hong Kong "in perpetuity,"* pay a large indemnity, and open five "treaty ports" to trade—one of which was the marshy land outside Nantao that would become Shanghai. Britain adroitly inserted a "most-favored nation" clause into a supplemental agreement signed in 1843, guaranteeing that any political or economic concession China granted to other foreign powers would automatically extend to British subjects. In turn, the United States and France forced treaties on China in 1844, and in them both countries insisted on becoming "most-favored nations," just like the British. It was a very astute arrangement, for it prevented China from playing the foreign nations against each other—any favor granted to one automatically extended to them all.

The Occidental incursions weren't the only problems faced by the Manchu dynasty. In the 1850s and '60s, three massive internal rebellions shook the throne. Muslims in the northwest provinces revolted, Nian bandits ma-

---

* The British received Hong Kong Island in the treaty settling the First Opium War, and Kowloon in 1860, following their victory in the Second Opium War, both "in perpetuity." The New Territories were added to the colony on a ninety-nine-year lease in 1898. The looming expiration of that lease motivated Britain to return sovereignty of the colony to China in 1997. The New Territories made up more than 85 percent of Hong Kong's area, and by the late twentieth century the colony wasn't independently viable without it.

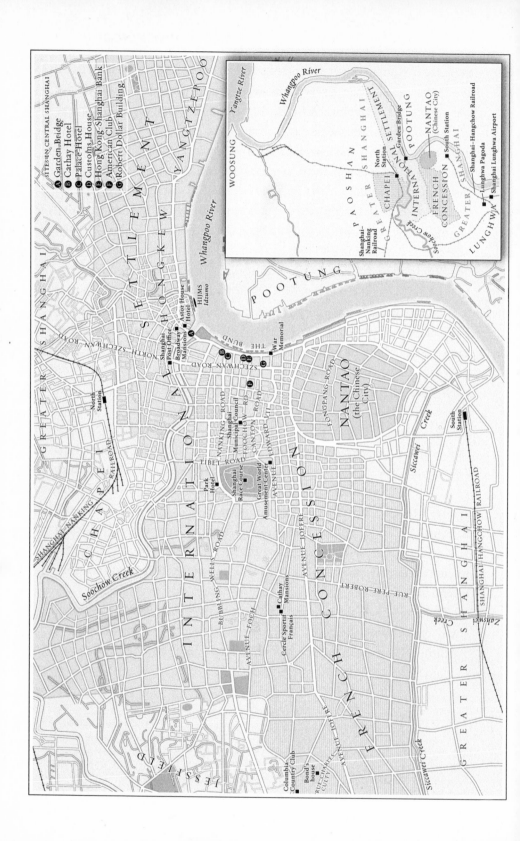

SITES IN CENTRAL SHANGHAI

Ⓐ Garden-Bridge
Ⓑ Cathay Hotel
Ⓒ Palace-Hotel
Ⓓ Customs House
Ⓔ Hong-Kong-Shanghai-Bank
Ⓕ American-Club
Ⓖ Robert-Dollar-Building

rauded from bases south of the Yellow River, and Hong Xiuquan, a failed Confucian scholar convinced he was the younger brother of Jesus Christ, proclaimed the "Taiping Heavenly Kingdom" and marched from south China into the Yangtze Valley at the head of an enormous band of followers. The "Taipings" established a capital at Nanking, and the civil war they fought with the Manchus may have killed as many as twenty million people. Opportunistically, the British, the Americans, and the French pressed for treaty revision. The British used a supposedly illegal search of a trading vessel as another pretext for war, and the "Second Opium War" (1858–60) was just as one-sided as the First. Britain dictated additional accords to complete the framework of the "treaty system" that governed China's relationship with foreign nations, and although China never appeared on the map as any country's colonial possession, the system cut significant chunks of commercial, social, and foreign-policy sovereignty from Chinese control. It was, in fact, the ultimate colonial arrangement: It allowed the foreign powers to leech the maximum economic juice from China without incurring much administrative responsibility.

The foreign traders headquartered in Shanghai managed to do themselves one better. British and American merchants merged their Shanghai fiefs into the "International Settlement" in 1863 and vested authority in a "Shanghai Municipal Council" elected by treaty-power taxpayers, which had the effect of removing foreign Shanghai from Chinese *and* home-country control. The French held their concession apart and managed it through their colonial administration in Indochina, but governed at such a long remove from Paris, it wasn't precisely a colony, either. The Western powers tolerated the arrangements, and protected them with military might, because Shanghai made such astonishing gobs of money.

Quick to recognize the advantage of living at arm's distance from their country's turmoil, Chinese "immigrants" flocked to the foreign concessions. By 1872, Chinese constituted the majority of the Settlement's population and paid the lion's share of its taxes. They remained disenfranchised, but they were freed from arbitrary taxation and Manchu tyranny, Western firepower protected them from China's internal strife, and, most crucially, their property rights were respected.

Understandably, China loathed the "treaty rights," which, among many indignities, forced the Chinese people to tolerate Christian missionaries spreading an alien religion in their communities, foreign gunboats patrolling their inland waterways, and, perhaps most onerous of all, the right of "extraterritoriality," a legalistic mouthful abridged to "extrality," which held that citizens of the treaty powers weren't subject to Chinese law, regardless of the crimes they might commit on Chinese soil. Foreigners compounded the insults by behaving badly. Most were abominably rude, many were downright abusive, and they saw it as their right to live and work in China. A strong, unified China would waste little time ridding itself of the detested arrangement, but the nation was far too weak to do so. The Manchu dynasty staggered forward, torn between the desire to cling to traditional customs and values and the overwhelming need to modernize if the country were to regain its lost sovereignty.

New menaces appeared toward the end of the nineteenth century. To the north, the Russian Czar began casting acquisitive eyes toward Mongolia and Manchuria, and west, across the China Sea, the island nation of Japan emerged from centuries of isolation and embarked on a disciplined program of modernization, industrialization, and militarization designed to make her a world power. Japanese nationalists dreamed of subjugating China into a colonial relationship such as Great Britain enjoyed in India.

Resurgent Japan took her first nibble in 1894. China had traditionally enjoyed preeminence in Korea, but when a rebellion menaced the Korean throne, both nations rushed forces to the peninsula, and Japan's newly modernized military crushed the Chinese. Among many painful concessions, the peace settlement granted Japan the full slate of treaty rights accorded Western nations—one of which made her yet another "most-favored nation."

Japan's victory exacerbated Chinese frustration and xenophobia, and just before the turn of the twentieth century, a violently antiforeign spiritual movement called "the Fists of Righteous Harmony"—dubbed "Boxers" by the foreign press—sprang up in north China and massacred some two hundred Christian missionaries and about twenty thousand of their Chinese converts. British, French, Russian, German, Japanese, and American regiments crushed the rebellion, killing thousands. Foreign forces occupied Peking.

A few years later, in 1904–5, Japan and Russia fought a war over control of Korea. Japan's decisive victory secured her suzerainty over the Korean Peninsula, greatly increased her influence in Manchuria, and put her on equal footing with the Western powers in the Orient. Japan had modernized and China had not, and China's failure kept her sprawled under the foreign heel. Attempting to spark change, a spontaneous anti-Manchu revolt spread across China in late 1911. The leading figure in the "Revolutionary Alliance," Dr. Sun Yat-sen, was elected provisional president of a Chinese republic, and the dowager empress abdicated, ending two thousand years of imperial rule. Republican dreams died quickly, however. Sun Yat-sen didn't prove capable of consolidating power, his government disintegrated, and he fled to Japan. China slipped into chaos, carved apart by regional warlords, each of whom paid lip service to a larger "China" but in reality ran his fief strictly for personal aggrandizement as they fought civil wars among themselves.

As in other periods of internal turmoil, the anarchy of the teens and twenties was Shanghai's boon. Rich Chinese flocked into the foreign settlements to secure their assets under the aegis of Western firepower. Peasants who lost their landholdings and refugees from the constant strife provided an endless reservoir of cheap labor. Silk filatures, brickworks, cotton mills, cement works, flour mills and noodle factories, paper mills, printing presses, metal smelters, tobacco factories, chemical refineries, shipyards, and munitions plants took root along the Whangpoo waterfronts. Banking institutions latched on to the industrial expansion, and Shanghai grew into a city of incredible wealth and unimaginable poverty, glittering nightlife and constant hunger, lazy indolence and ceaseless toil. The Shanghai proletariat slaved twelve and fourteen hours a day, seven days a week, twelve straight months, with only a day or two off to celebrate the Chinese New Year. Unscrupulous foremen demanded kickbacks as job-security payments. The cogs of unshielded machinery chewed off workers' fingers, rotten boilers scalded their skin, and lead, mercury, and chromium poisoned their bodies. Anyone sick, injured, or otherwise unable to work was almost inevitably reduced to begging. Thousands upon thousands of poorly fed people lived packed into unhealthy tenements and shanties, and the average life span of a Chinese living in greater Shanghai was twenty-seven years. Like mushrooms in manure, opium sales, gambling, prostitution, and organized crime flourished amid the suffering. A local aphorism described Shanghai as a thin band of heaven riding a thick slice of hell, and the iniquitous city inspired an American missionary to write that "if God allows Shanghai to exist, he owes an apology to Sodom and Gomorrah." It was, without doubt, the world's most merciless city, and it provided fertile revolutionary soil. In 1921, a dozen Marxists convened the first plenary meeting of the Chinese Communist Party in a girls' school in the French Concession; one of the twelve was an ambitious young delegate from Hunan Province named Mao Tse-tung. Intellectually appealing and promising better life to China's downtrodden masses, the movement flourished.

Returning from Japan, Sun Yat-sen reassembled the shards of his Chinese Nationalist People's Revolutionary Party, the Kuomintang, in Canton. By 1922, he was being aided by Chiang Kai-shek, a dark-eyed thirty-five-year-old who had risen through the violent, mercenary gutters of the Shanghai underworld. Hoping a united China would mitigate the threat Japan posed to Soviet Siberia, Moscow brokered an alliance between the Kuomintang Nationalist Party and the Chinese Communists, and although there was massive divergence between their long-run visions for China, they did share common ground—both saw the crying need to unify and modernize the country under a strong central government. Sun Yat-sen died in March 1925, and Chiang Kai-shek became one of the Kuomintang's leaders. A year later, he led the Nationalist Army north from Canton. He captured the tri-cities of Hankow, Hanyang, and Wuchang (modern Wuhan) and marched on Shanghai, where the Communists organized massive strikes to pave the way for his arrival, but Chiang had decided his wing of the party, drifting rightward, couldn't continue collaborating with the Communists on its leftward edge. He betrayed the strike leaders to his reactionary connections in the Shanghai Green Gang, a prime power in the city's underworld, and Green Gang assassins gunned down hundreds of left-wingers as they took to the streets. The army arrived and continued the purge. Thousands of Communists died in the treachery they came to know as "the White Terror" or "the Feast of Heads."

Chiang allied himself with one of China's wealthiest families in 1927 by marrying Soong Mei-ling, the younger sister of Sun Yat-sen's widow, having agreed to study Christianity to placate Mei-ling's mother's objections to her daughter marrying an unchristian divorcé known to keep concubines. Besotted by Chiang's supposed conversion and by his scourging of the godless Communists, American missionaries returned glowing reports about him to their stateside parishes. After the wedding, Chiang Kai-shek drove his army to Peking. The northern warlords made great protestations of fealty, and Chiang Kai-shek changed the name of Peking, "Northern Capital," to Peiping, or "Northern Peace." The Nationalist Government of China was formally proclaimed in Nanking, "Southern Capital," in October 1928, and by year's end, the green and gold gear-wheel banner of the Kuomintang flew over China from Indochina to the Amur River. Chiang declared that the Kuomintang would rule autocratically for a period of "tutelage" while its benevolent leadership cultivated Chinese democracy.

National political reality was much less monolithic, like the Kuomintang itself. Chiang's right wing held control through an unsteady balance of delicate alliances and personal allegiances, and he faced a multiplicity of conflicts in his struggle to establish his brand of the Kuomintang as China's new ruling dynasty: with recalcitrant warlords in the far-flung provinces, with the Communists whose bitter enmity he'd earned with the White Terror betrayals, with the foreign privilege ensconced in the unequal treaties, and with the increasingly belligerent Japanese.

Every aspect of Chinese society needed modernization. One of Chiang's biggest handicaps was the nation's atrocious transportation networks. "China is one of the largest countries in the world," Chiang pronounced at a conference, "but owing in no small degree to the lack of communications facilities, she is not yet thoroughly unified." Railroads and highways took years to build and required immense capital investment. Air travel offered a quick-fix alternative at much lower cost, and in 1929 and 1930 the Nationalist government sponsored the creation of a pair of airlines. One, the Eurasia Aviation Corporation, was formed with the German Lufthansa. The other was the China National Aviation Corporation, in partnership with Curtiss-Wright.

Taken together when William Bond reached China in 1931, Shanghai's French Concession and the International Settlement covered 12.66 square miles, about half the size of Manhattan. Some one million people lived in the concessions, including about 60,000 foreigners, half of whom were Japanese. Among the polyglot remainder were approximately 9,000 British and 3,500 Americans. Officially uncounted were 22,000 stateless White Russian refugees. Around two million Chinese lived in greater Shanghai outside the settlements, bringing the total into the neighborhood of three million, and, in effect, making Shanghai the fifth- or sixth-largest city in the world, behind London, New York, Tokyo, Berlin, and, possibly, Chicago.

As a new arrival, Bond received a steady stream of invitations to teas, parties, dances, and dinners, and he quickly found his place among the silk buyers, cotton tycoons, cigarette peddlers, opium dealers, speculators, refugees, fugitives, arms merchants, land barons, shipping magnates, insurance salesmen, bank executives, oil company officials, sewing machine salesmen, consular, Navy, and Marine Corps men, and other Westerners who made up foreign Shanghai. Bond's new friends proposed and accepted him for membership at the Columbia Country Club and the American Club, the former a sporting facility on the outskirts of Frenchtown with fourteen tennis courts, a softball diamond, a beautifully arcaded outdoor swimming pool, squash, handball, and badminton courts, a six-lane bowling alley, and a Spanish Revival clubhouse with a wide veranda for dining, cocktails, and dancing. The American Club was more of a businessman's institution, a six-story Georgian construction at 209 Foochow Road, a few blocks behind the Bund in the heart of the International Settlement's downtown, and although the club's lobby reminded most visitors of a well-decorated hospital, Bond enjoyed its relaxed, convivial atmosphere. It had a dining room, a reading room, a card and mahjong room, a billiards salon, and a bowling alley in the basement. The club's bar occupied most of the ground floor, and it always seemed full of gregarious young men eager to shake hands and raise a glass or two, which was legal in China, thank God, and should the alcohol raise the dander of a man's other passions, a few blocks farther along Foochow Road, at number 726, *Hui Le Li*—"the Lane of Lingering Happiness"—branched into a warren of opium dens, gambling establishments, and singsong houses where the temporary affections of a Chinese girl could be had for a smile and a few silver dollars. Shanghai had nightclubs, restaurants, cabarets, jazz clubs, horse races, dog tracks, and parties for tea, dinner, and tiffin (as lunch was known in the Far East), but despite the temptations and the frantic social whirl, Bond's primary occupation was work. It was a commercial city; people toiled hard.

Captain Westervelt left China at the end of May 1931, vesting Bond's authority, and Bond went to see his new superior, CNAC's Chinese managing director, the airline's top official, a Kuomintang general named Ho Chi-wu, whose brother was minister of war. (English-speaking airline employees invariably referred to the managing director as "the MD.") Speaking through an interpreter, Bond asked permission to fire Harry Smith, the doomsaying operations manager, and take over Smith's job himself, a consolidation of two positions that would save the airline money.

The general considered the proposal. "Those are your decisions to make, Mr. Bond," he pronounced.

Bond gave Harry Smith two months' pay to soften the blow and fired him as one of his first official acts.

"You won't be able to handle the pilots," Smith predicted. "You won't last sixty days."

"They won't give me any trouble," Bond countered. "I'll treat them like gentlemen, and if they don't respond to that, their problem will be how to get along with me."

3

"THIS AIRLINE IS A PARTNERSHIP"

Bond called a meeting of the airline's American personnel. He introduced himself as operations manager and explained why he'd sacked Smith. Next, he addressed two primary problems. "First is the damage raucous behavior does to the company image. You cannot be boisterous in the clubs and expect people to want to fly with you. Second, most of you seem to feel that treating the Chinese with common sense and courtesy means being superior and patronizing as hell. That will not do. This airline is a partnership. I expect you to start treating our Chinese *partners* accordingly."

Bond asked for questions. There were none.

He took up his new duties with relish. Vice President in Charge of Operations of an airline was exactly the sort of job he'd envisioned when he quit construction. He cut annual operating costs by U.S. $32,000 ($447,000 in modern dollars) and replaced American personnel who couldn't adjust to his philosophy of partnership with more cooperative and respectful men. On the asset side of the ledger, Bond counted chief mechanic O. C. Wilke and his half-dozen American pilots, led by chief pilot Ernest "Allie" Allison, who'd been flying since 1917 and had come to China with Curtiss-Wright's initial cohort in 1929. Allie and Bond were about the same age and height, but Allie was a much more powerfully built, formidable-looking man with a toothbrush mustache and a gruff bark. During the World War, he'd flown patrols along the Mexican border and served as an instructor for the Army Flying Service. Demobilized, he barnstormed around Philadelphia, and in 1920 he joined the United States Post Office's fledgling airmail service. Allison flew the airmail for seven years, pioneering air commerce and night flying alongside another young, then obscure aviator—his close friend Charles Augustus Lindbergh. By mid-1931, Allison had fourteen years of flying experience and more than eight thousand hours of air time in his logbook. Away from the airport, he was a warm, good-humored man; on duty, his pilots seldom saw him smile. Bond appreciated him as one of the world's most dependable aviators, and although the airline kept its head office a block behind the Bund in the International Settlement's downtown, Bond and Allison spent most of their time at Lunghwa Airport, near a thousand-year-old pagoda five miles south of town. It was a primitive facility on the banks of the Whangpoo River, where the airline had a hangar and some offices next to a runway and a ramp down which its seaplanes rolled into the greasy stream.

Through the middle of 1931, the two men pushed to extend service from Hankow through the Yangtze Gorges to Chungking, principal city of Szechwan, the most important interior province. They flew often to Hankow in one of the airline's six Loening Air Yachts, an ungainly biplane flying boat knit together by an intricate crosshatch of struts and wires, whose hull, slung beneath wings and fuselage with all the grace of an afterthought, protruded in front of the propeller and curled up at the toe like an elf's shoe. The Loening carried half a dozen passengers and cargo in a small cabin framed between hull and fuselage. The pilot and copilot sat side by side in an open cockpit over the passengers' heads, directly behind a single radial engine installed as high as possible to prevent the propeller from fouling the water. The plane cruised at about one hundred miles an hour (pilots said it had a built-in headwind), the cabin was so drafty passengers practically had to tie their hats in place, and water poured through its seams during takeoff and landing, but the Loening Air Yacht was rugged and dependable and economical to operate, crucial characteristics for an airline to consider if it hoped to do business successfully in China, and for a profit. China had few airports, but many rivers, and any flat-water stretch could serve as a base for flying boats, or, in a pinch, as an emergency landing strip. The Loenings were therefore the airline's prime moneymakers, moving passengers and mail up and down Route One, the Yangtze, the company's backbone as well as China's.

Aloft, flying inland, Bond took much comfort from the great river, an ever-welcoming landing strip, his twenty-ninth psalm—the voice of the Lord upon the waters. So new to Asia, he didn't yet comprehend the river's capacity for devastation. Far to the west, an unusually large snowfall melted under 1931's summer sun. Monsoon rainfall poured into the river's upper reaches, and deluges soaked its major tributary valleys. The Yangtze swelled, topped its dikes, and inundated a landmass the size of New York State, drowning tens of thousands of peasants. From altitude, the flood's havoc was impossible to comprehend. Reflections of cloud and sky shimmered on the surface of what looked like a large, peaceful lake. Only flying low could Bond make out the roofs of submerged villages and the bodies of drowned peasants bobbing in stagnant water. Hungry families floated listlessly on crude rafts tethered to rooftops and gawked at the passing airplanes. Days passed, then weeks. The disaster was so widespread there seemed nowhere to dent it. Only in the normal riverbed was the water deep enough for large vessels, and survivors were too scattered for large-scale relief. People starved to death in their rafts or on hilltop islands. Disease claimed untold thousands of others. Different sources touted divergent figures, but it hardly mattered; the numbers beggared imagination, and the awful truth was that nobody really knew how many people were lost, nor was there any way of knowing. China was like a whip. Fluctuation at the handle caused massive devastation among the millions of marginal lives at the tip. At a minimum, 145,000 people vanished, swept away and drowned, and a like number died from starvation and disease. Some 25 million people lost their homes. The calamity starkly demonstrated the fragility of life in China to Bond, while simultaneously revealing an aspect of the nation's strength—in its aftermath, life returned to normal with surprising speed.

Bond spent the rest of the year organizing the inception of air service from Hankow to Chungking, on the Yangtze River above its famous gorges, solidifying service on the rest of Route One, trying to spark up Route Two from Shanghai to Peiping, and laboring to keep the company's cash flowing in black ink. Although he wasn't successful in either of the last two endeavors, the gradual expansion of airline operations did materially contribute to China's political unification, knitting the profoundly provincial country's government and business practices closer to the Nationalist power base in Nanking and the lower Yangtze valley.

Nothing was more certain to ruin Japanese dreams of dominating Asia than a monolithic, modernized China, and with Chiang Kai-shek consolidating power, Japanese expansionists felt the time ripe to tear a chunk from the mainland, before the country became too strong to subjugate. The Japanese kept a force called the Kwantung Army in Manchuria to garrison the railroad concession won from the Russians in the 1904–5 war. On the night of September 18, 1931, a small bomb exploded under the railroad tracks in Mukden, a supposedly anti-Japanese attack that caught the Kwantung Army in a curious state of readiness—it occupied the city in less than eleven hours. Japanese reinforcements poured over the Korean frontier and seized all three Manchurian provinces.

Four days after "the Manchurian Incident," but unrelated to it, Britain defaulted on her gold payments, devastating the international gold standard and sparking bank runs in the United States. Nearly 2,300 American banks collapsed, dropping the nation into the worst economic abyss it had ever known. Gripped by such catastrophe, the United States cleaved to its isolationist tradition, and left to go it alone, the European League of Nations couldn't muster the will to take meaningful action against the Japanese aggression. Patriotic Chinese hit back the best way they knew how—by boycotting Japanese goods and businesses, which did immense damage to Japanese financial interests. Chiang Kai-shek didn't feel strong enough to provoke full-scale confrontation, but the quasi-independent Nineteenth Route Army marched into Shanghai in the last week of January to give teeth to the boycott.* At midnight on January 29, 1932, Japanese marines attacked Chinese positions under an intense barrage fired from warships in the Whangpoo. CNAC made one last round-trip flight from Shanghai to

---

* The Route Army's move might have had something to do with a CNAC extracurricular service—the Central Government had quietly commissioned Bond to fly an emissary to a meeting with the Route Army's commander. Shortly thereafter, the army struck its tents and marched on Shanghai.

Nanking and suspended service. Chinese infantrymen fought like devils in Shanghai's rubbled streets, but furious Japanese attacks and the weight of their naval gunfire and airpower gradually pushed them back. The fighting paralyzed river traffic and shut down the Shanghai–Nanking Railroad. Hating the idea of letting Japanese aggression dictate airline operations, Bond worried at managing director General Ho through eight days of combat, and finally, on February 8, was allowed to resume service. Bond had the planes flying the next day, and CNAC flew right over the problems, washing away any doubts about what civil aviation could do for China.

Both sides reinforced, and the fighting fronts extended northward. The mini-war fizzled in early March, having devastated many square miles of Shanghai's northern districts and killed some fifteen thousand civilians. Yet Shanghai made up in vigor what it lacked in moral fiber and quickly rebuilt the destroyed areas.

The China National Aviation Corporation survived 1932 under Bond's leadership, operating only its Route One up the Yangtze from Shanghai to Chungking. Politically, the Kuomintang consolidated power, struggled against the Chinese Communists, and howled in protest when Japan created the independent nation of "Manchuko" from the three Manchurian provinces. Toward the end of the year, elements of the Japanese Kwantung Army edged toward Jehol, one of the two provinces above the Great Wall that it didn't already control. Considering the threat, Bond thought the time opportune to establish CNAC's Route Two from Shanghai and Nanking to Tientsin and Peiping using the half-dozen single-engine, high-winged Stinson Detroiter monoplanes he and Allison hadn't yet been able to get into consistent revenue-producing service.* In Bond's mind, air communications would bind the northern provinces more tightly to the core of the nation. Realistically, however, the airline was barely covering its operating costs with the money it earned in the Yangtze valley. Bond didn't want to risk depleting its minuscule cushion by establishing a new line, and he couldn't solicit a subsidy through his Ministry of Communications

---

* The airline had already failed once to establish the route in late 1931, largely because its crop of Chinese pilots hadn't then been well enough trained to handle scheduled flying.

contacts—they'd already refused too many times. However, he had a new weapon in his arsenal who he hoped would help him take a different tack: M. Y. Tong, an executive at the Bank of Canton.

Tong spoke fluent English, having attended university in the United States. He and Bond were about the same age, shared many common interests, and they'd formed a genuine friendship. They played tennis and dined together regularly, and Bond appreciated the many insights into Chinese politics and culture his new friend provided. Tong had a ready wit that played well off Bond's drier humor, but he was a different man at the Bank of Canton, known to cynics as "T. V. Soong's bank," where Tong served as Soong's straitlaced right-hand man.

Bond didn't think there was a better-connected man in China than Soong Tse-ven—T. V. Soong—the Kuomintang finance minister, whose three sisters were every bit as influential as he was: Soong Ai-ling, wife of H. H. Kung, the president of the Legislative Yuan; Soong Ching-ling, widow of Sun Yat-sen, father of the Chinese revolution; and Soong Mei-ling, the beautiful and glamorous wife of China's Generalissimo, known the world over as Madame Chiang Kai-shek. Japan's effective employment of airpower in the "Shanghai Incident" the previous year had converted Soong into a staunch proponent of China's aviation development. Bond was reluctant to approach M. Y. Tong hat in hand, asking to be bridged across to T. V. Soong, but he felt the escalating developments in north China warranted emergency action.

Beyond that, the situation provided an opening for Bond to pursue what was, to him, a more important goal: to engage the Chinese government more closely in the development of its commercial aviation. Tong agreed to query Soong on Bond's behalf, and a small, temporary subsidy was granted the next day. Bond might have been able to establish the line without it, but he'd gotten what he really wanted—a toehold in the top echelon of China's governmental power.

Bond and chief pilot Ernie Allison sparked up the new line in the winter of 1933, and it progressed smoothly. William Bond met a new aviation man in Shanghai that February, probably over American Club martinis. His name was Harold M. Bixby, from St. Louis, Missouri, and he'd come to the Orient as an "aviation missionary" for Pan American Airways. Like Bond, Bixby was of average height, but Bixby was tomato-pole thin and seldom filled his suit. He was forty-two years old, two and a half years older than Bond, with a gaunt, lined face, a small, neat mustache, and wire-rimmed glasses. Both men had been businessmen before converting to aviation, although as an Amherst graduate and a former bank vice president, Harold Bixby was much more of an establishment type. Bixby had also made a crucial contribution to the most famous American aviation achievement since Kitty Hawk—his Saint Louis University Club cabal financed Charles Lindbergh's transatlantic solo, which Lindbergh honored by naming his airplane the *Spirit of St. Louis*. Later, Bixby's bank sold bonds for a real estate project crushed by the onset of the Depression, and although Bixby wasn't legally responsible, he must have felt his personal pledge part of the sales pitch, because he made good his investors' losses with funds out of his own pocket, a deed that sealed his hiring at Pan Am after his relationship with Lindbergh got his foot in the door. Bixby left four daughters and a wife behind him in the United States, and Bond tested the waters with a gentle tease, asking Bixby if he'd lamented the arrival of his fourth girl.

Bixby laughed. "I never held three queens and wanted to draw anything else."

Even in aviation, Harold Bixby was more "establishment" than William Bond. Working with CNAC, Bond struggled with obsolete equipment and primitive facilities on the farthest-flung fringe of commercial aviation, and he had a job only as long as he kept his airline solvent—behind him, Curtiss-Wright lay sprawled across the many horns of economic catastrophe. Bixby was a "made man" in the upper echelons of Pan American Airways, the risen star of international aviation, and he had the full confidence of Juan Terry Trippe, Pan Am's sphinxlike president, who'd built an empire pioneering international, over-water commercial aviation between North, Central, and South America, often buying and absorbing regional airlines. Trippe's dreams didn't stop at spanning such an oceanic millpond as the Caribbean, however. His vision focused on the Atlantic and the Pacific, the twin grails of international aviation, knowing he could change the world forever—and make millions doing it—if he could cast airlines across them.

It was a startlingly ambitious aspiration. Airplanes with the range, reliability, and load capacity to profitably cross such enormous expanses of water didn't exist, nor did the navigation systems crucial to finding mid-ocean islands. Pan Am took it on faith that this *could* be done, however, and the company was pushing forward with crossing projects for both the

Atlantic and the Pacific. Bixby's mission in Asia was to prepare the way for the coming service, and paramount among his assignments was persuading the Chinese government to grant Pan American the right to land its as-of-yet-nonexistent transpacific flying boats in China.

"With all due respect, Mr. Bixby, you're never going to get that right," Bond warned.

"No?" asked Bixby. Pan American Airways had twenty thousand miles of routes in operation, gross annual revenue exceeding nine million dollars, a million dollars of clear profits ($16.3 million in modern dollars), and it had dealt with a host of political problems in Central and South America and around the Caribbean. It was used to getting its way.

"I think you'll find the rub in the 'most-favored nation' clauses of the treaties the foreign powers signed with China in the last century," Bond explained. "If China gives an American company like yours the right to land in China, every other most-favored nation gets the right to land planes in China, and that means Japan, and China isn't going to give you anything that gives Japan the right to land airplanes in China. Not ever."

"That'll be negotiable, just like everything else," Bixby countered.

"I'm afraid you'll find it's not. You won't get permission to land American planes in China unless Japan abrogates her treaty rights or sinks into the ocean."

All American Club business was transacted via "chits," settled monthly. In accordance with Shanghai custom, Bixby gamely shook dice with Bond for the drink chits before he left.

That month, Japan's Kwantung Army at last stormed Jehol, but despite that ominous development, airline progress pleased William Bond. Air travel would become increasingly indispensable to China, he knew it, and he allowed himself to look into the future with increasing confidence.

A few days later, on March 31, 1933, Harold Bixby shattered Bond's settled outlook when he announced that Pan American Airways had taken control of Curtiss-Wright's 45 percent interest in the China National Aviation Corporation. William Bond was a China man, with a China focus. Pan Am was an American company with an international focus. Bond had no idea where he'd stand with his new corporate masters, and he feared for his job, a very grave matter indeed for an American in the spring of 1933.

4

CAKE AND CHAMPAGNE

If the sale worried William Bond, it shocked the airline's Chinese ownership. The company's founding charter clearly specified that neither the Chinese nor the Americans could sell their shares without the other partner's consent. The Chinese felt betrayed, and with good reason: Pan American had been sniffing at the China National Aviation Corporation for more than a year with Curtiss-Wright's full knowledge and cooperation, and a Curtiss-Wright gone sour on China had agreed to terms more than a month before. It was a legally dubious transaction, but Pan American did wriggle in without violating the letter of the contract, because Pan Am didn't actually buy CNAC and Curtiss-Wright didn't actually sell it. Instead, Pan Am bought an obscure Curtiss-Wright subsidiary, Intercontinent Aviation, which owned another mysterious entity, China Airways Federal, whose only asset was the American interest in the China National Aviation Corporation. Technically, the founding contract hadn't been violated, but its spirit of partnership most definitely had, and the airline's Chinese officials were furious—not because of any special relationship they thought they'd had with Curtiss-Wright but because they felt they'd been outsmarted. They'd lost face.

Shortly thereafter, in early April, chairman of the board K. C. Huang called a meeting to get acquainted with Bixby and Pan American. An extremely wealthy and shrewd businessman with rubber and shipping interests who'd grown up in the Dutch East Indies (modern-day Indonesia), Huang spoke Malay as his first language, was conversant in Dutch and English, and knew a smattering of Chinese. Another Chinese director took the lead in opening the meeting: The airline's revenues were $70,000 (Mex.) per month, against expenses of $120,000 (Mex.).* A third Chinese director moved to declare the company insolvent. That took some petrol out of Bixby's carburetor. There were four dark-suited Chinese seated opposite three Americans, and Bixby could count. Those men could vote the company out of existence and run an airline in partnership with somebody else.

Physically, Harold Bixby was far from imposing, and he urged the Chinese not to be hasty as he extolled the benefits of partnership with Pan American. Unlike Curtiss-Wright, Pan Am wasn't beholden to any manufacturing interest. It would always choose the safest and highest-performing aircraft and engines at the best price, regardless of who built them. Bixby assured the directors that Pan American did want to help China develop its internal airlines. It intended to link them to a visionary, "next step" air service spanning the Pacific Ocean, an ambitious plan, Bixby acknowledged, but Pan Am had proved its ability over the Caribbean. No other airline could do it. Transpacific service would bind China and the United States closer together, stimulate diplomatic and cultural intercourse, and capture the imagination of the entire world, making great "face" for everyone involved. Business between the two nations would boom. There was no downside. All CNAC's Chinese ownership had to do was arrange a reasonable airmail subsidy, open its undeveloped route from Shanghai to Canton, and allow Pan American to land in China.

The Chinese directors countered with a demand that Pan American grant CNAC an enormous, unsecured loan, an outrageous proposal that astonished Bixby. He reasoned and pleaded, but made no headway. All Bixby managed to accomplish was to convince the Chinese directors to withdraw their insolvency proposal—for the time being.

---

* Mexican silver dollars circulated freely in China, and "Mex." had become shorthand for Chinese currency.

Bixby was telling the truth when he said that Pan Am wanted to expand CNAC's operations within China. Pan Am did want to open a new route, one between Shanghai and Canton granted to CNAC in its founding contract. The company called it Route Three and, if developed, it would link two of China's principal cities. Route Three was a thousand miles long, however, a distance that mandated several intermediate stops, none of which would generate much additional traffic, over a mountainous coastline plagued by dense, unpredictable fogs. Although Canton was China's second city, and nominally subordinate to the Nationalist Central Government in Nanking (which controlled Shanghai), politics between the Canton government and Nanking ran to extremes of hot and cold, and flights between Shanghai and Canton would compete with efficient oceangoing steamships. Route Three promised such slim returns on invested capital that the airline had chosen to let it lie fallow. However, Route Three's theoretical existence was the prime reason Pan Am had bought into CNAC. Only Shanghai could profitably anchor the Oriental end of a transpacific airline, and only Route Three could link Shanghai to the mid-ocean islands across which Pan Am intended to fly the Pacific.* Intending to qualify for a generous U.S. airmail subsidy, Pan Am planned to operate Route Three in Pan Am livery.

A close reading of the founding contract granted CNAC exclusive rights to Route Three provided it flew mail on the route prior to July 8, 1933—just over three months away. The airline stood to lose that part of the franchise if it didn't, and after the crafty, shades-of-gray takeover he'd helped engineer, Bixby knew he couldn't expect a lenient interpretation. All the Chinese had to do was wait, and stall, and loss of the Route Three franchise would force Pan American into a massive renegotiation that the Chinese would presumably use to squeeze Pan Am dry. Route One, the Yangtze Route, and the newer Route Two, the Peiping Line, occupied all of the company's Loenings and Stinsons. Bixby couldn't divert any without making a lie of his rhetoric lauding Pan Am's commitment to China's internal airlines. Nor was either old, single-engine airframe the right machine with which to prosecute a long, dangerous route exposed to the open

---

* The geographically obvious straight line between Manila and Shanghai passed over the island of Formosa (Taiwan), which the Japanese had controlled since 1895.

ocean. Route Three required faster, longer-ranged, multi-engine seaplanes. A seven-man Pan American expedition had left Savannah, Georgia, on the Dutch freighter *Gertrude Maersk* with two twin-engine S-38 amphibians aboard, but the *Gertrude Maersk* wouldn't reach Shanghai until the end of June, just over a week before the deadline.

All through April and May, while Bixby wrangled with CNAC's Chinese ownership, fighting continued in north China. At times, the armies of the northern warlords fought well, but the Central Government didn't deploy a soul to help. Instead, Chiang Kai-shek launched the cream of his army into its "Fourth Red Bandit Suppression Campaign" against the major Communist base area in Kiangsi Province, south of the Yangtze.* The Japanese breached the Great Wall in May and attacked Hopei, Peiping's province. By the end of the month, citizens in Peiping and Tientsin could hear the booming of Japanese artillery. A humiliating truce ended the fighting, but Bixby still didn't seem to grasp the truth of what Bond had told him two and a half months before—that nothing on earth could induce the Chinese to grant foreign-flagged airplanes the right to land in China, given the certain knowledge that Japan would seize the most-favored nation opportunity to do it themselves.

Accordingly, Bixby's negotiations went nowhere. The unreasonableness of the Chinese counterdemands surprised him. He didn't yet understand this as a Chinese way of saying no. Pan American Airways' broader goals made Route Three far more important to Pan Am than it was to Chiang's government. The Kuomintang had other priorities. To them, CNAC was a tool to help cement the political unification and economic development of their country and a template for learning how to operate and administer an airline on their own. The company's Chinese leadership preferred to use their meager development capital to complete a long-standing plan to open service between Chungking and Chengtu, the two principal cities of Szechwan Province, both more than a thousand miles inland. Connecting

---

* Chiang's previous three extermination campaigns had failed miserably, largely because Central Government soldiery was profoundly vulnerable to Communist propaganda. The frequency of mass defections inspired *The China Weekly Review* to ridicule Chiang's bandit suppression campaigns as "red supply trains" (*CWR*, October 7, 1933).

these cities was utterly irrelevant to Pan American. Weeks passed, the north China fighting made headlines, and the deadline for carrying mail on Route Three crept closer. Pan American's two amphibians and seven flight personnel were somewhere on the oceans mid-route. There didn't seem to be much Bixby could accomplish until they arrived.

With two years in China behind him, William Bond understood from the start that Bixby needed wholehearted Chinese support to accomplish Pan Am's ambition. He also felt Bixby hadn't done much to deserve it. Bond shared Bixby's belief that partnership with Pan Am would prove a boon to China in the long run, but he saw what Bixby didn't—China's short-term problems outweighed its long-run considerations. Bond didn't think Bixby would get cooperation until he demonstrated Pan Am's concrete interest in China's immediate needs. Nor did Bond think Bixby appreciated the full profit-making potential of swift, efficient air travel within China and what it might do for national unification. He wanted Bixby to experience some of China beyond Shanghai, to get a feel for its complexities, charms, and difficulties, and to realize there was more to the company he'd bought into than the potential to anchor a transpacific line in Shanghai.

Bond also had a much more personal motivation: Even though nearly two months had elapsed since the takeover, he still didn't know where he stood with Pan American Airways. Contractually, CNAC's American partner had the power to hire and fire operations personnel. Bond was finished if Pan Am decided he wasn't useful, and a thousand-mile upriver journey with Bixby through the Yangtze Gorges to Szechwan to survey and open the Chungking-to-Chengtu line seemed a splendid opportunity to solidify his role. Bond marshaled his arguments and persuaded Bixby to join the expedition.

The airline's founding contract granted it the right to fly from Shanghai along the Yangtze River to Chungking, and from Chungking overland to Chengtu, the capital of Szechwan Province. Unfortunately, Central Government paperwork didn't hold sway in Szechuan. Warlord Marshal Liu Hsiang controlled the province. *His* blessing was the rights grant the airline needed if it wanted to operate the last leg of the line, and CNAC's business manager, Wharton School of finance graduate P. Y. Wong, had flown ahead to Chungking to initiate persuasion.

Szechwan was China's most populous interior province, but it was spectacularly isolated, rimmed by mountains. CNAC had been flying to Chungking, the province's largest city, for eighteen months, a permission the warlord marshal had only reluctantly granted, but Chungking's business community had clamored for the speed, efficiency, and convenience of air service more vociferously than he could afford to ignore. Even in the cloth and plywood single-engine string-bag Loenings, flying was actually the safest way to travel up- or downriver, since it eliminated the treacherous passage through the torrents of the Yangtze Gorges, which claimed upward of a thousand lives every year.

Flights between Chungking and Chengtu promised similar benefits. The overland route between the two cities was a three-hundred-mile-long path winding through rice paddies and opium fields and over mountain passes. Coolies carried more affluent travelers in sedan chairs, but those travelers also had to hire armed bodyguards. Alternatively, one could boat up the Yangtze (known above Chungking as *Jinsha Jiang*, "the River of Golden Sand") to its confluence with the Min and up the Min to Chengtu. However, steamers could navigate the Min only in summer high water. Otherwise, the voyage had to be made in junks hauled against its swift current. Either way, the journey between Chengtu and Chungking took about a fortnight.

The airline party left Shanghai for Hankow on May 26, 1933, in a Stinson Detroiter piloted by Ernie Allison. Aboard were Bond, Bixby, and Mr. A. M. Chapelain, the Shanghai postal commissioner. Foreigners were offensive, crude, uncultured, rude, and hairy, but they "squeezed" less money from the mail service than the Chinese, and in the early years of the century the dowager empress had begun inviting them to manage China's most important post offices.

Clustered around the mouth of the Han River at the head of deep-draft navigation on the Yangtze 585 miles west of Shanghai, joined to the north and south by important railroads and to points farther inland by the two rivers, the tri-cities of Hankow, Hanyang, and Wuchang* were a strategic intersection of river, rail, agriculture, and budding industry that made them China's Chicago. On the north bank of the Yangtze just east of the Han's mouth, Hankow was the biggest of the three cities, and for foreigners it was a microcosm of Shanghai. Western-style buildings in small British,

---

* Hankow, Hanyang, and Wuchang constitute the modern city of Wuhan.

Russian, French, German, and Japanese concessions presented their alien façades to the great river just downstream of the ramshackle jumble of the Chinese city, where new commercial buildings, factory chimneys, and a few ancient pagoda tiers protruded from old, dense-packed slums. Foreign Hankow had a racecourse, softball fields, golf links, a YMCA, movie theaters, a lending library, clubs, cricket pitches, a number of important missionary headquarters, a superb brothel run by a middle-aged White Russian madam, and Dump Street, a collection of cabarets and nightclubs that made it the upriver equivalent of Shanghai's notorious Blood Alley.

In Hankow, the expedition received a cable advising them to abandon their proposed extension because civil war had erupted in Szechwan. Mr. Chapelain had once been stationed in Chengtu, however, and he drily observed that Szechwan civil wars tended to feature combats a lot less ferocious than, say, Verdun. He didn't think rumor of another should cause CNAC to slow its expansion. They decided to continue, despite Bixby's misgivings.

The Yangtze took a long meander to the southwest above Hankow. Allison cut it off by flying straight west up the Han River over thick boat traffic and then cross-country over thousands of rice paddies to rejoin the Yangtze at Shasi. As they droned toward Ichang, hills appeared on either side of the river, dotted with picturesque villages among rice paddies, wheat fields, and citrus orchards. Beyond Ichang, the Yangtze's tawny waters spewed from the 3,000- to 5,000-foot Wushan Mountains, through which the river sluiced, confined to 146 miles of deep, turbulent gorges.

Clouds billowed atop the Wushan summits. Allison zoomed down to river level and slipped underneath the layer. Breezes in the gorge bottom nearly always kept open a few hundred feet of airspace. A thousand shades of green and gray painted the slopes rearing skyward from the riverbanks. An upriver junk seemed frozen in rapids below, held against the current by fifty or sixty naked "trackers" hitched to a tow rope, men who spent their lives hauling ships up the gorges, clawing upstream on the ancient towpaths worn into the riverbanks by the feet of their hapless ancestors. From the air, they looked like harnessed ants. Suddenly, a pair of downstream junks careened past, pitching over standing waves like twigs rushing down a storm-swollen gutter as they raced to maintain steerage way, for only at frightening speed would the vessels respond to their tillers. The upstream voyage was riskiest for the trackers. Many slipped into the current and drowned. The downstream journey was deadly to the junks themselves: Rapids and rocks damaged one vessel out of ten; one in twenty was lost entirely. Mists poured over limestone battlements and tumbled toward the moiling waters; flowers carpeted less precipitous slopes. A rock wall blocked the canyon ahead. Allison bore straight toward it, dead-center stream, on a certain crash course until he banked into a new reach of river, only to see it blocked a mile distant by another mountainside. It was like flying up a succession of blind alleys.

After more than an hour in the gorges, the mountains squeezed even tighter against the river, and the torrent made a mad rush through Qutong defile, known to Westerners as Wind Box Gorge. The shortest of the great gorges, Wind Box was only five miles long; nowhere in it was the river more than 500 feet wide, and in summer flood the Yangtze rose a staggering 165 feet, a maelstrom that had inspired a famous poet to write that it was as if "a thousand seas had been poured into one cup." At the upriver end, Allison burst through the Dragon's Gate, the two immense limestone outcrops confining the stream, and soared out over a gradually unfurling landscape of gentler hills.

Another hour upriver, Allison approached Chungking, a dense, medieval city straddling the steep sides of a wedge-shaped peninsula that jutted over the Yangtze's confluence with the Kialing River, 1,400 miles from the East China Sea. Five miles of thick stone walls girdled 600,000 inhabitants. The traditional trip upriver through the gorges from Ichang to Chungking in a junk took thirty to forty days; in the high-water season, it could take as many as fifty. The downstream trip commonly took a week. Even the most powerful modern river steamers needed a week to negotiate the upstream passage. CNAC had flown the gorges in about two hours.

In Chungking, May 29, 1933, dawned a typically gloomy spring morning. Rain and mist swirled through narrow, twisting alleys, wetting the raw sewage that putrefied in garbage-choked gutters. Chickens and squealing pigs dashed past open storefronts. The tangy smells of spicy Szechwan cuisine sizzling in alley-side cookeries mingled with the cloying scent of opium wafted by local addicts. Mr. Chapelain went off to conduct post office business. Four squads of sedan-chair coolies toted Bond, Bixby, Allison, and P. Y. Wong up and down dank, smooth-worn stone stairways, shouldering through morning crowds and yelling rudely for way until they reached one of Chungking's few wide streets, where the delegation trans-ferred to warlord Marshal Liu Hsiang's automobile, dispatched by their host to give face to his visitors and establish it for himself. A chauffeur drove them the short remaining distance to the marshal's fortress-like headquarters. Bodyguards flanked the doors. "Keep your eyes peeled," Bond said with a wink, stepping through. "He's supposed to have twenty concubines."

A chamberlain ushered the Americans into a gloomy audience cham-ber. Armed toughs lurked in every corner. Liu Hsiang appeared wearing a severe robe cut from midnight blue silk and made a slight, respectful incli-nation. Lamplight gleamed from the crown of his meticulously shaved skull. He smiled, spread his hands in welcome, and ushered the Americans into a smaller, less intimidating room. Bond found it difficult to reconcile the man's diminutive stature with the fact that he controlled the lives of somewhere between fifty and seventy million souls, the equivalent of about half the population of the United States. The warlord and the executives exchanged pleasantries as servants presented wedges of stale angel food cake and glasses of room-temperature champagne, Western delicacies in-tended to honor and impress the Americans, who would have preferred coffee at such an early hour, although they brimmed with the flowery com-pliments protocol required. The warlord murmured a few words in Chi-nese, translated by his interpreter: "The marshal wishes to tell you that he is very pleased that you decided, at his request, to fly a separate service from Chungking to Chengtu."

CNAC was happy to accommodate the marshal's wishes, Bond replied. The point had been a deal breaker. The marshal insisted the airline operate Chungking–Chengtu separate from the upriver flying boats that traveled from Hankow to Chungking so his men could search all in- and out-bound Chengtu airplanes to ensure they didn't carry military cargoes. Perhaps, thought Bond, every Chinese strongman rightly feared an armed peas-antry, but a lone, single-engine Stinson shuttling back and forth every other day to Chengtu couldn't carry enough arms in a year to threaten Marshal Liu's provincial stranglehold. Bond suspected another motive—to prevent the flights from carrying opium that hadn't paid the marshal's ex-port taxes. Bond wasn't privy to the warlord's finances, but he'd have wa-gered a year's salary the majority of his revenue flowed from his control of

Szechwan opium. Bond chose not to explain that the airline had no option *but* to fly a landplane service from Chungking to Chengtu. The rivers at Chengtu weren't suitable for flying boats.

The interpreter continued: "The marshal would also like to tell you how much he appreciates the service which the China National Aviation Corporation has been running between Hankow and Chungking. It is of very great benefit to the people and prosperity of Szechwan and Chungking."

True enough, thought Bond, air service *was* a boon—it had made Szechwan more accessible than it had been at any time in the four-thousand-year history of Chinese civilization, but Bond was equally certain the marshal would be delighted never to see another airplane buzz into his Szechwan stronghold. Every swift upriver flight knit Chungking closer to the seats of Nationalist power in the lower Yangtze valley.

The marshal casually mentioned his "disagreement" with Chengtu. Apparently, some wicked, misguided generals (who the Americans knew were Marshal Liu's men) were assaulting his uncle, holed up in Chengtu. The uncle resented Liu Hsiang's influence and might confiscate their Stinson. Nodding his head in rehearsed contemplation, the marshal gravely advised the Americans not to continue, at least not until he had Chengtu under control.

Bixby assured him their Stinson was a purely commercial airframe, useless for military purposes, and that the Nanking authorities were anxious to begin airmail service.

That last detail was something Bond wished Bixby hadn't mentioned. In China, one didn't bring unpleasantries to another's attention without intent to humiliate. It caused the marshal to lose face.

Fortunately, Liu Hsiang overlooked the "foreign barbarian's" breach of etiquette, and the visitors left the meeting and walked out into the rain and mist wrapping the Chungking headland. The warlord hadn't given much encouragement, but neither had he refused permission. They motorboated a dozen miles downriver to the military airfield where they'd left their Stinson, wanting to get airborne the instant the weather improved.

"Big" Chuan met them at the airport. He'd been a CNAC pilot in 1931, but the ignominious circumstances of a crash landing had caused him and the airline to part ways. He took his aviation skills to Szechwan, where he'd become "General-Admiral" Chuan, supreme commander of Marshal Liu Hsiang's land and naval air forces. The general-admiral gleefully toured his former employers through his headquarters in a commandeered Buddhist temple and the two hangars beyond the temple compound that sheltered his motley airplane collection. Quite understandably, the Nanking government refused provincial warlords permission to import airplanes, but a French arms dealer had smuggled a dozen biplanes into Szechwan from Indochina. Marshal Liu Hsiang controlled Szechuan Province with those airplanes and a standing army larger than that of the United States. Bond ran a finger over the wing surface of the best-looking airplane, a French Breguet 14 survivor of the Great War. It came away covered in dust.

The Americans spent the afternoon gathering information about Chengtu. An American trader recently returned from the city pegged a military parade ground inside its walls as Chengtu's best landing possibility. Allison cabled a truck salesman he knew in Chengtu and asked him to pace its dimensions. The answer came back: one thousand feet long, four hundred feet wide. Big enough, but only just.

Dank, dreary rain lingered over Chungking through the last three days of May, grounding the expedition and swallowing time the men had hoped to use making aerial surveys, but June 1 dawned with the cloud ceiling raised to the level of the mountaintops, and the party took off. Allison kept the controls until they'd passed a line of hills, then handed off to Bond, in the copilot's seat, over terrain more amenable to emergency landings. Bond knew how to fly, as did Bixby, but neither man was an ace pilot. Ernie Allison, by many thousands of hours the most experienced pilot aboard, made time, speed, and direction notations on a notepad and pored over three radically disagreeing maps, trying to orient them to the apparently unrelated terrain beneath and make amendments that would aid future pilots. It was challenging navigation, like most aerial navigation in China, where one impoverished hamlet looked much like the next in a land largely devoid of roads, railways, and telegraph lines.

An hour and forty minutes after takeoff, a solid mountain rampart appeared under the clouds ahead. White flowers covered the hillsides beneath, shivering in a gentle wind—opium poppies cultivated by upland farmers. Allison claimed the controls and scouted for a breach through the range, his hope fading until he spotted a tiny patch of cloud-free air at the base of a saddle. He angled across the pass, skimming treetops, into more roomy airspace over descending country beyond. Ahead lay the patchwork agriculture of the Chengtu Plain.

The walled city of Chengtu crept down from the northwestern horizon, a gray-walled island in a green rural landscape. The men scanned for troop concentrations, artillery bursts, trench lines, or any other indications of combat. Nothing abnormal disturbed the scene. Allison spotted the parade ground shoehorned between neighborhoods and the city's northeastern wall. It looked like a postage stamp, and they could see several hundred armed soldiers drilling on the field. Allison dived. If anybody aimed guns at them, the Americans agreed they'd scuttle back to Chungking, but the power dive on the clearing exposed no hostility.

Allison tightened his ovals and "dragged" the field. Two-story buildings and a line of telegraph poles at one end and the thick, thirty-foot-high perimeter wall at the other trimmed its usable dimensions, but Allison slicked the Stinson onto the field with hardly a bump, a landing that impressed Bixby with its precision. Bond smiled. Pan Am didn't have the best pilot in the world. CNAC did.

The plane rolled to a stop. Allison killed the engine, and Mr. Chapelain, the postal commissioner, broke the sudden quiet. The last time he'd traveled from Shanghai to Chengtu, in the early years of the century, he'd come from Shanghai to Ichang in river steamers, on a junk upriver through the gorges to Chungking, and overland to Chengtu in a sedan chair carried by coolies, and start to finish, without break, his trip had taken sixty-two days.

A double rank of soldiers formed around the plane, bayonets fixed to their rifle barrels. Curious civilians thronged behind them. Bond climbed out, and a soldier dashed forward and stopped beneath the wing, clicked his boot heels together and presented arms, raising his rifle before him with the one-two-three slaps of snappy martial salute, the last of which drove his foot-long bayonet straight through the Stinson's wing with a crisp, hollow thump. The soldier jerked out the blade and gawked at the damage, white with terror. Bond took him by the elbow and gently led him out from under the wing, receiving a look of pure, beatific gratitude. Enlisted men in Chinese armies could be shot for such transgressions.

As the four Caucasians pressed through the melee, an arm shot out and snatched Bixby's briefcase. Bixby swore and shouted, to no avail. The case disappeared into the crowd, along with all the special "first flight" covers he'd planned to mail from Chengtu—decorative envelopes, stamped and canceled and carried on the first airmail flight between two cities, much coveted by philatelists.

The Chengtu postal commissioner expected them, and he was waiting with his chauffeur on the outskirts of the crowd. He drove them to the old Manchu governor's yamen, converted into a military headquarters by General Liu Wen-wei, Marshal Liu Hsiang's rebellious uncle. An adjutant introduced them to the mayor, the Chinese secretary of the YMCA, and General Liu. Bixby mentioned his stolen briefcase and explained how the theft cost him face. Many people counted on him to post the first-flight covers, and he hadn't justified their trust. A staff officer copied a description of the case and its contents into a notebook and promised every official in Chengtu would do what they could to recover it.

Midafternoon, the Americans flew back to Chungking toting a few bags of mail. Based on postal statistics, flying airmail from Chungking to Chengtu would be immediately profitable, but CNAC's warlord politicking spotlighted Kuomintang impotence in Szechwan, and somewhere in their scramble to establish service, Bond and Bixby had neglected to kowtow sufficiently to Central Government eminence. A bull from Nanking ordered the airline to suspend the Chungking-to-Chengtu route. The edict came without explanation, but Bond recognized the face-making flex of Central Government muscle. In truth, Bond appreciated the delay, for they couldn't operate safely from the tiny parade ground. The Nanking decree wasn't made public, so he and Bixby cabled Chengtu authorities saying they couldn't begin until the city built a suitable landing facility. A month later, having made sufficient face, the Central Government instructed CNAC to resume service. Happily, the order coincided with Chengtu's speedy leveling of an airfield.

For Bixby, it had been a grand adventure; for Bond, it was business as usual in China. Bixby returned to Shanghai impressed by Bond's knowledge, competence, passion, and qualities as a travel companion, and although Bond's professional circumstances weren't tangibly improved, the expedition laid the foundation of a friendship. Strangely, Bixby's missing briefcase arrived in Shanghai with every first-flight cover inside, albeit with all the uncanceled stamps steamed off and stolen. A letter from Chengtu's mayor accompanied the case—written in Chinese, of course. Bixby asked his dinner companion, a Chinese general, to translate. Apparently, the mayor was out for a walk when he spotted the briefcase under a coolie's arm, a suspiciously amazing stroke of good fortune, and the mayor's escort clapped the coolie into handcuffs. The letter promised the coolie had been "appropriately punished."

Bixby asked what that might imply.

The general paused, a bite pinned between the points of his chopsticks. "They separated the coolie from his head, of course." He shrugged and popped the morsel into his mouth.

Bixby restamped the letters out of his own pocket and returned them to Chengtu, where they were officially airmailed with a small chit explaining the delay.

5

ROUTE THREE

Pan American's seven-man China expedition reached Shanghai aboard the SS *Gertrude Maersk* on June 28, 1933. Wearing a white tropical suit and a pith helmet to combat the sweltering heat, Harold Bixby met the arrivals with a galvanizing edict: If the airline was to retain the rights to the route they'd come halfway around the world to operate, the team had to assemble and test one of the S-38 amphibians they'd brought to China, fly to Canton, and return with mail within ten days.

Craggy-browed Zygmund "Sol" Soldinski, the expedition's hard-drinking Polish chief mechanic, supervised a gang of Chinese stevedores as they carefully transferred the wings, fuselages, engine crates, and other delicate aviation gear ashore from the *Gertrude Maersk* and then just as carefully stowed it aboard a barge for the shallow-draft tug up the Whangpoo to Lunghwa Airport. Soldinski spewed steady invective, his face flushed bright red, but he worked from first light until last, dripping sweat, and over the course of the next forty-eight hours, the first of Pan Am's strange-looking S-38 amphibians took shape under the thatched roof of a bamboo lean-to beside CNAC's Lunghwa hangar. Wingtip to wingtip, the S-38 spanned more than seventy feet. It was forty feet long and stood nearly fourteen feet tall, and visually, it had two distinct halves—an upper and a lower. The upper part was a large wing that jutted two booms rearward to a pair of vertical stabilizers and rudders joined by a long horizontal stabilizer. The lower half consisted of the airplane's hull, which looked as much like the hull of a small sailing yacht as it did a six-passenger airplane cabin. Less charitably, the hull could also have been described as a duck bill or a man's unmatched shoe. A stubby set of half wings protruded from the hull, with pontoons hung beneath to keep the plane stable on the water. At least eighteen struts and supports joined the upper and lower halves and held two 400-horsepower Pratt & Whitney Wasp engines in place between them. With broad upper wings and dwarf lower ones, the S-38 wasn't a monoplane, but it wasn't quite a biplane, either. Designed to bridge the gap between the Neanderthal Loenings and sleeker, more modern seaplanes, it seemed like a flying missing link. Pan American had used S-38s to good effect spanning the Caribbean, but they were obsolete by 1933, and Pan Am planned to use them in China only as stopgaps, until they could be replaced with one of the higher-performing seaplane types poised to emerge from the design sheds of Douglas, Sikorsky, or Boeing. In the meantime, the S-38 was the best option.

Along with the airplanes, engines, mechanics, pilots, radiomen, and rafts of sundry equipment they'd shipped to China, Pan American included its own operations man, William Stephen Grooch, a Germanic-looking Texan with brush-cut hair and wide, innocent eyes, known to everyone as Bill. He'd pioneered an airline between New York and Buenos Aires that Pan American bought in 1930, absorbing Grooch along with its other assets, and Pan Am sent him to China hoping to capitalize on his developmental aviation experience. Grooch test-flew the first S-38 on July 1, 1933, less than seventy-two hours after arriving. Two days later, he piloted it south toward Canton, with Bond, Bixby, business manager P. Y. Wong, and three other Pan Am personnel lounging in the passenger cabin. Comfort did not extend to conversation, however—it was almost impossible to hear beneath the two Wasp engines thundering above the un-soundproofed hull. The flight down the Chinese seaboard was magnificent, over a jagged, broken coastline and hundreds of islands, but William Bond studied it with trepidation. The islands would be difficult to recognize in bad weather or fog, and their rugged profusion and craggy hills prevented an airplane from safely hugging the shore beneath bad weather. They spent the night in

Foochow and flew the rest of the way to Hong Kong the following day, barely escaping disaster when the amphibian nosed over in soft dirt at Hong Kong's crude Kai Tak Airfield. Fortunately, the airplane wasn't seriously damaged, and they flew the final seventy-five miles to Canton on the morning of July 5, on schedule to return mail to Shanghai on or before the July 8 deadline.

All proceeded well until the Canton post office refused to give Bixby any airmail, and without mail Bixby couldn't fulfill the terms of the contract. It was hard to discern the decision's wellspring. It may have been the more or less independent Canton government making face at Nanking's expense; it could have been the Ministry of Communications fishing for concessions from Pan American; or Sino-German Eurasia interests scheming to seize Route Three for themselves. Bixby examined the contract. It specified that *mail* had to be carried prior to July 8. It said nothing about *airmail*. Bixby persuaded Canton's English postal commissioner to give him several sacks of ordinary mail, and the Americans stowed the sacks aboard the S-38, flew northeast, and delivered them to the Shanghai post office on July 8, securing CNAC's claim to Route Three on the last allowable day.

The mission saved the contractual rights to the Shanghai–Canton line, but it was a one-off stunt. From a practical perspective, Bixby didn't have an airmail contract or an operating agreement with Chinese officials, and the thousand-mile route couldn't support scheduled operations without mid-route mechanics, fuel depots, radio and weather stations, ticket agents, and terminals in cities far removed from the Chinese mainstream.

Trying to reach some mutually acceptable plan, Bixby wrangled with board chairman K. C. Huang all through the muggy summer of 1933. Since China would accrue so many of its benefits, Bixby wanted CNAC to share in Route Three's development costs, and he wanted the Chinese to allow Pan American to operate Route Three with Pan American pilots wearing Pan American uniforms in Pan American airplanes flying the American flag—the only way Route Three would earn American airmail subsidies.

K. C. Huang and the other Chinese directors shrugged and stalled, counterproposing that Pan American alone finance Route Three's development, furnish the planes and personnel, fly the route, do it in CNAC livery, under the Chinese flag, and remit a guaranteed portion of Route Three's revenues. They wanted a commission on all of Pan Am's transpacific tickets sold in the Middle Kingdom, and they steadfastly refused to let Pan Am land American-flagged planes in China. Bixby was gradually being forced to recognize the unalterable truth of what Bond had told him months before: Nothing on earth would induce China to grant that right.

Bixby's mission was to prepare the Asian end of Pan Am's proposed transpacific line, but he'd already been in the Far East more than six months, and besides buying into CNAC, he'd accomplished very little. Stymied, Bixby fished for creative solutions. He considered having Pan Am planes leave Manila under the American flag and change to Chinese colors before the flights crossed the mainland coast. The concept seemed sound until U.S. ambassador Nelson T. Johnson quietly reminded him that international law regarded changing flags on the high seas as an act of piracy.

Even though it was proving impossible to use Route Three to link Canton and Manila directly, the route's geography presented an intriguing opportunity to end-run most-favored nation complications. Pan Am's 45 percent stake in the China National Aviation Corporation was a minority holding. The airline was a *Chinese* company. CNAC flights could operate in and out of China without complications, and Route Three's Canton terminus was only thirty minutes of flying time from Hong Kong and Macau, the British and Portuguese colonies on opposite sides of the Pearl River Delta. Hong Kong was a piddling place compared to Shanghai in 1933, a few thousand Europeans planted among half a million Chinese, and Macau was smaller still, so neither place could profitably anchor the service, but if both CNAC and Pan American could secure permission to operate from either colony, then passengers could cross the Pacific to the mainland coast and transfer to CNAC flights for the last leg to Shanghai.

Unfortunately, gaining landing rights in Hong Kong or Macau promised another rash of complications. Grooch flew Bixby to Manila to try to secure Philippine landing rights for Pan American, but Bixby wasn't any more successful in the Philippines than he was in Hong Kong, Macau, or mainland China. The rights issues remained pitfalls that could crash the entire transpacific endeavor. Back in Shanghai, Bixby resumed his tug-of-war with CNAC's Chinese leadership. Not having his family in China kept him at a significant disadvantage, creating the impression he was in a rush. The Chinese waited, and the pressure mounted. The negotiations were contentious, but Bixby's calm demeanor, unimposing physical presence, and ready humor allowed him to press his case without giving offense, and he had the important Oriental knack of not arguing his opponents into positions from which they couldn't retreat with their dignity intact.

As Bond had already learned, and Bixby was discovering to his consternation, China was far from a nation of homogeneous millions marching in lockstep toward common goals. Quite the opposite, in fact: It was a tremendously complicated and ruthlessly competitive society in which individuals elbowed each other for the slightest scraps of advantage. Tiny margins could, and did, make the difference between life and death for the millions of Chinese lives on the razor's edge of survival. Ideology and geography fractured the national canvas, and each fragment struggled to dominate the country's destiny. Chiang Kai-shek's apparent sacrifice of north China raised the ire of many patriots, but nearly all Chinese political propaganda, from whatever source, espoused a patriotic, anti-Japanese, antiforeign agenda, most of it advocating a united front against the invaders. Reality didn't match the rhetoric, however, and the factions continued their bloody enmities without compromise.

The Kuomintang considered Communist Party membership a capital offense. Communist cells retaliated by murdering Nanking agents at every opportunity. A few minutes before midnight on August 25, 1933, a Kuomintang internal security officer—dispatched to exterminate Communists in cooperation with Shanghai's Public Safety Bureau—and his bodyguard entered the elevator of Shanghai's Sun Sun Hotel. Just as the newfangled automatic doors began to close, two men barged inside, drew guns, and disabled the bodyguard with a shot through the thigh. The triggerman paused, then pronounced the committee's sentence in clipped language and killed the Kuomintang agent with three bullets to the head. Both assassins escaped. The agent's predecessor had been murdered the previous year, but by no means was the Communist-Nationalist strife the only clash undermining national unity. Violence assailed most corners of the Middle Kingdom. In Szechwan, warlord Marshal Liu Hsiang quashed the last vestiges of his uncle's rebellion, and *The China Weekly Review* reported the Dalai Lama of Tibet "taking advantage of the Szechwan chaos to try and capture Sikang." Murderous corsairs plundered the coasts of Fukien and Kwangtung provinces, and no sensible captain steered his ship anywhere near the notorious pirate lairs of Bias Bay, sixty miles northeast of Hong Kong. The Nineteenth Route Army, heroic defenders of Shanghai in the 1932 war, rebelled against the Central Government, advocating stronger anti-Japanese resistance. The southern provinces of Kwantung and Kwangsi maintained their own governments and their own armies and didn't remit a penny of revenue to Nanking.

William Bond remained in professional limbo. He spent the summer and fall of 1933 in the background, apart from Pan American, overseeing CNAC operations on Routes One and Two. William Grooch was Pan American's operations manager in China. If CNAC and Pan Am merged more tightly, Pan Am would want its own man running the combined show. Bixby was combing the Shanghai aviation community for a permanent assistant and appeared fixed on Edward P. Howard, an aviation man on the staff of the Shanghai Trade Commission. Bond was improving his relationship with Bixby, but as far as Bond knew, he wasn't even being considered for the position.

Bixby became increasingly anxious as the clock ticked into autumn. Pan Am was in a hurry, China was not, and CNAC chairman K. C. Huang knew it. Huang held out for his terms, and at last the two men inked an agreement on October 8, 1933. Pan American Airways formed a wholly owned subsidiary, called *Pacific* American Airways, to develop and operate Route Three. Pan Am would provide the planes and personnel, and Pacific American would operate Route Three in CNAC livery under a charter arrangement crafted to deflect most-favored-nation complications. CNAC would get 20 percent of money earned from airmail carried on Route Three, 7.5 percent of passenger revenue, and 10 percent of all transpacific sales made in China. Pan Am would contribute $250,000 for Route Three's ground installations and airplanes. In return, the Ministry of Communications would loan CNAC $7,500 a month for three years, to be repaid out of net profits (4.1 million modern dollars from Pan Am; $122,000 per month from the ministry).

For China, it was a superb bargain. With no obligations and no capital investment, Huang secured Pan Am's commitment to develop a new Chinese airline, virtually guaranteeing CNAC a profit against negligible risk. Pan American also got what it wanted, however—the ability to construct an airline across the Pacific from San Francisco to Shanghai. Bixby and Huang attended a dinner party afterward, and Huang waxed on and on about how petrified he'd been on a tiger-hunting expedition in Indochina, perched in the crook of a tree with a lamb tied beneath. A tiger appeared! If he fell from the tree, he'd be eaten!

Bixby interrupted, waving for silence. "Stop, stop, stop! K.C., if you *had* fallen out of that tree, I'd have bet on you, and I'd have given the tiger first bite."

The party collapsed in hysterics, and Huang beamed. Nothing could entirely eliminate the frictions between Pan Am and CNAC's Chinese ownership, but the good-humored compliment represented an important step toward a collaborative atmosphere, and ever afterward, K. C. Huang was known as "Tiger Huang."

With an arrangement finally in place, Pan Am operations manager William Grooch rushed to get Route Three into action. Grooch and two other Pan Am men, Robert Gast and Bill Ehmer, flew the first airmail from Shanghai to Canton on October 24 and 25, 1933. The service operated without hang-ups for a month, and Grooch scheduled passenger flights to begin on November 24. The Pan American people were cocksure and confident, certain they were the best, most experienced aviation men in the world at over-water and coastal operations, and they didn't feel they had much to learn from a bush-league foreign outfit like the China National Aviation Corporation, including its chief pilot, Ernie Allison.

William Bond wasn't so sure. It seemed too rushed. Weather on the Chinese coast deteriorated after the middle of November, and he didn't think the Pan Am people were ready for it. The inception of airmail service had been tied to Bixby's negotiations, and their glacial pace prevented the Pan Am pilots from thoroughly familiarizing themselves with the route during the good-weather months. They had scads of experience flying over South America and the Caribbean, but China was different. For starters, the Caribbean didn't suffer much fog. China was plagued by it, and for airplanes flying in 1933, no weather was worse. Reliable radio navigation aids didn't exist. Airplanes absolutely had to fly underneath fog—they couldn't risk losing visual contact with terra firma for fear they would be unable to gently regain it. Allison seconded Bond's unease, and Bond especially didn't approve of the Pan Am people's attitude toward his seasoned, superb chief pilot, but every time Bond or Allison tried to broach the subject of reasonable caution, they were shut down by a "let us show you how it's done" attitude.

Inland, on the extension of Route One from Chungking to Chengtu, Bond and Allison's approach was very different—they wouldn't let the flights carry passengers until they'd proofed the route for *six months,* and compared with Route Three, Chungking to Chengtu was a much simpler flight. Route Three wasn't their show, however.

Bixby and Grooch sold all seven seats for Route Three's first passenger run and assigned George Rummel and copilot Bill Ehmer to the flight. November 24, 1933, was a damp, gray morning, and it was biting cold inside the S-38's cockpit and cabin, but it was flyable, and all the passengers were aboard by 6 A.M., including Lady Carlisle, niece of the British ambassador. Lady Carlisle's aristocratic manner raised democratic American hackles, but the ground crew strapped her into her seat for an on-time departure.

Bond was at the airport in connection with his duties managing the Peiping and Yangtze lines, and wearing long overcoats and their ever-present fedoras, he and Grooch stood outside the hangar and watched Rummel's S-38 take to the air, circle the field, and head south. Grooch remarked on the steady pace of aviation progress. Bond kept silent, but he couldn't shake his unease. Pan Am hadn't installed weather stations on the coast south of Shanghai, so there weren't many facts to work with, but Bond sniffed the air and thought the damp, cold autumn morning could easily presage coastal fog. With the plane away, Grooch figured his responsibilities ended, and he returned to his apartment. Bond was the only manager on site twenty minutes later when Rummel radioed that he was turning back over Hangchow Bay due to fog. Bond telephoned Grooch, but received no answer.

Deeply frustrated, George Rummel touched down back at Lunghwa at 6:50 A.M. Pan Am took pride in keeping its schedules, particularly on first flights, and he was anxious to get back under way. Rummel asked Bond for instructions. Bond reminded him that he was CNAC's operations man, not Pan American's, or Pacific American's, or whatever the hell they wanted to call themselves, and that Pan American had made the line exceptionally clear. Bond could, however, give Rummel advice. He was quite willing to do that. Rummel nodded, and Bond outlined CNAC's fog-flying policy.

Pilots regularly encountered fog in the Yangtze valley, and they'd learned never to fly through it over water without terrestrial reference. Over-water fogs could quickly become "zero-zero," zero visibility and zero ceiling, with gray water blending into gray fog so completely that a pilot couldn't tell where one began and the other ended and might unwittingly fly straight into the water. In Yangtze fogs, CNAC fliers flew along one of the riverbanks. If they couldn't continue, they executed their about-face over land, an axiom Bond and Allison considered so important that they allowed their pilots to deviate from it only in an emergency, so if Rummel wanted to fly in accord with CNAC policy, he should contour the north coast of Hangchow Bay and not cross it unless he spotted the opposite shore.

Two hours passed without word from Grooch, and Rummel decided to take off. Bond didn't like it, but he couldn't actually order Rummel not to fly. Instead, he asked Rummel to radio his position every half hour. Rummel agreed, and he left Lunghwa for the second time at 8:35 A.M. Thirty minutes passed without signal. Five more minutes ticked by, Bond's anxiety mounting with each passing second. Nine people were aboard the airplane. Bond telephoned Grooch again, and this time he answered. Bond *suggested* he return to the airport immediately. By the time Grooch reached the airport, there still wasn't word from the airplane, and it was obvious something had gone seriously awry. Grooch notified Bixby and took off to look for Rummel in Pan Am's other S-38. Bond and Allison joined the search in a Loening, taking a Chinese mechanic along to interpret if the need arose.

Bond and Allison flew south over canals, rice paddies, and vegetable patches until they reached Hangchow Bay, which was blanketed by fog. Allison skirted the northern shoreline until the fog thinned and he could see the opposite coast. He flew across and tracked east toward the bay mouth. The mist lifted to reveal the bulk of Seshan Island, the only serious obstacle in the bay, and Allison steered out to examine it.

The remains of Rummel's S-38 littered the island's four-hundred-foot hilltop. They buzzed the wreckage and saw no life. Bond radioed Grooch. Allison landed in a harbor and beached the airplane, and he, Bond, and the mechanic ran uphill. Torn and twisted metal lay strewn across the small peak at the end of a long gouge. Impact had bounced both engines across the landscape. Huge gashes rent the cabin. Bond and Allison reached it gasping, expecting carnage. Inside, they found no bodies. Several local fishermen appeared, and the mechanic interpreted: Many injuries, no one killed; the passengers evacuated to Minghong; the locals didn't think anyone would die.

Bond visited the victims in a Shanghai hospital that night. They'd been very lucky. George Rummel was crossing the bay in a thick fog when the island loomed out of the murk. He hauled on the yoke and zoomed up, but the plane hit just as it ran tangent to the hillside. Rummel had a deep cut in his scalp, but no broken bones. Three of the passengers' necks or backs were broken or fractured; none were paralyzed. After impact, Lady Carlisle, with two broken ankles, found herself under a heap of Chinese gentlemen. In typical British fashion, as bloody-minded as she'd been before the wreck, she'd been staunch and courageous afterward, and she was full of praise for copilot Bill Ehmer, who'd crawled through dripping gasoline to succor the wounded and shepherd them to safety despite his own pair of fractured ankles.* Several other passengers had broken bones. Everyone was bruised, cut, and shocked, but all things considered, the butcher's bill was amazingly light. Nobody died. Nevertheless, the Shanghai newspapers reveled in the disaster.

In the aftermath, CNAC held a directors' meeting. Although the pall of Rummel's crash hung heavy over the meeting, Chairman Huang didn't mention it. He solicited reports on the past year's earnings and expenses, listened to projections for the coming season, and ticked through his list, point by point. Bond felt more and more like a guest at the wedding of a six-months-pregnant bride. There it was; polite company just didn't mention it. Finally, Huang pronounced the formal agenda complete. Smoke from his cigarette curled toward the ceiling as he sat back in his chair. Suddenly, he turned on Bond. "You're the operations manager. I would like to hear your explanation of this accident."

Bond was stunned. He had nothing to do with Route Three! That was Pan Am's bag. He was in no way responsible. Just as he was about to protest, he caught himself. Considering the tensions between the Pan Am and Chi-

---

* Ehmer's heroism earned him a date with Lady Carlisle after their release from the hospital. Unfortunately, nothing came of the relationship.

nese factions, it was impossible to see who would try to profit from the accident and how, but either could crush him. He'd survive only if he proved valuable on both sides of the table.

Bond began, choosing his words with extreme care. "It was an unfortunate event. Everybody in the operations department is upset about it, nobody more so than me. But that doesn't answer your question." Huang nodded. "Several factors caused Rummel's accident. First, the weather. It was flyable at Shanghai. It wasn't over Hangchow Bay, which we didn't know because we haven't built a weather station there. Second, the airplane. It's inadequate. It was airworthy, of course, but the S-38 doesn't have the speed or range to give a pilot maximum safety on Route Three. We'll have next-step flying boats within a year, but we can't afford to wait another year for fear we'll lose the rights to a route which will probably grow into our most important."

As the meeting broke up, Harold Bixby discreetly gestured Bond to follow him from the room. Bixby closed his office door and sized up the middleweight Virginian. "You, Bondy, are a scholar and a gentleman. You took the rap for that accident, and you had nothing to do with it."

Bond shrugged. "Everybody in the room knew that, Bix, including old Tiger Huang. He probably expected me to deny responsibility. He might have wanted me to. Then he could have blamed Pan American. Who knows where he'd have gone with that?"

There was another plausible angle to the chairman's query. Chairman Huang might have deliberately given Bond a chance to make face with Pan American. Huang couldn't seriously have wanted to void CNAC's contract with Pan Am. No other airline could provide the same spectrum of opportunities. The Chinese directors were lobbying to integrate Routes One, Two, and Three under CNAC's umbrella, which would save money and boost efficiency, and a more thorough merge would amplify Pan American's interest in China's fate. Pan American had resisted such integration, however, not wanting to dilute the "Pan Am–ness" of Route Three. Huang must also have been aware of the arrogance of the Pan Am crew. They lorded it over the airline's Americans; they'd surely be worse with the airline's Chinese staff. As for the China National Aviation Corporation, Bond was their man. He'd proved himself in the last two and a half years. If Huang was contemplating a tighter merger, better one under Bond's direction than any other.

. . .

William Grooch flew reduced schedules on Route Three with the one remaining S-38. Bixby requisitioned another from the United States before sailing home in early January to report to the Pan Am leadership and make preparations to return with his wife and four daughters. Bill Grooch had his wife and their six- and seven-year-old sons, William and Thomas, already with him in Shanghai, but his wife's father was seriously ill back home. Financial anxieties, worry about her father, and a deep loathing of life in China drove her into a horrible depression. On the night of January 19, 1934, Mrs. Grooch took her two boys up to the rooftop garden of their fashionable apartment, ostensibly to enjoy the city lights. On top, she gathered both sons into her arms and leapt from the edge. All three died on the pavement, eight floors below.

Bond rushed to the scene and took charge of Bill Grooch's personal affairs. He moved Grooch into his own apartment, suspended both of their duties, and wouldn't let Grooch leave his sight, even refusing his bereaved associate permission to close the bathroom door. Grooch sat catatonic at Bond's dining table, bestirring himself only occasionally to pound the table with a fist and demand one reason that he shouldn't go to the roof and jump off himself. Bond couldn't think of a single one. Life was like that, that was all. Bond poured whisky to keep them both numb and stayed with Grooch for a week or ten days without break. A month later, Bond began taking him to the airport. Bond worked and Grooch sat in the car, his soul crushed, and although grief-stricken, he refused to relinquish his duties. The replacement S-38 arrived, and Grooch returned to work. Pan American group resumed its Route Three schedules.

It sold just one seat on April 10, 1934, to a Japanese businessman, who took off into mixed skies at 6 A.M. aboard an S-38 manned by Pan Am pilot Robert Gast and two crew members. Half an hour later, Gast radioed that he was aborting due to dense fog. He returned to Lunghwa, waited, and took off again at 8:12 A.M. Thirty minutes later, he sent a position report. An unsigned message arrived a few minutes after: *Turning back.* The plane never appeared, and the parallels were obvious. Bond and Allison searched for Gast in Pan Am's other S-38; Grooch used a Loening commandeered from the Yangtze line. Dirty, yellow-tinged fog over Hangchow Bay forced both aircraft back to Lunghwa.

The fog didn't lift until noon the following day. Grooch set off as soon as the ceiling raised a few hundred feet, flying the S-38 with CNAC captain Cecil Sellers; Hugh Woods, a Pan Am copilot from Winfield, Kansas; and one of the English-speaking Chinese mechanics. They flew south, but fog still lingered over Hangchow Bay. Frantic to do something, anything, to aid his missing airman, Grooch landed on the bay and searched on the sea surface like a ship. An hour before dark, he taxied toward a man on Lighthouse Island, cut the engines, and dropped their anchor. The man hadn't seen the missing plane, but a coastal steamer had gone by a few minutes before. Maybe Gast was on it? Unfortunately, the anchor wouldn't budge. Woods, Sellers, and Grooch heaved, the rope broke, and the fouled anchor stayed on the bottom, sinking their plan to spend the night anchored in an island's lee.

Grooch flew over and landed in front of the steamer that had just passed the island. The ship had no news of Gast, and the captain refused to give them a spare chunk of iron they might use as a replacement anchor. Just enough light remained to fly back to Lunghwa. Woods radioed for the weather: *Thick fog, visibility zero* came the reply.

Night fell and it began to rain, lightly at first, but before long it was "raining pitchforks" and blowing a near gale. Grooch started the engines and taxied twenty miles out to sea. He shut down the Wasps at ten o'clock, ordered Woods and Sellers to attach the engine covers, and had them knot a canvas sheet to the airplane's nose and toss it into the ocean to keep the plane pointed upwind. By midnight, a northeasterly gale was shredding the sea surface and choppy swells pounded the airplane, driving them toward the coast. They had a lighthouse dead astern an hour later. Grooch taxied back out to sea and the four men spent the rest of the night bailing for their lives.

Dawn found them wallowing toward another group of islands, beneath a ceiling raised a few hundred feet, enough to fly, but the huge swells prevented them from taking off. Grooch examined the charts. The nearest shelter was in the mouth of the Yung River, twenty-five miles to the south. Grooch taxied crosswise to the wind; a gust nearly capsized the plane. The only way to make progress was to motor several miles out to sea, cut the engines, toss the sea anchor, and let the plane make an angled drift inshore. Each drift gained the S-38 one or two southward miles. They repeated the process all day, until right before sundown, when the S-38 ended its final drift at the mouth of the Yung River, exactly as planned, but the river's outward current halted the plane's forward movement. The plane pitched up and down at the confluence of river and sea and edged laterally toward a shoal of lethal rocks. Grooch fired a distress signal.

A small steamship came alongside and tossed a towline. The fliers tied it to the S-38's tail, but the steamer started too fast, and the plane slewed. Its lower wings dipped into the waves, crumpled, and tore completely off. Three miles upriver, in utter darkness, the steamer captain made a sharp turn in a tight channel, and a gust of wind blew the airplane even farther out of line. One of its upper wingtips impaled the prow of an anchored junk, dragging it from its mooring. The junk crew ran forward with axes and chopped off the end of the S-38's wing to free their vessel. The steamer dropped anchor a short distance farther on, by which time Grooch's airplane was a mangled wreck, a complete washout. Miraculously, nobody was hurt.

Bill Grooch was stuck with his airplane carcass. It again fell to William Bond to do damage control for Pan American. He broke the news to chairman of the board K. C. Huang and Dai Enkai, who had succeeded General Ho as CNAC's managing director. Bond told it like it was; there was no hiding the totality of the Pan American fiasco. The MD was polite and sympathetic; K. C. Huang was rather less so. In six months, Pan Am had wrecked two airplanes, killed four, injured nine, and its vaunted air service was at a complete standstill. Dazed, his career in tatters, his family dead, William Grooch returned to the United States.

Seven days later, Harold Bixby cabled William Bond and summoned him to New York. A pair of mail sacks, a seat cushion, a few chunks of wood, and three report books were the only fragments of Gast's plane ever recovered. A fisherman pulled his badly decomposed body out of Hangchow Bay two months later.

6

A PAN AM MAN AND A WOMAN NAMED KITSI

Forty-year-old William Bond left Shanghai aboard the SS *President Hoover* in the last week of April 1934. He slept ten hours a day during the crossing, surprised by his exhaustion until he realized he hadn't had a vacation in three years. He swam in the ship's pool, played deck tennis, and socialized with the other passengers, but mostly he just relaxed with some of the better volumes in the *Hoover*'s library. Bond was acutely aware of his lack of higher education, and he'd acquired a taste for highbrow literature as part of an ongoing self-improvement campaign. The Pacific lived up to its name for once, and Bond felt much refreshed when the *Hoover* steamed through the Golden Gate into San Francisco Bay seventeen days after leaving Shanghai, past the enormous piers, trestles, towers, and anchorages under construction on both flanks of the strait. Cable spinning for what was intended to become the world's longest suspension bridge wasn't scheduled to begin for another year.

Ashore, Bond drank his first legal American cocktail since 1920, delighted that piece of civic stupidity had been excised from the U.S. Constitution, and flew overnight to New York City on United Airlines. Domestic aviation had made great strides while Bond was in China. A cross-country trail of beacons marked the nighttime portion of the flight route, the pilots flew dot-to-dot as if they were following Hansel and Gretel's bread crumbs, and Bond crossed the entire continent in less than twenty hours. Three years earlier, his transcontinental train journey had taken the better part of five days.

The excitement of the Pacific project electrified Pan American's offices high in the Chrysler Building in midtown Manhattan, and Bond spent three days in conclave with the corporate leadership. Technically, Pan Am could extend service only as far as Manila and claim to have spanned the Pacific, but the line wouldn't be profitable without Shanghai, and Bond was delighted to discover the standing that gave him in Pan Am boardrooms.

After New York, Bond visited his mother in Petersburg, Virginia, then embarked on an extensive tour of the Pan Am system that took him around the Caribbean and through the capitals of Central America. Pan Am chief engineer Andre Priester summoned him back to New York in August. A short, bald Dutchman with a thick old-country accent, Priester ran everything in any way connected to flying at Pan American. Bond stood in Priester's office and admired his immaculate desk. No surgeon would think twice about operating on such a pristine surface. Grief-stricken William Grooch would not return to China, Priester informed Bond. Two brand new Douglas Dolphin amphibians would replace the lost S-38s and reactivate Route Three, and henceforth, Route Three would be added to Bond's responsibilities. Pan American would provide financial and technical support, but Bond would be in charge. He was in "the System" at last, great news considering how long he'd struggled for job security, but Bond expressed no joy, unwilling to celebrate another man's misfortune.

Three years was the American businessman's standard tour of duty in the Far East, and Bond didn't expect to see his mother and brother again until he'd served another stint, so he swung through Virginia to make his goodbyes before heading to Vancouver to meet the SS *Empress of Japan*, the same vessel on which he'd sailed to China in 1931. The ship lay at the docks like a nautical greyhound, the fastest passenger liner in the Pacific, capable of sustaining twenty-two knots, and under any other circumstances Bond would have delighted in the velocity, but by the time the *Empress* got herself up to speed in open ocean beyond Vancouver Island, Bond found himself wishing she'd travel a whole lot slower. The reason was Miss Katharine Dunlop, a bright, witty, twenty-nine-year-old ray of sunshine with short, tightly permed brown hair that had a penchant to spring into sudden, intoxicating disarray. Miss Dunlop hailed from an old Washington, D.C., family, where her father was a successful, well-connected attorney, and she'd been educated at the elite Holton-Arms School before attending Vassar. The Dunlop estate, Hayes Manor, which had been in the family since 1792, was considered among the finest examples of Georgian colonial architecture in Montgomery County. Nearing thirty, Katharine Dunlop was a tad old for an eligible, high-society girl from such a prominent, well-heeled family, especially considering her gracious carriage, calm smile, and warm, intelligent eyes, but she carried a dark encumbrance that seemed forever destined to prevent her from marrying: Her mother was a holy terror as far as her daughter's romances were concerned and had already sabotaged several suitors. Katharine seized upon the idea of traveling to the Orient with Anne Covington Clark, a college classmate whose husband was a State Department officer posted to China, as the first step in a six-to-twelve-month round-the-world voyage designed to free herself of her mother's romantic subterfuges. So far, the plan seemed to be working— long before the *Empress* reached Honolulu, they had become "Kitsi" and "Bondy" to each other.

The charmed voyage continued beyond Hawaii. The two played bridge with other couples and swam in the pool on D deck. They watched movies in the ship's cinema, new "talkies" with sound, and wandered the six passenger decks, admiring the elaborately patterned floors and the dark natural-wood interiors. They chatted and smoked in the first-class lounge while a pianist played the latest tunes on an enormous grand. Bond's dedicated reading program stood him in good stead in his conversations with the charming Vassar girl, as did his store of witty, adventurous Oriental anecdotes. They dressed for dinner and sipped drinks against a curving bar in the cocktail lounge and danced on the beautifully sprung floor of the ballroom at the forward end of the promenade deck.

Kitsi badly wanted to avail herself of the opportunity to visit the thousand-year-old city of Kyoto while the ship was in Japan, an excursion that could just be managed by leaving the ship in Yokohama, taking an overnight train to Kyoto, spending a day sightseeing, and taking another train to rejoin the *Empress* at Kobe. Anne Covington Clark wasn't so enthusiastic about accompanying her. It seemed like an awful lot of rushing about with an eighteen-month-old toddler in tow.

Hearing of the conundrum, Bond proposed he escort Kitsi to Kyoto.

Kitsi stared at him as though he were about to sprout cloven hooves and horns.

"Wonderful!" Anne Clark chirped. "It's a beautiful trip. Bondy'll take good care of you."

Kitsi was equally astonished by her friend. Anne had given her no end of warnings about "China bachelors," whose fat paychecks and ready access to Shanghai's lurid pleasures allowed them to acquire significantly more experience than a well-bred society girl might want to associate with too closely. Anne Clark wasn't blindly tossing her friend to the wolf, however. The expatriate community was tight-knit. She'd checked among shipboard acquaintances and discovered generally fine impressions of the hardworking aviation missionary wooing her friend. Bond drank and smoked and had a good time, but all within reasonable bounds. If he'd committed any serious indiscretions during his three years in the Orient, he'd managed to keep them to himself.

In Kyoto, Bondy and Kitsi rambled through peaceful temples whose roofs soared through the forest tops. Sliding doors whispered open; in the hush, their feet squeaked on floors made intentionally creaky, and they wandered among wood and paper architecture of exquisite delicacy. Outdoors, among the Zen gardens, flowers and statuettes peeked through profusions of shrubbery, sublimely situated to enhance the natural mystery around them. They walked through a forest and along the shore of a small lake. Only the lazy seethings of the koi gathering at their feet disturbed the midnight velvet surface of the pond. Kitsi slipped her arm through Bond's, and a pleasing serenity settled onto his heart, entirely erasing his usual state of supercharged intensity.

The *Empress of Japan* reached Shanghai two days later. Shipboard romances were notoriously short-lived. Open-ocean magic rarely survived the realities of life on dry land. Anne Clark's husband flew down from Peiping. Kitsi may have been playing hard to get, but whether by design or not, the Clarks' social and diplomatic calendar dominated her slate for the next five days. She made time for only one date with William Bond.

He took her for cocktails, dinner, and dancing at the Little Club, an intimate and convivial nightclub near the Park Hotel on Bubbling Wells

Road, flavored with racy Shanghai spice by its American, ex-convict owner, peppy jazz combo, and a phalanx of splendidly turned-out White Russian dance hostesses, haughty beauties who demanded fistfuls of dance tickets before they'd deign to take a few turns around the floor with tipsy, toe-treading businessmen. Bondy and Kitsi's evening ended a scant few hours before sunrise.

The next morning, Bond saw her and the Clarks onto one of his Peiping-bound Stinsons. By the time the plane disappeared into the skies to the north, Bond admitted to himself that he'd fallen hopelessly in love with Miss Katharine Dunlop. He just had no intention of telling her quite yet.

Although Bond had had girlfriends before—his previous girlfriend, Stasia, short for Anastasia, was a stunning White Russian refugee—he'd been a bachelor his whole life, and as he crept toward his forty-first birthday, he found himself beginning to crave more permanent companionship. It was strange; for all its faults, Shanghai, so vibrantly alive, seemed a fine place to raise a family. But in his more realistic moments, Bond knew he couldn't responsibly court a woman without having a firm grip on his own future. While he'd been in the United States, Ernie Allison had temporarily replaced him as operations manager. Now that he'd returned, the airline's Chinese leadership wanted to keep Allison in that position. Allie had much more experience with the nuts and bolts of airline operations, and as a vastly experienced commercial flier he had standing with other pilots that Bond wouldn't ever possess. Fortunately, by mid-1934 Harold Bixby didn't think that he, Pan American, or the China National Aviation Corporation could afford to lose William Bond. Bixby made Bond a CNAC vice president, one of its American directors, and designated Bond his special assistant dedicated to nurturing Pan Am's China position when Bixby was in Manila, Hong Kong, or Macau. Looking further ahead, Pan American intended to call Bixby home once transpacific service was firmly established, and when that happened, Bixby wanted Bond to assume his place as Pan Am's Far Eastern representative. Both roles represented major strides for a former construction contractor without a college education. Granted, New York probably saw him as some sort of colonial administrator, but Bond had no problem with that—he was in the System, and his fief would anchor one end of commercial aviation's most ambitious undertaking. His professional circumstances felt secure for the first time in five trying years, and provided a newfound confidence that allowed him to concentrate on winning the permanent affections of a certain world-traveling brunette.

Transpacific requirements forced Bixby to spend much time away from Shanghai. Attending to business in his absence kept Bond furiously busy, and he had little opportunity to visit Kitsi. Instead, he wrote voluminous letters and sent cables composed in rhymed telegraphic baby talk that read like code and can't have made sense to anyone but their intended recipient. Bond couldn't plan trips in advance, but holes appeared in his schedule about once every three weeks, and he hopped up to Peiping aboard one of the company Stinsons.

Four or five dry-land months and six or eight trips to Peiping served only to strengthen Bond's feelings for Kitsi, although he still hadn't confessed his love. Bond had become good friends with Harold Bixby's entire family, and Bixby's wife, Debbie, and their four daughters began to smell a rat—they didn't think mere business could motivate Bond to fly north so regularly. Elizabeth Bixby, the second-oldest daughter, had found his previous girlfriend, Stasia, to be amazingly beautiful, but something seemed different about his attitude toward the girl in Peiping.

A letter from Kitsi announcing that she would be leaving China in three weeks to continue her around-the-world cruise spurred Bond to action: He cabled immediately, announcing a weeklong visit. In a Peiping hotel built against the south wall of the Inner City in the Legation Quarter, Bond washed and dressed in the tuxedo he'd brought north, then hired a rickshaw to tow him the two hundred yards to the Clarks' house. Just as he arrived, a gowned, bejeweled Anne Clark astonished him by emerging from the house with her husband on their way out for dinner and an evening of bridge. Mrs. Clark told Bond she'd arranged for their servants to prepare dinner. "Mind you," she said with a wink, "we won't be home until *very* late."

Too scared to smile, Bond promised to take good care of the house.

Anne Clark laughed in his face and spun off into the night, heels clicking on the cobblestones. A servant showed Bond into the living room, where three burning logs crackled in the hearth. Firelight trembled on the walls. Kitsi appeared wearing a graceful evening dress, with her hair perfectly coiffed, and for once, it stayed dutifully in place. Bond had never seen a woman so ravishing. She smiled, and a single brown ringlet tumbled from her temple. Bond took her hands, and they touched cheeks. A servant called them to dinner, which was superb, and artfully presented, although as soon as a houseboy cleared each course, Bond couldn't remember what he'd just eaten. Finally, the servants presented dessert and disappeared. Bond watched Kitsi savor every bite, then ushered her into the living room. They sat on a rug in front of the fire.

"Kitsi, I hope you know why I'm here."

She stroked the rug. "I think you'd better tell me," she murmured.

Bond reached forward and touched her hand. Their eyes locked, and Bond began the speech he'd rehearsed under the engine noise during the flight north. "Kitsi, ever since I met you I knew you were the girl I'd been dying to meet. That feeling got stronger every day on the boat. I've been completely and forever in love with you since Kyoto, and now, six months later, I feel the same. I haven't told you before, but I've tried to tell you without words. I'm sorry circumstances have made it impossible for me to see you more often, but now you're leaving, I can't delay." He put his hand to Kitsi's cheek. "What I'm trying to say is that I love you, Katharine Dunlop. Will you marry me?"

"Yes! Bondy, yes!" Kitsi threw her arms around him. "I knew you wouldn't let me leave."

She tilted her face to his, and they kissed in the firelight.

A flock of cables went stateside. A flurry returned. Bond wrote a long letter to Kitsi's father. Bond's older brother, Alan, a Norfolk insurance salesman, took his wife and children to Washington to meet Mr. and Mrs. Dunlop. The Dunlops drove to Petersburg to meet Bond's aging mother. There wasn't much money in the Bond clan, but they were hardworking, well-bred Virginians, and the families approved of each other. Perhaps seduced by the glamour of aviation and the prospect of having a son-in-law who was an executive for Pan American Airways—far and away the most exciting company in America—Mrs. Dunlop made no attempt to sabotage the match. However, she and her husband did insist on coming to the Orient for the wedding.

As the winter of 1935 turned to spring, William Bond found himself inundated by logistical complications that had nothing to do with air travel: Kitsi's parents had arrived in China, and Mrs. Dunlop tossed his and Kitsi's plans for a small, intimate wedding in a night soil bucket. Bondy and Kitsi were to be married in Peiping on May 15, 1935, as they'd intended, but Mrs. Dunlop moved the ceremony from the Clarks' house to the more suitable Anglican Church of England in the British Embassy compound, and there was nothing small or quiet about it. Rechanneling the energy she'd previously devoted to thwarting her daughter's marital prospects, she now resolved that the union would be the expatriate community's social highlight of 1935, sealed in the presence of a radiant international assemblage. Mrs. Dunlop corralled dozens of diplomats and military men into attendance and organized a squadron of ushers from the multinational potpourri of uniforms. The guests represented all the treaty powers—Britain, France, Denmark, the United States, Germany, Italy, Japan, and the Netherlands, among others—and Mrs. Dunlop surveyed them with immense satisfaction: They were good people, the right sort of people, splendidly dressed by meticulous Chinese tailors.

The church organ thrummed the first notes of the Wedding March and the company rose to their feet. Dressed in an immaculate tuxedo, Bond beamed from the altar, for Kitsi looked divine coming down the aisle on her father's arm. Anne Covington Clark was Kitsi's maid of honor. Harold M. Bixby held the rings. He was Bond's best man.

After the ceremony, Mrs. Dunlop held a reception on a clubhouse veranda overlooking the tiled rooftops of the Inner City and the Legation Quarter's polo ground. An orchestra sparked up music, and everywhere one turned, Chinese servants in starched white uniforms presented hors d'oeuvres and cocktails. The guests attacked their tipples with gusto. It was too early in the day for dancing, but not, apparently, for polo. An intrepid officer organized a chukker, the collected civilian embassy staffs versus the military officers of the various legation guards, and by the time the Chinese stable hands had collected and saddled the ponies, most of the participants were pickled like English walnuts and they decided to play in their cutaways, top hats, and dress uniforms, the same formal vestments they'd worn to the wedding. One English diplomat turned up his nose at treating polo so cavalierly and refused to participate, but most of the guests, British included, scoffed the man down the road and heaved themselves full-force into the bacchanalia. The Italian military attaché did marvelous duty, resplendent in his bemedaled cavalry uniform and so spectacularly inebriated that he could barely sit his horse. His steed drew wide arcs on the greensward, the attaché rolled and yawed in the saddle, and together they lined up long, preposterous charges at the white ball. The wedding guests howled with delight, goading the Italian to ever more ludicrous feats of horsemanship, and the other players soon realized it was better polo—and far less hazardous—to let Mussolini's cavalry charge and swing and then whack the ball in the wake of his many misses. The game wound down as the afternoon waned, and Chinese grooms cooled and stabled the horses.

The soft light of evening bathed the walls and rooftops of the ancient city. The sun fell below the Western Hills, and the heavens shone like taffeta, shimmering layers of vermilion, salmon pink, and mauve. Dinner was served. Later began the dancing, and the celebration continued far into the night, under the glitter of springtime stars.

7

THE LAST OF THE SALAD DAYS

The newlyweds settled at 279 Rue Culty, in a quiet villa in the backstreets of the French Concession, and Harold Bixby and Ernie Allison took great pleasure poking fun at Bond's Cheshire cat air in the months after the wedding, wondering aloud when they'd get the announcement of "little Bondy." At work, Bond and Bixby had leveraged Pan Am's bulk-buying power to get an excellent price on a Douglas DC-2, the best airliner in the world. Since the Pacific was being flown only as one-off stunts by pioneering pilots in the middle 1930s, the airplane crossed the ocean on a freighter. A Whangpoo lighter craned the pieces ashore in the spring of 1935. When they had it assembled and tested, the company mechanics rolled the all-metal, low-wing, twin-engine monoplane onto the concrete hardstand in front of the hangar. It had none of the crisscross mishmash of struts and spars that had knit together previous generations of aircraft, not a single one. It was a beautiful aircraft, a *gorgeous* aircraft, and the airline organized a gala to honor its arrival and coaxed Shanghai dignitaries to the airport with cloud-embossed invitations. A well-dressed crowd arrived on the appointed day. Newshounds snapped photographs of the sleek machine gleaming in the springtime sun, and little Shirley Wilke, the seven-year-old daughter of the chief mechanic, dashed back and forth under the wings in her prettiest flower print dress, amazed she could stand upright under the wing of such an enormous airplane. Late in the day, the airline gave aerial tours of the city in the new ship, winging sightseers through the Shanghai skies at 190 miles per hour. Something about the airplane's sleek lines inspired confidence; it looked the way an airplane *should* look. The airline used the DC-2's arrival to launch a marketing campaign spotlighting the prestige a person won using airmail and traveling by plane, a very successful selling point in face-conscious China. Within ninety days, passenger traffic increased 300 percent.

Keeping abreast of technological progress was crucial to corporate survival, but Bond, Bixby, and Allison recognized that people were the heart of an airline, and they felt confident facing the future with the superb collection of Caucasian, Chinese, and Chinese American mechanics, pilots, and ground personnel they'd recruited and trained to staff their operations department. Among the Caucasian pilots were Hal Sweet, Charles "Chili" Vaughn, Eric Just—a German who'd flown with von Richthofen's Flying Circus during the World War ("Just Eric Just," to the other fliers), Floyd Nelson, Frank Havelick, James McCleskey, Charles "Chuck" Sharp, and Hugh Woods, and they formed tight friendships. Hugh Woods and Chuck Sharp became best friends, a clear case of opposites attracting. A roguish little imp from Fort Worth, Texas, nicknamed "Apple Dumpling" on account of his plump, dimpled cheeks, Chuck Sharp had a fiery temper, a tall man's swagger, and he always seemed in relentless pursuit of his next laugh. Only three things could hold his attention: They either wore skirts and heels, held cards and cocktails, or had wings and engines. Hugh Woods— "Woody"—was much more reserved. He was taller, and darker, with thick, bushy eyebrows and the square jaw of a ship's captain, and he hailed from Winfield, Kansas. He'd come to China in the original 1933 Pan Am expedition. Sharp had made his own way to the airline. Both were bachelors, and excellent fliers, and for the most part, their jobs were routine, as flying essentially was everywhere. The difference for them being the strange, exotic country rolling beneath their wings. Their lives were punctuated by pointed seconds of difficulty and danger, but really, with the exception of Route Three's fogs, the job wasn't too demanding—five to eight hours of straightforward flying every working day. The relentless Shanghai social whirl was another matter entirely, at least for the Caucasian pilots, most of whom threw themselves wholeheartedly into its frenzy. Off duty, they ate, drank, bowled, or played cards at the American Club downtown; played tennis, golfed, swam, or lounged on the veranda at the Columbia Country Club on the outskirts of the Frenchtown; and attended teas, luncheons, and parties in rooftop gardens. They dined at Russian, Italian, French, Japanese, English, and Chinese restaurants, spooned up ice cream sundaes at the Chocolate Shop on Bubbling Hills Road, carved steak sirloin at Jimmy's American restaurant on Nanking Road, and danced and reveled to jazz combos at the Little Club, the Paramount, Saint Anna, or Vienna ballrooms like the Venus Café, the Ambassador, and the Tower Club on the fourteenth floor of the Park Hotel, famous for its splendid view of the city lights. They attended dramas and movies at theaters and cinemas, bet on horses at the International Settlement's racecourse and on dogs at a track in the French Concession. The salaries of the company's Caucasian contingent were good, and costs in China were ridiculously low. They lived impossibly well compared to how they'd have done back home, and they held the most glamorous jobs in the Orient.

Shanghai was a wide-open town, an absolute free-for-all, and the airline's unmarried Caucasian pilots roamed its bawdy orchards with delight. Fashionable Chinese girls flashed movie-star legs from the slits of high-throated chi-pao dresses. A monthly pittance retained a beautiful, heron-necked Chinese housekeeper. A meager surcharge hired a whole slew of benefits beyond housekeeping. Chinese variety could be enjoyed in hundreds of bordellos, and any intrepid pilot could poach a White Russian dance hostess from among the taxi dancers at the Del Monte, the Majestic Cabaret, or the Little Club. The White Russian influx had ruined Shanghai's round-eyed prostitution rackets. A man could keep a White Russian mistress for a month on a sum of money that a decade earlier would have bought him only a single night in the arms of a tawdry seductress boated across the Pacific from San Francisco, whose gritty, streetwise wiles would seem so gratingly coarse compared with those of a White Russian siren with the manners of a princess, who might well *be* a princess, speak four languages, and play the piano besides. The White Russian women were alluring, fascinating, exotic, and somehow able to gracefully tread the razor's edge between gold digging and the sale of intimate favors. A man could feel downright chivalrous lending a hand to such a courtly, refined beauty tossed on fortune's rocks. That the arrangements unweighted a pilot's pocketbook by agreed-upon cash sums discreetly tucked under the corner of a bedside bauble didn't necessarily undermine the tenderness of the affairs.

Upriver, the pilots enjoyed another rich field of round-eyed pickings in Hankow, among the wives of the U.S. Navy officers stationed with the Yangtze Patrol, whose husbands were often away from the city for months at a time, cruising the river and its navigable tributaries. Hugh Woods's bachelor roommate availed himself of exactly that opportunity with an underappreciated Navy wife, and their romance nearly rattled the apartment from its riverbank foundations.

Most of the airline's married men lived in French Concession villas with their wives, children, and three servants in attendance—number one houseboy, cook, and house coolie. With so much "help," the married pilots enjoyed a languid domestic existence, but they were easily infected by the ribald antics of their unattached brethren. A man on the upriver run could do as he pleased away from Shanghai, and in quickly developing "pilot away from home" tradition, many of them did, although the options became decidedly more provincial west of Hankow. It was all so *easy,* and so outrageously cheap.

For the pilots' wives, Shanghai was Easy Street. They lived like old-world aristocrats, without ever having to do any heavy lifting. They birthed babies, cuddled and kissed the newborns, and handed them to their Chinese amahs, who clothed, fed, bathed, walked, and played with the infants and swabbed their dirty behinds. Children ate the majority of their meals with the servants. Most parents spent a carefully choreographed hour with their offspring before bedtime, before departing, regally begowned and tuxedoed, for whatever social event the evening required. It was absolutely routine for Shanghai's Caucasian toddlers to speak their first words in Chinese, and before they started school most spoke better Chinese than English. The women joined clubs and drama societies and hospital boards or worked with orphanages, gave each other luncheons and teas, worried about exchange rates and dress shops and the state of the family back home, and they wound themselves into fantastic social fevers. There was little else to do. China was dirty, poor, smelly, and dangerous, and it was the very rare Caucasian girl who bothered to learn a word of Chinese beyond a few bastard phrases of pidgin, the half language with which most foreigners communicated with their servants. "My God," one wife quipped between sips of her country club cocktail, "at home I washed the clothes, cooked the meals, kept house, and everything else. Here, I haven't set foot in my kitchen in six months, and this morning I threw a fit because my amah didn't come in at the right time to put on my stockings."

Not to be outdone, with their husbands so often away, and not fools either, the pilots' wives also partook of expatriate Shanghai's libertine atmosphere. One afternoon, Woody called at the home of one of his closest friends. The servants didn't bother to announce his arrival, and he walked down the hall and knocked on the bedroom door. The door cracked, and his friend's head poked around.

Ah . . . yes . . . Woody . . . the club . . . I forgot. How about we meet down there later on?

That would be fine, answered Woody, not shocked enough to let surprise show on his face, but his friend had forgotten the mirror mounted to the bedroom wall behind his head. In it, Woody could plainly see the shapely, naked reflection of one of his fellow pilots' wives sprawled across a sea of tousled bedsheets. The door closed, and Woody grinned. It was Shanghai: These things happened, and he felt no obligation to rat her out. Her amorous infidelities were only quid pro quo for what Woody knew for a God-given fact were her husband's upriver dalliances.

The organization's Chinese and Chinese American personnel led much less rakish lives. Unfortunately, the tight friendships didn't generally cross racial lines, even though the various ethnicities worked together every day on flight crews or mechanic teams. Typical were Moon Chin, Donald Wong, and Joy Thom, the airline's star Chinese American fliers, all of whom had joined the airline when it opened Route Two in the winter of 1933. Barely out of their teens, the inseparable trio spent many evenings together at Moon Chin's house in the French Concession, studying Morse code and technical aviation manuals and socializing. All three honed their skills copiloting the airline's Stinsons, Loenings, "Tin Goose" Ford Trimotors, and its two Douglas Dolphin amphibians, and it gave twenty-one-year-old Moon Chin no small measure of pride that Ernie Allison had chosen him to be copilot of the airline's first DC-2 crew.

Moon Fun Chin was born on April 13, 1914, behind the sun-seared, windowless walls of a single-story, mud-brick house slowly crumbling back into the earth from which it had been raised, sixty miles up the Pearl River from Macau and a half a day's walk west of the riverbank in a tiny hamlet called Wing-Wa. Moon Chin wouldn't hear English spoken for more than ten years, but he'd been born an American citizen—courtesy of the worst natural disaster in American history.

Eight years before Moon Chin was born, in 1906, his father, Joe Chin, was working in the United States when a massive earthquake and subsequent firestorm annihilated San Francisco, destroying its birth and immigration records. An 1898 Supreme Court decision guaranteed the citizenship of ethnic Chinese born in the United States, and like most Chinese laborers then working in America—men barred from citizenship by the onerous Chinese Exclusion Laws of the last twenty-five years—Joe Chin swore he'd been born in the ruined city. Thus minted a citizen, he worked in the United States for another six years, sending money to his family in China. As was typical among Chinese working in America, Joe Chin returned to his homeland to see his wife and children once every ten years. Moon Chin was a result of his 1912–13 visit.

A decade passed, and Moon Chin grew into a healthy boy. Halfway through 1922, Moon's mother received a letter from her husband. Penned by a Chinese scribe in America, since Joe Chin could neither read nor write, and read aloud by one in China since Moon's mother was similarly illiterate, the letter announced that Joe Chin would come home in the spring of 1923, and that Moon Chin would return to the United States with the father he'd never met to capitalize on the economic opportunities his old man had discovered in a place called Baltimore.

Moon Chin, his father, and their single suitcase crossed the Pacific to Seattle jammed into the barracks-like hold of Asian steerage on a Dollar Line steamer. The Immigration and Naturalization Service welcomed the ten-year-old citizen to American soil by separating him from his father and locking him in the Seattle Immigration Detention Facility, a brick-built gulag looming over the waterfront whose main purpose was to allow the INS to question—and reject—Chinese immigrants. Moon Chin lingered in detention for six weeks, until he passed a grueling interrogation by three khaki-clad, jackbooted officers and a Cantonese interpreter.* Legiti-

---

* Thousands of Chinese had gained citizenship in the San Francisco earthquake, and like Joe Chin, at long intervals those men returned to their families in China. Nearly every one of them registered a

mized, father and son crossed the continent and settled in Walbrook, a quiet neighborhood northwest of downtown Baltimore, and spent the next few years running a laundry and a Chinese restaurant near Frederick Avenue's intersection with West Baltimore Street.

Charles Lindbergh's 1927 Atlantic crossing captivated Moon Chin, as it had William Bond. Moon dreamed of flight, but he was only thirteen years old. He finished grade school the following year, learned the rudiments of auto mechanics at a vocational school, and after he lost his job at a truck repair shop hammered by the onset of the Depression, he pestered his father for flying lessons. At first, Joe Chin wouldn't hear of it, but Moon Chin kept wearing at him. A practical man, like most Chinese, Joe Chin considered the costs, opportunities, and risks—his son getting killed paramount among them—but Moon needed a career and he'd do better at something he liked. Joe Chin committed the necessary funds, and Moon Chin learned to fly at the Curtiss-Wright Flying School,* beyond Baltimore's famed Pimlico racecourse. Aloft, listening to the engine roar, the green trees and emerald Maryland fields passing under his wings, Moon Chin felt the future in his hands, and he earned his limited commercial license in the autumn of 1932. In the waning days of the year, he received a letter from his father's younger brother in Shanghai, who wrote to pass the news that the "Middle Kingdom Space Machine Family"—as the China National Aviation Corporation was known in Chinese—planned to open a new route between Shanghai and Peiping, and that it was looking to hire Chinese aviators. "So, Moon," Little Uncle concluded, "do you want to come over and sign up?"

Moon Chin had seized the opportunity. Flying for CNAC was an excellent job, even if the Chinese and Chinese Americans were paid about one-third as much as their Caucasian counterparts for exactly the same work and responsibility, and by 1935 Moon Chin was dating Elsie, a comely young woman he'd met at a private gathering in Jessfield Park, far out Bubbling Wells Road beyond the boundaries of the International Settlement.

---

child with American authorities when they reentered the United States, and they claimed more than four hundred sons for every daughter. Among the Chinese, there was a brisk trade in official paperwork, and American immigration expended much effort to expose the "paper sons."

* The same flying school where William Bond had learned to fly in 1930.

They found each other attractive, but they had trouble communicating because Moon couldn't speak Shanghainese, and Elsie spoke neither English nor Cantonese. Regardless, when Moon was promoted to pilot-captain, Elsie wanted to get married. Bondy and Kitsi attended the ceremony in the Community Church at 53 Avenue Pétain, in the French Concession, along with much of the airline's staff.

The middle 1930s were good times for CNAC, decent times for China, considering the multiplicity of tensions rending the national fabric, and great times for Pan American Airways as it prepared to inaugurate transpacific service. The first commercial flight from San Francisco was scheduled for late November 1935, but the company still didn't have landing rights in the Philippines, and neither Pan Am nor CNAC had obtained rights for Hong Kong or Macau. Only at the eleventh hour did Bixby secure Philippine permission, after the country's first-ever presidential election settled the political landscape. Despite Bixby's and Bond's ongoing efforts, the problems of China remained unresolved, and U.S. Airmail contracts hung in the balance of proving the line's feasibility. Pan Am decided to begin service just as far as the Philippines.

Lustrous and aerodynamic, Pan Am's spanking-new, four-engine Martin M-130 *China Clipper* took off from the waters beside Alameda Island on the eastern side of San Francisco Bay on November 22, 1935. The San Francisco–Oakland Bay Bridge was under construction, its towers complete, but only one of its two suspension cables was finished. Bloated with fuel and more than one hundred thousand letters, *China Clipper* couldn't surmount the cables. She ducked under at the last second, thrilling thousands jammed along the San Francisco waterfront to witness her departure. The airplane banked between North Beach and the Alcatraz prison and flew down the Golden Gate, easily passing over the cable-spinning work that was beginning to bridge the strait between Fort Point and the Marin Headlands. The engine noise waned, and the airplane faded into the skies beyond the Farallon Islands. Twenty-one hours later, it reached Honolulu, and from there it jumped the isolated islands of the central Pacific on which Pan Am had constructed elaborate flying-boat bases—Midway, Wake, and Guam—one per day, until Harold Bixby was able to watch the enormous hydroplane settle into the waters of Manila Bay, a dream he'd labored to make reality for two and a half years. Two other M-130s, the *Philippine Clipper* and the *Hawaii Clipper,* joined the *China Clipper** on the transpacific run, and within a month the planes were hopping the Pacific every week. It was a brilliant accomplishment, and Pan Am had made it happen against the tide of the worst economic crisis in American history.

"I thrill to the wonder of it all," President Roosevelt cabled from the White House.

The first transpacific flights didn't carry passengers, but they instantly changed the nature of written correspondence. People on both sides of the ocean began timing their letter writing to coincide with Clipper departures, and the success of the venture pressured other governments to make the service available to their people. Bixby pressed the advantage, and in January 1936 he received permission for both CNAC and Pan Am to land at Macau. He preferred to operate through Hong Kong, a more economically significant place, but the British colonial government stubbornly refused to grant unilateral landing rights. It wanted Philippine rights from Pan Am, which only the Philippine government could grant, and the right to land British-flagged airliners in China from CNAC, which seemed to Bixby like "trying to trade a button for an overcoat," irrespective of the most-favored-nation complications that had thwarted Pan Am's efforts to land American-flagged carriers in the Middle Kingdom. Hong Kong's taipans saved the day—they didn't want the Crown Colony marginalized on the eve of the coming air age. His Majesty's Government relented, giving one-sided permission to both airlines. It had taken nearly three years, but the political cards for an air service from San Francisco to Shanghai had finally fallen into place.

A week before inaugurating passenger service, Juan Terry Trippe and his wife led a fifteen-person VIP tour across the Pacific as a dress rehearsal. Beyond Manila, they flew to Macau, Hong Kong, and Shanghai, and in the late afternoon of October 25, 1936, all CNAC turned out at the Tower Club on the fourteenth floor of the Park Hotel for a tea given in the Trippes' honor. It was a wonderful, vivacious soiree, far above the hectic streets, and a splendid afternoon, so warm the women didn't need shawls or wraps. Bond and Kitsi attended, along with Harold and Debbie Bixby, Ernie Alli-

---

* They were the only three M-130s ever built.

son and his wife, Florence, every pilot and mechanic not on duty, and all of the company's wives. The airline's Chinese staff was well represented, their wives sporting colorful, high-collared chi-pao dresses and quite stealing the show from their American counterparts. Only Kitsi Bond matched their radiance: She was pregnant, just beginning to show, and Bondy couldn't keep his hands off his wife's swelling tummy. Dusk fell over the racecourse, and from their perch high in the Park Hotel, the guests looked east into the gleaming neon canyon of Nanking Road, Shanghai's Broadway. Two days later, Pan American's first transpacific passengers landed in Manila. The airline and its subsidiaries stood at the apogee of international technological accomplishment. They'd changed the world.

However fair the fields of Asian prosperity were for CNAC, and China, where conditions had improved by most measures in the middle 1930s, company and country lived under constant threat of Japanese encroachment, and it was no imagined bugbear. Through those years, the Kwantung Army bit off chunks of the provinces adjacent to Manchuria and forced the extension of the zone demilitarized by a 1933 truce. Chinese patriots writhed under the humiliations, and several thousand Chinese students sparked an anti-Japanese riot in Peiping on December 9, 1935. The disturbances spread nationwide, but were quickly and violently suppressed by the Kuomintang. An antigovernment edge agitated the "December Ninthers." They wanted action against Japan, and the Central Government wasn't taking it.

Acquiescing to a Japanese demand, Chiang Kai-shek ordered the warlord of lost Manchuria, Chang Hseuh-liang (known to Westerners as "the Young Marshal"), to disengage his troops facing the Japanese and move west to lead a campaign against Chiang's old nemesis, the Communists, who'd been driven from their Honan base area in October 1934 and endured a seven-thousand-mile forced march through western China to reach the border country of Shansi, Kansu, and Shensi provinces. Now firmly under the control of Mao Tse-tung, the "Long March" survivors were building a new stronghold, but they were tenuously established, ripe for annihilation. Chiang intended to defer fighting the foreign foe until he'd crushed them, but his seemingly endless capitulations to Japanese aggression continued to anger the population. The Communists were Chinese, after all. Many, perhaps most, Chinese felt the factions should suspend their disputes and form a united front against Japan. Compounding the internal divisiveness, the in-fighting wasn't confined to the Nationalist-Communist schism. Anti-Japanese, antiforeign sentiment ran white hot in south China, and the southern provinces of Kwangtung and Kwangxi maintained an independent army and developed their own air force. Those governments sent an "Anti-Japanese National Salvation Army" north in June 1936, ostensibly to battle the Japanese, but fighting broke out between the southerners and Central Government troops. Chiang Kai-shek defused much of the southern ardor by inducing the Canton Air Force to defect to Nanking.

Toward the end of the year, it came to Chiang Kai-shek's attention that the Young Marshal and his exiled Manchurian troops were conducting the anti-Communist campaign with an exceptional lack of vigor. The Generalissimo flew to Sian and insisted they press the offensive. At about four o'clock on the morning of December 12, 1936, the Young Marshal's picked men stormed the Generalissimo's Sian headquarters and killed many of his bodyguards. Chiang leapt from a window and vaulted a wall. He fell thirty feet into a moat, clawed out of the ditch, and fled up a frozen hillside. He was taken captive a few hours later when one of the Young Marshal's officers found him shivering barefoot under a shelter stone wearing nothing but a gray silk robe and a long nightshirt.

The Young Marshal and a clique of malcontent generals pressed Chiang to abandon his anti-Communist obsession and lead a united front against Japan. The Generalissimo refused to abridge his freedom of action. News of the kidnapping spread, and rival factions scrambled for advantage—both inside and outside the Kuomintang. Madame Chiang flew to Sian to negotiate, accompanied by her brother, T. V. Soong, her Australian advisor William Henry Donald, and Dai Li, leader of the Kuomintang's Blue Shirt Society gestapo. The Young Marshal flew Mao Tse-tung's second-in-command, Chou En-lai, to Sian to join the wrangling. Many Communists wanted Chiang executed, but a telegram from the Comintern, possibly composed by Stalin himself, put them in the odd position of advocating Chiang's survival to the junta of officers who'd organized the kidnapping. Stalin needed China to help counter Japan's threat to Siberia, and he recognized Chiang as the only Chinese leader with sufficient face to lead a national coalition. Pressed from all quarters, the Young Marshal and his allies relented, releasing Chiang on Christmas Day.

The Generalissimo flew out of Sian piloted by an American flier named Royal Leonard, who would soon join CNAC, and a delirious multitude received him in Nanking on December 26. No written agreements emerged from the abduction—the Generalissimo had steadfastly refused to sign anything—but he'd obviously made significant promises in front of his wife, brother-in-law, chief foreign advisor, the Young Marshal, and a top Communist leader. The whole nation knew it. Ironically, the kidnapping made Chiang a symbol of China's greatest craving—unity—and the country expected him to cease scourging the Communists and lead a crusade against the Japanese. Many observers thought they were watching the endgame of Chinese unification, that henceforth the Chinese people would march together against the common foe.

Across the East China Sea, Japanese expansionists watched China's awakening with trepidation, under no illusions about their island's ability to dominate a cohesive, muscular China. If they were to rule the Middle Kingdom, and Asia, the time to strike was fast approaching, before China became too strong to subjugate.

However intense the political news that season, it took second place in the lives of William and Katharine Bond. Whatever gods ruled China smiled on the life growing inside her, and Katharine Dunlop Bond delivered a healthy boy on March 11, 1937. The proud parents named him Langhorne McCook to honor his grandmothers.

Tensions between China and Japan were high that spring, but Sino-Japanese hostilities had been at the vanguard of the news since Bond came to the Far East in 1931. Like Harold Bixby and most of the other China hands, Bond didn't think the Japanese would risk all-out war. He wouldn't have been planning a furlough if he'd felt otherwise, but with six years completed in China, he was overdue for his second home leave. The Bonds stayed in Shanghai for three months to ensure the health of mother and child, and by mid-June the family was fit to travel. Just before they left, the Ministry of Communications gave the company a new managing director, replacing Dai Enkai with Colonel Lam Whi-shing, a tough martinet from

Kwangsi Province who'd been vice-commander of the Canton Air Force and had been instrumental in orchestrating its defection to the Nanking government. For years, the Kuomintang Aviation Commission—which controlled the Chinese Air Force—had been trying to gain control of China's commercial aviation, run through the Ministry of Communications. Bond had only one meeting with the austere colonel before he left, but it seemed an ill portent for the airline's commercial independence to have a military man named its top executive.

Leaving Bixby and Allison in charge, Bond, Kitsi, and Langhorne flew the Pacific and took a transcontinental flight overnight from San Francisco, reaching Washington on July 1, 1937. Three-month-old Langhorne arrived fast asleep. Kitsi and Langhorne stayed with her family at Hayes Manor in Chevy Chase, Maryland, while Bond reported to Pan Am headquarters in New York. Four years before, Pan Am had bought into the China airline to anchor the western end of the transpacific line. Unexpectedly, it had become a profitable investment in its own right. The China National Aviation Corporation boasted thirty-four pilots and copilots and eighteen airplanes, including four of the superb DC-2s, and, like China, it seemed poised to enjoy years of steady growth and prosperity. Pan Am leadership was thrilled with Bond's accomplishments.

Back in Washington, Bondy settled in to enjoy his wife's company and their new son, keeping occasional appointments with his Washington acquaintances, notably Stanley K. Hornbeck, assistant secretary of state for the Far East, an old friend of his wife's family, and he twice drove Kitsi and Langhorne to Petersburg to see his mother and brother. At Hayes Manor, while a nurse watched the baby, Bond and Kitsi played tennis early, before the Maryland humidity suppressed activity. Afterward, they lounged in the cool, shaded rooms of the big house, sipping iced tea, reading, and playing parlor games, and at the end of the long Potomac afternoons Bond mixed an old-fashioned for his wife and a martini for himself—iced gin, straight up, with an olive, just the way he liked it. Bond relaxed with his cocktail and contemplated the enormous changes he'd wrought in his life since he'd cast away his construction career and joined Curtiss-Wright in the distant summer of 1929. With hard work and unswerving dedication, he'd earned top jobs in *two* of the most exciting flying companies on earth. His efforts made tangible contributions to human progress, and he'd played a part in the greatest commercial accomplishment of the decade. He'd seen Japan and the Philippines and much of China, and he'd lived in Shanghai, the world's most exciting city, for six years. Bond had powerful friends on both sides of the Pacific, and he was cordially acquainted with Charles Lindbergh, the most famous American besides the president. American financial markets were rickety again in 1937, and joblessness still plagued the country, but he'd weathered seven years of terrible depression without suffering a minute of unemployment, and he'd supported his widowed mother through all of it. He'd met and married the girl of his dreams, and she'd just birthed a healthy son. The future shone very bright.

PART

TWO

WAR

July 7, 1937, to December 31, 1937

Great battles, in which thousands of men are torn apart,
are forgotten as easily as last year's Olympics.

—Edgar Snow, *The Battle for Asia*

8

THINGS FALL APART

A dozen miles west of Peiping, the eight-hundred-year-old Lukouchiao Bridge crossed the Yongding River on eleven graceful stone arches. Marco Polo had admired the 770-foot bridge and the 485 uniquely carved stone lions adorning its railings, and Westerners knew it by his name, the Marco Polo Bridge. A railway trestle on the Hankow–Peiping line spanned the Yongding next to the venerable arches, and by the summer of 1937, the railway was the only overland route into Peiping not under Japanese control. A unit of Chinese infantry guarded the bridges from a nearby walled town, but Imperial Japanese Army elements regularly exercised in the area, as they insisted they had the right to do under their liberal interpretation of the 1901 Boxer Protocol. A Japanese infantry company maneuvering near the bridges clashed with Chinese guards on the night of July 7, 1937. One Japanese soldier went missing, and the Japanese commander demanded the right to inspect the Chinese garrison to determine if it harbored the uncounted man, as either deserter or prisoner. The Chinese refused. Larger-scale fighting erupted. Local commanders negotiated between skirmishes, and Reuters reported from Peiping on July 9 that both sides wished to localize the incident. Then greater forces seized control.

Across the sea, in Japan, the war minister argued that the Imperial Army could crush China's armies in a month. He took his case to Emperor Hirohito, and the emperor opted for war. Three homeland divisions mobilized on July 11; the Japanese Kwantung Army poured out of Manchuria; major combats blossomed, and in the open country around Peiping Chinese infantry couldn't match the tanks, artillery, airpower, and rapidly coordinated operational command of the Japanese Army.

Half a world away, in Washington, D.C., William Bond followed developments through *The Washington Post, The New York Times,* network radio broadcasts, in Spartan cables from Bixby in Shanghai, and in consultations with his friend Stanley Hornbeck in the State Department. Bond peered anxiously into the fog of war and distance and tried to divine how each scrap of news would affect China and, by extension, his airline. The Pan Am brain trust grew concerned as the fighting spread; unrest in China threatened the Transpacific Route, the crown jewel of the System. Bond telephoned New York every few days to interpret events. The fighting around Peiping forced CNAC to suspend one of its prime routes, but not its most profitable, which remained Route One in the Yangtze valley.

Unfortunately, tensions in Shanghai were escalating in parallel.

On July 24, the Japanese Navy in Shanghai reported a twenty-one-year-old sailor missing, and alleged that he'd been kidnapped. Despite denials by Chinese authorities, one thousand heavily armed Japanese marines fruitlessly searched Hongkew for the missing man, where the patrols had a legal right to be because it was part of the International Settlement, and they moved on through Chapei, a Chinese-run district, where they did not, stopping cars, rickshaws, and pedestrians at gunpoint. Most Shanghailanders thought the disappearance had been engineered by the Japanese secret service, and all could see the frightening parallel to Marco Polo Bridge. Five and a half years before, the 1932 Shanghai war devastated their neighborhoods. An exodus of Chinese inhabitants bolted from Chapei and Hongkew for the safety of the foreign concessions.

Three days later, a Chinese boatman fished the missing seaman out of the Yangtze a hundred miles above Shanghai. Chinese gendarmes returned him to the Japanese Embassy in Nanking the following afternoon. Apparently, another Japanese sailor had spotted him in a North Szechwan Road bawdy house that wasn't authorized by the Imperial Japanese Navy, and he'd deserted to elude punishment.

In north China, Japanese attacks continued for the next ten days, with a Japanese brigade ultimately occupying Peiping on August 8. In Shanghai, Sino-Japanese animosity mounted until the city seethed like an over-pressured boiler. Forty thousand people left Shanghai from North Station on August 6, jamming the third-class railway carriages as they scrambled to distance themselves from the explosive city. Twenty-five thousand others fled over the Soochow Creek bridges into the imagined safety of the International Settlement. Tens of thousands followed in the next two days, and they came with everything they could carry, push, or roll, their belongings piled into vans, rickshaws, carts, and wheelbarrows. Landlords in the settlements doubled rents. Rickshaw coolies charged outrageous hire. A thousand ticketless refugees swarmed aboard the Jardine steamer *Kutwo*, imminently scheduled to depart Shanghai, and sat on the decks and refused to budge. Squads of truncheon-wielding police cleared the ship.

The next day, an ex-CNAC copilot named Li struck the peace-shattering blow. Li had left the company of his own volition several years before and joined the Chinese Air Force, rising to the rank of major. In the summer of 1937, he commanded the Chinese Air Force base at Hungjao, a few miles west of the foreign settlements. That Monday, a Japanese Navy officer and his chauffeur motored to the gates of Li's aerodrome and tried to enter. Chinese sentries barred their way. The Japanese pair might have tried to force their way past. Major Li spotted the tussle and stormed over, his anger boiling into intense, personal outrage and hatred. A gunfight flared, killing both Japanese and one Chinese militiaman.

The Japanese insisted that their sublieutenant had a right to be at the airfield gate. The Chinese said he'd tried to force his way through and was obviously engaged in espionage.* Outraged, and perhaps wanting to share in the glory the Japanese Army was accruing in north China, the Imperial

---

* Regardless of the exact details, two uniformed Japanese at the gates of a Chinese military airfield, which they would certainly appear to be attempting to enter, was, in August 1937, either an intentional provocation or an act of mind-boggling stupidity.

Navy presented demands amounting to the complete Chinese abandon-
ment of Shanghai. Politically, in light of the Sian kidnapping and the United
Front, Chiang Kai-shek couldn't appease Japan without delegitimizing his
rule. Two viable alternatives presented themselves: to fight in the north, or
to expand the war into the Yangtze valley and fight at Shanghai. Chinese
military intelligence gathering embroiled CNAC as they debated which
course to pursue.

On August 11, the minister of communications ordered managing director Colonel Lam Whi-shing to send a DC-2 to Nanking for a charter
flight to a location he refused to divulge. Operations manager Ernie Allison objected. Colonel Lam stressed the importance of complying with the
minister's wishes, and Allison relented, sending pilot Floyd Nelson on assurances that the charter would be a short flight.

Nelson departed Nanking with General Mow of the Chinese Air Force
and a load of other officers. His radio signal faded throughout the day until
Lunghwa station lost contact. It reappeared the next day. He'd been tasked
to take the air force officers to inspect military airfields in north China,
landing at seven or eight small fields, all of them poor. Twice, Nelson's ship
stuck in soft sand; other airstrips had looked so bad he refused to touch
down. Nelson couldn't understand Chinese, but to his pilot's eyes it looked
as if the leadership was considering whether or not to stage an aerial offensive from the northern airfields. He didn't think it could be done from
such primitive bases. It was a dangerous flight, in threatened airspace, and
entirely military. Harold Bixby protested to Colonel Lam and the minister
of communications—Americans could not be used on such missions without violating U.S. neutrality legislation. The managing director and the
minister agreed not to authorize any more such "charters," but the next day
Colonel Lam sent another DC-2 pilot on a similar, albeit shorter, flight.
(American pilots were the only ones "checked out" as pilot-captains in the
DC-2s.) The China National Aviation Corporation was a Chinese airline.
China owned it. Pan Am held only a minority interest, and considering
the magnitude of the impending crisis, China didn't care a whit about its
"strictly commercial" status.

Up north, Japan had airfields, port facilities, rail lines, and many highly
mobile divisions. Only a few thousand marines guarded her interests in
Shanghai. The Imperial Navy could steam up the Whangpoo to bring reinforcements and lend gunfire support, but warships were supremely vulner-

able in such confined waters, and China's new air force, developed in the middle 1930s, expected to drive them to sea. Nelson's north China tour made it apparent that the new air arm would be most effective operating from their better-developed bases in the Yangtze valley within range of Shanghai. Close-quarters street fighting would minimize many Japanese strengths, and a battle fought in the city would play out in front of the world press. From the Chinese perspective, Shanghai had every strategic and tactical advantage. Two of Chiang Kai-shek's best divisions marched into the city on August 13 and fortified North Station, a stout, multistory building dominating the surrounding neighborhoods. Chinese regulars and Japanese bluejacket marines faced each other across the barricades. Inevitably, fighting broke out. In Chapei, patrols fought at the corner of Paoshan and Wangping roads. Small arms barked at Tientungnam Railway Station. A third battle erupted near the headquarters of the Japanese Naval Landing Party close to the Astor House and Broadway Mansions hotels at the northern foot of Garden Bridge.

Dense, sweating rivers of refugees continued to pour over the Soochow Creek bridges into the International Settlement, where food prices tripled. Everyone in the city needed money, and Chinese and Western civilians mobbed the banks, anxious to cash out their savings and change Chinese dollars into less threatened currencies. The flood of money leaving Shanghai paralyzed international currency exchanges. The banks faced collapse unless they could get cash infusions to satisfy the angry clamor at their teller windows. Finance Minister T. V. Soong ordered Colonel Lam to dispatch the DC-2s to the Nationalist air base at Nanchang, eighty-five miles south of the Yangtze in Jiangsi Province, and fly Nationalist banknotes as close to Shanghai as they could get. Colonel Lam passed the instruction to Harold Bixby, and Bixby accepted with enthusiasm. The mission was commercial, and critically important.

Shanghai passed a calm afternoon, but passengers landing on CNAC's last flight into Lunghwa spotted long trains packed with Chinese troops pouring into the city on the Shanghai–Hangchow railroad. Small-arms fire and artillery erupted before sunset, and dozens of buildings caught fire north of Soochow Creek. Flames lit the sky after dark, reflecting eerily in the smoke clouds billowing over the battle zones. Foreigners gathered on International Settlement rooftops, sipped cocktails, and watched the fighting, secure in their belief that the combat concerned only the Asiatic races.

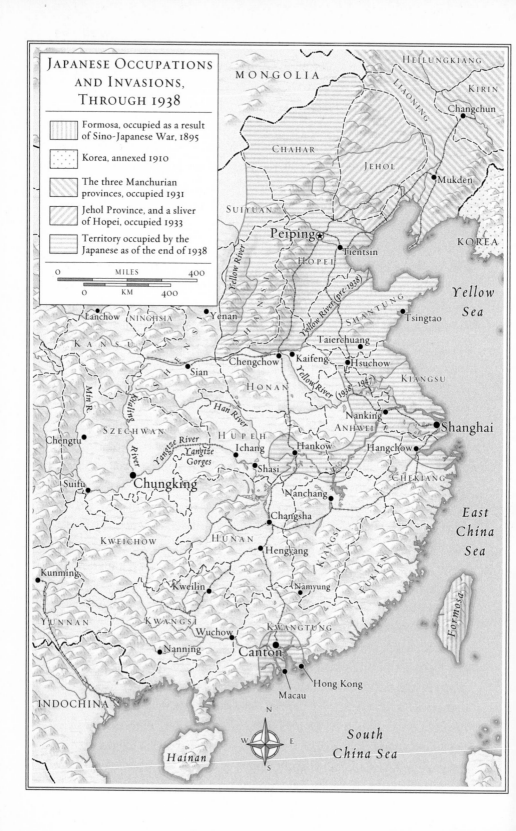

JAPANESE OCCUPATIONS
AND INVASIONS,
THROUGH 1938

Formosa, occupied as a result
of Sino-Japanese War, 1895

Korea, annexed 1910

The three Manchurian
provinces, occupied 1931

Jehol Province, and a sliver
of Hopei, occupied 1933

Territory occupied by the
Japanese as of the end of 1938

0   MILES   400

0   KM   400

It was Friday, August 13, 1937, and Asia's last hopes of peace vanished in the gunfire.

Tropical downpours sweeping in from the China Sea after midnight subdued the worst fires, but at sunrise Chinese shells pounding the Japanese Hongkew police headquarters sparked new blazes. Just before 10 A.M., Harold Bixby's office phone rang. It was Ernie Allison, calling from Lunghwa: "Bix! Three Chinese bombers just went over with loaded bomb racks."

Bixby had no doubt as to their target—the aging three-stack battle cruiser *Idzumo,* moored in the Whangpoo at the mouth of Soochow Creek, only a few hundred yards away from his office in the Shanghai post office. The *Idzumo* was the Japanese flagship, the most tangible symbol of Japan's presence in China, and easily the world's most despised warship. Bixby dragged the aging postal commissioner, A. M. Chapelain, to the roof. They reached it just in time to watch three Chinese bombers glide down through low-hanging clouds, as antiaircraft cannon and machine-gun fire rose to meet them from *Idzumo*'s decks, spewing shells, bullets, and shrapnel all over the city. Bombs plummeted from the planes. "Take cover!" Bixby yelled, tackling the hard-of-hearing postal commissioner when he didn't react. Two geysers erupted in the river; the third bomb crashed into a wharf-side godown. Detonations reverberated over the rooftop.

At that moment, as the bombs fell, Chuck "Apple Dumpling" Sharp was landing a DC-2 at Nanchang, having accepted the banknote assignment. The fiery Texan taxied to a stop near a knot of Chinese officials clustered beside an airfield shed, popped the side door, and raised a roguish eyebrow. There wasn't a banker in sight. These were *military* officers, wearing drab fatigues. Politely enough, they asked Sharp to fly a planeload of bombs, bomb racks, and machine-gun clips to a Chinese Air Force field at Hangchow, 140 miles southwest of Shanghai. Sharp refused. CNAC was a commercial operation, and he was a neutral, noncombatant American. He was sorry, but he couldn't fly outright military cargo. An officer drew a pistol and held it to Sharp's head. Sharp's eyes tightened to rattlesnake slits, but the pistol never wavered. Coolies loaded the "banknotes." The officer motioned Sharp back into the airplane and came aboard with a few compatriots. Aloft, Sharp radioed the news of the banknotes-for-bombs switcheroo to Allison at Lunghwa. Allison telephoned Bixby, who called T. V. Soong.

"It's out of my hands," Soong said. "The military has taken over. If they've threatened to shoot your pilot, then they will."

Their position hopeless, Allison and Bixby recalled the other DC-2s already in the air and ordered the airline to evacuate Shanghai. Brutal close-quarters melees raged in the dense neighborhoods north of the International Settlement, where more than thirty thousand Chinese infantryman battled to drive eight thousand Japanese marines into the Whangpoo. Japanese men-of-war belched gunfire point-blank into the fighting as mortar shell detonations and grenade blasts punctuated the small-arms fire ripping the streets. Driven by the storm winds, smoke whipped from battlefield infernos while Japanese planes swooped and dived on targets around North Station. Six Chinese bombers broke through the bottom of the cloud layer at 4:25 P.M. Antiaircraft fire fountained again from the *Idzumo*, joined by the guns of the other warships. The bombers held formation and pressed the attack, but none of their bombs hit the target. Two minutes later, four new bombers appeared from another direction, attacking across the wind, which shoved them wide of their intended bomb run. Antiaircraft guns chewed into them, and the pilots released their bombs far short of the *Idzumo*. The crosswind pushed the projectiles toward the International Settlement. Two bombs exploded in the river, throwing sheets of water over the jetty at the end of Peking Road. The third and fourth bombs detonated between the Palace and Cathay hotels at the intersection of Nanking Road and the Bund. Smoke, flame, and thunder consumed the concrete canyon, which was packed with refugees.

Yellowish high-explosive haze hung between the two hotels in the aftermath of the explosions. Glass shards and chunks of shattered masonry crashed to the street, unheard by deafened victims. Flames licked from ruined cars and trolleys as a slow anabiosis crept through the survivors. People moved again, amid unimaginable carnage. Tears streamed down the anguished visage of a Chinese woman as she staggered away from the devastation, herself unharmed, but the face of the two-year-old girl in her arms shredded to a bloody mask. A coolie shoved his hand into the remains of his lower leg, which spurted blood in time with his heartbeat. A decapitated Sikh policeman lay in the road where he'd been directing traffic. Aside from his missing head, his uniform was perfectly composed. Live electric wires writhed among hundreds of dismembered corpses: arms, legs, feet, hands, heads, chunks of infants, children, men, and women. Shreds of coolie clothing were everywhere, their usual blue blood-stained dark. The body of a young boy was plastered against the wall of the Cathay far above the sidewalk. Even skirting the grotesque heaps of corpses, it was impossible to walk without treading on chunks of human flesh. The smell of butchery mixed with the acrid nasal bite of high-explosive residue. A few European bodies lay among hundreds of Chinese dead. Seven hundred and twenty-nine people died at the intersection of Nanking Road and the Bund. Eight hundred and sixty-five others were badly injured.

Less than fifteen minutes later, a mortally wounded Chinese bomber winged over the French Concession. The pilot lined up an emergency landing on the Shanghai racecourse and jettisoned his bomb load, which hit the Great World Amusement Building, at the corner of Edward the VII Avenue and Tibet Road. The Great World had been converted into a refugee shelter; the bombs turned it into a charnel house. One thousand and eleven died in the devastation; 570 others were wounded. Taken together, the two "Bloody Saturday" bombings killed 1,740 civilians.

Harold Bixby, his wife, and their four daughters were staying in the Bonds' villa at 279 Rue Charles Culty in the French Concession that summer, where they'd thrown a number of successful cocktail and dinner parties in the two months since the Bonds went stateside. Bixby went through the Nanking Road bombing site on his way home, and he learned things he was doing his best to forget by the time he reached his badly shaken wife, who greeted him at the door. The Bonds' villa had screw-open living room windows, which had been open when a stray .50-caliber bullet whizzed through, ricocheted off the floor, and smacked into the rear wall of the living room. The spent round was sizzling hot, and slightly bent. Cooled, it fit neatly across Debbie Bixby's palm.

On the other side of the world, William Bond flew to New York, summoned by Pan Am president Juan Terry Trippe to discuss the crisis. Kitsi went north with her husband, but she wasn't included in the business council.

Fifty-nine floors above the lobby of the Chrysler Building, Bond met Juan Trippe and Stokely Morgan, Pan American Airways' vice president for the Orient. The news from China was dismal. The Japanese occupation of Peiping had cost CNAC one of its routes, which was bad enough. The Shanghai fighting put *all* of its routes in jeopardy. The three men rode the Chrysler's faûx-French elevator toward their lunch reservation in the Cloud Club, sanctum sanctorum of the New York elite housed in the building's stainless steel cap, and Bond struggled not to force nervous chitchat. A few words from Trippe could render meaningless the last six years of his life. Only Bond's mannerly Virginia upbringing and his tailored suit, done beautifully in Shanghai, hid the gulf of class and privilege dividing him from his companions, and if Trippe's blue-blood aura wasn't intimidating enough, he was six years *younger* than William Bond and physically much larger. A former Yale footballer, Trippe stood six feet tall and weighed two hundred pounds.

An attendant held a padded leather door opposite the elevator on the sixty-sixth-floor landing, and Trippe led the way through the Cloud Club's Georgian lobby, past its Tudor lounge and Bavarian bar, and then up a lavish marble-and-bronze Renaissance staircase to the main dining room. Juan Trippe was a Cloud Club member, of course, and a frequent patron, and he strode to a table against one of the fifty-four-inch windows: New York's other buildings, themselves giants, looked like upended matchboxes from the empyrean heights of the Cloud Club. The Empire State Building, some ten blocks away, was the city's only other thousand-foot skyscraper.

A waiter took lunch orders; another brought tycoon-sized martinis. "The China Incident" put a substantial amount of Pan Am capital in jeopardy, and CNAC's part in it threatened the company's relationship with the State Department. Trippe quickly put the talk on the business track. "Everything I hear from Bixby is bad. It looks to me like we're finished in China."

Bond didn't see things that way, not at all. He'd also been involved with Pan American long enough to know that a man crossed Juan Trippe at grave peril to his own employment, but Bond wasn't prepared to let war exterminate the airline he'd done so much to build because he was afraid to contradict Trippe. "Sir, with all due respect, I disagree. I think we should continue to operate. I think the Chinese can hang on for a long time, possibly years."

Trippe shook his head. "Impossible. They won't win. The State Department says so. And we can't run a commercial airline in the middle of a war.

You've seen Bixby's cables." Trippe wasn't negotiating. He wasn't exploring options. To him, the China venture was dead. "We're going to be opening a line to New Zealand, Mr. Bond. I want you to run that line."

The offer took Bond aback. He'd never envisioned a place for himself in the System beyond China. California to New Zealand would be the longest over-water route in aviation, longer than the transpacific flights. Running it held tremendous appeal—it would mean a raise and a big jolt of prestige. Best of all, it connected countries free of war, places he could take Kitsi and Langhorne.

However, to develop the New Zealand line Bond would have to turn his back on China and abandon everything he'd built. Bond sipped his gin, letting the liquor burn. He just couldn't stomach the disloyalty of it. Bond felt a debt to CNAC, Pan American, and China. He'd had a good job through the worst of the Depression. China needed air transportation as much, if not more, than any country on earth, it needed it now, and Pan Am had a million and a half dollars sunk into the endeavor (an investment worth about 22.2 million modern dollars). Nobody else in the system could recover that money, not even Harold Bixby.

"I'm flattered and honored by your offer, Mr. Trippe, and I'd dearly love to run that line, but I just can't do it. My place is in China. I need to go back."

"I'm going to tell Bix to fly whatever planes he has to Manila, and freeze whatever assets he can. We'll pick up in China when the war ends. It shouldn't last long." It was as if Trippe hadn't even heard Bond.

"Sir, the Chinese need our service *now*. If we don't help *now*, they won't want us back when the war's over."

"I've got the entire system to think about," Trippe continued. "This company does business in forty countries. We *cannot* afford to foul the State Department."

"I think we can continue to operate in China, sir, and China will still be there when the war ends."

Bond tried, but he couldn't make Trippe understand that as long as China had the will to resist, the Japanese wouldn't win, not in the long run. *Will* was the essential thing, not the modern arms and industry that balanced State Department calculations, and as long as the Chinese had will, they couldn't lose. The Japanese could take Shanghai, Nanking, Peiping, Hankow, Canton, or any other city, kill hundreds of thousands of soldiers, inflict a million horrors, and they still couldn't hold China. They were trying to grab a ghost the size of the continental United States. And as long as China resisted, whatever part of China remained free would need an airline. Bond couldn't think of a more powerful tool for developing and solidifying the internal and external communications so crucial to a besieged nation. China's greatest weakness wasn't industrial or technical. It was her lack of political unity, and aviation had a crucial role to play in that problem's remedy.

Bond and Trippe were extraordinarily tenacious men. Disciplined persistence was the key to whatever success both men had wrung from life, and neither would quit his position. Bond wanted to return to China and salvage his airline from the ruins of war. Trippe didn't think it could be done, that it wasn't worth the effort, and, more significant, the effort itself might be harmful to Pan American's crucial relationship with the State Department.

Lunch arrived, food was consumed, plates were removed, and they continued to go back and forth. Bond wouldn't agree to go to New Zealand; Trippe wouldn't let Bond return to China. One by one, the other tables emptied until their conversation ground to a halt, exhausted. Bond, Trippe, and Morgan rode the elevator to the Pan Am offices in tense silence. The Otis's doors parted, and Trippe walked away. Bond trailed him into his office. "Mr. Trippe, I would love to go to New Zealand, where I can have my wife and son, but I just can't do it. My job is in China. I must go back."

Trippe shuffled papers at his desk, clearly annoyed. He waved his hand without looking up. "Go on, go on," he said.

Only in the hall did Bond realize he had no clear notion of what Trippe meant. Did he have Trippe's endorsement for a return to China, or had Trippe merely wanted him to evacuate his office? Bond decided the question on the way to Stokely Morgan's desk. "Mr. Morgan, would you please reserve me a seat on the next transpacific Clipper? I've made up my mind. I'm going back."

"I suppose I don't need to tell you you're giving up a good thing and may injure your standing in the company."

"I realize that, but my place is in China."

.   .   .

Bond told Kitsi the whole story on the flight back to Washington, explaining he'd given up one of the best jobs in aviation by declining the New Zealand line, possibly damaged his position with Pan American, and might not be able to fix anything in Asia. "But it isn't just Pan Am's interest in CNAC that's at stake, Kitsi, it's China and the entire Far East. China has so little to fight with. An airline could make an enormous difference. And even if I can't do anything, at least I'll know that I didn't run away when things were bad."

Kitsi twined her fingers through her husband's and leaned her head against his shoulder. Bond kissed the top of her head. Her soft brown hair felt cool beneath his lips. Warmth flooded his chest, and gratitude for her support.

9

THE CAVALRY

At Hayes Manor, Bond packed a suitcase. Another painful downturn assailed the economy in 1937, even after five years of tortuous progress from the nadirs of 1932 and 1933, a depression within a depression that struck hard blows to Kitsi's family. Bond didn't think it right to add pressure by leaving his wife unsupported. He arranged to siphon $250 per month (about $3,700 in modern dollars) to Kitsi's family to cover her room and board for whatever period it took him to reestablish Pan Am's position in China.

Bond and Kitsi made their goodbyes, and he took the sleeper to San Francisco, an eighteen-hour flight on one of the Douglas Corporation's new DC-3s, then boarded the *Philippine Clipper* at Alameda and flew overnight again, eighteen hours to Honolulu. From Hawaii, the Clipper flew a leg a day across the islands of the central Pacific, and on Thursday, August 26, 1937, Bond jumped the South China Sea on the *Hong Kong Clipper*, the four-engine Sikorsky S-42 with which Pan Am did the leap to the Asian mainland. Five hours after leaving Manila, the twin-tailed seaplane gradually descended from its six-thousand-foot cruising altitude and winged up the Lei Yue Mun Channel west of Hong Kong Island. William

Bond peered through a porthole past the wing supports and the outboard pontoon and watched hazy, jungle-covered mountains scroll past. The plane burst into open sky over Victoria Harbor and lost altitude until its silver hull cut a white streak in the green water and settled into Kowloon Bay. The pilot taxied to the Pan Am pontoon at Kai Tak Airport, built on landfill a mile northeast of Kowloon, and Bond marveled at the speed of his trip: Eleven thousand miles of flying, Washington, D.C., to Hong Kong, and it had taken only eight days.

Ernie Allison met Bond on the dock, both sweating profusely in the August heat. Everybody in the airline was alive, Allison reported. After a frightening run down the Whangpoo River in a dangerously overloaded lighter—while shrapnel and stray bullets pinged off the hull—most of the American wives and children had taken the SS *President Jefferson* to Manila, where they'd been hit by the worst earthquake in thirty years. Allie's eight-months-pregnant wife was badly shaken—as much by the tremor as she'd been by the stray artillery shells that had hit their Shanghai apartment building—but judging from the cables she'd sent, she seemed okay. Debbie Bixby was taking care of her in Baguio, in the Luzon highlands 150 miles north of Manila. The majority of the staff was with Bixby aboard the SS *President Pierce*, due in from Shanghai the following day. So much for the good news; the rest of it was all bad. While Bond was flying, Pan Am's China position had collapsed entirely. Lunghwa Airport had been bombed; there was no hope of using it until the battle ended, and both sides were pouring reinforcements into the fighting. The airline's planes and people were scattered all over China. Overzealous Chinese antiaircraft gunners had riddled two airliners with machine-gun fire. A rattled pilot landing at Hankow had forgotten to put down a DC-2's landing gear. Belly-landed, the plane was out of commission until it got a new center section. Colonel Lam was running the company as an air force auxiliary, essentially press-ganging the American pilots into the Chinese military, and the State Department had formally warned Bixby that the airline's Americans were violating United States neutrality. Most of the Caucasian pilots had flown to Hong Kong in a DC-2, which Bixby ordered held in the colony against a $60,000 U.S. debt CNAC owed Pan Am for transpacific sales it had agented—an amount that almost exactly matched the value of a used DC-2 (worth about 900,000 modern dollars). Worst of all, except for the one DC-2 in Hong Kong, Colonel Lam and the Chinese Air Force had all the airplanes. That loss was an unexpected blow. Without planes, Bond had no tangible leverage. He grilled Allison for details. Allison told Bond everything he knew, but as far as he was concerned the China National Aviation Corporation was finished.

On Friday, Bond met the SS *President Pierce* at the ocean liner terminal on the Kowloon docks, and Harold Bixby came ashore carrying the recent ordeal in deep creases scored into his face. "Four years of hard work wrecked in ten days. Don't know why you came back. The airline's a total loss," he told Bond grimly.

Debarked and refreshed, the two friends reconvened in the bar of the Hong Kong Hotel, and Bixby told his tales of the airline caught astride the outbreak of war. As far as he was concerned, there wasn't a ray of hope.

"Bix, look, I've got *six years* of my life invested in this company. I'm not going to let it go down the drain without at least trying to save it," Bond pressed.

"I know how you feel. I've been at it for four. I just don't know how you'd do it. U.S. law won't allow military flying, and the Chinese don't want anything *but* military flying, and I think it's at least possible they used that lever to push us out and gobble our investment. Gauss* doesn't think we can operate without the Japanese shooting down one of our planes. Sooner or later. And he's right. He's in the State Department. They don't want us to operate, and we *cannot* cross the State Department."

"Trippe told me the same thing."

"So how in the hell are you going to get around that?" Bixby demanded. "Between State, the Chinese, and Trippe, you'll be getting it from three sides."

"You're forgetting the Japs."

Bixby tossed up his hands.

"I've got some ideas," Bond continued. "For one, I'll resign from Pan Am and go on the CNAC payroll. If the Japanese shoot down any of our planes, I'll say neither I nor anyone else in the company has any connection with Pan Am."

---

* Clarence Gauss, U.S. consul in Shanghai.

"What makes you think Trippe'll go for it?"

"Because he's got a million and a half dollars sunk into CNAC, and unless someone from Pan Am does something to help China *now*, when they need it most, that money is gone forever."

"How're you going to run an airline? Colonel Lam has all the airplanes. We've only got the one DC-2 here in Hong Kong, and as soon as we take that ship into Chinese airspace he's going to take it, too."

"It's not so easy to run an airline, Bix, you know that. Not on a schedule. Our Air Corps couldn't do it in '34, and I don't think Colonel Lam or anyone else in the Chinese Air Force can do it, either.* A few planes flying a few tons of military supplies isn't going to change the outcome of any battle, but the ability of the Chinese government to maintain communications and keep control and stay in contact with the outside world might affect the outcome of the whole war. Give it five or six weeks and they'll reach the same conclusion. Two months at the outside. All we have to do is wait."

"I was crowing the same story last week and no Chinese official would listen, not one, and personally, at this juncture, I just don't think it can be done without crossing the neutrality laws."

"Like I said, I won't be on the Pan Am payroll, and neither will anybody else. It won't be a Pan Am problem."

Bond chewed at Bixby's leg for the next forty-eight hours, and slowly, painfully, cautiously, Bixby came to see merit in Bond's point of view. It was, after all, an awful lot of money. As long as Bond could keep clear of the State Department, there wasn't anything to lose that wasn't lost already. Bixby's last concern was for Bond himself. "Bondy, if you fail, you're out. Trippe offered you New Zealand and you said no."

"Already done that," Bond rued.

"All right, it's worth a try." The men found a telephone. Bixby figured the time in New York. "Trippe'll be home. Let's see what he says."

Bixby lifted the receiver.

"Wait," Bond interrupted, "before you call, if it could be arranged, I'd be

---

* In the United States, in 1934, when an investigation had exposed corruption in the award of airmail contracts, President Roosevelt ordered the Army Air Corps to fly the mail. The Air Corps flew the airmail for seventy-eight days, had fifty-seven accidents, killed a dozen pilots, and destroyed thousands of letters. The post office invited civilians back to the job.

grateful if Pan Am would continue my life insurance. Nobody out here's going to take me with this job."

Bixby frowned and nodded, and the operator put the call through. Bond held his ear close. Bixby outlined Bond's arguments and told Trippe that despite his reservations, he thought there might be substance to Bond's position.

Trippe was silent. He wasn't the type to be rushed into a decision, no matter the excruciating cost of international telephone time. There were significant risks. The American public didn't want the country embroiled in any foreign wars. An "incident" could contaminate the System's relationship with the State Department, and Pan Am depended on its good graces. But if he didn't allow Bond to try, he'd have to swallow the loss of $1.5 million (about 22.7 million modern dollars), an investment that could conceivably blossom into something far more valuable. There was much at stake, and many uncertainties, paramount among them being William Langhorne Bond. Could he trust Bond to do the right thing? If Bond formally severed ties with Pan Am, only his word guaranteed the arrangement. Could he trust Bond with that much money? Bixby obviously thought highly of him. It all came down to Bond. The telephone was silent for a long time. At last, Trippe agreed—with conditions.

He wanted a written resignation. He'd send a written acceptance. And if anything should happen, however slight, he expected Bond to deny any connection with Pan Am and say that Pan Am had, at the insistence of the United States, reluctantly and completely withdrawn from CNAC.

Bixby turned to Bond. "You hear all that?"

Bond spoke clearly toward the mouthpiece. "Yes, sir, I did. I agree, and I fully approve."

Bixby continued. "Mr. Trippe, Bondy made one request, but I'm making it a condition: that Pan Am continue his life insurance. He's got a wife and a baby boy. It'll be impossible to replace."

Trippe agreed again.

"I have one more thing to ask for Bondy," Bixby added, "and I want to stress that it's something he has *not* mentioned. I'm asking for him. He's a member of Pan Am's executive stock purchase plan and the plan expires next summer. I'm making it a condition we include Bondy as a full participant in whatever extension or renewal we adopt, no matter the changes in his official status."

Trippe consented for a third time, and the deal was done. Bixby's spontaneous consideration touched Bond profoundly. Bix was trying to cement his family's future when uncertainty lapped at everything else.

Bond spent the rest of the day thinking, planning, attempting to ascertain the airline's current situation and plot a course ahead. In his mind, China's need for reliable, rapid, and dependable air transportation was a foregone conclusion, as was its need for Pan American know-how. Another five or eight years and the Chinese would be ready to go it alone, but right now they weren't. They still needed Pan Am, even if they wouldn't admit it. China's soldiers and leaders were proud, capable men trying to fight a war against a first-rate military power, and, apparently, holding their own in Shanghai, which was turning into a colossal battle, but Bond wouldn't be able to force-feed them arrogant foreign opinion. He could only show them the trough. They'd have to drink of their own volition.

After dark, Bond took the Star Ferry across the harbor to Kowloon. He rode upstairs, under the upper deck awning, and a burst of sea air washed over the open rails, a welcome salve after the stifling heat and humidity of Victoria town. Lights bobbed in the harbor and twinkled along the streets lining the waterfront and from houses on the peak behind. If one didn't concentrate, it was difficult to tell where the lights ended and the heavens began. Kowloon-side, a rickshaw hauled Bond a few blocks down the waterfront to the Peninsula Hotel, a luxurious establishment built in a square U shape, open to the front, directly across the street from the Hong Kong–Canton–Hankow railroad terminal. Seven stories tall, the tallest in Kowloon, the Peninsula towered over the mainland side of Hong Kong Harbor, perfectly positioned to take advantage of the aviation traffic beginning to boom at nearby Kai Tak Airfield. Shanghai's misfortune was proving to be Hong Kong's boon.

Bond's façade of dogged optimism lapsed in the privacy of his room. He slumped at the desk and wrote Kitsi on hotel stationery, outlining the many fiascoes besetting his airline:

Things here are at rock bottom, absolute zero. Bix thinks the show is impossible and finished. . . . It is a forlorn hope, but the present situation is so perfectly hopeless that I feel very cheerful about making an effort. If conditions were less bad I might not have the courage to try for fear I might make some fatal mistake and completely finish every-

thing. . . . I sent you a cable today asking for a reply. I just have to have
something I know is from you. . . . If ever I wished for you and needed
your inspiration and guidance, I do so now. . . .

I love you my angel, Your Bondy.

Bond signed his letter and stretched out on the bed, exhausted. Nobody cared about the company as much as he did—or, at least, no other American. Ernie Allison was an old hand in the aviation game, a true pioneer, a good man, and a dead-steady pilot, but he'd made his mark in flying long before joining the China National Aviation Corporation. Nor was the China airline quite so important to Harold Bixby, a made man at Pan American. CNAC was the sum total of everything Bond had accomplished in the industry. Bond had no special standing at Pan Am; he'd been grand-fathered into the System along with CNAC, and he had an inkling he'd never crack the top echelon of the Pan Am cabal. He simply didn't have the pedigree.

A torrent of loyalties squeezed Bond: to Pan Am, to CNAC and the people who worked for the company, to China, and to the United States. Above all was his loyalty to Kitsi and his infant son. His mind couldn't balance the competing interests. Sleep wouldn't come. He worried about pilots. Of the Caucasian pilots, only Hal Sweet and Harry Smith* had de-finitively elected to stay with the airline in defiance of State Department guidance. Bixby was going to Manila in the morning, where he'd base him-self while he tried to place the others elsewhere in the Pan Am System—where most of them hoped to catch on. Bond couldn't operate without pilots, even if he was successful with the Chinese, but he couldn't justify encouraging them to hang around in case he couldn't reestablish the American position. He'd lost the chance of making a big step by refusing the New Zealand line. He wouldn't have a job if he failed to restore Pan Am's role in CNAC. He hoped he'd made the right decision. His stomach hurt; he'd forgotten to eat.

In the morning, Bond took Bixby to the dock. Bixby wanted to pick a

---

* The same Harry Smith whom Bond had fired as operations manager shortly after arriving in China. Smith had returned to fly for the airline through the middle thirties.

bone with Colonel Lam. "CNAC owes us for the transpacific tickets they've sold, and the way things stand, we're never going to get it. The DC-2 here in Hong Kong just about exactly covers that debt. I want you to make sure he doesn't get that ship unless he pays."

"I can't do that, Bix! That ship is CNAC property. CNAC *owns* that airplane."

If Colonel Lam made any effort to take it, Bixby wanted Bond to have the Hong Kong courts "attach" the plane for payment of the debt—the method by which liens were handled in the colony.

"Don't make me do that," Bond pleaded. "You'll kill my chances."

"Bondy, I do not want that son of a bitch to get that airplane."

Bixby sailed on that sour note. The inseparable pilot duo of Hugh Woods and Chuck Sharp waylaid Bond in the Peninsula's lobby. Neither man wanted to leave the Orient. Bond wouldn't make promises or predictions, but, if they were serious about staying, Bond suggested they take a vacation and see how things developed. Woody and Sharp decided on a trip to the Dutch East Indies (modern-day Indonesia).

Bond bought three things before going to Kai Tak Airport to catch the Eurasia flight to Hankow for his meeting with Colonel Lam Whi-shing: a shoulder holster, shells, and a .22-caliber Colt automatic. They cost him U.S. $26 ($390 in modern dollars).

Eurasia's tri-motored Junkers 52 touched down on Hankow's dirt airfield on the last day of August 1937. William Bond stepped down from the airplane, adjusted his suit coat, trying to get accustomed to his Colt-carrying shoulder holster, and looked around the crude facility. It looked much the same as when he'd last seen it, a spare field, four thousand feet on a side, rimmed by a few ratty buildings, without designated runways, an airport tower, or traffic control. Toward the Yangtze, stolid bank buildings and the church spires of mission headquarters rose from the low red-brick and tile rooftops of Hankow, a noticeable departure from the usual dingy gray of Chinese cities. In other directions, coolie farmers labored in small rice paddies, protected from the savage August sun by wide-brimmed bamboo hats. Bond went straight to see Colonel Lam in the office CNAC kept in the Astoria Building on the French Bund. He'd met the colonel only once before his home leave, and what he'd learned since was unsettling. The colonel had roots in south China's Kwangsi Province, Kwantung's less prosperous neighbor. The two provinces often acted independently from the Nanking government. Kwangsi sponsored its own aviation school, which Colonel Lam had commanded, and from what Bond gleaned in Hong Kong he'd run the school as a pompous martinet and had a temper like a fuel explosion. Supposedly, he'd jailed a British instructor and spontaneously executed two of his Chinese subordinates.

A company receptionist showed him to a seat. Bond made himself comfortable, prepared for Lam to "make face" by keeping him waiting. To his surprise, Lam summoned him promptly. Bond stood, feeling awkward. He'd never carried a concealed weapon, but he was glad to have it as insurance.

Colonel Lam, a lean, leathery man in an immaculate uniform, received Bond with elaborate courtesy. He was tall for a Chinese, and had an inch or two on Bond. They inquired about each other's families and health and chatted about the weather. The receptionist brought tea. Colonel Lam asked Bond what he thought of CNAC's situation.

"I've only just arrived, so I think you can answer that question better than me." Bond paused. The colonel didn't react. Bond continued slowly, choosing his words with supreme care. "It does seem to me, however, that the company's prospects are . . . uncertain. In the last six years, we created an organization looked on as the ideal type for future foreign investment in China. Now, in thirty days, everything is different. There is no more faith, dedication, or goodwill, and precious little friendship."

"Whom do you blame for this, Mr. Bond?"

"No one." Bond excised the challenge from his voice. "Yet there *is* blame, and it should be borne equally by both partners. Both sides should have known that if war started, the U.S. government would pressure Pan Am to withdraw. A workable solution could have been arranged in advance. Not *after* fighting started. When it did, many unwise things were done, such as forcing American pilots to do military flying. But that's behind us. It's no longer important."

"What do you have in mind?"

"Only CNAC. I want to see it restored as an organized, viable, civilian company, operating on regular schedules to wherever the service is needed most. China's need for Pan Am is greater than ever, not only for its operating and organizational skill but also for the quality of its contacts within the American government. And yes, I'd like to take part."

"Good. The first thing I want you to do is return our DC-2 in Hong Kong."

Bond set aside his tea. "I said I would always tell you the truth, and I will. Mr. Bixby wants an attachment put on that plane until CNAC pays the debt it owes Pan Am for transpacific tickets."

The colonel sat bolt upright and clenched the arms of his chair. "Mr. Bixby is no gentleman!"

"I disagree," said Bond, dead calm.

Colonel Lam sprang to his feet. "What did you say?" he shouted.

Bond stayed rooted to his chair. Very cautiously, he undid his coat button. "I said I disagree . . . Colonel, would you please sit down." Bond spoke firmly, quietly, with extreme courtesy, the tone of a well-bred Virginian who expected to be obeyed. All the while, he kept his right hand ready to leap to his armpit. "There's been enough quarreling. I've been out of it, and I'm not going to get back in. Mr. Bixby is internationally known as a gentleman. He needs no defense by me."

The veins in the colonel's neck pulsed and contorted. Bond looked very deliberately at the wall beyond his cheek, not wanting to provoke him with a direct stare, nor allow his own attention to waver.

Colonel Lam lowered himself into his chair.

"Colonel, do you always get angry so quickly? You jumped before I could finish. What I was going to say was that I told Mr. Bixby that 'attaching' the DC-2 would be a grave mistake. I'll go to Hong Kong and do my best to get the plane out. If I succeed, I'll tell Mr. Bixby I didn't carry out his instructions, and I'll take the consequences."

Suspicious of Bond's intentions, Colonel Lam assigned business manager P. Y. Wong to travel with him to ensure that he pursued that goal with his usual vigor.

Bond had hoped to go to Nanking to reestablish his bona fides with Ministry of Communications officials, but an intestinal disorder leveled him in Hankow, and he spent the next week in a hospital. Staying healthy in China wasn't easy: Cholera, typhoid, smallpox, mumps, polio, diphtheria, measles, dysentery—all were well represented in the sprawling, destitute country, and even more so amid the ravages of war. The illness had run its course by September 8, and Bond flew instead to Hong Kong with P. Y. Wong and Donald Wong (no relation), one of the organization's star Chinese American fliers, who would be needed to fly the Hong Kong DC-2 back into China.

The silver Douglas continued to obsess Bixby. It represented the only tangible asset he held against the possibility of extreme Chinese malfeasance. Bixby wanted it flown to Manila, where he'd be in "a position where possession [was] nine-tenths of the law." Bixby pondered "clearing for Hankow and getting lost" and ending up in Manila, but the direction and terrain were too different and such outright "horsestealing" would cause complications in Nanking, Washington, and Hong Kong that Pan Am couldn't afford. Bixby consulted a lawyer, only to be told that there were no legal means to spirit the plane out of the colony. Increasingly bitter, Bixby considered forging an exchange of letters between himself and Colonel Lam in which Colonel Lam accepted a Pan Am offer to credit CNAC with $60,000 in exchange for the ship.

For William Bond, the Hong Kong DC-2 presented an extraordinarily complicated situation. Bixby wanted the plane for Pan Am, but it belonged to CNAC, bought with money earned in the Middle Kingdom. Bond was certain that Bixby's gaining possession of it would permanently ruin Pan Am's relationship with the Chinese.

Pilot Donald Wong sought out Bond the day after they arrived in Hong Kong and eased the immediate problem. "Mr. Bond, I was born in Chicago. I'm an American citizen, but Colonel Lam treats me like a Chinese. He'll shoot me if I don't do what he says, and I don't want to get shot so he can create an image of himself as some heroic anti-Japanese fighter."

Wong took the next boat back to the States, and the DC-2 couldn't leave without a pilot. Bixby returned from the Philippines and continued to refuse to relinquish the airplane. Colonel Lam wrote Bond from Hankow, "astonished to learn Mr. Bixby has taken such an action. If this plane will not be released immediately, I am afraid, nothing in the alternative, but to claim the return of the property through the Court in Hongkong [sic]."

Bixby relented—or at least gave that appearance. In the interest of preserving whatever shred of goodwill still existed between Pan American and the Ministry of Communications, he agreed to allow Bond to repatriate the captive airplane. However, at 2:15 P.M. on September 23, the Texas Company (Texaco) presented CNAC's Hong Kong office with a bill for $60,253.04 (Mex.) and required the airline to pay it within three-quarters of an hour or face legal action. Texaco filed suit at 3:00 P.M., asking the Hong Kong court to "attach" the DC-2 against a debt the airline refused to pay. The British court did Texaco's bidding.

William Bond and P. Y. Wong went to Texaco's general manager, "hat in hand," and begged him to release the plane. Their airline had always paid its bills promptly.

"We don't want your plane. Pay your bill, and you can have it."

Colonel Lam went apoplectic. According to Texaco's own statement, the bill wasn't overdue, and the airline had paid Texaco half of the owed money the day prior to the "attachment." Colonel Lam hired a lawyer.

Texaco had contracted to provide fuel for Routes Two and Three, both swallowed by war. Without them, Texaco had no outstanding relationship with the China National Aviation Corporation and nothing to lose by offending it. However, the Texas Company did do substantial business with Pan American Airways, all over the world. From Harold M. Bixby's perspective, Texaco's actions must have seemed awfully convenient.

In public, Bond put on a great show of working to free the airplane. In private, he might not have been working so diligently. He quietly consulted an English solicitor, an expert on maritime law, and the lawyer illuminated a variety of holes in Texaco's legal position. Colonel Lam's lawyer chose to take a different tack, and Bond opted not to share his solicitor's wisdom. The Hong Kong court heard arguments on September 27 and upheld the attachment.

Colonel Lam wrote Bond to thank him for his strenuous efforts and settled the issue by paying Texaco's bill. Bixby wasn't pleased, but on October 5, P. Y. Wong and William Bond flew to Hankow aboard the liberated airplane. It was a particular triumph for Wong. The episode made it seem as if he'd gone up against the American interest and won.

That was an impression William Bond was actively trying to create. He was beginning to ponder the levers he might pull to vault P. Y. Wong to the managing directorship in Colonel Lam's stead. The case had another important side effect, too. Bond thought Hong Kong had a critical role in the airline's future, and its rigid adherence to English court proceedings cemented the company's right to operate from the colony, which the loss of Shanghai made "Free China's" most important point of contact with the outside world.

The DC-2's release didn't go over so well in New York, as Stokely Morgan pointed out sharply in a letter to Harold Bixby: "[President Trippe] was quite upset when he realized the DC-2 had been flown away from Hong Kong after settling the Texas Oil claim without paying us anything. I had unfortunately assured him that we were going to hold that plane until we got $100,000 (Mex.) with balance promised." Bixby did damage control with New York.

Navigating such byzantine complexities, Bond struggled to play the desires of Pan American, Colonel Lam, the Aviation Commission, and the Ministry of Communications against what he felt was best for the China National Aviation Corporation, Pan Am, and China. Paramount among his short-run concerns was the need to calm the vitriol flying between Pan Am and the Chinese. Both partners' hopes for the airline had been dashed against the realities of war, and the recriminations were bitter: Pan American thought they'd been robbed; the Chinese felt they'd been deserted.

10

SHANGHAI NOVEMBER

Bond spent most of October bouncing between Hankow, Hong Kong, and Manila. He lamented to Kitsi that he spent all of his time commuting. Worse, he'd wagered his family's future on his ability to reinstate CNAC's American position, and in the nearly eight weeks that had passed since his return, he'd made no discernible progress. Bixby's hopes ebbed even lower, but Bond corralled him into making a final plea to every facet of the Nationalist government who might conceivably listen.

Quite understandably, the Central Government had other priorities. Japanese airplanes regularly bombed Nanking and other cities and military installations, and the Shanghai confrontation had escalated into an immense battle. China's August attacks had failed to shove the Japanese into the Whangpoo. Both sides reinforced, and by October, more than half a million men were engaged, and the front stretched from the north bank of Soochow Creek through Chapei, Yangtzepoo, and Kiangwan to Woosung and Paoshan and then west to Lotien and Liuho, more than twenty miles to the northwest. Inside the urban areas, it was a brutal close-quarters street fight. Outside the city, bloody combats surged through trench lines and muddy quagmires. Tens of thousands died in a Yangtze Verdun.

On October 25, with the battle raging and the Japanese rumored to be starting their long-anticipated "big push," Bond and Bixby lifted free of Hong Kong's ground haze aboard one of Eurasia's tri-motored Junkers Ju-52s.

The Ministry of Communications granted priority to Eurasia on the Hankow–Hong Kong run, and it was enjoying a commercial heyday. Although the Ju-52 carried only seven passengers, the Hankow foreign community had filled it to capacity with air express orders for "other necessities," chief among them cigarettes, coffee, butter, and whisky. The plane also carried 175 pounds of "antitoxin" consigned to U.S. ambassador Nelson T. Johnson.* Eurasia flew the medicine free of charge, just as Pan American had brought it across the Pacific the previous week, an altruistic use of aviation assets that greatly pleased William Bond, considering the devastation rained on China by airplanes in the last four months.

Bond and Bixby set aside the cold salads in their boxed lunches, fearing the cholera rampant in south China, and washed down fried chicken sandwiches and cake with a thermos of hot coffee. An Arizona-blue sky spanned the horizons. Bixby reclined his chair, enjoyed a smoke, and dozed. Bond stared out the window and watched a cavalcade of mountains parade underneath the plane. The ranges crammed together, refusing to follow an orderly plan, the highest summits rearing to within a thousand feet of the wings. Bond couldn't see the way ahead for his airline. Not that it was his anymore. Colonel Lam and the Chinese Air Force still lorded it over CNAC, and most of its flying was unscheduled "hey, you" missions in support of the military. Irregular schedules generated little revenue, and the only real airline flying being done was at the top of the old Route One, where Moon Chin, Joy Thom, Hal Sweet, and a few others were shuttling between Chungking, Chengtu, and Hankow, occasionally coming as far east as Nanking. Considering the rate at which Bond thought the airline's resources were being squandered, soon it wouldn't matter whether or not he regained control. He hadn't seen his wife and son in eight weeks, but there wasn't any point in bringing them to the Orient unless he could reinstate the American position and see the airline through to safer ground.

They landed in the late afternoon. Hankow seemed peaceful, orderly,

---

* Bixby wasn't specific about the type of the "antitoxin."

and quiet, despite recent air raids. The air held the fresh bite of autumn, and fall colors tinged the trees along the city Bund. Bond and Bixby went to meet Dr. Kung Hsiang-hsi, H. H. Kung, in the Ministry of Foreign Affairs. Titles and positions shifted constantly in the Kuomintang government, but they seemed to rotate through the same set of individuals. Kung was one of the innermost junta, currently serving as minister of foreign affairs and president of the Executive Yuan, positions foreigners regarded as China's foreign minister and prime minister. A plump, benign-looking man, Kung hailed from the northern province of Shansi, and he was supposedly the seventy-fifth lineal descendant of Confucius. His family had amassed a fortune managing Chinese pawnbrokers, and they'd educated him at an American mission school, at Ohio's Oberlin College, and at Yale University. In 1914, Dr. Kung married homely Soong Ai-ling, elder sister of Soong Mei-ling (Madame Chiang Kai-shek), thereby uniting two of China's largest fortunes. Madame Kung was reputed to be the mastermind behind the clan's internationally diversified portfolio. Financial savants thought the Soong family might be the world's wealthiest. It was hard to imagine one more powerful.

Dr. Kung received the Americans with distant courtesy, peering at them through wire-rimmed spectacles. When they'd been through the formalities and pleasantries, Bixby turned the conversation to business, hoping to persuade Kung to oust the Chinese Air Force from the airline and allow Pan Am to resume commercial services, free from military flying. Kung didn't budge, and the meeting progressed cordially until Kung dismissed Bixby's stories of American pilots forced to do military flying.

Bixby bristled. A Chinese officer had held a gun to Chuck Sharp's head! That was a fact. As he was about to respond, Bond gestured him down with a hand raised an inch from his lap and a tiny shake of his head. What he really wanted to do was kick his friend's shin. Dr. Kung was China's prime minister. If Bixby directly challenged his word, Pan Am's interest in China was deader than the last dodo. Fortunately, Bixby received the message and reverted to a more diplomatic tack.

"China didn't start this war," Kung replied, "but China has to fight it. CNAC is a Chinese airline. We have nothing to negotiate. There's nothing to discuss."

"We're sorry you feel that way, Doctor," Bixby said, recognizing their dismissal. "We hope you'll change your mind. We'll be ready when you do."

Outside, waiting for rickshaws in the dank autumn darkness, Bixby's frustration spilled over. He felt they'd accomplished nothing.

Bond disagreed. "We said our piece, and we didn't lose a thing."

"We don't have a lot to lose, do we?" Bixby grunted. "So where to next, besides bed?"

"Nanking."

A British river steamer carried the two executives down the Yangtze on October 28. They reached Nanking the next day and docked among the anchored hulks of the riverside trading district. A cloud ceiling rolled in close to river level, leaking drizzle, and, for once, nobody minded. In fair weather, Japanese bombers sometimes pummeled the city three or four times a day, relays of terror intended to break China's will to resist. The Chinese Air Force bravely contested the onslaughts, advised by a retired U.S. Army Air Corps major named Claire Lee Chennault and materially aided by several squadrons of Soviet fliers, but they weren't able to repulse the attacks. Thousands of civilians died proving that China's days of peaceful acquiescence to Japanese demands had ended.

The city center was about five miles inland. Bond and Bixby taxied through the Ichang Gate in the massive Ming dynasty walls and up a 130-foot-wide asphalt thoroughfare bulldozed through the city's ancient alleyways and dirt and cobblestone streets. The two Americans spent most of their five Nanking days in the Ministry of Communications building, drafting and redrafting proposals detailing the circumstances under which Americans could return to the airline. Dr. Chang Kia-ngau, Kuomintang minister of communications, couldn't—or wouldn't—make time to see them, but they did obtain an audience with the vice minister, Peng Sho-pei, the official who'd replaced K. C. Huang as chairman of the airline's board of directors. He received the two Pan Am emissaries with frosty politeness. His sentiments echoed Dr. Kung's: Nothing to negotiate, nothing to discuss, come back and fulfill your contract. Beneath his formal exterior, he was taut with anger.

Bixby glowered at Bond afterward. "Felt like old Peng blames the Americans more than the Japanese. This is ridiculous. We're beating the air with our fists."

"I've got one more idea," Bond offered. "I'd like to see Soong Tse-ven."

"T. V. Soong! For Christ's sake, Bondy, he's in Shanghai! How in the hell are we going to get there?"

"A few cars are getting through around Tahu Lake and across the Minghong ferry into the south side of the city." With the help of one of the girls at the U.S. Embassy, Bond had arranged seats on a car going through that night. If all went well, it would reach Shanghai just after sunrise. "We'll be safe once we get to the settlements," he said.

"Safe! It's the biggest fight since Flanders. And besides, what if Dr. Soong won't see you? And he might be difficult even if he does."

Bond didn't actually expect to see T. V. Soong, but he was sure he could see M. Y. Tong, his oldest and closest Chinese friend and still one of T. V. Soong's most intimate advisors. Bond occasionally mixed business with their personal relationship, as he'd done in 1933 when he'd convinced M.Y. to approach Soong about helping to finance Route Two's inception. "I just want to make sure we've turned over every stone, Bix. I can't give up until I've tried everything."

T. V. Soong was the Kuomintang finance minister, a staunch Chinese Nationalist, ardently anti-Japanese, and, aside from his brother-in-law Generalissimo Chiang Kai-shek, he might have been the most influential man in China. Soong had done much to develop the Chinese Air Force, and he'd long been a quiet backer of the CNAC project, but the Americans knew he was furious with Pan Am for running out when the war started.*

"You go ahead. M.Y.'s your friend. You can handle him better than me. I'd just slow you down."

Secretly, Bond was relieved. Alone, the trip would be more streamlined.

An hour before dark on the misty, rainy evening of November 3, 1937, Bond motored out of Nanking packed into the back seat of a dilapidated Model T Ford with two Chinese businessmen and another foreigner. Two burly Chinese chauffeurs traded driving duties and sped through the muddy, rutted darkness toward Shanghai with an urgency edging on panic. Fishtailing on the slick surface, they broadsided a tree, stuck in potholes twice, and reached the Minghong ferry over the Whangpoo River about ten miles south of the International Settlement just as a gray, inglorious dawn crept into the world. A dozen vehicles ahead of them waited to board.

---

* T. V. Soong was also the brother-in-law of H. H. Kung, who was married to T.V.'s sister Soong Ai-ling.

Bond's drivers nuzzled the Model T against the rear of the line and settled down to wait. Bond got out and walked to the ferry ramp. Thin fog clung to the flat landscape. Dull, irregular thuds drifted across the caramel-colored river, harsh artillery sounds William Bond recognized from his time in France during the Great War. He sniffed the dank air, knowing the fog well. It might cling and linger. It could clear just as easily. The ferryboat came over from the north bank, unloaded two truck chassis, and headed back empty.

Bond trod on his cigarette and asked his Chinese companions to find out why the ferry hadn't moved any traffic from their side. They learned that thirty trucks had jammed themselves against the far-side ramp without leaving space for anybody to unload. Therefore, the ferry intended to bring all thirty trucks over from the north side before any of the vehicles on the south bank could cross. The ferry took thirty-five minutes to complete a round-trip: They were in for an eight-hour wait! Under clear skies, or even a ceiling raised five hundred feet, a gaggle of trucks packed against a loading ramp would attract Japanese planes like a cesspit drawing flies. Bond looked around. There was no protection whatsoever, no solid buildings, no irrigation ditches, no holes, no berms, nothing, just flat, open ground. Bond huddled his companions. "Listen, if this fog lifts, Jap planes are going to blow this place to hell. It's a death trap. Forget the car. Let's go over to the other side and walk a mile down the road and wait for it to catch up."

All four travelers nosed into the fog aboard the next ferry. As they'd been told, the loading ramp on the far side was jammed with trucks and soldiers jostling for advantage. Bond cursed—rule one on page one of any military transport handbook said to keep roads unblocked.

A large truck piled high with heavy crates and a well-armed escort of six soldiers held position to load, but the overloaded truck couldn't mount the ferry's ramp. Bond and his friends helped the soldiers push it aboard. The Chinese lounging in the traffic jam hooted with delight to see a "foreign barbarian" heave like a coolie.

One of Bond's Chinese companions explained their problem to the soldiers they'd aided. A private suggested that the party accompany his group back to the other side, where he and his comrades would get the car loaded.

The private's idea sounded great to Bond, except for the traffic jam on the Shanghai bank. How would they get through?

"Just sit on the ferry and wait until these fellows back up and clear the road. What else can they do? They can't get on until they let you off."

Back on the south bank, the half-dozen armed men proved persuasive. The ferry officials loaded Bond's taxi. The soldiers on the Shanghai bank raised a tremendous ruckus, but after much vociferous complaining they reached the obvious conclusion and disassembled their traffic jam, exactly as the canny private had foreseen. As they motored off, Bond craned his neck and watched, flabbergasted, as the trucks swarmed back against the ferry ramp and re-blocked the road. The old American Expeditionary Force never-wish-someone-good-luck wisecrack leapt to his lips. "I hope all you bastards get killed," he muttered.

None of Bond's three servants or his gardener had been paid in two months, but his usual breakfast waited on the table of his home in the French Concession at 8:00 A.M., made to his exact standard of perfection. The house was immaculate, the grass was cut, and the garden meticulously weeded. Bond had the impression he was expected. Perhaps an embassy girl had called ahead? He had no idea. Bond had lived in the Far East for six years, but China was like an onion, always with another layer to reveal. He shook his head in awe of its "bamboo telegraph."

Artillery banging north of the International Settlement serenaded Bond's breakfast, a cacophony of combat that had punctuated the lives of Shanghailanders for more than eighty days. Bond rested through the morning. After lunch, he went to see M. Y. Tong.

Bond's appearance surprised his old friend, and he advised Bond to leave Shanghai immediately—advice to be taken seriously, given Tong's access to information on how the Central Army was truly faring.

Bond asked for an audience with Dr. Soong to discuss ousting Colonel Lam Whi-shing and the Chinese Air Force from the airline so Pan Am could return.

"Look, Bondy, we're old friends, and I'm sure you're sincere, but Dr. Soong wasn't pleased with your withdrawal."

"We weren't either. We only want to operate a commercial airline, free from military flying."

Upon reflection, Tong refused to interrupt Soong. "Don't forget who he is and that China is at war. You have no idea of the strain he's under. Write your concerns in a memorandum, and I'll present it to him, but not until I think he won't be angered. That might be a month. I make no promises."

Bond didn't think the airline could withstand another month. He spent the next two days drafting the requested memo in the airline's head office in the Robert Dollar Building at 51 Canton Road, a block inland from the Bund and around the corner from the Hong Kong Shanghai Bank. Built of reinforced concrete, the Dollar Building made no effort to rival its famous neighbor. Like much International Settlement architecture, it looked as if it had been rooted in Shanghai's mud for centuries, but in truth, it was only thirteen years old, and besides the offices of the Dollar Steamship Line and the China National Aviation Corporation, the tenant roster included the American Chamber of Commerce and the U.S. Navy's Asiatic purchasing office. Nothing truly outrageous could occur within such solid walls, a message the airline very much intended to communicate. The random detonations of war drifted through Bond's office window, along with the acrid smells of cordite and smoke, and while he labored in solitude, assault elements of three Japanese divisions landed on the north coast of Hangchow Bay, fifty miles to the southwest. Both sides rushed reinforcements to the new battlefield. If the Chinese sealed off the beachheads and divided the Japanese landing forces from their army in Shanghai, the Japanese would be vulnerable to piecemeal defeat. If the Japanese broke out, they would have an army corps loose in the rear flank of the Chinese Army, threatening it with annihilation.

The landings cut the overland route Bond had used to come to Shanghai, the one by which he'd hoped to escape. The airline's board of directors was scheduled to meet in Nanking three days hence, but as news of the landings spread, Bond realized he'd never make it. He closed the office at dusk on November 6, due at an American Club reception U.S. consul Clarence Gauss was giving for the commander of the Fourth Marine Regiment, America's contribution to the forces tasked to defend the International Settlement. The club was just around the corner from the Dollar Building, leaving Bond a half hour to kill. He detoured to the Bund, turned north, and used the twilight to pick his way through the mass of refugees cramming the waterfront. Tangles of barbed wire and sandbagged marine emplacements in the public park at the north end of the Bund guarded the foot of Garden Bridge. A few months before, it had been a popular civic rendezvous. Bond lingered, casually inspecting the fortifications as night descended. Suddenly, a thunderous belch of flame spewed from the guns of a Japanese cruiser anchored in the Whangpoo, warming his face and illuminating the decimated wharves of the Hongkew and Yangtzepoo waterfronts. Farther downstream, other warships joined the cannonade, their muzzle flames silhouetting the foreground cruiser as they heaved salvos inland. The barrage ended just as abruptly as it began. This wasn't an "incident," Bond thought, outraged; this was total war. He was furious with the do-nothing policies of the Western powers. This was the most savage and blatant international aggression since the end of the Great War, and the world was letting it pass without a whisper—or at least an active one. Manchuria in 1931 hadn't curbed the Japanese hunger for conquest; neither had Jehol in 1933 or Hopei in 1935. Four months ago, it was north China, and if the Japanese were successful in the Shanghai fighting, they seemed poised to take a massive bite out of the Yangtze valley. Nor did Bond think that would sate the Japanese appetite. Someday it would be Hong Kong, the Philippines, Malaya, and everything else in the Far East. Pacifist snivelings only stoked Fascist greed. Worldwide, Manchuria, the Rhineland, Ethiopia, much of Spain, and ever-larger chunks of China had been fed into the Fascist maw, all in the name of "peace," but peace for whom? And at what price? Clearly, the dictatorships respected nothing but muscle. Only a strong policy backed by force would deter them. Bond made his way to the party, still incensed.

In the morning, Bond reread his memo. He thought he'd made a good case, committed and professional, well grounded, and realistic. Nothing patronized the Chinese. They were rational, intelligent men trying to hold their country together in the face of the worst crisis in its modern history; they needed an airline, a civilian airline free of air force interference; and in the political, influence peddling, face-conscious bureaucratic culture of Chinese governments, the best way to ensure operational independence was through foreign partnership.

The Nationalists might not be able to hold their capital at Nanking if the Japanese broke out of Shanghai, but Bond didn't think its loss would necessarily force them to accept peace terms. It all came down to will, and if the Nationalist government had the will to resist and the people rallied behind them, a free Chinese government would need an airline.

M. Y. Tong hadn't given the impression he was going to put forth much effort, and since their meeting Bond had pondered how he might force M.Y. to act. Bond could think of only one way to do it, and it was fraught with risk. He sent a copy of his memo to T. V. Soong's sister Madame Chiang Kai-shek, who held real sway within the Aviation Commission, but it was impossible for an outsider to fathom the inner machinations of Soong family politics. Submitting his memo to Madame might cause friction between T. V. Soong, Madame, and the Generalissimo, but since the ability to influence events and outcomes defined power in the Middle Kingdom, Bond didn't think Soong would relish being cut from any decision-making. But neither would he appreciate having his hand forced. Bond risked incurring Soong's enduring enmity, and that could prove every bit as fatal to Pan Am as leaving the Chinese Air Force in charge. Bond presented his memo to Tong that afternoon and mentioned he'd sent a copy to Madame Chiang Kai-shek.

The implications were instantly clear to Tong. He couldn't risk *not* presenting it to Dr. Soong, which was, of course, precisely why Bond had done it. "I'm not sure that was wise," Tong warned. His expression betrayed nothing, but inside, Bond knew he was fuming.

Bond apologized. He and Tong said stiff goodbyes, and Bond made no further effort to see him, ashamed of having strong-armed his oldest Chinese friend.

That night, a gloomy Sunday, Bond sat down at the dining room table in his French Concession villa and penned a letter to his wife. Kitsi's silver gleamed on the nearby hutch. Li and his wife, the Bonds' two principal servants, kept it in a state of extraordinary buff, along with the home's richly carved dark walnut furniture. Pale peach walls softened the lustrous blue taffeta curtains Kitsi had hung over the bedroom windows. A beige-and-gold obi adorned her walnut dressing table. Kitsi's tastes and touches were everywhere, but the house felt colorless without her, lacking its most important dimension. He allowed himself to hope that positive resolution to the CNAC imbroglio and a quick end to the war would allow him to bring his family back to the Far East.

Sounds of combat broke his reverie. Bond gathered his thoughts and resumed writing:

As I sit here and write it is seven P.M., pitch dark outside, raining and dreary and every now and then the windows rattle and there is a big boom of artillery and then a tat tat tat of machine gun fire, but on the whole it is very quiet. What a mess. I hope the Japanese are getting slaughtered. Unfortunately, I learn they are not. The Chinese have their faults, but they didn't start and didn't want this war.

If you don't want to raise your boy to be a soldier then we must be prepared to join against nations who start such aggressions. I cannot see any other solution. I don't want any more wars, but I would rather face it again than see little Bondie have to go through what I have seen because his elders didn't have the intelligence and courage to put a stop to it.

In the northern districts of Shanghai, with their right flank anchored to the International Settlement, the Chinese had fought with stunning tenacity for three months as the front lengthened into the countryside to the north and west. The Japanese landings in Hangchow Bay changed everything. Chinese resistance south of the city collapsed in less than three days. Japanese columns racing north routed disorganized defenders. Their vanguard reached the Minghong ferry on the evening of November 8, threatening to surround the Chinese Army. Japanese units in Shanghai launched attacks to pin down the main force of the Central Army and prevent its escape.

At 8:50 A.M. on the morning of November 9, 1937, a bearded Japanese officer, samurai sword drawn, led an infantry detachment across Soochow Creek on the Jessfield Railway Bridge, meeting no resistance. The defenders had vanished. Armor and infantry spearheads poured across, sweeping around the western end of the foreign settlements and racing south along the tracks of the Hangchow–Shanghai Railway. Bitter combats erupted around Chinese rearguards, but Japanese artillery, air support, and flanking maneuvers quickly overwhelmed the covering forces. The Chinese had proved their mettle in the shattered streets and trenches of Shanghai, but they couldn't match the invaders in mobile warfare.

Relief flooded Shanghai's foreign community as sounds of combat faded from the settlements' boundaries. They longed for the old Shanghai, for normalcy, for business, and for an end to the miserable crush of refugees thronging their streets. Such hopes died quickly. Japanese dive bombers reappeared that afternoon, wheeling and plunging over the southern districts. Their ground forces captured Lunghwa Airport, a sudden advance that cast a cordon from the southeastern edge of the French Concession to the Whangpoo and trapped several thousand Chinese regulars, militiamen, and combat-hardened policemen in Nantao, the dense maze of alleys, homes, shops, stalls, and tottering buildings adjacent to the southern edge of Frenchtown that had been the original Chinese city on the Whangpoo. The Japanese called for their surrender. Chinese leaders vowed to fight to the last drop of blood. Tens of thousands of civilians remained in the district. Street fighting and wanton bombardment would turn it into a slaughter yard.

Father Robert Jacquinot de Besange, a one-armed French Jesuit priest, shuttled between the Chinese and Japanese commands in frantic efforts to demilitarize a "Nantao Safety Zone" north of Fongpang Road in the top half of the Old City oval. Both sides inked the Jesuit's plan at noon. The subsequent announcement failed to assuage civilian fears. Sixty thousand refugees crammed through the southern gates of the French Concession, the worst one-day upheaval in Shanghai's history.

Two Japanese planes dropped bombs near South Station that afternoon, supporting tanks and infantry tightening the Nantao choke hold. They closed on the west bank of Zahswei Creek, which flowed into Siccawei Creek at the south edge of the French Concession. Flames boiled skyward from a large spinning mill near the confluence of the two creeks.

Evening shadows lengthened, and the warplanes droned away. Japanese tanks rumbled into assault positions. Isolated gunfire crackled in the edges of the old city, and after dark the Chinese set fire to the Siccawei Creek bridges. Eerie reflections danced on the black waters. Chinese infantrymen lounged against the rear walls of hastily constructed blockhouses, hooding cigarettes with cupped hands. Distant artillery rumbles from the westward fighting rolled over the city, but Shanghai itself lapsed silent. The city passed the most peaceful night in three months.

William Bond slept well in his home near the western edge of the French Concession. He'd spent the last two days taking care of personal and professional business, and he'd missed the airline's board of directors meeting. At it, the Ministry of Communications granted Colonel Lam and CNAC the right to develop a route from Chungking to Hong Kong, news that Bond learned from an inquisitive Reuters correspondent. A cable from

Bixby instructed him to travel to Hankow via Hong Kong, but Bond had decided against such an enormous end-around, thinking it'd be reasonably safe and much faster to travel up the Yangtze. A first-class ticket for Butterfield & Swire's steamer *Wuseh*, scheduled to depart the Frenchtown Bund on the morning of November 11, lay in a silver plate atop the hutch. He rose early on November 10, his last day in Shanghai. He had much to do.

The Japanese command issued an ultimatum that morning: All Chinese would surrender by 2 P.M. or Nantao would suffer the consequences. An awful calm hung over the city as the hours and minutes ticked toward the deadline. Bond rushed about the foreign concessions, making departure preparations and squaring the affairs of his house servants and of the airline's skeleton staff who would remain in Shanghai. He had tiffin at the American Club on Foochow Road, and a few minutes before two o'clock, he walked three blocks to the Robert Dollar Building and climbed to the roof. True to their word, a squadron of Japanese dive bombers appeared as Bond's watch ticked up to the hour, cruising at four or five thousand feet. Above Nantao, they winged over and plummeted on targets. The whump of the bomb detonations rolled over the rooftops.

"That isn't war," Bond muttered. "That's murder, cowardly murder."

Covered by the bombing, a pair of Japanese tanks clanked forward into the smoldering remains of the cotton mill burned the day before, an infantry company advancing behind them. Japanese bluejacket marine infantry fixed bayonets and charged the creek. Chinese gunfire killed a dozen in the water; the survivors grabbed a toehold on the north bank. Reinforcements crossed the creek and clawed their way forward. Chinese regulars fought house by house, room by room, man by man, and the Japanese infantry paid in blood for every yard. It was chaos, the same sharp, savage urban combat that had racked Shanghai for eighty-nine days. The melee raged for hours. Men screamed, and they died.

Toward evening, the gales of gunfire faded to sporadic gusts until only lone shots and bursts punctuated the gloaming. Night fell, and calm draped the battlefield. Japanese artillery broke the silence, booming from positions beyond Jessfield Park. William Bond lay awake in the bed he'd shared with his wife and listened to the awful grunting of the guns. The shells passed overhead with the hiss and sizzle of frying bacon before exploding in the streets of Nantao, less than a mile away. The Chinese shriveled in their positions and absorbed punishment. Few held illusions about humane treatment they might receive at Japanese hands; they'd heard too many stories. One captured Chinese escaped after witnessing the Japanese rope together twenty prisoners, soak them in kerosene, and burn them to death.

A taxi collected Bond shortly after sunrise and drove him past the dense masses of displaced persons bivouacked throughout the concessions, although the worst crush still jammed the Bund from the foot of Garden Bridge to the French Concession's boundary with Nantao. The heavy cruisers USS *Augusta* and HMS *Cumberland* lay at anchor a hundred yards off the riverbank. Japanese guns thudded in the distance, and the shells crumped into nearby Nantao. The International Concession and the French Concession stood whole, sheltered oases, while the fires of Armageddon raged in greater Shanghai. Smoke plumes gushed from major conflagrations in Pootung, Chapei, Yangtzepoo, and Nantao.

Driven by desperate hopes, several thousand refugees crushed against barbed-wire barricades protecting the Butterfield & Swire pontoon on the Frenchtown Bund, clutching bundles, babies, and bedrolls and fighting toward gaps in the wire guarded by baton-wielding French police. Bond's pale Caucasian face and first-class ticket gained him easy admittance.

After locating his cabin, Bond took station at the upper rail, unable to tear his eyes from the refugee drama. Such a mob necessitated a firm, controlling hand, but the French police used far more force than was necessary. One mustachioed cop thrashed the heads, shoulders, and faces of the advancing Chinese with a leather-handled rattan cane, and he spared no one, beating them without regard for age or station, a rain of sharp, painful blows against the heads and faces of men, women, and children. A ten-year-old boy came forward gripping a cloth-wrapped bundle with both hands. The brutal cop shoved him to his knees. The boy toppled to the side without loosening his grip, and the cop bent and whacked three blows onto his face. The Chinese boy struggled to his feet. Fresh red welts streaked his face, and tears leaked from his eyes, but he pressed forward without a whimper.

Bond yelled from the rail, enraged by the cop's Cossack brutality. The crowd and the guns drowned his voice, and the onload continued. Finally, with the steerage compartments stuffed to the limits of toleration and beyond, the *Wuseh* cast off and made way downstream past the British and American cruisers. Immaculately turned-out sailors and marines stood guard on the afterdecks of both warships, beneath spry bunting and decorative flags. A few hundred yards upstream, two gunboats of the Imperial Japanese Navy fired point-blank into the Nantao waterfront, blasting Chinese snipers from hideouts in the waterfront godowns. Whole sections of Hongkew, Yangtzepoo, and Chapei lay in ruins north of Soochow Creek. Smokestacks and telephone poles protruded from the rubble, loosely bound by the telephone wires tangled through the wreckage. The vile sweet-cloying stench of decay hung over the ruined districts, and rats and dogs foraged everywhere. More than a quarter of a million dead lay among the devastation, 250,000 Chinese and 40,000 Japanese.

Twelve miles below the Bund, the Whangpoo merged with the Yangtze under the small hill at Woosung, and nearly a hundred Japanese ships hove into view over the bows—gun-laden cruisers, lithe destroyers, inshore gunboats, low-riding transports. A fresh breeze whipped the wave tops in the broad river and strung taut the patterned pendants and flags that fluttered from the superstructures of the gray-painted vessels. Under different circumstances, the armada might have been an inspiring sight, but all Bond could think as the *Wuseh* turned to port and made turns upriver was "God damn the Japanese, God damn the Japanese."

It was November 11, 1937, Armistice Day, the eleventh day of the eleventh month, and at eleven minutes past the hour of eleven o'clock, a group of Shanghai Municipal Council officials, blood-red poppies poking from the buttonholes of their dark suits, laid a wreath at the base of the war memorial opposite Number 1, the Bund, nineteen years to the day after the end of the war to end all wars. The International Settlement observed two minutes of silence.

In Chinese Shanghai, organized resistance collapsed. Less than a mile from the memorial, in Nantao, Japanese tanks pursued fleeing Chinese through burning streets, right to the Frenchtown wall, killing them as they ran. Japanese soldiers raped captured women and shot military-aged men, regardless of whether or not they bore arms.

High above the bricks and ashes of ruined Chapei, the Japanese raised a barrage balloon from which dangled a long streamer painted with self-laudatory characters. General Iwane Matsui, commander of the Japanese forces in Shanghai, held a press conference at 12:45 P.M. An austere, sixty-four-year-old reed of a man with a wizened, pitiless face, brush-cut hair, prominent ears, and a pencil mustache, and wearing a crisp, unadorned uniform, General Matsui received the journalists in what had formerly been a school classroom. He praised the courage of the Nantao defenders in a voice that seemed powerful coming from such a slight figure. "I am, at present, master of Shanghai," he informed the assembled correspondents, telling them he would feel free to take "any steps" necessary to secure Japanese interests. Matsui leaned forward, grinned, and showed a tooth gap in his upper jaw as he posed his own question, "Do you think the International Settlement is carrying out its duty of neutrality?"

A reporter quickly inquired what the International Settlement had to do to prevent General Matsui from feeling the need to "take steps."

The general relaxed. Nothing "brutal and foolish" would happen in Shanghai, he assured them. "The fundamental thing to understand is that Japan is not an aggressor but came here to restore order among the civilian population of China."

11

RESURRECTION

At dusk on November 11, 1937, ten hours after leaving the Frenchtown Bund, the *Wuseh* dropped anchor off Nantung, some miles below the barrier of vessels the Chinese had sunk across the Yangtze to prevent Japanese warships from attacking the upriver ports. William Bond was on his way upriver to meet Bixby in Hankow, and he chatted with other first-class passengers, smoked an evening cigarette, and watched the refugees emerge from below to gulp the cold November air. Bare bulbs lit the deck, harsh in the eyes of people who'd spent so many stifling hours in conditions Bond compared to the Black Hole of Calcutta, but the offload proceeded with much more order than the morning's melee on the Bund. A Chinese woman came up with her arms around an enormous package and a baby boy tied to her back. Her son was oblivious, smiling and cooing with the joy of living, delighted by the fascinations of the ship. The child looked about eight or ten months old, the same age as Bond's son, Langhorne, and he leaned over and yanked the twine binding a box atop a stack of luggage, then beat the box with both hands in pure, unadulterated glee.

Bond doffed his hat and winked at the infant, who smiled. "Sonny," said

Bond quietly, "you may live to be a coolie, and you may not live at all, but just now you are a man and I take my hat off to you."

Calm settled over the *Wuseh*. Outside, Bond smoked the day's final cigarette while the duty crewmen idly completed the day's chores. A steel halo ringed the moon, harbinger of foul weather creeping toward the China Sea. Last at the rail, Bond watched filtered moonlight gleam from current coils undulating past the ship: *Xie Jiang*, "the River," indifferent to the havoc that had wrecked Shanghai. Bond flicked the stub of his cigarette into the stream. He hadn't seen his son in three months, almost half the time he'd been alive. In his cabin, Bond propped a pad of paper against his knee and added the day's events to the serial letter he was writing to Kitsi. He had no idea when she'd read it, or how he'd send it, but he drew strength from the communication, even at such long remove.

Bond rose at dawn on November 12. It was his forty-fourth birthday, and he spent the next sixty tortuous, rainy hours leading a group of four foreigners and six Chinese businessmen around the Yangtze barrier by sampan, rickshaw, river barge, and canal boat. Above the obstacle, the party boarded another steamer and continued upriver to Chienkiang, forty miles below Nanking. The skipper docked and announced that he would remain there for three days. Bond disembarked his group to explore other options. The army had commandeered every bus and motorcar in town, but a train was scheduled to leave for Nanking at 6 P.M. Bond bought second-class tickets for his party, the only ones remaining, and led them to the station, where an infantry battalion waited to load the train among a crush of civilians. The soldiers were from the southern province of Kwantung, and although most appeared to be teenagers, they seemed well equipped and better fed than average Chinese infantrymen. On a whim, Bond bought all of the cigarettes in one of the station shops, some forty packs, and distributed them to the fighting men.

The men wouldn't have been more amazed if Bond had sprouted wings and flown around the station. The officers escorted Bond and his companions to a private station room and served them tea with their own hands. When the train was ready to leave—an hour late—armed soldiers held back the tide of other passengers and the officers escorted Bond's group through the gate onto the platform and installed them in the train's sole first-class compartment, irrespective of their second-class tickets.

Bond's gang basked in reflected glory, but Bond found the scene disturbing. Not because of what he'd done but because of what nobody else had. The station was a hive, and not a single Chinese civilian had made any tangible gesture of support to the departing infantrymen. Most hadn't given so much as a smile and a wave. Giving cigarettes to soldiers who'd soon be fighting struck Bond as perfectly natural, and it wasn't expensive, but of all the people present—and in Bond's party alone there were several prominent Chinese who talked like ardent patriots—a foreigner was the only one who'd done anything for the combat-destined soldiers. Bond realized with a shock that he didn't know a single Chinese official or well-heeled businessman with a son in the trenches. He hadn't even heard of one. They just didn't think wars were fought by men of their class. Coolies fought wars. The Chinese had a saying for it: You don't make good iron into nails, and you don't make good men into soldiers. China wouldn't accomplish much until its leaders learned to lead, Bond reflected gloomily. No nation ever had.

A thousand wounded soldiers sprawled in eerie silence on the platforms of the Nanking railroad station, their injuries wrapped in filthy, clotted rags, and not a single doctor or nurse worked among them. That afternoon, November 14, Bond stood on top of a shed in front of the U.S. Embassy compound and shared his CNAC laments with Marine major James McHugh, the U.S. naval attaché, as they watched six Japanese bombers fly long, lazy ovals over the Kuomintang capital interspersed with systematic, straight-line bomb runs, then repeat the process as though they were running a bus service. "Poor China," Bond thought, "what a licking she takes. And can take."

China was taking a licking far worse on the battlefields beyond Shanghai. Outflanked by the Hangchow Bay landings and unmoored from its urban anchor, Chiang's Central Army collapsed. The Japanese pursued the remnants toward Nanking, pouring across the most densely populated rural landscape on earth, pillaging cities, towns, and farms, and the population teetered toward panic as the Japanese advanced. Every civilian with means fled upriver, but there were hundreds of thousands—*millions*—with no such option.

Exhausted, Bond fell asleep early in the Metropolitan Hotel. He'd barely shut his eyes when the night telephone operator woke him. Would he care to take a phone call from Mr. W. H. Donald? A ruddy-faced, teetotaling, misogynistic Australian who spoke no Chinese tongue, despised their cuisine, and didn't smoke, William Henry Donald was Madame Chiang Kai-shek's most intimate and trusted personal advisor, and his gentle bluntness and utter incorruptibility had allowed him to win more influence in Chinese politics than any foreigner since Marco Polo. Bond sat up and cleared his head: "Bond speaking."

"What's all this trouble with CNAC?" Donald was a golfing buddy of Major James McHugh, and Bond had hoped for this exact connection when he'd talked to the naval attaché earlier in the day.

Bond sketched the details; Donald agreed to discuss them in person the next day.

At the meeting, Donald held the memorandum Bond had written for T. V. Soong and copied to Madame Chiang Kai-shek. Bond verbally outlined the salient points of what Pan Am wanted: freedom from military flying, a contract extension, full operational control of the airline, removal of Aviation Commission officials from the company's executive positions, and a change of managing director—any strong, intelligent, experienced Chinese *businessman* would do. In return, China would receive rapid, efficient, reliable air transportation and access to Pan American's contacts within the U.S. government.

"Makes sense to me. I'll go to bat for you."

Much heartened, Bond raced to the Nanking riverbank, where he hoped to find a berth for Hankow. The Jardine steamer *Kung Wo* was anchored three miles upstream with his friend and fellow CNAC director Max Polin already aboard. Nobody knew when the *Kung Wo* might sail, or how Bond could get to it, but at anchor off the Nanking Bund rode the USS *Panay*, a shallow-draft gunboat of the U.S. Navy's Yangtze Patrol. Aboard was Lieutenant Hank Jarrell, aide to the commander of the Yangtze Patrol, who'd been a groomsman at Bond's wedding. Bond hired a sampan to row him to the gunboat, where he explained his predicament. Jarrell practically tossed him into *Panay*'s motor launch, and Bond was racing upriver within minutes.

The steamer *Kung Wo* weighed anchor within the hour, having taken on three thousand passengers, but her load wasn't balanced. She limped upstream with a pronounced list. Rumors cut through the ship: The government was splitting up; the Generalissimo had accepted peace terms; the capital was moving to Changsha. Nobody knew anything for sure. The vice minister of finance camped on a couch in the lounge. More ominously, Bond noted a stunningly gorgeous, fashionable Chinese woman imperiously dictating to the crew from a nearby cabin. Bond directed Polin's attention. "See that moll? That's Sun Fo's number one concubine."

Sun Fo was the only son of Dr. Sun Yat-sen, father of the Chinese revolution, and an important member of the Kuomintang's ruling elite. In 1938, he was president of the Legislative Yuan, supposedly the lawmaking arm of the Central Government, and he had a degree from Columbia and another from the University of California. Sun Fo might have been the son of China's George Washington, but he was one of the few people William Langhorne Bond permitted himself to despise. Back in the first days of their China involvement, before Bond came to the Orient, Curtiss-Wright negotiated a contract and formed an airline with Sun Fo when he'd been minister of railroads. It was a disastrous episode, for the Railroad Ministry didn't control any aspect of the Chinese post office, and the post office refused to let the railway-sponsored airline fly any mail. In retrospect, it was either an attempt by Sun Fo to gain control of China's airmail or a bald-faced fleecing of naïve Americans ignorant of China's bureaucratic intricacies, and he'd done nothing to improve his reputation in the intervening years. "That's bad," Bond said. "It means something when number one concubines start moving."

Bond shared the details in his ongoing nightly letter to his wife:

There are several concubines, numerous nurses, and other women on board, and there is a suspicious lot of moving around going on. The boat has the air of a regular honky-tonk. But so far I have remained pure. . . . Right now it looks to me like China is on the verge of complete collapse, so I am afraid neither Donald nor anyone else is going to be able to accomplish anything. . . . However, if my seven years in China have taught me anything, it is that China seems to weather all storms and return to normalcy in a surprisingly short time.

Late in the afternoon of its third day on the river, the *Kung Wo* drew up to a Hankow dock in an ashen rain. Sunlight leaked away westward, behind slaty clouds. No place on earth was drearier than Hankow suffering a November rain, and Harold Bixby stood on the pontoon under an umbrella, waiting. They shook hands with few words. Bixby had made reservations for the two of them to fly to Kunming, take the narrow-gauge railway from Kunming to Hanoi in French Indochina, and thence fly to Hong Kong and the Philippines. "Let the Chinese worry for a while," he said. "We'll go to Baguio and play golf."

Bond told his friend about the memorandum he'd left for T. V. Soong and mailed to Madame, and about his meetings at the U.S. Embassy and with W. H. Donald. Bond felt he'd made progress, the first in months, and he wanted to stay in Hankow to maintain Pan Am's "squatter's rights," close to Colonel Lam, ready to jump to the airline's helm. Bixby agreed to stay a few more days.

The two Americans met with H. H. Kung again on November 22, without result. Disheartened, they flew to Hong Kong, and Bixby continued on to the Philippines. Days passed, then weeks, and Bond anguished over the loss of the New Zealand opportunity. The only real leverage he possessed was his conviction that the Chinese weren't yet ready to run an airline without American assistance. Chuck Sharp and Hugh Woods, two of his crucial pilots, returned to Hong Kong after bumbling around the Orient for two months, hoping for reinstatement, but their coffers were empty. They went home to seek other employment.

Colonel Lam remained in control of the airline. Ironically, Bond and Colonel Lam worked in much closer contact through the end of November and the beginning of December, and Bond's respect for his adversary grew as a result, although Bond never wavered in his desire to remove all Chinese Air Force influence from CNAC.

Chiang Kai-shek and his wife abandoned Nanking on December 8. The first Japanese artillery shells hit the city two days later, five weeks after the Hangchow Bay landings. Heeding a Japanese warning to "third-power warships" to clear the Nanking vicinity, on December 12, USS *Panay* was anchored twenty-seven miles upriver, near Hoshien. At 1:37 P.M., nine Japanese pursuit planes and fifteen bombers attacked the warship without warning. Twenty bombs fell on or near the gunship, wrecking her engines and pumps, and the crew abandoned ship. Two planes machine-gunned the survivors in the water. The *Panay* settled low, but American flags were still waving from her masts a few minutes after three o'clock, when two

Japanese patrol boats drew alongside the stricken vessel, raked it with machine guns, and sent a search party aboard. The *Panay* capsized and sank within an hour. Two seamen and an Italian correspondent were killed. Fifty other men were wounded, twelve seriously. (Bond's friend Hank Jarrell wasn't aboard.)

Attacking another nation's man-of-war was a belligerent act, a casus belli. Bond expected his country to fight, and he offered his sword to General John Beaumont, commander of the U.S. Marines in Shanghai, in a letter he wrote less than twenty-four hours after the attack: "During the World War, I held a commission in the Field Artillery, and for the past seven years I have been operating commercial air lines in China. . . . If at any time my services can be of any value to you, I will be glad if you will consider me entirely at your disposal." Bond sent a copy to Admiral Yarnell, commander of the U.S. Navy's Asiatic Fleet.* The "incident" was possibly the act of renegade elements in the Japanese military intending to expose the weakness of the Western powers; Japan apologized and paid an indemnity, and the threat of war passed.

The Japanese Army entered Nanking on December 13, 1937, and embarked on a grotesque, nihilistic orgy of intentional terror and devastation. Japanese soldiers raped thousands of girls and women and slaughtered civilians by the hundreds of thousands.** Japanese newspapers made no secret of the atrocities. The nation reveled in the murder and devastation, tracking the "score" between two army lieutenants racing to murder a hundred civilians. Western newspapers splashed the horrors across their headlines.

Shortly after Nanking's fall, W. H. Donald quietly asked Bond to make a list of three Chinese who could replace Colonel Lam. Thrilled, Bond mulled politics and possibilities and carefully crafted a reply, but Donald never asked for it. It seemed like one more fine chance cast onto the dung

---

* Two days before Christmas, Bond received a reply politely declining the offer: R. F. McConnell, Captain, U.S. Navy, Chief of Staff, USS *Augusta,* to Bond, CNAC, Hong Kong, December 23, 1937, WLB.

** The killings lasted six weeks. The exact number who died will never be known, but at the very least, Imperial Army barbarism killed 200,000 people. Reasonable estimates run to 377,400 killed. They quite possibly murdered more than 400,000. Iris Chang's *The Rape of Nanking,* an extraordinarily disturbing book, discusses the casualty figures in detail, pp. 99–104.

heap of unrealized potential. Bond's Christmas came and went, his son's first. It was an agony to be apart from his family, and the whole China affair seemed blanketed by permanent fog. His outlook brightened when a coded telegram from Major McHugh reached him through the American Consular Service on December 28:

> Please supply me with Chinese name in telegraphic code numerals of your nominees STOP Have been informed action possible upon receipt.

Bond submitted his suggestions. The first two were General Ho Chi-wu, CNAC's first managing director, and Dai Enkai, who had served in the position for five years after General Ho. Both were legitimate, qualified nominees, able and effective veterans who had done the job well. Bond was also certain neither would be appointed. General Ho's brother was the minister of war, and Bond didn't think the government would consolidate more power in Ho family hands. Bond wasn't sure why, but Dai Enkai seemed to have fallen out of favor. Bond pinned his quiet hopes on the third name he submitted—P. Y. Wong, CNAC's business manger.

The year drew to its dubious end, and Bond flew to Hankow yet again. Soon after he reached the city, Colonel Lam summoned Bond to his office. The colonel sat at his desk ramrod straight, his uniform tunic starched to immaculate perfection. "Mr. Bond, I am being replaced as managing director of the China National Aviation Corporation by Mr. P. Y. Wong. The reason given is that I have not been cooperating with the American partner."

A bubble of elation welled in Bond's chest. He suppressed it. "Colonel Lam," he said flatly, "you've known from the beginning I wanted the Chinese Air Force removed from the company and full control returned to the Ministry of Communications, with whom Pan American has a contract. You also know I've worked hard to that end. But I've never opposed you personally, only as an air force appointee. I wish you good luck in the future, and I hope we can be friends."

Colonel Lam studied the American. "There was only one time I felt like shooting you, Mr. Bond."

"I remember."

"You displayed extraordinary calm."

"I may surprise you again," Bond remarked. "I'd heard you had a violent temper, so before I went to see you, I steeled myself to keep absolutely still if you got angry. But I'm not so steady that I can keep quiet when I think I might be shot with no defense. Under my left arm I had a Colt automatic with eight shots ready to go. I didn't think you would shoot an unarmed man who offered no defense, but I was prepared in case I'd misjudged you. I haven't worn that gun since, until today, and it isn't loaded, so it's not a weapon."

Bond laid the pistol's magazine on the colonel's desk and unbuckled the shoulder holster.

"That was the only time in my life I've ever carried a concealed weapon. Now, I'd like you to have it."

Bond handed the holster and the unloaded automatic to the colonel.

Colonel Lam drew the pistol and turned it over in his hands. Bond detected the faintest trace of a smile. "You have been a good enemy, Mr. Bond." Colonel Lam put down the pistol and extended his hand. "I think we can be friends."

Bond shook the hard and proud colonel's hand with a stone face, careful not to shame him with the slightest show of triumph. He had an airline again.

PART THREE

GOING WITH THE WIND

January 1, 1938, to December 16, 1941

Our neutrality legislation is a snare and a delusion. It obscures our reasoning and renders us impotent. . . . It acts as an opiate, a soporific, a quicksand, and an alibi. . . . The sooner we scrap [it], the better.

—Stanley K. Hornbeck,
memorandum, U.S. Department of State,
October 19, 1938

12

THE PROVISIONAL CAPITAL

Only William Langhorne Bond's extraordinary efforts had rescued Pan American's China investment, and he'd done it for 600 U.S. dollars a month ($8,900 in modern dollars). In public, Bond held his emotions close, Chinese fashion. He allowed himself to gloat in a letter to his wife: "The new M.D. will be a Mr. P. Y. Wong," he gleefully announced. "Is Bond a good little Chinese policticator or is he a good little Chinese politicator?"

The executive changes formally occurred at a directors' meeting in early January, when a stunned P. Y. Wong accepted the board of directors' offer and ascended to the managing directorship.

In light of Bond's success, Harold Bixby thought the time ripe to make a slow fade from the China scene, if not completely into the sunset, then at least onto the golf links of Baguio, the idyllic American enclave in the highlands of Luzon. From there he could fiddle with transpacific details and keep a not-too-distant eye on events in China while Bond got himself on solid footing. "If you are going to run the Chinese show through the thick weather ahead," Bixby wrote, "you should have the controls as first pilot, and we should do everything possible to give you face. . . . I suggest therefore, you advise our Chinese associates . . . that you are in complete charge, subject only to orders from New York."

"I confess to feeling a little scared," Bond told his wife, "but I'll get over it."

The Shanghai fighting had forced the airline to move its headquarters to Hankow, where Chiang Kai-shek established an "interim" capital pending a jump 440 miles farther inland to Chungking, but Nanking's loss cast a threat toward Hankow, and P. Y. Wong uprooted the head office again and sent it upriver ahead of the Central Government. Complicating the government's retreat to Szechwan was the presence of General Liu Hsiang, the same warlord with whom Bond, Bixby, and Wong had negotiated the right to fly from Chungking to Chengtu in 1933. Kuomintang influence had waxed stronger in Szechwan with air service, Chiang Kai-shek's anti-Communist campaigns, and other financial and bureaucratic infiltrations, but Liu Hsiang had stubbornly resisted each encroachment. Politically, however, he needed to present a façade of patriotic unity, and he'd gone to Nanking to "assist in the direction of military operations" after the Japanese invasion. In January 1938, top Kuomintang figures summoned him to a conference to discuss the government's move to his province, an idea he'd met with singular lack of enthusiasm. At the conclave, the Kuomintang honored Marshal Liu with an elaborate feast. Afterward, Liu complained of stomach cramps. He died in a Hankow hospital the next morning. The Central Government staged an extravagant state funeral to mark his passing, but the Machiavellian convergence raised many eyebrows. Chiang Kai-shek appointed a trusted underling to the vacated provincial chairmanship, and the Central Government relocated without undue complication.

Given all his carping about Chinese operational ineptitude since the previous August, William Bond must have been surprised to discover that the airline was still operating in the black. Colonel Lam's regime had cleared a substantial profit (more than a million modern dollars), casting Pan Am's reinstatement against a much more starkly political background.

The change in Kuomintang attitude toward the airline closely mirrored their strategic situation. Forced to fight Japan by the United Front, Chiang Kai-shek had attacked in Shanghai because the urban battleground offered China the best chance of victory. Only air superiority and naval gunfire saved the Japanese in the August fighting, and even after the failure of their initial assaults, the Chinese fought the enemy to a bloody standstill. An ongoing stalemate and a fair, negotiated peace would have been a triumph for long-abused China. While events ran reasonably well, China had little interest in sharing the airline with the Americans, who, after all, had deserted at the war's outbreak. Also, ridding China of the onerous presence of all foreigners was a stated aim of the Kuomintang, and one of the prime reasons they'd created the CNAC partnership was to learn to run an airline for themselves. If China had shoved the Japanese into the river or won an equal peace, the subsequent explosion of national pride might well have expelled *all* the foreign powers. China had little interest in inviting the Americans back into the airline while those remained plausible outcomes.

However, Japan's risky Hangchow Bay landings broke the battlefield deadlock and disintegrated the main strength of Chiang's army. China suddenly faced a long war, one she would need friends to prosecute. Her two most potentially useful allies against Japan were the Soviet Union and the United States, and Pan Am president Juan Trippe nurtured his company's Washington ties with extraordinary care, particularly in the State and Navy departments, the two organs of American government most keenly interested in Far Eastern affairs. To China, Pan American's stake in the China National Aviation Corporation must have seemed an excellent tool with which to influence American policy.

As the dust of change settled, Hong Kong became the airline's base of DC-2 operations, and Harold Bixby warned Bond of a new problem he'd face as Hong Kong increased in relative importance—the British—and although Bixby was sure the two British officials who ran Kai Tak Airport had the same intentions as those "that pave the highway to Hades," he was equally certain their slow-as-molasses cruising velocity and "lack of horse sense" would provide Bond with many headaches, as they'd done for Pan Am. Heeding Bixby's advice, Bond quietly expanded the airline's flight schedules out of the colony without public announcement. The changes represented a major shift in the airline's flight patterns and altered Hong Kong's strategic relationship with both Japan and China, but Bond didn't petition the colonial government for new considerations. Exactly as he'd hoped, they accepted the changes without officially taking notice.

Bond threw himself into the work. Hundreds of issues competed for attention: maintenance, fuel supplies, spare-part shortages, enemy marauders, Chinese politics and bureaucracy, and a short, sharp Chungking storm that damaged four airplanes. Bond managed it all with an eye toward accomplishing his twin professional goals—maintaining China's air communications and recovering Pan Am's investment. Personally, he yearned for the stability that would allow him to return his family to the Orient.

Over in the Philippines, when he wasn't in Baguio, Harold Bixby stayed at the Manila Hotel, whose switchboard operator patched a telephone call through to his room in the wee hours of March 31, 1938, five years to the day after he'd announced Pan Am's takeover of CNAC's American interest. It was Juan Trippe calling from the other side of the world, and he spoke in glowing terms about William Bond's work. Bixby affirmed Trippe's sense that Bond could handle "the China Show," and Trippe ended by ordering Bixby back to New York. Bixby left for Baguio early on April Fool's Day, knowing he'd have "to break the news gently" to his wife, who had no desire to go home.

William Bond had exactly the opposite problem. He hadn't seen his wife in seven months, and he felt her absence like a sword through his gut. By March, Hong Kong seemed secure enough, and he persuaded Kitsi to leave their one-year-old son with her mother and a nurse and fly to Hong Kong for an experimental visit. If the Far East felt safe after she'd been out a few months, she'd go stateside and return with their son. If the political situation deteriorated, she'd go home to stay.

The Bonds rented Bungalow Number 1 at Repulse Bay, a charming seaside enclave on the south side of Hong Kong Island, and reveled in being together after more than half a year apart. Hong Kong was stuffy and provincial and very British compared with Shanghai, but Kitsi had friends among other families displaced from Shanghai. Harold Bixby flew in from the Philippines, ostensibly to sign a few papers, but mostly because he wanted one last *walla-walla* session with his best friend.

. . .

In the first half of 1938, the focal point of China's anti-Japanese resistance was the tri-cities of Hankow, Hanyang, and Wuchang, which Chiang Kai-shek made his "provisional capital." Bond was in Hankow on April 29, and after tiffin he visited longtime acquaintance Dr. Arthur N. Young at his apartment in the National City Bank of New York.* A jowly Californian who'd graduated from Occidental College in Pomona, earned an economics doctorate at Princeton, and was a concert-quality organist who'd performed regularly in the Shanghai Community Church before the war, Young had been T. V. Soong's closest American advisor since 1929. In the early and middle 1930s, Young had gained familiarity with the aviation business by helping Soong organize and maintain a detachment of ex-military American aviators who trained the fledgling Chinese Air Force. Bond wanted Young to fill Bixby's seat on the board of directors. The two men were talking shop when their conversation was squelched by the quickening howl of air-raid sirens, a mournful wail that had, in the last eight months, become the signature sound of life in war-battered China. Bond and Young hustled upstairs to the rooftop, drinks in hand. Visibility and ceiling were virtually unlimited. Apart from the sirens' dreary keen, it was a beautiful spring afternoon.

The sirens fell silent, replaced by the dull mechanical thunder of radial aircraft engines. Bond counted thirty-seven Chinese pursuit planes taking off from nearby military airfields. Half of them vanished to the north. The other contingent clawed to altitude over the city until they held positions high in the sun, so far overhead they were practically invisible, and the engine noise faded to a distant growl that occasionally oscillated louder as a quirk of atmosphere carried sound to the rooftop. Nothing happened for twenty-five or thirty minutes. The two men were on the verge of calling it a false alarm when Bond yelled and pointed at gun flashes across the river in Wuchang. The quick rolling up-tempo *tom-tom-tom* sound of antiaircraft cannon fire reached them a few seconds later. Young made out a formation of nine planes coming in at about twelve to fourteen thousand feet.

* Now Citicorp.

"Bombers!" Bond exclaimed. "Those're Japs."

Black flecks of exploding shells mottled the sky near the enemy planes. Young made out a second formation trailing the first by about a mile. April 29, 1938, happened to be the thirty-seventh birthday of His Imperial Japanese Majesty Hirohito, grandson of the Meiji and 124th emperor of Japan, and Japanese air forces clearly intended to honor the occasion with a grand assault on China's provisional capital.

Chinese planes joined the fight in full-power dives from high altitude, machine guns chattering. Escorting Japanese pursuit planes hurtled themselves at the Chinese interceptors, and the pursuit planes twisted and turned around the bomber formations, which cut across the river to attack the Hanyang arsenal near the mouth of the Han River, dropped their payloads, and turned for home. But the counterattacking Chinese had spoiled their aim. High explosives crumped into the town wide of the arsenal. The Japanese pursuits lingered to dogfight, preventing the Chinese from molesting the retreating bombers, and it became impossible to tell friend from foe in the chaos of pursuits pinwheeling like swifts in the sky east of Hankow. Sunlight winked from the wings of turning planes. Bond and Young could see machine-gun flashes, and distant gunfire rattles reached the edge of their hearing. A plane plunged from the heavens trailing a pillar of flame, and Bond and Young cheered like schoolboys, certain it was Japanese. The battle raged full-bore for thirty minutes, until the Japanese pursuits scattered eastward, low on fuel after the long stint of maximum power dogfighting. Chinese planes straggled to the tri-city airports in ones, twos, and threes. The release sounded not long afterward.

Bond walked to the edge of the roof and watched people pour from the Bund dugouts. Blue-shirted coolies hoisted the loads they'd laid outside the shelter entrances. Rickshaw men grabbed the poles of their simple conveyances and returned to business. Cars appeared. Bond felt the sun's warmth, and he marveled that the day could be so fine, knowing the scene was much different across the river in Hanyang, where the bombs had fallen. Bond wondered what the Japanese thought they'd accomplished. There seemed no point; it was so barbaric. As far as he could tell, all the Japanese military had done was honor their emperor's birthday by killing and wounding hundreds of civilians.

That evening, Bond sought out aviation advisor Claire Chennault, the tactician who'd masterminded the Chinese battle plan. Chennault's coarsely lined face radiated fierce pride. His pilots were claiming twenty-one to twenty-four kills for the day. So far, they'd found wreckage to prove seventeen, against seven of their planes destroyed, three damaged, and five dead pilots. Chennault had divided his forces, sending one group high into the bright sunshine over Hankow, and another north and east, away from the city. The first group attacked the Japanese bombers over Hankow and tangled their escorting pursuit planes in a dogfight crafted to use their fuel reserves and separate them from the bombers. The second squadron pounced on the retreating bombers, of which Chennault thought they'd shot down nine. It was the biggest air battle since the end of the Great War, and it was a resounding Chinese victory. Unfortunately, the air battle changed little, and neither had the actual battlefield triumph won earlier in the month by a well-led Chinese army at Taierhchuang, northeast of Hsuchow, a counteroffensive envelopment that had killed more than eight thousand Japanese. Both victories were widely celebrated, but the strategic momentum remained with the invaders. The Japanese secured the coastal provinces connecting Peiping and Shanghai, and thus free from the threat of flank attack, they continued to attack inland, up the Yangtze and Yellow rivers. Both prongs made progress, but their main effort went up the Yellow River toward Kaifeng and Chengchow, rail junctions from which they could strike down the Hankow–Peiping line toward the tri-cities, whose capture they hoped would force China to capitulate.

The Yangtze and the Han were wild rivers, unbridged and undammed, and in June of 1938 their summer currents swirled up level with the Hankow Bund. Junks, sampans, steamers, and gunboats jammed the swollen waters, a reflection of Hankow's teeming population, which had doubled since the fall of Nanking. The invasion had displaced sixteen million refugees, and the city's streets seethed with them, some leaving, some just arriving. Thousands of Chinese characters covered certain walls of the town, human lost-and-found notes left by those separated from their families. Journalists, photographers, arms traders, newsreel cameramen, revolutionaries, spies, war profiteers, foreign consuls, mercenaries, and prostitutes flocked to the city. Claims and counterclaims from the warring sides filled the newspapers, and in the middle months of 1938, as the Japanese advanced toward it from two directions, Hankow commanded the attention of the entire world.

To slow the enemy advance, in June Chinese soldiers dynamited the

Yellow River dikes near Kaifeng. Torrential rains swelled the river, and muddy water gushed through the breaches. A vast lake formed, a man-made catastrophe that drowned thousands of peasants, destroyed the homes and fields of millions, and swamped many hundreds of square miles of the lower Yellow River valley. The season's crops were ruined, condemning the region to famine, and the Japanese Yellow River drive stalled in the flooded landscape, but less than a month later, Bond explained to New York that although the flood had actually changed the course of the Yellow River—the stream now emptied into the Yellow Sea below the Shantung Peninsula, three hundred miles south of its pre-June mouth in the Gulf of Chihli—the floods hadn't significantly delayed the enemy advance. They'd simply shifted their main effort south and attacked up the Yangtze, beneath marauding screens of airpower.

CNAC planes and stations monitored the Chinese air-warning net designed by Claire Chennault to glean what information they could about Japanese aerial movements, but the margins thinned as the enemy advanced toward Hankow through the muggy summer of 1938. Bond considered cutting DC-2 service to the tri-cities entirely, but the pillaging of Nanking preyed on his conscience. As far as he was concerned, every person his airline evacuated was a life saved from Japanese bayonets and execution pits. Nevertheless, he worried constantly.

One of his prime concerns was money. His airline was making gobs of it, but the "considerable cash" it had on hand was in Chinese currency, which wasn't holding value. The official exchange rate stood at 29½ U.S. cents per Chinese dollar, but the Ministry of Finance wouldn't allow CNAC—or anybody else—to freely sell large quantities of Chinese money and buy foreign currency at the official rate. Each transaction had to be approved as a wartime necessity, and "gold" U.S. dollars trickled out of the Central Bank as if they were leaking from a pinhole.* Open-market rates were running about 40 percent less. More ominously, the Ministry of Communications' finances were a total shambles. "If their deficit continues to increase and our surplus continues to pile up, I am afraid the answer is going to be too obvious," Bond wrote to Stokely Morgan in the Chrysler

---

* It was common in the Far East to refer to U.S. dollars as "gold" dollars, and Chinese dollars as "Mex." dollars or "CN," for "China National."

Building. "Ask Mr. Bixby about his old mountaineer friend and how he kept his good-looking wife."

"Barefoot and pregnant" came Bixby's automatic answer. Both he and Bond felt that maintaining the airline in pauper's style was the only sure way of keeping the grubbing paws of Chinese officialdom out of its coffers. Still, Bond felt that a secret stash of U.S. dollars could serve as an important hedge against further decline in the value of Chinese currency, and he tried to persuade managing director P. Y. Wong to smuggle $100,000 (Mex.) out of China and convert it to U.S. dollars at whatever rate they could get. Wong was reluctant. He thought the Ministry of Finance would eventually release enough official rate exchange to meet their needs. Besides, Wong was a Chinese national subject to Chinese law. Such financial shenanigans would put a lot more than his job at stake.

Bond wore at his counterpart. Seeking guidance, he took Wong to call on M. Y. Tong, who'd moved to Hong Kong after the Shanghai battle and apparently bore Bond no ill will for the November strong-arming that had proved so critical in reestablishing Pan Am's position. The two friends were again on firm footing, and as president of the Bank of Canton and one of T. V. Soong's closest associates, Tong was perfectly positioned to give sound economic advice. Tong's analysis was an oblique masterpiece, but his implication was obvious—he expected the value of the Chinese dollar to decline substantially. P. Y. Wong agreed to Bond's scheme.

After a brief, unsatisfying stint with a Pan Am subsidiary in South America, Chuck Sharp and his pal Hugh Woods had returned to China on receiving word of Bond's reinstatement. Sharp flew the first $20,000 (Mex.) from Chungking to Hong Kong, but when Bank of Canton employees exchanged the notes they discovered the serial numbers had been recorded to track currency movements. M. Y. Tong aborted the transaction. Bond had another pilot smuggle the "hot money" back into China and exchange it for older, cooler bills. The second attempt went off without hitch, but Chinese currency was weakening so steadily that the delay cost the airline another few ticks on the currency exchange.

Gasoline was Bond's other enduring headache. Free China had no refining capability; every single drop had to be imported. The airline could get all the fuel it wanted in Hong Kong, but getting it into the interior was another matter entirely. The most reasonable way to get gasoline to Hankow in early 1938 was to send it up the Hong Kong–Canton–Hankow railroad, but the Japanese were bombing it nearly every flyable day, and the Standard Oil Company (Socony), through which Bond handled fuel shipments, insisted on receiving advance payment before it would ship a drop. If the cargo was destroyed en route, Socony kept the money and CNAC lost the gas. A few thousand gallons had trickled up the railway early in the year, but the airline's supply was dangerously low by mid-summer, and every military and civil organization in China squabbled to get freight cars allotted to its needs. Bond hadn't been able to move a gallon for four months. As the shortage became dire, Bixby and Morgan in New York suggested, stupendously, that Bond hire an army of coolies to *carry* gasoline 750 miles from Hong Kong to Chungking, a herculean labor they calculated would add only fifty cents to the cost of each gallon. Morgan's analysis of Oriental problems was often exactly what you'd expect from a man flying a desk in New York, but Bixby should have known better. Bond hoped he'd allowed Morgan to include his name in the proposal only because it would have been bad corporate politics to laugh in his face.

The rail-shipping situation was overripe for corruption, and it being China, some smart lad in the railroad administration refused to allot shipping space unless he was slipped hefty under-the-table payments. Nothing moved until he got his squeeze. He'd have gotten away with it if he'd been reasonable, but his outrageous rates caused several organizations to band together and publish a report. The super-squeeze artist was summoned to Hankow and shot.

Freight-car loading became much less complicated. Bond got eleven cars allotted in July, and a few weeks later he was astonished to report that he had got 110,000 gallons of fuel past Hankow, aboard ship, heading upriver toward the relative safety of Chungking.

Resolving the quandary earned him no reprieve. The circumstances were so volatile, and the problems were so widespread, that he could never fully solve them. The airline's demands never relaxed, and although having Kitsi in the Orient removed the worst ache of missing her, Bond spent far more than half of his time in the Chinese interior. He felt like a man juggling bricks over a glass floor, and it took a toll on his health. Harold Bixby airmailed a warning to the Orient:

I note you have only spent 23 days in Hong Kong during the last three months and want to remind you again that you have obligations to Kitsi, your family, and your friends which should not be overlooked in your desire to protect the best interests of the company. If you haven't sense enough to take care of yourself, we will probably give Kitsi a power of attorney and tell her to ground you in Hong Kong.

Ignoring instructions, Bond flew back into China in early August, cruising north at nine thousand feet with the passengers aboard a Hankow-bound DC-2 captained by Chuck Sharp, recently promoted to chief pilot. An hour southwest of their destination, the ship's radio operator reported a Japanese air raid heading for the provisional capital. Sharp banished his Chinese copilot to the passenger cabin and invited Bond into the vacated seat. Hankow air raids tended to last about an hour from alert to release, so Bond and Sharp decided it was reasonable to hold course and see what developed. Any other airline in the world would have considered it a perfect day for flying, but clear skies and unlimited visibility were dubious assets to an unarmed transport in contested airspace. Bond fished Sharp's binoculars from the flight bag behind the pilot's seat.

Forty-five minutes later, the raid still hadn't materialized, but neither had the release sounded. Any closer to Hankow and they risked being caught in an attack. Sharp veered to the west-northwest. Bond spotted black dots ahead and to the right, and through the binoculars he made out three single-engine pursuit planes tangled in mortal combat. Sharp banked left, then bent back right so Bond could keep the fight in view, but Bond's running narration didn't satisfy Sharp's curiosity. He kept leaning over to glimpse the action.

The details of the dogfight so absorbed Sharp and Bond that they didn't notice they'd turned and were following it until the adversaries reversed course and headed straight for the Douglas, but by then, Sharp was hooked. He couldn't stand to miss the spectacle. He flew a quarter circle and kept the fight off the right wingtip where he could watch it. It still wasn't enough. Sharp ordered Bond to change seats, and Bond flew the plane while Sharp studied the rhubarb through his field glasses. Eventually, it faded into the distance, and the release came over the radio.

Sharp returned to the captain's seat and resumed course for Hankow, whose airfield had been bombed in the meantime. A look-see orbit revealed that the damage was confined to a cluster of buildings northwest of the airport. The runway looked unharmed. Sharp curved away to line up an approach and spotted a single-engine pursuit coming in low and fast from the opposite direction. He and Bond passed a dozen high-anxiety seconds before they positively identified it as Chinese. The pursuit landed downwind, toward Sharp's DC-2, missing the best part of the field. Its wheels sank in soft ground, and it flipped over its nose and landed on its back. Sharp avoided the wreck, landing upwind at reasonable speed. The DC-2 passengers disembarked while a commandeered vehicle rushed the wounded pursuit pilot to the hospital. He had a bullet punched through his thigh. Bond led Sharp out of the passengers' earshot. "Chuck, back in the States, the Aeronautics Board would toss us in jail for flying like that."

"But we're not back in the States, are we now, boss?" drawled Sharp. He winked. "Gotta run. Big game going downtown."

The last Bond saw of Chuck Sharp that afternoon, he was promising a big bonus to a taxi driver to hurry him to the Hankow Bund, *chop, chop.* Since the women left, the hottest entertainment in town was a running high-stakes poker game in one of the riverfront hotels. Air raids enforced the only pauses, but only when bombs were actually falling. Aviation advisor Claire Chennault was another frequent player.

Bond wrote the matter-of-unembellished-fact details into one of his long letters to Pan Am (less Sharp's poker game, of course). "I hope I have not bored you with all this," he concluded, ". . . feel free to consign it to the waste paper basket if you so desire."

The letter wasn't so fated. Bond's breezy tales of the China war played brilliantly well in the upper floors of the Chrysler Building.

13

THE *KWEILIN* INCIDENT

The DC-2 rumbled at the end of the Kai Tak runway, morning sunshine sparkling from its shiny aluminum wings. In the cockpit, pilot-captain Hugh Leslie Woods and his Chinese copilot, Lieu Chung-chuan, ticked through the takeoff checklist. They tested the magnetos, left and right, and scanned the engine gauges. Everything hovered in the normal range. The yoke trembled in Woody's hands, and he tromped the rudder pedals, applying the brakes. At his nod, Lieu slid the throttles forward. The two radial Cyclones drank high-octane gasoline and roared in perfect tone, 1,750 horsepower of pure mechanical ecstasy. The propellers bit the summer air, and the marvelous Douglas, named *Kweilin*, pulled against the brakes like a Thoroughbred tugging at its reins.

Woods released the brakes. The plane crept forward, slowly at first, then faster and faster. The tail wheel rose, and the silvery plane blurred, not wholly terrestrial, not yet quite aloft. Woods eased back the yoke and lifted free. He gathered speed, banked right, and climbed over Victoria Harbor. The lush hillsides and rocky outcrops of the Crown Colony hadn't yet paled into the muggy haze of midmorning. Joe Loh, the ship's radio operator, keyed a departure message: *08:04 A.M.* It was August 24, 1938.

Woody had a full load, fourteen passengers, plus a steward, radio operator, and copilot, eighteen total, himself included, and most had their faces glued to the windows as the plane climbed, enjoying the magnificent views of Hong Kong Harbor. Woods set a northwestward course for the city of Wuchow, his first stop en route to Chungking and Chengtu in the heart of Szechwan Province, more than 750 miles to the northwest.

Twenty minutes after takeoff, he climbed through six thousand feet and crossed from Hong Kong territory into Chinese airspace. Dead ahead he spotted eight pontoon biplanes. Woody didn't recognize the type, but he assumed they were Japanese—they had a seaplane tender near Hong Kong, and he'd seen their warplanes in the vicinity before. No CNAC plane had ever been attacked, but the exact status of the company was pretty murky, and Woods was a careful, methodical pilot. He reversed course, flying back over Hong Kong's New Territories and losing track of the Japanese patrol in the process. Concerned, he climbed to eight thousand feet and gave them a few minutes to pass, then turned 180 degrees and reset his original course to Wuchow, 297 degrees magnetic. The DC-2 soared over the west end of the bay between Hong Kong territory and the Chinese mainland for the second time at 8:30 A.M. Woody scanned the skies in front, then skidded the plane and checked behind, just in time to see five Japanese biplanes diving on his tail at extreme speed from three or four thousand feet above, a textbook pursuit-plane attack. Worse, they cut him off from the safety of Hong Kong airspace. Perhaps it was Bushido bravado, but at the controls of an unarmed transport and responsible for the welfare of fourteen civilians, Woods didn't dare wait another second to find out whether they'd fire. He swerved left, dropped the nose, and streaked at more than two hundred miles per hour toward a cloud patch at three thousand feet. He might be able to elude the pursuit in the mists—if he could beat them there.

Woods won the race, but as he closed on apparent safety he realized the clouds were a false haven—they capped a minor mountain range. He banked tangent and skimmed their edges, ducking in and out of the vapor to take what protection he could. Beyond the clouds, he flashed into clear air, betrayed by the skies of south China, normally a cauldron of cloud creation. Now, not a wisp of cumulus marred the next hundred miles. His DC-2 was a clay pigeon under such cobalt heavens.

As Woods turned to make another pass through the cloud he'd just left, bullets shattered the instrument panel. Another flurry stitched his wings. Woods swore, throwing the plane into a tight diving spiral. He couldn't see the pursuit planes behind, but below, on the ground, the shadow of a Japanese plane slashed at the shadow of his DC-2 like a hunting falcon. Woods pulled out of the spiral at minimum altitude, flashing across rice paddies—which their spiderweb of raised dikes made bad terrain for an emergency landing. Jinking and jiving, Woods flew for a river to his right, twisting and hauling at the yoke and working the rudder pedals like a barnstormer. More gunfire chewed into the plane.

Sampans speckled the river, the fishermen gawking at the drama above. Woods swooped low over their heads, aiming for a clear stretch of water near the right bank as Joe Loh rapped a distress message. Killing his engines and cutting the magneto switches to disconnect battery power, Woods flared and bled off speed and stalled. The tail hit first, tossing a rooster of spray. A heartbeat later, the big plane plowed into the water holus-bolus, with an enormous splash. The Japanese biplanes roared in behind and riddled it with gunfire.

It was a perfect water landing, right next to the shore, but Woody hadn't factored in the strength of the current. By the time the splash water drained from the windshield, the current had swept the plane into center stream. Woods unsnapped his harness and clambered from his seat to check the passengers. Thankfully, not a single one was hurt. On Woody's orders, Joe Loh tapped out another Morse code message—*forced down, no one injured.* The steward popped the side door. The river swirled two feet below the bottom of the door. The passengers could leap and strike out for safety, but none moved. They stared at Woody with drawn faces, eyes blank with fear. *Jesus Christ,* he realized, *they can't swim!*

He popped the emergency hatch in the cockpit roof and poked his head into the sunshine as five pontoon pursuits curled into an attack run, radial engines screaming, red orbs prominent on their wings and fuselages. Japanese, there was no doubt. The lead biplane whipped a few feet above the conical straw hat of a fisherman in a tiny sampan oaring away from the floating plane as fast as his arms could work the sweeps. A burble of automatic gunfire staccatoed over the engine noise. Bullets clipped through the DC-2 fuselage, and a woman yelped inside. Woods spied an unoccupied sampan tied to the bank directly opposite.

Ducking back into the cockpit, Woods ordered copilot Lieu to tell the passengers who could swim to jump and get away from the plane. He, for one, was going for the sampan. Lieu shouted instructions, tore off his shirt, and dashed down the aisle to help a pregnant woman who had been shot in the neck. As he knelt to bind her wound, more bullets snapped through the airframe. Two hit Lieu in the head and chest, killing him with a meaty, butcher-shop *thwack-thwack*. The fifth fighter howled overhead, forty feet above the river, and pulled up into a swooping turn behind its fellows, readying another strafing pass. Woods wriggled through the hatch onto the top of the cockpit and flung himself into the river toward the sampan. He was a poor swimmer, wearing boots and clothes, and he was in trouble from the instant he hit the water. The six-knot current swept him far below the waiting sampan, and two Japanese pursuits bore straight for him, one behind the other. Woods took a breath and submerged as lead streaked the water around him. He ran out of breath in the middle of the second attack and surfaced with bullets still zinging close. The cycle repeated time and again, until he was too exhausted to dive. Panting and thrashing on the surface, he swallowed water in huge gulps as bullets slapped up geysers all around. Somehow, he wasn't hit. Woody reached the reeds along the riverbank with the last of his strength.

Retching and vomiting, he lay in the muddy waterline, hidden by the reeds. He checked his watch—waterlogged and frozen at 8:50 A.M. He'd been gone from Hong Kong just over forty-six minutes. Far downstream, the tail fin and horizontal stabilizers of his DC-2 protruded from the water behind its half-submerged fuselage. The nose had sunk, but the plane hadn't struck bottom. It should have floated for four hours, as designed, but water poured through dozens of bullet holes. It coasted around a bend and disappeared from sight. The pursuits machine-gunned it like a target on a practice range, swooping and diving above the reeds and rice paddies, guns barking. Eventually, they broke off the attack, gained a few hundred feet of altitude, and flew long ovals over the countryside to survey their handiwork. Time passed, perhaps as much as an hour. Woods couldn't summon the strength to stand. Eventually, the raiders flew away. The engine noise faded, leaving the quiet of an August morning. A bird chirped among the reeds. Woods pushed to his feet and wobbled along the riverbank in the direction of his downed airplane, gripped by cold fury. No civilian airliner in history had ever been shot down by hostile air action. It just wasn't done.

And those pilots had been waiting in ambush. There was no mistake: The attack—the murder—was premeditated.

Half a mile down the bank, Woods met a Chinese soldier. They spat questions at each other in a futile effort to communicate. The soldier spoke no English; Woods no Cantonese. Woody was near frantic to learn the fate of his passengers and crew, but the soldier had other ideas. He prodded the pilot down paddy dikes at bayonet point until they met his squad. Words, gestures, dirt drawings, and pidgin attempts failed to bridge the communications gap. The soldiers loaded Woods into a fisherman's sampan, detailed an escort, and shoved the boat into the river. The fisherman put them ashore an hour later. Sweating, Woods trudged with his guard on small paths through rice paddies and sugarcane for three or four miles and reached a barracks, but it had no interpreter either, and after still more fruitless communications efforts, a rickshaw coolie towed the very frustrated airman to the headquarters of General Chang Wei-chang, the district magistrate.

General Chang met Woods in his courtyard amid a slew of other eyewitnesses bringing reports of the attack. The general was terribly sorry, but as far as he knew, the only survivors were Woods, his radio operator, and one wounded passenger, both of whom were resting inside his headquarters. A few bullet-riddled bodies had been recovered, but General Chang was forced to presume everybody else aboard the plane was dead.

Dazed, Woody took a few steps, pirouetted, and slumped on a bench. Eighteen people on his airplane. Fifteen dead. It was hard to fathom. Sometime later, the general's chauffeur drove the three survivors to Macau.

Bond was in CNAC's Hankow office that morning, organizing materials for an 11 A.M. appointment with His Excellency Chang Kia-ngau, Kuomintang minister of communications. A clerk handed him a radiogram just as he was about to depart:

Woods forced to land on river by Japanese. Everybody safe.

A plane attacked! Bond grimaced. Sooner or later the Japanese were going to get the war they were asking for. Thank God nobody had been hurt. Bond looked at the message headers. It had also gone to the Ministry of Communications, who would run wild with the details of Pan American's participation and the foreign policy implications of the incident; their publicity bureau would sing propaganda like a church choir. The U.S. government was trying to maintain a neutral policy, in accordance with the national mood, and stories about American pilots flying in support of belligerent China might well backlash against Pan Am. It was the exact scenario most feared by Juan Trippe when he'd allowed Bond to re-engage in China. Worse, the Ministry of Communications had a head start. Adrenaline tingled his limbs. Bond needed a cool head in the ministry immediately—his own.

He forced himself to think. Kitsi was his first obligation, and she was in Shanghai, shipping belongings to the United States and Hong Kong from their former home in the French Concession. She'd be terrified when she heard a CNAC ship had gone down, and in a few hours word would be all over China. Bond couldn't afford to send her news that might later be held against him. His message was certain to be read by office staffs on both ends of the transmission, and any real information would quickly jump to the newspapers. He carefully worded a radiogram:

Do not worry. Do not change plans. Do not talk. Bondy.

A bit cryptic, perhaps, but the message itself would tell her he was alive, and Kitsi could ascertain his location from the sending station. She'd be appalled, but she'd be instantly reassured. And she'd know what to do. Next, Bond radioed Chuck Sharp to suspend flying out of Hong Kong and extend a gag order to all company personnel.

Messages away, Bond rickshawed to the ministry. The place buzzed like a newsroom, alive with the clack and ding of manual typewriters. Secretaries rushed back and forth clutching sheaves of paper. Bond sensed the tone right away: *Here's another* Panay *Incident and let's make the most of it.* The minister of communications swept Bond into his office and ordered him to prepare a speech and summon the correspondents.

Bond was taken aback by the minister's un-Chinese brusqueness. "Your Excellency, with all due respect, I think the publicity of this incident will take care of itself. Comments from me, six hundred miles away, will probably be lost."

"Mr. Bond, your part is to notify Admiral Yarnell and Ambassador Johnson, in that order, and emphasize the fact that CNAC is an American company with American pilots and American planes."

The minister was hoping for military action! Bond tried not to show surprise. Admiral Yarnell commanded the United States Navy's Asiatic Fleet, and he'd drawn tough anti-Japanese lines before, at least rhetorically. "Your Excellency, as you know, we're a Chinese company. Americans own shares in that company, yes, but it's a minority interest, and the U.S. Navy isn't going to fight for a Chinese company. However, I will notify Ambassador Johnson right away, and he'll be outraged, like everyone else."

Fretting, Bond slipped out of the minister's office. It was a precarious situation: To say nothing to Ambassador Johnson or to prevaricate about Pan American participation would deal a serious blow to Pan Am's fragile relationship with the Chinese government, but considering the high tide of pacifism and isolationism on the other side of the Pacific, the truth might damage Pan Am in the United States. Juan Trippe had Bond under strict instructions to disavow ties to the parent company in the exact scenario that had just occurred. But despite their best efforts, those ties weren't deniable. The Ministry of Communications' publicity bureau was already crowing about Pan Am's involvement, and Ambassador Johnson was no fool. Officially or unofficially, he certainly knew the gist of the relationship. Bad news doesn't improve with age, thought Bond. Much better to tell the truth, and without delay. He wired the details as he knew them in strong language: The Japanese had forced a plane to land on a river, everybody was safe, Americans were involved, and Pan Am had a minority interest.

Tied up on the Hankow Bund was the USS *Luzon* (PR-7), the shallow-draft, twin-stacked gunboat that carried the flag of the U.S. Navy's Yangtze Patrol and whatever prestige remained to the tiny inland squadron in the aftermath of the *Panay* sinking. Knowing that signals reached the ambassador faster via the Navy, Bond went to the *Luzon* and asked Admiral LeBreton, the Yangtze Patrol's commander, if he could use the ship's radio to resend the message via the gunboat at Chungking. The admiral acceded, and, also at Bond's request, he copied the message to Admiral Yarnell, who obviously needed to know, but who couldn't be compelled to officially respond to the Chinese government by notification coming through Navy channels. When Bond alluded to the horde of journalists and Chinese officials sure to dog his tracks ashore, Admiral LeBreton invited him to stay aboard. Bond was grateful, but he began to get a queasy feeling about the "everybody safe" aspect of the original message. Woody was a fine pilot with a level head. Bond could think of only one way the Japanese could force him to ditch in a river—with gunfire.

Bond confessed his fear to Admiral LeBreton. "Isn't *Mindanao* still in Hong Kong?"

She was. The USS *Mindanao* was the *Luzon*'s sister ship.

"I wonder if you'd have her run a few of my men over to Macau to see if they could collect specifics?"

Admiral LeBreton radioed instructions to Hong Kong, and at 4:30 P.M., the *Mindanao* reported that she was departing Hong Kong with chief station mechanic Zygmund Soldinski, a doctor, and a few other CNAC personnel aboard. She'd make Macau in three hours.

Five hundred and eighty-five miles to the south, the *Mindanao* raced across the Pearl River Delta toward Macau and the sinking sun, making sixteen knots, her top speed. An hour later, her lookouts spotted a warship lurking in the channel on the Macau approach. It was a blue-water destroyer, a much heavier class of warship. The *Mindanao* went to battle stations. The gunboat's full-speed approach spooked the suspicious stranger, which steamed for the open sea without showing colors. The *Mindanao* splashed anchor into the shallow waters of Macau Harbor at about 7:30 P.M. Hugh Woods was in the city, supervising his wounded passenger's hospital admission. He came aboard an hour later, and he went straight to the radio.

The gruesome details reached William Bond just as he sat down to supper in *Luzon*'s wardroom—fifteen people dead aboard one of his airplanes, including two of his own employees. Bond retired to an officer's cabin and flopped on a bunk. He dreaded the consequences of his afternoon message to Ambassador Johnson, a misinformed muddle that could have colored the ambassador's own response. By now, the true details were clattering over the newswires. Bond decided to fly to Chungking and speak to Johnson directly. If the attack portended a concentrated Japanese campaign against commercial aviation, his airline might not survive. The gentle susurrations of the great stream passing beneath the *Luzon*'s hull did nothing to ease his mind. He suffered a long, sleepless night.

Before Bond left the next morning, the minister of communications summoned him and expressed profound displeasure about the strength, volume, quality, and quantity of publicity he'd generated. Eurasia had also halted Hong Kong flights, and the minster was dead set against the airlines' knuckling to the Japanese aggression and canceling their schedules. Bond refused to reinstate them without safety assurances. The minister concluded the interview with a broad lecture about what, *exactly*, Bond and the United States should do, and why.

As soon as Bond set foot in Chungking, an airport clerk gave him a message instructing him to report to H. H. Kung immediately, but Bond couldn't afford to treat with Kung without knowing where he stood with the American government. Instead, he hired a boat to take him to Ambassador Johnson on the south side of the river. With Johnson, Bond came straight to the point, laying out everything he knew. He accepted responsibility for the lost plane—he hadn't thought the Japanese would do such a thing without a preliminary propaganda campaign. He apologized for his inaccurate message and asked the question burning at him ever since he'd learned of the attack: "Does Pan Am's involvement embarrass you or the American government?"

"Bondy, you're not supposed to hide and crawl! You don't embarrass us, not in any way. I cabled Washington, and they feel like I do, that you're a great service. We hope you can continue."

It took a moment for the ambassador's meaning to register: When fighting erupted in Shanghai, the State Department had ordered Pan Am to quit; now, a year later, the U.S. ambassador was actively encouraging Bond to press on. He had yet to face Dr. Kung, but knowing he wasn't laboring under a cloud of official American displeasure was a massive load lifted. He expressed trepidation about how things would go with Kung.

"Don't worry, Bondy. He needs you, and he needs your men."

Bond crossed the swift, tawny river on a leaky water taxi. Sedan-chair coolies carried him to the prime minister's office. Kung was well informed—he scolded Bond for detouring to see the ambassador. He wanted Bond to hold a rabble-rousing press conference.

Bond demurred.

"Doesn't it mean anything to you that it was an American company? Pan Am is practically the official airline of the United States."

"At best it's an unofficial, official airline, and all it has in CNAC is a minority interest. Pan American tried to get permission to land flying boats in China five years ago, unsuccessfully, because no foreign flying is allowed in China. CNAC flies in China precisely because it is Chinese, and the United States isn't going to war for a Chinese company." Bond paused, wanting a reply. He got none. "I'm sorry, Doctor, but I can't change that. I know you aren't pleased, and I understand why. The best I can do for China is to keep the airline flying. I'll do my best to do that. You have my word. With your permission, I'd like to be excused."

Bond's subsequent audience with vice minister of communications and board chairman Peng Sho-pei didn't progress with any pretense of courtesy. Peng subjected Bond to a high-volume rant elaborating his shortcomings, which Bond stood without comment. In the last forty-eight hours, every Chinese official he'd met had lectured him about what he should do, personally, what CNAC should do, what Pan Am should do, and what the United States should do. What they all wanted, thought Bond, was the United States to declare war on Japan. Which it wasn't going to do. Bond didn't like it, but considering that the *Panay* sinking and the Nanking butchery hadn't caused the United States to breach its precious neutrality, the destruction of an airplane filled with Chinese civilians, regardless of who owned it, wasn't going to impel his country to war. CNAC would just have to persevere and render what service it could to an embattled China.

The suspended Hong Kong flights forced Bond to travel an enormous arc back to the colony: a flight from Chungking to Kunming, a narrow-gauge railroad ride to Hanoi, and an Air France flight to Hong Kong. All told, the trip would take five days, when a direct flight would have taken five hours. By the time Bond climbed aboard one of his two still-functioning DC-2s at Chungking's Sanhupa Airport the next morning, Friday, August 26, 1938, newspapers all over the Far East had latched on to the shootdown drama, and another sinister twist had added itself to the intrigue—one involving Sun Yat-sen's only son, Sun Fo, recently returned from a seven-month trip to Europe and the Soviet Union, where he'd gone to drum up support for the Chinese war effort. No country in Western Europe had anything tangible to offer, but Sun Fo had promised "more active support from Russia" in a vehemently anti-Japanese speech made in Hong Kong. A colony newspaper had announced Sun Fo would travel to Hankow aboard CNAC on August 24, 1938—the very flight shot down. Many speculated it was an assassination attempt.

One British correspondent who'd interviewed Sun Fo found him to be "pleasant, capable, ambitious, and delightfully frank." William Bond's opinion wasn't nearly so charitable—he considered Sun Fo among the most venal officials in China and abhorred the very sight of him. Unfortunately, Sun Fo was an important man. Bond loathed official functions that forced him to shake his hand and put on a pretense of courtesy, and duty required him to attend enough of them that he'd recognized Sun Fo's number one concubine aboard the steamer *Kung Wo* during the upriver evacuation from Nanking the previous November. Bond was certain of a few things when he left Chungking that Friday morning: that eighteen people had been aboard Woody's airplane, that fifteen of them were dead, and that Sun Fo wasn't among either group. He'd left Hong Kong aboard Eurasia an hour earlier and reached Hankow unmolested; after landing, he'd spouted to the press about the "inevitability" of Chinese victory.

William Bond was equally certain Sun Fo never intended to be on the ill-fated airplane, and that he'd concocted the scheme to deceive the Japanese and served up Woody's flight as his sacrificial substitute. Directly questioned, Sun Fo said one of his secretaries had made a mistake, an excuse that held no water with Bond. Chinese secretaries didn't make that kind of error.

Despite Bond's suspicions, general outrage stayed focused on the Japanese. Journalists confronted the Japanese consul general in Hong Kong, who flatly denied the attack. He claimed the Japanese pilots had flown over to identify the plane and that Woody had become frightened and ditched in the river without provocation. The consul general told that story before it became known that a few people survived. "The Japanese seemed determined to kill everybody," related Mr. Liu Chai-sung, the sole surviving passenger. "Their planes returned again and again, machine-gunning us mercilessly, and I was hit by a bullet in the neck." The gunshot wasn't his worst wound. His wife and infant child had died in his arms, riddled with machine-gun bullets, before he swam to safety.

Concrete evidence corroborated Liu's account. Many dozens of bullet holes perforated the wreckage salvaged from the river bottom, and there were gunshot wounds in every one of the fourteen recovered corpses, including two women, a five-year-old boy, and Mr. Liu's baby. One victim had been hit thirteen times.

Different Japanese sources told different stories. Japanese newspapers in Shanghai announced the crash the result of "engine trouble," and an official Japanese spokesman told *The New York Times* the attack occurred because "the plane acted suspiciously and attempted to elude the pursuing planes." In Tokyo, Rear Admiral Kiyoshi Noda denied the navy fliers attacked with the deliberate intention of assassinating Sun Fo, but the most spectacular quibble appeared in a Japanese-language daily called *The Hong Kong Nippo*, which admitted that although Sun Fo was the object of the attack, "our wild eagles intended to capture [him] alive." U.S. secretary of state Cordell Hull cabled protest instructions to the ambassador to Japan, Joseph Grew; and the *North China Daily News,* the leading British newspaper in Shanghai, drily observed that "diplomatic circles were not certain which Japanese version of the incident would be cited in the rejection of the American protest."

Bond reached Hong Kong on an Air France flight from Hanoi on the last day of August. A *South China Morning Post* reporter met the flight. Bond had no comment about anything but flight schedules. Film producers compiled a newsreel about the "*Kweilin* Tragedy" using film taken at the salvage site showing the mutilated airplane, scattered mail bags, and bullet-riddled corpses. Hugh Woods commentated, and it showed to packed houses in Hong Kong's Queens, Alhambra, and Central theaters on the first three days of September. The extreme demand resulted in the addition of two more dates the following week.

Eurasia resumed daytime service from Hong Kong in the first week of September, and its number came up almost immediately. Japanese fighters shot up one of its tri-motored Junkers 52s near the Kwangsi-Kwantung border, and Eurasia suspended Hong Kong operations for a second time. Two days later, the Japanese shot down one of its planes twelve miles southwest of Hankow. No one was hurt in either incident, but both airlines received the message loud and clear—the Japanese were hunting China's civilian airliners.

Secretary of State Hull instructed Ambassador Grew to make a second formal protest and add forceful oral comments about the failure of the Japanese military to "exercise ordinary care to identify the object of their attacks or to manifest ordinary restraint and consideration with respect to human lives and suffering."

And to that, silence, perhaps the clearest message of all. There is no record of any response from Japan.

Ironically, at almost the precise time that the Japanese fighters were machine-gunning Woody's DC-2, Soong Ching-ling, Sun Yat-sen's widow, had stood at a microphone in Canton and broadcast a radio message to the United States.* She spoke fine English, with a trace of Southern lilt she'd acquired during her tenure at Wesleyan College in Macon, Georgia, and her impassioned speech laid some unpleasant facts before her intended audience:

> *Your country supplies 64 percent of Japan's petroleum. The raiders who horrify you are armed with products made by American labor, financed by American capital, loaded by American longshoremen, and often brought to Japan by American seamen in American ships.*

Some of that matériel support almost certainly propelled the attack on Woody's plane, and in relating the shoot-down and Madame Sun's address, an editorial in Hong Kong's *South China Morning Post* noted that

> *one of these days, the Great Democracies may find out that there is something, after all, for which no price can be fixed, they may learn that the only proper and wise way to deal with the aggressors is to demand an eye for an eye and a tooth for a tooth. In short, there will be a time when the peace-loving nations will be compelled to meet force by force. Until then, nothing can check Japan from her career of truculent destruction.*

The growing crisis over Hitler's obsession with Sudeten Czechoslovakia drove news of Woody's shoot-down from the front pages of the Far Eastern newspapers. Hitler ranted about the destiny of *Grossdeutschland,* "Greater

---

* She was Sun Yat-sen's second wife, not Sun Fo's mother, and the middle of the three famous "Soong sisters"—Soong Ai-ling (Madame H. H. Kung), Soong Ching-ling (Madame Sun Yat-sen), and Soong Mei-ling (Madame Chiang Kai-shek)—whose brothers were Soong Tse-ven (T. V. Soong), Soong Tse-liang (T. L. Soong), and Soong Tse-an (T. A. Soong).

Germany," before hundreds of thousands of rapt Germans at the Nazi Party's annual Nuremberg rally in the second week of September, and the continent teetered on the edge of general conflict. Prudent Britons dug air-raid shelters in their London gardens. To CNAC's foreign employees and their wives, the threat of war in Europe somehow seemed worse than the one they had on their doorsteps.

Central Government pressure mounted on the airlines to resume Hong Kong service. Night flying was a sure way to avoid the Japanese, but it was dangerous in the extreme, especially over a mountainous landscape devoid of lighted cities and roads and possessing no navigation aids. No airline in the world operated exclusively at night, but Eurasia embraced the dangers and landed its first commercial night flight from Hankow to Hong Kong a few minutes after midnight on the night of September 20–21. CNAC had fallen behind, largely because of Bond's reluctance to undertake nocturnal operations without permission from New York. Although nearly a month had passed since Woody was shot down, due to transpacific Clipper delays, Bond hadn't received a reply to any of the voluminous letters he'd written to Pan Am headquarters. He'd been navigating by guesswork.

The stack of letters that reached Hong Kong on September 22 assuaged his anxieties. The Chrysler Building suits offered nothing but encouragement. The *Kweilin* incident hadn't sparked any domestic backlash. Quite the contrary, in fact: Fifteen months of blatant aggression had evaporated whatever goodwill most Americans felt toward Japan. It had become obvious which side held the moral high ground, and why, and although the overwhelming majority of Americans had absolutely no interest in fighting *for* China, if a few of their compatriots were willing, the average citizen was quite prepared to allow them to do so.

Regardless of the friendlier political landscape, Bond remained uneasy about night flying. It seemed so gratuitously dangerous. A variety of forces contrived to change his mind. First was Eurasia's nocturnal service. CNAC stood to lose enormous face if it didn't offer one similar. The second was Ernie Allison, who had taken a job aiding the Chinese Air Force. Bond and Allison saw each other often in Hankow, Chungking, and Hong Kong, and Allison thought Bond was overestimating the risks of nocturnal operations, which Allie didn't think was unreasonable. Bond hemmed and hawed so much that Allison threatened to form a new airline, and to do it himself if CNAC wouldn't. The last consideration was the pilots themselves. Night flying was an obvious "next step," and they were eager to take it.

Eurasia's chief pilot trained Chuck Sharp to use Telefunken direction finders, an instantly responsive German system that allowed pilots to land at night or in bad weather. Using it, the pilot wore a headset that gave a null tone when he was "on the beam," flying directly toward the homing station. If the pilot deviated, the headset repeated either the Morse code letter "A," *dit dah, dit dah, dit dah, dit dah,* or "N," *dah dit, dah dit, dah dit,* to indicate needed left-right course corrections. Sharp was soon teaching CNAC's other pilots.

Bond worked like a fiend through all the drama. Most nights he didn't get home until long after Kitsi had gone to sleep. One night in the last half of September, he awoke to the sound of his wife crying on the pillow beside him. Kitsi buried her head in his chest and wept in the darkness. "I'm so scared," she sobbed. "Ever since they shot Woody down. And I want to see my baby. I haven't seen Langy in six months, and we can't bring him out here, not with the world acting like it is."

There it was, it was said. It must have been gnawing at her for days.

"I know, Monkey, I know, it's probably time for you to go. We can't let him grow up not knowing either one of us."

They'd been planning for her to return to the States for Christmas and bring Langhorne to the Orient after the New Year. Bond had been counting on the international situation smoothing out, but each day made that seem increasingly unlikely. They mulled things over in the darkness. Manila and Baguio were alternatives, but Japanese aggressions and the Czech crisis made the United States seem the only safe place on earth. It was agonizing; there just wasn't any reasonable alternative.

There was more. "Bondy, you haven't seen little Langy in nearly a year," Kitsi whispered. It was two-thirds of the time their son had been alive.

Bond absolutely refused to leave under circumstances that looked like he was running away. There was a war on, he had a role in it, and that was that, however much he hated it. No one else in the System could do his job, even though he wished someone would.

She was crying again. Bond hugged her tight. "I'll get you a spot on the next Clipper," he whispered. "Until then, I'm not letting you out of my sight."

As usual, Bond was as good as his word, glued to Kitsi's side until he put her on the big flying boat, savoring every bittersweet moment, but her departure left a tremendous void. In a letter to Bixby, Bond joked about Kitsi's Far Eastern adventures growing to "legendary proportions," but he hadn't fully recognized what a difference she'd made. However, hardships had to be endured, he told himself, and the Far East wasn't any place he wanted his wife. Not until things settled down. Maybe six months would make a difference. It was impossible to live without that hope.

In Europe, the Czech crisis climaxed with Neville Chamberlain's infamous Munich appeasement. Scant hours later, German soldiers goosestepped into the Sudetenland. Munich showed the dull teeth of democracy and, like tectonic effects, its ramifications rippled to the far side of the world. On October 12, thirty thousand Japanese troops stormed ashore in Bias Bay, sixty miles northeast of Hong Kong, and advanced toward Canton supported by more than a hundred airplanes. The invaders cut the Hong Kong–Canton railroad and closed tight against the colony's landward approaches, adding another layer of risk to CNAC's nascent night flying. Not only would the flights have to be made in darkness; henceforth they'd also have to be made over occupied territory.

With William Bond aboard, Chuck Sharp piloted the airline's first regular nocturnal schedule from Hong Kong to Chungking on the night of October 18. The night flying was off to an auspicious start, but Bond wasn't happy with the deteriorations apparent in China's general situation as the enemy closed on Hankow and Canton. He summarized his perspective in a letter to New York:

> I have been predicting the fall of Hankow so long that further comment will no doubt be taken as a false alarm. Nevertheless, I think [it] is going to occur. . . . The part that worries me the most is that while our grip on the situation seems as firm as ever, what we are holding on to seems to be dwindling away. I suppose there is nothing we can do about that, so I try not to worry over it.

In reality, William Bond never could achieve that grace note of Buddhist detachment, and the incessant stress nagged at his health. A persistent cold harried him, and over the last eighteen months his already thinning hair had receded far above and behind his temples, exposing his whole forehead. The lines in his face had deepened, and his stomach gave him constant pain. Bond wasn't a big man, but he'd lost nearly twenty pounds. A dentist extracted a tooth and constructed a bridge, but neglected to remove the entire root, which cost Bond many painful hours of reconstruction. An earache capped his ailments. The doctor discovered two boils close to his eardrum. Bond had them lanced and told Bixby that although "they hurt like the deuce," he was almost sad to see them go—they'd served as "strangely satisfying counter-irritants" to help take his mind off the airline's problems.

In Chungking on Friday, October 21, 1938, Bond received anxious messages from the minister of communications pressing him to add flights out of Hankow. The minister was there himself, and after swearing Bond to secrecy he confided that Hankow was to be evacuated on October 25. Bond promised his company's full commitment. Dozens of other telegrams snowed into Bond's office immediately after, a wispy blizzard of four- by six-inch carbon papers delivered through the commercial telegraph service—all urgent, personal messages from government officials frantic to arrange special, high-priority charters out of the provisional capital.

Bond hadn't been crying wolf after all.

14

THE EVACUATION OF HANKOW

In the middle 1930s, the airline had solved Chungking's "absence of flat ground" problem by building an airstrip on a sandbar island in the Yangtze below the city, where an army of coolies had fitted more than sixty thousand stone paving slabs into a 2,150-foot runway capable of withstanding a Yangtze flood, which in the high-water months of summer typically swooshed a thirty-foot head of current over its top at twelve knots. Floods came on in a matter of hours, and the only buildings ever erected on the sandbar were ramshackle bamboo-framed structures roofed in thatch and walled with woven mats that could be quickly dismantled and carried to higher ground. It was called Sanhupa Airstrip, it had the feel of a frontier colony, and Chuck Sharp and Royal Leonard, the airline's first two qualified night fliers, slicked a DC-2 on its cobblestones at about nine o'clock on the morning of Saturday, October 22, 1938.*

Leonard had flown ten hours since the previous afternoon, so Bond

---

* Nine or ten months of the year, the arrangement was fantastically convenient. In the flood months, the airline operated from the military airfield a dozen miles east of the city.

sent him to the room he borrowed in the Rappe family's Methodist compound to rest. Sharp stayed with Bond to finalize the evacuation plan. Thirty-six Japanese airplanes attacked the tri-cities that morning, the first bombing they'd suffered in several weeks. To have any margin of safety, the ex-Hankow flights had to be made at night, but because Yangtze bends at Chungking dictated a complicated sequence of approach turns, and a cluster of wires strung across the river close to the end of the Sanhupa runway mandated a dicey, eyes-required maneuver at the last minute, night landings at Chungking could be done only under a bright moon. In the third week of October 1938, the airline wasn't getting either celestial or meteorologic cooperation. The moon wouldn't show a sliver until October 26, four nights hence, and thick clouds wedged up by a Central Asian cold front blanketed the interior provinces. The flat countryside around Chengtu in the center of the Szechwan basin was more forgiving. Bond planned to send the DC-2s out of Chungking that afternoon, timed to arrive at Hankow just after dark. They'd immediately fly a load of passengers to Chengtu, fuel, and fly back to Hankow, and if things went well there'd be just enough time to escape Hankow with more evacuees, this time bound for Chungking, before daybreak brought Japanese warplanes. The predawn flight would reach the wartime capital before midmorning, and the pilots would snooze through the day before repeating the process late the following afternoon. It was an ambitious schedule. Any delay and they'd lose the window for the second flight. Ichang was closer, but its airfield was surrounded by foothills, and it wasn't yet prepped for night operations. Bond felt he'd be compounding substantial risks if he used it before it was ready.

Air-raid alarms shrieked just as Sharp prepared to cross the river to join Leonard for a few hours of shut-eye. He sprinted back to the DC-2 and took off, fleeing westward. The raiders hit a military airfield sixty miles downstream, but Sharp had to loiter for two hours before the all-clear sounded, It was well past noon before he got a chance to catnap.

One of the great lessons of the 1930s was that things could always get worse, and they did exactly that on the afternoon of October 22, 1938. News items rattling out of a teletype machine announced the fall of Canton. Scarcely a shot had been fired. The sullen clouds over Chungking matched the mood of a city that felt betrayed. The citizenry suspected treasonous generals and felt bitter resentment against Great Britain, which had promised "strong action" against any invasion of south China but, in the spirit of Munich, had done nothing to thwart the aggression. More disastrous news wasn't long in arriving: The Japanese had captured a strategic location forty-six miles downriver from Hankow. No natural obstacles remained between them and the provisional capital.

The second DC-2 came up from Yunnan. Sharp and Leonard were back at the airport after 4 P.M. Both were extraordinarily competent pilots. Royal Leonard, in particular, was exceptionally safe, but so locked into punctilious routine that it was nigh impossible for him to act expeditiously. The two planes took off a few minutes before 5 P.M., Sharp already in the lead. Bond climbed the 350-odd stairs above the airport to the "Pink House," the building in which the airline maintained its Chungking operations headquarters, and settled in to monitor the flight reports. The first relay went well. Both pilots got in and out of Hankow at around 9 P.M., but snow and mild icing conditions slowed their approach to Chengtu. Sharp dumped his passengers and got right back in the air. Leonard did likewise, but judging from the time span between Leonard's arrival and departure messages, he'd spent an extra twenty minutes on the ground.

Pushing hard, Sharp landed at Hankow a few minutes before first light and kept his propellers spinning. New evacuees hustled aboard, and Sharp climbed back into the graying sky. Leaden daylight crept under the cloud layer, and there was more than enough light to see as Leonard roared down the Han River into Hankow. Bluish fog tendrils clung to the ground, and Leonard noticed airplanes over the city. For the last year, China's air-warning net had been uniformly excellent. It had given no alarm, but to be safe, Leonard called Hankow control and asked if there was an air-raid alarm.

"No alarm," the station answered.

Leonard assumed the planes were Chinese warplanes assigned to cover the withdrawal. He kept coming in, but he worried. There were too many.

"Are those planes Chinese?"

"No."

Perhaps they were the Russian "volunteers" who'd been aiding China? A formation of pursuit planes peeled from medium altitude and made a low pass over the airfield. Black bursts of dirt and smoke spurted from the ground. Bombs! "Whose planes are those?" Leonard demanded.

"Those planes are Japanese, but there is no air-raid alarm."

Pouring on power, turning tail, and diving, Leonard zigzagged westward, practically flying between grave mounds. The air force alert service had evacuated Hankow without bothering to inform civilian aviation.

Leonard fled Hankow at full power, which used his fuel reserve. Throttling back after fifteen minutes, he no longer had enough gas to safely make Chungking, so he set course for Ichang. White panels on the Ichang airfield marked danger: ENEMY PLANES! DON'T LAND! Leonard goosed the motors down to minimum consumption and threaded low-altitude circles in the hills west of Ichang. The alert released after thirty minutes, and Leonard landed. Bond ordered him to Chungking, but Leonard needed gas. Unfortunately, Ichang was a satellite airfield. The airline stored its Ichang fuel in a riverside storage facility for the flying boats. The station manager had to truck fuel to the airfield, and Leonard didn't reach Chungking until well past noon.

Bond met Leonard at the airport, congratulated him on the tough night of flying, and asked why he'd fallen behind leaving Chengtu.

"I was out of the danger zone." Leonard said he'd had to wait for coolies to bring up a sufficient quantity of oil.

Bond was under a different impression. The Chengtu staff had told him Leonard wasted time getting breakfast.

Both men were frazzled; neither had slept. Bond asked if Leonard had given any thought to the fact that he was scheduled to repeat the same mission in two hours. Surprise flashed through Leonard's eyes—before he got angry. Leonard vehemently insisted he'd be ready.

Bond snapped. "Don't be foolish! I've canceled your flights. Those were twenty critical minutes. You've been awake for twenty-two hours. You flew all night the night before. You *can't* fly again in two hours. Sharp's been asleep for four hours, like you should've been."

Leonard objected. Bond cut him off. "Don't argue. I don't have time for it. The weather's getting worse. Go to the Rappes'. They'll put you up in my room. Stay there until tomorrow morning. Sleep. We'll need you again after you're rested."

The clouds thickened. The temperature at river level sank until it was only three degrees above freezing, virtually guaranteeing icing conditions in the clouds above. Thinking the ice rendered unsafe the midnight shuttle over the mountains to Chengtu, Bond decided to accept the risks of the hills around Ichang for future evacuations. It was a much shorter trip, but the field wasn't yet prepared for night operations. Bond radioed the minister of communications that the airline would manage only one evacuation flight that night, arriving after dark and leaving for Chungking just before dawn.

"Frantic" replies sizzled back from Hankow. Conditions were hotter than Bond imagined. To prevent the minister from forming the wrong impression, Bond decided to go to the provisional capital and explain the changes personally.

Simultaneous with the afternoon planning, Chinese pilot-captain Hugh Chen was lumbering down the Yangtze Gorges in one of the airline's two Consolidated Commodore flying boats,* supposedly on his way to Hankow as per Bond's plan to use the Commodores to evacuate the airline's own staff. Two years before, Chen had become CNAC's first Chinese-born flier to be "checked-out" as a full-fledged airline captain. He landed on the river at Ichang to refuel and radioed Bond to say he wasn't continuing.

Bond sent an irked message ordering Chen to complete his flight.

Chuck Sharp took off from Sanhupa Airstrip at 4:30 P.M. and held low altitude as he traced the river downstream. He had a copilot, a radio operator, and one passenger—William Langhorne Bond. The threat of icing conditions kept Sharp flying "contact" under the clouds, even if the decision crammed him into a 180-mile-per-hour race through a few hundred feet of clear air above the river.

In the Yangtze Gorges, Sharp wound the silver plane through the gloomy defiles, his concentration total, a perfect symbiosis of man and machine, and an unconscious smirk curled up from the corners of his lips, a man free in the practice of an exacting discipline, doing what he'd been born to do. The force of the turns lashed Bond from side to side in the passenger cabin. He might have been the only person in China who wanted to get into Hankow rather than out of it—except the Japanese Army, of course.

The aerial roller coaster lasted most of an hour, until Sharp shot from the gorges with the last of the daylight. The river looped away to the southeast, beginning a long southward meander, and Sharp set a divergent course eastward to cut off the bend, between clouds and flattening country and the darkening waters of numerous lakes. Sharp told his copilot to hold

---

* Colonel Lam had bought the Commodores from Pan Am the previous autumn.

course and altitude, to wake him when he raised the Hankow homing bea-con, and lolled his head against a bracing arm. The fellow nudged him awake forty-five minutes later. Sharp settled his earphones without fuss, tuned in the beacon, and "rode the beam" into Hankow, laying his Douglas alongside a line of tins filled with burning petrol that beaded a safe runway through the bomb-churned airfield.

On the ground, throaty airplane engines warmed in the darkness. Blue flames warbled from the exhaust pipes of a Eurasia Junkers 52. Pilots, me-chanics, and airfield coolies worked with a purpose, as dozens of other would-be passengers milled in the blackness, and an edgy whiff of panic mingled with the caustic tang of picric acid, the explosive chemical used in Japanese bombs, and the foul smells of charred buildings. In daylight, they would have been government officials, military officers, and promi-nent businessmen, men wealthy enough to afford airfares and important enough to merit priority. That night they were frightened civilians eager to avoid being spitted on a Japanese bayonet. Farther down the flight line, Bond and Sharp bumped into Ernie Allison shepherding a passel of evacu-ees onto a government-owned DC-2. They shouted and shook hands. A company chauffeur drove Bond and Sharp to the Hankow Bund, bucking a fierce tide of refugees. Tens of thousands of others camped haphazardly in the foreign concessions. Sharp climbed out at the Hotel Fienes and went to sleep. Bond had himself dropped at the U.S. Navy pontoon, where the USS *Luzon* was holding station despite a "suggestion" from the Japanese that third-power warships leave the tri-cities to avoid "unfortunate inci-dents." Neither the *Luzon,* the *Guam,* nor any of the British, French, or Italian gunboats had budged. The *Panay* had been sunk after she'd heeded a similar warning.

A mob of Chinese soldiery without semblance of organization crowded the Bund opposite the gunboat pontoons. On second glance, Bond realized most were wounded, too weak to withstand the rigors of an escape march and facing the future with "silent dread and numb resignation."

The *Luzon's* captain, Bond's old friend Lieutenant Commander Charles B. McVey, welcomed Bond aboard. Hank Jarrell, another close friend, was also on duty, but besides those two officers and a skeleton crew, the gun-boat was empty. Her other officers and men were out doing the fleshpots of Hankow's infamous Dump Street, as good sailors will, enjoying a last fling before the change of onshore management. The two officers presented

Bond with a whisky soda, and the men talked for ninety minutes, until Bond went on his way, "feeling very warm, and much cheered up."

The mood didn't last. Bond worked through the mob of soldiers and pointed himself toward the Hotel Terminus, where he expected to find the minister of communications. It felt odd to walk. Foreigners didn't walk in China, but Bond had no choice. The city's rickshaws were gone, along with every other cart, wheelbarrow, and jitney, hired by the affluent to ease the travails of evacuation. Beyond the knot of wounded soldiers, refugees bivouacked higgledy-piggledy through the foreign concessions, those awake gawking at him with listless, hungry eyes. The Hankow Bund, normally so clean and green and one of the finest streets in China, struck Bond as "the back alley of a poverty-stricken town." He strode carefully, unwilling to accelerate to his usual purposeful gait, for the Chinese had removed portable scrap iron from the city to fuel further resistance, including the sewer gratings, and Bond could imagine few fates worse than a nighttime plunge into a Chinese sewer. A huddle of children caught his attention. They were three to five years old, wearing rags, asleep, their heads on bare concrete, no possessions evident. Bond looked in vain for their parents and realized with horror that the children were marooned, abandoned. He gaped up and down the street and saw other bands of forsaken children. Guided by some innate compulsion, they'd gravitated to others of their own kind. This was China. They'd starve. None would survive. Bond straightened and smoothed his suit. There was nothing he could do. China forced a man to confront so much misery that he spent most of his time numb to it, but William Langhorne Bond was practically choking with outrage as he stepped into the lobby of the Hotel Terminus.

Astonishment dawned on Minister Chang Kia-ngau's face. Bond had told the minister he was coming, but he clearly hadn't expected the American to chance a Hankow rendezvous. Bond made light of his appearance, knowing he'd earned a great deal of face, and not only with the minister of communications, for loitering with Minister Chang were General Mow, head of the Aviation Commission, and several other Kuomintang elites, although after what Bond had seen in the streets, it was hard to care about placating politicians and spotlessly uniformed soldiers. Bond forced himself to the task, however, explaining the situation. The airline was doing its best; that was all.

About midnight, Bond rattled two Socony friends, Pete Dorrence and

Alfred Fitzsimmons, out of bed; both of them were staying through the occupation to safeguard company property. Bleary-eyed, they assured Bond that his gas had already been evacuated. Bond gifted them a bottle of whisky he'd brought up from Hong Kong: "Thought you fellows might need a drink when the Japs take over." Fitzsimmons thanked Bond from the bottom of his Irish heart.

Bond continued to the Astoria Building to explain evacuation procedures to the CNAC staff, and he learned that Hugh Chen and his Commodore were still floating on the river in Ichang—Chen hadn't completed his assigned flight, despite Bond's express orders. Furious, Bond didn't collapse into bed at the Hotel Feines until past one o'clock in the morning of Monday, October 24, strung too tightly to doze. He got up two hours later and walked back to the office, where the airline was rallying its departing passengers for the drive to the airfield through rivers of eleventh-hour refugees.

The ground staff precisely calculated the planeloads of the evacuating DC-2s, and after weighing passengers and baggage, they filled the remaining capacity with air-express shipments and government paperwork. One passenger toted a large electric fan in addition to his luggage allotment. The downtown traffic agent told him he couldn't take the appliance, but facing Chungking's notoriously stifling summers, he refused to abandon it. Aboard the airplane, he settled the treasured artifact on his lap. Exhausted, Bond was struggling to summon the bile to order him to jettison it when Chuck Sharp bounded into the airplane. As he hurried toward the cockpit, sight of the fan stopped him short. Sharp plucked the unauthorized appliance from the official's lap, spun on his heels, marched to the door, punched it open, and heaved the fan into the darkness. The man tried to fight past to recover it, and Sharp motioned to throw him out, too—a fate the bureaucrat wasn't prepared to meet. He scurried back to his seat. Sharp stalked up the aisle behind him, still having not said a word, yanked open the cockpit door, and glared up and down the cabin. The passengers sat in frozen silence. Sharp turned to the cockpit, winked at Bond, and ducked inside.

Sharp got the plane airborne a few minutes later, at 4:45 A.M., just as it started to rain. Temperatures had dropped overnight, and the airplane picked up a thin layer of ice. Sharp reached the gorges with the daylight and stayed beneath the cloud deck, flying "contact," as he'd done the previous evening. He landed in Chungking at 8:30 A.M. and went to bed. Bond checked in with the operations personnel on duty at the Pink House, had breakfast, and went to the company office to inspect arrangements for gasoline, oil, instrumentation, radios, and lighting needed to operate from the Ichang airfield through the coming night. Satisfied, he whittled away at paperwork piled on his desk.

At noon, intermittent rain was falling from a low, cold ceiling, and Moon Chin left Chungking in the other Commodore. Bond expected him to make two more trips ex-Hankow, the same as Hugh Chen. The Virginian descended to the sandbar airstrip at 2:30 P.M. Sharp and Leonard left an hour and a quarter later, about the time Moon Chin landed at Ichang, where Hugh Chen was still waiting with the other Commodore. Moon Chin took off again as soon as he'd refueled, without fuss, which proved more than Hugh Chen could stand. He followed Moon Chin to Hankow.

Bond had trouble concentrating as he tried to follow the reports. He hadn't slept the previous night; he'd only catnapped the night before that. At 5:00 P.M., he left assistant operations manager K. I. Nieh in charge and staggered off to the Rappes' Methodist compound, intending to sleep for a few hours and clear his head in preparation for any midnight decision-making the evacuation might require.

Chaos crept into Hankow that afternoon, Monday, October 24, 1938. Hundreds of corpses adrift from the bombing of a refugee-jammed steamship bobbed and eddied in the Yangtze's umber current. Several bumped gently against the CNAC pontoon, every bland thud underscoring the consequences of occupation. Japanese planes passed overhead all day, bombing and strafing west of the city, but the last of them had disappeared by the time Moon Chin and Hugh Chen droned in from the west and landed their flying boats in the final light of evening. Chen announced that he wouldn't be making another flight, but Moon Chin said he'd return the following evening, as per Bond's scheme, conflicting stories that gave the downtown staff a lot to ponder as they worked through the night of October 24–25, jolted by the crumps and booms of approaching artillery.

The first round of night flights went well from the landplane airfield west of the city. Sharp and Leonard arrived just after dark and left for Ichang with full loads. The Generalissimo, Madame Chiang, and the core of their entourage were still in Hankow, but they judged that night their last clear chance to escape, and they reached the airfield about 9 P.M. Former CNAC pilot Eric Just was piloting the Generalissimo's plane. Chiang wanted to go to Hengyang, south of the tri-cities, but Just didn't have much night-flying experience, he wasn't familiar with the Hengyang airfield, and he was reluctant to make his first trip there in the dark with such important passengers. Instead, the Chiangs and their inner circle climbed aboard Ernie Allison's Ministry of Communications' DC-2. Half an hour out of Hankow, Allison's electric system failed, rendering useless his airplane's cockpit lights, instruments, radios, and direction-finding equipment, and forcing him to return to the flaming city. The Chiangs' advisor W. H. Donald came forward after landing. "What next?"

"CNAC's got two planes going tonight. We'll get whichever one comes in first," Allison replied.

Predictably, Chuck Sharp was piloting the first flight in. Allie had no trouble enlisting him, but Sharp wouldn't just hand over his airplane. He insisted on flying it, allowing Allison to fly copilot. Sharp's departure message to the Pink House revealed only that he was ex-Hankow bound for Hengyang. He offered no explanation, made no mention of his passengers, and didn't respond to operations' steady inquiries, knowing that Japanese intelligence monitored the airline's frequencies. Sharp and Allison spelled one another at the controls and completed the flight without drama. Madame Chiang Kai-shek thanked CNAC on behalf of herself and the Generalissimo and promised Sharp a decoration.

Sharp pshawed her gratitude. He'd have cared only if it came with a cash honorarium.* Sharp and Allison returned to Hankow. Leonard was in from Ichang, and Allison's plane had been repaired. However, conditions at the airfield had deteriorated substantially in the wake of the unmistakable collapse telegraphed by the Generalissimo's departure. Mobs clamored against the airplanes. It took threats, shoves, and constant shouting, but Sharp, Leonard, and Allison eventually separated the passengers with legitimate priority from the frenzy and climbed their DC-2s out of Hankow at around 5:30 A.M. Cannon flashes hemmed the burning city behind them.

Moon Chin and Hugh Chen had spent the night at the airline's small

---

* Madame apparently forgot her promise. Sharp never received a medal: Bond, *Wings for an Embattled China*, p. 199.

seaplane station on Sha Hu Lake, outside the walls of Wuchang. They flew over to the Yangtze pontoon at first light. The dueling information from Chin and Chen had given the remaining ground staff the jitters. According to Bond's plan, most of the downtown staff weren't due to evacuate for another twenty-four hours, but Hugh Chen told them he wasn't coming back. Moon Chin insisted he was, but with Japanese artillery plainly audible, it seemed a poor risk to chance everything on his return. The staff boarded the Commodores and left, leaving eleven mechanics and radio operators working at the airfield west of the city. Moon Chin promised he'd return for them.

By eight o'clock, Bond was at the Chungking airport, bringing himself current, after sleeping twelve and a half hours straight and missing the whole night of flying. Try as he might, he couldn't comprehend why Sharp had gone from Hankow to Hengyang, 250 miles in the wrong direction, and then back to Hankow before making his sunrise evacuation flight. Neither could anyone else on the operations staff. Sharp's most recent message merely said he was coming upriver. He landed at 9:30 A.M., and a huge grin spread across Bond's face when he learned the reason. One didn't make greater face in China than by rescuing the Generalissimo. Sharp couldn't have made a better decision.

Earlier that morning, Moon Chin and Hugh Chen had landed their Commodores safely at Ichang, laden to their flying gunwales with evacuees. Hugh Chen sent Bond a message saying Moon Chin would handle the eleven staff members remaining in Hankow with the other Commodore, and Chen took off for Chungking without waiting for Bond's reply, eliminating the possibility that he'd be ordered to return to Hankow. While Hugh Chen droned upriver, Moon Chin waited in Ichang, killing the surplus daylight. He had his airplane fueled and his engines checked. Many times, his radio operator tried to raise the staff in Hankow, but they never replied. Best case, they'd dismantled their radio. Worst case could be a whole lot more grim. The drizzle leaking from low clouds would have grounded flights on any other day. The Generalissimo had abandoned the city eighteen hours earlier, but Moon Chin had given his word, and his boss expected him to go. At about 2:30 P.M., the twenty-four-year-old pilot-captain shrugged at his copilot, K. T. Yu, pressed the starter buttons, and headed for Hankow.

East of Ichang, Moon Chin skimmed rice paddies and fish ponds beneath the weather at the Commodore's leisurely cruising velocity, 108 miles per hour. Rain spattered the windshield. Close to the tri-cities, Moon flew over dense streams of people fleeing the Japanese. Ahead, smoke billowed into the clouds above huge conflagrations in Wuchang and Hanyang. Other fires burned in the countryside beyond the northern outskirts. Moon Chin skimmed Hanyang's rooftops and factory chimneys, cutting through scud and gushing smoke, arced over the waterfront, and descended toward the Yangtze. The river was at middle volume, the water as clear as it ever got, without the silt load of spring and summer, but flotsam jammed the middle channel—trees, railroad ties, human bodies, timbers of wrecked ships, the assorted detritus of devastation. Heading downstream, he laid the Commodore onto safe water close to the Hankow Bund, for once in history not having to worry about river traffic, because there wasn't any. Buildings afire on both sides of the river spewed smoke into the leaden sky. Moon Chin taxied downstream past the gunboats and steered the plane through a 180-degree U-turn to approach the company pontoon heading upstream, using the current to check his momentum.

The two happiest men in China stood on the end of the pontoon, waving and smiling. Otherwise, the dock was deserted. There should have been nine more. Moon Chin nosed the flying boat against the pontoon, the men caught hold, and Moon cut the engines. Artillery whumps were instantly audible, as was small-arms fire to the north and northwest. About forty-five minutes of light remained. The pair on the dock were company coolies, and Moon grilled them for information.

All eleven remaining members of the staff had waited through the day. Heavy dynamiting began around noon—retreating Chinese destroying military and industrial supplies and buildings that might aid the invaders—and the whole staff waited as the hours crept by, shaken by explosions, listening to guns draw closer, watching the tri-cities burn. Moon Chin's promise to return weighed against the drumbeat thunder of devastation, and any one of a thousand things could have thwarted his good intentions. It amounted to a lot of maybe weighed against the certainty of the approaching Japanese. Just over an hour earlier, nine mechanics, radio operators, and coolies had wedged into the airline's aging airport bus and fled. There simply wasn't any more room, and the two lowest-ranking coolies were left behind. They'd returned to the company pontoon, hoping for Moon Chin.

Westward, behind the clouds, the sun dropped below the flat Hupeh horizon. Explosions rocked the waterfront as crews in the city tripped demolition charges. Dusk gathered. Perhaps thirty minutes of gloaming remained. The airline's nearest station was at Shasi, 120 air miles to the southwest. Ichang was another 70 miles farther. Company seaplanes *never* made night landings, Moon Chin had *never* flown at night, and it would be dark in fifteen minutes. His Commodore didn't have a direction finder.

Moon Chin restarted his engines and flew over to the small facility on the shores of the lake outside the walls of Wuchang, where CNAC over-nighted its flying boats out of the Yangtze current, in case any other staff members remained there. It was deserted. He flew back to the Hankow waterfront, landed again, and taxied toward the stern of the USS *Luzon*, hoping to tie up for the night under U.S. Navy protection. An officer appeared on the *Luzon*'s taffrail, gesturing wildly. Moon didn't need to chop engines to hear the message: *No! Go away!*

He throttled back, and the current swept him away from the gunboat. He was running out of options. An immense explosion erupted in the former Japanese Concession, hurtling debris hundreds of feet into the air and shivering the Commodore. Dynamiters had blasted the posh Japanese Naval Club in the former Japanese Concession. Successive blasts wrecked the Japanese consulate and the consul's residence. Fuel and ammunition dumps exploded across the river in Wuchang, jetting fire into the twilight. Lambent flames danced on the water, and the Yangtze cut its calm arc through the pandemonium. The drizzle thickened to rain, and Moon Chin made up his mind. "We're getting out," he told his copilot.

He opened the throttles and turned downstream, the propellers whipping froth plumes into the dusk. The Commodore gathered speed and dragged itself onto "the step," a willing boat but a reluctant airplane. It reached sixty-five miles per hour, takeoff speed, but surface suction held the hull tight to the river. Moon Chin rocked the wingtips. One of the pontoons raised free, the seal broke, and the flying boat wallowed into the air in a rising turn. Moon Chin circled over the Hankow airfield and set a compass course for Shasi, subtracting a degree to ensure that he'd hit the river beneath the city, and flew into the gloom. Within minutes, the world faded into inky blackness, thick clouds above and no moon, and Moon Chin flew west-southwest at five hundred feet, his eyes flicking over the bare-bones instrumentation. More than an hour into the flight, a hint of gray ribboning through the landscape revealed the Yangtze, and the Shasi staff reported engine noise. Moon spotted a hurricane lamp burning at the end of a pontoon. He descended in a long, flat power glide, groping toward the river surface. Copilot Yu shined a flashlight out the side window and announced the distance to the river. "Forty feet! . . . Thirty feet! . . . Fifteen feet! . . . Ten feet!"

The underside kissed water, Moon chopped throttles, and the seaplane settled beautifully onto the river, a perfect landing, the first one Moon Chin had ever made at night. He'd earned his pay, all 450 Chinese dollars of it. Good pay, to be sure, but still only about a third of what his Caucasian counterparts were making, not one of whom was in the air that night.

And so it happened. Chiang Kai-shek wasn't the last person evacuated by air from China's provisional capital, as was widely assumed by the international press and was the impression-by-omission allowed by Kuomintang propagandists. That distinction went to two lowly coolies in the hierarchy of the China National Aviation Corporation who left Hankow in airborne splendor twenty hours after the Generalissimo, aboard a Consolidated Commodore piloted by a twenty-four-year-old Chinese American from an obscure south China village and the city of Baltimore.

Three Japanese destroyers and many transports anchored off the Hankow Bund shortly after sunup, ten months and fourteen days after Nanking's fall. Smoke wisped from vast swaths of wreckage on both sides of the river. Japanese warplanes circled overhead, while Imperial infantry debarked and occupied the tri-cities with the discipline befitting a civilized nation. International relief was palpable, and foreign newspaper correspondents soon felt comfortable reporting that Chinese civilians, including women, were moving freely through the streets.

Moon Chin flew upriver from Shasi while the Japanese took control. At Ichang, he filled his plane with evacuees and made the final leg of the journey to Chungking. William Bond had enjoyed another long night's sleep, and after assuring himself that Moon Chin was safely on his way into Chungking and learning that the station mechanics and radio operators who'd been at Hankow were making their way overland to Shasi, Bond had

Chinese "chow" with managing director P. Y. Wong. Hankow's loss forced
the reorganization of the airline's route structure, schedules, fuel supplies,
and finances, and after lunch the two executives discussed their options in
the company offices on the fourth floor of the Chien Yuan Bank Building.
Hugh Chen appeared, anxious to explain the choices he'd made in the preceding days, and a secretary showed him to a chair outside Bond's office. It
took all of Bond's self-control to stop himself from storming into the waiting room and chewing Chen's ass like a plug of Virginia tobacco, but he
forced himself to be rational. Hugh Chen was a valuable corporate asset
whose skills generated significant revenue. Unfortunately, Bond now knew
what else he was besides, and if he saw him he'd say it, and as a face-
conscious Chinese, Chen would never fly for him again. Bond balanced his
ire with thoughts of Moon Chin's splendid courage. As usual after weather-
ing a storm, Bond's mind turned to Kitsi. She'd be reading the newspapers.
He cabled to let her know the fact that everyone in the company was alive
and well, and that afternoon, while Hugh Chen waited outside his office
door, Bond wrote her an exquisitely detailed letter describing the events of
the preceding days. Finished, long after Hugh Chen had abandoned his
wait and left, Bond laid down his pen, exhausted, and peered out the window at Chungking's ugly rooftops feeling as if he'd been "beat all over with
a stick."

Chuck Sharp flew Bond and a full load of paying passengers to Hong
Kong on the afternoon of October 28. Bond stared out his window and
pondered the darkening continent, believing that Hankow's loss was a wa-
tershed. Many expected China to seek peace, but Bond wasn't so sure. He
thought the Generalissimo would keep fighting. Bond suspected that important voices in the government wanted to alleviate China's immediate
suffering by making peace, but continuing Chinese resistance, however
nominal, would leave Japan in an odd quandary, because Japan really had
nowhere else to go. The Japanese outclassed China in every measurable
military category, but they'd created a war they couldn't end. Chungking
was virtually unassailable, hundreds of miles farther westward and shielded
from ground assault by the thick mountainous fringe of Szechwan, and
there weren't any other important towns or geographic objectives toward
which they could work to mark decisive strategic progress. Nor was it
worth their while to scourge the Yenan base of the Chinese Communists,
Chiang Kai-shek's uneasy partners in the United Front—the Communists

would simply melt into the countryside, eschewing direct confrontation, and regroup elsewhere. Regardless, Bond expected the next sixty days to reveal the future, whatever it held, peace or ongoing war, although neither prospect offered much hope for his airline. He resigned himself to hanging on, which he felt he'd already been doing for a long, long time.

That night in Tokyo, hundreds of thousands of Japanese participated in highly choreographed victory parades. Chanting war songs, the multitudes converged on the War and Navy offices, the Yasukuni Shrine honoring Japan's war dead, and the Imperial Palace, where a lone couple appeared on a bridge over the palace moat, each holding a glowing lantern. A ripple swept the crowd as they recognized Emperor Hirohito and Empress Nagako. The murmur swelled into a deafening roar, and the august couple absorbed the jubilation for half an hour. If any of the assembled celebrants entertained hopes that Hankow's capture would bring peace, banners strung along the parade routes warned that military operations were not ended and that the future would require even greater sacrifices from the Japanese people.

15

MEETING MADAME

Kuomintang propagandists blathered on about "strategic withdrawals," Japanese "overextension," and noble Chinese resistance, but all of it was Central Government hooey designed to obfuscate the fact that, for China, the loss of Canton and Hankow culminated a year of incredible military catastrophe. The Central Army was a ghost of the force that had taken the field fourteen months before. Most of its best soldiers and junior officers had died in the Shanghai fight and the rout beyond Nanking, and the main strength of its new air force had been wrecked. The Japanese held China's resource-rich northern provinces, the bulk of its manpower and industry, and its Yangtze heartland, which had been the Kuomintang's main base of domestic support.

Forced out of Hankow, the Central Government completed the move to Chungking it had begun in early 1938, but although its wartime capital was insulated from overland attack, Szechwan Province wasn't a good place from which to fight a conventional war against a modern military power. It was entirely rural, devoid of industry—the nearest rail line was hundreds of miles away, in recently lost Hankow—and although Liu Hsiang's death allowed the Kuomintang to supplant the warlord at the top of the provincial order, it faced problems with local officials and minor militarists who resented its appointees as carpetbaggers. Kuomintang tax receipts plummeted. Chungking's best avenue of continued overland access to the Western world was through Yunnan Province, immediately south of Szechwan, but Yunnan was ruled by another powerful warlord, Long Yun, and although he paid nominal loyalty to the Central Government, as Liu Hsiang had done in Szechwan, Long Yun refused to relinquish the reins of power and successfully held the Kuomintang's internal security apparatus at bay. Mao's Communists based around Yenan in Shensi and other warlords in Kwangsi, Kwangtung, Kweichow, and Hunan further complicated domestic politics. Although all factions paid lip service to the United Front created after the Sian kidnapping and the Japanese invasion, Chiang was too weak to consolidate power, and he was plagued by the provincial divisions and ideological differences that had fractured China since the collapse of the Chin dynasty. He presided over what was, at best, a loose federation of rivals, forced to cajole, reward, and negotiate for loyalty and action.

Eurasia's prewar routes had hubbed from Hankow, and its capture wrecked the airline's route structure in the same way the loss of Shanghai had affected CNAC. A tussle for control of new routes in western China erupted between the two airlines. Managing director P. Y. Wong faced off against a fearsome bureaucratic infighter in Li Ching-Tsung, "German" Li, Eurasia's general manager. Li maintained tight contact with H. H. Kung and Minister of Communications Chang Kia-ngau, showered strategic authorities with extravagant gifts, and kept relatives of important people on his payroll—all things the China National Aviation Corporation refused to do. As testament to his potency, Li had held his post for seven years, during which time CNAC had churned through five managing directors, and his vicious cunning entirely overmatched P. Y. Wong. Eurasia captured 40 percent of the routes CNAC had developed in west China. Bond stalked to the Ministry of Communications and counterattacked. If the route reshuffle went through, he threatened, Pan Am would withdraw. The minister backpedaled and halved the damage, which helped, but Bond felt the real problem was P. Y. Wong's lack of political standing. Wong hadn't campaigned for his job. He had no feeling for the parameters of his power and consequently lacked confidence to push the airline's agenda.* Bond contented himself with the compromise, but Chinese business practices were so convoluted that he couldn't air his grievances at company board meetings: Mr. Molin Ho, director of the Bureau of Navigation, the branch of the Ministry of Communications under which the commercial airlines were organized, had a seat on CNAC's board, and he was also *chairman* of the Eurasia board of directors. Ho drew paychecks from both companies. Wearing his Bureau of Navigation hat, he'd been the primary arbiter between the two airlines, and Bond thought he made decisions solely in the interest of keeping them both alive.

In early December, Bond received a cable from Harold Bixby curtly demanding his return to New York. Bond recognized it for what it was, a typical Bixby consideration "ordering" him home for Christmas, and he flew to Chungking to clear departure with P. Y. Wong and board chairman Peng Sho-pei. As usual, he stayed in the Rappe family's missionary compound. One of the other guests was an American missionary advisor to Madame Chiang Kai-shek, to whom Bond mentioned his desire to make Madame's acquaintance. The man pulled a string and got Bond placed on her schedule.

Bond was readying for the interview when W. H. Donald burst into his office. "What's your problem?" the gruff Australian demanded. "M'issimo and G'issimo are giving a dinner tonight. She's tired. She sent me over instead. I hear you're disappointed with the support you're getting."

"My goodness, no! I'm not disappointed. Quite the contrary. I only wanted to meet Madame and tell her she can depend on Pan Am to do all it can to help China, no matter how long it lasts."

Donald slumped with relief. "Well, Bond, I'm delighted. I told Madame there must've been a misunderstanding. I'll get you rescheduled."

The big Australian barged into Bond's office the following day. "She wants to see you. Now."

---

* Bond couldn't make known how hard or through what channels he'd worked to secure Wong's installment: Knowledge that Wong had been elevated through American efforts would undermine his legitimacy in Chinese circles.

Bond rushed around gathering his briefcase and coat.

"That man you recommended for MD? How's he doing?" Donald asked.

Very well, Bond replied, asking his secretary to fetch P. Y. Wong. When he appeared, Donald presented a thick antipodean paw. "So, Bond, this is the man you recommended so highly. I'm glad he's doing well."

P. Y. Wong clutched the Australian's hand with a look of absolute confusion, until the astonishing reality dawned and he realized that his appointment to the managing directorship had come from the absolute apogee of the Kuomintang government—and that Bond had engineered it. The Generalissimo and Madame Chiang had all-important face invested in his success. He gawked at Bond with awe. He had *much* more political strength than he'd imagined.

"Come on, Don," Bond said, grinning. "We mustn't keep Madame waiting."

After seven years in China, Bond had heard a thousand stories. Led by the publishing empire of Henry Luce, owner of *Time, Fortune,* and *Life* magazines, the American press fawned over Madame Chiang Kai-shek, lauding her as queen empress of China, who, with her austere, disciplined, Methodist husband, would lead the Middle Kingdom into a gilded age. Bond's personal picture was less shiny; he'd had too much day-to-day contact with Kuomintang officialdom. Like the majority of Americans working in China in 1938, however, he still believed the Chiangs and the Nationalists presented the best hope of unifying China and leading her to modernity.

Bond was nervous as he waited to be announced. At last, Donald ushered him in, and Madame stood from her writing desk. The photos didn't do her justice. He wasn't braced for such beauty. Her hair shone like polished obsidian; her eyes sparkled with genial intelligence. She was exquisite in every detail. And then she spoke, in perfectly accented American English. The effect was breathtaking. She settled Bond on a couch and sat beside him.

He apologized for any misunderstanding and repeated what he'd told Donald—that he'd merely intended to use his interview to assure her that Pan American would do its part to maintain China's air communications for the duration of the war. Bond was a realist, but also an optimist, and he told her that although China's situation was difficult, he thought that "the future will be worse for Japan than it is for China."

Pursed, her painted lips were like a flower bud. She smiled, and they blossomed into a heart. "Let me see if I can get the Generalissimo to break away for a minute. I'd like you to tell him what you just told me," she murmured.

Bond stood. Chiang Kai-shek appeared wearing an immaculate, starched uniform, a compact, lean man with a shiny bald pate. He'd shaved the back to complete the effect, and skin stretched taut over his bare skull. He gave a thin smile, showing no teeth. A dictator's mustache rode his upper lip, and his handshake was a three-second iron clasp. He nodded and responded *"Hao, hao"* to Bond's pleasantries—"Good, good," or "I see, I see."

Madame gestured Bond to a seat against the arm of the couch. The Generalissimo sat as well, canted toward Bond, hands on his knees, his spine as stiff as a musket ramrod. Madame perched between them to interpret. It was a heady experience, cloistered with two of the most celebrated personages on earth, and Bond's mannerly Virginia upbringing served him well. He reminded himself to be measured, and responsible, and not to gush, and he did what he'd been asked to do, repeating what he'd told Madame about Pan Am's commitment. "And, General," Bond finished, "during that time, Pan Am won't ask for anything for itself."

Chiang Kai-shek's gaze was cold, and it came with lingering silence. Finally, he uttered a few words, which his wife rendered into English. "He says we only get that from Americans."

The Generalissimo expressed "deep gratitude" to Pan American Airways for connecting the two countries, and for the efforts they made as the American partner in CNAC, actions he considered typical of "the feeling of friendship between China and the United States." The Generalissimo hoped ties between them would improve after the war.

"I think I should add," Bond said, "that we hope to serve you so well that when it's over, Pan Am can recover its investment and, hopefully, a reasonable profit."

"I'll see you do. If you ever have a problem you can't solve, bring it to me, directly. I'll issue instructions for you to see me with minimum delay."

"Thank you, General, I appreciate that, but I think you have enough problems without me adding to them."

"Your problems may not be so big for me."

They stood and shook hands again and the Generalissimo left.

"He meant what he said, Mr. Bond," Madame reiterated. "Just remember you must also have a reasonable solution in mind when you bring him a problem."

Bond wondered if there was anything he could do for her in the United States. She asked him to mail some personal letters, and her secretary produced pen, paper, ink, and a writing table. When she'd readied herself, Madame turned to W. H. Donald, who hadn't left the room, and asked him the date.

"December twelfth," Donald intoned.

"Oh! December twelfth," she said in a strange voice.

The two foreigners waited while Madame penned a few notes. She swept out of the room, and Donald showed Bond out. "What was that bit with the date?" Bond inquired.

"December twelfth. The Generalissimo was kidnapped two years ago today."

Leaving chief pilot Chuck Sharp in charge of day-to-day operations and Arthur Young covering his strategic business responsibilities, Bond reached Baltimore on December 22, overnight from Chicago on the Baltimore & Ohio Railroad. A "Windy City" blizzard had grounded his cross-country flight. Kitsi was on the platform, waiting, and her embrace warmed his heart on a gray, blustery day. Kitsi rushed her husband home, shocked by his haggard appearance. He'd lost more weight since she left China, and aside from the Chevy Chase Club's annual holiday ball, an event she'd attended since her college days, she kept the Christmas swivet to a level of manageable mayhem. William Bond finished the year at Hayes Manor, enjoying friends and family, the Christmas hearth, and the son he hadn't seen in sixteen months. He and his airline had had their backs to the wall that entire time. Bond had no idea what the long run held, or if his company would succeed, but he knew one thing for a God-given fact as he sat contemplating a holiday fire in the waning days of 1938—it deserved to.

16

BOMBING SEASON

Life calmed after the New Year. Kitsi's ministrations and the Hayes Manor cooking did wonders, and Bond packed weight onto his emaciated frame. He wasn't a man to sit idle, however, and his mind never really left the affairs of the China National Aviation Corporation. The contract between its Chinese and American partners was a looming question. It didn't expire until July 1940, but it had an automatic renewal clause that triggered six months hence, on July 7, 1939, and extended the contract another five years provided neither partner gave written notification of termination. Assuming the Chinese wanted to continue the arrangement, it would eliminate an element of Pan American uncertainty to extend it as soon as possible. Bond had politicked on the subject before leaving Chungking: with managing director P. Y. Wong and the board of directors; through Arthur Young to T. V. Soong; with vice minister of communications and chairman of the board Peng Sho-pei; and with Finance Minister H. H. Kung. In Washington, Bond made overtures through the Chinese Embassy. Conveniently, announcement of a $25 million U.S. credit to China (albeit for nonmilitary purposes, worth about $387 million in modern dollars) came on the heels of Bond's efforts, and P. Y. Wong appended a copy of a proposed extension to a letter he sent Bond shortly thereafter.

Bond thought he had the situation in hand, but no formal notification followed. Instead, the Chinese began pressing for an infusion of Pan Am capital. It took Bond some time to realize he'd touched a nerve in the Chinese business psyche. Contract renewal was automatic. If Pan Am wanted an early extension, there must be a *reason,* and if there were a reason, the Chinese thought they'd be foolish to allow it without finding out what the Americans would pay. Bond responded by going mum, but the chiseling left a bad taste. If one thing was 100 percent certain, considering the war in China and the state of Pan American finances, heavily burdened by debt incurred in a decade of relentless expansion, it was that Pan American wasn't going to pour more capital into China. Bond's strategic recommendations to Juan Trippe, Harold Bixby, and Stokely Morgan were simple: "Do not put up more capital. Hold on as long as we can. Hope for the best."

A glance at any situation map showed Free China holding few resources, and in the last days of 1938, one of the Kuomintang's elites, former president of the Executive Yuan Wang Ching-wei, had appeared in Hanoi, purportedly on his way to Hong Kong to discuss truce terms. On New Year's Eve, a Japanese news agency in Hong Kong issued a message from Wang to the Generalissimo that urged peace and collaboration with Japan—on Japanese terms. Chiang Kai-shek categorically rejected the overture, vowing continued resistance and decrying Wang's treason, but the defection seemed to expose major divisions inside the Nationalist government.* Subsequent news stories told of violent purges of Wang's associates from the ranks of the Kuomintang, and Japan announced that it would no longer treat with Chiang's government.

All of it seemed to make "the best" in Bond's recommendation an increasingly ephemeral hope. Nothing seemed to slow the predatory marches of the Fascist nations. In mid-February, Japan invaded Hainan Island at the mouth of the Gulf of Tonkin, undermining the security of the railroad from French Indochina into Yunnan that was one of China's few remaining

---

* A year later, on March 30, 1940, Wang Ching-wei formed a Japanese-sponsored puppet government in Nanking, branding him China's Quisling.

routes of external supply. Hitler annexed the rest of Czechoslovakia in mid-March and began haranguing against Poland. Recognizing the likelihood that they'd soon be defending their interests with armed force, Britain and France placed enormous airplane orders with American factories, and, in an indication that even the United States was rousing itself from its long slumber in "legislated neutrality," it ordered 1,500 aircraft for its own military. CNAC had a DC-3 on order at Douglas Aircraft, not due off the assembly line until July, and Wong told Bond to add another, but such small orders had plummeted in relative importance, and the airline needed planes immediately. Professionally, a largely futile quest to acquire additional aircraft consumed the rest of Bond's home stay. He was able to buy only one used DC-2.

Much refreshed, Bond flew back to China in the third week of March 1939. On his way through Hong Kong, he had another quick meeting with Madame Chiang Kai-shek, and long, detailed discussions with M. Y. Tong and W. H. Donald about strategies going forward. He reached the island airstrip below Chungking on a typically overcast April morning. Japanese air raids had done "comparatively little damage" to the city while he was away, Bond observed, but when the weather improved, he had "little doubt Chungking [was] in for some very painful experiences."

Mists and light rain wreathed the city through the rest of the month. The gloom broke in early May, and hillsides across the Yangtze from the city glimmered with the lush greens of the Szechwan spring. That afternoon, Bond intended to return to Hong Kong, but he owed Harold Bixby a letter, so in the meantime, he sat at his desk next to a window on the fourth floor of the Chuen Yien Bank Building and reflected on his first month back in China, fighting the temptation to bum a cigarette and enjoy a smoke. He'd quit at the New Year and had a one-hundred-U.S.-dollar bet running with a friend, the loser being the first man to light up in 1939. If both survived a twelvemonth, the stakes rose to $500 and the term extended to five years (wagers worth about 1,600 and 7,800 modern dollars, respectively). So far, Bond was hanging tough. He examined the operational data. On paper, the airline was doing surprisingly well, which Bond thought meant very little. The situation was "ethereal," a lucky bombing raid might wipe out half the airplanes, and the war showed no sign of end-

ing. Although Bond felt the Chinese were "going to come out of [it] in better shape than anyone expected," he was less roseate about what the
prospect of a drawn-out conflict boded for him personally. He'd already
lost nine of the seventeen pounds he'd gained in Washington, and August
would mark the completion of two years of war, so much of it crucifying
time apart from his wife and son. Kitsi had been a "good sport" thus far, but
the situation wasn't fair, and he worried about how much more she could
stand. "I hope you will not think I am getting soft," he wrote, finishing his
letter to Bixby, "but this war can easily last two more years." Bond wasn't
sure he could tolerate two more years. He signed and dated the letter and
left for the airport. It was May 3, 1939.

Chinese Air Force advisor Claire Chennault stopped him on the street
outside the Pink House, CNAC's Chungking operational headquarters.
"Bombers just left Hankow. Don't know where they're headed yet."

Bond thanked the Louisianian and examined the cerulean sky. It was
the first clear day in weeks, and Free China's wartime capital would surely
rank high on the Japanese target list. Bond pounded down the steps to river
level, across a rickety footbridge to the sandbar airport, and passed Chennault's warning in the operations shed. A passel of passengers and well-
wishing friends clustered around the passenger terminal, the usual mix of
officials and businessmen, mostly Chinese, but salted with a few European
faces. Traffic agents made out the manifests for several flights while coolies
stowed baggage and airmail. Bond took DC-2 pilot Hal Sweet aside and
quietly told him about the Japanese bombing raid aloft. Inconspicuously,
Sweet sauntered to the plane and set about readying for takeoff while Bond
casually ordered his other pilots to take the same steps.

At 12:55 P.M., the telephone in the passenger terminal rang. The clerk
who took the call shot up from his desk and shouted, in Chinese, "The Japanese are coming!" just as air-raid sirens keened in the city. Pandemonium
erupted. A woman screamed, and for an awful second Bond thought the
raid was right on top of them. He roared for order, stunning the passengers
and his traffic agents into a tenuous calm. Things happened briskly from
that point. Agents shooed those not traveling up the steps to the shelter cave
in the cliffside seventy-five feet below the Pink House and hustled passengers aboard the waiting airplanes. Engines rumbled to life. In the DC-2,
Bond took his usual seat in the first row to the left of the cockpit door. The
moment ground crews yanked chock blocks from the plane's wheels, Sweet

bounced toward the end of the runway, stomped a rudder pedal to swing the plane into line, rammed the throttles forward, and began his takeoff roll.

Sweet had the DC-2 in the air less than a minute later, curling away from the airport, following a river bend and gaining altitude. Bond leaned into his window and looked back. Chungking looked like an overturned anthill, with civilians swarming down the hillsides toward the ferries that would shuttle them to imagined safety on the South Bank. In a second DC-2, Joy Thom, one of the airline's three original Chinese American pilots,* was just lifting off the runway. Moon Chin, another of the trio, was halfway down the strip behind him, gathering speed in an eight-passenger de Havilland Dragon Rapide biplane on loan from Madame Chiang Kai-shek. A Stinson swerved into position behind Chin. A Loening was on the step in the river, tossing froth at takeoff speed. The Commodore cast off from its buoy, both engines churning. It was an awesome sight. Bond sat back, proud of his men. He checked his watch. The entire scramble had taken six minutes. He doubted any air force in the world could duplicate the feat.

Ten minutes after takeoff, forty-five Japanese bombers came over Chung-king with the "buzzing of a million bees," wingtip to wingtip in a line spanning the horizons. The first bombs landed in the river, thundering up waterspouts, before the explosive strings climbed the hill into the city. More than fifty hit downtown Chungking, destroying dozens of bricolage constructions and burying scores of inhabitants. Fires took hold in the devastation. At least thirteen major conflagrations burned an hour later, shooting flames far above the rooftops. Black smoke palls merged above the city, clouding the otherwise bright day. Not until nightfall were fire-fighters able to douse the worst blazes. Three to five hundred Chinese civilians died in the attack, slaughtered without discrimination. Everybody on the company payroll survived unscathed, but their families weren't so fortunate. Mrs. Wei, wife of a company welder, fled the city with their three small children on a grossly overloaded river ferry, which capsized when a bomb exploded alongside. Only one of the Wei children survived. Mr. Wei's wife, two of his children, and most of the other passengers drowned. That wasn't all. The terrors of the raid caused the pregnant wife of one of

---

* Joy Thom, Moon Chin, and Donald Wong (who'd resigned in the autumn of 1937).

the radio operators to miscarry. She never stopped bleeding and died a week later.

The raids were over by the time Sweet landed at Kweilin in the mid-afternoon, 381 miles south of the wartime capital. He waited out the daylight and passed north of Canton well after dark. With his head under the Telefunken headphones and lighted by a full moon, Hal Sweet greased the Douglas onto the Kai Tak runway at 8:40 P.M. Forty-seven minutes later, the earth's shadow sliced into the beautiful orb, and it swallowed the moon's last bright sliver at 10:39 P.M., a total lunar eclipse. The moon's lightless disk hung in the sky like a dark penny, an orb of negative space. It seemed the worst possible omen.

Twenty-seven Japanese bombers attacked Chungking again at dusk the next day, sweeping in from the north and surprising thousands in the open. The first demolition bombs and incendiaries hit buildings on the Kialing River waterfront, then pounded all the way across the spine of the city to the banks of the Yangtze. Fires overwhelmed the emergency crews. By midnight, flames engulfed an eighth of the city, incinerating hundreds. Visible from the German Embassy, more than eighty women, children, and elder citizens burned to death against the base of the city's thirty-foot walls. Estimates hovered at about five thousand killed, the most devastating raid on any Chinese city since the beginning of the war, trumping Guernica as history's bloodiest aerial terror attack to that date. The Generalissimo and Madame Chiang Kai-shek stayed in the Chungking vicinity through the raids, sitting them out in underground bomb shelters and touring and speaking from among the wreckage in their aftermath.

The Japanese gave Chungking an eight-day reprieve, then bombed it again on May 12, killing another two or three hundred civilians. Afterward, Bond returned to the city, where everyone regaled him with stories of the raids, some lucky, some tragic, others comic, all shot through with outrage that the Japanese would inflict such agony on a civilian population. One of the most gut-wrenching tales concerned a six-year-old boy who'd been carried to the Methodist Hospital with a femur broken by the bomb that had killed his parents in the May 3 raid. A harried, blood-soaked surgeon working triage through the carnage set the bone, sank a pin through the child's heel, and used it to anchor the leg to a medieval traction device of ropes and pulleys on the third-floor children's ward.

For much of the next fortnight, muggy clouds shrouded the wartime capital in safety, but on May 25, Chennault's air-warning service announced a bombing squadron heading westward from Hankow. Bond joined his staff in the cave below the Pink House. Minutes clicked past. At 6:30 P.M., Bond left, thinking the raid had gone elsewhere.

Urgent alarms started wailing when Bond and his chauffeur were a quarter mile short of the Methodist compound. People flooded the streets, in flat sprints for shelter caves. There wasn't enough underground space for the entire population, and it was first come, first served, the devil take the hindmost. Other residents raced for the city gates, fighting for safety outside the walls. The gates of the Methodist compound were locked, the gateman long gone. The only feasible route over the wall was via the gate itself, a twenty-five-foot-tall iron grillwork affair. Bond climbed it, in suit, tie, shoes, cuff links. His chauffeur left the car under a tree and followed him over.

Inside, the two hustled through the deserted school campus toward the large cave near the main house, where Bond could see white-uniformed nurses crowded around the shelter entrance. Beside him, movement in the school's doorway caught his eye. A Chinese boy crab-crawled through the front door, pushing a splinted leg in front of him, dragging a traction harness behind that had fouled the doorway. Bond stopped short, realizing it was the six-year-old whose story he'd heard. The boy's tear-streaked face was a knot of pain, and he was trembling with terror, but he wasn't making a sound. Bond soothed the boy and scooped him into his arms, his chauffeur gathered the traction harness, and the two men carried the emaciated lad to the big shelter and laid him on a wooden board. Arthur Young was staying in the Methodist compound as well, and he led in a Chinese man whose arm had been blown off at the shoulder in the May 12 raid. Once they'd situated the wounded, Bond went topside to await developments.

On the surface, Bond met two journalists, F. Tillman Durdin, Chungking correspondent for *The New York Times*, whom he knew well, and a younger man with whom he wasn't acquainted. Durdin introduced Teddy White, a self-assured Harvard graduate recently arrived in Chungking to write propaganda for the government-sponsored "China Information Committee." Evening deepened, and the three men watched sunlight flashing from the wings of six Chinese pursuits turning circles high over the city, then heard the "unmistakable heavy drone" of twin-engine bombers. Bond spotted them almost immediately, twenty-seven bombers coming on in two lines abreast at about ten thousand feet. Tracers carved across the sky from the Chinese pursuits as they made frontal attacks. Bright streaks spouted back from the bombers' defensive guns. Shells arced upward from ground batteries and flashed against the quarter moon gliding the purpling sky. It was a spectacular display, almost beautiful, and the bombers didn't seem to threaten the Methodist compound, so Bond and the newsmen remained aboveground. As always during air raids, it was a comfort to be among friends. Suddenly, Bond heard a whispering swish. He whirled, spread his arms, and charged, clotheslining Durdin and White into the dugout. All three tumbled down the stairs as a bomb detonated nearby. Dozens of others exploded in the nearby district. The three Americans untangled at the bottom of the steps.

Bond apologized, "No time to talk."

"How did you know it was coming?" White asked.

"I heard it."

White brushed himself off. "I must learn to distinguish the sound."

The raiders bore off into darkness. Bond, Durdin, and White returned to the surface, joined by Mr. Rappe. Acrid smoke spread from fires burning downtown. Notwithstanding their missionary companion, Bond whispered the mantra he'd recited on the deck of the steamer *Wuseh* off Woosung eighteen months before, leaving Shanghai on Armistice Day, 1937. "God damn the Japanese, God damn the Japanese."

"Amen," Mr. Rappe answered, sotto voce, "Amen."

The cave was safe, but it wasn't comfortable; it was damp and claustrophobic and rank with the smell of cigarettes, the waft of dense-packed, unwashed bodies, and fear's sour odor. The Americans moved the boy with the broken leg and the other children back to their beds in the third-floor children's ward of the former school building. Night had fallen by the time they finished, and the men chatted outside the dugout, awaiting the release siren. A few rifles cracked in the city—police summarily executing looters. Simultaneously, the men heard a new engine drone, the unmistakable harbinger of another attack wave. Bond directed people back toward the shelter cave. He was about to go down himself when he remembered the boy and the other children, spun on his heels, and sprinted toward the children's ward, 150 yards away, his chauffeur and Teddy White trailing him. Bond bounded up the stairs two and three at a time and burst into the ward, stumbling over confused, frightened youngsters. The nurses had fled. Sure enough, Bond's little boy had again clambered out of bed and was scooting toward the stairwell, trailing his harness. There wasn't time to get the children to a cave, but the building was sturdy. Staying in it seemed best. The men restored order and herded the children to their beds. Bond and Teddy White scooped up the broken-legged boy, laid him in his bed, and sat at its foot as the engines droned closer. The bombs hit a military airfield near the city; the release finally sounded at around nine o'clock. Before he left the hospital, Bond issued the returning nurses explicit instructions on expected air-raid comportment, then ate dinner and went to bed. As for the little boy with the broken leg, William Bond never did learn his name.

After sunrise, Bond toured company installations. First, the airport and the Pink House; both were undamaged. Next the booking office: It had taken a direct hit and was a smoldering shell. Happily, it had been evacuated at the first alarm. Last, Bond went to Shensi Street and the head office in the Chuen Yien Bank Building. The bank had taken a direct hit on its roof, but it hadn't collapsed. Ten other bombs had landed within two hundred feet. Bond's office was a shambles, desk overturned, chairs flung around the room. Papers fluttered among wood splinters; glass shards crunched underfoot. Bond picked his way to the window. Greasy smoke wisped from gutted ruins. Cleanup crews worked amid street debris, loading bodies; Bond had the office coolies move his desk to the center of his office so it wouldn't get wet in a rain, and set about reorganizing his files.

A few days later, Bond collected a check from the friend with whom he'd made the no-smoking bet—he'd been done in by the anxious hours in the underground dugouts, waiting for the bombs to fall. Bond still hadn't cracked, but he soon would.

It was hard to imagine a more uncomfortable climate than the boiler-room heat and humidity of Chungking's summer. Most nights, Bond had his cot and mosquito netting carried onto the Methodist compound's lawn in the hope of catching a tiny breeze. He was outside on the night of July 6–7, trying to sleep beneath a glowering bombers' moon, bright silver and just past full. Chungking's air-raid sirens screamed a few minutes before midnight. Bond spent three hours in a shelter while enemy bombers pounded the city, not regaining his cot until 3:15 A.M. He'd hardly shut his eyes when Joy Thom shook him awake. "Mr. Bond, Mr. Bond, please wake up."

"What is it?" Bond grumbled. It was 4:45 A.M. He'd been asleep for only ninety minutes.

"I hate to bother you, Mr. Bond, so sorry, but Joe Shen got hit pretty bad."

Bond sat up and shook his brain clear. Shen was another one of his pilots. "You're not bothering me. What happened?"

Joy Thom explained that he and Shen and some of the other Chinese and Chinese American pilots had taken to passing the air raids in one of the fourth-floor interior hallways of the eight-story Chuen Yien Bank Building, which had acquired a reputation for being sturdy since surviving the direct hit on May 25. During the just-completed raid, a fluke bomb had exploded against the steel frame of a building under construction directly opposite the CNAC office, blasting a metal sliver through a glassless window, a room, and an open door into the hallway, where it tore into the small of Joe Shen's back. The uninjured pilots stuffed a washroom towel into the wound to stanch the gushing blood, propped Shen in an office armchair, and carried him to a coarse, underequipped, hard-pressed city hospital. "He's still alive," Joy Thom concluded, "but the doctor won't do anything, says it's hopeless."

Bond had already dressed. "Take me to him."

Due to his seat on the board of an organization responsible for distributing American aid to Chungking charities, Bond was all too familiar with the deplorable state of the city's hospitals. The best was a Canadian infirmary on a hilltop a mile or two beyond the South Bank of the river, which had Dr. Allen, an excellent surgeon who usually came to Chungking to do trauma work after air raids, but Dr. Allen wasn't in his usual aid station. Bond and Thom continued to the city hospital. Joe Shen was conscious and in extreme pain, but his doctor lamented that there wasn't anything he could do, and he didn't think Shen would survive the trip to the Canadian hospital, where Bond proposed to take him.

"How do you know that?" Bond demanded. "He was hurt two hours ago. He's alive now."

"I'm giving you my considered opinion, and I'm sure he suffered a great deal getting here."

Bond didn't have any doubt about that. Nor did he doubt that Joe Shen would suffer a great deal more getting across the river, but what was an hour or two of agony against a chance for life? It would have been easy to agree with the doctor and do nothing, but Bond knew what he'd want his people to do for him if he were on the litter.

First, they had to find Dr. Allen and secure his help. Bond and Thom crossed the Yangtze in a hired sampan and raced uphill to Allen's hospital, where they learned the doctor had just gone to bed after treating casualties all night. Bond woke him. Groggily, Dr. Allen said that rather than having him travel back to the city to treat Shen, it'd be better to bring Shen to the south side, where he had an X-ray machine and a sterile operating room.

Bond and Thom ran to the riverside anchorage of the USS *Tutuila* (*PR-4*), the American gunboat in Chungking to serve the U.S. Embassy, and secured the loan of a sturdy metal basket stretcher and *Tutu*'s motor launch. A sailor steered them to the stairs beneath the Pink House. Bond and Thom puffed up all 350 stairs with the litter, rousted the driver of the company passenger bus, and drove to Joe Shen's side. By the time they arrived, it was after 8 A.M., six hours since Shen's wounding, but he was still alive, and still conscious, although gray with pain and blood loss. The doctor didn't think he would last much longer. Bond thanked him for his concern and helped ease Joe onto the Navy stretcher. Thom, Bond, and four hired coolies stood in the back of the bus and held the stretcher aloft to smooth the ride, then manhandled it down the stairs and into the Navy launch, crossed the river, and hired another coolie gang on the South Bank. Joe squeezed his eyes shut and endured the hellish journey without a sound. They reached the Canadian hospital at ten minutes to ten.

Shen opened his eyes as Bond bent over his stretcher. They were watery and unfocused. "Thank you, Mr. Bond," he whispered. "I'm so sorry . . . to cause . . . so much . . . trouble."

That a man in such soul-grinding agony would, before anything else, be *courteous* brought tears to Bond's eyes. That was pure Chinese courage. It made them great.

Dr. Allen's explorations in Shen's blood-saturated abdominal cavity revealed a ruptured right kidney. The metal splinter had torn through it and lodged in Shen's liver, but Allen couldn't get an X-ray picture clear enough to guide its extraction. Fortunately, Shen's intestines weren't damaged, and neither were any other organs. Shen and Thom had the same blood type, so Dr. Allen had Thom give Shen a blood transfusion and pronounced that Shen had a good chance if the wound didn't become infected.

Some hours passed before Bond realized it was July 7, 1939, the magic day—it had arrived without notice from the Chinese government. The contract between Pan Am and the Ministry of Communications had automatically been extended, committing Pan Am to China for another five years.

By the summer of 1939, it was clear to the most important American in China, Ambassador Nelson T. Johnson, that Bond's exertions reflected great credit on the United States, and Johnson raved about Bond's qualities in a letter to Stokely Morgan, Pan Am's vice president for the Orient. The letter went from Morgan to Harold Bixby, who sent copies to Kitsi and Bond's mother, another to Juan Trippe, and one to Bond in China, quipping that "most letters of this type are deferred for delivery with the flowers." Still, he worried about Bond's deteriorating health, a concern heightened by three other letters from mutual friends lamenting Bond's poor condition, all of which reinforced Bixby's desire to get the hard-toiling Virginian home.

Bond wanted out, too, but in a larger sense. The airline was functioning well and making steady progress, and he wanted to use the contract extension as a landmark accomplishment that would allow him to bow out of China and turn his responsibilities over to a younger man. He wasn't comfortable making the request—it smacked of quitting—and he'd waited "until all things important to Pan Am's interest had been made as secure as possible." He pinned his hopes on Chuck Sharp, who was on stateside leave. "I think he can handle the job," he wrote.

Bixby and Morgan didn't agree. As a top-shelf pilot, Chuck Sharp could handle the operational aspects of the position, but the duties of Pan American's "number one" in China were much more than flight management—their most crucial aspects were political, and required a sophisticated, mannerly, mature judgment that Chuck Sharp just didn't have.

Unfortunately for William Bond and his family, nobody in the System could replace him. The Joe Shen story was a microcosm of why. Tragically rare was the foreigner who was willing to make such exertions to save a Chinese life. "What you did for [Joe Shen] shows why the Chinese . . . are so loyal to you," Bixby explained. "Such considerations will not soon be forgot." Bond's connections were impossible to replicate in a country where long-term relationships were the rollers that moved the entire society. Bond had been correct in the summer of 1937—his place was in China. Two years later, it was a fate he couldn't escape.

The Japanese attacked Chungking on the night of August 1. After a few hours in a shelter cave, Bond went to bed just past midnight feeling perfectly well. He awoke weak and light-headed. He held himself together long enough to manage an operational emergency at the Pink House, then doubled over and vomited. Two minutes later, he lost control of his bowels. Violent eruptions from both ends of the gastrointestinal system were a prime symptom of cholera, a disease that had scourged unsanitary Chungking since the bombings began. Bond had himself carried to the hospital that had treated Joe Shen. The ailment didn't prove to be cholera, but five days later he was still bedridden, without concrete knowledge of what had afflicted him. Once he was ambulatory, Bond did what he always did—he went back to work.

Dawn broke bright and sunny in Szechwan Province on the morning of August 19, 1939. As the morning sky paled to a hazy blue, the air-warning net reported Japanese bombers heading for Chungking. Sanhupa Airport, on the sandbar below Chungking, was submerged beneath the Yangtze's summer flood, so two of the airline's DC-2s were on the military airfield west of town, where Methodist mission leader Mr. Rappe was on hand to see a friend off. The Chengtu flight took off with its full load of passengers. Hugh Woods was to take the other DC-2 to Hong Kong that evening, but it was far too early in the day to depart. He had to scramble west until the raid passed, and he asked Mr. Rappe if he'd like to join him for a scenic tour around Mount Emei, one of China's four sacred mountains. It was a life goal of many Chinese Buddhists to watch the sun rise and set from the Golden Summit Temple perched on the mountaintop. Rappe and his wife had spent two months in a resort at its base when they'd first come to China in 1909, and he was thrilled by the opportunity to see it for the first time in thirty years.

Ninety-five minutes into the flight, they passed Kiating, a small provincial city. Woody orbited the summit of Mount Emei shortly thereafter, gawking at the elaborate temple perched atop gray cliffs soaring from the dark, conifer-covered slopes of the lower mountain. Westward, sunlight gleamed from the snows and glaciers of the twenty-three-thousand-foot Minya Konka massif. Mr. Rappe enjoyed himself thoroughly—until he happened to look in the direction of Kiating and saw smoke clouds towering above it. The enemy was bombing the city.

Woody took one glance and dived just as a Japanese pursuit escorting the raiding bombers spotted the Douglas. Woody plunged to minimum altitude and skimmed the bungalows of the foreign colony at the base of the mountain, racing south. Six Christian missionaries summering at the resort watched the airliner roar past, its propellers practically churning the rice paddies as Woody wove through the valley bottom ahead of a lead-spitting Japanese plane trying to close within killing distance. Woody's plane probably would have gotten the worst of it if the cat-and-mouse game had gone on much longer, but his pursuer was a long way from its Hankow base, and dwindling fuel supply forced it to break off.

Woods flew south across the Yangtze and put some distance between himself and the river, which any Japanese returning from farther westward would be using to aid homeward navigation. He stayed low and wove among the hills south of the river until he felt safe, then turned west toward the military airfield at Suifu, cautiously relieved until his copilot spotted twelve or fifteen planes at altitude above them, flying east, exactly like a homeward-bound bomber formation. Woody slammed over the wheel and raced south again. The formation above broke apart, and half the planes continued east. The others dropped toward the DC-2, holding every advantage. Among so many mountains, Woody couldn't see anywhere to execute a forced landing. Mr. Rappe's prayers were answered when the group proved to be part of a Chinese training flight, and Woods touched down at Suifu unholed and unharmed. The release sounded after thirty minutes, and he soon had the missionary safely back in Chungking. Mr. Rappe went straight home, so wrung out he couldn't sleep that night. Woody loaded passengers and made the nocturnal run to Hong Kong. Aloft in the darkness, droning through the night skies of China, he decided he'd had enough. He was earning superb money, but the close shave hammered home the obvious—getting killed in a war that wasn't your own wasn't worth *any* sum. He found Bond and resigned the next day.

Bond valued loyalty above almost all other qualities, and Hugh Woods had been flying for him faithfully since 1933. Woods was a good man for whom Bond felt great personal and professional affection, and considering his own uneasy commitment, Bond couldn't fault Woody's desire to get out. Bond promised to do what he could to place him elsewhere in the Pan Am system, and Woods was soon in Miami training to fly four-engine flying boats.

Twelve days after Woody tendered his resignation, on September 1, 1939, German forces crashed into Poland, and Britain and France declared war. For Europe, "peace in our time" had lasted a few days longer than eleven months.

Claiming that Pan Am needed Bond for direct consultations, Harold Bixby asked managing director P. Y. Wong to send Bond to New York. Cleared by the airline's board of directors, Bond flew across the Pacific with all the stress he'd bottled in China.

17

VENTRICULAR TACHYCARDIA

It was a fine morning in the second half of September 1939. The Dunlop family nurse was tending young Langhorne, and after coffee and a Hayes Manor breakfast William Bond followed his wife upstairs to their bedroom. Suddenly, his world wobbled. He barely managed to get a foot on the upstairs landing. "Kitsi," he gasped, "something's wrong with my heart."

Kitsi turned. "You're all white!"

Bond collapsed into bed, panting, his heart racing like an ungoverned engine. He couldn't catch his breath, and tears streamed down his cheeks.

When the doctor Kitsi summoned arrived, he found Bond's heart fluttering like a bird's, more than two hundred nearly powerless beats per minute, and Bond was still assailed by a powerful urge to cry, itself confusing and frightening, because crying was something the sharp-elbowed Virginian just didn't do.

Bond's heart had lost its normal rhythm, its chambers firing out of sync at a wildly accelerated pace, circulating only a small volume of blood. The doctor diagnosed ventricular tachycardia, a serious heart condition with the potential to degenerate into ventricular fibrillation, the disorganized quivering that presaged sudden cardiac death. Not enough oxygen was reaching Bond's brain, which untethered his emotional control. Prolonged periods of strain and nervous tension were thought to contribute to the onset of the condition. Kitsi nodded in vigorous agreement.

The doctor jabbed Bond with morphine. His heart rate relaxed with the drug, then lurched forward and accelerated before it re-calmed, a pattern that repeated itself through the remaining daylight. The episode took ten full hours to play out. The freedom to breathe easily, without fear, came as a tremendous relief, but it left Bond feeling like a puddle of spent candle wax. The doctor prescribed absolute rest. Bond wasn't allowed to talk— a particular agony for such a garrulous man—or listen, not even to the radio, and Kitsi enforced the dictates with grim satisfaction, allowing no appeal.

Seven days passed before Bond felt well enough to totter downstairs clutching the banister and a supporting arm. Drenched in clammy sweat, he slumped onto a sitting room sofa. He hadn't spent an October in the United States since 1930, and he'd been looking forward to the World Series radio broadcasts, but his doctor forbade him to listen, fearing the excitement the baseball would generate. Bond considered listening to the games surreptitiously, but he lacked the energy to combat Kitsi's religious adherence to the doctor's edicts and contented himself with newspaper reports, just as he'd done in China. Playing without "the Iron Horse," Lou Gehrig, for the first time in sixteen seasons, the New York Yankees of Red Ruffing, Monte Pearson, Charlie Keller, and twenty-four-year-old Joe DiMaggio swept a quartet of games from the Cincinnati Reds to capture their fourth consecutive championship.

Bond made progress every day and was soon worrying about how things were going in China under Chuck Sharp's operational management. Despite the confidence in Sharp's abilities he himself had professed, by the end of the month he was agitating with his wife, doctor, and Harold Bixby for permission to return. Pan Am wanted him to work, but it wasn't in the corporate interest to push him unto death—his relationships in China were irreplaceable. Bixby allowed him to return only after he promised to submit to a strict medical regime dictated by his cardiologist requiring him to "take it easy" and spend three or four months of every year relaxing at home in Washington.

Bond reached China before Christmas. His Chinese personnel assiduously avoided speaking to him, their grim faces presaging something terrible. Those with whom he interacted briefly smiled, nodded, welcomed him back to China, and bustled off. He finally discovered the cause: Joe Shen had died, and nobody wanted to break the bad news.

Five months had passed since Shen had been hit by the bomb shard, and he'd recovered nicely. His doctors expected him to live a normal, productive life, even with the shrapnel embedded in his liver. He just couldn't fly. The metal chunk had to come out if Shen ever wanted to do that again, and the surgery to extract it was extremely risky. However, flying for CNAC was one of the best jobs in the Middle Kingdom. Apart from the glamour, the pay was excellent, even though Chinese pilots continued to earn only a third of their Caucasian counterparts. Flying, Joe Shen provided opportunities for his entire clan that vanished when he was grounded. Besides, he loved it. In December, Joe Shen decided he'd found a British surgeon in Hong Kong who was good enough to do the job. The doctor teased the sliver out of Shen's liver, but the act of removing it split a major artery, and Joe Shen bled to death on the operating table.

The loss cast a pall over the Christmas season. Bond couldn't forget Shen's stoic courage, and he stuck with him, even in death. At the next board of directors meeting, Bond and P. Y. Wong made certain the company considered him killed in the line of duty and granted a generous death benefit to his family.

Apart from that tragedy, things were running smoothly. The stalwart Woody was gone, but Chuck Sharp was doing a fine job orchestrating flight operations in the absence of his best friend, and nobody was more pleased than William Bond, who gratefully relinquished the burden of day-to-day operational management and made Sharp's position permanent. Company mechanics had finally completed repairs to plane number 32, the *Kweilin*, the DC-2 in which Woody had been shot down, more than a year after it had been hoisted off the bottom of the river near Macau.* Reconstructed and reconditioned, the plane was quietly rechristened *Chungking* and given a new number, 39, without the public fanfare that might dissuade supersti-

---

* There had been huge problems getting U.S. dollars to pay for the necessary spare parts. Strangely, Dr. H. H. Kung and the Ministry of Finance were extraordinarily slow releasing U.S. dollars for spare parts, even though they were reasonably prompt releasing foreign exchange for the airline's other routine purposes. On several occasions planes sat idle for want of spares that had already reached the Orient but were being held by the Hong Kong shipping agent pending payment.

tious Chinese from flying in an airplane in which fifteen people died. The airline had begun scheduled flights from Chungking to Rangoon, Burma, but by far the most exciting event that occurred on Sharp's watch involved an entirely new piece of equipment, one the airline had never used before— the Douglas DC-3. Long delayed, CNAC's first DC-3 had finally arrived, in pieces, aboard a rare ship sailing from the West Coast that didn't touch Japan. (Moral issues notwithstanding, the United States was still doing brisk business with Japan in 1939.) Douglas engineers had stretched the DC-2 fuselage, added wingspan and wing area, increased the size of the tail, mounted more powerful engines, and in the process created a new airplane. The DC-3 was larger, faster, more powerful, carried more pay- load, and had a longer range than its predecessor. Remarkably, it was even easier to fly. The DC-3's elongated and widened passenger cabin carried twenty-one people in comfort, and the additional capacity bumped reve- nue 50 percent with little additional cost. It was the first airplane in history that could profitably carry passengers without the de facto subsidies of government airmail contracts. Assembled, the airline's first DC-3, number 41, the *Chiating,* entered service on November 17, 1939.* Chuck Sharp had checked out in "the Three" during his last home leave, and now that CNAC had one of its own, he could barely tear himself away from the cockpit. The pilots and mechanics loved it, and the squints in the finance department smiled over improved ledgers. The DC-3 alleviated other pressures as well. With small auxiliary fuel tanks, it could fly round-trip from Hong Kong to Chungking with only 250 gallons of fuel added inside China, significantly reducing the drain on interior gasoline supplies. The airline's first DC-3 was such a boon that P. Y. Wong wanted to order two more.

A strange lull hushed the world that winter. "Sitzkrieg" paralyzed the armies of Europe, where there'd been little combat since the fall of Poland, and status quo held the Orient. Assuming things didn't deteriorate, Bond imagined it safe to bring Kitsi and young Langhorne to Hong Kong. His and Kitsi's relationship was suffering, and since his new, post–heart attack

---

* The DC-3 had entered service in the United States in June 1936, and it had been an instant success. Orders swamped the Douglas Corporation.

medical regime mandated that he spend three or four months in the United States each year, he elected to spend his 1940 quota right away, after about thirty days in the Orient, and escort his family back to Hong Kong in the early spring.

Back in Washington, Bond borrowed his mother-in-law's car and took Kitsi and Langhorne to Florida via visits to family and friends in Virginia. To bring himself current on the System's latest procedures, he toured Pan Am's main flying-boat base at Miami's Dinner Key, where he ran into Hugh Woods, looking uncharacteristically grim, devoid of his usual quiet, square-jawed confidence. He'd been grounded.

Woody had come home, taken the paid leave he'd been due, and trained as pilot-captain in Pan Am's Eastern Division. Only the supposed formality of a flight physical remained before he began flying regular schedules, and Woody had passed a rigorous medical examination soon after he'd returned from China. Unfortunately, a new test had been added, an electrocardiogram that measured heart performance, and Woody's T wave zigged when it should have zagged, and the pattern repeated in a series of retests. Woody was healthy in every other respect, but the mysterious EKG wrecked his flying career as far as commercial aviation in the United States was concerned. He'd been flying for fourteen years, professionally for more than twelve. He didn't know anything else. Although he was only thirty-four years old, he was within his rights to retire and demand a disability pension from Pan Am, especially because the doctors felt his China traumas likely caused the errant T wave, but Woody felt fine, and he wasn't the type to exploit such a dubious opportunity. He'd asked for a nonflying job, and he was languishing at Dinner Key awaiting an opening.

William Bond thought the T wave was medical malarkey. He didn't think it affected a man's ability to fly, but it would be bad corporate politics to announce his skepticism at Dinner Key or in the high-and-mighty halls of the Chrysler Building. In writing, Bond offered Woody a ground position with CNAC; verbally, he promised him that he could go back to his old job, with all his former seniority. Hugh Woods had just left China, however, and although he had no desire to return, Pan Am didn't seem able to find him a ground job. After much internal debate, he accepted Bond's offer.

From Washington, William and Kitsi Bond, three-and-a-half-year-old Langhorne, and Hugh Leslie Woods flew to Los Angeles on April 22, 1940, and all three adults were exceedingly glum—the Nazi invasions of Denmark and Norway eroded hopes for a bloodless resolution of the European conflict, and not one of them was enthusiastic about returning to China, but after a decade of economic depression, terror of unemployment outweighed their fear of war. The foursome sailed from Los Angeles to Honolulu on the SS *Lurline,* flew the hops across the mid-Pacific, and arrived in Hong Kong on May 6, 1940.

Little had changed. Woody moved back into his old digs with Chuck Sharp, and Sharp wasted no time putting him on regular schedules. The Bonds reoccupied their former rooms at Repulse Bay. The stable international situation William Bond hoped would allow him to enjoy an extended run of peace with his family lasted all of four days.

On May 10, Europe's "Phony War" came to a sudden, violent end when German forces slammed into Holland, Belgium, and France. Widespread combat in Western Europe changed the balance of power in the Orient, and Japan didn't hesitate to press her strategic advantage, threatening France and Britain in a concerted effort to close Free China's routes of external supply and choke the life out of the Nationalist regime.

Free China had four lifelines to outside support in the spring of 1940—from Rangoon, Burma, up-country to Lashio and thence over the mountains to Kunming on the Burma Road, constructed by an army of conscripted coolies in 1937 and 1938; north from Indochina to Kunming on a narrow-gauge railway; from Alma Ata in the Soviet Union across the central Asian deserts to Lanchow; and in and out of Chungking by air on the airplanes of Eurasia and the China National Aviation Corporation. Of the four, the last was arguably the most important, because the air routes allowed the Nationalist government to function on the world stage. With air service, Washington, London, Moscow, and Paris were fewer than ten days from China's wartime capital; without it, the trip would have taken months.

The three overland routes presented appalling difficulties. Supplies for China that came ashore in Rangoon had to travel 618 miles up-country before they reached the *beginning* of the Burma Road. From there, they crept across Burma and Yunnan for another 712 mountainous, unpaved miles to reach Kunming. Transportation experts pegged the road's capacity

at 30,000 tons per month, but erratic fuel supplies, inadequate maintenance, and incompetent management precluded anything more than a
fraction of that sum from reaching Kunming. No fewer than sixteen separate bureaucratic entities shared responsibility for the road, and in keeping
with China's endemic corruption, the various agencies seemed primarily
concerned with protecting their fiefdoms and squeezing whatever profit
they could from the traffic. One observer discovered that 14,000 tons
left Lashio for every 5,000 tons that arrived in Chungking—a whopping
64 percent of the road's traffic was being sold, stolen, grafted, or hijacked en
route.

Equally horrendous geographic and bureaucratic obstacles assailed the
thirteen hundred Russian trucks hauling supplies across the deserts
of northwest China. The route to Kunming from Haiphong and Hanoi in
Indochina wasn't beset by such appalling terrain, but the rail line in northern Vietnam didn't physically connect to the one that ran down from Kunming. A gallon of gasoline going to Chungking from Haiphong had to be
transshipped to the Yunnan line, then trucked onward from Kunming to
the wartime capital, a total transportation distance of 1,461 miles. Both
routes into Kunming passed through territories controlled by Long Yun,
the Yunnan warlord, who, although loosely allied with Chungking, always
extracted a layer of squeeze. Worst of all, the flow of supplies over any of
the overland routes depended on the European powers' willingness to resist Japanese pressure. Considering the colossal obstacles, moving freight
by air presented an attractive alternative, and since the beginning of the
year Bond, P. Y. Wong, and other aviation experts had been discussing how
it might best be done with the authorities in Chungking.

Realizing Free China's fears, the French colonial government suspended
the movement of war matériel on the Haiphong–Kunming railroad. Aviation gasoline was naturally on the list of banned items, and adding menace
to the diplomatic pressure she was applying to Great Britain to close the
Burma Road, Japanese combat units closed on the landward frontiers of
the Hong Kong colony's New Territories. The British military command
destroyed strategic bridges on the mainland and unspooled barbed wire on
the beaches of Hong Kong Island, including the one at Repulse Bay directly
across the street from the Bonds' bungalow as Katharine Dunlop Bond
held her three-year-old son's hand and watched. She didn't find the sight
the least bit reassuring. Heeding State Department advice, she took Lang-

horne to the Philippines aboard the SS *Coolidge,* relieved to have her son protected by American guns and at what felt like some remove from the frightening events churning the Asian mainland. Bond was despondent. There had been so many partings.

On the day Germany attacked France, Winston Spencer Churchill had replaced Neville Chamberlain as British prime minister, promising unbending resolve in the fight against the dictatorships. Churchill's intransigence didn't extend to the opposite hemisphere, however. On July 17, 1940, with the Luftwaffe raiding British shipping and ports and the Wehrmacht massing for an invasion of England, Churchill kowtowed to the Japanese and imposed a three-month ban on military cargoes traveling the Burma Road, ostensibly done, as Churchill explained, to allow diplomats to reach a "just settlement," although some members of Parliament decried the agreement as an "Asian Munich." In Japan, an even more hard-line cabinet assumed power four days later, vowing to end the "China Incident," align Japan with European fascism, and to seize by force the spoils the new leadership thought would cement Japanese hegemony in the western Pacific.

Not surprisingly, Churchill's closure of the Burma Road had catalyzed no Sino-Japanese reconciliation. However, Britain's position improved as the summer of 1940 waned and her air force held its own against the Luftwaffe in the skies of England. By mid to late August, the Japanese must have concluded that Churchill wouldn't extend the ban on military supplies being freighted out of Rangoon and began pressing the Vichy French government to grant them the right to base land and air forces in northern Indochina, less than two hundred miles from the road's Kunming terminus. The French acquiesced. American Secretary of State Cordell Hull protested, and the Japanese Foreign Office counterclaimed that Japan had "no designs upon the French Colony." The United States Congress approved a massive re-armament program. President Roosevelt embargoed scrap iron and steel exports to Japan on September 26, and Japan signed the "Tripartite Pact" with Italy and Germany the next day. Britain announced that the Burma Road would reopen when the three-month ban expired, and Japan rushed air forces to Lao-kai Airport in northern Indochina, planning to attack the reopened road from a drastically shortened distance. Hoping to deter further aggression, President Roosevelt made permanent the move of the U.S. Pacific Fleet from San Diego to Pearl Harbor, Hawaii, and the State Department warned American civilians to leave the Far East. Katharine Dunlop Bond took the announcement at face value. She wanted out. Bond made a transpacific reservation for her and Langhorne and flew to Manila to spend two final weeks with his wife and child.

The airline gave its pilots enormous latitude to decide when planes should take off and what routes they would fly—a practice intentionally designed to foster unpredictable operational patterns. Flights in and out of Kunming, the provincial capital of Yunnan, had been dangerous prior to September 1940. Japanese air forces in northern Indochina considerably worsened the peril. Since the company didn't have enough aircraft to allow a plane to sit idle for a full day and still complete the schedule of flights the Kuomintang government demanded, it used the plane coming up from Hong Kong to make a continuing daylight flight from Chungking to Kunming. But Japanese air forces at the newly occupied Lao-kai Airport, just over the border in Indochina, could fly to Kunming in less than sixty minutes, and they could loiter for hours. In some capacity, Japanese airpower was active nearly every flyable day. Nor was the Chinese air-warning net as well developed in Yunnan as it was around Chungking, where excellent reports allowed the airline to sardonically time its departures for "fifteen minutes before the first raid," and its arrivals for "thirty minutes after the third." Pilots received less comprehensive reports in the southwest. Those heading for Kunming needed to wait until the pattern of each day's Japanese operations over Yunnan became apparent before departing Chungking. Some handled the waiting better than others, and many were tempted to fly to Kunming before Japanese intentions came clear. If raids went to the Yunnanese capital, they could orbit in the hills north and east of the city or divert to one of the three or four auxiliary fields within a hundred-mile radius. With full fuel tanks, the DC-2s and the DC-3 could have tarried half a day, but with gasoline in such short supply in the interior, the planes carried only minimum fuel weights.

Hugh Woods and Royal Leonard were the most cautious of the Caucasian airmen. Woody waited when the warning net announced Japanese planes leaving their bases. His passengers groused and whined about crucial business that couldn't stand delay, but Woody wouldn't take off until he had a solid understanding of Japanese activity around Kunming or until raiders approached Chungking and forced him to flee. Walter "Foxie" Kent, a fiery redhead who had flown for the airline before the war and had recently returned, poked fun at what he thought was Woody's excessive caution, dismissing it as overreaction caused by Woody's trauma of August 1938. Even after the Japanese forced down, strafed, and bombed a Eurasia flight near Kunming on October 16, 1940, badly wounding its chief pilot, Kent didn't think the risks extreme. In the wee hours of October 29, he brought DC-2 number 39, the *Chungking*, up from Hong Kong. Resurrected, renumbered, and renamed, it was the same airframe in which Woody had been shot down two years before. Kent landed at Chungking at 7:00 A.M., scheduled to continue to Kunming, but an air-raid alarm radioed from Yunnan delayed his departure. Two hours later, Sanhupa Airport received a report of Japanese planes passing Ichang, heading up the Yangtze toward the wartime capital, and Kent was forced to leave. He flew upriver to Suifu with five company personnel and nine Chinese civilians aboard.

Foxie Kent was from Kentwood, Louisiana, a tiny town on the Mississippi border north of New Orleans named for one of his ancestors, and he was two days shy of his thirty-sixth birthday. Big, fast, and aggressive, he played the best shortstop in the history of the Hong Kong baseball club. He landed at Suifu at 11:05 A.M. and left an hour and a half later, under exactly the conditions that he'd mocked Woody for fearing—knowing that Japanese raiders were aloft in Yunnan, but without understanding where their attention would be focused, or for how long, or how many of them were in the air, or in how many groups they were operating. Kent reached the Kunming vicinity two hours later, with the air-raid alarm still in effect, and he circled among drab hills northeast of the city, but at the end of a four-hundred-mile flight begun without full fuel tanks, Kent didn't have much reserve. Each spent gallon diminished his options, eliminating the more distant alternate fields from his landing possibilities until only Changyi remained, an obscure secondary airfield about eighty miles northeast of Kunming.

Creeping in low, hopping hills and sliding down valleys, Kent spotted two Chinese planes on the Changyi field. Assuming they'd have scrambled if Japanese planes were in the vicinity, he lined up an approach and had his radioman key out a message: *Landing Changyi. Remaining here 14:25.*

Changyi didn't have a radio station and therefore wasn't able to advise Kent that five Japanese pursuit planes were climbing away from the field, having just finished strafing the two grounded airplanes, which were, in fact, wooden decoys built to draw enemy fire. The departing Japanese spotted the silver Douglas, wheels down, on final approach, and the raptors winged over, diving and gaining speed, scenting an easy kill.

Kent touched down, and the *Chungking* rolled in a straight, slowing line, coming to a complete stop just as the lead pursuit bore down on its tail. The first twenty-millimeter cannon shell ripped through the fuselage, the rear cockpit wall, and the pilot's seat and slammed into Kent's back, rupturing his heart. The big shortstop hurtled against the instrument panel, killed instantly.

The copilot leapt from his seat and shouted for the passengers to run. The stewardess was twenty-six-year-old Lu Mei-ying, a delicate Nanking native working out her two-week notice before returning to Hong Kong to marry a young engineer. The round trip with Kent was her last turn on the schedule. Miss Lu popped the side door and tried to hustle the passengers onto the field. Only four obeyed. Paralyzed with fear or perhaps thinking the plane offered protection, the others remained glued to their seats. More bullets snapped through the fuselage. The left wing caught fire; flames enveloped the engine. The crew shouted a last round of exhortations and fled themselves, leaping into the dust and sprinting for bushes at the field's edge. The Japanese pursuits machine-gunned them as they ran. Last through the door was Lu Mei-ying. Her immaculate white uniform shone against the brown field as she cut and wove across it. A plane peeled toward her, engine screaming. She jinked in the dust. A bullet clipped through one of her legs, and she collapsed halfway between the burning plane and the field's edge. The Japanese pursuits loitered to complete the massacre, making more strafing passes at her where she lay, severing her ankle with a cannon shell. She died eight hours later.

A CNAC staff member aboard, Mr. Hwang Chi, was also killed, as were six of the nine passengers, including an expectant mother and her ten-month-old child. There would be no third shoot-down for the ill-starred airplane. The *Kweilin/Chungking* burned to unsalvageable slag, roasting Kent's body. At the exact moment he died, his pregnant wife had been sitting at a marble countertop in the Hong Kong office of the National City Bank of New York, chatting with other well-dressed American wives while she filled out the paperwork necessary to arrange evacuation to Manila.

William Bond rushed back from the Philippines and spent the first ten days of November dealing with the disaster's fallout, arranging Mrs. Kent's affairs, counseling the pilots, and trying to ensure that the tragedy wouldn't be repeated. The obvious flaw was the Yunnan air-warning net, and Bond secured Claire Chennault's commitment to improve it. The airline flew Kent's, Lu's, and Hwang's remains to Hong Kong, and Bond delivered a eulogy for his fallen employees. No matter how badly Bond personally wished to escape the Orient, he was 100 percent certain the China National Aviation Corporation was on the side of righteousness. China was flawed, and Bond knew it, but the Japanese aggressions were blatant, and unconscionable, and the only way to make sense of the deaths of Kent, Lu, and Hwang was to put their loss in the context of the "vitally important" service they rendered unto China and renew his pledge to struggle on until the Japanese militarists were destroyed, even though it was demanding sacrifices of him and his family that he wasn't entirely willing to make. "I'm too old and have too much family responsibility for all this mess," he'd tell Ernie Allison in a letter written after the funeral.

Woody served as one of the pallbearers of Kent's sealed casket, and his comrade's death hit him like a blow to the solar plexus; he was so distraught that Bond and Sharp had no choice but to ground him for a week, until he pulled himself together. This time, however, he had no thought of leaving Asia, for a powerful new force anchored him in Hong Kong—he'd fallen in love with Alva "Maj" Majors, a secretary in the American consulate.

Two years before, the attack on Woody's plane had splashed through the newspapers in Hong Kong and Shanghai for weeks and had received detailed attention in almost every Western newspaper. In late 1940, in a world growing ever more inured to violence, Kent's demise didn't even play for a week in Hong Kong. The company shipped his body home, and family and friends laid him to rest alongside the body of his father in the Kentwood cemetery.

Thirty-nine months of war had hardened the airline. It didn't miss a single schedule in the wake of Foxie Kent's death. Struggling to arrange the affairs of Mrs. Kent and the airline in the aftermath, Bond wasn't able to return to Manila to see his wife and son off, and Kitsi and Langhorne left the Philippines on November 7, 1940, eastbound on a transpacific Clipper. Among the other passengers were two hush-hush travelers using assumed names—aviation advisor "Colonel" Claire Lee Chennault and Chinese general Mow Pang-tzo, P. T. Mow, operations director of the Chinese Air Force, on their way to New York and Washington for clandestine meetings with top officials in the Roosevelt administration. They, along with T. V. Soong and Arthur N. Young, who'd gone stateside earlier in the autumn, were planning to push a proposal to form and equip a volunteer band of American pursuit pilots to break Japan's domination of China's skies. Kitsi knew them both personally, and the rugged Chennault, his face cracked and weathered by years in open cockpits, made what chivalrous Southern gestures he could to ease the difficulties of an acquaintance's attractive wife making such a long trip with a small child. Kitsi was relieved to have her son out of the Orient, but she didn't have much appetite. She was pregnant with Bondy's second child, and worry about her husband and their family circumstances wasn't helping her first-trimester discomfort.

18

A WING AND A SPARE,
NO PRAYERS NEEDED

Proving the adage about clouds and silver linings, the collapse of France had created an opportunity for the China National Aviation Corporation. Air France had ordered a new DC-3, and Douglas Aircraft had built it, but after the French capitulation, the U.S. government wouldn't grant an export license sending the plane to what had become the commercial air arm of the Vichy government, Hitler's ally. Air France had already paid for the plane, however. They *owned* it, and the United States wasn't at war with France, Vichy or otherwise, and no court in the land would have authorized outright confiscation. Air France's interest in the plane was represented by a Major Brun. He offered to sell the plane to CNAC for $160,000, a $35,000 premium on the standard list price, on condition the money was paid, in cash, in Buenos Aires. Pan American eyebrows shot skyward reading the terms, but William Bond didn't care a whit where the money went so long as his airline finished with another spanking new DC-3. CNAC sent cash to Argentina, took possession of the plane in Santa Monica, and an official in the Treasury Department greased approval of the airplane's export license, but the circumstances of the sale and the "French DC-3's" eventual destination worried the Douglas Corporation's legal department so much it demanded, and got, Harold Bixby's signature on a series of exonerating documents.

Fronting the Bay of Bengal and sequestered behind the Malacca and Sunda straits, Burma seemed far removed from Japan, and most people believed it was free of the immediate threats gripping Hong Kong, China, and the Philippines. Bond wasn't so sure, however. He understood too well how vulnerable the Burma Road and his airline's route into China from Rangoon were to air interdiction from the new Japanese bases in Indochina, and an actual ground attack on Yunnan or southern Burma no longer struck Bond as beyond the pale of possibility. To hedge against those risks and the possibility that Japan would close his access to Hong Kong, Bond wanted to develop a less vulnerable air route from Kunming across the top of Burma to Calcutta, but if the proposed route was to function safely, it needed an intermediate airport. A glance at a map revealed the best place to be Myitkyina, a trading center on the Irrawaddy about 450 miles north of Mandalay, and Bond made the arduous journey from Chungking to Myitkyina by plane, automobile, and train in the days following Thanksgiving to investigate the feasibility of building an airport there.

An air reconnaissance was just as important as one from the ground, and after Bond had finished his ground examination, Hugh Woods met him in Lashio with a DC-2. They flew to Myitkyina, and Woody examined the various options Bond presented from the air, then flew a straight line back to Chungking, passing over the tail end of the mountains that fishhooked around the northeastern corner of Burma and ran south down the Burma-China border, gradually shrinking from clusters of 18,000- to 22,000-foot summits in the north into the smaller mountains of the Shan Highlands at the juncture of Burma, China, and Indochina. No aircraft had ever flown the route, but it seemed viable. The air was surprisingly smooth over the mountains, considering the clouds and mild icing conditions, although it was easy to imagine conditions much more treacherous. If the British built an airfield at Myitkyina, Calcutta–Myitkyina–Chungking could serve as a valuable alternative to the more exposed routes from Chungking and Kunming through Lashio and Rangoon and from Chungking to Hong Kong. North Burma seemed as secure as any place in mainland Asia, and in the coming months Bond raised the matter with two successive governors of Burma. Through those efforts, the airfield was built.

The year turned without fanfare. CNAC operations were still expanding, with special charters flown for China's Central Bank accounting for much of the growth. Ironically, the inflation that caused such difficulty for the company fueled the rise in bank charters, since China needed larger and larger volumes of money as the inflation accelerated, especially in the wintertime as banks stockpiled cash for Chinese New Year celebrations. Because no print shop in China could be trusted, "China National" currency was produced by a British concern in Hong Kong, and CNAC flew it into China by the ton, in heavy bales wedged between seats in the passenger cabins. On the night of January 20, 1941, Bernard Wong, one of the Chinese pilots, was carrying currency into China, and he got caught in a storm that he couldn't climb above while at the controls of the airline's last tri-motored Ford. The "Tin Goose's" direction-finding gear wasn't as powerful as the sets on the DC-2s or the DC-3, so Wong was navigating by dead reckoning, with no means to discern how far off course a strong crosswind was blowing his airplane, and by the time Wong estimated that he should be receiving the Kunming signal, he'd been blown laterally out of its range. He flew back toward the coast, trying to raise the more powerful Hong Kong beacon, but he never heard it. He turned inland again, thoroughly lost, far off course, over rough terrain, in darkness, with a shriveling fuel supply. Wong's outbound communications capacity functioned perfectly, however, and every CNAC station in China monitored his plight as the hours crept by. The Goose ran out of gas shortly before sunrise. After that, silence held the airwaves; Wong was never seen alive again.* Three weeks later, pilot Joy Thom, copilot Paul Chinn, and radio operator C. N. Pau tried to slip under an icing condition in a storm, and they crashed too, killing all aboard. Thom's death left Moon Chin as the only one of CNAC's

---

* One of the company's radio operators, P. L. Chang, survived the crash.

three original Chinese American pilot-captains still with the airline. Thom, Chinn, and Bernard Wong were all close friends of Moon Chin's, as were the lost radiomen. It had been a bad run, but they were in a war, and such things happened. Moon Chin stifled his emotions and kept flying.

For more than a year, William Bond had been involved in schemes to air-freight supplies into China. The concept was sound; the problem was obtaining adequate aircraft with which to do it—extreme worldwide demand had swept the market clean of first-class transport aircraft—but a used-aircraft dealer in Glendale, California, discovered five large, slow, ungainly Curtiss Condor biplane transports languishing on a pier in Tampico, Mexico, and brought them to the attention of the Chinese government.* Acting for H. H. Kung and his Ministry of Finance, Bond had negotiated their purchase while he was last in the United States, and Kung had intended to lease them to CNAC so the airline could use them to operate a freight service from French Indochina to Kunming, a relatively low-altitude flight route. Japan's closure of French Indochina torpedoed the scheme, and it was replaced by hopes for a Burma–Yunnan airlift, over much higher terrain. The first two Ministry of Finance Condors arrived, and Hugh Woods and Chuck Sharp put the assembled biplanes through their paces. Fully loaded, they needed fifty-five minutes to climb to fifteen thousand feet, and their maximum speed at that altitude was 120 miles per hour. Over the mountains of the Burma-China frontier, they'd regularly encounter head-winds half that strong. The conclusion was obvious: They were totally unsuited to freight service between Burma and China, a worry that had gnawed at William Bond since the previous summer. "Since then, many things have changed," Bond wrote, "except the Condors." The planes sat idle at Kai Tak Airport.

China's minister of economic resources rescued the undertaking. Free China exploited substantial reserves of tin and tungsten, both crucial primary ingredients of wartime industry. China had promised to repay its

---

* The Condors had been intended to fly supplies in the Spanish Civil War, but the war ended before they could be transshipped.

American loans through mineral sales, and the United States was stock-piling tungsten, fearing shortfalls.* The minister arranged to use the idle Condors to fly tungsten and tin to Hong Kong from an airfield at Namyung,** two hundred miles to the north, paying the freight charges in U.S. dollars. Service began in March 1941, but CNAC couldn't locate any nonmilitary inbound cargo, and the freight service lost money until P. Y. Wong found a tobacco firm that wanted to import cigarettes into China. Wong insisted they pay their freight in Hong Kong's readily convertible currency, and CNAC was at long last paid in hard currency for flights in *and* out of China. Apart from the Condors' lease fees and spare-part costs, all the freight line's expenses were in Chinese currency, and money poured in from both direc-tions of airlift. It was legit, and secure, and the lucre the airline stashed in a New York account was a world away from the war and the grubbing paws of Chinese officialdom. For the first time in its history, the China National Aviation Corporation made a killing.

By the middle months of 1941, Axis aggressions had thawed the glacier of American isolationism. President Roosevelt's Lend-Lease bill passed Con-gress in March. His economics advisor, Lauchlin Currie, had visited China the previous winter, flown to and from meetings in Chungking by CNAC, of course, and he'd formed a very positive impression of the airline, its Chinese and American personnel, and of William Langhorne Bond, with whom he discussed options for airfreighting supplies into China. On Cur-rie's recommendation, President Roosevelt extended Lend-Lease to China, and he ordered Currie to figure out what China needed and how to get it there, an assignment that expanded Currie's relationship with T. V. Soong, who had been in Washington for nearly a year as Chiang Kai-shek's per-sonal representative precisely in order to drum up American support. Soong immediately requested trucks, railroad equipment, tractors, cars,

---

* China produced about 50 percent of the world's tungsten. Tungsten alloys greatly increased the hardness of steel, making "high-speed steels" needed in precision milling and turning tools, valves and valve seats, armor plate, armor-piercing projectiles, and corrosion-resistant gun liners. Smaller gross quantities went into lamp and radio filaments, telephone parts, X-ray targets, and electrical contact points.

** Also spelled Namyang and Nanshiung.

machinery, gas, oil, munitions, and weapons and equipment for thirty Chinese infantry divisions. The enormous bottleneck was transportation, and many of Soong's ideas revolved around improving surface communications into China's southwestern back door: constructing a narrow-gauge railroad from Burma to Yunnan, hacking a highway to China across the jungles and mountains of north Burma from Assam, in northeastern India, and paving the Burma Road. None of those projects could be accomplished rapidly, however. The only immediately viable alternative was airfreight, and that line of thinking led straight to William Bond. The actual cable summoning him to Washington came from Harold Bixby at Pan American, but it was T. V. Soong who had requested his return.

The timing couldn't have been better for Bond. Operationally, Chuck Sharp seemed to have it all under control. Personally, Bond was due for the annual rest mandated by his cardiologist, and, most important, Kitsi was entering the third trimester of her pregnancy. He'd be at her side for the birth of their second child. In Washington, T. V. Soong tasked him to write a proposal for airlifting freight into China from Burmese airfields, a project Bond had been pondering for a long time. The need to get war supplies to China was "so obvious that little need be said to emphasize its urgency," Bond declared in his "Air Freight Service into China" memorandum.

He considered two factors paramount to the airlift's success—planes and pilots. He wanted "men of responsibility, determination, and character," and he expected the U.S. Army and Navy to supply them by releasing multi-engine-rated fliers willing to volunteer for China. As for airplanes, Bond wanted DC-3s or he wanted nothing at all, and for once he wasn't worried about financing, assuming the details would be arranged between the American and Chinese governments. Although the proposed Burma-to-Yunnan air route involved "every obstacle known to aviation, in a blockaded country subject to constant air attacks," it was with obvious pride that Bond concluded that "CNAC has shown, after nearly four years of such operations, that [they] can be done successfully." Bond dated his proposal May 8, 1941, and with guidance from Pan Am and T. V. Soong, he presented it to Lauchlin Currie later in the month. Bond's plan was much like the one Arthur N. Young had drafted for Chennault's "American Volunteer Group" (the AVG)—with American planes and American volunteers financed by American loans to China—except that it was intended for DC-3s and airfreight instead of P-40s and aerial combat. Currie approved, and under his umbrella of sponsorship Bond shopped the proposal at the highest levels of the United States government. The China National Aviation Corporation, Pan American Airways, and William Langhorne Bond had become exactly what T. V. Soong, H. H. Kung, W. H. Donald, Madame Chiang Kai-shek, and other influential members of the Kuomintang had envisioned when they allowed Pan Am to reinstate its interest in China's airline at the beginning of 1938—a tool with which to influence the policy of the world's most powerful democracy.

As usual, spring brought fine weather to Szechwan. It also brought Japanese bombing squadrons. They blasted substantial holes in those parts of Chungking that were still standing, killing hundreds of civilians. The China National Aviation Corporation kept operating, regardless, as it had for the previous four years. On the night of May 20, 1941, Hugh Woods piloted "the French DC-3" from Hong Kong to Chungking. The moon was full, and Woody was pleased with the substantial bands of overcast at cruising altitude, cover in which he could elude any Japanese patrols aloft in the moonshine. The flight went without incident, and he landed at Chungking after daylight and quickly got back in the air, heading for Chengtu with twenty-two passengers.

Fifteen minutes out of Chungking, Woods received notice of Japanese planes flying into Szechwan, threatening Chengtu and Chungking. He peeled from his route and winged up the Yangtze to the airfield at Suifu, where he landed and disembarked his passengers. The air defense radio operators reported no Japanese west of Chungking, and Woody rested easy—until the officer in charge of the airfield sprinted up and screamed about enemy planes over Luchow, a nearby city, bearing straight toward them and precluding escape. Woods hustled his passengers into a bamboo copse on a hillside above the field, while twenty-four Japanese bombers droned overhead. Bombs boomed around the precious airplane. One punched through its right wing. Dirt and fire blasted skyward, and only a mangled spar kept the trailing edge of the nearly severed wing attached to the main body of the airplane. Outboard of the number two engine, the right wingtip pointed straight up, its undersurface rotated forward like an aluminum spinnaker. Amazingly, the plane didn't catch fire.

Woody was absolutely furious: With timely notification, he could have easily escaped. He also knew the Japanese would come back to finish the job, and he organized a coolie gang to manhandle the twenty-thousand-pound airplane three miles down a dirt road and camouflage it in a bamboo forest. Royal Leonard retrieved Woods and his stranded passengers the next morning, just before four Japanese pursuit planes spent twenty minutes strafing the Suifu airfield, hunting the stricken Douglas.

Figuring out how to recover the airplane fell to Zygmund "Sol" Soldinski, the airline's meaty, squinty-eyed maintenance chief. Once he'd gathered the facts, Sol took the problem to managing director P. Y. Wong. In time-honored colonial fashion, they repaired to the nearest bar. They didn't have to go any farther than the fully stocked drinkery the British airport administration kept in the hangar, which could have been kept in business by Soldinski's patronage alone. The twosome mulled the situation over a few glasses of White Horse, a blended Scotch whisky popular with Hong Kong expatriates, P.Y. in a dark suit, Soldinski in soiled dungarees.

Replacing a wing on a DC-3 was a big repair, albeit a routine one. Problem was, Soldinski didn't have a replacement wing for a DC-3, and even if he did, how could he get it to Suifu, 860 miles distant? A spare wing wouldn't fit *inside* another airplane. The prewar solution would have been to ship it up the Yangtze, but the Japanese held the lower six hundred miles of the river. The only overland route to Suifu was to ship a wing to Rangoon and truck it up the Burma Road, but a thirty-foot section of airplane wing traveling fifteen hundred miles over dirt roads through thick jungles and rugged mountains would almost certainly be ruined. Besides, it'd take months.

Soldinski watched a gang of mechanics overhauling a DC-2. The Two had eleven feet less wingspan and a lot less wing surface area, but Soldinski couldn't help but wonder—would a DC-2 wing fit on a DC-3? The mechanics thought Soldinski had gone mad, but they did as they were told and dismembered the right wing of the airline's other DC-3 and tried to mate a DC-2 spare in its place.

The wing fit. Not perfectly, but pretty well. Credit Donald Douglas's Scottish thrift—his engineering team had used the jigs from the DC-2 to form the DC-3 wing butt attach angles. But the hybrid side was five and a half feet shorter than normal, with much less lifting surface. Would it fly? Would it tolerate a six-hour flight from Suifu? And that was only half the problem. Soldinski still had to get the wing to Suifu. CNAC was an airline, and the obvious answer was to fly it, but how? He decided to mount the wing *underneath* one of the DC-2s, but he'd still need a man willing to fly it to Suifu. Soldinski summoned Hal Sweet, one of the airline's veterans, a former barnstormer who Soldinski thought was a little more mature than the other pilots.

Soldinski laid out the concept to him in the hangar bar: Mount the spare wing underneath the fuselage of a DC-2, butt first, build a fairing to streamline it in place, and fly the contraption to Suifu. As long as the underslung wing didn't cause a dead-air bubble that destroyed the plane's flight characteristics, Soldinski didn't *think* the center-slung wing would do much besides reduce speed and rate of climb, but the final word was always the pilot's.

The plan seemed reasonable after a few rounds of White Horse. "If you say it'll fly, I'll fly it," Sweet said, nodding.

Mechanics spent the night slinging the wing beneath a DC-2. The plane ended up looking pregnant, but considering the magnitude of the external modification, by and large, Sweet thought it looked pretty good.

Evening closed in with darkness and rain, perfect conditions for a Hong Kong departure. Soldinski handpicked the mechanics for the field repairs. Then came one last nasty surprise: Soldinski and Wong exploded when they learned that traffic control had sold a complete load of passengers and freight for the flight—which by company definition was 2,200 pounds *more* than the maximum load specified by the Douglas Corporation's engineers—without considering the wing slung beneath.

Sweet calmed them down. "Load it," he said. "I'll fly it all."

The plane wallowed into the sky at the end of the longest, most sluggish takeoff roll Sweet ever experienced. Aloft, the plane strained to maintain flying speed, but Sweet delivered the passengers and cargo safely in Chungking and flew the wing and the mechanics to Suifu. Relieved of the third wing, Sweet returned to Hong Kong. Suifu repairs took several days, and when they were finished, coolies pushed the plane back to the field. Another pilot took Sweet back to Suifu, where he inspected the hybrid. "Fair enough," he thought, "this thing'll fly." He fired up the engines, loaded the mechanics, and took off for Chungking. In the air, the DC-3 wing generated much more drag and lift than its junior counterpart, and the "DC-2½" pulled hard to the left like a car whose wheels were out of alignment. Sweet hassled to keep the plane on course, even with full aileron trim and a constant stomp on the rudder pedal. He didn't fancy wrestling it all the way to Hong Kong. Sweet had a mechanic pass a heavy aircraft spanner into the cockpit, and he lashed it to a wheel spoke, which balanced the yoke, and from then on he flew without strain, admiring the flight characteristics of his asymmetric aircraft, albeit with lots of added rudder.

In Chungking, the traffic agent asked Sweet if he could carry any passengers.

Sweet considered the airplane. Given the spanner counterweight, the DC-2½ flew pretty well. "Hell, gimme a full load," he said with a shrug, and he carried passengers to Hong Kong "without incident." Magazines and newspapers all over the world latched on to the story, a surprise propaganda coup for Nationalist China, Pan American, and the China National Aviation Corporation. There was, however, an odd casualty of the episode. The "French DC-3" died forever. Ever after, DC-3 number 46 was known as "the DC-2½," even once the arrival of a new wing restored its normal configuration.

William Bond spent the summer in Washington, waiting for his wife to give birth and pushing his freight service concept, which he presented in the Commerce, Treasury, Army, Navy, and State departments, while conferring regularly with Lauchlin Currie, T. V. Soong, Arthur Young, and Stanley Hornbeck, and he hashed over the plan with Marine Corps captain James Roosevelt, the president's eldest son, who had just returned from a world tour that included China. Everyone was "sympathetic" and "anxious to assist." The problem wasn't finances; money was readily available. The problem was aircraft. The Germans had captured Crete in May solely with troops parachuted and landed from transport aircraft, a spectacular success that caused a mad rush for comparable airframes in the British and American militaries at a time when the Douglas Aircraft assembly line was completing only three DC-3s per week. Douglas was making an immense effort to expand capacity, tooling up assembly lines in new factories and training hundreds of men, but production wouldn't significantly accelerate until year's end. Bond's initial proposal called for thirty-five DC-3s to fly freight from Myitkyina over the mountains to Yunnan. Currie asked Bond to cut it to twenty, then ten. Assuming planes could be found, the service was intended to begin in early 1942, and one of its prime purposes was to fly mission-critical supplies to the group of American volunteer pursuit pilots being organized by Claire Chennault for combat in China.

Theoretically, Bond was relaxing, but his anxiety mounted as Kitsi approached full term. She had her first contraction on one of the summer's most sweltering days, July 12, and before the day was over she'd given birth to their second son, Thomas Dunlop. Mother and son came home from the hospital ten days later, both doing well, an event that triggered a few happy, sleepless nights for the "old man."

Concurrent with Thomas Dunlop's homecoming, Japan strong-armed the Vichy government into allowing its ground forces to occupy bases in Indochina. The first troops debarked on July 26, threatening actual land invasion of Yunnan, Burma, and Malaya. Hoping to counterbalance the menace in addition to what he'd already okayed for Chennault's volunteer pursuit group, President Roosevelt approved a plan to equip, train, and maintain a five-hundred-plane Chinese Air Force that could act in concert with American airpower in the Philippines to threaten both flanks of any southerly Japanese aggression. The administration froze Japanese assets in the United States and required the issuance of export licenses for all Japan-bound cargoes. In practice, no licenses were granted for oil shipments, and the restriction evolved into an embargo. Claire Chennault's American Volunteer Group* and its P-40C Tomahawk IIB pursuit planes began reaching Rangoon in the late summer and autumn, and Chennault instituted rigorous courses in gunnery and tactics needed to ready the force for combat. Lauchlin Currie was deeply entwined in every evolution of the anti-Japanese policy, and he was proud of what he'd wrought. "I was checking back the other day on the list of commissions and messages the Generalissimo gave me on that memorable last evening at your house," he would write to Madame Chiang Kai-shek toward the end of the year. "I find they have all been more or less discharged. The hardest to accomplish was the freezing order."

Bond spent six weeks getting to know his new son, wedged around a two-day trip to New York to see Bill Pawley, an aircraft trader of long acquain-

---

* Chennault's group would become famous as the Flying Tigers.

tance who coordinated Chennault's logistics, and a two-week hospital stay
to have a throat operation. The time was too fleeting. William Bond said
goodbye to his wife and sons in September and returned to Asia. The China
National Aviation Corporation had functioned perfectly in his five-month
absence, testament to the strength of the organization he'd done so much
to build. The cigarettes-and-minerals freight service to and from Namyung
continued to mint money, having already netted close to a million American dollars ($14.7 million in modern dollars). It was superb revenue, and
even better experience. The airline learned to handle heavy cargoes efficiently and to keep aircraft in near-constant operation in foul weather and
at night over occupied territory, expertise it expected to use to help clear
the backlog of China-bound supplies piled in Rangoon and Lashio when
the new DC-3s began arriving in early 1942. Bond selected Hugh Woods to
manage the operation. Promotion to management responsibilities gave
Woody the courage to propose marriage to his girlfriend, "Maj" Major,
who accepted.

Among the few negatives Bond found on his return was the condition
of his managing director. The stresses of running the airline had broken
P. Y. Wong's health, and like Bond, he'd developed a serious heart condition. The long-tenured managing director, the best the company had ever
had, wasn't well enough to get out of bed, let alone to perform his normal
duties in Hong Kong or travel to Chungking. William Bond picked up the
slack and hoped he'd recover. Off duty, Bond played tennis and socialized
with M. Y. Tong, his oldest and best Chinese friend. Bond spent two weeks
in Hong Kong, two weeks in Chungking, and then flew to Burma, where,
sparked by his efforts of 1940, construction of an airport at Myitkyina was
nearing completion. From Burma, Bond continued to New Delhi to try to
negotiate the inception of air service to India.

In the fourth week of November, Chuck Sharp took Bond and a passel
of Royal Air Force officers and other CNAC leadership on a reconnaissance flight from Dinjan, in Upper Assam, to Kunming, across the wild
jungles of north Burma and the rugged sixteen-thousand-foot mountains
of the Three Gorges country, where the eastern Himalayas wrapped around
the northeast corner of Burma and the Salween, Mekong, and Yangtze rivers ran in parallel through colossal gorges down the Burma-Yunnan border, in spots separated by a mere thirty or forty miles, before diverging
across Asia, defining civilizations, and ultimately emptying into three dif-

ferent seas two thousand miles apart. Sharp touched down in Kunming just before dark, 505 miles east of Dinjan. It had been a gorgeous, inspiring flight. Bomb craters on the Kunming airfield brought the men back to objective reality. The route they'd just flown would be extraordinarily difficult to fly on a schedule, pummeled by South Asia's volatile weather. It was higher and rougher and farther northward than the Myitkyina–Kunming route Bond had explored with Woody the year before, but both he and Sharp felt the Dinjan–Kunming run could be done, even in foul weather, and that meant the China National Aviation Corporation could fly supplies into China regardless of what happened to Burma.

Bond did a week of business in Chungking and returned to Hong Kong on the first day of December. Disquieting stories of Japanese military movements appeared in the newspapers. Even more disturbing details reached the airline's managers through their contacts in the British intelligence community, but there was hope, too, in the ongoing negotiations between the Japanese and American governments. Correspondents reported an exchange of proposals that might afford temporary accommodation, ostensibly conceived as first steps toward a reasonable settlement that would remove the threat of war. Most company pilots thought the prime danger had passed, feeling that the Japanese had waited too long, that the window of American vulnerability was closing as re-armament programs took hold. Lauchlin Currie, for example, after "heartbreaking delays," had secured a commitment to provide five Lend-Lease DC-3s *per month* to Bond's proposed Burma-to-China freight service, beginning in January or February 1942 and continuing until the airline had thirty-five in operation. Bond was sure those planes would do much to bolster China's fortunes. The first of them was due to load ship in San Diego on December 7, 1941.

19

"THOSE PLANES ARE JAPANESE!"

Monday, December 8, 1941, dawned a day like any other on Hong Kong Island. Below scattered clouds, the sun broke the rim of the South China Sea at 6:50 A.M., gilding the lush hillsides above Repulse Bay, whose south-facing waters lay calm and dark in shadow cast from the eastern headland. The air was fresh and cool, and it smelled of the sea. Rain had fallen overnight. The sunrise caught William Bond, ever an early riser, puttering around his bungalow, expecting a servant to appear with tea, breakfast, and the newspaper. Instead, the telephone rang.

It was Pan Am captain Fred Ralph, calling from Kai Tak.

Ralph, of Northeast Harbor, Maine, was pilot-captain of the *Hong Kong Clipper,* the aging four-engine Sikorsky S-42 flying boat that shuttled passengers and airmail over to the Philippines to meet the transpacific flights. Gassed and serviced, the big plane was moored at the Kai Tak pontoon, due to depart that morning for Manila. "I'm in a bind, Mr. Bond. I've got a radiogram from Manila in my hand telling me not to go there, but Mr. Moss wants me to leave Hong Kong immediately and he won't tell me why. What do you make of it, sir?"

Bond pondered the news. Moss was the airport manager. "It must be serious. That probably makes Hong Kong more dangerous than Manila. . . . Moss must know something. Make him tell you."

The servant appeared with breakfast as Bond hung up and checked his watch. It was 7:10 A.M. A zephyr ruffled the bay. Bond shook open the newspaper and sipped his tea.

The phone rang again five minutes later. "It's war!" exclaimed Captain Ralph. "Japan declared war on the U.S. and Great Britain."

"Then you can't take off at all!" Bond blurted.

War. It was hard to comprehend. So they'd actually gone and done it, forced a war on the United States, the one so long apprehended, the one for which he'd sometimes hoped, and here it was, ready to visit its horrors on his countrymen. What fools the Japanese were: Did they actually think they could win? They'd certainly discovered how to end American vacillation, although Bond knew it'd take time to marshal his homeland's power. In the meantime, he and his airline had immediate problems, and he staccatoed instructions to Captain Ralph: "The Japs will be over Kai Tak in a few minutes. I say again: Do not take off. Get your passengers and crew off the field. Tell Sharp and Soldinski to get our people off the field. Get the mail off the Clipper if you get a chance. The first raid will go after the planes. If your Clipper survives, we'll give you one of our pilots to navigate you to Kunming tonight. There's a lake there. Good luck. I'm on the way."

Bond threw on his clothes, shoveled a few changes and sundries into a suitcase, and rushed into the corridor, calling for his car. The newspaper abandoned on the breakfast table contained a message from an official of the Hong Kong government. "There will be no war," it declared.

Word of an attack on Pearl Harbor reached other members of the airline at about the same time. One of Madame Kung's daughters called mechanic Troy Haynie. "The Japs just blew up Pearl Harbor," she said. Haynie called maintenance chief Zygmund Soldinski. "Call Sharp," Soldinski instructed. "We'll probably get it soon. I'll get down to the field."

Number 24, the *Nanking,* and number 26, the *Chengtu,* two of the airline's three DC-2s, gleamed on the packed dirt and stubbled grass in front of the

Kai Tak hangar. Taken together, in six years of stalwart service the two planes had given CNAC more than twelve thousand hours of productive flight time and had flown the equivalent of seventy-eight equatorial circumnavigations of the globe. Alongside the DC-2s sat three Curtiss Condor biplane freight carriers leased from the Ministry of Finance. The previous night, the maintenance staff had fueled and serviced all five airplanes. Farther down the flight line, three Eurasia planes waited in similar states of readiness—two tri-motored Ju-52s and a much older single-engine machine. Pan Am's S-42 *Hong Kong Clipper* floated on the placid waters of Kowloon Bay, tied against the Pan Am pontoon. Inside the hangar, CNAC had DC-2 number 31, the *Chungshan,* and two DC-3s (numbers 41, the *Chiating,* and 46, the *Omei,* a.k.a. "the French DC-3," a.k.a. "the DC-2½"); Eurasia had a third Ju-52. Bill McDonald was in Burma with number 47, "the Irish DC-3," CNAC's newest airplane.

Soldinski found Mr. Moss at the Pan Am dock trying to convince Captain Ralph to fly the Clipper out of Hong Kong. Moss didn't care where. The plane had enough fuel to make Rangoon or Calcutta. Ralph refused. There weren't enough clouds in which to elude pursuit, and his cumbersome flying boat would be easy prey. He argued that there'd been no official confirmation of attacks at Pearl Harbor and Manila, which seemed far-fetched to him. Soldinski had the distinct impression that Ralph was awaiting instructions from Pan Am's Pacific Division headquarters in San Francisco. Whatever the case, Ralph had missed his opportunity and he knew it. Soldinski turned his back on the arguing officers and headed for the hangar, his office, and a telephone.

The six-man Clipper crew, immaculate in their handsome Pan Am uniforms, hustled airmail sacks down the dock.[*] Ralph ducked inside the Clipper to help. Chen Teh-tsan, T. T. Chen, a member of the ground staff since October 1939, was unloading the busload of Pan Am passengers he'd escorted to Kai Tak from the Peninsula Hotel, the sumptuous lobby of which the airline used in lieu of a bona fida passenger terminal. Suddenly, the drone of airplane engines sounded in the distance, growing louder by the second.

---

[*] Two letters written by William Bond on December 5 were in the sacks. They were delivered four years later: *Wings,* p. 306.

"Look!" A passenger pointed to a gaggle of aircraft bearing down from the north at medium altitude.

"They're British," someone said dismissively.

Chen had been in Chungking a few weeks before. He squinted at the formation. "No! Those planes are Japanese!"

Panic hit the passengers; they scattered into bedlam. Four of them followed Chen across the street at a dead run and leapt into a drainage culvert along with a bunch of blue-coveralled airport coolies. Soldinski sprinted to his car and raced for home. The Clipper crew took shelter in the sturdy dock house and shouted for Captain Ralph, who was still in the plane.

The formation broke into attack groups and descended to strike altitude. Twelve single-engine Ki-36 bombers banked toward Kai Tak, escorted by nine single-engine, fixed-undercarriage Nakajima Ki-27 "Nate" pursuit planes. With no RAF opposition aloft, the nimble pursuits peeled out of formation into a straight line and swooped to fifty feet, heading directly toward Pan Am's flying boat.

Captain Ralph scrambled out of the Clipper and sprinted down the dock as bullets chewed into the plane behind him. The New Englander flung himself over the side into three feet of water and splashed behind a concrete piling. One after the other, six Japanese pursuits riddled the Clipper and screamed overhead to attack targets farther down the field. Bullets from a seventh ignited a fuel tank. Safe behind a pillar, Ralph watched his flying boat erupt in flame, heat searing the dock.

The bombers cruised in level at five hundred feet, engine roar changing tone as they passed overhead. Black cylinders fluttered earthward and boomed in rapid-fire succession among the parked airplanes, where hot shrapnel ripped into full fuel tanks, igniting massive secondary detonations that annihilated the airplanes.

The attack ended as abruptly as it started, the Japanese vanishing into the distance only about three minutes after they'd first been sighted. In front of the hangar, the mangled remains of eight airplanes raged aflame under roiling palls of oily black smoke—three Curtiss Condors, the three Eurasia planes, and CNAC's two DC-2s. Another greasy smudge jetted skyward from the ruins of the Pan Am Clipper. The Royal Air Force's contingent of pathetic biplanes—three Vildebeest torpedo bombers and two Walrus amphibians—burned at the other end of the field.

Advised of the spread of war by a call from Mr. Moss even before Haynie phoned, Chuck Sharp was headed for the door of his Eu Gardens apartments at 158 Argyle Street when an airplane engine screamed in at low altitude. Huge explosions quaked the building and drilled craters in the pavement directly in front, rocking Hugh Woods and Maj Majors out of bed—the bombs missed the apartment complex by less than thirty feet. Enemy spies had discovered that most of CNAC's American pilots lived in the complex, and it was targeted for destruction in the first wave of attack. Sharp, Woods, and the other staff members in the building sent their wives or girlfriends to shelter among boulders on a hillside above the apartments.

Moon Chin had intended to sleep late that Monday morning. About a month before, he and his wife had moved into a new flat on the second floor of a three-story apartment on the uphill side of Prince Edward Road, about a mile from the airport. They'd almost finished furnishing the new place, and Moon had been up late on Sunday night, struggling to anchor a light fixture to the concrete ceiling. Awakened by the growl of multiple airplane engines, he sat up in bed and tried to make sense of the noise. He could see most of the Kai Tak hangar through the bedroom window. The tail of DC-2 number 24, the *Nanking*, poked from behind an intervening building. Farther away, the rear half of the Pan Am Clipper protruded past the hangar, floating low. Gentle harbor swells rocked its outboard wingtip and most distant propeller in and out of Moon Chin's vision. He'd heard a Canadian infantry regiment was moving up to the Gin Drinker's Line built across the Kowloon Peninsula and thought the engines were British planes escorting them forward. A formation of pursuit planes dropped into the frame of his window, dipped to low altitude, and raced toward the Pan Am Clipper like dragonflies skimming the surface of a pond. The Clipper burst into flame an instant later. *My God, those planes are Japanese!* he realized. The level bombers came into view, promptly followed by explosions tearing through the airplanes parked around the hangar. Moon watched number 24's tail crumple and burn. He'd been flying it regularly since 1935. Ugly billows of jet-black smoke plumed above the devastation. From Moon's perspective, it looked like CNAC's entire air fleet had been annihilated and that he'd just been bombed out of a job. He had his wife and mother to think about. He sprang out of bed, dressed, and drove to the market to buy rice, soft fish, and other supplies before prices rose. Market vendors didn't yet know what Moon Chin had seen with his own eyes—that the war had come to Hong Kong.

William Bond gunned his car across the spine of Hong Kong Island and descended into Victoria town like a bootlegger with G-men on his tail, covering six miles in minutes. The streets were strangely deserted. An air-raid warden flagged Bond to a halt and ordered him off the road. Bond insisted on going through. No sooner had he circumvented the first warden than he had to repeat the process with a second, and then a third. Bond was furious: The Japanese were almost certainly trying to bomb his airline out of existence, if they hadn't done so already, and he was wasting time with stuffed-shirt colonial air-raid wardens.

In central Hong Kong, Bond curbed his car in front of the Gloucester Hotel, where CNAC had an office in the corner of the outdoor walking arcade. Inside, Bond jogged past the mural of the world showing "The Routes of the Flying Clippers," bounded upstairs, and barged into his office on the mezzanine. He had the telephone in his hand before the door drifted shut, but he couldn't get through to the airport, finally slamming the phone into its cradle and sprinting four hundred yards downhill to the Star Ferry terminal, only to find that it wasn't running. Angry people anxious to get to their families crowded against the barred entry. Bond approached a uniformed police sergeant waiting in the throng. "My duty station is Kowloonside too," the sergeant explained, "but regulations prohibit boat traffic during air raids."

"But you're a police sergeant! Use your authority to make one of the motor launches take us over." Across the harbor, Bond could see smoke rising from Kai Tak.

Nothing was allowed to move until the release sounded, the sergeant reiterated.

"But there's a war on! And we're both supposed to fight it in Kowloon."

"I'm sorry, sir, but I can't do that. It's against regulations. I might be demoted."

"That sounds like an excellent idea," Bond snapped.

Without the policeman, and despite the fistful of Hong Kong currency he was waving, Bond couldn't persuade any of the small launches milling about the ferry terminal to take him across.

He spied a Canadian officer and three soldiers and surmised that they belonged to one of the units defending the Gin Drinker's Line. The three rifles, the officer's pistol, and Bond's wad of cash at last persuaded a *wallah-wallah* sampan owner to ferry them across. No Japanese planes were visible during the trip, but Bond couldn't tear his eyes from the smoke pillars above Kai Tak.

The ferry terminal on the Kowloon side seethed with Chinese civilians frantic to get to Hong Kong Island. People needed food, water, and cash to survive the crisis, and their life savings were on the island, where most of the colony's banks were located. British police forbade the Chinese residents of Kowloon to cross the harbor, and the mob was furious. Bond flagged a taxi and rode the short distance to the Peninsula Hotel. One of his employees in the lobby broke the news: nobody hurt, three Condors, two DC-2s, and three of Eurasia's Junkers destroyed. Amazingly, the hangar hadn't been bombed. Inside, DC-3s number 41 and number 46 and DC-2 number 31 had escaped damage. Plus, McDonald had DC-3 number 47 in Burma. Four airplanes, and three of them were DC-3s. William Bond still had an airline. At 9:35 A.M., Bond radioed McDonald orders to fly to Chungking, and from there, pending developments, to continue to Hong Kong after dark.

Moon Chin got a call from company operations when he returned home from the market.

"Get ready to leave tonight."

"But the planes burned up. How're we going to get out?"

"The hangar didn't get hit. Two of the Threes were inside. McDonald's got the other in Burma. Number 31's okay. You're flying it tonight. Get your wife ready. We're getting out."

At the airport, Bond found Chuck Sharp, Zygmund Soldinski, Hugh Woods, five other pilots, and a gang of mechanics and airport coolies working feverishly to tractor the surviving transports from the hangar to positions on the dirt road that rimmed the interior of the airport fence, spread about three hundred yards apart. The air-raid alarm shrieked, and everybody scattered. The dispersals weren't good: The Japanese were sure to spot the airplanes. Vegetable patches tended by Chinese peasants beyond the road *outside* the perimeter fence and tucked against the base of Kowloon Peak promised the best camouflage and were geographically difficult to bomb or strafe due to the steep contours of the adjacent escarpment, but there was the fence, a berm, and a ditch to get across, and the villagers weren't at all enthusiastic about hosting the cumbersome prize targets in their cultivations. After fifteen minutes with no raid materializing, the men went back to work. Soldinski gave bolt cutters to one of his mechanics and told him to cut the chain-link fence in two places. Bond went to get permission from Mr. Moss, who, predictably, refused to let the airline destroy Crown property, but by then it was too late—Soldinski had hitched the tractor to the cut section of fence and torn it away.

On the far side of the road, Soldinski used the tractor to shove a section of the dirt berm into the drainage culvert. Airport coolies smoothed and finished the job with hand tools and, one by one, Soldinski tractored the three surviving transports through the fence gap and across the road and his hastily built bridge to dispersal positions in the vegetable patches. Coolies sloshed mud on the wings and fuselages and sprinkled the aircraft with armloads of straw as the peasants swore and ranted and threatened to burn the planes. Sharp and Soldinski persuaded Moss to deploy armed guards, and, facing the inevitable, most villagers decided to spend the day elsewhere. Once the precious airplanes were camouflaged and the guards posted, there was nothing else to do to safeguard them except hope, and wait for darkness.

Inside the hangar, the maintenance and storeroom staffs prioritized people and spare parts for evacuation: radios and communications gear, instruments and spare tires, engines, ailerons, rudders, tools, and all the rest. Few people in Hong Kong were as valuable to China as CNAC's operations staff. It took years to train technical aviation specialists. An aircraft mechanic was harder to replace than a Chinese general. There were certainly fewer of the former—and a lot more demand for their services.

Bond, P. Y. Wong, Soldinski, and Sharp had roughed together an evacuation plan more than a year before, but it was predicated on being able to use the freight-carrying Condors to shuttle parts, equipment, and tools to Namyung while the DC-2s and DC-3s evacuated company personnel, families, and important Chinese and foreign officials to Chungking. The Japanese bombs had blasted the plan out of relevance. Bond, Sharp, and Soldinski made the best of the leftovers.

A radioman handed Bond a message from H. H. Kung asking him to ensure the evacuation of his family. Madame Kung and their two daughters were in Hong Kong, and so was Madame Kung's sister, Soong Ching-ling, widow of Dr. Sun Yat-sen. Bond recognized rescuing Soong family members as his top priority. A plethora of messages from Chinese, British, and American authorities arrived on the heels of Dr. Kung's request, all instructing Bond exactly what he should do and when. He sorted through them a few times. Each seemed more inane than the last. He tore them to pieces and dropped the shreds in a wastebasket.

He surveyed the hangar. Sharp and Soldinski seemed to have the evacuation preparations in hand. To Zygmund Soldinski, it seemed utter chaos, too many people milling about without specific tasks to accomplish. Soldinski dragged Chuck Sharp into his office. "Get your goddamned pilots out of here. There ain't anything for 'em to do. They're just getting in the way."

Sharp summoned the flight personnel—pilots, copilots, and radio operators. He made flight assignments and described the evacuation procedures. "Staff and families fly out tonight. Ten kilograms of baggage per person. Go home and get organized. Be here before dark. Bring your children, wives, and girlfriends. We'll probably have to put 'em on the same flight, so let's hope they get along." That won a few chuckles. He might not have been joking. "Most of the staff is going to Namyung with the spares and tools. Each DC will shuttle twice to Namyung and return. The third flight goes direct to Chungking. Tomorrow night we'll come back here after dark, fly a round-trip to Namyung, then return to Chungking. We'll keep doing that, in and out of Hong Kong at night, just like always, until the Japs start dropping shells on Kai Tak. Questions?"

There were a few, after which all the pilots except Hugh Woods and Hal Sweet were banished. Those two culled essential flight and maintenance paperwork. Soldinski detailed mechanics to the vegetable patches to work on the number one engine, the left, of DC-3 number 41, which had a bad main bearing. The mechanics had been prepping a replacement engine but hadn't finished when the attack hit. Changing an engine was too big a job to tackle that Monday, but Soldinski thought his men could jury-rig the bad one into temporary utility. He ordered other mechanics to try to get the lone surviving Condor into flying condition. It had been given to Eurasia by the Ministry of Finance, but hadn't been put into service and was now the only plane in Hong Kong with a cargo door big enough to admit CNAC's two spare DC-3 engines.*

Bond felt a surge of pride as he watched his men operate. Only a few hours had passed since the Japanese sucker punch, and the airline was already off the canvas. Every man had a job and was doing it beautifully. Bond left Sharp and Soldinski to sweat the details. He needed to see Madame Kung, who had a suite at the Gloucester Hotel on Hong Kong Island, above the CNAC office he'd rushed through early that morning. There didn't seem to be any Japanese planes aloft, and a mechanic agreed to ferry Bond across the harbor in a motor launch Pan Am maintained to service the flying boats, but the launch's water pump malfunctioned a few hundred yards from shore, and at about one-thirty in the afternoon, they turned back to Kai Tak. Bond had just put his foot ashore when the air-raid sirens wailed.

The foreign pilots and ground personnel vanished in the pilots' cars. Bond loaded the Chinese staff into the company truck and sent them away from the airport, directing two Chinese mechanics who couldn't fit to the drainage culvert beyond the airport fence. He stayed at the hangar, loitering near a ditch in case an attack materialized. Airport manager Moss drove by and swerved to a stop. "Hop in, Bondy! I've had the office sandbagged. We'll be fine unless the Nips drop one through the roof."

Two tripod-mounted machine guns manned by Indian soldiers flanked the gatehouse where Moss kept his office. Two English riflemen, their sergeant, and several members of the airport staff crowded inside. The dreaded sound of airplane engines heralded a new attack wave flashing in and out of broken clouds over the New Territories. This time, there was no doubt. They were Japanese. Antiaircraft fire boomed from batteries around the colony, without discernible effect. For twenty minutes, the bombers focused on targets in Kowloon and the harbor. Then a flight swerved for Kai

---

* Two 1,000-horsepower Curtiss-Wright R-1820 G103 Cyclone engines.

Tak. Bond crossed his fingers and willed the Japanese not to see his airplanes. He could start fighting this war if the transports survived until dark. The Indian machine gunners rattled through belts of ammunition—cha-cha-cha-cha—as the planes roared overhead. Bond heard the telltale swish of falling bombs. "Take cover!"

The Indian gunners continued blasting away as the bombs fell. Everyone else in the gatehouse threw themselves to the floor. The nearest bomb hit the edge of the field three hundred yards away. Most fell beyond the fence, nowhere near the camouflaged airplanes. The bombers disappeared around Kowloon Peak, but the release didn't sound. Finally, at 2:30 P.M., Hong Kong colonial governor-general Sir Mark Young came on the radio to announce to the general population what had been obvious at Kai Tak Airport for more than six hours, that a state of war existed between Great Britain and the Empire of Japan.

Another Japanese bomber formation attacked the airport at ten minutes to three, flying above the range of light-caliber guns. Eight large bombs exploded around the hangar, and the release sounded soon after. Bond and Moss inspected the damage. The bomb divots blasted in the field proved of little consequence, but daylight shone through a hole in the hangar roof. Thick yellow dust covered the floor, spiked with jagged chunks of bomb casing. In the middle of the mess, a mauled aileron hung from a wing of Eurasia's sole surviving tri-motored Junkers. A Japanese bombardier had dead-centered the hangar with a one-hundred-kilogram dud that clipped the Junkers' aileron a millisecond before it shattered on the concrete floor.

Bond and Moss couldn't resist the impulse to fiddle around in the bomb detritus. Bond should have known better. The yellow dust was picric acid, the compound used in Japanese explosives, which stained his shoes and clothes and triggered a poison-ivy-like rash on his hands. Worse, he inhaled some acidic dust and developed a painful, persistent cough.

Late in the afternoon, Bond fought through mounting chaos to the Star Ferry terminal, intending to try again to cross to Hong Kong Island to see Madame Kung. Lacking the newly required police permit to go over, he returned to the airport among lengthening shadows.

Pilot Billy McDonald reported leaving Chungking in DC-3 number 47. The sun vanished at 5:40 P.M., and Bond's heart soared as darkness gathered. The China National Aviation Corporation had survived the day. Soldinski towed the three Douglases back to the hangar front, parked them among the airplane wreckage, and the staff rushed loads on board. Number 46 was the first off the field, at 7 P.M., with Frank Higgs,* of Columbus, Ohio, at the controls, taking parts, company personnel, and family members to Namyung. Soldinski checked the work his mechanics had done on the main bearing of DC-3 number 41's left engine and judged it rigged well enough for takeoff. Soldinski explained the situation to Chuck Sharp. He was pretty sure number 41's left engine would stand takeoff, but nothing more. It would have to be shut down at cruising altitude. After that, it was a single-engine airplane. Both men understood the risk. If Soldinski proved wrong, takeoff power failure would cause a crash. They summoned Hal Sweet, the man who'd flown the DC-2½.

Sweet listened to the explications. "Get it ready. I'll fly it."

Sharp asked Sweet how much load he could handle.

"Full load."

Soldinski's final tweaks to the engine caused a short delay. Sweet took off fifteen minutes behind Higgs, without incident. Aloft, he killed the number one engine, feathered its prop, and cruised to Namyung with fifty-four passengers on board, two and a half times normal capacity.

Radio trouble delayed the DC-2 even further. Specialists worried at the problem under hooded floodlights. Airline people and their families filled every seat and crammed the aisles, clutching small bags. Young children sat on their parents' laps; babies clung to their mothers' shoulders. Spare parts, tools, and sundry aviation gear filled every cranny. Moon Chin fought through the throng to the cockpit and settled into the pilot's seat, and Pop Kessler squeezed in beside him. Nothing had been officially weighed. Moon had no idea exactly how much load he had on board, but his gut told him the plane would fly, and that was enough. He lifted off at 7:45 P.M.

William Bond finally raised Madame Kung on the telephone seventy-five minutes later. He'd been trying to reach her all afternoon. He told

---

* Frank Higgs was a fraternity brother of cartoonist Milton Caniff and served as the model of Caniff's character Dude Hennick in Caniff's iconic comic strip *Terry and the Pirates*.

her about the message he'd received from her husband, and that he had four planes in action. He wanted her and her family evacuated as soon as possible.

Madame Kung declined, thinking it too dangerous. "The Japanese just committed hara-kari," she informed him. "The governor said he can hold Kowloon for a month. The American fleet will be here in three weeks and the war will be over."

Bond was incredulous. He'd thought her far too canny to be such an ostrich but was careful to keep his skepticism to himself. In any event, it was too late to get her to the airport that night. Bond suggested she wait and see how everything proceeded. If all went well, perhaps she'd consider getting out the following night. Afterward, Bond drove to the Peninsula Hotel, where he tried to convince important officers of the Central Bank, other high officials, and members of the joint Chinese-American Currency Stabilization Board to evacuate. Only Emmanuel Fox of the stabilization board seemed to appreciate the urgency. Like Madame Kung, the others wanted to wait.

Frank Higgs's return from Namyung in number 46 triggered another air-raid alarm, until he switched on his cabin lights and was recognized. On the ground, Higgs passed word from Namyung: Hal Sweet had landed safely, but as feared, he'd burned up the left main bearing. Number 41 was stuck, needing a new engine. The false alarms repeated when Moon Chin and Pop Kessler came in with the DC-2.

There were other pilots available to fly, but Moon Chin had more "time in type" and an order of magnitude more time in China than any of the other DC-2 pilots, Caucasian or otherwise, and nothing could pry him loose from number 31's left-hand seat. There was face involved, and the emergency gave him another chance to drive home a point he'd been trying to make with steady service since the winter of 1933—that he was the equal of any of the Caucasian fliers.

The Socony employees had fled with their fuel trucks at the first false alarm. Fortunately, the airline had an emergency stash of high-octane fuel in five-gallon tins. Soldinski, his ground staff, and the crew of the stranded Clipper carried cans until their arms felt as if they would fall off, enabling the planes to make a second trip to Namyung.

. . .

Billy McDonald brought the last DC-3 in at about 1 A.M., triggering yet another air-raid alarm. Considering the logistics of loading, unloading, and fueling time, there wasn't enough darkness remaining to get McDonald back and forth to Namyung. He loaded for Chungking instead.

The situation was fluid; anything could happen. Bond considered Hugh Woods "shockproof," and he wanted Woody in Chungking to manage incoming traffic and handle emergencies. He ordered Woody to fly to Chungking with McDonald.

Mr. Fox of the Currency Stabilization Board, eight members of his staff, K. P. Chen and Tsuyi Pei* of the Central Bank, one Chinese general, and a few others presented themselves for evacuation. CNAC ran them aboard McDonald and Woody's DC-3 and maxed out the remaining load with company personnel and family members. Many more important officials could have been evacuated. None appeared. Most of the spares and tools went aboard with eyeball calculations, but Woods had charge of the departure scales for individual baggage to make sure no one left with more than the ten allotted kilograms. With each plane loaded to the absolute edge of capacity, a few kilos of uncalculated load could mean the difference between successful takeoff and fiery disaster. Woody's fiancée, Maj Major, was manifested aboard. Technically, Maj wasn't company family, but Bond had given Woody permission to get her out.

Maj wore a dark pantsuit and her favorite string of pearls. Woods hefted her suitcase onto the scale. The suitcase sank, slowly, a bare fraction too heavy. "Please, Hugh," Maj pleaded quietly. Everything inside was necessary or sentimental.

"Sorry, Maj," Woody muttered. "Ten kilos."

Maj's eyes blazed. Surely a few grams wouldn't make any difference?

"Maj, I'm sorry," Woods said gently. "There's nothing I can do."

She snatched her suitcase from the scale, yanked out a beautiful evening gown, and held it up for inspection. It was his absolute favorite. She dumped it on the oily concrete, resealed her suitcase, and boarded the plane without further comment.

Woods and McDonald left at 2 A.M. Higgs and Moon Chin returned

---

* Father of famed architect I. M. Pei.

from Namyung with their Douglases a second time and were loaded and dispatched to Chungking. Moon took his wife. His mother had opted to stay and look after her Kowloon apartment. As many as sixty people went out on each of the Threes, planes designed to carry twenty-one. Bond drove Woody's Mercury sedan to the Peninsula Hotel and limped to his room. One of his legs throbbed with what he assumed was a charley horse; he couldn't remember how he'd gotten it. He collapsed into bed at 5:30 A.M. without undressing or bothering to examine his aching leg and tossed for more than an hour, hacking and coughing, finally relaxing toward sleep. The air-raid sirens wailed at quarter to seven. Bond stayed in bed. The fourth floor of the Peninsula Hotel seemed as safe as anywhere in Kowloon and he wanted sleep so badly. The release shrieked fifteen minutes later, and the alarm howled fifteen minutes after that. It was useless. Bond went downstairs for breakfast and walked to the police station and got a permit to cross the harbor. The alert was still on when he reached the Star Ferry, but the boats had received permission to run during alerts and crossed without attracting the enemy planes bombing coastal fortifications on Hong Kong Island. The island seemed more secure than Kowloon. Aside from distant bomb detonations, conditions in central Hong Kong didn't strike Bond as too far from normal.

Madame Kung received Bond in her Gloucester Hotel suite. The night's flying had gone well, he told her, and he urged her to get out. If she went, she said, she'd have fifteen people in her party and they'd require their own fully dedicated, private airplane.

Bond didn't protest. He was too exhausted, and it wouldn't help. All he cared about was getting her to the airport.

M. Y. Tong's office in the Bank of Canton was in the same block. Bond tried to find his old friend, but the bank was closed, and he couldn't raise Tong on either his office or home telephone. Considering how close he was to T. V. Soong, Bond felt certain Soong would want to evacuate Tong and his family.

Bond went to the hospital near the Happy Valley Racecourse, where managing director P. Y. Wong was being treated. A nurse showed him in to see his partner, asking for quiet. After all they'd been through, Bond loathed the thought of leaving Wong behind. He'd concocted a plan for a series of ambulances and stretcher relays to take Wong, his wife, and daughter to the Star Ferry, the Peninsula Hotel, where Bond would give them his room, and thence to the airport. Woody would have a stretcher meet the plane in Chungking. Wong could recuperate in the wartime capital.

Both Wong and his wife felt he was too ill to travel. He'd stay and chance occupation, promising to do what he could to safeguard company assets left behind.

Dismayed, Bond ferried back to the mainland as the afternoon waned. Reams of messages awaited him at the Peninsula, among them a radiogram from vice minister of communications and chairman of the board Peng Sho-pei ordering Bond, Sharp, and Soldinski to "come out tonight unless you have strong reason to the contrary" and a telephone message from one of Madame Kung's daughters. Bond returned the call immediately. The younger Kung courteously informed Bond her mother would fly that night. Bond asked them to be at the airport by 2 A.M.

The phone in Bond's room rang incessantly. A parade of people came seeking advice. In the lulls, Bond tried again and again to reach M. Y. Tong, horrified to think he was on the verge of losing both P. Y. Wong and M. Y. Tong, his two closest Chinese friends. He drove Woody's Mercury to the airport. Clouds hid the quarter moon. Blacked-out Kowloon was "dark as the inside of a whale," and Bond hadn't slept in more than forty hours. Twice, he got badly lost. At the airport, Mr. Moss told him the Hong Kong command feared a Crete-style air landing and intended to blow up the airfield the next day. Flabbergasted, Bond begged Moss to leave a three-hundred-foot-wide strip from which his airline could operate. The *crump-pause-boom* of distant artillery interrupted their conversation. Were the thuds creeping closer? It took a lot of pleading, but Moss finally agreed to leave a strip, although with such little enthusiasm that Bond feared he might renege. That meant the airline had to get out of Hong Kong immediately. That night. He and Sharp chose a skeleton staff to stay in Hong Kong. Everybody else had to be taken to Namyung and Chungking.

The three planes coming in from Chungking didn't arrive until after 10 P.M. Fortunately, Standard Oil was back in action, albeit without its Chinese staff. Three of its top Western executives drove the fuel trucks.

Madame Kung's party arrived three and a half hours earlier than expected, at 10:30 P.M., with mountains of baggage and 1,200 pounds of documents she considered essential to Central Government survival. She insisted on leaving immediately, aboard the first available plane, and her imperious dictates lit operations manager Chuck Sharp's short Texas fuse. He'd scheduled himself to fly the Soong party later that night. Soldinski dragged him aside just before detonation, and William Bond stepped into the breach. The evacuations were proceeding according to plan, he explained. She'd leave for Chungking at about 3 A.M., after the planes shuttled to Namyung.

"I want to go now, on that plane," she said, indicating the nearest DC-3.

"I'm sorry, madame. You'll go on that plane, but at three o'clock. It has to go to Namyung first."

"Let it go to Chungking now, with my party."

"We can't do that, madame. I'm sorry, but if it goes to Chungking, it can't get back here before daylight and we lose the Namyung trip."

"Then let it remain in Chungking and return tomorrow after dark."

Madame Kung's teenage daughter took her mother's arm. "Oh, Mummy, let Mr. Bond handle it. They know what they're doing."

Bond excused himself to other business. The three flights went to Namyung, and the airline loaded the Kungs into McDonald's DC-3, the first to return. The ground staff got them strapped down with their most critical items of hand luggage, then four pilots riding to Chungking came aboard. Behind them, mechanics loaded crate after crate of greasy spares and heavy tools until they'd gotten the plane stowed far beyond "max." Chuck Sharp had his ire under control when he boarded with his hand luggage and two pet dachshunds.

"My documents?" Madame Kung asked. They seemed on the verge of being forgotten.

Sharp assured her that he'd taken care of them and loosed his dogs inside the plane.

Pulling seniority, Sharp nudged Bill McDonald into the copilot's seat. McDonald eyed the load behind them. "No way this son of a bitch'll take off."

Sharp flashed his rogue's grin. "You're right. It won't. But it'll fly."

They restarted the engines, proofed the controls, and checked the instruments. Sharp released the brakes, slid the throttles forward, and steered the plane downfield. The harsh floodlight glared across the stubbled grass. The engines wailed, and the Douglas slugged to flying speed. Sharp got the tail up, but the plane was lead-heavy on its main wheels, hurtling toward the seawall at the edge of the grass at ninety miles per hour.

McDonald edged back in his seat. "Chuck?" The plane wasn't going to take off.

Number 47 smacked the dirt berm angled to meet the back of the rock seawall at the end of the field and vaulted into the darkness. The props clawed for purchase, the Douglas dropped from the apogee of its bounce, and Sharp fought to keep the nose level. McDonald yanked up the landing gear. The plane fell until it caught the cushion of air trapped between the water and the underside of the wings. The prop blades nearly sliced the water, but the ground effect provided an extra iota of lift and saved the plane. Sharp climbed into "the Gap" between the mainland and the western edge of Hong Kong Island inch by full-power inch.

William McDonald was a tough man to ruffle, a vastly experienced aerobatics pilot who had flown dozens of hours quite literally roped to his wingmen John "Luke" Williamson and Claire Lee Chennault as part of their "Three Men on a Flying Trapeze" stunt-flying act in the early and middle 1930s, but the launch from Kai Tak was a first. Sharp was a hothead, without doubt, but after that takeoff, whenever someone commented on Sharp's volatility in McDonald's presence, he would say, "Yeah, maybe, but in the cockpit that guy pisses ice water."

The last plane at Kai Tak Airfield was Moon Chin's DC-2, number 31, the *Chungshan*. William Bond's gimpy leg had deteriorated, and he limped around the hangar in substantial pain, but he still hadn't bothered to drop his trousers and examine it. There seemed no point: He couldn't capitulate to it. His acid-burn cough had worsened, too. Nearing the end of his second consecutive night without sleep, he found it increasingly difficult to reason coherently. He'd be useless to the airline unless he could get some rest. He resigned himself to the fact that he'd never get any in Hong Kong. Besides, Peng Sho-pei's instructions made sense. He'd be able to do more from Chungking. Moon Chin was cool in the clutch; Bond decided to evacuate on his plane. A Pan American employee named Charles Schafer volunteered to stay in Hong Kong and coordinate outbound traffic.

Moon and Elsie Chin had lost their entire household in Shanghai in 1937. They'd rebuilt their possessions in Hong Kong, but they were on the verge of losing everything a second time. They were doing well compared with most of the evacuees as far as saving personal belongings—they'd each taken a bag to Chungking, and Moon had taken a bag to Namyung on each of his other flights. There was, however, one last thing Moon Chin wanted to rescue. While the flight loaded, Moon drove home. He returned to the airport, abandoned his car, and waddled toward the waiting airplane toting a suitcase-sized Telefunken short-wave entertainment radio.

Most of the operations staff had already evacuated. Most of the leftovers were shoved aboard number 31. The last mechanics perched on their heavy toolboxes and clutched personal baggage. The plane was ready, but where was Moon Chin? William Langhorne Bond stood on the top step at the passenger door and waited for his pilot. Moon Chin staggered out of the darkness lugging the Telefunken. Bond limped down the ladder. He coughed, forced a smile, and shook his head. "That's too much," he said. "You can't take that."

Moon Chin couldn't afford to cross Bond. He'd secreted his daughter-in-law in the plane's radio compartment. Bond might or might not have known, but without official permission, Moon couldn't chance her fate on Bond's ire, so he set down the Telefunken, climbed the stepladder, and forced his way to the cockpit. He and his copilot soon had the engines running and the plane bouncing across the surface of Kai Tak at full throttle, accelerating toward flying speed. Moon Chin got the tail up, but just like Sharp, he couldn't break contact with the earth. The ground staff had mistakenly filled number 31's cabin fuel tank. That unexpected burden and the mechanics' heavy toolboxes threw the plane far past takeoff weight. The dirt berm piled against the seawall at the field's edge chucked Moon's Douglas into the air, just as it had for Chuck Sharp, and just as coolly, Moon Chin held the nose level as the plane leapt and fell. The ground effect caught the plane above the water, but Moon's plane was so absurdly overweight that it wouldn't climb at all. Moon Chin threaded through "the Gap" down the Lei Yue Mun and Tathong channels between Hong Kong Island and the Chinese mainland a few feet above the water. The engines burned fuel and the plane lost weight. Moon eked his way to altitude over the South China Sea, turned, and made for distant Chungking.

An hour or two after daybreak on Wednesday morning, Chuck Sharp greased Madame Kung and Madame Sun Yat-sen onto the cobblestone airstrip below Chungking. Officials and journalists astute enough to realize

Madame Kung and Madame Sun Yat-sen would likely be among the evacuees had gathered to meet the plane, bundled against the December chill, for the Soongs always made good copy. The plane's Hamilton Standard propellers windmilled to a halt in front of the crude passenger terminal, and a ground crew pushed a ladder against the plane. As the passenger door popped open, two frightened dachshunds burst through, bounded down the steps, and tore dusty circles amid the horseshoe of onlookers. The two grand ladies appeared in the doorway and were bundled off by their entourage without public comment.

The pressmen touched off a mini-storm with snide remarks about Madame Kung evacuating dogs when so many important people were trapped in Hong Kong, and the truth that the dogs belonged to Charles Lamar Sharp of Fort Worth, Texas, operations manager of the China National Aviation Corporation, never overtook the rumor. Sharp hadn't lied to Madame Kung, either. He *had* arranged to take care of her papers. The staff left behind in Hong Kong soaked them in aviation fuel and burned them to cinders.

Frank Higgs brought in the second DC-3. Moon Chin came in last, in the DC-2, carrying William Bond and many others. Expecting to fly again through the coming night, Moon catnapped in the passenger cabin after his passengers dispersed. Bond, Woods, and Sharp huddled over the operational details. Sharp planned to go back as a passenger and fly out the surviving Condor with the two spare DC-3 engines that were too big to fit through a Douglas passenger door—the few mechanics still in Hong Kong were trying to get the Condor airworthy. As the scheme solidified, they received a message from Mr. Moss ordering them not to return. Moss gave no explanation, but the wording was clear. CNAC stood down the airplanes.

Every room at the Rappes' Methodist compound had at least three occupants. Bond crossed to the South Bank, where U.S. naval attaché James McHugh lent him a bed. Bond's left leg throbbed with pain, and he sat on the edge of the bed and eased off his trousers for the first time since Monday morning. His leg was an ugly, swollen mess, tinged a sickening grayish yellow below the thigh and darkening toward his foot and ankle, both of which were as "black as a bowler hat." Sometime on December 8, he'd burst a pack of blood vessels without realizing it. Bond hadn't slept in fifty-three hours. He heaved the hurt leg onto the bed, lay down, settled his cough, and blacked out. He slept from one-thirty Wednesday afternoon until eight o'clock Thursday morning.

The Chinese government pressured the airline to resume evacuation flights, and Bond visited the British ambassador to China, Sir Archibald Clark-Kerr, to see what he could arrange. Clark-Kerr rushed a message to the Hong Kong command and got permission to make two flights between 9 P.M. and midnight. Bond asked to make more, but received no response. Frank Higgs, Bill McDonald, and Moon Chin left Chungking in the three operational Douglases at 4 P.M. An hour into the flight, Moss ordered them to desist, again giving no reason. The pilots diverted to Namyung and began the more leisurely process of bringing the company employees who'd been evacuated there the rest of the way to Chungking.

Five Japanese pursuits attacked the Namyung field at daybreak, too late to snare the evacuation flights, but the marauders caught DC-3 number 41 on the ground, stuck with its useless engine. The Japanese made dozens of strafing passes. Drained of gas and oil, the plane didn't burn, but by the time the Japanese flew away, ammunition expended, number 41 was holed in hundreds of places. Bullets ruined engines, propellers, and landing gear, shredded tires, shattered instruments, snapped control cables, and punctured the ship's hydraulic lines and fuel tanks. Mechanics dismantled the wounded carcass and carted the parts to camouflaged positions in rice paddies several miles from the airfield. The initial damage summary estimated that it would take five or six months to return the plane to service.

By that point, Kowloon was in chaos. Mobs plundered the town. The British command issued orders to abandon the peninsula, and the last of the Punjabi rear guard crossed the Star Ferry to Hong Kong Island in the wee hours of Friday morning. The British weren't under pressure from anything except gangs of Chinese thugs venting their hatred and looting in the city. Later on Friday, the Japanese entered Kowloon without resistance. Only in retrospect did Moon Chin realize that Hong Kong was the second Chinese city out of which he'd piloted the last evacuation flight.

The U.S. government listening post in Ventura, California, received a radiogram for Katharine Dunlop Bond on Saturday, December 13, 1941, the first she'd heard from her husband since Pearl Harbor. "I am safely in

Chungking and feeling fine," it said. "All our Americans are here. Have plenty of everything I shall need until we win this war and that will not be long. Everything is fine and the goose is hanging high. Love Bondy."

The man himself wasn't feeling so jaunty. On doctor's orders, he spent Sunday in bed. His leg improved, but he moved around too much on Monday and had to return to the infirmary. Chuck Sharp was using the airplanes to recover the evacuated tools, spares, people, and sundry equipment from Namyung. Coolies carried Bond to the office on Tuesday. He forced himself to stay seated and wrote a detailed letter about the evacuation to Harold Bixby, hoping it would serve "for reference in the future." Typed by one of the company secretaries, it ran to ten single-spaced pages and, disseminated by Bixby, it would be read throughout the American government.*

In summary, Bond was characteristically self-critical. "It was a bad show," he wrote. ". . . CNAC got badly caught . . . [but] after the hell broke loose we did our best to save the pieces. . . . We were doing alright until the Hong Kong government stopped us. . . . If you think this is a lousy alibi, I would like you to know that I think so too." Bond felt he should have seen it coming. His men, however, had been humblingly magnificent. "Each pilot wanted to fly every flight." The only way to stop fights between the senior pilots had been to assign two of them to each flight. "Sharp was a wheel horse and as steady as a rock. Soldinski, as usual, rode herd on everything in sight. . . . It is difficult to pick out outstanding cases, however. Every man did his job." And that, coming from William Bond, was high praise, indeed. A man did his job, and that was all. It was hard to swallow the loss of five airplanes and such a large quantity of stores and spare parts, not to mention P. Y. Wong and M. Y. Tong—he'd had no news of Tong whatsoever—but to Bond's eye, they were in better shape than they'd been in after losing Shanghai in 1937 or Hankow in 1938.

---

* That letter (Bond to Bixby, December 17, 1941, the San Diego Air & Space Museum), along with the author's interviews with Moon Chin, Frieda (Chinn) Chen, and T. T. Chen is the cornerstone primary source of this chapter. It is excerpted in *The Morgenthau Diaries*, Vol. 1, pp. 622–23, the entry making it clear that the letter was read by Lauchlin Currie and by members of the State and Treasury departments. Frieda was the sister of Donald Wong and the wife of pilot Paul Chinn, who was killed in early 1941, after which she served as P. Y. Wong's secretary and then Bond's. She married T. T. Chen in 1943 and resigned from the airline in 1948.

. . .

The airline's performance wasn't anywhere near as sorry as Bond imagined. Weeks would pass before Bond understood events and came to appreciate the multiplicity of disaster that had beset the Allied militaries in the Far East and the Pacific over the last ten days. Their armies and navies had fared infinitely worse: At Pearl Harbor, eight battleships and eleven other warships sunk or badly damaged, two hundred planes destroyed on the ground and another hundred damaged, 2,400 Americans killed; a hundred planes lost in the Philippines, most on the ground, even though the American military command had received notice of the Pearl Harbor attack at 2:30 A.M. local time, nearly ten hours before the main Japanese air raid, a grotesque negligence; the Royal Air Force smashed on the ground in Malaya; the HMS *Prince of Wales* and *Repulse* sunk by torpedo bombers in less than an hour on December 10; Japanese armies ashore on the Malay Peninsula and in the Philippines; Guam lost; Shanghai's international settlements stormed and occupied; Wake Island besieged. Most Allied military commands took weeks to function at peak efficiency. The China National Aviation Corporation operated at full surviving capacity within eleven hours of the attack, and even then it had only been waiting for darkness to shield its unarmed operations. Bond grew increasingly angry as he gleaned details of the attacks. Pearl Harbor had been ravaged many hours before Hong Kong. The U.S. government knew. The Army and Navy knew, as did Pan American's base in Honolulu. The British colonial government had learned in the wee hours of the morning. Not one of them had bothered to notify CNAC. Properly informed, Bond and Sharp could have saved all their airplanes. It was a bitter irony, but the December attacks left two civilian entities as the most functional and professionally competent facets of Allied airpower in the Far East: Claire Lee Chennault's American Volunteer Group and William Langhorne Bond's China National Aviation Corporation. Both would play enormous roles in the campaigns yet to come.

The New York Times and *The Washington Post* released news of the Hong Kong evacuation on December 15, 1941, hailing it as "the most perilous bit of work in the history of commercial aviation." The CNAC pilots relished the notoriety, as most pilots do, but they weren't overly impressed. Their terse operational prose described the evacuation flights as "without incident."* The loads were larger and more chaotic and the Japanese were closer and Kai Tak had gotten bombed, but the flights weren't substantially different from the hundreds of others they'd made in and out of Hong Kong at night and in foul weather in the last three years. No other airline in history had faced such difficulties. None ever would again.

---

* The *Times* and the *Post* listed the names and hometowns of all the Caucasian pilots who'd participated. Moon Chin wasn't mentioned, even though he was an American citizen, from Baltimore, and he'd flown as much as any of the named pilots and more than most.

PART FOUR

THE HUMP

December 17, 1941, to December 31, 1949

CNAC originated this idea and pioneered the service.

—William Langhorne Bond, April 19, 1944

20

IN THE FIGHT

By December 16, 1941, Chuck Sharp had orchestrated the retrieval to Chungking of the company stores and personnel flown from Hong Kong to Namyung. Only the machine-gunned and dismantled hulk of DC-3 number 41 remained behind. The war was nine days old for the United States of America. The China National Aviation Corporation had been embroiled for four and a half years, and its people were exhausted from the go-go push of the evacuations. William Bond stood down the company for two days. Few people in the airline did much of anything. Bond used the pause to take stock.

The United States was in it, finally, awake, incensed, united, flexing the muscle of the world's most powerful industrial infrastructure, at last bent on Fascist extermination. Bond delighted to have his countrymen in the fight—he'd been in it so long without them—but elements of America's sudden ardor sat poorly with the lean Virginian. He thought it to his country's everlasting shame that it hadn't been able to discern—in either hemisphere—any principle or outrage worth fighting for prior to the December attacks. The stark issues of right and wrong had been obvious for years, and at so many junctures the united democracies might have confronted the aggressor nations and forestalled the current catastrophe. Instead, the United States had fiddled with the subtleties of its "neutrality," Britain and France had waffled through years of appeasement, and the militarists had clawed to the brink of dominance on two continents.

The airline had been ten years of unrelieved struggle for William Bond. He was worn by the constant setbacks. Aviation was a young man's industry; CNAC was a youthful company. Bond had passed his forty-eighth birthday the previous November. Hal Sweet, aged thirty-six, was next oldest person in operations. Most were substantially younger. Kitsi, Langhorne, and six-month-old Thomas were settled into the Potomac winter on the other side of the world. The war was costing him so much of their lives. He was tired of it. He'd been tired of it for years.

Financially, four and a half years of war had destroyed nearly thirteen million dollars (Mex.) of his airline's assets, and that didn't account for a penny of lost opportunity, the business the airline would have developed in an uninvaded China. The December 8 raids reduced the company to four airplanes, only three of which could fly, and the loss of Hong Kong severed its steady supplies of fuel and spare parts and its most lucrative revenue streams. The newly widened war was sure to recast the company's obligations entirely. It had already cost the services of P. Y. Wong, the best managing director the airline had ever had. Bond dreaded rebuilding the airline's logistic chain and reinventing its income sources at the same time he had to deal with a new managing director exploring the parameters of his power and responsibilities. As from the start, whoever held the managing directorship of the China National Aviation Corporation would wield tremendous influence at the controls of China's most important Sino-American partnership, and the vacancy was sure to spark a bureaucratic dogfight. An unethical character at the helm would hinder the coalition war effort and sully the reputation the airline had earned with loyal, honorable service. Unfortunately, the tangled web of alliances, debts, influence, intrigue, patronage, and favors that moved Chinese society could easily install such a person, and Bond might find himself disagreeing with the new man or riding roughshod over his inexperienced judgment, things potentially fatal to their long-run relationship. He begged vice minister of communications and chairman of the board Peng Sho-pei to delay appointing a new man until he'd established the airline's new foundation.

Gravely, Mr. Peng said his search for a new managing director could possibly take as long as ninety days. It was an extraordinary measure of the trust Bond had built in the Middle Kingdom that the Chinese would give him, a foreigner, free hand to operate one of their most vital strategic assets at such a critical time.

Besides the China National Aviation Corporation, the three pursuit squadrons of Claire Chennault's American Volunteer Group constituted the other strategically significant, American-flavored civilian aviation entity on the Asian mainland. Nicknamed "the Flying Tigers," they'd been spared the surprise attacks. The AVG was created to safeguard the Burma Road, but the assault on the British Empire expanded the scope of what needed protecting, so Chennault tasked one of his squadrons to augment Burma's air defense. He wanted the other two moved to Kunming. Getting their P-40 Tomahawks to Kunming wasn't complicated; they and their pilots could fly, but the squadrons couldn't function without mechanics, armorers, and other technicians, and it would take two weeks to drive them to Kunming over the Burma Road. Other than one dilapidated twin-engine Model 18 Beechcraft able to shuttle a few people and light cargoes, the AVG didn't have its own dedicated air transport. Fortunately, it enjoyed the services of the China National Aviation Corporation.

William Bond and Chuck Sharp put their people back to work on Thursday, December 18, in support of the AVG. Just before nightfall, Moon Chin and two other pilots landed the company's three airworn Douglas transports at Toungoo, Burma, and flew contingents of Chennault's ground staff to Kunming. Successive relays moved enough ammunition, oxygen, and sundry supplies to support a fortnight of combat operations.

Aside from "special charters" for the AVG, Bond and Sharp wasted no time reorienting operations to Burma, but lower Burma was supremely vulnerable, and any Japanese action that closed Rangoon, Burma's principal seaport in the Irrawaddy River delta, would make Free China's best line of communication to the outside world an air route across north Burma to Assam, India, and from there downcountry to Calcutta at the head of the Bay of Bengal. At the end of 1941, the airline needed Calcutta in the same way it had needed Hong Kong in the autumn of 1937, but Bond still didn't have permission to fly in and out of Calcutta, even though he'd been trying to get it for months. Contemplating the byzantine subtleties of His Britannic Majesty's colonial government, Bond decided forgiveness would be easier to obtain than permission. He sold tickets for an inaugural passenger flight from Chungking to Calcutta, and telegrammed the director of Indian civil aviation to meet him at Calcutta's Dum Dum Airport. The director met Bond without a raised eyebrow and granted his every request. For all the stuffy bureaucratic proceduralism and hoity-toity social airs that so irritated Americans in the Far East, the British weren't fools. Anything that helped China hindered Japan's ability to threaten India.

The AVG squadrons scored widely publicized victories over Kunming and Rangoon, the best pieces of Allied news west of the date line, buoying spirits at a time when it took concentrated will to contest the calamities battering the cause elsewhere in Asia and the Pacific. Bond returned to Chungking and spent the last short, dark days of December working in the airline's head office. The year 1942 brought the Allies no respite. Shanghai, Hong Kong, and Wake Island had surrendered; in the Philippines, American and Filipino forces abandoned Manila and retreated to the Bataan Peninsula. The enemy made steady progress in Malaya, threatening Singapore, and occupied sites on Borneo and in the Celebes. They captured the fine harbor at Rabaul, on the island of New Britain, and a major Japanese offensive swept into Burma on January 20 through a jungle-covered mountain range on the Thai border that British Army planners had considered impassable to a modern army. Overhead, Japanese air forces tangled with the civilian-manned P-40s of Chennault's AVG, and the China National Aviation Corporation toiled through the first month of 1942 with the three flyable Douglas transports saved from Hong Kong.* The planes labored constantly, moving the airline's scattered support structure to Calcutta, making passenger and mail runs in and out of China, and flying support for Chennault. CNAC and the AVG were the most effectively engaged aspects of Allied airpower in the entire Pacific war. Prodigious exertion, mechanical and meteorological good fortune, and enemy neglect allowed the airline to complete its reorientation by month's end. Looking forward, its biggest problem was lack of airplanes, as it had been for years. Two DC-3s

* Two DC-3s (number 46 and number 47) and one DC-2 (number 31).

stripped from domestic service were going to be air-ferried to China for the airline, a far cry from the promises of November, but global circumstances had changed enormously, as everyone recognized. The only other airplane procurable in the short run was the machine-gunned hulk of DC-3 number 41 languishing in the Namyung countryside. Maintenance chief Zygmund Soldinski took a team to ascertain if field repairs could cobble it together soundly enough to survive a 1,500-mile flight to Calcutta. They counted nearly two thousand holes in its wing, fuselage, and tail surfaces. "It looks like a noodle strainer," someone quipped.

True restoration would take weeks in a first-class repair shop, which Namyung most definitely was not, but Soldinski judged number 41's bones solid. Coolies carted the pieces back to the airfield, where mechanics reassembled it under camouflage. One of its Wright Cyclone G103A engines was repairable; the other was not. The airline had lost its two spares at Kai Tak. Six engines of the type were aboard ship from the United States, but they weren't due into India for another two months. A "loaner" engine came from Bill Pawley, aircraft salesman associate of H. H. Kung and president of the business front for Chennault's volunteers, but Pawley's engine proved to be a spavined 950-horsepower variety cannibalized from a wrecked Chinese pursuit plane, far less robust than the Wright Cyclone. Soldinski hung the dinky engine without second thought, blasé about such improvisations after the DC-2½ episode. Mechanics spliced severed control cables, patched ruptured hydraulic lines and cylinders, replaced mangled radios, shredded tires, and the shattered cockpit windshield, and rigged a makeshift instrument panel, mounting four of the usual forty-one instruments. Soldinski had the perforated fuel tanks removed and flown to Chungking, repaired, and returned to Namyung. Coolies pasted canvas patches over the bullet holes with homemade glue. Last, the mechanics discovered that the shaft of Pawley's engine was too small to accommodate the DC-3's Hamilton Standard propeller. Soldinski installed a smaller prop borrowed from the Chinese Air Force and deemed the plane just barely airworthy. He detailed the Mickey Mouse repairs to operations manager Chuck Sharp and asked Sharp to give him a pilot for the fly-out.

Not surprisingly, Sharp assigned himself.

On the ground in Namyung, number 41 didn't look as solid as Soldinski had made it sound. The beetle-browed chief mechanic detected Sharp's skepticism. "She'll fly," Soldinski assured. "I'll bet a month's pay on it."

If there was anyone in the company who appreciated a gambling proposition, it was Chuck Sharp, even one as hard to collect as Soldinski's. Hal Sweet had done it with unmatched wings in the DC-2½. If Soldinski pronounced it flyable, there probably wasn't any reason he couldn't do it with a puny engine, an undersized propeller, and a cheese-grater airframe.

The chief mechanic suggested a test flight to probe the airplane's shortcomings, but Sharp overruled him. Namyung was only fifty miles from Japanese lines. Assembled and in the air, the plane was too likely to attract enemy attention. The faster he got westward, the safer he'd feel. The unmatched engines set up a strong vibration as the plane bumped and shuddered down the field toward takeoff. Sharp eased the plane aloft and retracted the undercarriage, but a hydraulic line burst and the landing gear refused to budge. The wheels hung in the breeze, two gigantic sea anchors cutting even more speed from the underpowered airplane. Sharp twisted the wheel and pushed on a rudder pedal to begin a gentle climbing turn. A spliced rudder cable snapped, and Sharp's foot mushed to the floor. He instantly began steering with ailerons and throttles, a much more difficult procedure. Sharp crept toward Kunming into a thirty-mile-per-hour headwind, average ground speed sixty-six miles per hour; he'd be helpless as a crawling baby if he was caught by a Japanese patrol. Further complicating matters, the four cobbled-together instruments failed, and it took Sharp eleven hours and fifteen minutes to cover the 743 miles to Kunming. As he touched down, the left brake failed, and only his lightning reactions averted a smashup. Refueled, and with the control cable, brake hydraulics, and instruments repaired, Sharp hopped 375 miles to Lashio, Burma, still unable to hoist the landing gear. Most military experts thought the British could hold central and north Burma even if they lost Rangoon. Many civilians weren't so confident, and people hoping to evacuate mobbed the Lashio airport. Hal Sweet had flown a full load on the DC-2½. Sharp didn't see any reason he couldn't do the same in number 41, and so he left Lashio with the company's usual overload, a metric ton more than the Civil Aeronautics Board would allow a domestic American airline flight to carry on a perfectly sound DC-3.

A rainsquall pelted the plane over central Burma, dissolving the homemade glue securing the canvas patches over the myriad bullet holes. One after another, the patches peeled away, each one's release adding a new tone to the discordant keening of the airstream racing over the exposed holes.

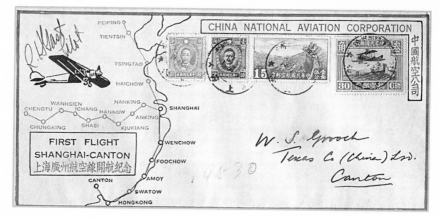

First flight cover, Shanghai to Canton, signed by Robert Gast, addressed to William Grooch. *Courtesy of Tom O. Moore, Jr., www.cnac.org*

The Loening Air Yacht on the banks of the Whangpoo River. *Courtesy of Nancy Allison Wright*

CNAC hangar at Lunghwa Airport, early 1930s. *Courtesy of Nancy Allison Wright*

William Langhorne
Bond. *Courtesy
of Thomas and
Langhorne Bond*

Katharine Dunlop Bond.
*Courtesy of Thomas and
Langhorne Bond*

The maiden flight of
CNAC's first Douglas
Dolphin, 1934. *Photo
by Edward P. Howard*

The Yangtze Gorges over the tail of a Loening, early 1930s. *Courtesy of Judith M. Ferguson*

Lunghwa Pagoda, 1930s. *Courtesy of Tom O. Moore, Jr., www.cnac.org*

Returned from fruitless search.

Ernie Allison, just returned from a fruitless search for Robert Gast, April 1934. *Courtesy of Nancy Allison Wright*

The Shanghai post office on the north bank of Soochow Creek. *Photo by Edward P. Howard*

CNAC's head office in Shanghai, just a block off the Bund. *Courtesy of Shirley Wilke Mosley*

CNAC's first Chinese American pilot-captains, Joy Thom, Moon Chin, and Donald Wong, in front of a Stinson Detroiter. *Courtesy of the Family of Donald S. Wong*

CNAC's first DC-2 over the Shanghai Bund on its maiden flight, 1935. Garden Bridge and the mouth of Soochow Creek are below the Broadway Mansions Hotel, prominent on the right; the Cathay Hotel is just below the left wingtip; the War Memorial is the obelisk below the center of the right wing; leaving Shanghai on November 11, 1937, Bond boarded the Butterfield & Swire's steamer *Wuseh* on the French Bund at the bottom of the photo. *Courtesy of Edward P. Howard*

CNAC's first DC-2 gets craned ashore at Lunghwa Airport, 1935. *Photo by Edward P. Howard*

Hand fueling DC-2 number 26, probably at Chengdu. *Courtesy of J. L. Johnson, Jr.*

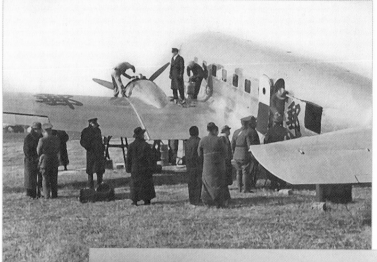

Loading DC-2 number 26, probably at Chengdu. *Courtesy of J. L. Johnson, Jr.*

Lunghwa Airport in 1937. On the hardstand in front of the hangar are two S-43B amphibians that the airline used briefly on Route Three, two DC-2s, and a Ford trimotor; on the grass are a Stinson Detroiter and a Loening Air Yacht. *Courtesy of Tom Moore, www.cnac.org*

Hugh Leslie Woods. *Courtesy of Shirley Wilke Mosley*

Sylvia Wylie and Charles Lamar Sharp. *Courtesy of Shirley Wilke Mosley*

Harold M. Bixby at the Customs Jetty on the Shanghai Bund, tending to the evacuation of his wife and four daughters, August 17, 1937. *Courtesy of Shirley Wilke Mosley*

Carnage in the streets of Shanghai, August 1937. *Courtesy of Shirley Wilke Mosley*

Consolidated Commodore flying boat in the Yangtze River at Sanhupa Airport below Chungking, 1938. *Courtesy of Shirley Wilke Mosley*

The ramshackle, temporary buildings of Sanhupa Airport on the Yangtze River sandbar below Chungking, 1938: the carcass of a Loening in the foreground, a Stinson Detroiter on the left, two DC-2s in the distance. *Courtesy of Shirley Wilke Mosley*

Hong Kong's Kai Tak Airport in 1938: one of Pan Am's M-130s is barely visible at the end of the pontoon. *Courtesy of Shirley Wilke Mosley*

Hong Kong Harbor, 1938; the Peninsula Hotel is the biggest building in the foreground. *Courtesy of Shirley Wilke Mosley*

The Gloucester Hotel, location of CNAC's Hong Kong office. *Courtesy of J. L. Johnson, Jr.*

Salvage operations under way at the wreck of number 32, the *Kweilin*, after it was shot down in August 1938. *Courtesy of the Pan Am Historical Foundation and the University of Miami Libraries*

CNAC people in Hong Kong, 1938. In front: Foxy Kent. First row, left to right: Sylvia Wylie, Kitsi Bond, Katie Wilke, Mrs. Kent, Chuck Sharp, Mary Margaret Pottschmidt, Hugh Woods. Second row: Hal Sweet, Erin Havelick, Mabel Sweet, Maxine Leonard, Mr. Owens, Royal Leonard, Bob Pottschmidt. *Courtesy of Shirley Wilke Mosley*

CNAC director Max Polin, pilot Chuck Sharp, and maintenance chief Zygmund Soldinsky, 1939. *Courtesy of Shirley Wilke Mosley*

Moon Fun Chin, 1941; behind him is DC-3 number 46, "the French DC-3," soon to become famous as "the DC-2½." *Courtesy of J. L. Johnson, Jr.*

Number 46 with its wing blown off at Suifu, May 1941. *Courtesy of the Pan Am Historical Foundation and the University of Miami Libraries*

The DC-2½, a DC-3 flown with a DC-2 wing attached outboard of the right engine; on its flight back to Hong Kong from Suifu, via Chungking, it carried a full load of paying passengers. *Courtesy of the Pan Am Historical Foundation and the University of Miami Libraries*

One of the Curtiss Condors with which CNAC conducted the cigarettes, tin, and tungsten airlift between Hong Kong and Namyung in 1941. *Courtesy of the family of Bill Price*

December 8, 1941. CNAC people shelter among boulders above Kai Tak airfield during one of the Japanese air raids. Left to right: Operations Manager Chuck Sharp holding one of his dachshunds, Pan Am pilot Fred Ralph (in white hat), pilot Paul "Pop" Kessler, Elva "Maj" Majors, and pilot Emil Scott. *Courtesy of the family of Bill Price*

One of the CNAC DC-2s destroyed during the initial Japanese attack on Hong Kong, December 8, 1941. *Courtesy of the family of Bill Price*

CNAC's pilots'
hostel in Dinjan,
1943. *Courtesy
of Gifford Bull*

Pete Goutiere, 1944.
*Courtesy of Pete
Goutiere*

Likiang Mountain, north of the Dinjan-to-Kunming flight path. *Courtesy of
Gifford Bull*

The snowy mountains of the Hump. *Courtesy of Janet Dalby Mars*

Early morning over the Three Gorges country. *Courtesy of Gifford Bull*

Jimmy Fox's plane wreck. *Courtesy of Pete Goutiere*

Ridge Hammell and Joe Rosbert after their epic trek out of the mountains—in borrowed clothes. *Courtesy of the Pan Am Historical Foundation and the University of Miami Libraries*

Bob Jenkins, Elmer the bear, and Ridge Hammell in Ballygunge, Calcutta, 1943. *Courtesy of Pete Goutiere*

CNAC number 50, a C-53, flying downcountry from Dinjan to Calcutta. *Courtesy of Janet Dalby Mars*

The Bond family in 1943 or 1944: William Langhorne, Langhorne, Thomas Dunlop, and Kitsi. *Courtesy of Thomas and Langhorne Bond*

CNAC veterans in the cargo bay of a C-46 at their 2002 reunion: Dick Rossi, Fletcher Hanks, Moon Chin, Carey Bowles, Bill Maher, and Pete Goutiere. Between them, they flew *at least* 2,400 Hump trips—truly remarkable, considering the Army Air Corps deemed one hundred trips to be a full tour of duty. *Courtesy of Tom O. Moore, www.cnac.org*

The last patches blew away, and the atonal chorus rose to an eerie, howling crescendo. Sharp landed in Calcutta some hours later.

A British airport official examined the plane in disbelief and asked, "How did you get that here, in a truck?"

In a letter to Harold Bixby, William Bond hailed Sharp's flight as "probably the most spectacular and dangerous flight of this nature ever made by CNAC," remarkable laurels considering the airline's accomplishments since Marco Polo Bridge.

Allied strategy decreed a main effort against Hitler, but the sudden totality of Japanese success menaced India and Australia, considered cornerstones of eventual victory. The Combined Chiefs of Staff felt compelled to take immediate countermeasures, and buttressing the Chinese war effort was a core principle of Allied strategy, on the presumption that China's active belligerency prevented a major portion of the Japanese Army from deploying elsewhere. Supporting the Chinese meant getting supplies to China, and the enemy's offensive into Burma added urgency to ideas that might augment, reorient, or supplant the Burma Road. Assigned to determine how best to help China, White House advisor Lauchlin Currie told President Roosevelt that he was exploring the feasibility of building a road from Assam through northern Burma to link with the existing Burma Road, and of establishing an airfreight service from Calcutta to northern Burma and China—a concept that William Langhorne Bond had been explicitly advocating to him for more than seven months.

T. V. Soong was still in the United States—he'd been made China's minister of foreign affairs just before Christmas—and he relentlessly advocated both projects. "It is necessary that a new life line to China be opened," Soong wrote to President Roosevelt and Major General Joseph W. Stilwell on January 30, 1942, following Stilwell's appointment as the senior American officer in the Far East. "Miraculously enough," he continued, "that life line is conveniently at hand." The miracle Soong had in mind was a variation on the "Airfreight Routes into China" proposal Bond had written in the spring of 1941, although Bond's memorandum described the difficulties in somewhat different terms. What Bond considered a route "over some of the highest and most rugged country in the world" prosecuted against "every obstacle known to aviation"—over a shorter and lower-altitude Myitkyina–Yunnanyi flight route—Dr. Soong's letter morphed into seven hundred miles of "flying over comparatively level stretches." Bond's proposal had studiously refrained from making exact promises about freight quantities the service could deliver. Soong blithely announced that 100 DC-3s could haul 12,000 tons of war matériel into China per month, or 4 tons per plane, per day.* "There are of course competing demands for transport planes," Soong concluded, "but we venture to submit that nowhere else in the world could 100 transport planes be placed to greater advantage."

White House intimate Averell Harriman took the letter to the president, having added a caveat about the geographic obstacles between Assam and Kunming. President Roosevelt met with General Stilwell on February 9. Afterward, Stilwell discussed the China aviation program with Lauchlin Currie and General Henry Harley "Hap" Arnold, commander of the Army Air Corps, and that very day, President Roosevelt radioed a specific promise to the Generalissimo: "I can now give you definite assurance that even though there should be a further set back in Rangoon . . . the supply route to China via India can be maintained by air. The whole plan seems altogether practical and I am sure we can make it a reality in the near future."

The president was probably receiving technical assurance on airlift plausibility from Lauchlin Currie, who, in turn, had gotten his information from William Langhorne Bond.

It would take far more than plans and pontifications to prevent the situation in Asia from worsening, however. Only hard, intelligent fighting and grim determination could do that, and, for the Allies in early 1942, those qualities were in perilously short supply. The British surrendered Singapore on February 15—to a Japanese assault force less than half the size of their garrison—and in Burma aggressive Japanese infantry cut off most of a British infantry division from a railway bridge on the six-hundred-yard-wide Sittang River. Afraid the Japanese would capture the bridge intact, the

---

* A figure that operational realities would prove as absurdly optimistic as Soong's assessment of South Asian geography—the U.S. Army Air Corps's India-China Wing of the Air Transport Command wouldn't get 12,000 tons over the Hump until December 1943, when it was operating 178 airplanes, many of which were C-87s and C-46s with much greater payload capacity than DC-3 variants.

division commander ordered it blown before dawn on February 23, but only one of three hastily wired spans dropped into the river. It was the worst of both worlds: the broken bridge doomed the brigades on the far shore, but the damage wasn't severe enough to greatly impede the enemy. Fewer than half of the stranded men escaped across the Sittang, most without rifles, many without clothes or boots. The division was eviscerated, and the road to Rangoon lay open.

William Bond was asleep in a well-kept bed in Calcutta's Great Eastern Hotel when the sappers blew the ill-fated bridge. He awoke in the white-washed hotel on Old Court House Street, just off Dalhousie Square, feeling as if he'd successfully navigated the major changes forced on his company by the events of December 8. He'd established a business office in Chowringhee Square; Sharp and Soldinski had built the rudiments of a fine base at Dum Dum Airport, nine miles from the city center; spare parts, replacement engines, and a pair of airplanes were on the way from the United States; and under Woody's supervision, construction of the base at Dinjan in Upper Assam was progressing smoothly. Peng Sho-pei had kept his promise not to name a new managing director until Bond accomplished the reorientation; now that the groundwork was complete, Peng filled the vacancy with Colonel Wang Cheng-fu, an "upright and efficient" aeronautical engineer, educated at the Massachusetts Institute of Technology. With the immediate situation controlled, it seemed that the most important battles governing the company's future would be fought in strategic debates in Washington, D.C., the outcomes of which would have a decisive impact on the airline's ability to acquire airplanes and find a role in the war effort. Bond pressed for permission to return to the United States so he could participate. As before, it was T. V. Soong's desire to capitalize on Bond's expertise with American policy-makers that tipped the scales in favor of his return, but true to Oriental good form and protocol, rather than simply announcing his departure, Bond gave face to the new managing director by formally requesting permission to leave, which Colonel Wang immediately granted. Bond flew west from Calcutta on February 25, the beginning of a two-week aerial odyssey that took him across India, Arabia, central Africa, and the South Atlantic to Brazil, and then up the South American coast, across the Caribbean to Miami, and up the Eastern Seaboard to Washington.

·   ·   ·

Newly promoted Lieutenant General Joseph Stilwell looked in on CNAC's Dum Dum Airport operation on March 3, his first wartime encounter with a company he knew well from his 1935–39 stint as military attaché to China.* Chuck Sharp showed him around the airline's Calcutta facility and talked him through the ongoing repairs to number 41, the Noodle Strainer. "Sharpe [sic] working on the DC-3 shot up at Hong Kong," Stilwell noted in his diary. "Over 500 shots hit it, —2,000 holes. Okay in a week." CNAC flew Stilwell from Calcutta to Lashio and Kunming that afternoon and evening, and took him the rest of the way to Chungking the next morning.

In Burma, nimble Japanese infantry swept over the Sittang River, outflanked road-bound British defenders in the boggy rice and delta country of lower Burma, and occupied Rangoon on March 8, pillars of smoke darkening the ruin of another great Asian city. All six of CNAC's planes were busy that day, flying gasoline to Myitkyina, banknotes and Red Cross supplies across the mountains to Kunming, and carting passengers and mail between Calcutta and Chungking.

On March 11, General Stilwell flew back from Chungking to take command of the Chinese divisions newly assigned to help defend Burma. For the British, thrice-wounded Great War veteran Lieutenant General Sir William Slim took charge of the Anglo-Indian fighting forces in Burma. Freed from Malaya by the Singapore surrender, Japanese reinforcements poured into Rangoon. The RAF and the AVG defended central Burma with 38 planes; against them, the Japanese arrayed 223. Massed Japanese airpower hammered the main Allied airbase at Magwe on Saturday and Sunday, March 21 and 22. Only four AVG P-40s and eight RAF Hurricanes escaped destruction, and with Allied air resistance broken, the major cities of central Burma suffered the merciless "bus service" bombing the Japanese had inflicted on China's population centers. Japanese ground forces attacked north from Rangoon in central Burma, making steady progress.

In the United States, portraits of Pan American Airways' China man graced enormous, full-page ads in *The Washington Post*, and William Bond

---

* Stilwell had reached India on February 24, twelve days after leaving the United States, and had been in Calcutta since February 26, the day after Bond's departure. The date of Stilwell's promotion was February 25.

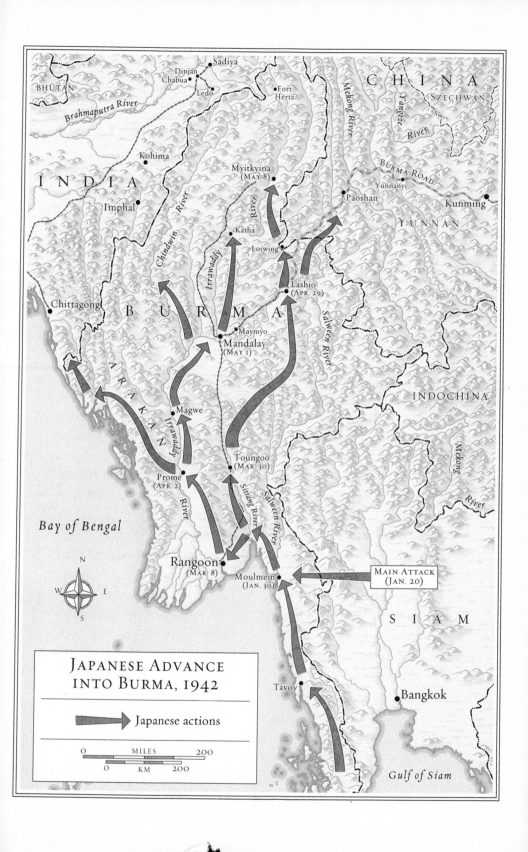

BHUTAN

Brahmaputra River

INDIA

Kohima

Imphal

Chittagong

B U R M A

ARAKAN

Chindwin River

Irrawaddy River

Magwe

Irrawaddy River

Prome
(APR. 2)

River

Bay of Bengal

Rangoon
(MAR. 8)

Sadiya

Dinjan
Chabua

Ledo

Fort
Hertz

Myitkyina
(MAY 8)

Katha

Loiwing

Maymyo

Mandalay
(MAY 1)

Lashio
(APR. 29)

Salween River

Toungoo
(MAR. 30)

Sittang River

Salween River

Moulmein
(JAN. 30)

Tavoy

C H I N A

SZECHWAN

Yangtze River

Mekong River

BURMA ROAD

Yunnanyi

Paoshan

Kunming

Y U N N A N

INDOCHINA

Mekong River

MAIN ATTACK
(JAN. 20)

S I A M

Bangkok

Gulf of Siam

JAPANESE ADVANCE
INTO BURMA, 1942

Japanese actions

0   MILES   200
0   KM   200

N
W   E
S

looked worried, even in print. A dismal succession of defeats and disappointments dogged the Allies. The only bright spots the American public could look to with any sort of pride were the defenses of Wake Island, long since lost, and Bataan, which, barring a miracle, obviously soon would be, and the exploits of Chennault's AVG, in which the China National Aviation Corporation played a critical supporting role. A joint Army-Navy operation that had sought Bond's advice in Washington was soon to provide another.

In mid-March, an Air Corps officer approached Harold Bixby in New York City with a slate of technical questions about flying conditions in eastern China. Bixby gave what specifics he could, but said that for precise, accurate, and current information, the Army should query "our Mr. Bond," recently returned to Washington.

The officer took Bixby's suggestion. He was evasive, but he told Bond the Army planned to bomb Tokyo between April 10 and April 20 and wanted to land in China afterward. Based on landing-weight parameters, Bond surmised the Army was planning to use medium bombers, and he disabused the officer of hope that there was a suitable spot north of the Yangtze. But CNAC's airfield at Namyung was just barely within the radius the officer indicated. It was fifty miles from the nearest Japanese garrison and wasn't difficult for skilled navigators to find in daylight. Bond told the man everything he knew. He never heard from the officer again, but extrapolating from what he'd been told and knowing the Air Corps didn't have any medium bombers in China, the realization grew on him that the military must have figured out how to launch them from aircraft carriers, after which they'd raid Japan and carry on to China. Considering the value of the assets the Japanese could annihilate if the operation was compromised, Bond was amazed the officer hadn't extracted a formal secrecy pledge—concrete proof he was trusted as much in Washington as he was in China.

His instincts were correct. In mid-April, a Navy task force built around the aircraft carriers *Hornet* and *Enterprise* plowed through the North Pacific toward Japan. Spooked aloft by a fishing boat 170 miles short of their intended takeoff point, sixteen U.S. Army B-25 bombers commanded by Lieutenant Colonel James H. Doolittle staggered off the *Hornet's* flight deck, attacked targets in six Japanese cities, and fled west, across the East China Sea. Short on fuel, in foul weather, and at night, the raiders couldn't find Namyung. All fifteen crews bailed out or crash-landed. Three men died. The enemy captured eight others, three of whom they executed. The survivors struggled westward on foot. Chinese villagers and an American missionary named John Birch sheparded Doolittle and his crew to safety.* "TOKYO BOMBED!" screamed headlines across the United States, an enormous boost to American morale even though the raid did little material damage. The B-25s had been intended to join Chennault after the raid, but not a single one survived. Tragically, the raid had terrible consequences in China—the Japanese scourged the areas where the bombers had crash-landed and put thousands of villagers to the sword for helping the Americans.

The raid made no impact in central Burma, where Japanese infantry had sprung upon the Chinese division anchoring the eastern end of the Allied line. The Chinese disintegrated, and Slim's and Stilwell's defense collapsed. Japanese infantry plunged forward, capturing Lashio on April 29. Mandalay fell on May 1, and the Japanese hustled north toward Myitkyina, against negligible resistance, pressing to capture its crucial airfield before the monsoon closed the campaigning season.

Hugh Woods had been orchestrating the steady retrieval of men and matériel from Myitkyina to his new base at Dinjan, a short-haul 250-mile route over rugged mountains and jungles. On May 4, military authorities ordered the airline to concentrate all available resources on the evacuation.

Moon Chin was piloting a regular flight from Chungking to Calcutta the next morning, scheduled to make intermediate stops at Kunming and Yunnanyi, and he had only six passengers aboard, one of whom was a very haggard-looking American Air Corps major wearing a battered flying cap, torn khaki trousers, and a ragged flight jacket. Yunnanyi wasn't on CNAC's normal itinerary, but the Army had a meteorological outpost and radio station there in need of resupply. The landing was difficult, and Army planes had twice failed to deliver. Predictably, Moon Chin got in and out without difficulty. Westward, he climbed for the altitude he'd need to get over the mountains of the Three Gorges country, through substantial turbulence, but the thick clouds piled over the ridges promised shelter from

---

* Yes, *that* John Birch. Birch was killed by Communists in a violent misunderstanding near Sian in August 1945. Considering him the first casualty of the Cold War, right-wing groups in the United States founded an anti-Communist society in his name. People who knew Birch personally always felt he'd have been appalled by the use of his name.

any Japanese air patrols marauding north of their usual haunts. Moon's radio operator passed forward signals between the planes going in and out of Myitkyina, and Moon decided to help. The major in the passenger cabin felt the plane divert and asked what was happening. He was shocked to learn of the unscheduled stop. In Chungking, Ambassador Gauss* had told him Myitkyina would be in Japanese hands before nightfall. He wrote a note and passed it to the cockpit. Moon sent one back reassuring the major that the airline's Myitkyina station wouldn't be transmitting if the Japanese had captured it, and he soon had his plane safely on the airfield, which swarmed with despairing refugees. Moon counted twenty-four people aboard, bringing the total to thirty, and the disheveled officer raised an eyebrow. DC-3s were designed to carry twenty-one. Worried, the major watched the count swell to fifty, and still Moon Chin kept bringing on people, finally slamming the door when he had sixty-six people sardined inside. Appalled, the major at last protested.

Turning his smooth face to the scruffy officer, Moon Chin said, "Calm down, Major. I, Moon Chin, know how much people a DC-3 can carry, and this one can carry sixty-six."

"Christ, I should've gone back the way I came," the major muttered.

Takeoff was sluggish, the plane more tail-heavy than anticipated, but Moon Chin got the nose level at cruising altitude and flew to Calcutta as usual, "without incident." At Dum Dum, Moon discovered six additional stowaways in the rear baggage compartment. He'd flown seventy-two.

He also learned the identity of his mysterious passenger. It was Jimmy Doolittle, commander of the Tokyo Raid and one of his boyhood aviation heroes, recently promoted two grades from lieutenant colonel to brigadier general. Doolittle had been so busy organizing and planning the Tokyo Raid that he hadn't bothered to change his insignia to account for his promotion to lieutenant colonel, let alone his recent ascension to the rank of general.

The Japanese captured Myitkyina that night, and for once, Moon Chin hadn't made the last evacuation flight.** The Royal Air Force did that, and

---

* Clarence E. Gauss had replaced Nelson T. Johnson as U.S. ambassador to China in 1941.

** Between April 8 and May 5, the airline evacuated 2,400 people and fifty tons of cargo from Myitkyina.

kept at it one relay too long. The Japanese destroyed two of its transports on the ground.

The British remnants retreated westward to India, "outmaneuvered, outfought, outgeneraled," in the blunt assessment of Sir William Slim. An emergency meeting of the airline's board of directors authorized Chuck Sharp to evacuate Calcutta for Allahbad if the situation deteriorated any further. Chinese forces in eastern Burma retreated across the Salween River into Yunnan. Three Chinese divisions farther west could have escaped west to India most easily, and one of them did, but Chiang Kai-shek didn't seem to know what to do with the other two: order them out to India and allow them to fall under Stilwell's training program and operational control until Burma was recaptured, or send them eastward through the horrendous country of the Three Gorges, which would return them to service in China—if they didn't starve or die of exposure in the process. Instead of choosing one course or the other, the Generalissimo's bizarre orders sent them marching farther and farther into the jungles of north Burma on increasingly slim margins of supply. Six weeks later, their plight would catch Bond in a trap between the Chinese government and the U.S. Army that had the potential to ruin his relationship with both institutions.

Although few could see it at the time, the Chinese retreat offered a glimpse of the basic, underlying problem that would dog the partnership of the three Allies fighting on the Asian mainland through the entire war— they all had fundamentally different aims. The British wanted to protect India and, in the process of defeating Japan, re-exert control of their prewar colonial dominions in Burma, Malaya, Singapore, and Hong Kong. The Americans intended to crush Japan and eliminate her ability to threaten the stability of postwar Asia but had no interest in propping up the British Empire. Chiang Kai-shek nursed bitter resentment against Great Britain, and he was content to let America and Britain do the fighting required to defeat Japan. His primary goal was to emerge from the conflict as the dominant political force in China, possessing the military power to crush the Communists and bring China's recalcitrant warlords to heel, an objective that left him concerned that three well-equipped, American-trained divisions—of uncertain loyalty—would represent a force to be reckoned with in postwar Chinese politics. The disparity of aims didn't bode well for the Allies' ability to accomplish meaningful anti-Japanese action on the Asian mainland.

21

"FOR US IT STARTED FIVE YEARS AGO"

The loss of Burma drove a Texas-sized wedge between China and India. Japanese forces inside the salient threatened offensives into both countries and severed the Middle Kingdom from overland supply.* American leadership feared China would quit the war. Time and again in recent years, they'd been told what China could accomplish given modern means, often in personal letters from Madame Chiang Kai-shek written on "Headquarters of the Generalissimo" stationery, and a steady flood of Kuomintang propaganda sold the public the same story. China was America's darling, the favorite ally—the United States' intrinsic anti-European resentment always tempered its pro-British feelings—and popular opinion demanded action to help China immediately. Much civilian sentiment believed Chinese manpower wedded to American matériel and know-how was the easiest, fastest, and least expensive manner to hit Japan. Not surprisingly, considering their sensitivity to public opinion, China enthusiasm ran hot-

---

* Free China's Central Asian supply route from Alma Ata to Lanchow had withered when Hitler invaded the Soviet Union.

ter in Congress, the White House, and the State Department than it did in the Department of War. Vermont senator Warren Robinson Austin publicly demanded that more be done to support China's war effort.

Chief of naval operations Admiral King, the Navy's top officer, deplored Senator Austin's pronouncements. "If such conception [as Senator Austin's] is seriously held by those controlling high strategy it is fatally defective. . . . China's [lack of] offensive spirit, physical and political, and difficulties of transportation were continuously reported before the fall of Rangoon. The simple truth is that we will be well on [our] way toward defeating Japan by the time [meaningful] lines [of supply] can be opened."

Chairman of the Joint Chiefs of Staff General George C. Marshall concurred with the Navy's assessment. The U.S. ambassador to China, Clarence Gauss, had been sending home sobering evaluations of Chinese capabilities and intentions, and an Army officer on a liaison mission in China had presciently surmised that the Nationalist Chinese would "shun offensive action, wait until their allies had won the war, and then use their jealously husbanded supplies for the solution to the Communist problem." Despite their uneasy public alliance in the United Front, for both Kuomintang and Communists, the fight to control China was the paramount conflict.

However, the American people lacked such a subtle understanding. They believed in China, and so did President Roosevelt. A self-admitted Sinophile due to Delano family roots in the China trade, he and many influential members of the State Department expected China to play an important role in Japan's defeat and, as a strong, stable nation, to help guarantee peace in postwar Asia. Besides, on the eve of Rangoon's loss two months before, President Roosevelt had specifically promised Chiang Kai-shek that American support would continue to reach China regardless of whether or not Japan closed the overland route, and as recently as April 28, President Roosevelt had assured the "gallant people of China that . . . ways will be found to deliver airplanes and munitions of war to the armies of Generalissimo Chiang Kai-shek."

Burma's loss left airlift as the only means by which aid could be delivered, but considering the horrendous intervening topography and the impending monsoon, it wasn't clear whether an airlift to China was feasible. Given unlimited resources, no professional air officer would have shied from the challenge, but the same shortage of transport aircraft that had hampered the China National Aviation Corporation since 1939 dogged Allied logisticians in the middle of 1942. Transport aircraft were extremely valuable assets that significantly enhanced the combat power of the units they supported, and there simply were not enough of them to satisfy the demands of every theater. Committing to China a major portion of those projected to come available meant shorting the fight against Hitler, the most dangerous enemy.

President Roosevelt made his position clear in a May 5 memorandum that he wrote to Lieutenant General H. H. "Hap" Arnold, commander of the U.S. Army Air Corps: "It is essential that our route [to China] be kept open, no matter how difficult."

The memo stayed in the White House overnight. It was delivered to General Arnold with a note appended by Harry Hopkins on May 6: "The President is very anxious that you see Soong today sometime."

General Arnold duly summoned the Chinese foreign minister. To balance Arnold's experience, T. V. Soong wanted his own aviation expert at the meeting, and later that day, in carefully tailored suits, William Langhorne Bond and the rotund foreign minister presented themselves in the "temporary buildings" lining the National Mall that had been built to house the War Department during the Great War, twenty-five years before.* Uniformed aides escorted Bond and Soong to a situation room. Chairs semicircled a wall-mounted map of Asia and the Pacific that illustrated a dismal story—the enemy had won a hemisphere in six months. Capping the gloomy mood, banner headlines across the morning's *New York Times* and *Washington Post* announced the surrender of Corregidor, America's last toehold in the Philippines. A flock of officers milled about at the back of the room, waiting to begin a staff meeting once General Arnold dispensed with T. V. Soong, which Bond interpreted as a reflection of the relative importance the Air Corps assigned China. General Arnold appeared, his remaining white hair sheared so close it made his ears protrude beyond stern, fleshy cheeks. Without pleasantries, Arnold hoisted two chairs over to the map, keeping one for himself and motioning Soong into the other. Bond hesitated, then took another chair forward and settled himself off the minister's shoulder as Arnold began a lecture on the difficulties of getting

---

* The Pentagon was under construction on the opposite shore of the Potomac, in Arlington, Virginia.

war matériel to China, citing the lengthy voyage to India at a time when an agonizing shipping shortage was the single biggest damper on America's ability to deploy combat power. Each round-trip to India occupied a ship for four months. Matériel unloaded in Calcutta, Bombay, or Karachi spent weeks mired in the Indian rail network before reaching Assam, and those were only some of the more serious frictions wearing at the logistic chain *before* supplies reached the *beginning* of an airlift. Arnold then sank his teeth into that topic, lamenting aircraft shortages, un- and underdeveloped airfields and facilities in India and China, and the region's atrocious geography and meteorology. The highest summits of the eastern Himalayas soared into the middle reaches of the stratosphere, past twenty-three thousand feet, altitudes unattainable by loaded transports. Hundreds of peaks towered over fifteen thousand feet, none of the passes dipped below ten thousand, and the southwest monsoon blanketed South Asia from mid-May until mid-October, dumping constant rain. Violent thunderstorms plagued the area in the months before the monsoon. Only in late autumn and winter was the weather predictably clear, and those conditions were hardly benign—the cold at altitude was paralytic, invisible winds tearing over the mountains could actually move a plane backward,* and there were no clouds in which to hide from marauding Japanese pursuit squadrons.

Bond found General Arnold remarkably well versed in reasons the airlift wouldn't succeed, considering he'd never visited the area or flown the route. When Arnold railed on about how impossible it would be to fly across a region washed by five hundred inches of annual rainfall, Bond couldn't contain himself any longer. "Sir, I've heard about these five hundred inches from lots of people, but I've never actually met anyone with direct knowledge. Supposedly, it's just one place. We keep schedules in the monsoon without undue difficulty."

General Arnold plowed ahead, deploring the state of radio navigation facilities on the Asian mainland. Bond noted that his airline was installing three-hundred-foot radio navigation towers at Kunming, Calcutta, and Dinjan, all of which would be in operation within ninety days.

Undaunted, the general soldiered forward. His discourse was generally accurate, but in Bond's mind the data didn't support the conclusion Arnold

---

* The meteorological phenomenon of the jet stream wasn't yet properly described or understood.

had obviously already reached—that flying a strategically significant quantity of supplies to China wasn't worth the effort it would entail. Arnold seemed devoid of sympathy for China's predicament, and his brusque condescension embarrassed Bond on Soong's behalf. The Chinese foreign minister sat through it in stony silence, until Arnold stood and terminated the meeting. Soong barely spoke until they were outside the War Department. "You did your best, Bondy, and you were wise not to persist."

"It's depressing. He should realize we know more about flying over there than anybody else."

"The interest isn't there."

After extensive lobbying in the War Department, the State Department, the White House, and the Lend-Lease Administration, which was headed by Edward Stettinius, father of Juan Trippe's wife Betty, Bond, Bixby, and Soong had received assurances of airplanes for CNAC. The initial deliveries were to be DC-3 passenger liners stripped from domestic service and converted to cargo use, officially making them C-53s. Later would come C-47s, the military version of the DC-3 constructed specifically for carrying freight. "Dr. Soong, if you make sure we get those Lend-Lease planes, we'll demonstrate so clearly the route can be flown he'll have to do it," Bond vowed.

The first of the promised planes had already begun arriving in eastern India, along with increasing numbers of Army airplanes, personnel, and equipment, but as the Army Air Corps stepped up its operational pace, its general level of competence failed to impress the professional aviators of the China National Aviation Corporation. There were scores of examples. Moon Chin had had trouble flying into Lashio because a raw Army radio operator could handle only one incoming flight. The airline's Chinese radio operators, vastly more experienced men, routinely handled multiple aircraft simultaneously. An Air Corps pilot flying passengers from Chungking to Kunming had gotten so badly lost that he ran out of fuel and crashed 150 miles from Canton, closer to Japanese lines than to his intended destination. Chuck Sharp rescued one of the eight B-17 heavy bombers the Air Corps had managed to get to India after it made an emergency landing on a Hooghly River sandbar because the Air Corps was unwilling to undertake a high-risk, short-field takeoff from the soft surface, and AVG ground crews had had a series of near disasters attempting takeoff from Kunming in an Air Corps Douglas piloted by an inexperienced lieutenant. Finally—and barely—aloft, the volunteers demanded to return to Kunming and insisted that CNAC fly them instead.

Since Pearl Harbor, Chennault's AVG—the Flying Tigers—had spent more time in combat than any other American pilots in the world, by far, and they'd been phenomenally successful, but they were also an extremely awkward outfit to fit into the overall war effort. Air Corps enterprises would soon dwarf the AVG, and Army morale couldn't tolerate fighting alongside a band of highly paid civilians. However, Chennault, his fliers, and the Chinese government wanted to keep the volunteers operating as currently constituted, extolling their motivation, skill, and flexibility. What to do with the volunteer group, how to support and employ it, and whether or not to induct it into the U.S. military had been subjects of lively debate in China and Washington from the moment America entered the war.

Heading the Army's aviation efforts on the Asian mainland was forty-six-year-old Brigadier General Clayton L. Bissell, commander of the Tenth Air Force, and one of Bissell's many responsibilities was implementing, executing, and managing the China airlift, which President Roosevelt had required the Air Corps to undertake. A War Department favorite who'd compiled an excellent record as a staff officer, Bissell was expert in unglamorous but essential logistics. Chennault coveted his job, but Generals Marshall, Arnold, and Stilwell worried that Chennault's extremely close, long-running relationship with China compromised his ability to act in U.S. interests, nor did any of them think he could handle the required staff work. On paper, Bissell and Chennault seemed an excellent combination: expert logistician and cunning tactician. In reality, it was an unfortunate pairing, because Claire Chennault loathed Clayton Bissell.* Nor was Chen-

---

* Ironically, although Chennault had the fighting reputation, Bissell was the one who had actually fought in air combat, shooting down six German planes during the last summer of the Great War. Chennault earned his wings five months after the Armistice (Ernie Allison had been his flight instructor), and although there were whispers that he'd single-handedly engaged the Japanese over Nanking in 1937, like most higher-ranking Air Corps officers in the Second World War, he led the AVG from the ground.

nault's opinion unique. Most people found Bissell extraordinarily unpleasant, but since he had responsibility for airlifting supplies to China, he was one of the officers with whom CNAC was required to work most closely.

Bond had promised that an airlift to China was possible; he hadn't promised that it would be easy. A host of problems hampered initial efforts: shortages of airplanes, personnel, and spare parts; difficulties getting supplies to Assam for transport to China; muddy, underdeveloped airfields—Dinjan was improving rapidly, but its condition still dragged on performance; and the monsoon rains that had dogged the region since mid-May grounded Air Corps transports for eight days in late May and for thirteen days of June. Complicating everything was the terrain of the route itself—leaving India, the planes had to climb over the 10,000- to 12,000-foot summits of the Patkai Range on the Burma-India border, cross the trackless jungles of north Burma, and then surmount the 15,000-foot summits of the Three Gorges country, high, rugged mountains that had acquired a fearsome reputation, and a nickname—pilots were calling them "the Hump."

Arthur Young was covering Bond's responsibilities while Bond was in Washington, and Bissell summoned him to a meeting in Chungking because Bissell didn't think the airline was using its airplanes efficiently or doing its best against the monsoon weather, and he implied CNAC was making no effort to fly out a large quantity of tin and tungsten waiting in Kunming for outward shipment. He demanded an explanation as to why two of the airline's nine Lend-Lease airplanes were grounded. Young received the dressing-down with consternation, not expert enough to parry the attacks and, back at his office, Young wrote a letter to Chuck Sharp loaded with Bissell's criticisms.

Sharp didn't appreciate the condescension from a bookish economist, not one bit, nor the relay of criticism from General Bissell, the head of an organization that Sharp regarded as barely competent. In Sharp's judgment, the Army had made very few flights into China relative to the quantity of equipment it had on hand. To him, it looked like the Air Corps was in over its head, which, in his eyes, was demonstrated conclusively—and tragically—in early June, when, intending to add an offensive nucleus to Allied airpower in China, the Air Corps sent a batch of B-25s to the Orient to replace those lost in the Doolittle raid. The first six had reached Calcutta as May turned into June, commanded by Major Gordon Leland. The major planned to fly to Dinjan on June 2 and then over the Hump to Kunming the next day, announcing his presence in-theater by bombing Lashio en route.

Chuck Sharp was at the airport while the Air Corps readied the crossing, and he offered to brief the Army pilots and navigators regarding terrain, charts, radio stations, routes, and procedures, sharing the wisdom of his ten years of Asian flying. Major Leland rejected Sharp's advance, adamant that he and his fliers had all the information they needed.

Grossly overloaded with personal equipment, extra fifty-caliber ammunition, and full loads of ordnance—so much "essential" weight that they opted to fly without much reserve fuel—the flight left Dinjan and bombed the Lashio airfield, blowing up one Japanese plane. Two enemy pursuits jumped the six bombers immediately afterward. Four of the B-25s firewalled their throttles and dashed for a cloud bank. The enemy mauled the two bombers that kept to cruising speed in order to husband their fuel supply, killing a radio operator. A few minutes after reaching the imagined safety of the clouds, three of the four escaping bombers crashed full throttle into a mountainside. The fourth was lost over unfamiliar, cloud-covered terrain. Panicked, the Army tried to get CNAC's Kunming direction-finding station to give bearings to the disoriented plane—but with none of its own planes inbound, the airline's Kunming staff had gone off duty. The lost bomber ran out of gas, and its crew bailed out near Changyi, where Foxie Kent had been killed in October 1940. Of the six B-25s, only two badly shot-up planes reached Kunming. The Army lost four bombers—and nineteen men.

Enraged, General Bissell blamed CNAC for the fiasco, at least partly. Chuck Sharp refused to bear one iota of responsibility. He'd come to China in 1933 because his one thousand hours of flying experience wasn't enough to land him a job as a copilot in a domestic airline, and since then, he'd amassed some ten thousand hours of sky time. Most Air Corps higher-ups hadn't flown in years, and as for the junior ones, Sharp didn't think many of the three- or four-hundred-hour "experts" arriving in the Far East at the controls of multi-engine aircraft could tell an elevator from an earflap. The inexperience of the Army pilots was excusable considering the Air Corps's astonishing expansion; the attitude of their leadership was not. Most mid- and upper-echelon Air Corps officers struck Sharp and the rest of the company's people as amateur blowhards, hell-bent on showing the civilians how things were done, Army fashion—an extraordinarily unintelligent attitude, considering that the airline had *five years* of wartime experience. Sharp dashed off a letter and "jumped right down Bissell's throat [wearing] hob-nailed boots and spurs," laying fault where it fairly belonged—on Air Corps arrogance and incompetence.

Wonderful as it was to be in Washington with his wife, their two sons, and the extended relations, William Bond never felt completely comfortable at Hayes Manor. Events in Asia and the Pacific worried him too much. The complete loss of Burma made an airlift seem the only hope of keeping China in the fight. With the exception of the four Japanese aircraft carriers recently sunk in the waters off Midway Island, the war wasn't going well, and Midway was many thousands of miles from the regions of Asia that concerned his airline. T. V. Soong had held Bond in the United States through April and May, using Bond's practical expertise to counterweigh the Air Corps' "can't do" attitude with regard to a China airlift, but Washington's commitment to the project seemed to solidify in late May and early June, and Soong decided that he could afford to let Bond return to Asia.

Bondy and Kitsi had dinner with Lauchlin Currie and his wife as part of his predeparture round of social engagements, both business and pleasure. The foursome had just sat down to dinner when they were interrupted by a telephone call from Stanley Hornbeck, ordering Bond to a morning meeting with General George C. Marshall, chairman of the Joint Chiefs of Staff and the de facto commander of the entire Allied war effort. At the War Department, Marshall was upright and proper and immaculately uniformed, but he was also scrupulously polite and considerate, the picture of professional courtesy and mutual respect, all in marked contrast to the impression Bond had formed of General Arnold a few weeks before. Inside his office, Marshall explained that he needed an informal envoy to carry a message to the Generalissimo, and that Stanley Hornbeck had recommended Bond. Of course, Bond agreed without hesitation, flattered to have the confidence of the Allies' top-ranking military man. Marshall summarized what he needed conveyed, acknowledging that the war hadn't gone well since Pearl Harbor. Setbacks in the Middle and Far East had forced Marshall to divert Lend-Lease resources intended for China to help the

British defend Burma, India, and Egypt. Burma and India had to be given higher short-run priority, since China couldn't contribute as an active ally without India. Marshall knew that Chiang blamed Britain for those decisions, although Marshall had made them with no goal in mind but the quickest possible defeat of Japan. Marshall wanted his strategic thinking explained to the Generalissimo, but he couldn't do it through official channels without provoking howls of formal Chinese protest and demands for return concessions.

Soon after the meeting, Bond began the two-week odyssey back to Asia, and he delivered Marshall's message to Madame Chiang in Chungking. Madame received it politely and assured Bond that the Generalissimo understood entirely.

Unfortunately, Chuck Sharp had done much to sour the airline's relationship with General Bissell and the Air Corps while Bond was in the United States. As Bond noted in a letter to Bixby after he'd reached Asia, "There was some justification for his wanting to do this, but no justification for him actually doing it." Bond made General Bissell's acquaintance, discussing needs for direction-finding equipment, and before long, he too was experiencing some of the aggravations that had unhinged Sharp. General Bissell challenged his every statement, apparently on general principle. Bond thought he enjoyed such conflict, and came to consider it typical of interactions with Bissell in particular and the Army in general. "However, CNAC is and will continue to cooperate one hundred percent," he informed Bixby. "Whether it will be because of or in spite of the General remains to be seen."

Part of the Army's resentment seemed due to the statistically unarguable qualitative gap between the two organizations. The Army flew 106 tons to China in June 1942; the China National Aviation Corporation flew 91 tons, with one-third the number of aircraft. If the Army had kept the airline consistently supplied with cargo, it could have flown much more.

The two Chinese divisions retreating northwest from Myitkyina had spent the last half of May and most of June thrashing north-northwest through thick jungles and monsoon downpours toward the head of the Chindwin Valley, from which they could escape over the Indian frontier to Ledo, in Upper Assam. The increasingly wretched survivors were only fifty miles from safety when the Generalissimo changed their orders. He allowed one division to march out to Ledo, but he ordered the other to make a 90-degree eastward turn back to China across the jungles of north Burma and the rugged heart of the Three Gorges country, condemning the soldiers to months of indescribable misery in some of the world's most punishing terrain.

Intermittently, U.S. Army planes flying under the monsoon cloud cover had dropped supplies to the unfortunate infantrymen, but not enough food was getting through. Chiang Kai-shek wanted CNAC on the job. The minister of communications passed the order to William Bond, and Bond went to see General Bissell, who blew up when Bond explained his instructions. It was a waste of effort, Bissell roared. The Chinese division was going to starve walking out to China instead of taking the shorter route to India.

Bond said he could understand why the Generalissimo wanted his army in China instead of India, even if the terrain was more difficult. All he wanted to do was help the Chinese soldiers.

Daily, for the next four days, the minister of communications telephoned Bond and asked why support wasn't reaching the starving infantrymen. Over the Hump in Dinjan, Hugh Woods had airplanes ready to go, but the Army wasn't supplying any food.

Bissell's cussedness forced Bond into an untenable position: Either lie to a ministry of the Chinese government with which he'd been honorably conducting business for eleven years or tell the truth—that an American general so disagreed with Chiang Kai-shek's policy that he was willing to let Chinese soldiers suffer when he had the means to alleviate their plight, which was sure to damage Sino-American relations at the highest levels. To the Chinese, Bond hemmed and hawed, citing imaginary operational difficulties. After the fourth day, he at last confronted the general. "I can't assume this blame any longer. I've got to make an intelligent report to the minister. We're ready but can't get food. What can I report?"

Food appeared the next day, CNAC began making airdrops, and the Chinese infantry continued its awful journey to China. "That doesn't sound reasonable, and it isn't," Bond wrote to Bixby, describing the imbroglio, "but it is far more reasonable than many things I see being done."

Aside from the difficulties of dealing with the U.S. Army Air Corps, Bond's biggest problem in the middle months of 1942 was pilots. Given the two-per-month rate of Lend-Lease airplane deliveries he and T. V. Soong had secured, the airline needed to add four to six aircrews every month in order to operate the new planes efficiently. Bond had lured a handful of pilots to Asia while he was in the United States, but he needed far more, and the Air Corps' massive expansion was hoovering most qualified men into uniform. The airline's obvious short-run solution was to sign on the pilots and ground technicians of Claire Chennault's American Volunteer Group—Chennault had lost his campaign to maintain his pursuit group's civilian-flavored independence, which the Army simply couldn't tolerate, and the group was going to be disbanded when their yearlong contracts started expiring in early July. Ironically, the Air Corps needed the services of Chennault's men, and it hoped to entice them to uniformed service, but unfortunately for the Army's suit, General Bissell fronted its recruitment efforts, and his threats, bluster, and bravado could hardly have been better calculated to offend the volunteers. Aware of CNAC's allure, the Army tried to prevent the airline from hiring any AVG personnel. Messages from Bixby in New York and from Army commanders in India and China expressly prohibited the airline from recruiting Chennault's people, but the messages contained no threats serious enough to dissuade Bond, Sharp, and Woods from keeping quiet feelers out among them.

The American Volunteer Group disbanded on July 4, 1942, having compiled one of the best combat records of any fighter group in history. They'd "raised hell on a shoestring," as one AVG pilot boasted to *Life* magazine, and Madame Chiang Kai-shek honored the volunteers with a party on the last night of their official existence. Bond attended, and he greatly amused Her Eminence by taking two turns through the receiving line, joking on his second pass that he "couldn't resist the opportunity to pay his respects twice." Inside, Bond dipped into Madame's nonalcoholic punch, the stiffest tipple she served, and glad-handed among the AVG personnel. Madame Chiang made her guests play musical chairs, an unanticipated diversion for hard-carousing fighter pilots on bellies full of virgin fruit juice, and she made a formal ceremony of presenting Chennault with an oil portrait of himself standing with the Chiangs. The party ended early, its only mercy. At 11 P.M., Bond's chauffeur drove him through steady rain to the Methodist compound.

Predictably, the Air Corps wasn't yet prepared to assume the AVG's responsibility for the air defense of China. Chennault asked for volunteers from among his volunteers to hold the fort for the two additional weeks it would take the Air Corps to get a pursuit group combat-ready. Eighteen AVG pilots agreed to serve the extra time, including Camille Joseph "Joe" Rosbert, a black-haired, blue-eyed, middleweight Philadelphian who'd signed on with Chennault in 1941 to escape the tedium of flying Navy patrol planes. It wasn't light duty: One of the holdovers died in action over central China on July 10. When Rosbert finished his extended service, he went to talk to CNAC in Calcutta. Unlike the Air Corps, Bond, Sharp, and Woods pitched it straight and level. Starting salary would be eight hundred dollars per month, for sixty hours of flying, they said, with ten dollars an hour for hours between sixty and seventy, and twenty per for hours above seventy. He would stay in Calcutta for a week or two, then go up-country and fly until he got his hours in, then back to Calcutta. One of the things that had really stuck in the AVG men's craw was that the Army wouldn't give them the home leave promised in their contracts. The airline couldn't send them home right away, either, but it was receiving an average of two DC-3 types a month in the States and needed people to fly them to Asia. Based on the delivery schedule, the company promised to send the AVG men home two at a time for three months' leave and have them each fly a plane back at the end of their furloughs.

Good pay, continued flying, home leave, organizational competence, freedom from uniformed annoyances, luxury living in Calcutta, the hope of postwar employment with Pan Am, and, most important of all, an honorable and important way to contribute to the war effort: Joe Rosbert had heard enough. "Give me the papers," he said. "I'll fly for you."

For Joe Rosbert, it was a fateful decision, one that would cost him untold agony, and very nearly his life, but the airline was hard to resist, and when the dust of disbandment settled, the Army Air Corps got five pilots from the American Volunteer Group. The China National Aviation Corporation got sixteen.

The tussle did nothing to ease relations between the U.S. Army and the airline, and considering how closely his company was working with the military, and the perils of the relationship's becoming overtly adversarial, Bond wanted to cultivate a favorable impression with Lieutenant General Joseph Stilwell, the Army's top man in Asia. There were a number of operational questions he hoped Stilwell could resolve, and Bond arranged to meet him at the general's Chungking headquarters, a flat-topped, modernist villa overlooking the Chialing River originally built for T. V. Soong that in its ascetic design meshed well with Stilwell's Spartan proclivities.

Stilwell had walked out of Burma five weeks before, and he looked as thin as barbed wire, and about as spiny, tinged pale yellow by jaundice he'd contracted from defective yellow fever serum. The day before, his doctor had diagnosed blood worms, and his debilitating physical ailments compounded the grinding frustrations of his job. Although the airline's allotment of Lend-Lease airplanes came from the highest echelons of the American government, Stilwell wasn't pleased, feeling that all military equipment sent to the area should be subject to his command. He demanded that Bond justify the allocation.

CNAC was a Chinese company, explained Bond, organized under Chinese law, and most of its officers were Chinese. Lend-Leasing those planes to the airline told China it hadn't been forgotten when most Allied decisions sent the opposite message.

Military considerations outweighed diplomatic ones, Stilwell countered.

"General, I'm going to be frank. You're a West Pointer and you're not going to like my explanations, but I can back everything I say with facts. Point-blank, there is no officer of any rank, nor any unit in the United States Army, capable of operating over the Hump as well as the China National Aviation Corporation. None of the Air Corps officers in the Far East think it's feasible. They won't attempt it wholeheartedly unless they're forced. You *need* us to have those airplanes so we can prove it's possible."

Bond left the meeting without having gotten his operational questions answered.

The rains of the southwest monsoon soaked Assam and Burma through the summer, as they'd done since the middle of May, and the steady downpours turned unimproved roads and runways into quagmires. Water condensed in fuel tanks and carburetors, and it was instrument flying most of the way from Dinjan to Kunming. The vile weather near-grounded the Tenth Air Force's newly formed India–China Ferry Command—the unit with which it intended to prosecute the Hump airlift. CNAC flew regardless, carrying much heavier payloads. General Stilwell noted the difference in his diary: "No attention to capacity. CNAC 4,700 lbs., USA, 3,500 lbs.

CNAC flying regularly when weather keeps us grounded." Ferry Command had 35 planes, and it flew 73 tons into China in July; CNAC flew 136 tons, using 9 aircraft.

Despite the initial efforts of the airlift, a few hundred tons delivered were but a drop in the ocean of Free China's need. Hemmed into poor western provinces and juggling for power, prestige, and position with Mao's Communists and various regional warlords, Nationalist China was under immense pressure, and the stress manifested in the value of its currency. Prices in September of 1942 were running thirty to sixty times higher than they'd been in mid-1937, and the inflationary pace was quickening, accelerated by the monetary policies of His Excellency Dr. H. H. Kung, Kuomintang minister of finance, whose primary answer to paucity of revenue, fiscal deficits, and the arbitrary, enormous, unbudgeted sums the Generalissimo lavished around China was to print more paper money to cover the shortfalls—which, of course, did little but devalue the paper and render increasingly worthless bank deposits, bonds, and the small quantities of cash squirreled into the walls of peasants' hovels. In distant Chinese history, the Sung dynasty and the Mongol Empire had collapsed in inflationary whirlwinds. By the summer of 1942, another such storm was beginning to batter the supports of Nationalist China. Practical Chinese saw two ways to safeguard their wealth: hoard commodities and own gold—the Central Government made both illegal. Regardless, black markets sprang up like weeds: for medicines, clothing, rice, milk powder, and other foodstuffs, cosmetics, toothpaste, jewelry, cigarettes, nylon stockings, perfume, flashlights, Parker pens, wristwatches, typewriter ribbons, envelopes, gasoline, tires, spark plugs, and scrap metal—any tangible commodity seemed certain to hold value better than Nationalist currency. CNAC had about thirty qualified or soon-to-be-qualified pilot-captains on its roster in September 1942, by far the most it had had in its thirteen-year history, and with their unique ability to get in and out of China, the company's flight crews and mechanics were the men in Asia most perfectly positioned to exploit extracurricular fund-raising opportunities. The corporate leadership hoped its generous salaries were sufficient to dissuade employees from smuggling, and sometimes they were. There were less scrupulous men who reached for ever more lucrative opportunities, however, and for them, the excellent pay provided a tidy amount of venture capital. In the late summer of 1942, an intrepid airman could buy an ounce of gold in Calcutta for 180 rupees, fly it over the Hump, sell it to a Kunming gold bug for 6,300 Chinese dollars, and use that wad to purchase 406 rupees from any black-market currency trader.* In simple financial terms, an airman buying gold in India and selling it in China earned a 125 percent return on invested capital per successful trip, a market inefficiency with the power to quickly turn small fortunes into large ones.

On September 2, 1942, the Kunming Airport Inspectorate stormed aboard a flight piloted by Captain J. A. Porter and found 410.8 ounces of gold—twenty-five and a half pounds—stashed under his seat, worth more than two and a half million Chinese dollars on the black market. For the single flight, Porter stood to profit approximately 14,500 U.S. dollars, a year and a half's salary (worth about $180,000 in modern dollars). Customs confiscated Porter's gold; Hugh Woods terminated his services. Three Chinese mechanics had exposed his scheme—Porter must have treated them badly, or else refused to cut them into his profits, both dangerous courses of action, considering mechanics controlled the flightworthiness of the airplanes.

Later in the month, inspectors found twenty-two pounds of gold hidden under a C-53's washbasin in the lavatory at the rear of the airplane. The crew denied knowledge of it. The gold probably belonged to Dinjan mechanics sending it across to Kunming coworkers. Attempting to stifle the smuggling, William Bond prohibited his flight crews from wearing new clothes, more than one watch per man, or any gold jewelry besides wedding rings. He barred them from taking bedrolls, sleeping bags, or blankets on ordinary flights, and no crew member other than the flight captain was allowed to carry a fountain pen.

There were other irregularities. Left behind in a Hong Kong bank, the airline had 148,000 U.S. dollars that Bond hadn't been able to evacuate (worth about $1.85 million in modern dollars). He presumed it lost for the duration. Much to his amazement, the money "turned up" in Chungking in mid-September. Obviously, it suited the company to have access to the cash, but its return stank like a Chungking sewer—someone, somewhere

* One Indian rupee for 15.5 Chinese dollars, the black market rate in September 1942.

in the upper echelons of the Nationalist government, was doing business in enemy territory. Bond wondered what quid pro quo had been provided.

In continuation of the tungsten freight-flying business conducted from Namyung prior to Pearl Harbor, minister of economic affairs and chairman of the National Resource Commission Wong Wen-hao had pledged to supply fifteen thousand tons of tungsten to the United States in 1942—a point of leverage applied to the United States government when the Chinese were trying to persuade it to commit airplanes to the China airlift. At the time, America's tungsten shortage was so acute that the U.S. Army was detailing soldiers to work in stateside tungsten mines. Bond had helped deliver the message. But in mid-August the National Resources Commission claimed that tungsten supplies were "temporarily exhausted," and pressed the Americans to fly out tin instead. Bolivia supplied the bulk of American tin, however, a much less logistically complicated source that didn't bamboozle the United States into buying metal at an artificially inflated price by insisting on a twenty-to-one "official" exchange rate while actual currency values fluctuated from eighty to one hundred to one. Not wanting to set a precedent, the U.S. Metals Reserve Company, a quasi-corporate government entity established to coordinate the supply of metals to the American war machine, didn't want to fly tin in tungsten's stead. Only a handful of Americans realized what caused the tungsten shortfall. Colonel Frank Dorn, one of General Stilwell's closest associates, considered it indicative of the state of China's belligerency—or lack thereof. "There exists what amounts to an undeclared peace," Dorn wrote, "with mail and a considerable trade going back and forth between occupied and unoccupied China. That is why tungsten shipments have not been as large as had been expected. The Japs pay a little better." The Metals Reserve Company solved the shortage by raising the price it paid for tungsten.

Most Americans operated under the mistaken assumption that ridding their country of invaders topped Chinese priorities. Only extreme realists like Stilwell, Dorn, and Ambassador Gauss perceived that expelling the Japanese didn't head the policy agendas of either the Nationalist or the Communist factions vying to control China, no matter how loudly they each rattled the anti-Japanese saber. Japan's bid for Far Eastern hegemony had given China powerful proxies. Both Communists and Nationalists were quite content to allow the United States to crush Japan. They were already looking beyond Japan's defeat, maneuvering to amass the military, economic, and political capital for the fight for what was, to them, the greatest prize—the right to unify and rule China.

The monsoon began petering out in October. Solid overcast and steady rain fragmented into broken skies and intermittent downpours, becoming more widely scattered as the month progressed. Bond, Sharp, and Woods knew the better weather would bring the return of the Japanese, and as far as they could discern, the Army Air Corps and the Royal Air Force hadn't made any meaningful efforts to upgrade the Assam air-warning net while they'd had the monsoon's protection. Predictably, a Japanese raid caught Dinjan by surprise on Sunday, October 25, but the airline took no damage because all of its eleven Lend-Lease C-53s had left at daybreak and weren't due back till dusk.* On Monday, Hugh Woods got ten of the planes away at dawn. One pilot was refreshing his flying procedures in the eleventh, making practice landings on the Dinjan runway, when he saw the gray-black plumes of bomb-burst eruptions on the field. He hammered his throttles, hauled his wheels, and roared out of Dinjan at minimum altitude, not having caught sight of the attacking planes, nor of the three Japanese Zeros diving onto his tail.** An Army P-40 pilot swooped to his aid and shot down the lead Zero, only to be shot down and killed by the other attackers. The airline pilot escaped and flew his empty airplane over the Hump to Kunming, where he learned how close he'd been to death.*** An airline work gang recovered the body of the P-40 pilot who'd died saving their pilot's life and returned it to the Air Corps. Although inexperienced, there was noth-

---

* Actual deliveries of Lend-Lease aircraft hadn't quite kept pace with the promise made earlier in the year.

** Technically, the planes weren't Zeroes (Mitsubishi A6M2s), which was a Japanese Navy airplane, but probably Nakajima Ki-43 Hayabusas—code-named "Oscar" by the Allies—a similar-looking but different airplane flown by the Imperial Japanese Army Air Force. However, Bond referred to the planes as "Zeros" in an October 29, 1942, letter to Harold Bixby, and the CNAC fliers routinely called any Japanese fighter planes "Zeros" during the war and still do to this day, so "Zeros" they shall remain in this story.

*** The CNAC pilot was Donald Wong, Moon Chin's best friend and one of the airline's three original Chinese American pilots, who'd rejoined the airline after Pearl Harbor.

ing wrong with Army pilots. Most were uncommonly courageous. It was their leadership that left so much to be desired.

CNAC suffered no losses in the three days of raids, but the Air Corps lost two fighters shot down in the air and four other fighters and ten transports destroyed on the ground, and the attacks rattled the Army command in Delhi. They instructed their military mission in Chungking to determine CNAC's intentions. A telephone call summoned Bond to Army headquarters, where a group of excited officers huddled around the airline executive, eager to ascertain if his company intended to keep operating.

"Yes, I suppose so. Why do you ask?"

"Well, it looks like this war has finally started," gabbed their spokesperson, telling Bond to keep his chin up, to soldier on against the difficulties, and assuring him they'd win through in the end.

"For us it started five years ago," Bond monotoned icily. As politely as he could manage, he thanked the Army officers for their concern. Their breathless arrogance would have been so much easier to tolerate if they were getting their jobs done.

Neither had the Army yet paid anything for the use of CNAC's Lend-Lease planes. Bond was negotiating an operating contract for their services, and although he knew that his company would get paid eventually, the Army's glacial accounts payable were wreaking havoc with the airline's cash flow. The only thing keeping the Lend-Lease planes in the air was Standard Oil Company's very generous agreement not to make the airline pay for gas and oil until the Army settled its bill. A reprieve came in the form of Mr. Kusminsky, the Soviet Union's trade representative, who'd bought eighty tons of mercury in China.* He asked Bond to fly it to India.

"Why don't you have the Army fly it?" Bond asked. "They'll do it for free."

"So they've been telling us for two weeks, but they haven't moved a ton."

Sensing opportunity, Bond arranged to fly the quicksilver for five hundred U.S. dollars per ton, and his airline got all of it to India in four days.

---

* Mercury was another crucial primary ingredient of modern war, and the Germans had captured Russia's principal mercury-producing region in the Donets Basin. Fiercely embattled with the Nazis in the Volga River city of Stalingrad, the Russians were trying to make good their shortage with purchases around the world.

The Soviets immediately wired payment to New York. Two weeks later, the airline flew three hundred tons of Russian tin, and the Communists paid just as promptly, keeping the airline solvent while it waited for the Army to make good on its promises.

On the other side of the Hump, in Assam, to house the pilots serving their up-country rotations, the airline had established a hostel in a tea planter's bungalow a few miles from the Dinjan airfield. Like every other structure in the region, it stood on eight-foot stilts to protect it from monsoon floods. It was a hundred feet wide with a roof of steeply pitched thatch, and steps rose to meet a wide veranda stretched across the building's entire front. Tall, leafy trees cast pleasing shade into the compound. Compared with the atrocious living conditions to which the Army Air Corps subjected its Assam-based personnel, the CNAC employees were living high on the hog, but the airline was still dogged by the same pilot shortage that had hampered it since the Lend-Lease planes started arriving early in the year. Trying to draw experienced fliers to Asia, the airline had feelers out in all corners of the aviation world.

One man who heard the whispers was Pete Goutiere, who, since Pearl Harbor, had been flying for Pan American Airways–Africa, a Pan Am subsidiary formed to ferry planes and supplies across that continent, which he'd joined because the Air Corps considered twenty-seven-year-olds too venerable for military flying. The Army had revised its opinion in the last eleven months, but so had Pete Goutiere, and he'd spurned their ham-handed attempts to recruit the Pan Africa pilots and traveled to Assam hoping to catch on with Pan Am's China partnership. An inch or two shorter than six feet, with a leather flying jacket draped over an arm, and a studiously smushed flying cap perched on his head when he pushed through the hostel's rough wooden gate in late October or early November, Goutiere positively dripped casual pilot glamour. Out back, he discovered Hugh Woods playing badminton with his fiancée, Maj. She'd been hired by the airline to manage the hostel.

"I heard you were looking for pilots," Goutiere said.

"I don't believe it," Woody said, chuckling. "We've been looking all over for pilots, and here you come, slouching out of the tea patches."

Woods inquired about his experience, and Goutiere gave a quick verbal résumé: about eight hundred hours, the last three hundred hours as a DC-3 copilot.

"You'll do, but I warn you, this ain't what you're used to," Woods cautioned. The airline had lost its first plane on the Hump recently, missing without trace. Woody summoned Suklo, the hostel's Indian housekeeper, and asked him to show Goutiere to one of the bunks inside.

And Goutiere proceeded to ask Suklo, in fluent Hindi, if Suklo would be pleased to draw him a hot bath?

Woods nearly dropped his racket.

"Sahib," mumbled the astonished servant, "Hindi you're speaking almost like a native. How come you're speaking so good?"

Goutiere answered in Hindi, grinning slyly. He'd learned the language taking pretty little Hindu girls to bed.

Suklo roared with laughter and hurried off to draw the bath and share the story with the other servants. Pete Goutiere had spent his childhood in India, and now, after fifteen long years in America, he was ready to renew his love affair with the Orient.

Woody had Goutiere flown to Calcutta to formalize his employment, and Goutiere started making Hump trips as copilot to the airline's more experienced fliers. Off duty, Goutiere began palling around with Jimmy Fox and Charles Sharkey, two other recent arrivals. Six feet tall and tomato-pole thin, swarthy, and sporting a small mustache, Fox was from Dalhart, Texas, where he'd learned to fly as a teenager and been president of his high school class. Before the war, he'd earned a degree from the University of California at Berkeley and he'd migrated to the airline from Pan American Air Ferries.* Charles Sharkey, of Lawrence, Massachusetts, had joined the airline a month before the other two, and although Goutiere didn't think Sharkey looked old enough to drink, let alone pilot an airplane, he'd recently checked out as captain, making him the new clique's veteran. At only twenty-two years old, Sharkey was the youngest pilot-captain in the China National Aviation Corporation by a long measure, but he'd been flying since his early teens, when he'd saved enough spare change and allowance to pay for flying lessons, then for gas and aircraft hire to build his experi-

* Another Pan Am subsidiary formed to fly military aircraft to the theaters where they'd be employed.

ence. He'd come to Asia from Canada, where he'd spent 1940 and 1941 teaching flying to Commonwealth pilot candidates, and he absolutely refused to let anyone call him Chuck, or Charles, for that matter. He insisted on "Sharkey," and with his pockets full of airline money, he'd built himself a reputation for wild gambling and carousing on Calcutta's Kariah Road.

Goutiere, Fox, and Sharkey all did one or two flying rotations in the late autumn and, as most of the airline's new hires did before they settled into permanent Calcutta accommodations, when they were downcountry they stayed in the Grand Hotel or the Great Eastern, opulent constructions of the British Raj. The Grand faced onto Chowringhee Street and the Maiden, central Calcutta's long, thin park running along the east bank of the Hooghly River. The Great Eastern was a few blocks away, at the intersection of Old Court House and British India streets. Sharkey, Goutiere, and Fox were off duty for the holidays, and they gravitated to the Grand's lavish Christmas banquet. Civic leaders blacked out the city to confound Japanese bombardiers and navigators, but behind lightproof curtains, the Grand Hotel was spectacularly lit for Christmas. American, British, Canadian, Australian, and CNAC uniforms clustered against the bar. Brass insignia gleamed from the turbans and white caftan coats of the servants bustling through the hotel, their midriffs wrapped in red and blue cummerbunds. Right on the stroke of eight o'clock, the uniformed and liveried majordomo stepped into the bar and announced, "Gentlemen, dinner is served."

More than a hundred guests filtered into the dining room and stood behind their seats, contemplating tables heaped with turkeys and hams, salads and side dishes, towering plum puddings, candelabras, and holly twigs. The majordomo gave the order to sit, the orchestra struck up a Christmas carol, and deep booms outside the hotel interrupted the band's second stanza. Then came whistles and yells: "Air raid! Air raid!"

The banquet room disintegrated into a chaos of fleeing servants, fear-stricken band members, and military men dashing off to join their units. The electricity failed and the hotel went dark, leaving the gentle glow of the dining room candles illuminating the CNAC men and the two dozen assorted uniforms who'd stayed at their seats. Engines droned, sirens wailed, and more bomb detonations echoed over the city.

"What the hell," said a voice, "let's help ourselves before dinner gets cold."

A British officer found a carving knife and set to work on a turkey, loading plate after plate. Another Englishman poured brandy over a plum pudding and lit it up, the flames quickly subsiding to a blue glow. Sharkey vaulted the bar and liberated an armload of whisky bottles. After dinner, one of the Brits played Christmas carols on the hotel piano as the men drank and sang into the wee hours.

Downstairs the next morning, British Boxing Day, Goutiere picked a path through the prostrate bodies sprawled among the festive debris. Thirty woozy steps beyond the dining room and through the foyer and onto the sidewalk, Goutiere came face-to-face with the hard poverty of Calcutta's streets. A naked woman lay motionless on the sidewalk, her thighs wet with her own menstrual blood, attended by a cloud of fat, hovering flies and two gaunt dogs. Beggars accosted him. The contrast with the genteel colonial splendor of the Grand Hotel couldn't have been more extreme.

A few blocks away, Goutiere checked the airline's flight schedule posted on a board outside the bar in the Great Eastern. Another pilot asked him if he'd heard about Privencal and Lane, two other recent hires.

Apparently, James "Skippy" Lane and Al Privencal had finished their flying on Christmas Eve and were enjoying a booze session in the lounge of the Dinjan bungalow. Soon, they were feeling no pain, and Privencal prattled on about how he'd become a crack shot testing pistols for Colt Firearms before the war. Eventually, Skippy Lane couldn't stand it anymore. "Okay, Pri, let's see how good you really are," he called from the other side of the lounge. "I got ten rupees saying you can't hit my foot."

And so twenty-nine-year-old Albert Joseph Privencal from Mount Tabor, Vermont, whipped a Colt 1911 automatic from his flight holster and blasted a .45-caliber hole in Skippy Lane's foot.

The strain of the Hump flying was beginning to tell.

22

CLIPPING THE EDGE OF BEDROCK

Unhappy with results, the War Department relieved the Tenth Air Force of responsibility for the China ferry on December 1, 1942, and reorganized the airlift into the India-China Wing of the Air Transport Command (the ATC), the Air Corps agency responsible for global airlift. General Stilwell tasked the new wing to get 5,000 tons over the Hump in February 1943. It quickly became apparent that the new wing wouldn't come close to hitting the benchmark. "Ferry line is falling down," Stilwell grumbled into his diary.

In contrast, the airline was setting an excellent example. Inclusive, August 1942 through January 1943, CNAC flew 1,185 round-trips between India and China, and it had made at least one flight over the Hump every single day since July 1, a feat the Army hadn't come close to duplicating. Since August, the airline had flown 465 tons of paper money into China, 140 tons more than any other type of cargo, a perfect reflection of China's inflationary malaise,* as well as significant quantities of copper ingots and

---

* Banknotes constituted 9 percent of all eastbound Hump tonnage between September 1942 and February 1943: R&S I, p. 314.

zinc slabs, aviation supplies, automobile parts, heavy machinery, printing ink and papers, copper and steel wire, smokeless gunpowder, brass and steel caps, medicines, tires, tubes, assorted war matériel, and 268 Army personnel—all in support of the Chinese war effort. Outbound, the airline had flown 1,203 long tons of tungsten, 7.4 percent of the total quantity consumed by U.S industry, tin and mercury for the Soviet Union, silk for Allied parachutes, wood oil, tea, 6,784 Chinese soldiers to flesh out the divisions in India training for a counteroffensive into Burma, and 87 tons of bristles shorn from Chinese hogs, much valued by the Navy for use in marine paintbrushes. The statistical results in both directions would have been even more impressive if the airline hadn't been so hamstrung by spare-parts shortages and lack of cooperation.

Foul weather plagued the Hump at January's end. Bucking hundred-mile-per-hour headwinds, the planes returning to India hit severe icing conditions climbing into a cloud layer at 14,000 feet. Cockpit temperatures fell into the negative twenties, Fahrenheit, and if they were lucky, the pilots could just barely get their DC-3 types into the sunshine at 20,500 feet, where they flew blind beneath the ice hoods frozen over their windshields for four or five hours, until they could let down into warmer air. Nobody in the world was flying regularly in worse conditions, but the airline hadn't lost a plane since November. Bond tapped wood whenever he thought of it.

Of course, it was too good to last. A DC-3's right engine caught fire forty minutes out of Chungking on February 13, and the pilot force-landed on a Yangtze River sandbar. Everyone aboard escaped unscathed and took a boat downriver to the wartime capital. The plane was DC-3 number 46, the airline's most famous, "the DC-2½," a.k.a. "the French DC-3," and it had been flying faithfully since its notorious wing replacement. The great river rose and swept it away. Worse wasn't long in arriving, as the approach of spring brought even more volatile weather.

In Dinjan on the morning of March 11, Suklo, the head bearer, woke the pilots as he always did, blaring Glenn Miller's "Under Blue Canadian Skies" on the hostel's gramophone about ninety minutes before sunrise. After breakfast, copilot Pete Goutiere and his pilot-captain, Russell Johnson, flew drums of aviation fuel over the Hump for General Chennault. On the ground in Kunming, they lounged with Charles Sharkey, Jimmy Fox, and Orin Welch, each of whom had brought an airplane over from Dinjan. The men gossiped and talked flying, watching coolies unload gasoline drums and strap tin ingots into the planes for the outbound flight. Welch said he'd discovered a pass where you could slip through the mountains under the cloud layer at less than eleven thousand feet, an attractive option given the horrendous turbulence and icing. He offered to show it to the others on the return flight.

West of Kunming, the planes gathered in loose trail formation. Welch in the lead, then Sharkey, then Jimmy Fox. Last came Russ Johnson and Pete Goutiere. The quartet climbed to ten thousand feet, skirting Paoshan and Tali mountains, and the going was easy until they bounced through turbulence over the huge ridge dividing the Mekong Valley from the Salween. Dead ahead, a massive cloud roll buried the highest peaks on the route. Rocks, bare trees, and dull white snows showed on the lower flanks of the mountains. The V of a pass cut below the cloud layer, and Welch made straight for it, leading the little formation under the thick edge of gray. Loosely supervised by pilot Johnson, Goutiere had control of their airplane. Suddenly, snow pelted the windshield. Welch went through the pass, and Goutiere lost sight of Sharkey in the squall. He could barely see Fox, a mere seven hundred feet in front of him. Turbulence buffeted the plane, and Goutiere chanced a glance at his instruments—caught in a downdraft on the leeward side of the pass, the plane was down to ninety miles per hour and losing altitude at five hundred feet per minute. Goutiere shoved power and mixtures forward and banked away.

Just ahead, Jimmy Fox clawed for power and altitude as he made the same realization too late to turn around. He skimmed the trees, and for a few seconds it looked as if he'd make it, but his left wing hooked a treetop and the twenty-eight-thousand-pound airplane cartwheeled through the forest, smashing trees in a cloud of snowy debris.

Goutiere barely managed to slot himself into a gulch plunging down from the pass. He silently prayed that Fox was okay, but he'd seen the crash and knew he wasn't. In the valley bottom, Goutiere leveled out, turned south along the Salween River, and began climbing. Johnson hadn't seen Fox's wreck; Goutiere told what he'd witnessed. Soon they were in clouds and snow again, flying blind. They turned west once they'd gained enough altitude to clear the peaks.

Since arriving in India, Jimmy Fox had been one of Goutiere's best friends. Goutiere pretended to dry moisture from the yoke with his hand-kerchief, hoping Johnson wouldn't catch him wiping tears. In Dinjan, Hugh

Woods met them on the flight line, his face etched with relief and worry. Welch, Sharkey, Goutiere, and Johnson were home; Fox was not. Woods did his best to appear gruff and tough, but to his pilots his war face was utterly transparent. He heard the story and turned away from the sunset, casting shadow across his eyes. "You two go back to the hostel. I'll stick around and wait a little more, just in case."

Two days later, Goutiere, Welch, Weldon Tutwiler, and George Huang were again flying back to India from Kunming. The Hump was gentle, and they buzzed smoothly over the mountains west of the Salween. Roiling thunderheads athwart the route across north Burma guaranteed the rest of the flight wouldn't be so benign. It didn't appear possible to end-run the squall line. Goutiere spiraled to the deck and squeezed between the jungle and the base of the clouds, where he flew for half an hour, buffeted by heavy rain and strong winds, before emerging into stable weather beyond. George Huang, Weldon Tutwiler, and Orin Welch opted to fly straight through the storm.

Huang plowed into the cumulonimbus at fifteen thousand feet, and updrafts skyrocketed his airplane. Horrendous turbulence nearly shook it apart. He reversed course, a difficult maneuver to execute in such angry air, and popped out of the storm at twenty-three thousand feet with such violence it snapped the ropes securing the tin ingots in his cargo bay. The hundred-pound metal bricks bucked into the air and crashed down like cannonballs, smashed the floor, and burst through the aluminum skin of the airplane. Luckily, the free-flying projectiles didn't sever any control cables. Weldon Tutwiler had the same experience. Badly shaken, Huang and Tutwiler followed Goutiere's example, circled to low altitude, and sneaked under the storm. Such good fortune didn't smile on Orin Welch. He and his crew never reached Dinjan.

Two fatal accidents within forty-eight hours plummeted morale among the freight pilots. For weeks, they'd flown through atrocious weather when common sense dictated otherwise. Bond and Colonel Wang flew to Dinjan to impress upon the pilots the importance of their efforts to the war effort. The airline's rapid expansion and the four months he'd spent in Washington hadn't allowed Bond to form the close relationships with the new pilots he'd enjoyed with the men who'd flown for him during the Shanghai and Hong Kong years and, frankly, many of the freight pilots didn't like him. He was a "suit" in their eyes, a politician, even a "dishrag," an old man counting down the months to his fiftieth birthday. Most of them were in their mid to late twenties and, like pilots everywhere, they couldn't imagine he did anything important, since he wasn't flying or maintaining an airplane. The old, prewar personnel held Bond in high esteem, but their influence was increasingly diluted.

Whether or not Bond's encouragement had any real effect, the pilots kept flying despite the icing conditions and the seven and a half inches of rain that fell in the Assam Valley in the third week of March, and CNAC's freight kept making it to China in per-plane quantities that dwarfed Army deliveries.

The airline had kept its word to ex-AVG ace Joe Rosbert and sent him home for three months of leave in the autumn of 1942. He'd piloted a new Lend-Lease plane back to Asia after the New Year and flown several Hump rotations spaced around seven- to ten-day spates of rest and recreation in Calcutta. Rosbert was in Dinjan in early April, edging toward the 100- or 120-hour total that would earn him another stint downcountry. Quite frankly, he was making such superb extracurricular money that he wasn't in a hurry to get back to Calcutta. Airline personnel had recently discovered another illicit Golconda in China, where government bondholders would sell the paper for a fraction of its printed value. Pilots who flew those bonds over the Hump to India could deposit them with the Bank of China's Calcutta branch and wire them to the United States, where family could redeem them at face value for U.S. currency, and the Bank of China in the United States honored the *official* twenty-to-one exchange rate, which added icing to an already thick cake. The pilots were doing so well with the arbitrage they'd begun referring to Chinese paper as "gold bonds," a moniker that would have flabbergasted the original bondholders, who'd thought the pilots fools for believing they'd ever get any return on a bond issued by the Chinese government. Many Chinese had been coerced into buying Nationalist bonds in the first place. Using profits gleaned smuggling gold into China compounded a third round of outrageous gain. There were other opportunities, too: In China, the pilots were exploiting the unofficial/official exchange rate situation by purchasing U.S.-dollar-denominated savings certificates sponsored by the Bank of China as anti-inflation vehicles—at official exchange rates with Chinese money obtained at black-market rates.

Again, it was the pilots' ability to take the paper out of China that provided the gold-plated opportunity, because in China they were for all practical purposes impossible to redeem. In March, Joe Rosbert had subscribed to $4,450 worth of the savings certificates (worth $55,400 in modern dollars), deposited them in Calcutta, and telegraphed them to the United States, where they were redeemed by his family at the official exchange rate. Several of his freight-flying cronies had bought many thousands of dollars more. The Ministry of Finance quietly banned the practice as soon as it understood the scheme, not wanting to draw much American government attention to the official/unofficial exchange rate discrepancy because it had insisted that the U.S. military finance its purchases in China at the official exchange rate, an even more astronomically lucrative racket.

Pilots were assigned to airplanes at the last minute. Their sub-rosa fund-raising was confined to what they could sneak into easily searched hand luggage. Company mechanics enjoyed larger-scale opportunities. To the pilots, their planes often seemed more sluggish than could be accounted for by the weights detailed in their cargo manifests. They suspected the Chinese mechanics of dangling chains of gold bars in the oil sumps and fuel tanks, and there were rumors they forged engine cowlings from gold, painted them drab, and installed them in place of the usual parts, with Chinese character codes tipping their Kunming associates about which items to swap.

For his current rotation, Rosbert had been assigned a new copilot, lanky, black-haired Charles Ridgley Hammell, popularly called "Ridge," who, like Pete Goutiere, had come to the airline from Pan Africa. Rosbert and Hammell hadn't had much time to get acquainted, but they had much in common besides flying. Rosbert hailed from the South Philadelphia neighborhood between Seventeenth Street's intersections with Ritner and Porter. Hammell grew up ten miles away, in nearby Germantown. Quite a lot more social distance separated middle-class Quaker and Protestant Germantown from Catholic, blue-collar South Philly, but that distance hadn't affected their working relationship. Rosbert was the senior pilot, with enormous ex-AVG fighter-pilot cachet Ridge Hammell couldn't help but admire. Together, they were flying fine.

As usual, Suklo rousted them long before first light on April 7, 1943, and after breakfast they bumped through the tea patches to the airfield in the back of a company truck. Hugh Woods assigned them radio operator

Li Wong and one of the Lend-Lease C-53s. The weather report predicted strong southwest crosswinds, storms, and possible icing conditions over Burma, par for the course in recent weeks.

Dawn spread along the flight line, and Rosbert and Hammell gave their plane the usual once-over, opened its fuel tanks' drain sumps to bleed out accumulated moisture, kicked its tires, and pissed on the tail wheel for luck—widely considered the most important preflight ritual. Crates of heavy machinery packed the cargo bay. Neither Rosbert nor Hammell did anything besides check the gross weight statistics on the load manifest and glance at the tie-downs. They didn't care what they were flying. Ground crews in Dinjan loaded the planes; ground crews in Kunming did the unloading. The only important cargo to Joe Rosbert was a gallon-sized cask of Coca-Cola syrup he stashed in a corner of the radio operator's compartment—a present for a well-to-do Chinese friend who liked mixing Coke syrup with Scotch whisky. It was a handsome gift. Such luxuries were unobtainable in wartime China.

Springtime conditions concocted a cauldron of violently unstable weather in Upper Assam and north Burma, and once they were aloft, Rosbert added a slight southward deviation to his eastward course for Kunming, compensation for what he figured would be a forty- to seventy-five-mile-per-hour southwest crosswind.

Thirty minutes out of Dinjan, at sixteen thousand feet, they hit rough air and dark clouds. Flying blind, they continued on instruments for the better part of another hour. Suddenly, intense turbulence pounded the airplane. A blur of snowflakes whisked past the windows, which, combined with their inability to raise the Fort Hertz direction-finding beacon, made Rosbert suspect they'd been blown north of their intended course, nudging into cold air flowing over from Tibet, and over much higher mountains. He added a few more degrees of southing to their eastward flight path and tried to climb free of the storm, but the overloaded C-53 couldn't win more altitude.

Rosbert gave Hammell the controls, and Hammell fought the pummeling, impressing Rosbert with his competent handling of the ship. It was tough flying, but they'd make it if they could push through to the halfway point, past the highest summits and the worst of the weather. Sharp thwacks banged the aluminum skin of the airplane, crisply audible against the engine roar, as ice shards flung from the whirling propeller cracked against the fuselage. Rosbert swore and switched on the propeller de-icer, which dispensed an alcohol-based antifreeze from the propeller hub onto the spinning blades. Rosbert peered out the side window into the gloom. Ice glazed the wing and engine nacelle and would be accumulating on every other exposed surface as supercooled water droplets froze on contact with the aluminum. Unfortunately, the airline's C-53s didn't have inflatable rubber de-icer boots along the leading edges of their wings—some fool, somewhere, had stripped them from the planes before they left the United States in a misguided effort to reduce weight. Thousands of pounds of ice formed on the wings and fuselage in the next five minutes, eroding the aerodynamic properties of the airplane, cutting lift, adding weight, increasing drag. As they lost speed, Rosbert applied emergency power, but it wasn't enough, and in order to maintain flying speed, Hammell had to nudge down the nose. They lost altitude, and they didn't have much to spare—mountaintops en route rose to within a few thousand feet of their cruising altitude, and that was if they'd managed to stay in the normal flyways. They were among much higher summits if they'd been driven any distance north.

"Controls are getting sloppy," Hammell noted.

Out the left-side window, the wing looked like a white-frosted Popsicle. "There's five inches of ice on the wing." Rosbert cursed. "We ain't gonna get over. Turn around."

Hammell nursed the plane through the turn, doing what he could to conserve speed and altitude.

Such serious icing conditions could choke a carburetor intake, and Rosbert strained his ears to catch any hesitation in the engines, but the big radials roared steady, the situation's only constant. Buffets walloped the plane, and the altimeter sank below sixteen thousand feet. Ice glazed the windshield, and Rosbert pulled off a glove and held his bare hand against the glass in an attempt to defrost a viewport. The altimeter slumped through fifteen thousand feet. If they were north of their projected course, they were among mountains easily that high. "Let me and Li dump the load," Hammell pleaded.

Rosbert denied him. A jolt of turbulence might bounce an untied load to the rear of the cargo bay while Hammell and Wong wrestled it to the door, and such a sudden disturbance of their center of gravity might stall the plane, a terminal calamity. Rosbert ordered Wong to tell Dinjan control they were in trouble. Wong stood in the gangway and tapped out a Morse code message, but received no response. He stayed at his post and kept trying.

The grayness outside the ice sheathing the windscreen seemed to lighten, which made Rosbert think the storm might be breaking. He peeled his hand away from the tiny hole his bare hand had melted. "Jesus Christ, a mountain!"

Rosbert grabbed the yoke and banked right, tramping hard-right rudder. Hammell did likewise. The plane veered away from the high point, barely missing it, but a tremendous grating jolt slammed Rosbert's head against the instrument panel as their airplane's belly clipped the rocky saddle connecting the outcrop to an adjacent crag, tearing both propellers and one of the engines from their mounts. On the far side of the saddle, the plane whumped into a snowfield and careened through the whiteness. Joe Rosbert sagged in his harness, unconscious.

Seconds passed, perhaps as much as a minute. Rosbert opened his eyes, thoroughly disoriented. The engines had roared steady for more than two hours. Now there was only silence, tomblike and overwhelming. The plane felt like it was in a gentle dive, but there was no power. Rosbert puzzled at snowflakes settling on the instrument panel and heard a distant voice.

"Joe! Joe! Get the hell out before it catches fire!"

Snowflakes pitter-pattered against the airplane's metal skin, and Rosbert's dazed brain registered an odd fact: The crash had torn the ice from the wings and fuselage. Training took hold. He reached up and switched off the magnetos, standard crash procedure to cut electrical power and minimize fire danger. Frigid air gusted into the cockpit. Rosbert craned his neck, wincing. Snowflakes whirled through a gaping hole torn in the airplane's skin above and behind the pilots' seats. Tenebrous clouds churned beyond. Rosbert didn't think the plane would burn. If it was going to, it would have already.

"Hell with that," Rosbert croaked. "Get back in here before you freeze to death."

Hammell made his way forward, swinging from the ceiling struts to favor an apparent ankle injury. The radio operator's compartment was crumpled like wadded paper. Li Wong lay sprawled in the aisle, dead, his head lolling to one side.

Rosbert tried not to gawk at his copilot, who looked as if he'd done a dozen rounds with Joe Louis. A three-inch cut oozed blood from under his left eye, which was already purple-black and swollen shut. Rosbert fumbled with the seat belt's release and tried to stand. A searing pain shot up his right leg and dropped him back into the seat. His right foot jutted to the side at an impossible angle, his ankle clearly broken. He gingerly steadied himself in the gangway; the damaged leg wouldn't support an ounce of weight. "We ain't gonna get warm up here. Let's get in the back where there ain't so much goddamned cold air blowing around."

Hammell limped past with a parachute and pulled its rip cord; cream-colored silk billowed into the back of the airplane. Rosbert arrived panting, in excruciating pain. The two aviators ruffled into a silk nest and examined themselves. An ugly bulge of bone pressed against the skin on the inside of Rosbert's right leg. It didn't hurt so much if he didn't move. Hammell's right ankle was also badly mauled. Certainly sprained, perhaps broken. He couldn't tell. "Hard right rudder," Hammell snorted. "And it kicked back."

The passenger door dangled from a hinge against the side of the plane, and snow swirled through the opening. Hammell hobbled to the radio compartment, hopping over Li's graying body, and returned with their flight bags, the flight chart, and the plane's survival kit, which had only a single C ration inside. The rest had been looted, either in Dinjan or Kunming, and likely sold on the black market. The men stared at the one meal and decided not to eat. Rosbert and Hammell scrunched together in the silk, scrutinized the chart, and tried to ascertain their location. If the altimeter had read true, they couldn't be plastered against anything in the Patkai Range. None of those peaks exceeded 11,000 feet, and they'd clipped the edge of bedrock above 14,000. Stronger-than-anticipated crosswinds, outbound and after they'd turned around, might have turned their flight path into something of a reverse C shape ending on a mountainside somewhere in northern Burma or Assam, the only locations with peaks at or above their crash altitude besides the Hump itself, which they hadn't flown far enough to reach. Just exactly where they'd hit was a whole lot harder to pinpoint. The entire region was mountainous; there were hundreds of possibilities. Their best guesses kept putting them in a group of 13,000- to 17,000-foot peaks astride the northernmost border of India and Burma. If accurate, the nearest inhabited place they could positively identify was the town of Sadiya, the frontier of civilization in Upper Assam, and that wasn't necessarily good news: Sadiya was at least seventy-five straight-line miles distant, and the intervening terrain was extraordinarily rugged, hills and precipitous gorges swathed in trackless jungles reputed to be inhabited by headhunting tribes untouched by modern civilization. "We are so god-damned lucky," Rosbert said, laughing. "We hit a mountain at a hundred and ten miles per hour and here we are talking about it."

"Lucky? Think about it," Hammell sneered. "We don't know where we are or if anybody will find us or how'n the hell we're going to get out of here if they don't. We might wind up wishing we smacked that mountain straight on."

Hammell fished a deck of cards from his flight bag, and the pair played gin rummy, their breath frosting over the cards. Rosbert jotted the score in the margin of the flight map. "Being optimistic," he noted.

The game continued into the late afternoon, and they were beset by the first pangs of hunger. Neither wanted to break into the precious C ration, so Hammell retrieved the gallon of Coca-Cola syrup stashed in the radio compartment, which was still intact, and dribbled some over mouthful-sized snowballs, yielding "snow Cokes," a concoction that anesthetized their stomachs and dulled the worst aches of thirst and hunger.

The storm intensified. Renewed gusts whined around the airplane, blasting jets of snow through the wrecked door. Wrapped in parachute silk, Rosbert and Hammell passed the night huddled together against the rear of the cargo area. The storm broke before dawn, and the sun rose into clear skies, but the wreck stayed in shadow. Frigid hours later, the sun cleared a ridge and light streamed through the open door. Hammell wriggled from the silk and hobbled to the door. Outside, piercing white reflected from fresh snowfields. He blinked back tears and drew the scene into focus. Two feet of new powder covered the wing. On the surrounding peaks, ice gullies cobwebbed through dark bands of rock to join snowy ridges. Below them, westward, beyond the treeless alpine fingers reaching from the mountains' base, line after line of rugged, jungle-clad hills faded into a gray-green horizon. Nothing besides the wrecked airplane marred the wilderness.

Hammell leaned out the door and reconstructed their flight path. He pointed rearward, saying, "So, if we'd been flying five feet *lower,* we'd have smacked head on into the rocks on the other side of that saddle and that would have been the end of us." He pointed forward. "And if we'd have been flying five feet *higher,* we'd have missed the saddle and smacked head on into that mountain." He gestured toward the many other high points in the vicinity. "And if we'd have been flying a few hundred feet to either side, we'd have smacked one of those other crags and *that* would have been the end of us. You couldn't land in here on a *perfect* day and expect to live."

There was no wind, no sound. The silence had substance. Rosbert rapped his knuckles against the skin of the airplane, knowing they'd be hearing engines if they were anywhere near the normal flight paths. Back in the rear of the plane, they played cards and talked of home. It was funny, they'd grown up so close together in Philadelphia and Germantown, but only crashed against an Asian mountainside did they find time to get more than casually acquainted. Clouds built around the summits in the afternoon, and by evening thick snow was falling once again. The wind rose after dark, and avalanches grumbled around them.

The following morning, Rosbert and Hammell basked again in sunshine at the door. The silence wore on, unbroken, and it contained a clear message: No help was coming. They discussed the practicalities of abandoning the plane. Somewhere to the west lay the valley of the Brahmaputra and safety, but the region's major rivers flowed north–south, and although it would be easier to follow them downstream, if they strayed too far south, they'd likely end up captured by the Japanese, an appalling prospect. Rosbert thought their only realistic chance was with the help of native tribesmen, but Hammell worried about the rumors that they were headhunters.

"I'd rather take my chances with them than with the Japs," Rosbert replied.

The inventory was spare: flight jackets and the clothes on their backs, a map and pen, Hammell's cigarette lighter, a knife, and the lone C ration. Realistically, their chances were very poor, but there was hope in taking action. Waiting, doing nothing, led to an obvious end. Pilot pride demanded action. They decided to leave the following day.

Their first escape attempt was a profound failure. Awake in a biting dawn, they waited a few extra hours for the morning sunshine to hit, and although Hammell's ankle could support some weight, he sank to his hips in the sun-softened snow. Rosbert hadn't adequately braced his ankle, it couldn't bear any load, and he struggled to keep pace, in excruciating pain. They wallowed for three hours and barely managed five hundred yards of progress. Rosbert could see the snow line they intended to reach beyond many undulations of slope below, but it seemed hopelessly distant. Facing the prospect of a night on the snow in wet clothes—which neither thought they'd survive—they returned to the wrecked airplane.

After another long night huddled in the parachute, Rosbert carefully shucked his boot and examined his damaged ankle, which he hadn't done since the hours immediately following the accident. Blackish discolorations striated swollen flesh. In succession, he pinched each toe and felt corresponding sensation, proof that blood still reached them all. He poked and kneaded the injury, which was very painful. Not splinting it properly prior to their escape attempt had been a serious neglect. Rosbert put his mind to constructing something substantial enough to bear a little weight.

Their plane was a C-53, a civilian DC-3 stripped of seats and passenger amenities, and, left over from its days of fancier service, ⅛-inch plywood paneling lined both walls. Rosbert tore off a chunk, broke it into two-inch-wide strips and snap-folded the pieces to brace his mangled ankle, binding them in place with silk ribbons torn from the parachute so that they fit tight but didn't impinge blood flow. It was a vast improvement.

The airplane's snow-crusted door, torn almost completely free of its hinges, lay angled against the side of the airplane. Despite dents, it retained the basic curve of the fuselage, and Rosbert and Hammell worked it loose, thinking to try it as a toboggan. It was awkward to propel, but it did slide. After a few tests, they propped it up against the fuselage and killed the remaining daylight playing gin rummy. And keeping score.

"In the morning, we have to go," Hammell said. "If we stay up here any longer, we're gonna stay up here forever."

The two Pennsylvanians awoke at first light and dribbled generous syrup doses over little snowballs until the last of it was gone, ingesting all the snow Cokes their stomachs could tolerate. Rosbert tightened the boot over his splinted ankle, nodded to Li's frozen body, and lowered himself out the door. The sun still hadn't risen and crucifying cold numbed their hands and feet, but it was easier going over snap-frozen snow. They dragged the door into position, braced themselves aboard, and pushed again and again with their good legs, creaking over the snow and drifting a few yards with each surge. Thus they struggled through most of the day, until they reached a point where the slope below steepened considerably.

They searched out the best grips on the door and kicked, and the sled leapt past the lip of the incline. Within seconds, they were beyond braking, white-knuckling the door, bucking and slamming. A rock on the slope below drew the sled like a lodestone. The door clipped the rock, chucked both pilots into the snow, cartwheeled twice and righted itself on its sliding surface, and disappeared down an even steeper slope below.

They slid the rest of the way down the five-hundred-foot slope on their backsides. At bottom, the battered pair shuffled off the snow into a boulder field, where a tiny black bird danced among the talus, the first living thing they'd seen in seven days.

They groped through the rocks to the top of a canyon. Hammell, with his lesser injury, could have traveled much faster. Time after time, he scrambled ahead, then waited for Rosbert to catch up. They struggled into the canyon as the afternoon waned. The pain in their damaged ankles was bearable, a known adversary. Far and away their greatest burden was *not knowing*. As the daylight faded, they huddled together under the lip of an overhanging boulder, and the hard, rocky ground and freezing air leeched warmth from their wet clothes. Racked by shivers, they spent the longest night either had ever known.

Dawn arrived slowly. Rosbert and Hammell rationed themselves a single bite of C ration and hobbled away from their campsite. All that day, and the next, they worked downcanyon, each day making a mile or two of tortuous progress, generally keeping to the right bank of a snowmelt torrent that kept adding volume from many side streams.

Scrub vegetation and vines began to crowd the canyon walls as they lost altitude, an alpine pre-jungle that hindered progress, and the torrent beside them continued to grow. Each night they shared a single bite of C ration and huddled beneath a shelter stone, clutching each other for warmth. Toward the end of the fourth day below the plane, the country ahead and below seemed to be opening in broader forests and jungles, even as their canyon tightened upon itself. Steeper and steeper side walls forced them toward the river until Rosbert and Hammell were thrashing over and around boulders at its edge, often splashing through the water itself. A bass vibration tickled the edges of their hearing, the canyon walls closed further in, and the water accelerated. The vibration became a whisper, then a roar, increasing in volume with each step forward until it filled the entire canyon with apocalyptic thunder.

Ahead, the river fell over a series of vertical steps into a tumultuous, mist-filled gorge. It was impossible to descend the waterfalls. They collapsed in a riprap of boulders, numbed. They were trapped. Their families would never learn their fate; no one would know what they'd endured.

23

"WE'LL BE TALKING ABOUT THAT
FOR THE REST OF OUR LIVES"

The losses appalled William Bond. His airline had flown so well, for so long, and then, in the space of twenty-eight days, it had scattered three planes across the South Asian landscape, killing, as far as Bond knew, nine men. It was the worst spate of accidents since the Hangchow Bay calamities of 1933. Never one to wriggle from responsibility, Bond racked his brain to pinpoint the contributing flaws.

The Hump was the hardest flying in the world, without rival, and the urgency of the mission meant flying it in conditions peacetime safety standards wouldn't have tolerated. The weather was "nearly always bad and [often] a great deal worse," Bond wrote, and the high-altitude terrain stretched the performance envelopes of the airplanes. Those were the givens, like the sunrise, and the war. They could only be accepted, not changed. Beyond them, Bond surmised that a confluence of three factors accounted for the accidents, the first of which was pilots. The size of his pilot roster had doubled *twice* in the last nine months, from fifteen or sixteen in the first half of 1942 to the fifty-eight the airline had on its rolls before losing Rosbert and Hammell. The original fifteen had been vastly experienced commercial pilots who'd flown with the airline before Pearl Harbor. Sixteen pilots from Chennault's AVG joined in the summer of 1942, men with "better than average training" who'd learned the Hump route during the relatively benign conditions of late summer and early fall. (Competent instrument pilots didn't consider monsoon flying particularly difficult.) CNAC had recruited twenty-seven more since October and had "checked out" most as pilot-captains. Under normal conditions, new hires should have flown a route like the Hump as copilots for six or eight months before becoming captains responsible for their own ships. Wartime expansion forced the airline to promote the new men beyond their experience, and even then, they'd done well until the weather soured in February and March. Second, the airline knowingly overloaded its airplanes, "grossing them out" at 27,000 pounds, sometimes more, even though Douglas designed the planes to fly a "maximum gross load" of 24,400 pounds. The overload chipped away at safety margins. Third, they'd flown on many foul days when they should have stayed grounded. "From a purely technical view," Bond considered all three "serious errors," he wrote in a letter to managing director Wang Cheng-fu, and he took his "full share of responsibility." The airline hadn't flown out of carelessness or indifference, but because it was so important to get "urgently needed supplies into China at a critical period [of] serious uncertainty as to whether it was possible" to do so. "The only way to stop these accidents is to stop flying the Hump," Bond wrote, and that "cannot be done and must not be considered. We are doing military flying and must take certain and unavoidable risks. CNAC is actually fighting in this war and losses are unavoidable. We have experienced some and we can expect more."

The airline's example was crucially important. In neat statistical terms, it demonstrated what expert air operations could accomplish against the hazards of the Hump. Only fifty-nine Army flights landed in China in the first ten days of April, and they had more than a hundred airplanes. During the same period, the China National Aviation Corporation made 102 flights with twenty-one airplanes. The civilians had landed nearly twice as many flights in China with one-fifth the number of airplanes. "In spite of our tragic losses, I think our efforts have been worthwhile," Bond concluded. Focusing on their contribution to the war effort was the only way to justify the extinction of nine young lives. Considering the atrocious weather, the dearth of available aircraft, the imperative of freight carrying, and the colossal quantity of trackless terrain into which they'd vanished, there wasn't any way to conduct coherent searches for the missing men.

Bond's estimate of his airline's body count was two men too high. Joe Rosbert and Ridge Hammell were still alive when he wrote those words, if barely, trapped in a remote canyon above a series of undescendible waterfalls. They'd fought for life for days, not daring to hope but hoping nevertheless, and they sat above the cascades, overwhelmed, their filthy flight clothes hanging from their shriveled frames like jute sacks. They shivered, and minutes turned to hours, the roar of the waterfalls filling the amphitheater around them.

Hammell's eyes drifted along the canyon walls, defeated until he noticed a sturdy vine hanging down one wall. "Joe, look! Wonder if we could get up that thing?"

Rosbert studied the slope. It appeared to have been used before.

Braced by the vine, Hammell hauled himself up, passing a bulge at sixty feet. Rosbert ascended after him, in many agonizing intervals having to trust weight to his broken ankle. Up top, the vine was secured to a notched sapling, and a faint trail led away from it. They clung to the derelict trail like drowning men and followed it up gentler slopes into the country above the gorge. That evening, they ate the last two bites of their C ration.

For three more days, they made a few miles of progress and passed each night on heaps of vegetation, cold and miserable in steady rain. They crossed a small creek late in the afternoon of the third day since they'd left the canyon, nearly a fortnight since the crash. Hammell followed the trail uphill on the far side of the stream and disappeared over the crest of a rise. Rosbert limped behind, focused on the ground in front of him, carefully picking steps to favor his broken leg, and practically stumbled into Ridge Hammell on his knees in the middle of the trail, gesturing forward, speechless. The trail sloped gently downhill alongside a rivulet of water that ran into a clearing, and in the clearing, on four-foot stilts, was a long rectangular hut made of bamboo and roofed in thatch. A thin column of smoke rose from the roof.

Inside the gloomy, smoke-filled structure, the pilots found two frightened old women beside a fire, clothed in rags, blinded by cataracts, and sheltering six naked children behind thin, knotted arms. The famished Americans were soon stuffing their mouths with handfuls of popcorn and cakes of rough polenta.

Rosbert and Hammell spent two days gorging on polenta on the hut's porch, taking in the view that stretched down the valley over hills and jungles and watching the naked boys and girls play with the metal zippers of their flight jackets and tromp gleefully around the hut wearing their boots. On the third morning, Rosbert observed that the two oldest boys were missing.

"Should we worry?" Hammell asked.

"Don't know what the hell we'd do about it if we did," Rosbert said, flopping back on the porch. "It's out of our hands."

The older boys returned midafternoon with a group of teenage tribesmen who guided them to a larger village farther downhill the next morning. Three inactive days had unnumbed Rosbert's broken leg, and even with help, every step was a jarring agony. In the late afternoon, they reached another long bamboo hut in a hillside clearing, the first structure they'd seen since abandoning the upper camp.

The hut housed an entire village. Native men swarmed around the two stranded fliers; the women hovered at the rear of the throng, dark dresses falling to their ankles, black, inquisitive eyes peering between the bodies of their menfolk. The headman's name was Dayno, and Rosbert and Hammell spent many days lazing around a fire in the new hut with the native men, eating cornmeal mush, drinking a meadlike concoction of fermented corn, and smoking opium through a bamboo water pipe. Desperately missing his Lucky Strikes, Hammell enjoyed smoking with the natives. Rosbert didn't smoke, but he partook regardless, not wanting to offend their hosts. After so much time in their company, Rosbert felt that he was beginning to comprehend the gist of the native conversations and thought they were calling themselves "Mishmi." On their flight chart, they found the Mishmi Hills in the extreme northeastern corner of India, near its confluence with Burma and Tibet, a good fifty miles north of their intended flight path, which explained why they hadn't encountered any Japanese.

Once the novelty of their arrival wore off, the Mishmis treated Rosbert and Hammell as part of their enormous family. Every morning, the women went to work in little corn patches, where they stayed most of the day while the men lounged in the hut. The days were cool and cloudy, with intermittent rain. Both pilots swore they didn't feel any effects from the opium, and so they passed the days in the bucolic vale, effortlessly and without pain. Rosbert found it hard to comprehend that the rest of the world was tearing itself apart and that he had fought and killed and seen friends die in the same South Asian sky that rode so indifferently above the valley. Days passed, perhaps as many as eight or ten, until one day two native men walked out of the jungle, one of them carrying an ancient blunderbuss.

The locals rushed to greet the newcomers, their deferential manners making it obvious the new pair were men of consequence. The man with the blunderbuss, whose name was Ah Shaw, had small quantities of rice and tea in his shoulder pouch, which he shared with the stranded fliers, further evidence that he'd touched the outside world.

The younger of the pair, named Ma Lon, spied Rosbert making notations on the back of his map. He pointed to the words Rosbert had written, speaking rapidly and gesticulating. Rosbert couldn't discern what it was he so passionately desired. Confused, he wrote a short note in the corner of the map—*To Ah Shaw and Ma Lon from two pilots crashed in the mountains*—tore it off, and handed it over. Ma Lon sprang to his feet, spoke a few words to Ah Shaw, tucked the scrap into his pouch, and bounded off the porch like a black buck antelope, at a flat run.

The whole exchange so surprised Rosbert that it took him a few minutes to realize he'd made a grotesque error. "Ridge, this is gonna sound pretty goddamned dumb, but I didn't put our names on that note."

Ma Lon reappeared four days later, gestured Rosbert and Hammell to a seat next to the fire, and, from inside his pouch, retrieved four hard-boiled eggs. The Americans consumed the eggs with the inevitable bowls of cornmeal gruel. Ma Lon next produced rice, which was cooked and consumed. After the rice, Ma Lon withdrew tea, and something in the pouch caught Rosbert's eye. "Ridge, look!"

A broad grin split Ma Lon's round face, and he passed across an official Indian Telegraph Service envelope, sealed with red wax.

"How long was this guy going to hold out!" Rosbert exclaimed, tearing it open.

Inside was a handwritten telegram:

To pilots Ashaw and Malon STOP Sending rations with message STOP Doctor arriving two days later with aid STOP Major Pfeiffer and Captain Lax STOP

The story emerged from pidgin and pantomime communication: Ma Lon couldn't read, but he knew about writing, and he took Rosbert's note to a British scouting party camped four days' march away, running the whole way, sometimes traveling at night, and he made the trip in less than two, delivering the note and reporting the lost and injured fliers. Major Pfeiffer, leader of the scouting party, sent Ma Lon back with the written telegram and dispatched his doctor at the head of a slower-moving relief column.

Two days later, a thirty- or forty-person column snaked into the clearing. At its head was the promised doctor, tall and thin, ten years older than Rosbert or Hammell, and unmistakably British in tan fatigues. The doctor extended his hand. "Dr. Lax, North East Frontier Agency. I say, you chaps are bloody lucky. We haven't had a patrol go through this area in four years." They were on a survey to determine if it was feasible to build a road to China through southeastern Tibet.

Examining Hammell's foot, Dr. Lax diagnosed a severe sprain. He thought Rosbert's ankle was dislocated and broken in several places, and he wouldn't predict how properly it would heal, bad news for a man who hoped to make his life in aviation. Worse was Dr. Lax's announcement that the only way out was to walk, news that hit Rosbert like a body blow. "How far?" he asked.

"Well, that depends," the doctor mumbled.

"On what?" Rosbert demanded.

"Major Pfeiffer is hacking a landing strip out of the jungle next to our camp at Minzong. That's four days away. With any luck, we'll be able to get you out from there on a small plane, but the monsoon's coming, and the weather's iffy already."

"Four days! And what if the plane can't get in? How much further if it can't?"

"Oh, it's quite a bit further from there."

"How much further?"

"Almost a hundred miles," Dr. Lax muttered.

"What?" Rosbert gasped.

"I said it's almost a hundred miles. I'm sorry, I really am, but I'm afraid there just isn't any alternative. If we can't get you out on a plane in the next couple of days, you are going to have to walk."

"I can't possibly walk a hundred miles."

"The other bit of news is that we need to leave first thing in the morning. Things are going to get rather a lot worse once the monsoon breaks."

The doctor's party included Tibetans, Hindus, and Muslims, some of whom spoke smatterings of the Mishmi tongue, and with their aid the communication barrier disintegrated. Across three-language bridges, the two fliers could truly express their gratitude to the local tribesmen. Their first gesture was to share all of the supplies brought by the doctor's rescue party: cigarettes, matches, salt, rice, tea, canned goods, and other sundries. Everyone feasted on the British rations, and the natives broke out a copious supply of their corn-mash mead. Rosbert and Hammell partook wholeheartedly. Dr. Lax put a hand on Rosbert's forearm when he spotted him reaching for a pipe and said, "I say, you do know that's opium?"

Rosbert nodded.

"How much have you been smoking?"

"Dunno, couple times a day, I guess."

"For how long?"

"Couple weeks."

"I think you'd better stop."

"What's the big deal? Neither of us feels a thing."

"No, I don't suppose you would. You do know what they say about opium, don't you?"

Rosbert had no idea.

"They say that if you smoke more than three pipes a day, you're an addict."

"Hell, Doc, we're smoking way more than that and we don't feel a thing."

"Like I said, I think you'd better stop."

Departure held an edge of sadness, for it meant saying goodbye to the highland people who'd saved their lives. Unable to bear the pain of parting, Ah Shaw, Ma Lon, and Dayno decided to walk out with the Americans.

Three days of hard travel wound down into the gorge of the Gulum River and brought them to the village of Minzong at the junction of the

Gulum and Tullo rivers, where the tents of the Anglo-Indian base camp dotted a jungle clearing. Unfortunately, a small plane trying to land couldn't breach the cloud cover, condemning the injured Americans to the long walk.

Assisted by the Mishmis, Rosbert and Hammell tracked day after day through rugged, mountainous country on single-file trails, up and down steep slopes above precipitous ravines cut by rock-choked rivers. Major Pfeiffer drove the column from dawn to dusk, pressing to escape the highlands before the monsoon rendered the watercourses uncrossable, and the small-framed hillmen carried Rosbert and Hammell over the worst parts, which the stout fellows never seemed to think was a chore.

The monsoon broke eight days out of Minzong. Rain fell in sheets, streams swelled to torrents, and the moisture added leeches to their litany of sufferings. At every break, Rosbert and Hammell had to pinch off half a dozen latched to their lower legs.

After eight more days of painful slogging through the downpours, they escaped a river gorge and climbed to a hilltop on a long ridge. Atop it, they met an American Signal Corps unit manning a long-range radio station, and the GIs treated the two errant pilots to a bona fide American feast—Southern fried chicken, coffee, and apple pie. Before them, the valley of the Brahmaputra spread beneath clouds of monochromatic gray. The river coiled in the distance, and a muddy road reached through a patchwork of tea plantations to a Frontier Agency outpost at the foot of the hills. Southwestward, the two fliers could just discern the bend in the Brahmaputra near Dinjan, the base they'd left nearly seven weeks before. The Mishmis refused to descend to the outpost, and the parting tempered the joy of imminent arrival.

That night, the two fliers took hot baths, an ultimate luxury. A truck took them to Sadiya and a small plane flew them to Dinjan on May 24, 1943. Joe Rosbert and Ridge Hammell had been lost for forty-seven days. After dinner, they held court in the lounge in the pilot hostel, regaling the other fliers with their epic narration.

Flown to Calcutta, Rosbert taxied and crutched to the apartment he'd shared with Dick Rossi since the summer of 1942, and he found his roommate upstairs. Both aces, they'd been squadron mates and best friends in the AVG, a relationship they'd continued in the airline. They shook hands, and Rosbert glanced around. Another pilot had already moved in. "At least my key still works."

"Kinda didn't think we'd be seein' you again," Rossi mumbled. "Can I fix you a drink?"

Rossi fumbled with tumblers, and Rosbert scouted for his music collection. "Come on, Dick, where are my Latin albums?"

"What albums?" Rossi deadpanned.

Rosbert's temper boiled. Rossi was his best friend! After all they'd endured, after all the friends they'd seen die, Rossi had gone and sold his favorite stuff! Then Rosbert laughed, and his anger faded as suddenly as it had appeared. Such were the ways of war: Rossi hadn't made its grim rules. In Rossi's shoes, he'd have done the same damn thing. Desi Arnaz, Schmezi Arnaz, it didn't matter a damn. It just felt good to be alive.

Rosbert and Hammell lodged separately at the Great Eastern. Hammell's ankle had improved enough to allow him to return to the Hump, which he planned to do after a stint of R&R in Calcutta. Rosbert's ankle was an entirely different affair, requiring a major surgical reconstruction that could be done only in the United States. His war was finished, and he was imminently due at the airport to catch a plane for Karachi, the first leg of the long journey home. Waiting for the taxi, Rosbert and Hammell nursed drinks in the Great Eastern's bar. A bellhop announced its arrival, and they clicked and drained their last round. A servant held the massive doors, and Hammell walked his hobbled friend across the portico. Curbside, Rosbert loaded his crutches and turned to his partner. They shook hands awkwardly.

Rosbert grunted and raked a hand through his black hair. "I wouldn't have made it alone, Ridge. Not a chance. If I had to do it again, I'd want to do it with you."

"I feel about the same way." Hammell rocked forward and cuffed Rosbert's shoulder. "Come on, pal, we'll be talking about that for the rest of our lives."

Hammell watched the taxi merge into traffic, spun on his heel, and reassumed his station at the Great Eastern's bar.

24

NOT THE WORST WAY TO
FIGHT A WAR

Flight operations kept off-duty behavior somewhat sober in Dinjan. When they weren't flying or sleeping, the pilots on rotation gathered on the hostel's veranda to drink tea, smoke a cigarette or pipe, crack jokes, and gabble about home, girls, and airplanes. Somebody might produce a bottle of gin or much more precious whisky and pour a few cocktails, the most common mixes being soda water, grapefruit juice, and ginger beer, but ten to fifteen hours in the cockpits over the Hump dampened festivities. Dinjan entertainments centered on minor hunting expeditions and gambling. Craps games at 200 rupees a throw created huddles of dice-tossing airmen that commonly gathered pots in excess of 2,000 rupees (835 and 8,350 modern dollars, respectively). One game's heavy action accumulated more than 30,000 rupees, equivalent to *10,000* U.S. dollars, nearly a year's pay (about 125,000 modern dollars). The men were just as likely to deal gin rummy or acey-deucey, and CNAC's group of high-stakes chronics played no-limit poker with a U.S. $5,000 buy-in, a colossal hazard intended to scare "shoe clerks" from the table, as went airline slang for pikers and unsteady pilots.

Downcountry in Calcutta, second city of the British Empire, where the pilots were off duty for ten days or a fortnight between Hump rotations, the airline had three Link Trainers, flight simulators in which the pilots rehearsed the letdown procedures for the various airfields, which the more diligent of them ran through religiously, but once they'd had their fill of practice they were free to enjoy the town. Calcutta's contrasts of wealth and poverty were appalling, even to people who'd come of age during the Depression, but the CNAC personnel lived squarely on the easy side of the have/have-not divide. They taxied or rickshawed through chaotic streets to drink at the British-American Club, the Great Eastern, the Grand Hotel, and patronize the 300 Club at 38 Theatre Road, Calcutta's most fashionable, expensive, and racially integrated private club, operated by Boris Lissanevitch, a White Russian impresario. Boris's best customer was the maharaja of Cooch Beher, a swarthy Lothario who befriended many airline pilots and took them tiger hunting in his princely state in the Himalayan foothills three hundred miles north of Calcutta. There were dances with Red Cross and USO girls and WACs. Men outnumbered women by comic margins, but the money-flush pilots did remarkably well, although patriotically inclined women did their bit for Allied morale by spreading the wealth of available dances. American-style steaks could be had among the marble columns, lofty ceilings, crystal chandeliers, and gilded mirrors of Firpo's, an Italian restaurant on Chowringhee Road a few doors from the Grand Hotel, and the fliers whiled away afternoons at the Calcutta Swim Club's pool until a polio scare put it off limits.

Hoping to dispense with hotel living and improve the quality of their off-duty time, Pete Goutiere and five of the airline's other former Pan Africa pilots rented a four-bedroom bungalow a few blocks south of Park Street in Ballygunge, a Calcutta suburb some two miles southeast of Chowringhee Street and the Grand Hotel. The pilots hired three Indian bearers, a cook, a dishwasher, a gardener, and a sweeper boy to staff their new base of social operations. Behind the house, a six-foot wall enclosed a modest garden, which was overlooked by a veranda. On it one muggy Calcutta afternoon, Goutiere slouched into a rattan chair alongside his girlfriend, Allison, the young and vivacious fair-haired stepdaughter of a British sergeant, while a yellow-eyed brain-fever bird serenaded the supine couple from a nearby tree with its persistent, rising whistle, a signature Indian sound. On the other side of the world, Goutiere's wife had recently delivered him a son, but she was in Maine, and he hadn't seen her for the entire course of her pregnancy. He'd been flying for Pan Africa for most of it, and now he was even farther away. A commotion among his housemates shook the handsome flier from his reveries, and a very boozy Ridge Hammell reeled into the backyard from around the side of the house leading a live Himalayan bear, a jet-black creature with a white V stripe in its chest fur.

Astonished, Goutiere sat up, laughing. "What the hell, Ridge?"

"They weren't treating him too good at the New Market. Besides, he only cost forty bucks."

"W-well . . . what's his name?"

"Elmer."

"What the hell're you gonna do with him?"

"I dunno, take him up to Dinjan, I guess."

Elmer's former owners had kept him caged in his own filth, so Hammell drew a tubful of cool water in one of the baths and the sixty-pound bear climbed in and made no fuss while Hammell soaped and rinsed its thick fur. The wetting revealed that Elmer was a she, not a he, but her name stuck, and Elmer she remained. Afterward, Hammell leashed her to a pole in the back garden.

That afternoon, Pete Goutiere, Ridge Hammell, and their other housemates threw a party—no great hassle, considering the house staff did all the work—and iced beer and Carew's gin flowed in wide streams. A fierce Bengal cloudburst drove the party indoors and cooled the bear, who'd have much preferred frigid altitudes to humid, sea-level Calcutta. Midafternoon, Goutiere spirited young Allison off to his room and they made love under the mosquito netting until teatime. The single fellows infuriated Hammell by tipping cocktails into a bowl and getting Elmer sloppy drunk. It wasn't the worst way to fight a war.

True to his intention, Ridge Hammell took Elmer up-country to Dinjan. He kept her leashed in the shade outside the hostel, and although he spoiled the beast rotten, no amount of attention could make the bear enjoy the Assam Valley's sweltering climate. She was lethargic and morose. Much of the time, she seemed too uncomfortable to sleep. One night when he didn't have a copilot, Hammell took Elmer out to the airfield and settled the bear in the empty seat.* She stared at him with weepy eyes, too miserable to be bothered by the engine noise, but by the time Hammell had climbed to sixteen thousand feet, Elmer was curled up in the right seat, fast asleep, looking more content than at any time since he'd purchased her. She made the round-trip without fuss. That made Elmer official—she'd flown the Hump. The pilots adopted her as their mascot and did their best to keep her in the air. Before long, she'd begun to amass some serious flight time, and the flying bear provided excellent opportunities for entertainment at Army expense.

One pilot had Elmer aboard when he was bringing a group of military passengers back to India, and the uniforms had settled behind the crew compartment at the forward end of the cargo bay. The pilot was flying without a copilot, and Elmer took the vacant seat, as she'd grown accustomed to doing. When she wasn't sleeping, the bear sat on her haunches and looked out the window. She seemed to enjoy the views, and granted, they were often spectacular. The C-47s had primitive toilets in their tail sections, and once the pilot got the plane through the rough air over the "Rockpile" (another of the Hump's many nicknames), he had to answer a call of nature. He engaged the autopilot, unstrapped his seat belts, and picked his way aft.

"Who's flying the airplane?" an Army guy exclaimed.

"Elmer the bear," the pilot answered.

The fellow's head snapped forward. "My God, the bear *is* flying the airplane!" As she sat on her haunches with the autopilot making the yoke wiggle beneath her paws braced on the window ledge, it did look like Elmer had the controls.

"Yeah, and she's better'n anybody you got in the Air Corps," the pilot noted.

CNAC expanded 150 percent in 1943, from 445 employees to 1,075. Most of the new people were Chinese, but the airline also had a substantial ap-

---

* The airline didn't have enough copilots and radio operators to provide full crews for every flight, but since it was important to have a second set of hands aboard to jettison cargo if the plane lost an engine or caught a load of ice, Hugh Woods made sure he assigned one or the other to every Hump flight.

petite for American pilots and technical personnel. In the States, military needs were drawing most available Americans into uniform, leaving the airline to hire virtually every qualified man it could lure to Asia. Plenty of stable, wholesome personalities joined the outfit. Many others were added who would never have found employment in William Bond's peacetime airline. It was excellent work for both Chinese and Caucasians, but for the flight crews it was also extremely dangerous, for even with a far better safety record than the Air Corps, fifteen CNAC pilots and copilots were killed in 1943, which, considering the monthly average of about fifty-five on the roster, constituted an annual mortality rate of about 25 percent.

Men facing those odds generally don't invest heavily in tomorrow, and company leadership concocted schemes to discourage the freight pilots' "riotous living," imploring them to "breathe more oxygen and drink less whisky," but no approbation shackled the airline's new breed of wild spirits. Chief among the hellions was a round-faced, curly-haired Californian named Jimmy Scoff, who never stopped blessing the luck that tossed him into a corner of the war with such a plethora of booze and pretty girls. Disregarding his wedding ring, Jimmy Scoff spent so much time with Margo, the luscious-lipped, midnight-haired, green-eyed bombshell who maintained a moss-dripping, beautifully staffed seraglio at 57 Kariah Road, that he stored his passport and personal effects there and used it as his mail drop. (Most Americans flying to the China-Burma-India theater of the war [the CBI] had Margot's address memorized before they cleared West Africa.) Scoff was a discredit to his company, nation, and race, and he wouldn't have been taken on by the peacetime airline if he'd lived for a thousand years, but a Calcutta bender with Jimmy Scoff was an experience most company men would remember for the rest of their lives. One balmy night, Scoff was wallowing through just such a bacchanalia, drifting between nightclubs. Well past midnight, he headed for Kariah Road, but business was slow, and the girls had closed shop. Frustrated, the reeling airman hauled his .45-caliber pistol from its holster, blasted a shot through a whorehouse lock, and crashed down the door.

Jimmy Scoff regained consciousness on the cold, filth-encrusted concrete floor of the Calcutta jail. He had an enormous goose egg on the back of his head—the brothel's night watchman had sapped him with a club. The police ordered Scoff to report to the magistrate that afternoon and released him on his own recognizance. He appeared disastrously inebriated. The judge scowled, but there wasn't much that could be done to a man who was, in fact, risking his life for the future of the free world. The judge fined Scoff 1,500 rupees, about 500 American dollars (6,000 modern dollars), and sent him back to Dinjan to continue flying the Hump.

Toward the end of his magistrate-enforced rotation, Jimmy Scoff had one of the airline's Lend-Lease C-53s on a night flight to Kunming. It was a routine flight until Scoff was one hundred miles from Kunming and the Army switched off all its radio navigation outposts to confound Japanese raiders homing on them and harassing the Kunming airfield. Scoff circled for an hour, and when the stations came back on the air, an inexperienced Army radio gave him a reciprocal bearing, 180 degrees opposite his actual azimuth to the station. Scoff didn't detect the error until he'd flown a hundred miles in the wrong direction, by which time he couldn't raise any navigational aids. He was lost over a mountainous landscape on a moonless night. ATC crews commonly bailed out when they had difficulties far less grave. No CNAC crew had ever done it, but by 0400 Scoff's engines were sucking fuel fumes. Scoff held course while his copilot and radio operator jumped, then raced aft and hurled himself into darkness, but instead of the expected fall, he got a tremendous jerk in the opposite direction— a parachute strap had fouled the door handle. The pilotless airplane hauled Scoff across the sky, the slipstream battering him against the tail section. The airplane nosed into its final dive, and a colossal jolt of adrenaline gave Scoff the strength to pull against the flying breeze. The offending strap came loose and he tumbled free, yanking his rip cord. The parachute slammed open, and a few seconds later Scoff smacked into a Chinese hillside. His plane exploded a mile or so farther on.

Eventually safe again in Dinjan, Scoff described his life flashing before his eyes.

Someone asked if he had any regrets.

"Hell yes," he said, nodding with sudden gravity. "I had two paychecks I hadn't spent."

The Allies had made their first forays back into Burma before the 1943 monsoon, and they didn't go well. A British attack from India into the coastal province of Arakan was repulsed with heavy casualties, as was the long-range infiltration of the "Chindit" brigade, commanded by Orde

Wingate, which had attempted to create chaos in Japanese rear echelons. Through the first half of 1943, the China-Burma-India theater was the only theater of the war where the Allies didn't seem to be making substantial progress, but despite its host of political, logistical, and geographic complications, it did have one distinct advantage over the Pacific fighting, where the Indonesian archipelago, New Guinea, and the Pacific islands kept the Allies at immense strategic distance from Japan. No such barrier existed between China and the home islands, and General Chennault argued that a small, aggressive air force operating from Chinese bases could cripple the enemy's shipping lanes in the East and South China seas, force Japan to withdraw from her outlying conquests, and bomb Japan, incinerating her wood-and-paper cities.

As everywhere, it was a question of priorities. Executing a stepped-up air offensive meant devoting the vast majority of Hump tonnage to Chennault's air force and neglecting reform of the Chinese Army, the raison d'être of General Stilwell's mission, and although Stilwell appreciated Chennault's fighting desire to hit the enemy, he thought it premature to invest in a major air campaign until the Chinese Army was capable of defending the airfields. Chennault felt no qualms about exploiting political connections to push his agenda, however, and he went over Stilwell's head and expounded his theories directly to the Generalissimo and in letters to Harry Hopkins, T. V. Soong, and Madame Chiang Kai-shek, who'd gone to the United States the previous November to get medical treatment for stomach pains and a skin condition and to press the American people and government to send more aid to China. Madame was often quartered in the White House, and she and Soong clamored for more transports and Hump tonnage and advocated Chennault's ideas to every American official who would listen. The Generalissimo backed Chennault's plan, and President Roosevelt acquiesced.

In May 1943, at a Washington conference code-named Trident, the British and American Combined Chiefs of Staff continued hashing out the war's strategic framework. It was perhaps no coincidence that William Bond returned to Washington that month, ostensibly for his annual health-related sojourn, but Bond always seemed to find his way home when major decisions loomed that might affect China's supply line. Presumably, as before, he'd been quietly summoned by T. V. Soong, who would have wanted Bond's wealth of experience, knowledge, and factual achievement on hand to counter any Air Corps claims the Hump couldn't be prosecuted. Major agreements were reached pertaining to the war in the Mediterranean, Europe, and the Pacific, and as for the China-Burma-India theater, after much deliberation the Combined Chiefs scrapped plans for a full-scale invasion of Burma and substituted a limited offensive designed to liberate a ground route from Ledo, India, across north Burma to link to the old Burma Road.*

While she was in the United States, Madame Chiang Kai-shek cajoled President Roosevelt and other top American leaders into immediately deploying to the Hump the Curtiss C-46 Commando, whose five-ton payload, improved high-altitude performance, and large portside cargo door pointed toward a revolution in Hump capacity. The India-China Wing put the first C-46s to work in early May and soon had thirty in operation. Unfortunately, the new plane hadn't been proved in rigorous circumstances. The Hump had those in abundance, and it quickly exposed serious shortcomings. By July, the ATC had lost six C-46s, evaporating enthusiasm for the new airplane.

Stateside business complete, Madame Chiang Kai-shek returned to Asia, due to arrive in China on July 4, 1943. Security considerations kept her exact itinerary secret, however. The Generalissimo had stayed in China, and not even he knew precisely where and when she'd arrive. Since she was flying in a DC-4, he expected her to arrive in Chengtu, the field closest to Chungking that normally handled four-engine traffic. Intending to personally greet his wife, Chiang Kai-shek left Ku Lung Po Airfield outside Chungking on the morning of July 4 aboard a twin-engine Douglas of the Aviation Commission and had himself flown 170 miles to Chengtu. While he was away, Madame Chiang's plane landed at Ku Lung Po, the airfield he'd just left. Madame discovered no greeting party and burst into tears. Her niece commandeered a station wagon from two CNAC mechanics and hustled Madame off to Chungking.

Embarrassed, furious, and losing face by the second, Chiang Kai-shek ordered his pilot back to Ku Lung Po. The Generalissimo's contagious im-

---

* Eliminating the major offensive into Burma freed enough shipping to transfer 215,000 men and their equipment to the United Kingdom to prepare for the cross-Channel assault at a time when shortage of shipping capacity was the single biggest drag on the Allied war effort: *Strategic Planning, 1943–1944*, p. 81.

patience inspired his pilot to land straight in, downwind, without circling the field to make an upwind approach. Simultaneously, Captain Lin, the Aviation Commission's number one pilot, was landing another plane upwind, after circling the field, as was standard and proper. Aboard, Lin had Chiang Ching-kuo, the Generalissimo's only son, inbound from Kweilin for the family reunion.* Neither airplane was aware of the other's presence. Only after Captain Lin's wheels touched down did he notice the other plane barreling toward him. He rammed forward emergency power, hauled his yoke, and vaulted the Generalissimo's plane.

Once both planes were safe on the ground, the Generalissimo vented his wrath. Irate, he summoned the head of the Aviation Commission and CNAC managing director Colonel Wang Cheng-fu. Warned, the former slunk off to his second home outside the city walls and had a servant make excuses. Colonel Wang received no advance notice and followed the summons to the Generalissimo's headquarters. "Who is your man at Ku Lung Po Airfield?" Chiang Kai-shek demanded.

"Mr. T. Y. Tsai," the colonel responded.

"What sort of man is he?"

Tsai had been with the company for twelve years. Colonel Wang considered him a good man.

How could that be? raged the Generalissimo. Tsai almost got him and his only son killed—in the same accident! If Mr. Tsai was a good man, what sort of men did CNAC have? The company was a hotbed of incompetence! Colonel Wang ran the airline, he was the responsible man. He ought to be shot! Chiang threatened to call in his guards and summarily do the job.

Mortified, Colonel Wang struggled to betray no emotion, determined to preserve his own dignity. His airline bore no responsibility: The Aviation Commission, Central Air Transport Company (CATC),** the U.S. Army, and CNAC all used the airfield. There had never been an overall traffic manager. Both planes involved belonged to the Aviation Commission. No CNAC plane had even been in the vicinity.

---

* Chiang Ching-kuo was the son of the Generalissimo's first wife, not of Mei-ling Soong (Madame Chiang Kai-shek).

** The Central Air Transport Company had been formed from Eurasia's assets on June 1, 1943, an attempt to rid Eurasia of its German taint so it could receive American aircraft.

The Generalissimo cooled enough not to administer kangaroo justice, but someone needed to be punished. He dismissed Wang Cheng-fu and told him to expect arrest and court-martial.

Arthur N. Young rushed to the head office and found the ashen managing director with a volume of the Encyclopaedia Britannica, reading the Magna Carta's entry with serene resignation. Colonel Wang drew Young's attention to the seven-hundred-year-old document's thirty-ninth clause: "No freeman shall be taken, or imprisoned, or desseized, or outlawed, or exiled, or in any way harmed . . . save by the lawful judgment of his peers or by the law of the land." But this was China. Colonel Wang expected no such consideration. He anticipated the firing squad.

Deliverance came from Madame Chiang, Dr. and Madame Kung, and the new minister of communications, all of whom interceded on Colonel Wang's behalf. The Generalissimo rescinded his arrest order. CNAC's Ku Lung Po Airport manager didn't receive the stay. Three days later, T. Y. Tsai still languished in jail. Arthur Young's impassioned letter to H. H. Kung secured his release, but only after the poor man had endured more than a week of incarceration.

Face allowed the Generalissimo to be merciful; it did not permit him to be wrong. He awarded Colonel Wang Cheng-fu a "very serious demerit," an intentional shaming that forced him to resign the managing directorship. He was succeeded by K. C. Lee, who would prove an able replacement, but the arbitrary, unfair nature of Wang Cheng-fu's fall from grace and the extralegal threats levied against him raised some worrisome flags among the more thoughtful members of the airline's leadership.

General Chennault began his promised offensive against enemy shipping while Colonel Wang was reading the Magna Carta on the morning of July 6, and in the coming weeks his air forces pummeled Japanese-controlled harbor installations and shipping in Chinese rivers and in the East and South China seas. Attrition wore down his force, and he clamored for reinforcements, his results indecisive, claiming with some justification that Hump inefficiencies and tonnage shortfalls had hamstrung the scope, ferocity, and impact of his campaign.

Air Corps commander General Hap Arnold considered the Army's airlift results "disappointing" and "unacceptable." Granted, the India-China

Wing's rapid expansion and its sheer scale wore into its per-plane efficiencies, and it was hampered by spare-parts shortages, poor maintenance, rudimentary airfields, and low morale worsened by the dismal living conditions it inflicted on its people, but its performance was woefully inadequate compared with CNAC in tons moved per plane, round trips per plane, accident rates, utilization hours, or any other metric used to evaluate the efficiency and competence of an airline. In September 1943, after completing many airfield improvements, the Army moved 5,198 tons over the Hump with 225 planes, well over half of which were C-87s and C-46s capable of hauling nearly 5 tons. CNAC delivered 1,132 metric tons with 27 planes, all of which were DC-3 types with 2- to 3-ton payloads. Per plane, the airline got 42 metric tons to China. The Army managed to fly only 23 tons with each of its airplanes despite a much larger gross capacity. General Stilwell tersely compared the organizations in his diary. "The over-promoted Air Corps is sunk when it comes to administration and management. Just a bunch of aerial chauffeurs . . . The C.N.A.C. has made them look like amateurs."

As bad a season as it was for the ATC, it was exponentially worse for the destitute citizens of Bengal and the Chinese province of Honan. The loss of Burma had cut eastern India from its most important foreign food source, a Bay of Bengal cyclone ruined the rice harvest in coastal regions, and worries about a Japanese invasion motivated the Indian government to confiscate shipping, fishing boats, and local transport, compounding distribution problems. Rumors of shortages caused hoarding and speculation, and food prices skyrocketed. Much of the populace couldn't afford crucial staples. Hordes of landless laborers and ruined farmers forced from foodless villages flocked to Calcutta, and they died in the streets. In all of Bengal, perhaps two and a half million people died of hunger.

Inconceivably, conditions might have been worse in Honan Province, astride the Yellow River north of Hankow, where severe drought withered the year's wheat. Indescribable misery greeted the few Western journalists with the courage to venture to the stricken region. Unmoneyed peasants paid tax in weights of grain, and venal Kuomintang magistrates forced them to pay with their last hoarded food, often at gunpoint. Central Government administrators and Chinese Army officers dined at loaded tables and blandly denied calamity, outrageous conduct that put lie to the conceit that the Kuomintang was genuinely working to further the interests of its own people. The aroused peasantry revolted—without Communist inspiration. The war inflicted apocalyptic misery worldwide; in Asia, it was somehow compounded.

The CNAC pilots sharing the house in Ballygunge continued to live relatively well through the middle of 1943, although they weren't insulated from the suffering of the Indian famine. Starving beggars and hungry children accosted them constantly as they pushed through the streets of Calcutta, the stench of death and filth clogging their nostrils. They literally stumbled over dead bodies, and they commonly witnessed pariah dogs and vultures feasting on human carrion. Pete Goutiere had checked out as pilot-captain in April, Ridge Hammell had done it in July, and the promotions bumped their base pay from $400 to $800 per month, with generous bonuses earned for hours flown in excess of seventy. In July, they both cleared about 1,200 U.S. dollars (nearly 15,000 modern dollars). Pilots further up the seniority chain earned even more. Associated risk accompanied the fat paychecks, of course. Sam Anglin was one of the pilots sharing the bungalow, and he took a Hump flight out of Dinjan on August 11 in number 48, the airline's oldest C-53, which, like all the C-53s, had two pairs of levers for the carburetor and oil heaters on the control pedestal between the pilot and the copilot. Each pair had small accompanying lock knobs. Anglin was a meticulous man, healthily obsessed with checking his planes before takeoff, and as part of the C-53 preflight run-up the pilot watched his engine temperatures climb into the normal range. Once there, he switched on the carburetor and oil heaters and made sure the temperatures continued to rise. Satisfied with the heaters, he closed them to the "off" position and engaged the lock levers to make sure the heaters didn't accidentally engage. What Anglin either didn't know or didn't remember was that company mechanics had rigged experimental superchargers into number 48's engines and connected the "blowers'" on/off control to the plane's oil and carburetor heater lock-levers. For some unfathomable reason, the mechanics hadn't put a sign in the cockpit explaining the modification, and Anglin took off without realizing he'd engaged the superchargers. Running them at low altitude dangerously elevated the engine temperature, and fifty-eight minutes out of Dinjan, over north Burma's Fort Hertz Valley, the engines started misbehaving. Anglin reversed course for India. An Army pilot spotted smoke trailing from his left engine and advised him to parachute. Anglin opted to nurse the plane for Dinjan. The smoking engine caught fire. Anglin killed the engine, feathered the power-less prop, and triggered the fire extinguisher, spraying carbon dioxide into the engine nacelle—to no effect. Fanned by 150 miles per hour of flying breeze, the inferno ate through the firewall behind the engine. An explosion snapped the wing. The broken airplane fluttered out of the sky and blew up in the jungle, killing Anglin and his two Chinese crew members. The entire disaster unfolded in about 120 seconds.

Sam Anglin had earned a few more dollars than Pete Goutiere in July, unaware that he'd have a scant eleven days in which to spend his last paycheck. More than a few Ballygunge glasses were raised in his honor, and Pete Goutiere dipped his wings every time he flew over the blackened patch of jungle marking his comrade's end. He'd flown number 48 the day before Anglin, and it had worked perfectly.

The monsoon that had started during Joe Rosbert and Ridge Hammell's epic struggle out of the Mishmi Hills continued through the summer, suppressing most Japanese air activity over north Burma and Assam, but it began to break up in early October, and on October 13 the sun finally rose into a crisp autumn sky. Recently checked-out pilot-captain Marshall Schroeder took off, climbed to sixteen thousand feet, and joined a group of Army pilots flying east at 115 degrees magnetic, the direct course to Kunming. It was the first truly clear day in months, and a glorious panorama of gorges, jungles, rivers, and snowy mountains filled the cockpit windows. Over Sumprabum in north Burma, a flight of Japanese Ki-43 "Oscar" fighters jumped the gaggle of transports.

Word of the air battle shot around the Dinjan airfield, and airline personnel flocked to the radio shack, where Schroeder's voice broke the background static. The transports scattered, but several enemy planes latched on to Schroeder's tail. He turned and twisted and dived while the crowd in the radio shack hung on his staccato narrations, but he couldn't shake the pursuit. The one-sided fight ran on for fifteen minutes, until the static crackled, unbroken. Seconds clicked into a minute, then two. The men dispersed with few comments. An hour later, a damaged military plane came screaming into Dinjan shot up like a sieve. The army pilot got out and fainted.

Schroeder's death crushed Pete Goutiere. Although Schroeder was a latecomer to CNAC, he was another man with whom Goutiere had flown in Pan Africa. He'd flown in Goutiere's right seat for the better part of a month during the monsoon, and if there was one piece of Hump wisdom Pete had tried to impart, it was *Don't fly across Burma at high altitude in clear weather—you'll be easy prey for any patrolling Japanese fighters.* In clear weather, Goutiere had told Schroeder to bend north, stay low, and hold tight to the mountains, which made the transports much more difficult to spot, gave them canyons and valleys in which to elude pursuit, and forced the enemy to operate at a greater distance from their bases. Schroeder paid a steep price for neglecting the advice, but Goutiere felt his share of responsibility. A ground party of Allied infiltrators operating with Kachin tribesmen behind Japanese lines found Schroeder's wreck, and three sets of human remains were buried at the site. Marshall Schroeder, from Buffalo, New York, was twenty-four years old.

William Bond had just worked his way over to Kunming on his way back to Chungking from the United States when the Japanese attacked the Hump transports. He immediately returned to Dinjan. If the Japanese attacks presaged a serious post-monsoon campaign designed to sever the airlift, the airline's best defense was to switch to night flying, just the way it had after Woody was shot down leaving Hong Kong in 1938. CNAC instituted the change that very night. Bond stayed two nights in Dinjan, doing what he could to help organize the transition. "As usual, CNAC is leading the way and demonstrating that this work can be done," Bond wrote. "The Army will have to do it."

The Army didn't follow the civilian example fast enough. Most Army pilots weren't well enough trained to handle an immediate shift to night flying, and the Japanese post-monsoon attacks evolved into a major effort against the Hump. The Oscars shot down three A-36A fighter-bombers (an unhappy variant of the P-51 Mustang) patrolling over Sumprabum in broad daylight on October 16. In the next ten days, they destroyed five C-46s. The Air Corps countered with strikes against Japanese airfields in Burma, and the tit-for-tat fighting continued through November and December. The Japanese bombed and strafed Dinjan on December 13, driving the airline's field personnel into muddy, fetid slit trenches. No company planes were harmed, but bombs destroyed the operations office and the storeroom. Woods had a table and chair set up in front of the wreckage, phone lines and radios connected, and he was back in the groove within fifteen minutes, both buildings afire behind him. The enemy suffered heavy attrition through the autumn, and once the Army had regained a measure of air superiority, CNAC went to round-the-clock operations. In spite of the attacks, South Asia's volatile weather remained the biggest drag on the airlift's success. CNAC was flying in all weathers and at night, its pilots far more experienced than their Army counterparts, who were fresh out of flight school. Army crews routinely scrubbed missions if they felt the weather too foul. Hoping a command shakeup would improve performance, the Air Corps had installed damn-the-torpedoes martinet Colonel Thomas O. Hardin in charge of the India-China Wing. Hardin thought his flight crews were taking advantage of lax policy. "There will be no weather on the Hump," he decreed, ordering them to fly regardless. Army tonnage deliveries increased. Predictably, so did the number of accidents. The India-China Wing had thirty-eight major crashes in November; CNAC had one. The Army suffered twenty-eight in December; CNAC had two fatal accidents that month, both on the foggy morning of December 18, when someone in the Chinese Air Force moved a landing beacon a few hundred feet without informing the airline, an act of negligence that cost two planes, two cargoes, and six lives.

The airline had to deal with the situation without the full attention of William Bond, for he'd spent several weeks laid up in the Rappes' Methodist compound with a terrible fever, joint agony that made him feel as if his bones were breaking, and a sledgehammer headache, fighting dengue fever. The sickness didn't prevent him from enjoying a joke in the inaugural issue of *The Chungking Edition of The Shanghai Evening Post and Mercury*, which hit the damaged streets of China's wartime capital that fall. In it, a China National Aviation Corporation advertisement invited readers to the gala opening of its new Shanghai airport, date "to be announced later"—a touch of optimistic irony that provided sure evidence that William Langhorne Bond was still operating in China.

25

TO LOSE A FRIEND

In most of the world, 1943 had gone well for the Allies. The Russians won decisive victories at Stalingrad and Kursk. Anglo-American campaigns expelled the Fascists from North Africa and Sicily and invaded Italy. Pacific offensives in New Guinea and the Solomon Islands made significant progress, and the Navy opened its campaign across the islands of the central Pacific. With unswerving perseverance, desperate fighting, and agonizing losses, the Allies had wrested the strategic initiative from the Axis. The only battlegrounds on which the Allies hadn't made major advances were in Burma and China. In late November, in Cairo, the Allied Combined Chiefs of Staff convened for the year's third strategic conference. In keeping with his intention to nurture China into a keystone of postwar Asian stability, President Roosevelt invited Generalissimo and Madame Chiang Kai-shek to attend. Despite the gesture, attitudes on China's importance in the world war were changing. Although Kuomintang propaganda continued to bamboozle American public opinion, Allied leadership—including President Roosevelt—was all too aware that the Chinese Army hadn't done any meaningful fighting in eighteen months. The Chiefs pressed Chiang to launch his Yunnan armies across the Salween River into Burma. Chiang cagily evaded formal commitment, and the Generalissimo's reluctance to take action to aid himself made it easy for the Allies to attach less importance to breaking China's blockade. Chiang's discussion of the potential "collapse of the China theater" did little to create the impression that he was sincerely working toward defeat of the common foe. The blossoming success of Pacific operations made China seem less crucial as a component of Japan's defeat than it had at any time since Pearl Harbor, and the Allies' strategic conception of twin drives crushing the Japanese Empire from east and west was giving way to one that envisioned a main effort from the Pacific defeating Japan without much help from the Chinese mainland.

The Cairo meetings had been held in secret. "The several military missions have agreed on future operations against Japan," a joint Allied statement declared in their aftermath. The truth wasn't so accordant. Chiang Kai-shek had made a poor impression on British and American leaders. In one of his many demands, he asked President Roosevelt for a billion-dollar loan; to stabilize the Chinese currency, Madame Chiang Kai-shek claimed they needed $200 million of it in gold bars. In post-conference telegram exchanges, a decidedly cooler President Roosevelt informed Chiang Kai-shek that he'd referred the loan request to the Treasury Department for "consideration." The aftermath of Cairo tended to relegate the war in China, Burma, and India to a supporting role, leaving the Hump airlift as the highest-priority American effort in Asia, primarily intended to keep China in the war and to supply air attacks against the enemy.

Just before Cairo, at the end of October 1943, the "Chinese Army in India" had crossed the Naga Hills and the Patkai Mountains and slogged into the pestilential jungles of north Burma, the beginning of the offensive decided upon at the Trident conference the previous May. Created by General Stilwell's training program from the survivors of the Chinese divisions that had retreated to India after the collapse of Burma in mid-1942, it advanced beyond the head of the road construction being pushed forward from Ledo and probed into the Taro Plain and the Hukawng Valley. Elements of a Japanese infantry regiment assigned to cover the region counterattacked with characteristic intensity. General Stilwell was in the Middle East for the Cairo meetings, and without him the Chinese regiments couldn't find their offensive fire. A stalemate ran through November and the first half of December. Stilwell flew into Burma on December 21. Three days later, the Chinese attacked effectively and spent the last days of December and all of January clawing into the central Hukawng Valley, aiming for the ridge at the head of the valley over which they'd have to fight to gain entry to the Mogaung drainage and the town of Kamaing on the far side, waypoints en route to the Irrawaddy riverside town of Myitkyina, the key to controlling north Burma. The north Burma campaign gave CNAC a new mission—airdropping supplies to the advancing Chinese, which it executed with characteristic daring and efficiency, kicking rice sacks into jungle clearings through the side doors of its cargo planes from low altitude. A new weapon joined the fracas in late February—the 5307th Composite Unit, a brigade-sized American long-range penetration group designed along the lines of Wingate's Chindits. Commanded by General Frank Merrill, the unit was called "Merrill's Marauders" by the press.

Concurrently, British general Orde Wingate mounted a second Chindit expedition. One of his brigades infiltrated overland. Beginning on March 5, the others were flown deep into Burma and blocked the Mandalay–Myitkyina railroad, partially isolating the north Burma battlefields from enemy reinforcement and resupply and attracting a great deal of Japanese countermeasures. Wingate died in a plane crash on March 24, but his Chindits fought on without him.

In parallel with the north Burma actions, three Anglo-Indian divisions had advanced into the Burmese coastal province of Arakan in December of 1943, a larger-scale repeat of the offensive they'd attempted a year earlier. The British pounded at a Japanese defensive line without result for most of December and all of January. The Japanese counterattacked on February 4, a right-hand envelopment through terrible jungles and mountains that cut off two divisions—a maneuver similar to the one they'd used to such good effect the year before. But General Sir William Slim issued "stand-fast and fight" orders to the isolated units, sustained them with aerial resupply, flew in reinforcements, and launched his own riposte. The encircling Japanese now found themselves surrounded, and they were wiped out in detail in the last half of February. The British bludgeoned forward again in early March. They were on the verge of breaking through when a developing emergency compelled Slim to abandon the campaign—the Japanese had launched their own massive offensive through the mountains of the Burma-India frontier aimed at driving the British from the Imphal Plain and the town of Kohima in the Manipur highlands, which would deny the British the only bases from which a major army could attack into central

Burma. It was an imitation of the Chindit infiltration Orde Wingate had executed before the 1943 monsoon, but with 155,000 men instead of 3,000, an extraordinarily daring plan whose success depended on capturing British supplies in the offensive's initial rush. Heedless of the risks, Japanese infantry began crossing the Chindwin on the night of March 7.

General Slim had anticipated the Japanese move, but he was amazed by the ferocious velocity of their advance, and he rushed reinforcements to the battlefields with air transports diverted from the Hump. The enemy swept a hundred miles through the Naga Hills and cut the Imphal-Kohima road on March 29. Soon after, they invested the bulk of an Anglo-Indian corps in Imphal and a smaller garrison at Kohima, the decisive point. If the British lost Kohima, the Japanese could flood into the Assam Valley and undermine every major Allied effort on the Asian mainland, including the Hump airlift.

With the Japanese at full surge, General Stilwell conferred with General Slim on April 3. Stilwell's Sino-American force had just fought into the Mogaung Valley, but with disaster threatening at Imphal and Kohima, Stilwell expected the Britisher to ask him for reinforcements that would derail his north Burma undertakings. However, Slim assured Stilwell that he could handle the situation with the forces he had at hand, and Slim's confidence freed Stilwell to begin planning a phenomenally audacious stroke of his own.

Time and again through the middle of April, Japanese assaults nearly overwhelmed the Kohima defenders. Just over a hundred miles from the fighting, and well aware of the enemy's propensity for sweeping envelopments, CNAC pilots in Dinjan were sleeping with their guns during those tenuous days. In desperate combat, the British held Kohima for two weeks. Slim's rescue mission fought through to Kohima on April 20, relieving the battered garrison. With the immediate emergency ended, Slim directed his energies to attacking south, toward the divisions besieged at Imphal, where intense fighting still raged.

Well positioned as he was, William Bond wasn't privy to the shift in Allied strategic thinking that had taken place at Cairo, and neither were most of the men fighting in the CBI. Once Bond had shaken the dengue fever, he appraised the state of the Hump airlift in early 1944 with tremendous sat-

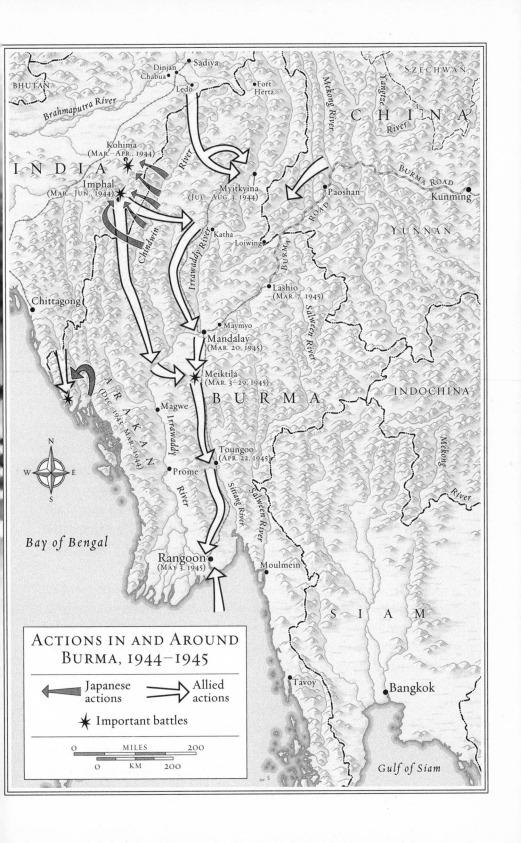

BHUTAN

Brahmaputra River

INDIA

Chittagong

Bay of Bengal

Dinjan
Chabua
Ledo
Sadiya
Fort
Hertz

SZECHWAN

CHINA

Mekong River

Yangtze River

Kohima
(MAR.–APR., 1944)

Imphal
(MAR.–JUN, 1944)

Chindwin River

Myitkyina
(JUL.–AUG. 3, 1944)

Paoshan

BURMA ROAD

Kunming

YUNNAN

Irrawaddy River

Katha
Loiwing

BURMA ROAD

Lashio
(MAR. 7, 1945)

Salween River

Mandalay
(MAR. 20, 1945)

Maymyo

Meiktila
(MAR. 3–29, 1945)

BURMA

INDOCHINA

A R A K A N
(DEC. 1943–MAR. 1944)

Magwe

Irrawaddy River

Prome

Toungoo
(APR. 22, 1945)

Sittang River

Salween River

Mekong River

Rangoon
(MAY 3, 1945)

Moulmein

S I A M

Tavoy

Bangkok

Gulf of Siam

N
W   E
S

ACTIONS IN AND AROUND
BURMA, 1944–1945

Japanese
actions

Allied
actions

★ Important battles

0   MILES   200
0   KM   200

isfaction. It was growing into a colossal undertaking, and the Army's struggles were at last bearing fruit. Taken together, the airline and the Air Corps were landing more than a hundred flights in China every day, and that number kept rising. They'd registered a major success in December 1943, when they carried more than twelve thousand tons to China, surpassing the ten-thousand-ton goal established by President Roosevelt. The India-China Wing got a Presidential Unit Citation for the achievement; CNAC was having a hard time getting paid—its invoices to the Army were running nearly six months in arrears. However, in light of the successes, there seemed no limit to the quantity of tonnage that might be moved. Bond felt responsible, and justifiably proud, even if he and his airline weren't receiving many public accolades. The China airlift was ripening into one of the war's great efforts, and he knew it probably wouldn't have been attempted without the pioneering efforts of his airline. To Bond, it seemed that China was finally being accorded the place in the war he'd long thought it merited. He took it for granted that belligerent China kept a significant portion of the Japanese Army tied to the Asian mainland, that Allied airpower operating from bases in east China could do tremendous damage, and that Chinese manpower welded to American equipment and know-how would prove decisive in the final battles. It seemed as though the United States was finally doing exactly what Bond had been explicitly advocating since 1937—expending a massive effort to supply the means of modern war to an embattled China—and doing it in the manner that he'd been specifically championing since the spring of 1941, with an airlift over the Hump. William Bond expected that the verdict of history would judge CNAC's work a fulcrum of Japan's defeat.

And like the good businessman he most definitely was, Bond was already planning for peace. Pan Am's contract with the Ministry of Communications expired on July 8, 1945, a year and a half into the future, and it was high time to start considering what would happen when it did. Bond wrote a memorandum to clarify his thinking. Although the Central Government's autocratic tendencies concerned him, as did its careless economic policies, corruption and callousness, unfair judicial practices, and the irredeemable hostility that existed between it and the Communists, Bond still believed the Kuomintang would likely be the force to continue and complete China's unification after the peace was won, and he presumed that the Kuomintang would eventually deliver on its oft-repeated pledge to liberalize Chinese society and lead the country forward to democracy and the rule of law, all of which he considered essential to China's long-run success. He foresaw "a great period of activity and development" taking hold in China when hostilities terminated, and he was carefully positioning his airline to exploit the immense opportunity he saw coming—he intended to grow the China National Aviation Corporation into Asia's dominant airline.

Although T. V. Soong still served as China's foreign minister, he hadn't exercised any real power since he returned to China in the autumn of 1943 and launched an unsuccessful campaign to remove General Stilwell. The obstreperous West Pointer had proved incorruptible, "show me" realistic, and impossible to manipulate, and the Chinese wanted him replaced. Surprisingly, Soong's maneuverings had escalated into a major family in-fight that apparently pitted him against Madame Chiang and Madame Kung, both of whom crusaded for Stilwell. Soong convinced Chiang Kai-shek that his personal appeal to the U.S. government could compel the issue. It didn't. Relations smoothed back into business as usual, but being forced to recant cost the Generalissimo a great deal of face. He blamed his foreign minister, and a schism grew between the two men, exacerbated by what Chiang and other right-wing members of his inner circle perceived to be T. V. Soong's alarmingly autonomous tendencies. The Generalissimo clipped Soong's power base, most notably when H. H. Kung replaced Pei Tsuyi, T. V. Soong's protégé, as head of the Bank of China. T.V. immediately issued a diplomatic passport to his younger brother, T. L. Soong, and sent him to the United States to retain control of the American end of the foreign-aid apparatus that was the key to his influence. Although T.V. remained foreign minister, he was conspicuously absent from the Cairo Conference. Soong spoke too frankly at a family meeting afterward; the enraged Generalissimo supposedly threw a teacup at his head. The U.S. ambassador to China, Clarence Gauss, reported that Soong had gone into social and official "retirement," a disappearance from public life that seemed tantamount to house arrest. Other omens indicated vicious scuffling behind the Nationalist throne. Rumors hinted at marital troubles between China's first couple and elaborated on the apparent hostility between T. V. Soong and H. H. Kung and between T. V. Soong and his two sisters. The influence of the whole Soong clan suffered.

Bond didn't know what to make of the Praetorian melee. It was extremely hard to fathom the political maneuverings in the dark closets of the Kuomintang, and it was at least possible that the squabbling among the Soong clan was strictly for show, masking some larger, more subtle objective—which wasn't an unheard-of practice in Chinese politics.* The levelheaded businessman neither believed everything he heard nor dismissed the rumors entirely. Following the dictates of business, William Bond bounced back and forth over the Hump as the fighting intensified around the Burmese periphery in the first half of 1944, and during one of his Chungking stays Bond received an invitation to dine with T. V. Soong. Bond was a loyal man, and he was too fully aware of how much of his own and Pan American's success in China he owed to Soong's influence to let Soong's eclipse dissuade him from accepting. Besides, Bond genuinely liked and admired the foreign minister.

At the door, a valet asked Bond to follow him upstairs to Dr. Soong's bedroom. That struck Bond as odd, but he did as asked and found the portly foreign minister sprawled back in a chair, his face covered in shaving lather, being tended to by a barber. His round spectacles lay on a side table. Ministrations complete, the barber departed. Dr. Soong and Bond exchanged brief pleasantries, after which Soong said nothing for a long while, and when he did speak it was to mutter some brief, commonplace remark demanding no reply. Bond held his tongue, for it was clear that Dr. Soong was deeply troubled, and rather than feeling insulted or dismissed, he felt privileged and sympathetic at the unexpected intimacy as Soong wrestled with an obviously difficult problem. Bond sat quietly, keeping T. V. Soong company.

Finally, a servant came up and announced dinner.

"Tell them to wait fifteen minutes," Soong instructed.

When the time had elapsed, Bond brought it to Soong's attention.

"Go on down, Bondy. Tell them to send mine up."

Downstairs, Bond was seated with one Chinese official he knew well, but to his great surprise there were two other guests at dinner whom he'd never met: Chiang Ching-kuo—Chiang Kai-shek's son—and another Chi-

---

* Harold Bixby had once suggested that Bond and P. Y. Wong stage a vociferous, public row to quell suspicion that they were working too closely.

nese Bond suspected of being a major player in a secret police organization.

Dinner was uncomfortable, without much conversation in any language, and it needed no great intuition to perceive a connection between T. V. Soong's internal struggle and the pair downstairs with whom he refused to dine. A very serious matter must lie behind such calculated discourtesy. Afterward, Bond hurried home and pondered the strange evening, wondering futilely why he'd been included and what role his presence had played.

The airline's business manager, Alfred Kao, came into Bond's office a day or two later and said, "Mr. M. Y. Tong called for you and requested me to ask you to call him when you arrived."

M. Y. Tong! Bond hadn't seen his best Chinese friend since before the Japanese attacked Hong Kong, when he hadn't been able to find Tong during the crucial days of the evacuation and had been compelled to leave him behind. Although he'd since received word that his friend was okay, Bond was delighted that Tong was safe in Chungking—and filled with curiosity. Why was he here? What were conditions like in occupied Hong Kong? How had he escaped? Tong was an extremely prominent banker, president of the Bank of Canton, and well known as one of T. V. Soong's closest associates. Surely the Japanese would have kept close watch on such an important man? His friend would have a great story. Bond asked Kao to bring him to the office for tea.

Kao returned alone. Mr. Tong was being "detained."

That surprised Bond, but he assumed it was surely the result of some misunderstanding, easily resolved. He pushed it from his mind and returned to his mountain of paperwork.

A few days later, still not having heard from Tong, Bond asked Kao to get him on the telephone.

Alfred Kao shuffled into Bond's office a few minutes later. He seemed confused. "What on earth is it, Mr. Kao?"

"Mr. Tong has been executed for treason," he murmured.

Bond was shocked into silence. Then the questions came in a flood. "Why? In God's name, why?"

Kao had no details and hurried from the room, driven by more than the Chinese horror of delivering foul tidings.

Bond paced the room, stunned. A kind and considerate man—his dear friend—had been executed without public trial, charges, lawyer, judge, jury, or warning. He might have been tortured. Bond clutched the window-sill and surveyed the dingy city. Rancid smells rose from its ramshackle neighborhoods. A child relieved herself in a gutter. It was awful, ugly be-yond words. True composure was a long time coming. Bond made inqui-ries in the coming days, choosing his questions and contacts carefully, asking only those of his Chinese associates he thought might have seen his friend, might have heard something, or might have some insight into *why*. Bond received no real answers, and the anxious manner in which everyone denied knowledge and changed the subject made him realize he was on dangerous ground. Not for him, he was an American, nothing would hap-pen to him. It was his Chinese friends who considered the subject danger-ous and took care to demonstrate disinterest.

A rage grew in Bond, a quiet, soul-grinding anger that refused to be ignored. He couldn't shake the vision of his best Chinese friend crumpled at the base of a dingy wall, blood and brains spattering the boots of some Kuomintang enforcer. The terrible image compelled him to reexamine his faith in the Kuomintang, and it couldn't withstand the scrutiny. Bond forced himself to acknowledge that he'd been naïve, seeing what he wanted and hoped for Nationalist China rather than what existed in the real world. Beneath the propaganda blather, "Free China" was a police state, devoid of justice, most keenly interested in preserving its own power and position, close kin to the enemies the Allies were expending so much blood and treasure to exterminate elsewhere in the world. Bond kept his mouth shut, but he couldn't stop asking himself questions as he tried to make sense of the murder, for he knew in his bones that any allegation of treason against M. Y. Tong was false. Bond concocted theory after theory, but it wasn't until he connected Tong's murder with his odd evening with T. V. Soong that one of them acquired a plausible aura.

Tong clearly hadn't escaped Hong Kong. Escape was for the obscure. An aristocratic financier couldn't disappear without seriously endangering his family and the staff at his bank, and Tong was too much of a suit for harebrained endeavors. The Japanese must have freed him for their own purposes. Bond could think of only one reason that would motivate them to release such a man, and that was peace. The Japanese government and military had never been a monolithic structure. Divisions and factions within it had been noted in the years before Pearl Harbor, and for all their visible fanaticism and willing self-sacrifice, by early 1944 it must have been apparent to many Japanese that they were losing the war. The Americans would soon crack Japan's inner defense ring, exposing the home islands to attack. There must have been some Japanese who were anxious to avoid the annihilation of their island and culture or hoped to win a peace settlement more favorable than unconditional surrender. Rumors said they'd been trying to find someone to mediate between them and the United States. Some claimed the Swiss had been approached, others said it was the Soviets. Face wouldn't allow the Japanese to send a peace overture through the Generalissimo, since they were trying to establish their puppet regime as China's legitimate government and therefore didn't officially recognize Chiang's leadership. However, they could seek mediation through T. V. Soong. He was a perfect man to approach. No other Chinese was closer to the American government, and therein lay the danger for M. Y. Tong, because it wasn't peace negotiations that threatened the Generalissimo. Many Kuomintang elements had been doing business with the Japanese in ways most Americans would have considered treasonous since before Marco Polo Bridge. It was the *who* that threatened him. If Bond's theory was correct, peace negotiations brokered by T. V. Soong would bring him considerable credit and prominence, and Soong's international reputation, lock-tight control of American financial and military aid, and respected position within China's educated elite made him one of the few men who could conceivably challenge Chiang for control of the Kuomintang. Upon reflection, Bond didn't think it was a coincidence that Tong had arrived in Chungking as the peace rumor was making the rounds. He suspected the Japanese had sent Tong to Chungking to try to persuade Soong to approach the American government about opening peace negotiations.

Chiang didn't dare jail or execute T. V. Soong. Aside from being his brother-in-law, Soong was too close to the Americans, and his elimination would curtail the regime's aid from America, support it most definitely needed. Chiang and his internal security chiefs could, however, send an unmistakable signal to the Soong family by putting a bullet in the brain of the messenger.

Bond suspected that T. V. Soong was in the throes of this morass when he had Bond to dinner. Indeed, Bond may have been summoned precisely in order to emphasize the quality of Soong's American relationships to the others at the table. Bond surmised M. Y. Tong was barely ahead of the Generalissimo's police when he reached Chungking and called the CNAC office seeking Bond. Public friendship with a well-respected, governmentally connected American would have made him awkward to eliminate, but between the time of Tong's call and Bond's dispatch of Alfred Kao, Tong was intercepted by Chiang's enforcers and "detained," an event that had terminal consequences.

Bond mulled his scenario. It proved plausible and withstood examination. His anger mounted with each review. He probed the well-concealed emotions of his Chinese associates, and to his consternation, he discovered fear, even as the Allies climbed to the brink of victory. Indeed, Tong's murder could have been a message to a whole class of educated Chinese, increasingly disgruntled with the Kuomintang, and for Bond it lifted the veil of Chinese "potential" he'd worn for so many years. A good man had been summarily executed without trial, without murmur, his life and works swept under an Oriental rug as if he'd never existed. Chiang and his cronies had been paying lip service to fostering democracy for seventeen years and he'd fallen for it the whole time, when they were nothing but a gang of Fascist thugs ruling behind a ruthless Gestapo. It was so extralegal, so far removed from personal liberty, inviolate rights, the rule of law, and all the other values for which Bond imagined the Allies were fighting, principles that Bond believed were crucial to China's postwar stability and prosperity. He sensed his closest Chinese associates losing confidence in their country's future. Graft, corruption, terror, self-interest, and incompetence had delegitimized the Kuomintang, and if it came to civil war with the Communists or another warlord faction, Bond was no longer convinced they'd win.

It was also an exceptionally awkward epiphany, for Bond was still responsible for Pan American's investment in the China National Aviation Corporation, a very substantial asset. However, he was now beset by the growing feeling that China was doomed, or rather, that Chiang's China was doomed, and although CNAC's contract was with "the Government of China," Bond had little faith that his airline's odd partnership could survive a change of government. He forced himself to acknowledge the likelihood that the airline he'd labored so long and hard to build was flying toward a mountain with its controls locked—and that changed his priorities entirely. Pan

American's contract with the Chinese expired on July 8, 1945. The time was ripe to start negotiating an extension, and, considering the fate he now felt likely awaited Kuomintang China, the coming contract renewal was the time to extract Pan Am's investment—and its return—no matter how perfectly the airline seemed poised for postwar expansion. Nor could he allow his Chinese partners to get even the slightest glimmer of his intention. They made no secret of their desire to increase the Chinese portion of the airline, but if they realized Pan Am wanted out, they wouldn't pay true value for the American share. Bond also knew there was someone else he'd have to convince in order to do this, someone long considered the most stubborn, tightfisted man in aviation—Juan Terry Trippe, the very man he'd browbeaten into giving him the opportunity to save Pan Am's China investment in 1937.

If M. Y. Tong's execution contained a general message to all educated Chinese, its direct imperative to the Soong family was undeniable, and they were afflicted by a sudden desire to leave China. H. H. Kung eased out of the Finance Ministry and attended an economic conference at Bretton Woods, New Hampshire. Afterward, he quietly joined his brother-in-law T. L. Soong, T.V.'s younger brother, in residence at the family mansion in Riverdale, New York. Madame Chiang and her sister Madame Kung made a hush-hush trip to Brocoió Island in Rio de Janeiro, Brazil, along with Madame Kung's son Louis and his wife. After eight weeks in South America, the entourage quietly flew north and disappeared into seclusion in Riverdale.

The exodus seemed to confirm Bond's interpretation. It also left T. V. Soong as the only politically active clan member on Chinese soil.* With his closest blood relatives beyond the reach of the Generalissimo's secret police, T. V. Soong began to use his not-inconsiderable resources to fight his way back into the corridors of power.

---

* His third sister, Madame Sun Yat-sen, also stayed in China, but her uncorrupt stewardship of Sun Yat-sen's legacy made her unassailable by any faction.

26

GETTING HIS

Notwithstanding the political infighting in Chungking, there was still a war to win, and it raged to a climax in Burma and India in the spring of 1944. Freed by General Slim's confidence in his ability to handle the Imphal and Kohima fighting, General Stilwell concocted an operation designed to seize Myitkyina, which was still far behind enemy lines. Beginning in late April, attacks in the Mogaung Valley masked a seventy-mile end run through the six-thousand-foot peaks and passes of the Kumon Range by Merrill's Marauders, two Chinese regiments, and a force of Kachin tribesmen. Beyond the crest of the range, the columns marched south and burst onto the Myitkyina airfield on May 17, taking the Japanese by complete surprise. Air transport rushed hasty reinforcements to the scene. Chinese and American infantry held the airfield, but lacked the punch to oust the Japanese from the town. The Japanese fortified defensive positions but were themselves too weak to break the Allies' tenuous grip on the airfield. The monsoon broke, and the miserable, rain-soaked opponents jabbed at each other in vicious seesaw fighting. As soon as William Bond appreciated the gravity of the Myitkyina stalemate, he volunteered his airline's services, and the company shuttled men and supplies to Myitkyina alongside regular Air Corps transport squadrons.

During the airlift, a CNAC pilot named Donald McBride stood in line outside an Army mess tent at the Myitkyina airport, waiting for a sandwich in a drenching rain while his plane was unloaded. A gaunt, aging soldier emerged from the tent, ducking through the sheet of water pouring off the tent roof. He had a Colt .45-caliber pistol strapped to his waist, usually the provision of officers, but the old man wasn't wearing a speck of insignia, he looked like a common private, and the creases in his face were as deep as those in a worn-out combat boot. "My God," McBride muttered, "have things gone so bad in this war that they're sending old men like that over here to fight?"

An Army sergeant snickered nearby. "Don't you know who that is? That's Vinegar Joe."

The unpretentious Yankee general made a habit of eating the same fare as his enlisted men.

The Imphal battles continued concurrent with the Myitkyina fighting, and in a series of hard-fought, carefully managed attacks, Slim's Anglo-Indian army steadily chewed through the Japanese, turning the Imperial Army's near-victory into a crushing defeat. The Japanese had never captured the supply depots on which so much depended, and by the middle of June they were starving. Slim's relief force opened the Imphal-Kohima road on June 22, ending Imphal's three months of encirclement. In the following weeks, Slim's army shoved the enemy back into Burma. In India, the Japanese Army left sixty-five thousand dead, the worst defeat it had ever suffered.

Buoyed by constant aerial deliveries of men, munitions, and food, and by the Chindits' and his Chinese divisions' destruction of the Japanese positions in the Moguang Valley, Stilwell's Sino-American force finally captured Myitkyina on August 3. The Hump airlift had felt the benefits of the campaign since the day the Myitkyina airfield was overrun—its capture largely eliminated Japanese fighters from the skies of north Burma, allowing the transports to fly the more southerly, lower-altitude route William Bond had envisioned in the freight service proposals he'd authored before the fall of Burma. Tonnage deliveries jumped from 13,686 tons in May to 18,235 tons in June and to a hitherto unimaginable 25,454 tons in July. Sometime that summer, CNAC made its twenty thousandth trip over the Hump.

In almost every part of the world, the Allies were gaining, inflicting and suffering terrible losses in fighting that grew increasingly savage as they crunched toward the Axis homelands. Amphibious assaults ejected the Japanese from the Marshall Islands, completed the isolation of Rabaul, and captured bases in the Marianas from which B-29 bombers could hit Japan. In Europe, colossal Anglo-American bomber raids pulverized German cities. The Western Allies occupied Rome on June 4, and two days later they landed eight divisions in Normandy, opening the main effort against Hitler that had been envisioned by American strategists since the day they'd entered the war. On the Eastern Front, the numbers of killed and wounded—on both sides—beggared imagination, but the Red Army expelled the Nazis from the Ukraine, and by the end of August Soviet divisions were within sight of Warsaw. Only in the Middle Kingdom did the Allied cause continue to fare poorly.

Nineteen forty-four was a terrible year in China. Fiscal mismanagement fueled outrageous inflation that was eviscerating the country. CNAC had flown *244 tons* of paper money into China in April alone, 68 more tons of money than it had flown in any previous month. A picul of rice that had cost 9 Chinese dollars in Chungking in 1938 cost $9,000 in May 1944, and prices were rising so fast that merchants preferred to hoard goods rather than sell them. Items of tangible value sold for "good" currency at exorbitant prices. Parker pens went in seconds for 100 U.S. dollars. Used suits of clothes fetched twice their original price. The inflationary heat evaporated the last vestige of the community spirit that had thrived in Chungking in 1939, leaving only China's savage dog-eat-dog competitiveness. Grotesque corruption flourished at all levels of society, and the bald-faced cynicism of China's war effort appalled most knowledgeable foreign observers: Chiang's best troops weren't even deployed against the Japanese but were in the north blockading Mao's Communists; most consumer goods on sale in Chungking came from trade conducted with Japanese-held regions; and the Ministry of Finance insisted that the United States military finance its purchases in China at the official 20-to-1 exchange rate rather than at black-market rates of more than 250 to 1, which reflected the currency's true value, creating the strong impression that China expected the United States to pay a 90 percent premium for the privilege of fighting Japan from

Chinese soil. Criticisms mounted. Secret police made midnight visits to would-be dissenters. More than a few suffered the fate of M. Y. Tong.

Since the Cairo Conference, American leadership had grown increasingly exasperated with Chiang Kai-shek's reluctance to order his forces forward on the Salween River front between Yunnan and Burma, where five Chinese armies faced one depleted Japanese division.* President Roosevelt had sent a blunt message to Chiang Kai-shek in early April. A few days later, General Marshall gave Stilwell permission to link continued American aid to tangible anti-Japanese results. Stilwell had a subordinate inform the Chinese military that the United States would withhold Lend-Lease and cancel CNAC's contract and reassign its freight-carrying aircraft unless the Chinese advanced. Within a month, the Chinese vanguard had crossed the Salween, fought over the passes beyond the river, and threatened to do its part in squeezing the Japanese out of north Burma with converging attacks from east and west. Unfortunately, inept generalship bungled the opportunity. A counterattack by fifteen hundred Japanese infantrymen sent ten thousand Chinese reeling and ruined hopes that the Yunnan force could aid the Chinese and Americans then embattled at Myitkyina. Events vindicated other aspects of General Stilwell's judgment. China-based airpower had finally started inflicting the damage Chennault had long claimed it could, battering Japanese merchant shipping and airfields and impinging Japan's free use of China's rivers. B-29s based in India and staging through China bombed the Japanese home islands. The result was exactly what General Stilwell had predicted two years before. The Japanese mounted a ground campaign to capture the airbases.

The main Japanese offensive broke south from Hankow in May, and the Chinese armies proved incapable of stopping it. Changsha fell on June 18. Hengyang repulsed several attacks, but succumbed on August 8. Thereafter, the Japanese drove south at will. Claire Chennault begged Stilwell to divert Hump tonnage from his air force to buttress Chinese ground units, a monumental irony. Warlord politics hamstrung defensive efforts. "War zone commanders" in east and south China existed at the fringe of Central Government authority, and Chiang Kai-shek didn't want American arms strengthening potential rivals. Nor would the war zone commanders

---

* Chinese armies were about the size of a Western corps.

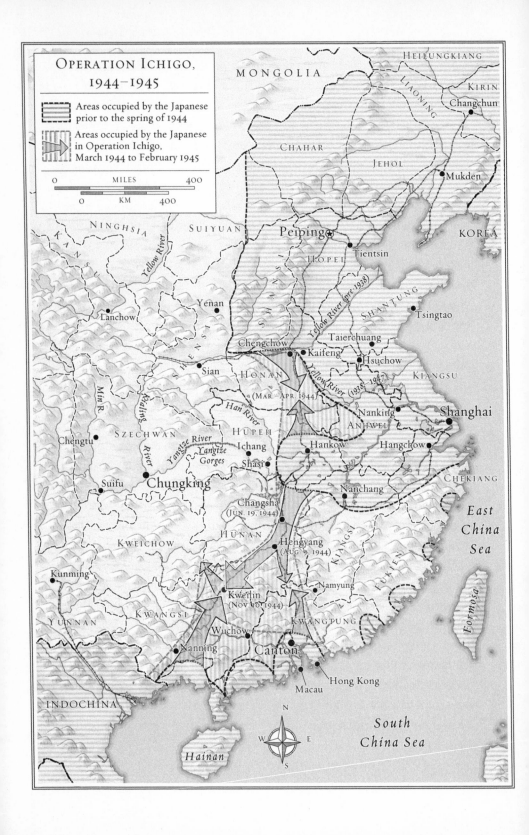

HEILUNGKIANG

MONGOLIA

LIAONING

KIRIN

Changchun

CHAHAR

JEHOL

Mukden

KOREA

NINGHSIA

SUIYUAN

Yellow River

KANSU

SHANSI

Peiping

HOPEI

Tientsin

SHANTUNG

Yenan

Lanchow

Yellow River (pre-1938)

Tsingtao

Chengchow

Kaifeng

Taierchuang

SHENSI

Sian

HONAN

(MAR.–APR. 1944)

Yellow River (1938–1947)

Hsuchow

KIANGSU

Han River

Nanking

Shanghai

Min R.

Chengtu

SZECHWAN

Yangtze River

HUPEH

Ichang

Langtze Gorges

Hankow

ANHWEI

Hangchow

Pei River

Shasi

CHEKIANG

Suifu

Chungking

Nanchang

KWEICHOW

Changsha (JUN. 19, 1944)

HUNAN

KIANGSI

East China Sea

Kunming

Hengyang (AUG. 9, 1944)

FUKIEN

Formosa

YUNNAN

KWANGSI

Kweilin (NOV. 10, 1944)

Namyung

Wuchow

KWANGTUNG

Nanning

Canton

INDOCHINA

Macau

Hong Kong

Hainan

South China Sea

N
W   E
S

risk their armies in pitched battles for fear their destruction would eliminate their domestic political influence. Provincial authorities and war zone
commanders from Kwantung, Kwangsi, Yunnan, and Szechwan approached U.S. military officers and State Department officials to ascertain
whether they'd get American support if they ousted Chiang. A State Department official reported that the Generalissimo had made agreements
with the Japanese. Another source had the potential usurpers negotiating
with the enemy. The "Dixie Mission" of U.S. Army and State Department
officials met with the Chinese Communists in Yennan, exploring the possibility of supplying American arms to the Red Army in return for its services against the Japanese, a mortal peril to Chiang Kai-shek. The Allied
war effort in China verged on collapse. Hoping to stave off disaster and
stimulate meaningful anti-Japanese action, President Roosevelt and General Marshall maneuvered to install General Stilwell in charge of the Chinese Army, with full command authority guaranteed by the Generalissimo.
President Roosevelt's personal representatives General Patrick Hurley and
Donald M. Nelson, along with General Stilwell, haggled toward a solution
with senior Chinese Army officers, the Generalissimo, and T. V. Soong,
who'd successfully clawed back to influence after nearly a year in the political wilderness. Meanwhile, Japanese forces advanced toward the crucial
airfield nexus around Kweilin. Chiang Kai-shek stalled and wrangled for
Chinese control of Lend-Lease on par with that enjoyed by Great Britain
and the Soviet Union, apparently less concerned about the disaster threatening the anti-Japanese war effort than he was about appointing a foreigner
to command his armies, being forced to recognize the Chinese Communists, and scuttling Stilwell's plans to supply Lend-Lease arms to the east
China warlords and the Red Army. Exasperated, President Roosevelt sent
the Generalissimo a blunt communiqué on September 19, an ultimatum
demanding that Chiang act. General Stilwell delivered it in person, as he
thought he'd been instructed to do, in front of Chinese and American officials with whom Chiang was conferring, including members of China's
National Military Council. In appearance, it was General Stilwell giving
orders to Chiang Kai-shek. The Generalissimo received the message with
no outward emotion, but its contents and the method of its delivery were a
resounding slap to his face in front of some of his government's principal
actors. The Generalissimo's reply to President Roosevelt squarely laid

blame for China's woes on Stilwell's lack of "military judgment." Chiang demanded his recall.

Since Chiang's riposte made it clear that he wouldn't continue to work with and cooperate with Stilwell, President Roosevelt had two options: bring Stilwell home without replacement—for all practical purposes, folding the American military tent in China—or install a new man and try to muddle through. Reluctant to abandon his China efforts after so much investment, Roosevelt recalled Stilwell on October 19, and the War Department split the CBI into two component theaters, India-Burma and China, gave General Albert Wedemeyer charge of the newly created China theater and Stilwell's former role as Chiang Kai-shek's chief of staff, and scrapped its push to give the Chinese Army an American commander. The Generalissimo "categorically" promised General Wedemeyer that the Chinese could hold Kweilin for sixty days. The Japanese overran the city and its airfields about a fortnight later, forcing the Army to destroy tens of thousands of tons of aviation supplies that had been flown over the Hump at such astonishing cost.

Chiang Kai-shek made face in Chinese politics by forcing General Stilwell's ouster, but he reaped an expensive backlash in the United States, where China took a hard fall from the pedestal Kuomintang propaganda had so assiduously constructed. Returning newspaper correspondents penned articles beyond the arm of Chinese censorship, breaking stories of Kuomintang official malfeasance and incompetence along with news of the east China military collapse. No less a billboard than the front page of *The New York Times* described Stilwell's recall as "the political triumph of a moribund anti-democratic regime more concerned with maintaining its political supremacy than in driving the Japanese out of China." Other stories lamented China's disunity, the brutalities of Chiang's secret police and their concentration camps, and implied that an undeclared truce existed with the Japanese in most parts of China.

William Bond wasn't in China to bear firsthand witness to the accelerating decay. In June, the stress of running the airline and the accumulated horror of his friend's execution had given him another ventricular tachycardia attack, the worst he'd ever suffered, and it nearly killed him. Harold Bixby summoned Bond home as soon as he could travel, and Bond spent the last half of 1944 recuperating with his family at Hayes Manor.

Notwithstanding the feelings and thoughts that had been sparked by M. Y. Tong's execution, Bond defended China against the torrent of negative articles in a letter he wrote to Harold Bixby. "In practically all of these articles the Chinese have been criticized for lack of effort, lack of cooperation, lack of unity, and poor staff work," he wrote. ". . . I am sure the Chinese are not only hurt over it, but resentful." Bond proceeded to emphasize the strategic value of China, the difficulties the Chinese had faced since 1937, and the role China might yet play in Japan's defeat. In his letter, Bond claimed it was "well-known that [the Generalissimo] didn't have sufficient strength to hold [east China]," although in Bond's defense, he was certainly unaware that American military policy had been based on Chiang Kai-shek's explicit guarantee that it could. It was a strange letter, a grand white-wash of China's domestic situation and wartime performance, infected with naïve, wishful thinking, and it was, without doubt, the most speciously reasoned strategic summary Bond had authored since he'd gone to China in 1931. Perhaps it was difficult to abandon the strategic concepts he'd espoused for years, but Bond's letters to Bixby often made extensive rounds in New York and Washington and the letter might well have been calculated to stroke an entirely different audience—a Chinese audience—one with whom Bond would soon be negotiating to reduce Pan Am's stake in the airline. Bond would have certainly wanted them feeling magnanimous toward him when it came time to discuss price.

In truth, victories in the Pacific continued to evaporate the military value of Burma and China; everything that could have been done from China was being done better and easier from that theater. Unfortunately, the incredible investment of resources to mount the Hump airlift had its own momentum. Whether or not the U.S. government was garnering a worthwhile return on its investment wasn't something most participants were in a position to judge, unaware that the true cost of the Hump had been paid elsewhere, in Europe. The United States had used one of its highest-leverage assets—transport aircraft—in a low-leverage role, supporting the "war effort" of Nationalist China. General Marshall and Secretary of War Henry

Stimson recognized that a grave mistake had been made: "The amount of effort which we have put into the 'Over the Hump' airline has been bleeding us white in transport airplanes," wrote the secretary of war. "... [It] bids fair to cost us an extra winter in the main theater of the war."

In northwest Europe, after the Normandy landings, the Allies hadn't been able to open a significant port on the English Channel or the Bay of Biscay in the summer and fall of 1944, and nearly three hundred miles separated the Normandy beaches from the advancing spearheads, which, for want of supplies, stalled against the German frontier. The Air Transport Command's India-China Division carried 23,675 tons into China in August and 22,314 tons in September, and the Lend-Lease airplanes of the China National Aviation Corporation added more than a thousand tons to those totals—at the same time the Allied dash across France was grinding to a halt for want of gasoline. A major portion of America's air transport capability had been committed to the Hump. Those same planes, in better weather, making shorter hauls over flat terrain from easily supported bases in the United Kingdom to northern France and the Low Countries, would have delivered vastly greater quantities, and that logistical support might have propelled the Western Allies' armies into the German heartland in the autumn of 1944, and would certainly have hastened Hitler's demise, the Allies' primary objective for the entire war. They'd been committed to India and China early in the war. It was impossible to redeploy them to Europe. The Hump transports kept doing what they'd always done and flew supplies to China.

None of which made the Hump flying any less dangerous, as CNAC wild man Jimmy Scoff learned landing a C-47 in a Dinjan downpour. One of Scoff's brakes locked, and the plane ground-looped, careening in a wild circle. Its outside wingtip hooked the nose of a B-25 assigned to an Air Corps general. Both planes crumpled in aluminum mutilation, totally destroyed. Incredibly, nobody was hurt, and neither plane burned. Scoff clambered from the wreckage, fumbling to spark a cigarette under cupped hands.

The general stalked through the rain to the accident. "Do you know who I am?" he fumed.

"No," Scoff said, exhaling a drag.

"I'm General Old!"

Jimmy Scoff stared blankly at the officer through a few long heartbeats, then clicked his heels together, snapped to attention, and whipped up a salute. "And I'm Field Marshall Scoff," he mocked over his dangling cigarette.

Scoff was a civilian, beyond the reach of the general's ire. Off duty again after yet another near-fatal accident, Jimmy Scoff tore through Calcutta like a Viking. It was his last campaign. That autumn, as he left Dinjan with a cargo of smokeless powder and one-hundred-octane gasoline, a violent thunderstorm tore a wing off his C-47. The plane tumbled out of the sky like a shot duck and exploded in a swamp twenty miles west of Sadiya. The only human remains recovered at the site were the soles of Scoff's boots and a few scraps of his favorite sweater. Everything else was swallowed by the fetid Indian mire, although a persistent company rumor claimed that an Assamese native had pried the gold teeth from his jawbone. His friends' only solace lay in the knowledge that Jimmy Scoff hadn't missed a party in more than a year and that he'd been a king on Kariah Road.

Some days later, Suklo drew a hot bath for Pete Goutiere, who'd just finished a trip and a half, three times over the Hump: Kunming to Dinjan, Dinjan to Kunming, and Kunming back to Dinjan. Goutiere soaked for thirty minutes, until Suklo startled him from a half sleep with a note from Hugh Woods at the airport: *Pete, special flight to Kunming tonight. You're the only pilot available, so please make it.*

Goutiere groaned. He'd already done fifteen hours of flying, but he had never refused a flight, and he wanted his apple well polished when it came time for management to choose whom to keep in the postwar airline. Back at the airport, Woody stepped from a group of Air Corps officers gathered around a C-47 and presented a woman from inside the huddle. "Didn't think you'd mind the extra flight."

Fatigues couldn't hide her beauty. "You're a lucky girl," Goutiere told her. "There's a first-class seat waiting for you in the cockpit."

The cowls and flap controls were on her side of the cockpit. Goutiere taught her to operate them before takeoff, and they soared into the night sky. She was British, daughter of a tea planter, and she'd grown up near Digboi Mountain. Goutiere indicated its dark bulk slipping under the wings. A small vibration rattled the airplane, so Goutiere asked her to reset the cowl flaps, but she couldn't remember how. Goutiere unsnapped his seat belt, put his hand on her right shoulder, and reached across with his left to adjust the lever. She leaned forward and kissed him. And then kissed him again. Goutiere had planned to cruise across Burma at ten thousand feet before climbing over Foxy's Pass. Considering the new circumstances, he climbed to sixteen thousand, fired up the cockpit heater, and set the autopilot.

Goutiere rigged their jackets across the cockpit opening so that his radio operator couldn't see forward and switched off the instrument lights. A million stars jumped into the cockpit. He hadn't realized the night was so lovely. He slid his seat back and boosted the girl into his lap. Flight clothes and fatigues slithered to the floor. Yoke, pedals, levers, limbs—the cockpit was a fantastic tangle. Goutiere felt the woman go woozy in his arms. He fumbled for the oxygen mask and held it across her face, then took a few sucks himself. Periodically, he dialed up the instrument lights and checked the course. The flight was as smooth as silk; he'd never had one better. Gingerly, the girl unwound herself from Goutiere's lap, and they squirmed back into their clothes. They crossed over the navigational beacon at the Kunming airport and Goutiere spiraled down to a routine landing, past one o'clock in the morning. The ground crews were fast asleep. Goutiere winked at his Chinese radioman and led his amorous companion to an empty room in the pilots' hostel. They surfaced around noon the next day for a late breakfast. Feeling smug, as any pilot would, Goutiere smiled at his ravishing companion and asked why she'd come to China.

"I came out to marry a lieutenant in the Air Corps."

Goutiere went numb. "W-w-well . . . ," he sputtered, as they burst out laughing. "I . . . I . . . I wish you every happiness in the world."

27

THE GOLD MISSIONS

William Bond stayed in the United States through Christmas 1944, the first time he'd spent the holiday season with his wife and sons in six years. The war had forced so much hardship on his family; he was so tired of the long separations. Pan Am president Juan Trippe invited Bond to dinner at the house he kept on F Street in Washington, D.C., intending to discuss the looming contract negotiation and chart the course of CNAC's future. Trippe was amazed with what Bond had accomplished, and he was delighted with Pan Am's prospects in the Orient. The China National Aviation Corporation was ten times bigger than it had been before Pearl Harbor. In the United States, it would have been among the five largest carriers. Like most industry observers, Juan Trippe expected it to dominate Asia's aerial commerce after the war, paying excellent dividends on Pan Am's dozen years of investment and encouragement.

In light of what had happened to M. Y. Tong, William Bond now held exactly the opposite opinion. Tong's execution had convinced him that Nationalist China was doomed, that CNAC would share its fate, and that *right now* was the time to extract whatever return Pan American could get. Ironically, it was a near-exact reversal of the positions they'd held during their fateful Cloud Club conversation in the summer of 1937, when Trippe had been prepared to write off Pan Am's investment entirely and Bond had been determined to salvage it. Now, eight years later, Trippe wanted to retain all of it. Bond felt that Pan Am should sell most of its 45 percent share to the Chinese. True to form, the two men batted arguments back and forth without budging the other's position. Unable to sway Trippe with reason, Bond played his last card. "Mr. Trippe, maybe you're right, but you can't make a success of something you don't believe in. I'd be criminally disloyal if I didn't oppose this with everything I've got. I'll have to resign."

Trippe scrutinized his China man for signs of bluff. "You feel that strongly about it?"

"If I didn't feel that way, I wouldn't say so. I like working for Pan Am and I need my job, but I'm not going to agree to do something I know will lead to disaster."

Bond left dinner with permission to sell 35 percent of the airline for 2.5 million U.S. dollars, retaining a 10 percent stake in the reorganized company for Pan Am.

When Bond returned to Asia in early 1945, the Allies had essentially won the wars in both Europe and the Pacific. All that remained was the grim task of crushing the last fires of resistance from fanatic enemies, final bloodbaths in which tens of thousands would lose their lives. Hitler's remaining forces were being crushed between armies advancing from east and west. In the Orient and the western Pacific, the Japanese fought with a tenacity that defied Western comprehension. Eventual victory seemed secure but still distant. Conventional wisdom expected Japan's end to come sometime in 1946. President Franklin Roosevelt didn't live to see either enemy's defeat. He died on April 12, succeeded by Harry S Truman, and on the last day of the month Adolf Hitler committed suicide. A week later, on May 8, 1945, Germany surrendered unconditionally, ending six years of European war. British general Sir William Slim's Anglo-Indian Army had spent the first half of the year ousting the Japanese from Burma, recapturing Mandalay and Rangoon. Overhead, the Air Transport Command delivered more than forty-six thousand tons to China in May, and the quantity was still growing. The Army had finally mastered the Hump—with airline-style operating procedures implemented by Brigadier General William H. Tunner, who had been installed in charge of the airlift in the middle of 1944. Every person in CNAC wondered what the Army might have accomplished if it had employed such commonsense techniques from the beginning.

Like Bond, Charles Ridgley Hammell, survivor of the epic 1943 trek out of the Mishmi Hills with Joe Rosbert, had spent a sizeable chunk of 1944 at home, and Hammell made good use of his time, romancing and marrying an attractive woman named Jean. Duty called, however, even to civilians working for CNAC, and Hammell returned to Asia, bringing with him a modern hunting rifle. He was working through the North East Frontier Agency to get it to the Mishmis who'd saved his and Rosbert's lives. On May 9, 1945, the day after Germany's surrender, Hugh Woods assigned Ridge Hammell to take a C-47 to China.

For the last three years, company freight pilots had been left entirely to their own devices from the time they were released from Dinjan control until they came under the command of the traffic controllers at Kunming. They picked their own routes and altitudes, flying alone or in loose company with one or two of their brethren. Not so in the spring of 1945. The skies between Assam and Yunnan had become so jammed with transport aircraft that the brass hats in the Air Transport Command established prescribed airways to contain the traffic, and they insisted that CNAC flights join the general pattern. To get into it, airplanes leaving Dinjan actually began their flights heading west, away from China, passing at prescribed altitudes over radio beacons that guided them through a long, climbing U-turn and into the proper air corridor. The new procedures required the radio operators to switch frequencies shortly after takeoff, and as usual, the airline was shorthanded. The freight pilots were rationed either a Chinese radioman or a copilot, and they preferred the radio operators, who were well trained and spoke passable English. Not so the Chinese copilots the airline enlisted late in the war. Woefully undertrained, most weren't fit to do much besides respond to commands like "Wheels up!" and "Flaps down!" and Ridge Hammell had one such "hydraulic secretary" in his right seat on the morning of May 9. After takeoff, he circled the field, climbed to three thousand feet, and set the autopilot, not trusting his right-seater with the controls. Hammell clambered out of his seat into the radio compartment to tune in one of the upcoming air-traffic-control stations. It was all hunky-dory until one of the engines failed. A well-trained copilot would have handled the emergency, but Hammell's wasn't, and didn't, and the airplane tipped into a spin. Centrifugal force pinned Hammell against the wall of the radio compartment.

Pete Goutiere and the other pilots on the Dinjan airfield doing preflight checks stood paralyzed by the high-pitched whine of Hammell's plane. It *whoomped* into the ground a few miles from the airport and burst into flames. Goutiere couldn't bear to visit the crash site. So many of his friends had died. He buttoned the agony and kept flying. They all did. Ridge Hammell had flown the Hump more than four hundred times. Joe Rosbert got word in Los Angeles, California, where he'd parlayed the Hollywood connections of his actor uncle, Elmer Goodfellow Brendel, known onscreen as comic actor El Brendel,* into a job at Paramount Pictures advising development of a motion picture about the Hump. He was working on one of Paramount's Marathon Street soundstages when someone got his attention. "Ridge went in."

Rosbert grimaced and heard the particulars. "That's a damn shame," he said, blowing out a long breath. There wasn't much more to it. He was a pilot, and it was 1945. Friends died all the time.

Hammell's mascot Elmer the bear came to an end just as ugly. Fearing foul luck, few pilots would fly her after Ridge got his. They kept Elmer chained to a pole outside the airline's Kunming hostel, and the bear grew so much that her metal collar dug into her neck. Discomfort made her ornery, and she lunged at those who dared approach. One day, the bear disappeared. That night, the men ate a delicious sweet-and-sour dish vastly more meaty and satisfying than their normal Kunming fare. A pilot asked the cook what it contained. "Elmer," the cook said with a grin. The pilots pushed back and digested the information, put off their appetites. On second thought, it seemed a shame to waste the bear's last service. Most cleared their plates.

---

* El Brendel was most well known for his comic portrayals of Swedish immigrants—notwithstanding his German-Irish heritage.

. . .

When Ridge Hammell was killed, William Bond was in China, in the thick of contract negotiations. Like much Chinese business, many of the exploratory maneuvers were social, and he was invited to a party with CNAC's Chinese directors by General Yu Fei-peng, Chiang Kai-shek's porcine cousin and rapacious "chief of supply," newly installed as Kuomintang minister of communications. Copious alcohol consumption was de rigueur at such events, and General Yu and the others ganged up on Bond. *"Gom-bey, gom-bey"*—"Bottoms up"—they toasted Bond in succession, each iteration requiring Bond to empty his glass. To do otherwise would be to lose face with his corporate peers. Unless he could divert their purpose, Bond had a face-first date with the floor. He saved himself with a matchbox drinking game remembered from his younger years. Taught the rudiments, Yu Fei-peng roared with delight, and Bond's meticulous flips stood the matchbox on end time and again. Minister Yu howled and guzzled the required whisky. Before long, Bond had the minister pie-eyed, and he focused on his other companions. Most were soon just as soused. When it was over, Yu Fei-peng's aides had to summon four coolies and a sedan chair to get their "old water buffalo" downstairs. Bond's hangover seemed a small price to pay for the great face he'd made with his fellow directors, the very men with whom he was negotiating the reduction of Pan Am's stake in the airline, and the means by which Bond envisioned getting Pan Am's investment—and himself—out of China.

After breakfast, Bond met with T. V. Soong and General T. H. Shen, a relatively new managing director. It was a delicate dance. For years, the Chinese had made clear their expectation that the 1945 contract renegotiation would make the airline "more Chinese" by reducing the American share. Bond put on a façade of great regret and reluctance, stressing everything Pan Am had done to nurture the company since 1933 and the aviation community's expectation that CNAC would become exceptionally profitable after the war and that it would be grossly unfair to squeeze out Pan Am on the verge of such success. General Shen gave his estimate of the company's value. Bond examined Shen's asset and liabilities sheet and pointed out several omitted items. Shen raised his appraisal. They went back and forth over a few other aspects of the valuation until Dr. Soong cut in and ended the dispute—Bond had been met more than halfway. Bond uncapped his pen, leaned forward, and signed. He pushed the papers across to General Shen and watched him do likewise. They forwarded the signed agreement to Minister Yu for approval, and with Dr. Soong's sponsorship there was little doubt that it would be accepted. Bond smiled reluctantly. Inside, he backflipped with joy. The exact mechanics of the sale weren't yet settled, but the deal was shaping up to be much better than the one Juan Trippe had authorized him to negotiate. All Bond needed to finalize the sell-down was for Pan Am's corporate attorney to come to Chungking and sign the contract. He'd been promised the lawyer's prompt appearance. He pestered Bixby, but he heard nothing in return, and the silence had him sick with worry. Days ticked by, then weeks, and the Chinese started chiseling on price. Bond was terrified that the deal would collapse. Fully a month passed without word from Pan Am. A persistent cold nagged Bond's throat and sinuses. Stomach troubles stopped him from eating. He couldn't sleep.

Bond never did hear from New York. Another ventricular tachycardia attack waylaid him instead. He was in Calcutta, unconscious for more than an hour, and the attack derailed his work on the new contract. He recuperated slowly, and it remained unsigned. The July 8 expiration date came and went and the airline continued operations without a formal arrangement between the two partners, a state of uncertain flux that did little to lessen the strain on the airline's indispensable China man.

China's economic malaise had continued to worsen, black-market exchange rates ballooning to three thousand to one. To help quench the inflation, the United States had promised tens of millions of dollars of financial assistance. The Chinese government continued to insist on a large chunk of it in gold. The Treasury Department had dithered since the Cairo Conference, frustrated with China's war effort, internal corruption, and hard-line official/unofficial exchange rate bargaining for payment of American in-country construction costs, but Secretary of the Treasury Henry Morgenthau, Jr., finally authorized gold shipments in May 1945. The United States dispatched an oceangoing freighter from New York with a generous allotment of precious metal in a secure hold. It docked in Calcutta on July 17, blanketed by heavy security. Armed guards escorted a gold-bearing truck convoy to Dum Dum Airport. The gold came stowed in little barrels resembling beer kegs. CNAC employees rolled the kegs into ten transports and lashed them in the cargo cabins in two rows on either side of the center line, three tons of it per plane, each load worth about $2.5 million (some $96 million in modern dollars). Pete Goutiere and nine other reliable pilots flew the gold to Dinjan, refueled inside another tight security curtain, and took it over the Hump to China, required to make position reports every thirty minutes. They landed at Ku Long Po, the dusty military airstrip outside Chungking where a near-collision had come close to killing the Generalissimo in 1943. There was no security at all in China, nothing. Coolie gangs rolled the gold-stuffed barrels to the airplane doors and dropped them onto receiving beds of worn-out tires. Other teams rolled the barrels up ramps into the beds of open trucks. Pete Goutiere sat on a fuel drum, watching dust whip from the truck wheels as they drove the gold off the airfield. It looked to him like the Chiangs had just conned the United States out of thirty tons of gold. "Americans," he muttered, "the rubes of Asia."

Goutiere climbed off his perch and flew back to India. Since the end of 1942, he'd flown the Hump more than 650 times.

In August, the maharaja of Bamra invited several airline personnel and some Army officers on a hunting expedition in the forests of his princely state in central India. Chuck Sharp and Pete Goutiere were among those who attended, along with two generals in the Army's Service of Supply. They hunted antelope and sambars from tree stands, but they weren't bagging much game, and after about a week of hunting the group was enjoying an afternoon soiree in the raja's palace garden, trying to fathom the nature of the atomic bombs just dropped on Hiroshima and Nagasaki. President Truman said they were powered by the same force that fired the sun. A plane buzzed low overhead and dropped a packet, trailing a small parachute. Bearers fetched the package, which contained a note. Chubby General Hackett peered at it through spectacles and looked up. "Gentlemen, the Japs surrendered," he announced, beaming. "The war is over."

28

ENDGAME

Nothing in China went smoothly in the aftermath of the Japanese surrender. The enemy's capitulation caught the Nationalist regime without detailed plans for economic and financial reconstruction, for disease and famine suppression, for refugee return, for the surrender and repatriation of nearly four million Japanese soldiers and civilians, or for asserting political control in eastern and northern China. Confusion, corruption, and incompetence marred its efforts, the surrender took months to accomplish, and, as usual, the Kuomintang seemed more interested in Communist suppression than in public welfare. Racing to fill the power vacuums, the Central Government allowed many Japanese collaborators to remain in positions of authority in areas where the alternative was to allow Communists to take control. After a few months of uneasy financial stability, another round of inflation took hold, compounding China's mind-boggling misery. The Kuomintang's popular support eroded, and the Communists' violent land-reform strategies consolidated their political control of the countryside, at the peasant level, bringing vast areas under their influence. Chiang Kai-shek moved his capital back to Nanking, but, without pausing to solidify his traditional power base in the lower Yangtze valley or improve his sway in southern China, he sent a large army north to reckon with the Communists in Manchuria, where they'd moved large forces, having adopted Mao's "defend in the south, develop toward the north" strategy after the Japanese surrender. They had taken possession of large weapons stockpiles from the Russians, who had declared war on Japan two days after the Hiroshima bomb and immediately poured into northeastern China. Secure between Korea and Mongolia and with their rear flank anchored against Soviet Siberia—from where they received military, technical, and economic assistance—the Chinese Communists developed Manchuria into a substantial stronghold, one from which dynastic change had emerged at other junctures in the long history of the Middle Kingdom.

President Truman dispatched General Marshall to China to attempt to forestall civil war, but despite Marshall's immense personal prestige and the good relationships he cultivated with Communist negotiator Chou En-lai and the Generalissimo and Madame Chiang Kai-shek, he quickly ran into an impasse: The Communists wouldn't countenance giving up their army until they'd been admitted to a national coalition government, and the Kuomintang wouldn't consider forming a coalition government until the Communists had integrated their armed forces into the Central Government's military. General Marshall brokered several short-lived cease-fires, but neither side trusted the other, and they jockeyed for advantage, unwilling to compromise. Efforts to foster democratic institutions and constitutional government through an assembly of delegates representing the Kuomintang, the Communists, the new Youth Party, and the Democratic League appeared to resolve a host of major problems until the Central Committee of the Kuomintang forced through ex post facto changes designed to secure Chiang Kai-shek's presidential powers. The assembly disintegrated, and Chiang Kai-shek's state security enforcers added the persecution of liberals, intellectuals, students, and artists to their usual anti-Communist obsession. The Chinese Communist Party's suppression of dissent was almost certainly worse, but its thuggery generally occurred far from journalistic eyes.

By June 1946, in Manchuria, the Nationalist Army had occupied Changch'un and established a bridgehead across the Sungari River, leaving it in control of the most important cities in southern and central Manchuria, but with its lines of communication dangerously exposed to counterattack by Communist forces still safely ensconced in the Manchurian hinterlands. In July, Chiang Kai-shek opened a major offensive designed to drive the Communists from their base area in Shensi and gain control of north China.

The Japanese capitulation had also forced massive change on the China National Aviation Corporation. Fuel scarcity, government interference, and the herculean task of moving ten thousand tons of aviation equipment and nearly a thousand people from Calcutta and Chungking back to Shanghai's Lunghwa Airport greatly hampered its efforts to reestablish the prewar route structure. Against the background chaos, William Bond wasn't able to wrap up the new contract and the sell-down of Pan Am's interest until December 1945, when, through a series of byzantine financial and legal maneuverings, Pan Am sold its entire 45 percent share of the China National Aviation Corporation to the Chinese government. The old company was disbanded, and a new one formed with the same name. Pan Am bought a 20 percent stake in the new company and recorded "a non-recurring profit" of $4,460,036 for the transaction. Juan Trippe had given Bond permission to sell Pan Am's stake in the original CNAC for $2.5 million and retain a 10 percent stake in the reorganized company. Bond's negotiations had done substantially better than authorized. Trippe was delighted, and he acknowledged that it was largely Bond's visionary dedication and ceaseless toil that secured such an excellent profit, cash in hand, from an investment he'd once been willing to write off entirely. In modern terms, between 1937 and 1945, William Bond created $53.5 million of value for Pan American.

But even with the contract finally settled and the long war at last ended, William Bond still couldn't escape the Middle Kingdom. It was his old curse: Neither Pan American nor the airline's Chinese leadership wanted him to leave, and Bond's highly developed sense of loyalty wouldn't allow him to quit without his superiors' blessing. A seat-of-the-pants, combat-expedient attitude had infected the company during the Hump years, a spirit of quick and dirty improvisation that ran contrary to the "safety first" principles of civil aviation, and the airline had a hard time readjusting to peacetime conditions. Greatly expanded by the Hump airlift, the organization was bloated and inefficient, with many dissatisfied personnel, both Chinese and Caucasian. Mechanics and flight crews threatened strikes. As one of the senior pilots, Moon Chin had spent the Hump years doing specialty missions within China and flying passengers and mail between Calcutta and Chungking, and during the eastward stampede from Chungking after the Japanese surrender, a prominent Chinese banker asked him to fly a hoard of cash from Chungking to Shanghai.

Moon Chin protested. He was one of the few pilots who weren't scheduled to fly east. The banker assured him that he'd be more than happy if Moon would just deliver it at his first opportunity. When Moon reluctantly agreed, the banker returned with a footlocker stuffed full of money. It was so heavy that Moon couldn't lift it by himself. Afraid of being hijacked, he never told any of his helpmates what it contained.

For several weeks, Moon Chin flew routes in western China, lugging the footlocker wherever he went with the help of his houseboy and airport coolies—never whispering a word about its contents. One morning, he got an assignment to fly T. V. Soong and his entourage to a small place in the mountains west of Suifu, where T.V. spent the night in conference with the Generalissimo. Moon overnighted in the plane with the footlocker strapped across the back row of seats, fairly sure Dr. Soong was unaware of its contents.

In the morning, Dr. Soong ordered Moon to fly him to Nanking and asked if he had a map.

"Dr. Soong, I don't need a map to find Nanking!" Moon exclaimed. "Just fly downriver until we get there."

East of Chungking, cruising at eight thousand feet, Moon flew over the Wushan Mountains and the Yangtze Gorges—geography through which he'd threaded at low altitude many dozens of times copiloting Loenings in the middle 1930s—then passed Ichang and Hankow, a place he hadn't seen since his last evacuation flight in October 1938. The Yangtze widened below its confluence with the Han—*Xie Jiang,* "The River," the implacable heart of the Middle Kingdom, ribboning through the agricultural patchwork of central China. Just over two hours later, Nanking's Purple Mountain scrolled off the horizon.

Typhoon weather had assailed the Chinese seaboard through much of August and September, but it wasn't a factor when Moon Chin landed at Nanking and, after an overnight stay, flew Dr. Soong on to Shanghai. The resilient city had rebuilt itself from the 1937 battle. Few physical scars remained, and American bombers had largely spared the city. A strange cocktail of jubilation and uncertainty possessed Shanghailanders as they shed the yoke of the eight-year occupation. Consumer goods unobtainable in Chungking stocked the stores, and prices seemed fantastically low. Currency of the Japanese occupation still circulated freely, even though more than a month had passed since the A-bombs, and armed Japanese soldiers still policed the streets. They were gradually being disarmed and prepared for repatriation. Out at Lunghwa Airport, bullet holes perforated CNAC's two old hangars, but, happily, neither had taken any bomb hits. The Japanese hadn't used the field much: Tall weeds grew in the runway. Moon Chin delivered the money without "squeezing" a single dollar; he supposed it went to recapitalize a Chinese bank.

A day or two later, the general manager of Eurasia's successor, Central Air Transport Corporation (CATC), quietly invited Moon Chin to meet him in the Astor House, Shanghai's oldest Western hotel, whose five-story, gray stone, Baroque façade rose on the north bank of Soochow Creek, just across Garden Bridge. In the last half century, former American president Ulysses S. Grant, physicist Albert Einstein, philosopher Bertrand Russell, and actor Charlie Chaplin had all stayed in the hotel. Moon Chin met the CATC general manager in the smoke-filled coffee shop just inside the main entrance.

Even with the 1943 name change designed to erase the stain of its German partnership, CATC hadn't been able to acquire any aircraft besides three low-performing Lockheed Hudsons, and it was struggling to gain traction in the postwar environment. However, a number of Japanese L2D "Tabby" transport aircraft had been captured in China, exact knockoffs of the DC-3—Douglas Aircraft had sold the plans to the Japanese in 1938. The Kuomintang government wanted to give the clones to CATC, but CATC had never used the type. The general manager hoped Moon would train his pilots to fly it. The airline had a time-sensitive deal in place with a Chinese general to haul a stockpile of medical supplies from Kunming to the eastern cities. Long deprivation had grossly inflated the price of medicine in the regions that had been held by the Japanese, but prices would return to normal when oceangoing ships discharged similar cargoes.

Moon Chin advised the man not to accept the Japanese DC-3s. Their engines were grossly underpowered. Surplus American engines could be bought, but transporting and installing them would burn valuable time, and airfields in India were wingtip to wingtip with U.S. Army surplus C-47s and C-46s available for about twenty thousand U.S. dollars apiece. Moon Chin suggested CATC buy them instead.

The general manager lamented his company's lack of foreign-currency reserves, but he wondered if Moon Chin could find out if T. V. Soong would authorize CATC to buy foreign exchange with its Chinese dollars.

The aides who had traveled to the United States with Dr. Soong during the war usually returned with their luggage stuffed with luxury goods, particularly the wristwatches and fountain pens that circulated as hard currency in Chungking, but with such intense demand for India-to-China passenger space, not all of them were able to fly the Hump into China with Dr. Soong on his periodic trips. When they couldn't, Moon Chin carried their loot over and personally delivered it to their families. Again, Moon Chin hadn't squeezed any personal profit from the venture, but the accumulated favors allowed him to contact one of T. V. Soong's aides and ask if he could see the foreign minister. Back in Chungking, some days later, the man told him to come by before Soong went out to dinner.

At the appointed hour, T. V. Soong descended the stairs of his residence and noticed Moon in the entry foyer. "What are you doing here?" he asked, surprised.

"I came to ask about the possibility of CATC getting foreign exchange," Moon said.

"Why are you worried about them? You work for CNAC."

"They want me to help train their pilots to fly the Japanese DC-3s, but those planes can't carry much load," Moon explained. "I suggested they get some foreign exchange and buy surplus planes from the U.S. instead."

"Don't bother with it," Soong said, "there's only going to be one airline," apparently planning to consolidate China's airlines into one corporate entity.*

"What if they get the exchange on their own?" Moon asked.

Dr. Soong paused. "If they do that, then okay."

---

* Although it was much discussed, nothing came of Soong's plan.

On his next trip to Shanghai, Moon Chin gave the news to the general manager at the Astor House coffee shop. CATC was stymied. The general manager had no idea how to get foreign currency.

Someone in the crowded coffee shop overheard their conversation and interrupted, offering to find out if a banker he knew might be able to help.

Forty-five minutes later, the man returned with the banker, and by incredible happenstance it was the same man for whom Moon Chin had carted the trunk of money around China earlier in the month. Once he understood the situation—and the opportunity—the banker asked how much money they needed.

To do it properly, considering airplanes, spares, and operating costs, Moon Chin estimated 400,000 American dollars (about 4.8 million modern dollars).

The banker wrote a check and pinched it between his fingers, looking back and forth between Moon Chin and the CATC general manager. "If I'm going to do this," he said, "Moon Chin, you have to come to CATC and run their operations . . . you personally."

"But I've been with CNAC for twelve years," Moon protested.

"No. You have to come to CATC."

Moon forced himself to think. He'd come a long way with loyalty. With Chuck Sharp and Hugh Woods in management and the two other pilots who'd been ahead of him on the roster recently returned to the United States, he was the China National Aviation Corporation's most senior pilot, its number one man. But he was also up against an impenetrable ceiling—he'd never make operations manager. Contractually, the Operations Department was under American direction. The position would always go to a Pan American appointee, and he didn't think they'd ever install a Chinese person. Looked at objectively, he'd come as far as he was ever going to get with the China National Aviation Corporation. Perhaps it was time to seek higher-ceiling opportunities. "Some people in your company will object if I come over," Moon said to the CATC general manager. "If I do, you have to give me a free hand to do as I see fit."

"If we get the money, you get the free hand," the CATC man promised, and that cemented the deal. Everyone shook hands.

Moon Chin flew to Calcutta and deposited the check, but he couldn't buy the airplanes until it cleared, which would take a fortnight. A tremendous opportunity was slipping away. Fortunately, Moon Chin met an old acquaintance—Colonel Lam Whi-shing, the leathery colonel who'd been CNAC's managing director and William Bond's prime adversary during the desperate days of 1937. Eight years later, in 1945, Colonel Lam was managing the Calcutta purchasing agency of the Chinese Air Force. As such, he had ready access to large quantities of money, and he fronted Moon Chin U.S. $400,000, in cash, on Moon's word alone. Moon bought the airplanes CATC needed, the jump start allowing him to get them into paying service two weeks ahead of what would otherwise have been possible. Moon returned the money the minute his backer's check cleared.

The new airplanes and Moon Chin's influence revitalized the Central Air Transport Company. Flying the Kunming stockpiles to east China proved exceptionally profitable, and the airline repaid its backer's investment within six months, with significant profit. Moon Chin paid Chinese employees the same as Caucasian ones, and many of CNAC's best-trained Chinese personnel followed him to CATC. William Bond admired Moon Chin's operation and never bore him any ill will for jumping ship. Moon Chin had come a long way from the mud bricks of Wing-Wa village in the coastal lowlands of south China, where he'd been born. He had an airline, his own airline.

Chuck Sharp had been an excellent wartime operations manager, but he had difficulty adapting to the new peacetime realities, and he most definitely did not possess a diplomatic personality. His temper played poorly with Chinese officialdom. Sharp resigned and returned to the United States, having served the company for thirteen years. Hugh Woods replaced him, and in what seemed to have become an annual event, China stress gave Bond another ventricular tachycardia attack. He recuperated with his family in Florida in the autumn of 1946. Pan Am tried a new executive in his place, but the new man lacked Bond's experience and savvy, and the airline drifted. Standards slipped. Little had been done since the war's end to improve the antiquated conditions of Chinese domestic aviation, which needed more and better meteorological stations, runway lights and surfaces, air traffic control, night and foul-weather landing equipment, and radio communications. The Chinese government expected the airlines to front the development costs. CNAC, CATC, and Civil Air Transport (CAT), a new airline formed by Claire Chennault, wanted the government to finance the improvements, as was common in other countries. Predictably, little got accomplished until seventy-one people died aboard two CNAC planes and one CATC flight that crashed trying to land through a pea-soup Shanghai fog on Christmas night, 1946—which could have been avoided if the latest aviation technology had been in place. Less than a fortnight later, former Hump pilot Charles Sharkey hit a mountainside near Tsingtao, killing himself and forty-three passengers. Eighteen people died in an accident outside Chungking on January 25. Twenty-five more lost their lives three days later in a wreck one hundred miles west of Hankow.

The government grounded all civil aviation. Operations manager Hugh Woods resigned, and Pan Am rushed William Bond back to China. Bond replaced Woods with his old compatriot Ernie Allison, and "Allie" set about retightening the airline to his exacting professional standards. Operations and morale improved. Unfortunately, the fortunes of the Nationalist government were plunging in the opposite direction.

To many observers at the end of 1946, the Nationalist Army appeared to have scored important victories against the Communists, but although Chiang's armies overran most of Kiangsu, Jehol, and Hopei provinces, they couldn't pin important elements of the Communist army—newly renamed "the People's Liberation Army" (the PLA)—into any decisive engagements. Secure in the countrysides of Manchuria and north China, the Communists gathered strength. It was obvious to both sides that the United States lacked the will to intervene militarily, and therefore possessed no meaningful leverage to employ against the Communists. After thirteen fruitless months in China, General Marshall returned to the United States in January 1947, having found no common ground between the Nationalists and the Communists. He criticized both sides, but in trying to reconcile two such implacable foes he'd probably been "beating the air with his fists," as a Chinese proverb had it. Fighting intensified, particularly in Manchuria, and the Nationalist currency skittered yet farther up the inflationary parabola, increasing popular discontent. In mid-March, the Nationalist offensive against the Shensi base captured Yenan, the Communist capital, but Mao Tse-tung remained at large in the surrounding terrain. Elsewhere, the Communists seized the initiative. Better motivated, organized, and disci-

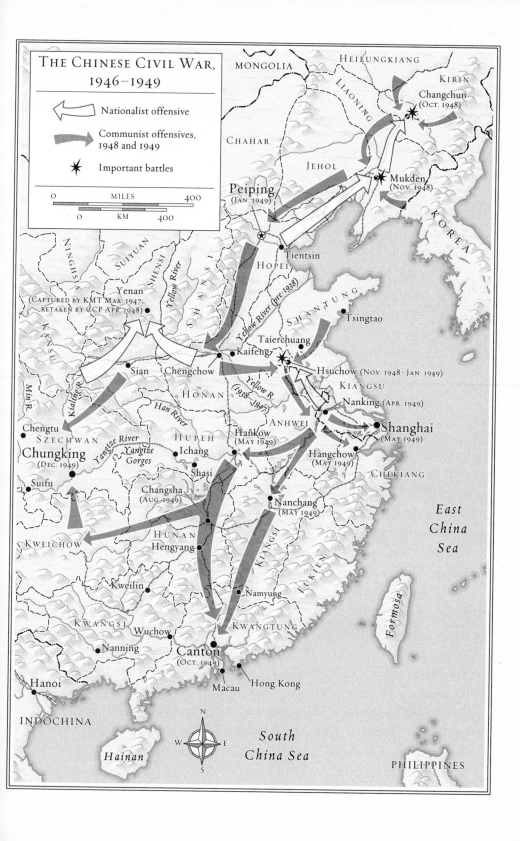

The Chinese Civil War, 1946–1949

← Nationalist offensive

← Communist offensives, 1948 and 1949

★ Important battles

MILES 400

KM 400

MONGOLIA

HEILUNGKIANG

KIRIN

Changchun (Oct. 1948)

LIAONING

CHAHAR

JEHOL

Mukden (Nov. 1948)

KOREA

Peiping (Jan. 1949)

Tientsin

HOPEI

Yellow River (pre-1938)

NINGHSIA

SUIYUAN

SHENSI

Yellow River

SHANSI

SHANTUNG

Tsingtao

Yenan (Captured by KMT Mar. 1947, retaken by CCP Apr. 1948)

Taierchuang

Kaifeng

KANSU

Sian

Chengchow

HONAN

Yellow R. (1938–1947)

Hsuchow (Nov. 1948–Jan. 1949)

KIANGSU

Nanking (Apr. 1949)

Min R.

Kialing R.

Han River

Hankow (May 1949)

ANHWEI

Shanghai (May 1949)

Chengtu

SZECHWAN

Chungking (Dec. 1949)

Yangtze River

Yangtze Gorges

HUPEH

Ichang

Shasi

Hangchow (May 1949)

CHEKIANG

Suifu

Changsha (Aug. 1949)

Nanchang (May 1949)

East China Sea

KWEICHOW

HUNAN

Hengyang

KIANGSI

FUKIEN

Formosa

Kweilin

Namyung

KWANGSI

Wuchow

KWANGTUNG

Nanning

Canton (Oct. 1949)

Macau

Hong Kong

Hanoi

INDOCHINA

Hainan

N

W E

S

South China Sea

PHILIPPINES

plined, more aggressively and creatively led, and emphasizing mobile warfare, the Communists pushed the Nationalists onto the defensive. The Kuomintang armies holed up in towns, their command structure riddled with spies. When they sortied, they were often savagely ambushed by well-informed elements of the People's Liberation Army. In May, in Manchuria, Communist general Liu Biao launched a conventional campaign across the Sungari River, involving perhaps as many as 400,000 men, backed by captured artillery. It was a major departure from the guerrilla tactics previously employed by the Red Army, and savage seesaw fighting raged through the summer of 1947 around the Manchurian cities of Changch'un, Kirin, and Szeping. The Manchurian operations were coordinated with other Communist offensives that cut the rail lines near Kaifeng, severing the main artery of overland supply for Chiang's armies in north China and Manchuria. Beginning in September, Liu Biao swept around the Nationalists' important Manchurian strongholds, aiming to isolate them from north China. The three domestic airlines flew supplies to beleaguered garrisons as the tide of war turned steadily against the Nationalists.

None of it stopped CNAC from scoring another major aviation accomplishment in the last half of 1947. Using U.S. Army surplus C-54s converted to plush passenger use (turning them back into DC-4s), CNAC inaugurated transpacific flights on October 7, 1947, Shanghai to San Francisco across the islands of the mid-Pacific in forty hours. Using Chinese and mixed Chinese and American crews, it flew the route in direct competition to Pan American, and it did a better job of keeping schedules than its parent, much to Juan Trippe's astonishment. The hard-currency revenues earned on international routes kept the airline solvent when astronomical inflation was almost instantly devaluing its Chinese currency earnings. Bond's health, always a concern, really seemed shattered by the end of 1947. He and Harold Bixby had been grooming a replacement and, wanting to lessen the strain on his friend and reward him for so many years of toil, Bixby had his hand in Pan American World Airways Executive Memorandum Number 107, dated December 3, 1947, which elevated William Langhorne Bond to Pan Am's "vice president for the Orient," and although Bond would continue to make his office in Shanghai, Bixby hoped the promotion and its broader responsibilities would distance him from the day-to-day anxieties of the China airline. The plan worked, and Bond stepped away from the airline in the spring of 1948, succeeded by Quentin Roosevelt.

Quentin Roosevelt was the perfect replacement—young, brilliant, energetic, popular, diplomatic, knowledgeable about China, and the grandson of former president Theodore Roosevelt. He'd been wounded and decorated in the North Africa campaign, he sported the most prestigious American surname, and he was very enthusiastic about representing Pan American. Relieved by the change, expecting the promotion to keep him in the Orient for years to come, and fed up with the long separations, Bond brought Kitsi and their two sons back to Asia, to Shanghai.

Fighting in Manchuria raged through the end of 1947 and into 1948. Relentless Communist pressure wore away Nationalist capabilities and drove them from Kirin and Changch'un, and by October, the People's Liberation Army had the Nationalists hemmed into Mukden, the principal northeastern city. CNAC and the other airlines had been airlifting supplies into the city ever since Quentin Roosevelt assumed Bond's position. Hard, aggressive Communist attacks and relentless political propaganda ravaged the Nationalist defenders. Exhausted, hungry, and thoroughly demoralized, they surrendered on November 1, 1948. Chiang Kai-shek had lost nearly half a million men in his misguided Manchurian adventure—and all their American-supplied equipment. The victorious Communists flooded through the Great Wall and invested Peiping. Several emergency airstrips were constructed inside Peiping's walls, including a hasty enlargement of the polo ground that had echoed to the drumbeat thunder of racing ponies and flapping coattails at the Bonds' wedding reception in 1935. At the end of 1948 and the beginning of 1949, it roared with aircraft flying supplies to the isolated city. By and large, however, it was a peaceful siege, without much fighting. A major battle was already being fought farther south, near Hsuchow, between the Yellow and Yangtze rivers, and it looked to be the one that would decide the fate of China.

A 300,000-person city at critical north–south and east–west rail junctions in Jiangsi Province, Hsuchow shielded the Nationalist heartland, and Chiang Kai-shek deployed a large army to defend it. If the Communists destroyed the Nationalist army guarding it, Nanking, Shanghai, and the lower Yangtze valley would lie open to invasion. Sensing opportunity, two Communist thrusts converged on Hsuchow—one from the west, from around Kaifeng; another hammered down from the northeast, from the Shantung Peninsula—and the fight grew into a massive battle, each army deploying about 600,000 soldiers. Communist political commissar Deng Xiaoping* organized several million peasant laborers to aid the People's Liberation Army, carrying supplies and digging trenches and tank traps to counter Nationalist advantages in heavy weapons, armor, and airpower. The battle began in early November 1948, and the aggressive Communist commander, attacking from Shandong, surrounded and decimated a 100,000-man Nationalist force a dozen miles west of Hsuchow. At the same time, the Communist army attacking from the west drove the Nationalists out of a fortified town south of Hsuchow and established a blocking position that cut the Nationalist supply lines. Kuomintang forces attacked the Communist blocking position from north and south, hoping to crush the Communists between their attacks, but utilizing interior lines of communications, better organization, and their faster operational tempo, the Red Army separately defeated each effort, in the process encircling another large Nationalist force. In early December, the Nationalist force isolated at Hsuchow attempted to break out to the west. Its effort began well, but contradictory instructions, exhaustion, and operational incompetence paralyzed the escape attempt, and by December 7 it was again tightly surrounded. The Communists focused their efforts on the southernmost Nationalist pocket, completing its destruction by mid-December. The Nationalist remnants west of Hsuchow held out for another four weeks, but in the end they, too, were totally destroyed. The Nationalists had lost five armies and more than half a million men in the campaign. Peiping and its 200,000-man garrison surrendered in late January, leaving the Communists in firm control of all China north of the Yangtze. Chiang Kai-shek's combat power had been eviscerated, and the Nationalist heartland lay open to invasion.

·   ·   ·

---

* Deng Xiaoping rose to become China's supreme leader after Mao's death.

The airline had already been beset by its own tragedy. A few days before Christmas 1948, in marginal weather, the pilot of a flight into Hong Kong had inexplicably deviated from standard letdown procedure and smashed into a mountaintop, killing everyone aboard—including Quentin Roosevelt. He was only thirty years old, and he left behind a wife and three daughters. Bond was forced to resume his former role.

The Nationalists disintegrated in the aftermath of the Hsuchow debacle. For three months, the Communists solidified their incredible gains. On April 20, the People's Liberation Army crossed the Yangtze, virtually unopposed, and captured Nanking two days later. Nationalist vestiges fled to Formosa (Taiwan) with their gold, silver, foreign-currency reserves, and the masterpieces of Chinese art, although they'd formally moved their capital to Canton.* Bond sent his family back to Washington, CNAC evacuated Shanghai for Hong Kong, and the Communists captured Shanghai at the end of May. Afraid to anger the power consolidating control of mainland China, the Hong Kong government reneged on its promise to allow CNAC use of Kai Tak Airport—for all practical purposes putting the airline out of business. Its fifty-six airplanes sat idle at Kai Tak.

On October 1, 1949, Mao Tse-tung stood atop the Imperial Palace's Gate of Heavenly Peace in Peking (formerly Peiping) and announced the creation of the People's Republic of China. Embracing the new reality, eleven airplanes, their flight crews, and many airline personnel with family left behind flew from Hong Kong to China on November 9, 1949, led by managing director C. Y. Liu. Communist overtures hinted at allowing Pan Am to continue its participation in the airline—Pan Am's contract was, after all, with the "Government of China," and China had a new government, but the prospect was sure to appall the new breed of anti-Communist crusaders gaining influence in America. Claire Chennault and his business partners schemed to win control of CNAC's assets for the Nationalists. Exploring options, Bond flew to Washington, where he and Bixby heard the

* Before the end of 1949, the Nationalists would move their capital from Canton to Chungking, and then to Chengtu, before finally formally moving it to Formosa (Taiwan).

opinion of Livingston Merchant, assistant secretary of state for Far Eastern affairs. Merchant painted a bleak picture. Anti-Communist fervor was beginning to grip the American populace and, with China gone red, the United States government wanted Pan Am to divest itself of the China National Aviation Corporation. That didn't leave Pan Am many options, or much leverage. Bond went to New York to negotiate a price with T. V. Soong.

Bond, a Pan Am lawyer, and two attorneys associated with Chennault assembled in T. V. Soong's luxurious Fifth Avenue apartment. Bond paid no attention to Soong's marvelous view of Central Park, infuriated as he was by Chennault's machinations. "For every year that Chennault has served China, Pan Am has served two," Bond scoffed, "and for every hour he's had in combat areas in the air, I've had ten. Which I have." Point-blank, he refused to sell "his" share of CNAC directly to Chennault. He'd sell it only to the Nationalist Chinese government. After that, they could do with it as they pleased.

An independent survey of the Pan American system had recently valued its 20 percent ownership of the China airline at $1,970,000, an appraisal that made no attempt to account for the seventeen years of goodwill, training, and advocacy Pan Am had sponsored.

Soong offered one million dollars.

"I can't go back and report that," Bond said. "I'd rather tell Mr. Trippe I failed."

Dr. Soong thought for a long time. "Bondy, I'll give you a million and a quarter and you can tell Mr. Trippe I wouldn't give that to him. I wouldn't give it to anybody else in the world."

Bond took Soong's offer to the Chrysler Building, and Trippe approved. (It was worth 11.3 million modern dollars.) T. V. Soong wasn't in the government, however. He couldn't make explicit promises on its behalf. He could only "suggest" and "advise," and the deal could be legally consummated only by the airline's board of directors, so Bond flew to Hong Kong on December 24, losing Christmas with his family yet again. The company's Chinese directors and Chennault's representatives wanted to settle the sale immediately, but Bond stalled. Pan Am hadn't yet been paid. Acting on behalf of the Chiangs' government, newly confined to Taiwan, one of Chennault's men in New York handed a Pan Am lawyer an ordinary bank draft for $1.25 million. Pan Am demanded a certified check. Chennault's man returned with the required instrument, and Pan Am wired confirmation to Hong Kong.

And so it happened on the last day of December 1949: William Langhorne Bond convened with the airline's other directors in Room 231 of the Hong Kong and Shanghai Bank Building in central Hong Kong and signed the China National Aviation Corporation out of existence, thus dissolving the most successful Sino-American partnership of all time.

EPILOGUE

The great adventure had at last ended.* But what a run it had been: high-stakes business, intrigue, and politics; high-risk flying; and total war played out over two of the more crucial decades in the long, agonizing history of the Middle Kingdom. Copiloting with a variety of Chinese managing directors, William Bond had held the controls through most of it. Always a civilian, Bond had manned a critical position for eight full years of war, combating the Japanese more than twice as long as most of his uniformed countrymen, and alongside Bond, men like Hugh Chen, Chuck Sharp, Hugh Woods, and Moon Chin—Chinese and American and Chinese American—had fought with the airline through all of it. Many company personnel had given their lives to the cause. It's hard to imagine any other civilians, anywhere else in the world, who'd had such a long-running, active role in the Second World War.

---

* Legal tussles over the fate of CNAC's airplanes would drag on for another two and a half years, however, until October 1952.

Amazingly, in retrospect it seems that all concerned parties got what they wanted from the China National Aviation Corporation. For William Bond, the China airline had certainly provided the adventure he'd been craving when he went to the Orient in 1931—a clear case of be careful what you wish for, for he'd gotten all of that and more. CNAC had also taken him from obscure construction foreman to vice president in Pan American World Airways, the world's most admired company, and if he'd endured crucifying difficulties through the terrible depression and the Second World War, he'd never suffered a minute of unemployment—professional stability that had allowed him to marry and start a family.

Aside from Bond, Pan American and China also got what they wanted from the China National Aviation Corporation. The China airline had played its role in the creation of the Transpacific Route, Pan Am's crowning accomplishment, proved an exceptionally lucrative investment, aided in the anti-Japanese war effort, and contributed to the unification of the Middle Kingdom, one of the most significant events of the twentieth century. And although the Chinese spent the entire duration of the partnership frustrated by the slow pace with which Pan Am trained and promoted Chinese personnel, people trained in the company went on to found China's domestic aviation industry on Taiwan and in mainland China. For the vast majority of the people who worked for the company, it was the experience of a lifetime.*

If the Transpacific Route was Pan Am's crowning achievement, then the equivalent for CNAC was undertaking and mastering the Hump airlift, another one of the greatest aviation accomplishments of all time. The Hump was the world's first strategic airlift, and it had evolved into America's main effort of the Second World War on the Asian mainland. CNAC proved the Hump could be done, and by the time the airlift was officially closed after the Japanese surrender, the airline had flown it more than thirty-five thousand times and carried approximately 10 percent of the total cargo. The Hump airlift's deepest roots tangled into the "Air Freight Service into China" memorandum that Bond wrote in the spring of 1941, and Bond himself

---

* The author counts himself as the most recent in the long line of people who have gotten what they wanted from the China National Aviation Corporation.

perhaps best summarized the airline's influence on the undertaking in the spring of 1944, when he wrote, "It is not an exaggeration to say that CNAC originated this idea and pioneered the service."

But was it worthwhile? That's a much larger question, and one of strategic consequence far beyond the purview of William Bond and his airline. In retrospect, it seems the United States reaped little tangible reward for the colossal effort it expended, and the transport aircraft committed to the operation could have done much to ameliorate the supply shortages that stalled the Allied advance toward the German frontier in the late summer and fall of 1944. However, no historian seems to have measured—or perhaps even considered—the impact of the raw material the airlift brought *out* of China. Through the war years, China supplied a significant percentage of the tungsten consumed by American industry. How important was that metal and the silk, hog bristles, tung oil, and tin brought out of China for the Allied war effort? What contribution did Chinese mercury make to the Russian cause? Could other sources have filled the vacuum left by the absence of Chinese supply? An exact accounting of the airlift's value needs to answer those questions. Ironically, the United States reaped the biggest dividends of the Hump three years *after* the Japanese surrender, during the Berlin airlift, when the lessons of maintaining, prosecuting, and managing an around-the-clock, all-weather airfreight operation had decisive impact on success—all of them retained and reapplied by the same General Tunner who had been the last and most successful American commander on the Hump.

Standard airpower histories credit the Hump as the foundation stone of the modern American military's strategic airlift capability, a crucial component of the country's ability to project power to any point on the globe. But the roots of strategic airlift go deeper, to the professional Chinese, Chinese American, and American aviators of the China National Aviation Corporation, without whose trailblazing efforts the China airlift probably wouldn't have been attempted. Indeed, considered even more carefully, the roots go down a little bit further still, to the tin, tungsten, and cigarettes airlift flown between Namyung and Hong Kong in 1941, before Pearl Harbor, when the China National Aviation Corporation gained the operational expertise the Hump would require.

. . .

For CNAC's people, the airline's dissolution was the end of one era and the beginning of another, and they scattered to the corners of the earth. Many caught on with different aviation concerns. Others changed industries, founded businesses, or bought farms and ranches. Most prospered, some foundered, but with the passage of time nearly all of them would come to recognize their time with the China airline as the highlight of their lives. They began holding annual reunions in the 1950s, a tradition that continues to this day.

Moon Chin served as operations manager of CATC until the end of 1949, and through the Chinese civil war his company flew many of the same missions and suffered many of the same complications as CNAC. After the Nationalist collapse, Moon relocated to Taiwan and founded Foshing Airlines, which flew domestically in the Republic of China and to a few international destinations around the peripheries of the China seas. He proved his flying expertise yet again in 1954, when a C-119 crew flying supplies to Dien Bien Phu parachuted into the South China Sea, which was running a fifteen-foot swell. Seaplanes from Okinawa and the Philippines circling the downed men didn't have the courage to land. The drama seemed sure to have a tragic end until Moon Chin arrived over the scene at the controls of a PBY Catalina amphibian. Unruffled, Moon landed and rescued the five imperiled men.* Moon expanded his business in the late 1950s, becoming the Taipei agent, airport ground handler, and food caterer for a number of airlines, which proved a shrewd and lucrative diversification.

Moon Chin sold Foshing in 1983 and returned to the United States—after all, he'd been an American citizen since the day he was born.** A kind, generous, entertaining man who has surely traveled one of the most unlikely and fascinating life arcs of the twentieth century—from barefoot Chinese peasant to owner of his own airline—Moon currently lives in a beautiful home in the hills of Burlingame, above the San Francisco airport, drives a jet-black Mercedes, hosts a marvelous party during CNAC's annual reunion, and commands a respect among his fellow airline veterans that simply cannot be exaggerated.

* The daughter of one of the rescued men regularly attends the CNAC reunions to pay homage to Moon.

** Foshing changed its name to TransAsia in 1992, the moniker under which it still operates.

Home from China, Chuck Sharp took up with Pan Am, where he was allowed to retain the seniority he'd earned in China, and he flew for the airline for the rest of his career. He and Sylvia Wylie went their separate ways after the war. Sharp married Grace Douglass on July 30, 1949, and they raised four children, the first two of whom were born in Rio de Janeiro when Chuck was based in South America. Chuck and Grace eventually settled in Miami, and Chuck continued to fly routes in Central and South America and around the Caribbean. Through the years, Chuck Sharp took great delight in tinkering with his boat and taking friends fishing—and in the collections of stamps and coins he'd amassed in his world travels. His truest friends always remained those he'd made in China, and he and Hugh Woods maintained their close relationship through the rest of their lives. Completing a professional circle, Chuck Sharp's last routes were 707 flights into Hong Kong's Kai Tak Airport. He retired in 1968, having amassed a colossal quantity of lifetime flight hours, and died in Houston in 1974.

Hugh and Maj Woods also settled among the palms and balmy breezes of South Florida, where they ran a successful real estate sales and development business. They were made for each other, and their marriage always prospered. Hugh Woods died in 1979; his beloved Maj joined him a few weeks later. Close friends said she'd died of a broken heart.

Harold Bixby served with Pan Am until the late 1950s. He and his wife, Debbie, enjoyed a delightful retirement, spending much time with their four daughters and seventeen grandchildren at the family retreats on Lake George, New York, and on Captiva Island, Florida. Like the rest of the Americans who'd served with CNAC, he never got over China. One of the great unsung executives of aviation's golden age, Harold Bixby died in 1965.

Not wanting to leave Asia, Pete Goutiere asked his wife to come to the Orient after the Japanese surrender. She refused, and they divorced. He married again in 1947 and left CNAC the following year. He piloted around India and the Middle East until 1952, returned to the United States, and flew for National Airlines. Not liking the monotony of domestic aviation, by 1955 he was back in the Middle East, divorced for a second time, and flying out of Beirut. He married a third time in 1956 and had two children. In 1962, he took a job as an air-carrier operations inspector with the Federal Aviation Administration (FAA). His third divorce hit in 1968. In the late 1970s, he worked for another Bond—Langhorne Bond, William Bond's elder son—when Langhorne headed the FAA during the Carter administration. Pete Goutiere retired in 1990, and he seems to have gotten it right with his fourth wife, Evelyn. They currently live in Katonah, New York. Ninety-six years old, Pete occasionally and expertly mixes cocktails like the gin and ginger beer he used to enjoy in the Orient and seldom misses a CNAC reunion.

Toward the end of the war, Joe Rosbert, his great friend Dick Rossi (who had flown the Hump 735 times, more than anybody else), and eight other ex-AVG, ex-CNAC pilots pitched in ten thousand dollars apiece and formed an airline. Blending their fighter-pilot cachet with the skill they'd learned flying for CNAC, they named it the Flying Tiger Line—and dedicated it to flying freight. After a sketchy beginning, the company gained traction and thrived.* Claire Chennault lured Rosbert back to China in the summer of 1946, and Rosbert flew for Chennault's airline, CAT, rising to become its operations manager. He followed the airline to Taiwan after the Communist takeover, and continued working for "the old man"—as Chennault was always known to his AVG fliers—until Chennault died of lung cancer in 1958. Repulsed by what he regarded as incompetent and nefarious CIA incursions into the airline, Rosbert resigned and moved to Majorca, where he and his wife refurbished a dilapidated castle into a hotel, which they operated until they found themselves on the losing end of an underhanded takeover putsch and returned to the States, close to broke, in 1972. They lived in Florida for a time, then operated a campground and hotel in the Great Smoky Mountains of western North Carolina until their eldest son died of cancer in 1980. After another round of quieter adventures, Joe Rosbert died in Katy, Texas, outside Houston, in 2007, eleven days shy of his ninetieth birthday, and if the old ankle injury had pained him at times, he delighted to the end in all the borrowed time he'd had since that fateful day in April 1943, when he and Ridge Hammell came so close to dying against an obscure Asian mountainside.

Back in California after the Nationalist collapse, Ernie Allison founded

---

* The ten founders of the Flying Tiger Line were Bob Prescott (the front man), William "Bill" Bartling, Cliff Groh, Tommy Haywood, Robert "Duke" Hedman, C. H. "Link" Laughlin, Ernest "Bus" Loane, Robert "Catfish" Raine, Joe Rosbert, and Dick Rossi. Federal Express bought the Flying Tiger Line after Prescott's death, thus establishing its own little-appreciated connection to the AVG, CNAC, and the Hump.

Allison Aircraft Export in Arcadia and coordinated the supply of airframes, engines, spare parts, and aircraft accessories to a variety of worldwide aviation concerns from an office attached to the family carport. During one Washington trip early in the history of Allison's business, William Bond spent several days introducing him to his contacts in the State Department, whose approval Allie needed to obtain export licenses. One of Allison's best clients proved to be Peacock Airlines, formed in Burma by a group of his ex-CNAC associates, which provided aircraft and training to the Indonesian Air Force. When he retired, Allie bought an alfalfa farm twenty-five miles from Barstow, California, and although his pilot's license (number 1,285) had expired years before, in his mid-seventies he found himself longing to return to the cockpit. Rather than submit to the FAA's lengthy renewal process, he took up glider flying, twice a week soaring above the Mojave Desert, which always left him feeling rejuvenated and reconnected to his roots in early aviation. He died in 1976, at the age of eighty-one.

As for William Bond, he wrapped up his Pan Am career not long after CNAC's end. He'd served long and well, in trying times. It's hard to imagine family circumstances more difficult than those endured by William and Kitsi Bond from July 1937 to the end of 1949. For a dozen years, their marriage was conducted primarily at long distance. They'd found each other relatively late in their lives, in 1934, when Kitsi was nearly thirty and Bond forty-two, and they'd just started a family when the Japanese invasion of China shattered their optimistic beginning. Through the years of war against Japan, both before and after Pearl Harbor, Bond had done his best to be a good father to his two sons, albeit often from the far side of the globe. But if he wasn't always able to be there in the flesh, solving daily problems, he was supporting his family financially and setting an example of how a man comports himself with discipline, dedication, responsibility, and honor few have the courage to match. He was a man, and he stands tall upon his accomplishments. Kitsi never wavered in her support of her husband, and as a love story, theirs has a happy ending, as the best ones do.

After Bondy's return from the Orient, for the rest of their lives he and Kitsi were seldom parted. They bought Picket Mountain Farm outside Warrenton, Virginia, and raised their sons straight and true. Bondy kept Hereford cattle and grew hay, discovered that he loved farming, and threw himself into the work with characteristic intensity. Despite being in his late fifties when he purchased the farm and having been told by a doctor after his most recent tachycardia attack that he shouldn't live in a house with a set of stairs, on Picket Mountain Farm Bond religiously rose before 7:00 A.M. to check on his two hired hands, returned to the house for break-fast with his family, then spent the rest of the day working out of doors, often in the hot sun, running a combine or a baler and heaving forty-pound bales up onto hay wagons. He also served on the board of the Kentucky River Coal Company through the 1950s and '60s, eventually becoming its chairman, and he came to appreciate the monotony of the coal business after the "constant and kaleidoscopic" difficulties he'd faced in China. McCarthyism, red scares, and the rabid anti-Communist policies of the postwar decades struck him as nearly as counterproductive and foolish as the isolationism of the 1930s, even when balanced against the genius of Lend-Lease, the Marshall Plan, and Containment.*

In Warrenton, Kitsi and Bondy developed a wide circle of friends, and they took great pleasure in entertaining. They discovered a mutual love of gardening and always nurtured beautiful plantings, both at Picket Moun-tain Farm and after advancing years persuaded them to move into town. Kitsi maintained her community work, as she'd always done, volunteering with the Red Cross, the local hospitals, and in the local garden club, even-tually becoming its president. She was intelligent, energetic, articulate, and determined; friends and family always said she'd have made an excellent lawyer.

It was a great source of pride to William Bond that both of his sons earned the excellent university educations he'd never had the opportunity to pursue. Thomas earned a bachelor's degree from Princeton and master's degrees from Middlebury and the University of Virginia, and he taught at two of the best schools in the country—Governor Dummer Academy in Byfield, Massachusetts, and Virginia's Woodberry Forest School. Lang-horne studied law at the University of Virginia, and after graduate work at the McGill Institute of Air and Space Law and at the London School of Economics, he started his public service career during the Johnson admin-istration, in the Commerce Department, and became special assistant to the secretary of transportation. Fired by President Nixon, he led a non-

---

* Bond truly loathed Senator McCarthy, and was convinced that McCarthy's rabid, anti-Communist witch hunts had unfairly ruined the careers of many of his State Department friends.

profit until he was appointed Illinois's secretary of transportation. President Carter tapped him to head the Federal Aviation Administration, and after Reagan's election returned him to private enterprise he practiced aviation and transportation law and consulted on regulatory policy.

Once Langhorne and Thomas had left home, Kitsi and Bondy developed the habit of spending the winter months in Ponte Vedra, Florida. Bondy's heart trouble never quite left him, but it never got the better of him, either. He kept himself in fine fettle with hard physical work, daily exercise, and a healthy diet, having quit smoking years before. No man escapes the march of time, however, and he suffered a number of tachycardia episodes and a few small heart attacks, but he worked diligently to get his stamina back after each one, determined to "stay alive so that he could take care of Kitsi."

Bondy's deteriorating hearing and Kitsi's soft voice caused some comic episodes and occasional irritation during their twilight years, but as always, they remained devoted to each other, taking great delight in their sons and four grandchildren and in their broad group of friends until July 17, 1985, when Bondy, at the venerable age of ninety-two, had a fainting spell after shaving and was soon gone. True to the pattern of their postwar lives, Kitsi, twelve years his junior, was in the house when he died, but it was downhill for her after his death, and she lived only another three years, taking leave of this world on October 1, 1988.

Nobody would have predicted it watching Bond battle his own health through the trying years of Hong Kong, Chungking, the Hump, and the Chinese civil war, but he'd outlived the China National Aviation Corporation by more than thirty years. To his dying day, Bond always felt that he'd held the most interesting, exciting, and challenging job in the entire history of commercial aviation, and that he'd had a crucial hand in guiding the most successful Sino-American partnership that has ever existed.

Many things could have happened. These were the ones that did.

ACKNOWLEDGMENTS

First and foremost, I'd like to thank the men and women of the China National Aviation Corporation. *China's Wings* is their story, and I wouldn't have been able to write it without their wholehearted cooperation. Neither would I have been able to do it alone—this is the most difficult endeavor I've ever undertaken. Dozens of people helped make this book possible, and I'm deeply grateful to all of them.

My own personal adventure with the airline began with an email from Charlie Fowler, a climbing buddy with whom I'd adventured in Patagonia. Charlie's other major expeditionary obsession was unclimbed mountains in China. "Greg," he emailed after one trip, "I keep hearing stories about World War II American plane wrecks in the eastern Himalaya. You're a climber, a writer, and a military history guy. You should spark up a story."

I recognized a good idea, but I was then on an assignment that took months to complete, and I wasn't able to sniff after Charlie's suggestion for the better part of a year. When I did, Web searches led me to cnac.org, a website maintained by Tom Moore, the nephew of a CNAC pilot who was killed while flying number 31, the airline's last DC-2, in March 1942.* Although not exactly Charlie's topic, Tom's website drilled home the excellence of an untold story. Through the years, I'd read much about the

---

* The DC-2 that Moon Chin had piloted during the Hong Kong evacuation.

aviation tales around the airline's edge—the transpacific flights, the Flying Tigers, and the Hump flying—but I'd never even heard of the airline itself. As I perused Tom's reunions page, I realized that the airline's annual reunion was only three weeks hence, in San Francisco, about twenty miles from where I live in Walnut Creek. (People with souvenirs, photographs, and personal remembrances of the China National Aviation Corporation should consider submitting their images and stories to Tom at cnac.org; it's the clearinghouse of CNAC history. I'd also love to post them on my China's Wings blog at gregcrouch.com.)

CNAC Association president Bill Maher, one of the Hump pilots, responded to my nervous telephone inquiry asking whether a curious writer could attend with an enthusiastic "Hell, yes! We've got some great stories."

He was right, of course, and I was physically shaking as I drove away from the reunion at the end of the weekend. Beyond doubt, I'd discovered a fabulous story, one I felt I'd been born to tell. Bill and every other member of the association have offered nothing but staunch support every step of the way, although I'm sure they wish I could have finished sooner. (Sadly, Charlie Fowler can't enjoy the fruit of the seed he planted, he was killed by an avalanche in China in 2006, and neither can Bill Maher—he passed away in the summer of 2011.)

Through the years, I've spent dozens of hours interviewing company veterans, time that not only proved professionally fruitful but also produced memories I'll treasure for the rest of my life. Among the many veterans I interviewed, I owe a particularly enormous debt to Moon Fun Chin, who was generous with many hours of his time through years of research, and is one of the most remarkable men I've ever had the honor of meeting. A singularly fascinating experience was the day spent reviewing the extraordinarily well-remembered events of the Hong Kong evacuation with Moon and Frieda and T. T. Chen, two other ex-CNAC employees I'd like to thank. (When I apologized for taking so much of their time, Frieda, ever sassy, shot back, "Don't worry! This is all we sit around and talk about anyway.") Not less are my debts to the rest of the airline's family: Shirley Wilke Mosley, daughter of chief mechanic O. C. Wilke, whose photo albums, charming conversation, and detailed remembrances opened my eyes to the richness of the airline's story before Pearl Harbor; Nancy Allison Wright, daughter of Ernie Allison, who granted me unfettered access to the archive of relevant letters, diary entries, and photographs she's collected over a lifetime—and in the process became a valued friend; Joe Rosbert, with whom I spent a long weekend in Katy, Texas, and his son Bob, who facilitated the interview; Peter J. Goutiere and his wife, Evelyn, with whom I stayed in Port Richie, Florida; Donald McBride, with whom I spent three days in Omaha, Nebraska, and his daughter Elaine McBride and her husband, Joe Ramirez, who put me up while I was there; Dick Rossi and his wife, Lydia, who hosted me at their home in Fallbrook, California; Harold Chinn and his son Craig Chinn, for interviews here in Walnut Creek, California. The list goes on and on: brothers Al Mah and Cedric Mah, Fletcher Hanks, C. K. Tseng and his wife, Theresa, Elizabeth "Bo" Bixby, Hugh Grundy, Bob and Audrene Sherwood, Carey and Cynthia Bowles, Bill Maher, Ilse Shilling, Jeanne Holder, Martha Conrath, Oliver and Rosemary Glenn, Bill and Camille Gilger, John Lee, Catfish Raine, Y. H. Yu, Gifford and Grace Bull, John Parish, Hsiang-Lai Wen and his wife, Grace Wen, Margaret Mun Soong and Dr. Kenneth Soong, Anson Lisk, Gene and Mitzi McHale, Francis Lee Tong, Elizabeth Chan, Starr Thompson. And I bow my head in gratitude to Katharine Dunlop Bond and William Langhorne Bond, neither of whom I had the honor of meeting.

I'm also indebted to CNAC's younger generation, generally, but not exclusively, sons, daughters, nieces, and nephews of company personnel. William and Kitsi Bond's two sons, Thomas Dunlop Bond and Langhorne Bond, and Langhorne's wife, Enriqueta, have been incredibly helpful and cooperative throughout this whole process, supplying their father's correspondence, providing family photographs, answering questions, and granting me permission to use their father's writings. Tom Moore again deserves special mention for his years of assistance and enthusiasm, the loan of many crucial books, and for the quality of his friendship. At various points, all of the following provided valuable assistance: Lisa and Robert Mitchell, Dolly Wong (P. Y. Wong's daughter), Renee Robertson, Valerie Kendrick Parish, Eve Coulson, Karol Nielsen, Dona Wong (Donald Wong's daughter, Frieda Chen's niece, and a Ph.D. researcher at Harvard—and a perfect three-generational Chinese American success story), Elise Petach, Cora Quisumbing-King, Clayton Kuhles, John Stahly, Louis Stannard, Kai Freise, Peggy Maher, Royal Leonard, Jr., Carol Slade and Charon Sharp (Chuck Sharp's daughters), Patti Gully, Stephen Loane, Pam Biederstedt, Patty Lee, John H. Anderson, Tom Watson, John Lisk, Bob Willett, Lee Harrison, Frances Pengra, and the rest of the Bixby clan, and all the rest.

One of the great rewards of the publishing industry is being able to associate with the fascinating people who constitute it, and I'm deeply indebted to the team assembled around this book. My agent, Ronald Goldfarb, believed in it from the moment I outlined the bones of the story. Farley Chase, an agent then working with Ronald, rescued the *China's Wings* proposal from the dung heap of good ideas poorly executed, and with keen editorial guidance shaped it into a compelling—and salable—story. Without Farley, I doubt this book would have grown wings. It found a home at Bantam Dell, where I owe much to Nita Taublib and John Flicker, my commissioning editors. John's sage advice shepherded *China's Wings* through its first five years, but he left Bantam before I completed the book. With John's departure, Tracy Devine inherited the project, and her good humor, keen intelligence, and laser guidance lashed me through its final years. She's been a real delight, and the final manuscript owes much to her talents. Others in the Random House Publishing Group universe also richly deserve thanks: assistant editor Angela Polidoro, executive managing editor Benjamin Dreyer, production editor Janet Wygal, senior art director David Stevenson, who designed *China's Wings'* book jacket, senior designer Liz Cosgrove, who designed its interior, and copy editor Deborah Dwyer, who saved me from errors too numerous to mention and set what must be a publishing industry record by copyediting this entire manuscript in six days—due to my need to spend a month in the Islamic Republic of Iran. Thanks also to Evan Stone and Carol Anderson for their fine proofreading work.

Along the way, many friends read and commented on the manuscript at various stages, and I'm grateful to them all. Most tireless were Kathryn Townsend, Diana McSherry, and Evie Skoda, each of whom suffered through several versions and offered many excellent suggestions. Kathryn, the busiest human being I know and one of my oldest friends, always found the time to help. Evie contributed major assistance during my initial research and through a few long sessions in the Hoover Institute's archive and was an inspiration through several years of writing. Diana's emails and conversations have provided so much thoughtful inspiration—and the story's walk-off. Kudos also to Phil Krichilsky, Eric Verwaal, Paul Marks, and Bill McDowell for their constructive comments, and to Jennifer Prior, the lovely and talented copy chief of *Wired*, who, along with many excellent suggestions, served up a crucial piece of advice: "Greg, if you're going to write a book about flying, you're going to have to learn the difference between 'hangar' and 'hanger.' One is for airplanes. The other is for coats."

I'm grateful for so many other people, all of whom in some way helped: In no particular order, Mr. Wong How Man of the China Exploration and Research Society, Christine Harris and John Hall at the San Francisco Airport Commission Aviation Library and Louis A. Turpen Aviation Museum, Mary Dixie Dysart at the Air Force Historical Research Agency at Maxwell Air Force Base, Alabama, Taiwanese aviation historians C. W. Lam and Fu Jing-ping (Clarence Fu), Roland Joynes, a photo printer associated with the University of Miami, Craig Likeness, Rochelle Pienn, Laura Cupell, and Jennifer Lea in the Pan Am Archive at the Richter Library at the University of Miami, Craig M. Berry, Arvo L. Vercamer, Lennart Anderson, Martin Best, Wen Liang-yen, Andy Dawson, Catherine Bunting Spinks, Tom Strickler, Norman Fritz, Bruce Oestler, Robert Cassidy, and Chandra Jackson, serials librarian at the University of Georgia Libraries.

I'm blessed with incredible friends and family. They've kept me afloat through the writing process: my mother, Janet Crouch, who, sadly, didn't live to see the finished product, my father, Robert L. Crouch, who provided an excellent economic sketch of the Great Depression and much other advice; my son, Ryan Crouch; my cousins John and Bruce Crouch and Linda Cameron; Steve Gully, Dave Saunders, and John Sprague—the three best friends a guy could have—and Michelle Taylor and Kim Sprague, Steve's and John's wives; Laura Borden; Dina Bernstein Howard and her husband, Edward P. Howard IV (whose grandfather almost landed William Bond's job); Leesl Herman, who always has my back; her son, Sam; Todd Zimmerman; Elizabeth Macken and her heart of pure gold; Andrew Lindblade and Jennifer Macfarlane; Hans Florine and Jackie Adams Florine; my surfing buddy Theo Emison and his wife, Carrie; Tim and Nora Dolan; Lizzie and Roger Udwin; Emily Lydgate; Sharon Donovan; Emily Brewer; Steve Johnson; Rolando Garibotti; Lori Loriero; Patrick Poe; Ana Paula Siquiera; Serena Lourie and Alan Baker; Gillian Penitente; Amy Sillers; Diana Sanson; Amy Bennett; Ted Barker; Clark Argeris; Darja Koehler; Eliza Moran; Claudia Walther; Stephen and April Alvarez; Larry Adams; Mark and Susan Robinson; Randy Leavitt; Jim Cope; Marian Cope; Sabrina Lamb; Roberta Raye; Leslie Robertson; Kristen Reif; Mark and Susan Croshaw; Bud and Melba Sprague; Cindy Mallot; Dolores and Bill Pollock; Tina Messineo; Helena Hill; Patti Smart; John and Heidi Frost; Rob and Sheryl

Lowe; Randy and Eden Jasiorkowski; Bill and Missy Macfadyen; and everyone else in my mother's Marymount crew and those other of her friends who were so stalwart during her ordeal; Kimberley Puckett; Ken Larson; Ross and Sylvia Payne; Andy Dawson; Lili Weigert; Tammy Owens; Betty Voyko Groom; John and Deb McLauchlin; Steve Brophy; Brian Coppersmith; Paul and Adele Skoda; Pom and Kristie Skoda; Fred and Cynthia Skoda; Viju Mathew; Valerie Martin; Elena Mauli Shapiro; Yvon and Melinda Chouinard; Doug and Kris Tompkins; Jim Donini and Angela Goodacre; Joanne Goldfarb. The list goes on. I thank you all.

Last, but certainly not least, comes Tina Rath, for helping bring the project, and me, home.

BIBLIOGRAPHY

Abend, Hallett. *Chaos in Asia*. New York: Ives Washburn, 1939.

———. *My Life in China: 1926–1941*. New York: Harcourt, Brace, 1943.

Allen, Louis. *Burma: The Longest War, 1941–1945*. London: Phoenix Press, 1984.

Angle, Chrystal. *Reflections of Chrystal*. Waterbury, CT: Network Communictions, 1993. (A self-published memoir by the wife of CNAC pilot Bob Angle, in the collection of Tom Moore.)

The Army Almanac: A Book of Facts Concerning the Army of the United States. Washington, DC: U.S. Government Printing Office, 1950.

Arnold, H. H. *Global Mission*. New York: Harper and Brothers, 1949.

Auden, W. H., and Christopher Isherwood. *Journey to a War*. London: Faber and Faber, 1939.

Augustin, Andreas. *The Most Famous Hotels in the World: The Peninsula, Hong Kong*, 5th ed. Singapore, Vienna, and London: Treasury Publishing, 1996.

Background of the Shanghai Troubles. New York Office of Japanese National Committee of the International Chamber of Commerce, 1932.

Baker, Barbara, ed. *Shanghai: Electric and Lurid City*. Oxford University Press, 1998.

Barraclough, Geoffrey, ed. *The Times Concise Atlas of World History*. London: Times Books, 1982.

Baxter, Walter. *Look Down in Mercy*. London: Heinemann, 1951.

Bayly, Christopher, and Tim Harper. *Forgotten Armies: The Fall of British Asia, 1941–1945*. Cambridge, MA: Belknap Press of Harvard University Press, 2006.

Bender, Marylin, and Selig Altschul. *The Chosen Instrument: The Rise and Fall of an American Entrepreneur*. New York: Simon and Schuster, 1982.

Berg, A. Scott. *Lindbergh*. New York: G. P. Putnam's Sons, 1998.

Bickers, Robert. *Empire Made Me: An Englishman Adrift in Shanghai.* New York: Columbia University Press, 2003.

Bixby, Debbie, "H. M. Bixby Family in China, 1934–1938." Privately published pamphlet compiled by Debbie Bixby from her diary and the diary of her daughter Frances, provided to the author by Harold Bixby's second-eldest daughter, Elizabeth "Bo" Bixby.

Bixby, Harold M. "Top Side Ricksha." Unpublished manuscript in the San Francisco Airport Commission Aviation Library, 1938.

Bjorge, Dr. Gary J. *Moving the Enemy: Operational Art in the Chinese PLA's Huai Hai Campaign.* Leavenworth Paper Number 22. Fort Leavenworth, KS: Combat Studies Institute Press, 2004.

Bonavia, Judy, and Richard Hayman. *Yangzi: The Yangtze River and the Three Gorges from Source to Sea.* Hong Kong: Odyssey Publications, 2004.

Bond, Charles R., Jr., and Terry H. Anderson. *A Flying Tiger's Diary.* College Station: Texas A&M University Press, 1984.

Bond, William Langhorne. *Wings for an Embattled China.* Edited by James Ellis. Bethlehem, PA: Lehigh University Press, 2001.

Borg, Dorothy. *The United States and the Far Eastern Crisis of 1933–1938.* Cambridge, MA: Harvard University Press, 1964.

Bowyer, Chaz. *The Encyclopedia of British Military Aircraft.* London: Bison Books, 1982.

Boyington, Gregory. *Baa Baa Black Sheep.* New York: Putnam, 1958, reissued by Bantam, 1977.

———. *Tonya.* New York: Bobbs-Merrill, 1960.

Boyle, John Hunter. *China and Japan at War, 1937–1945: The Politics of Collaboration.* Palo Alto, CA: Stanford University Press, 1972.

Bradley, James. *Flyboys: A True Story of Courage.* New York: Little, Brown, 2003.

Brereton, Lieutenant General Lewis H. *The Brereton Diaries: 3 October 1941–8 May 1945.* New York: William Morrow, 1946.

Brewer, James F., ed. *China Airlift: The Hump.* Dallas: Taylor, 1980.

Burdsall, Richard, Arthur Emmons, Terris Moore, and Jack Theodore Young. *Men against the Clouds: The Conquest of Minya Konka.* New York: Harper and Brothers, 1935.

Byrd, Martha. *Chennault: Giving Wings to the Tiger.* Tuscaloosa: University of Alabama Press, 1987.

Carr, Caleb. *The Devil Soldier: The American Soldier of Fortune Who Became a God in China.* New York: Random House, 1992.

Chang, Iris. *The Chinese in America.* New York: Penguin, 2003.

———. *The Rape of Nanking.* New York: Basic Books, 1997.

Chang, Jung, and Jon Halliday. *Mao: The Unknown Story.* New York: Alfred A. Knopf, 2005.

Chiang Kai-shek. *President Chiang Kai-shek's Selected Speeches and Messages, 1937–1945.* Taipei, Taiwan: China Cultural Service, 1946.

Churchill, Winston S. *The Gathering Storm.* Boston: Houghton Mifflin, 1948.

———. *Their Finest Hour.* Boston: Houghton Mifflin, 1949.

Clubb, O. Edmund. *Twentieth Century China*. New York: Columbia University Press, 1964.

Coffee, Thomas M. *Hap: The Story of the U.S. Air Force and the Man Who Built It, General Henry H. "Hap" Arnold*. New York: Viking Press, 1982.

Conrad, Barnaby. *Pan Am: An Avaition Legend*. Emeryville, CA: Woodford Press, 1999.

Cornelius, Wanda, and Thayne Short. *Ding Hao: America's Air War in China 1937–1945*. Gretna, LA: Pelican, 1980.

Craven, Wesley Frank, and James Lea Cate, eds. *The Army Air Forces in World War II*. Vol. 1, *Plans and Early Operations, January 1939 to August 1942*. University of Chicago Press, 1948.

———. *The Army Air Forces in World War II*. Vol. 4, *The Pacific: Guadalcanal to Saipan, August 1942 to July 1944*. University of Chicago Press, 1950.

———. *The Army Air Forces in World War II*. Vol. 5, *The Pacific: Matterhorn to Nagasaki, June 1944 to August 1945*. University of Chicago Press, 1953.

———. *The Army Air Forces in World War II*. Vol. 7, *Services around the World*. University of Chicago Press, 1958.

Culbert, Tom, and Andy Dawson. *PanAfrica: Across the Sahara in 1941 with Pan Am*. McLean, VA: Paladwr Press, 1998.

Curie, Eve. *Journey among Warriors*. New York: Doubleday, Doran, 1943.

Cuthbertson, Ken. *Nobody Said Not to Go*. New York: Faber and Faber, 1998.

Dahl, Roald. *Going Solo*. New York: Penguin, 1986.

Daley, Robert. *An American Saga: Juan Trippe and His Pan Am Empire*. New York: Random House, 1980.

Dallek, Robert. *Franklin D. Roosevelt and American Foreign Policy, 1932–1945*. Oxford University Press, 1979.

Davies, John Paton, Jr. *Dragon by the Tail*. London: Robson Books, 1974.

Dillon, Richard, Thomas Moulin, and Don DeNevi. *High Steel: Building the Bridges across San Francisco Bay*. Berkeley, CA: Celestial Arts, 1979.

Dong, Stella. *Shanghai: Gateway to the Celestial Empire, 1860–1949*. Hong Kong: FormAsia Books, 2003.

———. *Shanghai: The Rise and Fall of a Decadent City*. New York: William Morrow, 2000.

Dorn, Frank. *The Sino-Japanese War, 1937–1941: From Marco Polo Bridge to Pearl Harbor*. New York: Macmillan, 1974.

Dupuy, R. Ernest, and Trevor Dupuy. *The Encyclopedia of Military History*. New York: Harper and Row, 1986.

Eltscher, Louis R., and Edward M. Young. *Curtiss-Wright: Greatness and Decline*. New York: Twayne, 1988.

Fairbank, John King, and Merle Goldman. *China: A New History*. Cambridge, MA: Belknap Press of Harvard University Press, 1992.

Farmer, Rhodes. *Shanghai Harvest: Three Years in the China War*. London: Museum Press, 1945.

Feis, Herbert. *The China Tangle: The American Effort in China from Pearl Harbor to the Marshall Mission*. Princeton, NJ: Princeton University Press, 1953.

Fenby, Jonathan. *Chiang Kai-shek: China's Generalissimo and the Nation He Lost.* New York: Carroll & Graf, 2004.

Ferguson, Ted. *Desperate Siege: The Battle of Hong Kong.* New York: Doubleday, 1980.

Ferrell, Robert H. *American Diplomacy in the Great Depression: Hoover-Stimson Foreign Policy, 1929–1933.* New Haven, CT: Yale University Press, 1957.

Finch, Percy. *Shanghai and Beyond.* New York: Charles Scribner's Sons, 1953.

Folsom, Kenneth E. "The China National Aviation Corporation, an Affiliated Company of Pan American Airways System." (BA diss., Princeton University Department of History, 1943, copy in the Pan Am Archive in the Richter Library, University of Miami, Box 21, File 1.)

Ford, Daniel. *Flying Tigers: Claire Chennault and the American Volunteer Group.* Washington, DC: Smithsonian Institution Press, 1991.

Foreign Relations of the United States, Diplomatic Papers, 1938. Vol. 4, *The Far East.* Washington, DC: U.S. Government Printing Office, 1955.

Foreign Relations of the United States, Diplomatic Papers, 1942, China. Washington, DC: U.S. Government Printing Office, 1956.

Foreign Relations of the United States, Diplomatic Papers, 1943, China. Washington, DC: U.S. Government Printing Office, 1957.

Fraser, George MacDonald. *Quartered Safe Out Here: A Recollection of the War in Burma.* Pleasantville, NY: Akadine Press, 2001.

Frater, Alexander. *Chasing the Monsoon.* New York: Alfred A. Knopf, 1991.

Friedman, Milton, and Anna J. Schwartz. *A Monetary History of the United States, 1867–1960,* Princeton, NJ: Princeton University Press, 1963.

Frillmann, Paul, and Graham Peck. *China: The Remembered Life.* Boston: Houghton Mifflin, 1968.

Galbraith, John Kenneth. *The Great Crash: 1929.* Boston: Houghton Mifflin, 1954.

Gann, Ernest K. *Fate Is the Hunter.* New York: Simon and Schuster, 1961.

———. *Flying Circus.* New York: Macmillan, 1974.

———. *Soldier of Fortune.* New York: William Sloane Associates, 1954.

Gellhorn, Martha. *The Face of War.* New York: Simon and Schuster, 1959.

———. *Travels with Myself and Another.* New York: Putnam, 1978.

Genovese, Flight Captain J. Gen. *We Flew without Guns,* Philadelphia and Toronto: John C. Winston, 1945.

Glines, Carroll V., and Wendell F. Moseley. *The Legendary DC-3.* New York: Van Nostrand Reinhold, 1959, 1965, 1979.

Goodwin, Doris Kearns. *No Ordinary Time: Franklin and Eleanor Roosevelt: The Home Front in World War II.* New York: Simon and Schuster, 1994.

Goutiere, Peter. *Himalayan Rogue: A Pilot's Odyssey.* Paducah, KY: Turner, 1994.

Greenlaw, Olga. *The Lady and the Tigers: Remembering the Flying Tigers of World War II.* New York: E. P. Dutton, 1943.

Grooch, William Stephen. *Winged Highway.* New York: Longmans, Green, 1938.

Hahn, Emily. *China to Me: A Partial Autobiography.* Philadelphia: Blakiston, 1944.

————. *No Hurry to Get Home.* Seattle: Seal Press, 2000.

————. *The Soong Sisters.* Garden City, NY: Garden City Publishing, 1941.

Hanks, Fletcher. *Saga of CNAC #53.* Bloomington, IN: AuthorHouse, 2004.

Hemingway, Ernest. *Islands in the Stream.* New York: Charles Scribner's Sons, 1970.

Hoyt, Edwin P. *Japan's War.* New York: McGraw-Hill, 1986.

Hsu Long-hsuen and Chang Ming-kai. *History of the Sino-Japanese War, 1937–1945.* Taipei, Taiwan: Chung Wu, 1971.

Huxley, Anthony, ed. *Standard Encyclopedia of the World's Mountains.* New York: G. P. Putnam's Sons, 1962.

Keane, Fergal. *Road of Bones: The Epic Siege of Kohima.* London: Harper Press, 2010.

Kennedy, David M. *Freedom from Fear: The American People in Depression and War, 1929–1945.* Oxford University Press, 1999.

Koenig, William. *Over the Hump: Airlift to China.* New York: Ballantine Books, 1972.

Koginos, Manny T. *The Panay Incident: Prelude to War.* West Lafayette, IN: Purdue University Studies, 1967.

La Farge, Oliver. *The Eagle in the Egg.* Cambridge, MA: Houghton Mifflin, the Riverside Press, 1949.

Lam, Robert P. F. *The Hong Kong Album.* Hong Kong: Urban Council, 1982.

Lan, Alice, and Betty Hu. *We Flee from Hong Kong.* Grand Rapids, MI: Zondervan, 1944.

Lanier, Henry Wysham. *The Far Horizon: Twenty Years of Adventure, Development, and Invention on the New Air Frontier, the Life Story of Birger Johnson.* New York: Alfred A. Knopf, 1933.

Leary, William M. *The Dragon's Wings: The China National Aviation Corporation and the Development of Commercial Aviation in China.* Athens: University of Georgia Press, 1976.

Leonard, Royal. *I Flew for China.* New York: Doubleday, Doran, 1942.

Levy, Daniel S. *The Life of Shanghai.* Tokyo: Shobido Printing Office, 1934.

————. *Two-Gun Cohen: A Biography.* New York: St. Martin's Press, 1997.

Lindbergh, Anne Morrow. *City of Gold, Hour of Lead.* New York: Harcourt Brace Jovanovich, 1973.

————. *North to the Orient.* New York: Harcourt Brace, 1935.

Liu, F. F. *A Military History of Modern China: 1924–1949.* Princeton, NJ: Princeton University Press, 1956.

Lu, David J. *From Marco Polo Bridge to Pearl Harbor: Japan's Entry into World War II.* Washington, DC: Public Affairs Press, 1961.

Lyttle, Richard B. *Ernest Hemingway: The Life and the Legend.* New York: Atheneum, 1992.

Malraux, André. *Man's Fate.* New York: Harrison Smith and Robert Haas, Inc., 1934.

Mason, Daniel. *The Piano Tuner.* New York: Vintage, 2002.

Matloff, Maurice. *The United States Army in World War II: The War Department: Strategic Planning for Coalition Warfare, 1943–1944.* Washington, DC: Office of the Chief of Military History, Department of the Army, 1959.

Matloff, Maurice, and Edwin M. Snell. *The United States Army in World War II: The War*

Department: Strategic Planning for Coalition Warfare, 1941–1942. Washington, DC: Office of the Chief of Military History, Department of the Army, 1953.

Maugham, W. Somerset. *On a Chinese Screen.* New York: Paragon House, 1990 (originally published 1922).

McBride, Donald. "The Wartime Diary of Donald McBride." Unpublished, provided to the author by Donald McBride.

McKenna, Richard. *The Sand Pebbles.* New York: Harper & Row, 1962.

Moldrem, LaVerne J. *Tiger Tales: An Anecdotal History of the Flying Tiger Line.* Clearwater, FL: Flying M Press, 1996.

Molesworth, Carl. *P-40 Warhawk Aces of the CBI.* Oxford, UK: Osprey, 2000.

Moreira, Peter. *Hemingway on the China Front: His WWII Spy Mission with Martha Gellhorn,* Dulles, VA: Potomac Books, 2006.

Morgenstern, Karl, and Dietmar Plath. *Eurasia Aviation Corporation: Junkers & Lufthansa in China 1931–1943.* Munich: GeraMond, 2006.

Morgenthau Diary (China), Vol. 1 and Vol. 2. Washington, DC: U.S. Government Printing Office, 1965.

Morison, Samuel Eliot. *The Oxford History of the American People,* Vol. 3. Oxford University Press, 1965.

Morton, Louis. *United States Army in World War II, the War in the Pacific: The Fall of the Philippines.* Washington, DC: Center of Military History, United States Army, 1953.

Natkiel, Richard. *Atlas of 20th Century History.* London: Bison Books, 1982.

O'Neil, Paul. *Barnstormers and Speed Kings.* Alexandria, VA: Time-Life Books, 1981.

Oong Chao Haun, Brigadier-General. *Forward—China!* Shanghai: China Aero Institute, 1932.

Pakula, Hannah. *The Last Empress: Madame Chiang Kai-shek and the Birth of Modern China.* New York: Simon and Schuster, 2009.

Payne, Robert. *Chungking Diary.* London: William Heinemann, 1945.

Pearcy, Arthur. *Fifty Glorious Years: A Pictorial Tribute to the Douglas DC-3.* New York: Orion Books, 1985.

Peers, William R., and Dean Brelis. *Behind the Burma Road.* New York: Avon Books, 1963.

Pehrson, E. W., and C. E. Needham, eds. *Minerals Yearbook, 1942.* Washington, DC: Bureau of Mines, 1943.

Peissel, Michel. *Tiger for Breakfast.* Sevenoaks, UK: Hodder and Stoughton, 1966.

Powell, John B. *My Twenty-five Years in China.* New York: Macmillan, 1945.

Rea, George Brownson. *The Highway to Hostilities in the Far East.* Shanghai: Japanese Association in China, 1937.

Rees, David. *Harry Dexter White: A Study in Paradox.* New York: Coward, McCann and Geoghegan, 1973.

Rees, Lawrence. *Horror in the East.* London: BBC Worldwide, 2001.

Ristaino, Marcia R. *The Jacquinot Safe Zone: Wartime Refugees in Shanghai.* Palo Alto, CA: Stanford University Press, 2008.

Roberts, Edith. *Sketches of Nanking, Revised and Enlarged Under the Auspices of the Literary Section of the Nanking Woman's Club*. Nanking, China, 1933.

Rohwer, Jürgen. *Chronology of the War at Sea, 1939–1945: Naval History of World War Two*. Annapolis, MD: Naval Institute Press, 1972.

Romanus, Charles F., and Riley Sunderland. *The United States Army in World War II, China-Burma-India Theater: Stilwell's Mission to China*. Washington, DC: Office of the Chief of Military History, Department of the Army, 1953.

———. *The United States Army in World War II, China-Burma-India Theater: Stilwell's Command Problem*. Washington, DC: Office of the Chief of Military History, Department of the Army, 1956.

———. *The United States Army in World War II, China-Burma-India Theater: Time Runs Out in CBI*. Washington, DC: Office of the Chief of Military History, Department of the Army, 1959.

Rosbert, Camille Joseph. *Flying Tiger Joe's Adventure Cookbook*. Franklin, NC: Grant Poplar Press, 1985.

Rosholt, Malcolm. *Flight in the China Airspace, 1910–1950*. Amherst, WI: Palmer Publications, 1984.

Rowan, Roy. *Chasing the Dragon*. Guilford, CT: Lyons Press, 2004.

Saint-Exupéry, Antoine de. *Night Flight*. New York: Harcourt Brace, 1932.

———. *Wind, Sand and Stars*. New York: Harcourt Brace, 1992.

Salisbury, Harrison. *The Long March*. London: Harper and Row, 1985.

Samson, Gerald. *The Far East Ablaze*. Sevenoaks, UK: Knole Park Press, 1945.

Samson, Jack. *The Flying Tigers: The True Story of General Claire Chennault and the U.S. 14th Air Force in China*. Guilford, CT: Lyons Press, 1987.

Scott, Colonel Robert L. *God Is My Co-Pilot*. Garden City, NY: Blue Ribbon Books, 1943.

Seagrave, Gordon S. *Burma Surgeon*. New York: W. W. Norton, 1943.

Seagrave, Sterling. *The Soong Dynasty*. New York: Harper & Row, 1985.

Selle, Earl Albert. *Donald of China*. New York and London: Harper and Brothers, 1948.

Sergeant, Harriet. *Shanghai*. London: Johnathan Cape, 1991.

Service, John S. *Lost Chance in China*. New York: Random House, 1974.

Sevareid, Eric. *Not So Wild a Dream*. Columbia, MO: University of Missouri Press, 1995. (First published in 1946.)

Shanghai: City Guide. Lonely Planet Publications, 2004.

Sherwood, Robert E. *Roosevelt and Hopkins: An Intimate History*. New York: Harper and Brothers, 1948.

Shilling, Erik. "Destiny: A Flying Tiger's Rendezvous with Destiny." Self-published, 1993.

Shirer, William L. *The Rise and Fall of the Third Reich*. New York: Simon and Schuster, 1959.

Shore, F. M., ed. *Minerals Yearbook, 1941*. Washington, DC: Bureau of Mines, 1942.

Simpson, Joe. *Touching the Void*. London: Jonathan Cape, 1988.

Slim, Field-Marshal Viscount William. *Defeat into Victory: Battling Japan in Burma and India, 1942–1945*. London: Cassell, 1956.

Smith, Felix. *China Pilot: Flying for Chennault during the Cold War.* Washington, DC, and London: Smithsonian Institution Press, 1995.

Snow, Edgar. *The Battle for Asia.* New York: Random House, 1941.

——. *Far Eastern Front.* New York: Harrison Smith and Robert Hass, Inc., 1933.

Snow, Phillip. *The Fall of Hong Kong.* New Haven, CT: Yale University Press, 2004.

Spence, Jonathan D. *The Search for Modern China.* New York: W. W. Norton, 1990.

Spencer, Otha C. *Flying the Hump: Memories of an Air War.* College Station: Texas A&M University Press, 1992.

Springweiler, Max. *Pioneer Aviator in China.* Translated by Larry D. Sall. Dallas: CAT Association and the Air America Association, 1998.

Stanley, Roy M. *Prelude to Pearl Harbor.* New York: Charles Scribner's Sons, 1982.

Starks, Richard, and Miriam Murcutt. *Lost in Tibet: The Untold Story of Five American Airmen, a Doomed Plane, and the Will to Survive.* Guilford, CT: Lyons Press, 2004.

Stettinius, Edward R. *Lend-Lease: Weapon for Victory.* New York: Macmillan, 1944.

Stilwell, General Joseph W. *The Stilwell Papers.* Edited by Theodore H. White. New York: Sloane Associates, 1948.

Stimson, Henry L., and McGeorge Bundy. *On Active Service.* New York: Harper and Brothers, 1947.

Taleb, Nassim. *Fooled by Randomness.* New York: Random House, 2008.

Taylor, Jay. *The Generalissimo: Chiang Kai-shek and the Struggle for Modern China.* Cambridge, MA: Belknap Press of Harvard University Press, 2009.

Terkel, Studs. *Hard Times.* New York: Avon, 1971.

Theroux, Paul. *Sailing through China.* Boston: Houghton Mifflin, 1983.

Thomas, Gould H. *An American in China, 1936–1939.* New York: Greatrix Press, 2004.

Tolley, Kemp. *Yangtze Patrol: The U.S. Navy in China.* Annapolis, MD: United States Naval Institute Press, 1971.

Tuchman, Barbara. *Stilwell and the American Experience in China, 1911–1945.* New York: Macmillan, 1970.

Tunner, William H. *Over the Hump.* New York: Duell, Sloan, Pearce, 1964.

Tyson Li, Laura. *Madame Chiang Kai-shek: China's Eternal First Lady.* New York: Atlantic Monthly Press, 2006.

Vaughn, Charles S. "The China Memoirs of Charles S. (Chillie) Vaughn." Unpublished manuscript written in 1978–79, provided to the author by Nancy Allison Wright.

Webster, Donovan. *The Burma Road.* New York: Farrar, Straus, and Giroux, 2003.

Wei, Betty Peh-T'i. *Old Shanghai.* Oxford University Press, 1993.

——. *Shanghai: Crucible of Modern China.* Oxford University Press, 1987.

White, Colonel Edwin Lee. *Ten Thousand Tons by Christmas.* New York: Vantage Press, 1970.

White, Theodore H. *In Search of History.* New York: Harper and Row, 1978.

White, Theodore, and Annalee Jacoby. *Thunder out of China.* William Morrow, 1946.

Willett, Robert L. "An Airline at War: Pan Am's China National Aviation Corporation and Its Men," Self-published, 2008.

Wiltshire, Trea. *Hong Kong: Pages from the Past*. Hong Kong: FormAsia Books, 2003.

Winchester, Simon. *A Crack at the Edge of the World*. New York: HarperCollins, 2005.

———. *The Man Who Loved China*. New York: HarperCollins, 2008.

———. *The River at the Center of the World*. New York: Henry Holt, 1996.

Wings over Asia. Vol. 1, *A Brief History of the China National Aviation Corporation*. China National Aviation Association Foundation, 1971.

Wings over Asia. Vol. 2, *A Brief History of the China National Aviation Corporation*. China National Aviation Association Foundation, 1972.

Wings over Asia. Vol. 3, *A Brief History of the China National Aviation Corporation*. China National Aviation Association Foundation, 1975.

Wings over Asia. Vol. 4, *Memories of C.N.A.C.* China National Aviation Association Foundation, 1976.

Wu Liang. *Old Shanghai: A Lost Age*. Beijing: Foreign Languages Press, 2001.

Young, Arthur N. *China and the Helping Hand, 1937–1945*. Cambridge, MA: Harvard University Press, 1963.

———. *China's Wartime Finance and Inflation, 1937–1945*. Cambridge, MA: Harvard University Press, 1965.

———. *Cycle of Cathay: A Historical Perspective*. Vista, CA: Ibis, 1996.

NOTES

Abbreviations

AFHRA = Air Force Historical Research Agency, Maxwell Air Force Base, Alabama

ANY = Arthur N. Young Papers, the Hoover Institution Archive, Stanford University

C&C I = Wesley Frank Craven and James Lea Cate, eds., *The Army Air Forces in World War II*, Vol. 1, *Plans and Early Operations, January 1939 to August 1942*

C&C IV = Wesley Frank Craven and James Lea Cate, eds., *The Army Air Forces in World War II*, Vol. 4, *The Pacific: Guadalcanal to Saipan, August 1942 to July 1944*

C&C V = Wesley Frank Craven and James Lea Cate, eds., *The Army Air Forces in World War II*, Vol. 5, *The Pacific: Matterhorn to Nagasaki, June 1944 to August 1945*

C&C VII = Wesley Frank Craven and James Lea Cate, eds., *The Army Air Forces in World War II*, Vol. 7, *Services around the World*

CWR = *The China Weekly Review*

FRUS = *Foreign Relations of the United States*

LBC = Lauchlin B. Currie Papers, the Hoover Institution Archive, Stanford University

NAW = The private collection of Nancy Allison Wright

NYT = *New York Times*

PAA = Pan American World Airways Inc. Records, Special Collections Division, University of Miami Libraries

R&S I = Charles F. Romanus and Riley Sunderland, *The United States Army in World War II, China-Burma-India Theater: Stilwell's Mission to China*

R&S II = Charles F. Romanus and Riley Sunderland, *The United States Army in World War II, China-Burma-India Theater: Stilwell's Command Problem*

R&S III = Charles F. Romanus and Riley Sunderland, *The United States Army in World War II, China-Burma-India Theater: Times Runs Out in the C.B.I.*

Strategic Planning, 1941–1942 = Maurice Matloff and Edwin M. Snell, *The United States*

Army in World War II: The War Department: Strategic Planning for Coalition Warfare, 1941–1942

Strategic Planning, 1943–1944 = Maurice Matloff and Edwin M. Snell, *The United States Army in World War II: The War Department: Strategic Planning for Coalition Warfare, 1943–1944*

SCMP = *South China Morning Post*

SDASM = San Diego Air & Space Museum

SKH = Stanley K. Hornbeck Papers, the Hoover Institute, Stanford University

SWM = The private collection of Shirley Wilke Mosley

WLB = William Langhorne Bond Papers, the Hoover Institute, Stanford University

Chapter 1: Saint Patrick's Day, 1931

7–10   A ragged wind (Bond's arrival in Shanghai): Robert W. Moore, "Cosmopolitan Shanghai, Key Seaport of China," *National Geographic,* September 1932; Hewitt Mitchell Diary, the private collection of Lisa and Robert Mitchell; *All about Shanghai and Environs: A Standard Guidebook,* 1934–35 edition; Debbie Bixby, "H. M. Bixby Family in China, 1934–1938" (privately published, supplied to the author by Elizabeth "Bo" Bixby); William Langhorne Bond, *Wings for an Embattled China,* pp. 29–30; Stella Dong, *Shanghai: The Rise and Fall of a Decadent City,* pp. 94–95, 194–200; Rhodes Farmer, *Shanghai Harvest,* pp. 34, 44; William Stephen Grooch, *Winged Highway,* p. 173; Henry Wysham Lanier, *The Far Horizon,* pp. 177, 181; William Leary, *The Dragon's Wings,* p. 50; Harriet Sergeant, *Shanghai,* pp. 10–11, 49; Kemp Tolley, *Yangtze Patrol: The U.S. Navy in China,* p. 209; Simon Winchester, *The River at the Center of the World,* pp. 38–39; author's interviews with Langhorne Bond, January 27 and September 14, 2005; author's visit to Shanghai, April 2005.

7   Close-cropped strands (Bond's appearance): "Japan Doomed to Fail, Says Virginian on Return," undated clipping from an unidentified newspaper, WLB, 1938 file; Martha Gellhorn, "Flight into Peril," *Collier's,* May 31, 1941; Theodore White, "China's Last Lifeline," *Fortune,* May 1943; Grooch, *Winged Highway,* p. 179; George Robertson, "Append 322," *C.N.A.C. Cannonball,* in the 1970s, exact date uncertain; many period photos of William Bond.

10   Bond had been: Bond, *Wings for an Embattled China,* pp. 19–20; Leary, *The Dragon's Wings,* pp. 49–50.

11   Wall Street big: Harold Bixby, "Top Side Ricksha," p. 3; Louis R. Eltscher and Edward M. Young, *Curtiss-Wright: Greatness and Decline,* pp. 3, 39–40; John Kenneth Galbraith, *The Great Crash,* p. 46; Lanier, *The Far Horizon,* p. 211; Leary, *The Dragon's Wings,* p. 17.

12   Bond spent 1928: Bond, *Wings for an Embattled China,* pp. 20–21; Bond interview, October 23, 1972, PAA, Box 19, Folder 3, p. 5; author's interview with Langhorne Bond, January 27, 2005.

12   "Could you finish": Bond interview, October 23, 1972, PAA, Box 19, Folder 3, p. 5.

12   First things first: Bond, *Wings for an Embattled China,* p. 20.

12   **Curtiss merged with:** "$70,000,000 Air Deal Combines Keystone, Wright, and Curtiss," *NYT*, June 27, 1929; Theodore White, "China's Last Lifeline"; Eltscher and Young, *Curtiss-Wright: Greatness and Decline*, pp. 3, 39–41, 51–52; Leary, *The Dragon's Wings*, pp. 8, 40, 69.

12   **Unfortunately, the gilded:** Galbraith, *The Great Crash*, pp. 88, 141; David M. Kennedy, *Freedom from Fear*, p. 38.

13   **For Curtiss-Wright:** Bond interview, October 23, 1972, PAA, Box 19, Folder 3; White, "China's Last Lifeline"; Bond, *Wings for an Embattled China*, pp. 20–21; Eltscher and Young, *Curtiss-Wright: Greatness and Decline*, pp. 51–59; Leary, *The Dragon's Wings*, pp. 48–50.

13   **One of Curtiss-Wright's:** Bond interview, October 23, 1972, PAA, Box 19, Folder 3; *CWR*, August 6, 1932; William Leary, "George Conrad Westervelt, Captain USN: At the Beginning of Chinese Aviation," *American Aviation Historical Society Journal*, Summer 1972; Bond, *Wings for an Embattled China*, pp. 19–23, 29–30, 39; Leary, *The Dragon's Wings*, pp. 33, 35, 39, 43, 49–50.

Chapter 2: "You Won't Be Able to Handle the Pilots"

15–18   **The Bonds were:** Bond to General John Beaumont, December 13, 1937, WLB; Bond interview, October 23, 1972, PAA, Box 19, Folder 3; author's interviews with Langhorne Bond, December 2, 2004, January 27, 2005, and September 14, 2005; "Japan Doomed to Failure, Says Virginian on Return," unidentified newspaper clipping, WLB, 1938 file; Martha Gellhorn, "Flight into Peril," *Collier's*, May 31, 1941, p. 87; Theodore White, "China's Last Lifeline," *Fortune*, May 1943.

18   **"Don't take a":** William Langhorne Bond, *Wings for an Embattled China*, p. 32.

18   **Bond's capacity to:** author's interview with Langhorne Bond, January 27, 2005.

18   **While Westervelt remained:** Bond, *Wings for an Embattled China*, pp. 31–32.

18–25   **Perched near China's** (history overview, China and Shanghai. All cited sources were studied in their entirety; the listed citations are for specific instances of fact): *All about Shanghai and Environs: A Standard Guidebook, 1934–35 edition;* W. H. Auden and Christopher Isherwood, *Journey to a War*, p. 237; Harold Bixby, "Top Side Ricksha," chap. 3, p. 6; Stella Dong, *Shanghai: The Rise and Fall of a Decadent City*, pp. 11–13, 83–84, 94–95; John King Fairbank, *The Great Chinese Revolution: 1800–1985*, pp. 182–84; Jonathan Fenby, *Generalissimo: Chiang Kai-shek and the China He Lost*, pp. 142–48, 161–71; Percy Finch, *Shanghai and Beyond*, p. 12; Edwin P. Hoyt, *Japan's War*, pp. 16, 26–27, 35–37; Harold Isaacs, "The Peasant War in China," *New International*, pp. 25–27, www.marxists.org, accessed August 2005; Marius B. Janson, *The Making of Modern Japan*, pp. 432–33; Robert W. Moore, "Shanghai, Key Seaport of China," *National Geographic*, September 1932; John B. Powell, *My Twenty-five Years in China*, pp. 153–54; Harriet Sergeant, *Shanghai*, pp. 14–26, 74, 89, 96, 151, 166, 210–11, 218–22; Jonathan D. Spence, *The Search for Modern China*, pp. 122–23, 131, 149, 157, 161–62, 165–81, 184–93, 222–24, 230–35, 239, 271, 298,

310–19, 323, 348–54; Barbara Tuchman, *Stilwell and the American Experience in China, 1911–1945*, pp. 35, 40, 58, 73–74, 116, 152, 167; Theodore White and Annalee Jacoby, *Thunder out of China*, pp. 20–30, 116.

25   National political reality: *CWR*, October 28, 1933; Bond interview, October 23, 1972, PAA, Box 19, Folder 3. "When I first got there, there wasn't such a thing hardly as China."

25   One of Chiang's: *CWR*, May 2, 1931, and October 7, 1933; *The Shanghai Evening Post*, February 3, 1934; Westervelt's address to the U.S. Chamber of Commerce in San Francisco, May 19, 1932, SDASM; White, "China's Last Lifeline"; William Leary, "George Conrad Westervelt, Capt., USN, at the Beginning of Chinese Aviation," *American Aviation Historical Society Journal*, Summer 1972; Tuchman, *Stilwell and the American Experience in China, 1911–1945*, p. 168.

25   "China is one": *CWR*, May 2, 1931.

25   Taken together when: "Shanghai," *Fortune*, January 1935.

25–26   As a new: Bond, *Wings for an Embattled China*, p. 31; author's interview with Elizabeth "Bo" Bixby, January 24, 2006; http://www.earnshaw.com/shanghai-ed-india/tales/t-all08.htm, accessed February 16, 2006; "Shanghai," *Fortune*, January 1935; author's trip to Shanghai, April 2005; http://bbs.zanhei.com/showthread.php?t=101, accessed September 10, 2005.

26   Captain Westervelt left: Bond, *Wings for an Embattled China*, pp. 44–47.

27   "Those are your": Bond, *Wings for an Embattled China*, p. 45.

27   "You won't be": Bond, *Wings for an Embattled China*, p. 46.

Chapter 3: "This Airline Is a Partnership"

28   "First is the": William Langhorne Bond, *Wings for an Embattled China*, p. 47; William Leary, *The Dragon's Wings*, p. 51, citing Bond to Leary, March 20, 1969; author's interview with Langhorne Bond, January 27, 2005, and with Frieda and T. T. Chen, October 5, 2005.

28   Ernest "Allie" Allison: author's interview with Moon Chin, September 15, 2005; author's interviews with Allison's daughter, Nancy Allison Wright, October 6–9, 2005; William Bond, "E. M. Allison," and an unidentified newspaper obituary, both in the *C.N.A.C. Cannonball*, 1976; Leary, *The Dragon's Wings*, pp. 68–69.

29   the two men pushed: Leary, *The Dragon's Wings*, p. 18; Harold M. Bixby, "Top Side Ricksha," chap. 4, pp. 1–10; Bond, *Wings for an Embattled China*, pp. 25, 32, 51; Richard I. Hope, "Developing Airways in China," *Chinese Economic Journal*, January 1930, ANY.

30   Aloft, flying inland: Ernest M. Allison, "Story of Another First Flight," *Wings over Asia*, Vol. 3, p. 11; Bond, *Wings for an Embattled China*, pp. 50–60; Percy Finch, *Shanghai and Beyond*, pp. 219–21; Anne Morrow Lindbergh, *North to the Orient*, pp. 112–14, 117–24; *CWR*, Summer and Autumn 1931. The mortality statistics vary: The

China page of the World Bank says the floods killed 400,000: http.worldbank.org.cn /english/content/427n1214549.shtml, accessed September 29, 2005; Tuchman, *Stilwell and the American Experience in China,* p. 166, claims 2 million dead; Hallett Abend, *My Life in China, 1926–1941,* pp. 154–55, says 30 million people lost their homes; Jonathan D. Spence, *The Search for Modern China,* p. 434, claims 14 million refugees.

31   Nothing was more: Frank Dorn, *The Sino-Japanese War: From Marco Polo Bridge to Pearl Harbor,* p. 28; Edwin Hoyt, *Japan's War: The Great Pacific Conflict,* pp. 80–97; John B. Powell, *My Twenty-five Years in China,* p. 190; Stella Dong, *Shanghai: The Rise and Fall of a Decadent City,* pp. 212–13; Marius B. Jansen, *The Making of Modern Japan,* pp. 577–86; Earl Albert Selle, *Donald of China,* pp. 267–68; Spence, *The Search for Modern China,* pp. 391–94.

31   Four days after: David M. Kennedy, *Freedom from Fear,* p. 77.

31   Patriotic Chinese hit: Dong, *Shanghai,* p. 213.

32   Hating the idea: Ernest M. Allison, "Story of Another First Flight," *Wings over Asia,* Vol. 3, p. 11; Bond, *Wings for an Embattled China,* pp. 42–43, 65–70; Leary, *The Dragon's Wings,* pp. 55–60; Leary, "George Conrad Westervelt, Capt., USN, at the Beginning of Chinese Aviation," *American Aviation Historical Society Journal,* Summer 1972; "CNAC Story Prepared for Southern Flight," September 7, 1943, PAA, Box 205, Folder 11; Theodore H. White, "China's Last Lifeline," *Fortune,* May 1943; *CWR,* October 7, 1938. George Westervelt had returned to China to represent Curtiss-Wright and help guide Bond.

32   edged toward Jehol: Bixby, "Top Side Ricksha," chap. 10, p. 29; Selle, *Donald of China,* p. 280; Spence, *The Search for Modern China,* p. 394.

32–34   Considering the threat: Bond, *Wings for an Embattled China,* pp. 73–75.

33   Japan's effective employment: Evan S. Young to Arthur N. Young, April 13, 1933, ANY.

33   Harold M. Bixby: Bixby, "Top Side Ricksha"; Bixby interview "Airline Operations," PAA, Box 20, Folder 1; Frederic MacMaster, "Pan Am's China Man," *Air Line Pilot,* August 1976; "Harold Bixby, a Chief Supporter of Lindbergh's '27 Flight, Dies," *NYT,* November 20, 1965; Robert Daley, *An American Saga: Juan Trippe and His Pan Am Empire,* pp. 119–20; Marilyn Bender and Selig Altschul, *The Chosen Instrument: The Rise and Fall of an American Entrepreneur,* p. 206; A. Scott Berg, *Lindbergh,* pp. 95–96, 98; many period photographs.

33   "aviation missionary": Bixby, "Top Side Ricksha," p. 4.

34   "I never held" and "establishment": author's interview with Langhorne Bond, January 27, 2005.

34   Pan American Airways: Trippe to Morgan, February 7, 1933, SDASM; Bond interview, October 23, 1972, PAA, Box 19, Folder 3; Daley, *An American Saga,* pp. 119–20; Bender and Altschul, *The Chosen Instrument,* pp. 158–64, 236–39; Bond, *Wings for an Embattled China,* p. 83.

35   **"With all due"**: Bond interview, October 23, 1972, PAA, Box 19, Folder 3.

35   **twenty thousand miles**: Leary, *The Dragon's Wings*, p. 72.

35   **gamely shook dice**: Henry Wysham Lanier, *The Far Horizon*, p. 180.

35   **stormed Jehol**: Spence, *The Search for Modern China*, p. 394; Tuchman, *Stilwell and the American Experience in China, 1911–1945*, p. 175; Selle, *Donald of China*, p. 280; Abend, *My Twenty-five Years in China*, p. 203.

35   **March 31, 1933**: Some sources say Pan Am bought China Airways Federal, Inc., on April 1, 1933, but preferred to publicize the acquisition as having occurred the day before because of Oriental superstitions. Bixby apparently didn't think the distinction particularly important. He notes that Pan American acquired China Airways Federal on April 1, 1933, in a very exacting letter he wrote at a critical point in company history (Bixby to Peng Sho-pei, September 13, 1937, WLB), but in a memorandum titled "Acquisition of the China Airways Federal, Inc., USA by Pan American Airways" (PAA, Box 58, Folder 8, undated, but certainly written after August 8, 1941), he says the acquisition date was March 31, 1933, as does "Contract between the Ministry of Communications, National Government, Republic of China and Pan American Airways Corporation, December 21, 1945," ANY. In this story, March 31 wins the tiebreaker—it happens to be the author's birthday.

Chapter 4: Cake and Champagne

36   **If the sale**: Cyril McNear to Juan Trippe, April 1, 1932; Morgan to Trippe, February 1, 1933; Trippe to Tom Morgan, February 7, 1933; Trippe to Morgan, January 26, 1933; Trippe to Robert Payne, February 20, 1933; all letters in PAA, Box 20; CAB Docket No. 1706, "Brief History of Pan American Airways, Inc.," PAA, Box 205, Folder 14; Arthur N. Young to Evan S. Young, March 17, 1933, ANY; "Acquisition of China Airways Federal, Inc., USA, by Pan American Airways," SDASM; "High Rates Cheap on China Airline," *NYT*, August 6, 1946; William Langhorne Bond, *Wings for an Embattled China*, pp. 78–79; William Leary, *The Dragon's Wings*, pp. 72–74. Pan American closed the deal without spending a penny of company cash, fobbing three thousand shares of stock on Curtiss-Wright in exchange for Intercontinent Aviation, Inc. (Pan Am's stock then traded at $28 per share), and including an option to buy ten thousand Pan Am shares at $25 before March 31, 1935. Pan Am recorded its initial investment as $282,258.69, worth about 4.6 million modern dollars.

37   **Shortly thereafter**: Bixby interview, 1957, PAA, Box 20, Folder 1; memo titled "C.N.A.C.," dated August 7, 1942, PAA, Box 58, Folder 8; Bond, *Wings for an Embattled China*, p. 82; Harold M. Bixby, "Top Side Ricksha," chap. 4, p. 5; Leary, *The Dragon's Wings*, pp. 75–76.

38–39   **Bixby was telling**: Bixby to Arthur N. Young, April 18, 1933, ANY; Bixby, "Top Side Ricksha," chap. 6, p. 58; William Stephen Grooch, *Winged Highway*, pp. 166, 176;

Leary, *The Dragon's Wings*, p. 76; *CWR*, October 7, 1933; and *Shanghai Evening Post*, February 3, 1934. Route Three was 1,628 kilometers long—1,008 miles: "Aviation in China," Vol. 3, No. 12, *Consul of International Affairs*, Nanking, May 1, 1937, ANY.

39   All through April: Hallett Abend, *My Life in China, 1926–1941*, pp. 204–5; Barbara Tuchman, *Stilwell and the American Experience in China, 1911–1945*, p. 175.

39   Bixby still didn't: Bixby, "Top Side Ricksha," chap. 6, pp. 75–85.

39   Chinese way of: Bond, *Wings for an Embattled China*, p. 82.

40–41   With two years: *CWR*, October 7, 1933; Bixby interview, 1957, PAA, Box 20, Folder 1; Ernest M. Allison, "Landing in a Walled City," *Wings over Asia*, Vol. 1, pp. 40–41; Leary, *The Dragon's Wings*, pp. 87–90; Bixby, "Top Side Ricksha," chap. 3, p. 6, and chap. 6, pp. 1–57; Bond, *Wings for an Embattled China*, pp. 49, 79–81; author's conversations and emails with Nancy Allison Wright, November 4 and 5, 2005.

41–42   clustered around the: Bond's letters, WLB; *See China by Plane*, CNAC travel brochure, 1934 or 1935, the private collection of Lisa and Robert Mitchell; Rhodes Farmer, *Shanghai Harvest*, pp. 153–58; Paul Frillman and Graham Peck, *China: The Remembered Life*, pp. 3–46; W. H. Auden and Christopher Isherwood, *Journey to a War*, pp. 49–71; author's interviews with Moon Chin, January 7, 2005, and April 19, 2006.

42–43   146 miles of: *Shanghai Evening Post*, February 3, 1934; *See China by Plane*, CNAC travel brochure, 1934 or 1935; author interviews with Moon Chin, September 17, 2004, and July 15, 2005; Judy Bonavia and Richard Hayman, *Yangzi: The Yangtze River and the Three Gorges*, p. 331; Richard L. Burdsall, Arthur Emmons, Terris Moore, and Jack Theodore Young, *Men against the Clouds: The Conquest of Minya Konka*, pp. 18–23; Farmer, *Shanghai Harvest*, p. 212; Bixby, "Top Side Ricksha," chap. 6, pp. 4–5, 15, 16, 21; Theodore White and Annalee Jacoby, *Thunder out of China*, p. 4; Simon Winchester, *The River at the Center of the World*, pp. 262, 284.

43–44   a dense, medieval: *See China by Plane*, CNAC travel brochure, 1934 or 1935; Emily Hahn, *The Soong Sisters*, pp. 297–98; W. Somerset Maugham, *On a Chinese Screen*, pp. 231–35; Gerald Samson, *The Far East Ablaze*, pp. 160–66; Edgar Snow, *Battle for Asia*, p. 155; Bixby, "Top Side Ricksha," chap. 6, pp. 30–33; White and Jacoby, *Thunder out of China*, pp. 3–5. "Opium was everywhere. The smell was everywhere": author's interview with Moon Chin, July 15, 2005.

43   The traditional trip: *CWR*, October 7, 1933.

44   "twenty concubines": author's interview with Moon Chin, July 15, 2005.

44   fifty and seventy million souls: The numbers vary. Bixby says seventy million in "Top Side Ricksha," chap. 6, p. 4; White and Jacoby say fifty million in *Thunder out of China*, p. 5; Bond, in *Wings for an Embattled China*, p. 49, says fifty million; Edgar Snow uses the figures given, between fifty and seventy million, in *Battle for Asia*, p. 166; the 1930 census gives the U.S. population as 123,202,624: http://www.census.gov/population/censusdata/table-2.pdf, accessed August 24, 2005.

44 "The marshal wishes": Bond, *Wings for an Embattled China,* p. 79, Bixby, "Top Side Ricksha," chap. 6, pp. 39–40.

46 White flowers covered: Bixby interview, 1957, PAA, Box 20, Folder 1; author's interview with Moon Chin, July 15, 2005; Percy Finch, *Shanghai and Beyond,* p. 278.

46 the patchwork agriculture: Walter C. Lowdermilk, "China Fights Erosion with U.S. Aid," *National Geographic,* June 1945.

49 "They separated the coolie": Bixby, "Top Side Ricksha," chap. 6, pp. 51–52.

Chapter 5: Route Three

50–52 Pan American's seven-man: Bixby interview, 1957, PAA, Box 20, Folder 1; Bond interview, 1972, PAA, Box 19, Folder 3; Harold M. Bixby, "Top Side Ricksha," chap. 6, pp. 57–75; William Langhorne Bond, *Wings for an Embattled China,* pp. 84–85; William Stephen Grooch, *Winged Highway,* pp. 174–200; William Leary, *The Dragon's Wings,* pp. 77–78; author's interviews with Peter Goutiere, January 22 and 23, 2005, and with Joe Rosbert, August 14 and 15, 2004. Bixby must have complained to Pan Am leadership, because on July 13, 1933, Acting Secretary of State Phillips telegrammed Nelson T. Johnson, the American ambassador to China, to say that "Pan American [in Washington] informs Department that . . . it attempted . . . to inaugurate . . . a postal service between Shanghai and Canton but that project failed due to certain unreasonable demands of Minister of Communications following pressure upon the latter from the Sino-German Eurasia Company which is aggressively interested in obtaining similar rights": secretary of state's telegram to China, *FRUS,* 1933, Vol. 3, p. 603.

52–53 Trying to reach: Trippe to Wood Humphrey, August 23, 1933, SDASM; "Aunt Merly to Folks," August 17, 1933, NAW; Marylin Bender and Selig Altschul, *The Chosen Instrument,* pp. 207–8; Leary, *The Dragon's Wings,* pp. 76, 83–84; Bixby, "Top Side Ricksha," chap. 6, p. 72, chap. 8, pp. 41–45; Bond, *Wings for an Embattled China,* pp. 83, 85–86; author's interview with Elizabeth "Bo" Bixby, Bixby's second-oldest daughter, January 24, 2006.

53 Stymied, Bixby fished: Bixby interview, 1957, PAA, Box 20, Folder 1.

53 Not having his: Debbie Bixby, "H. M. Bixby Family in China, 1934–1938," p. 1.

54–55 The Kuomintang considered: *CWR,* September 2, September 9, and October 28, 1933.

55 William Bond remained: Edward P. Howard to his mother, September 6, 1933, the private collection of Edward P. Howard IV. Howard was first in line for the job: "Pan American Airways: This is what I want more than anything as it is purely constructive [developing airlines in the Pacific]. I know their chief in China [Bixby] quite well and he wants me over here to act as No. 2 and to be ready to take over the whole show when he returns to the U.S. The Pan Am heads in N.Y. have approved me for the particular job but can do nothing further about it until the political situation in China gives some indication as to how their affairs in China are to turn. The chances of my getting this are pretty good." As stunning luck would have it, the letter is in the possession of Edward P. Howard IV, the husband of Dina Bernstein Howard, a preschool classmate of mine and one of my lifelong friends. Dina and I discovered the China connection during our carpool to our twentieth high school reunion.

55   **the two men inked:** Bixby, "Top Side Ricksha," chap. 6, p. 57; Bond, *Wings for an Embattled China*, p. 83; Leary, *The Dragon's Wings*, pp. 79–80; there is some discrepancy about the date: Leary, *The Dragon's Wings*, p. 79, says it was signed on October 8, 1933, citing Pan Am records, but P. Y. Wong to Arthur N. Young, January 6, 1939, ANY, says it was signed on October 14, 1933.

56   **"Stop, stop, stop":** Bixby interview, 1957, PAA, Box 20, Folder 1.

56–59   **With an arrangement:** author's interview with Moon Chin, April 19, 2006; "Crash Victims Tell Story of Thrilling Escape from Death" and "Condition of Injured," November 26, 1933, clippings from an unidentified Shanghai newspaper, SWM; Bixby, "Top Side Ricksha," chap. 6, pp. 98–101; Bond, *Wings for an Embattled China*, pp. 87–90; Leary, *The Dragon's Wings*, p. 82; Grooch, *Winged Highway*, pp. 207–14; Henry Wysham Lanier, *The Far Horizon*, p. 181. The injury details in *Wings* and *Winged Highway* are not in accord with contemporary newspaper accounts. I have cleaved to the more contemporary sources.

59–60   **In the aftermath:** Bond, *Wings for an Embattled China*, pp. 90–91; CWR, October 7, 1933; Dai En-kai, "Many Obstacles Overcome since Beginning; 3,050 Miles Operated," clipping from an unidentified Shanghai newspaper, 1934, SWM.

59   **"You're the operations":** Bond, *Wings for an Embattled China*, p. 90.

60   **"You, Bondy":** Bond, *Wings for an Embattled China*, p. 91.

61   **before sailing home:** Bixby, "Top Side Ricksha," chap. 7, p. 2. (Bixby left Shanghai on January 2, 1934.)

61   **Grooch had his:** "Wife and Two Children Die in Fall in China," *NYT*, January 20, 1934; author's interview with Elizabeth "Bo" Bixby, January 24, 2006; Bond, *Wings for an Embattled China*, pp. 97–99.

61–63   **It sold just:** Bond, *Wings for an Embattled China*, pp. 99–100; Grooch, *Winged Highway*, pp. 234–40; "Big C.N.A.C. Sikorsky Lost in Hangchow Bay," *The China Press*, April 11, 1934; "Sikorksy Search Party Battles Seas in Day-and-Night Ordeal," April 14, 1934, clipping from an unidentified Shanghai newspaper, SWM; "Remnants of Lost Plane Picked Up," April 19, 1934; "C.N.A.C.'s Man Ending Survey of Channels," April 20, 1934; "Missing Pilot's Body Found," clippings from unidentified Shanghai newspapers, SWM.

62   **"raining pitchforks":** "Sikorksy Search Party Battles Seas in Day-and-Night Ordeal," April 14, 1934, clipping from an unidentified Shanghai newspaper, SWM (quoting Grooch).

Chapter 6: A Pan Am Man and a Woman Named Kitsi

64   Bond left Shanghai: William Langhorne Bond, *Wings for an Embattled China*, p. 101; author's interview with Langhorne Bond, January 27 and September 14, 2005. There was no Golden Gate Bridge to sail under—construction began on January 5, 1933, and cable spinning between the two completed towers began in August 1935: www.goldengatebridge .org, accessed August 26, 2008; Richard Dillon, Thomas Moulin, and Don DeNevi, *High Steel*, pp. 79–165.

65   The excitement of: Bond, *Wings for an Embattled China*, pp. 101–2; Robert Daley, *An American Saga: Juan Trippe and His Pan Am Empire*, pp. 36–39; Marylin Bender and Selig Altschul, *The Chosen Instrument*, p. 157; Bixby to Nellie, April 6, 1938, WLB.

65   After New York: Bond, *Wings for an Embattled China*, pp. 102–7.

65   Three years was: Bond, *Wings for an Embattled China*, pp. 106–10; author's interviews with Langhorne Bond, December 2, 2004, and January 27 and September 14, 2005, and with Frieda and T. T. Chen, October 2005; 1930s photos of Kitsi; photographs in WLB; "These Fascinating Ladies," undated newspaper clipping in the 1938 file, WLB; *Empress of Japan:* http://college.hmco.com/history/readerscomp/ships/html/sh_030800_empress ofjap.htm; http://www.simplonpc.co.uk/EmpressOfScotlandPCs.html#anchor1289727; http://www.angelfire.com/pe2/pjs1/index.html; all accessed October 2005; http://hhmi .org/news/090902.html, accessed July 11, 2005. Deepening Hayes Manor's connection to early aviation, it was bought by the Hughes Foundation—of Howard Hughes fame, he of transcontinental speed records, TWA, and "the Spruce Goose." Also, for those hoping to read about their romantic "slow boat to China," please note that songwriter Frank Loesser didn't pen his famous song until 1945. Before that, "I'd like to get him on a slow boat to China" was a gambler's expression used to describe a steady loser.

67   "Wonderful!": Bond, *Wings for an Embattled China*, p. 108.

67   the Little Club: http://users.adelphia.net/~jharland/familyfolder/johnbrownehome folder/johnbrownehomepage.html; http://www.constantnoise.com/stage6.htm, both accessed September 10, 2005; "Shanghai," *Fortune* magazine, January 1935; author's interview with Elizabeth "Bo" Bixby, January 24, 2006: "That was the best nightclub in town!" The opening sequence of the movie *White Countess*, an evocative and romantic drama set in 1930s Shanghai and starring Natasha Richardson and Ralph Fiennes, mentions the Little Club by name.

68   Although Bond had: author's interview with Elizabeth "Bo" Bixby, January 24, 2006; author's correspondence with Nancy Allison Wright.

68   Allison had temporarily: Bond, *Wings for an Embattled China*, pp. 110–11. Bond's new job was the same position Bixby had been intending to offer to Edward P. Howard in the late summer of 1933. See note **William Bond remained** to page 55.

68   colonial administrator: author's interview with Langhorne Bond, January 27, 2005.

69   Transpacific requirements forced: author's interview with Langhorne Bond, December 2, 2004; Bond to Kitsi, October 27, 1937, WLB, which differs from Bond's description in *Wings for an Embattled China*, pp. 115–17. I've cleaved more closely to the 1937 account.

69   **rhymed telegraphic baby talk:** cable addressed "to Kitsi, c/o Lewis Clark, American Legation, Peiping," WLB.

69   **began to smell:** author's interview with Elizabeth "Bo" Bixby, January 24, 2006.

69   **"Mind you":** author's interview with Langhorne Bond, January 27, 2005.

70–72   **As the winter:** Bond, *Wings for an Embattled China*, p. 117; author's interview with Langhorne Bond, December 2, 2004.

Chapter 7: The Last of the Salad Days

73   **"little Bondy":** Florence Allison to her family, July 20, 1935, NAW.

73–74   **Douglas DC-2:** William Leary, *The Dragon's Wings*, p. 95; author's interviews with Moon Chin, September 17, 2004; author's interviews with Shirley Wilke Mosley, June 2004, and conversations at the various CNAC reunions, 2003–2008. There is an invitation to the event and many photographs in the Edward P. Howard collection.

74   **marketing campaign:** Stokely Morgan, "Memorandum to J.T.T.," September 13, 1935, PAA, Box 20; *CWR*, December 21, 1935.

74   **Hugh Woods:** Hugh Woods, *Wings over Asia*, Vol. 4, p. 1; many photos in SWM.

74–77   **relentless Shanghai social whirl:** Mary Howard to Mother Howard, November 29, 1932, private collection of Edward P. Howard; Hugh Woods, "Pre-War Shanghai and Hong Kong," *Wings over Asia*, Vol. 4, pp. 4–10, 12, 13–15; 1957 Bixby Interview, PAA, Box 20, Folder 1; *All about Shanghai and Environs: A Standard Guidebook*, 1934–1935 edition, text online at http://www.earnshaw.com/shanghai-ed-india/tales/t-all.htm, accessed November 7, 2005; Harold M. Bixby, "Top Side Ricksha"; Harriet Sergeant, *Shanghai*; Stella Dong, *Shanghai: Rise and Fall of a Decadent City*; Emily Hahn, *China to Me* and *No Hurry to Get Home*; Ken Cuthbertson, *Nobody Said Not to Go*; Percy Finch, *Shanghai and Beyond*; John B. Powell, *My Twenty-five Years in China*; Hallett Abend, *My Life in China, 1926–1941*; Kemp Tolley, *Yangtze Patrol: The U.S. Navy in China*; *CWR*, 1929–41; author's interviews with Shirley Wilke Mosley, Nancy Allison Wright, Elizabeth "Bo" Bixby, Moon Chin, Frieda Chen, T. T. Chen, and Langhorne Bond: "Dad always said it was a wide-open town, and that the guys flying for him were a freebooting bunch."

77–80   **Moon Fun Chin:** Moon Chin's Oral History at the Louis A. Turpen Aviation Museum; author's interviews with Moon Chin, September 10 and September 17, 2004, and January 7, July 15, and November 1, 2005; many telephone follow-ups; Bond to Kitsi, Saturday, August 28, 1937, WLB; Iris Chang, *The Chinese in America*, pp. 137–39, 145–47; Simon Winchester, *A Crack at the Edge of the World*, pp. 343–50. Moon Chin's birth certificate shows his birthday as April 13, 1913, but that's due to the Chinese custom of considering an infant to be one year old on the day he or she is born.

79   "So, Moon": author's interview with Moon Chin, September 10, 2004.

80–81   inaugurate transpacific service: *CWR,* December 7, 1935; CAB Docket Nos. 851 et al., "History of the Transpacific Air Services to and through Hawaii," written August 12, 1944, Louis A. Turpen Aviation Museum; Marylin Bender and Selig Altschul, *The Chosen Instrument,* pp. 244–57; Barnaby Conrad, *Pan Am: An Aviation Legend,* pp. 81–104; Robert Daley, *An American Saga,* pp. 165–90; Richard Dillon, Thomas Moulin, and Don DeNevi, *High Steel,* p. 23. The San Francisco–Oakland Bay Bridge's first cable was completed on November 12, 1935, the second on January 20, 1936.

81   "I thrill": Conrad, *Pan Am,* 87.

81   Bixby pressed the: Memorandum, Bixby to Young, January 22, 1936, ANY; "The British Ambassador (Lindsay) to the Secretary of State," *FRUS,* 1936, Vol. 4, p. 643; CAB Docket Nos. 851 et al., "History of the Transpacific Air Services to and through Hawaii," August 12, 1944, the Louis A. Turpin Aviation Museum.

81   "button for an": Bender and Altschul, *The Chosen Instrument,* p. 255.

81–82   A week before: the corrected manuscript of Betty Trippe's diary, pp. 21–22, PAA, Box 30, Folder 9; Florence Allison to her sister, Merly, October 29, 1936, NAW. The first passengers flew from California to Manila on October 21, 1936: CAB Docket Nos. 851 et al., "History of the Transpacific Air Services to and through Hawaii," August 12, 1944, p. 23, Louis A. Turpen Aviation Museum.

82–84   However fair the: Hallett Abend, *My Twenty-five Years in China,* pp. 197, 231–34, 245; Bixby, "Top Side Ricksha," chap. 8, p. 50, chap. 9, p. 16; Jonathan Fenby, *Generalissimo: Chiang Kai-shek and the China He Lost,* pp. 276–77, 283; Royal Leonard, *I Flew for China;* Earl Albert Selle, *Donald of China,* p. 324; Jonathan D. Spence, *The Search for Modern China,* pp. 420, 422–24; Barbara Tuchman, *Stilwell and the American Experience in China, 1911–1945,* pp. 203–4; author's interviews with Moon Chin; W. H. Donald to Stanley K. Hornbeck, January 23, 1939, SKH, Box 150: "The reaction was much like that after the release of the Generalissimo from Sian—a sweeping cry for the continuation of resistance." The long run of history is likely to view the Sian kidnapping as a turning point of the twentieth century—it prevented Chiang from exterminating Mao's Communists.

84   by mid-June: *CWR,* July 3, 1937.

84   Colonel Lam: Bond, *Wings for an Embattled China,* pp. 141–42; Bond to Bixby, July 3, 1938, WLB: "The aviation commission has been trying for years to get control of commercial aviation." Simple as it seems, Colonel Lam Whi-shing's name presents a perfect quandary for those fascinated with producing a "correct" English spelling for Chinese names. Moon Chin, in interviews, seems to pronounce the colonel's name "Lam." Bond spells it "Lem Wei-shing" in *Wings,* but "Lam" in a letter to John C. Leslie on January 6, 1975, and "Lam Wai Shing" in a letter to Lam himself on September 7, 1937. Bixby spelled it "Lum" in a letter to Stokely Morgan on October 11, 1937, but "Lam Wei-shing" on December 3, 1937. The colonel's signature is clearly "Lam Whi shing" at the bottom of letters to Bond on September 26 and 28, 1937, both times without a hyphen, and both times without a third capital letter. I have allowed the colonel to spell his own name, although I suspect a secretary did the signing—the handwriting is loopy and rounded and looks like it was penned by a woman's hand. I added the hyphen because it seems to me most Chinese names at the time—in English—used the hyphen, and of all the options, it is the one that most pleases my eye.

85   Pan Am leadership: unidentified newspaper clipping dated July 1, 1937, WLB; Bond, *Wings for an Embattled China,* p. 122.

Chapter 8: Things Fall Apart

89   A dozen miles: *CWR,* July 17 and August 7, 1937; Hallett Abend, "Japanese Planes Bomb the Chinese in New Outbreak," *NYT,* July 26, 1937; "Human Toll Heavy," *NYT,* July 30, 1937; *NYT,* August 9, 1937; *SCMP,* August 9, 1937; Chiang Kai-shek, *President Chiang Kai-shek's Selected Speeches and Messages, 1937–1945,* p. 5; O. Edmund Clubb, *Twentieth-Century China,* pp. 213–20; Jonathan Fenby, *Generalissimo: Chiang Kai-shek and the China He Lost,* pp. 287–89; Edwin P. Hoyt, *Japan's War,* pp. 142–49; F. F. Liu, *A Military History of Modern China,* pp. 197–98; Jonathan D. Spence, *The Search for Modern China,* pp. 445–46; Barbara Tuchman, *Stilwell and the American Experience in China, 1911–1945,* pp. 207–11; http://www.china.org.cn/english/features/beijng/31253.htm.

90   Half a world: William Langhorne Bond, *Wings for an Embattled China,* p. 130.

90–91   On July 24: *CWR,* July 31, 1937; "Outstanding Events of the Sino-Japanese War at Shanghai," *CWR,* September 11, 1937; *SCMP,* August 6 and August 9, 1937; Rhodes Farmer, *Shanghai Harvest,* pp. 34–36; author's interviews with Moon Chin: September 17, 2004, January 7, 2005, and April 19, 2006.

91–92   The next day: "Two Slayings Investigated," *NYT,* August 12, 1937; "32 Tokyo Warships Mass at Shanghai; Guns Fire Nankow," *NYT,* August 12, 1937; "Clash at Airdrome Results in Deaths of Two Japanese, Two Chinese," *CWR,* August 14, 1937; Bond, *Wings for an Embattled China,* pp. 129–30. (Bond remembered Li as a colonel, but *SCMP, CWR,* and *NYT* all rank him major.)

92–93   On August 11: Bixby to Morgan, August 25, 1937; Bixby to Mr. Peng Sho-poi [*sic*], September 13, 1937; both in WLB.

92   China didn't care: author's interview with Moon Chin, April 19, 2006.

93   China's new air force: Jack Jouett, one of the principal American aviation advisors who'd worked in China, certainly thought so, and so he told Bond, as Bond reminded his wife in a letter written three months later: "Do you remember Jack Jouett saying the Chinese were going to win this war because their air force was so much better and I disagreed with him?": Bond to Kitsi, "Aboard the S.S. *Changsha,* I think it is November 14," 1937, WLB.

93   Two of Chiang: *SCMP,* August 14, 1937; Farmer, *Shanghai Harvest,* p. 42; photographs of the refugees taken by Swiss photographer Karl Kengelbacher, photos posted online at http://www.japan-guide.com/a/shanghai/image.html?5, accessed April 24, 2006.

93   Dense, sweating rivers: Anna to Mother, cc Kitsi Bond, August 14, 1937, WLB; author's interview with Moon Chin, April 19, 2006.

93   flood of money: *SCMP,* August 14, 1937; "Chinese Banks in Shanghai Close," *NYT,* August 14, 1937.

93   Soong ordered Colonel Lam: Bixby to Morgan, August 25, 1937, WLB; Memorandum, "C.N.A.C.," August 7, 1942, PAA, Box 58, Folder 8; Bixby interview, 1957; undated Bixby interview, "Bixby in China: Personal Tales"; both in PAA, Box 20, Folder 1.

93–95   Shanghai passed: Anna to Mother, cc Kitsi Bond, August 14, 1937, WLB; *SCMP,* August 14, 1937; Farmer, *Shanghai Harvest,* p. 39; Emily Hahn, *China to Me,* pp. 52–60.

95   "Bix! Three Chinese": Bixby interview, "Bixby in China: Personal Tales," PAA, Box 20, Folder 1.

95   Bixby had no: Bixby to Morgan, August 25, 1937, WLB; "Warships Targets," *NYT,* August 15, 1937; Farmer, *Shanghai Harvest,* p. 43; photo of *Idzumo* by Swiss photographer Karl Kengelbacher, posted in an online portfolio at http://www.japan-guide.com/a/shanghai/image.html.

95–96   At that moment: Bixby to Colonel W. S. Lum [*sic*], August 15, 1937, NAW; Bixby to Morgan, August 25, 1937; Bond to Kitsi, August 28, 1937; Bixby to Mr. Peng Sho-poi [*sic*], September 13, 1937; all in WLB; Memorandum "C.N.A.C.," August 7, 1942, PAA, Box 58, Folder 8; http://cnac.org/pottschmidtletter01.htm, accessed May 2006; Leary, *The Dragon's Wings,* p. 113.

96   "It's out of": 1957 Bixby interview, PAA, Box 20, Folder 1.

96–97   Brutal close-quarters: Florence Allison diary, August 15, 1937, NAW; "Chinese Surprised," *NYT,* August 16, 1937; "Shanghai Experiences Horrors of Modern Warfare in Pronounced Degree," *CWR,* August 21, 1937; Walter "Foxie" Kent, "Wings for China," *The Atlantic,* November 1937; Farmer, *Shanghai Harvest,* pp. 44–49; Percy Finch, *Shanghai and Beyond,* pp. 252–57; photographs taken by Chief Mechanic O. C. Wilke, SWM; photographs taken by Ernie Allison, NAW; photographs taken by Swiss photographer Karl Kengelbacher posted at http://www.japan-guide.com/a/shanghai.

97   Harold Bixby, his wife: handwritten postscript addressed to Kitsi in Anna to Dearest Mother, cc Kitsi, August 14, 1937, WLB. "The Bixbys are enjoying your house. Have been to some very nice dinners and cocktail parties there this summer."

97   Bixby went through: "Notes Written before May 1957 Interview with Bixby at Bolton Landing," PAA, Box 20, Folder 29; "Notes 10: Bixby in China—Personal Tales," PAA, Box 20, Folder 1.

97   his badly shaken: Bixby to Morgan, August 25, 1937, WLB; author's interview with Elizabeth "Bo" Bixby, January 24, 2006. Bo was in the house when the bullet flew in the open window. The bullet is still in the Bixby family's possession. Duly mounted, it's the centerpiece decoration in a bathroom in "Topside," the Bixby family retreat at Lake George, New York.

97   **Fifty-nine floors:** David W. Dunlap, "Juke Joint in the Sky," *NYT,* May 26, 2005; Michael J. Lewis, "Dancing to New Rules," *NYT,* May 26, 2005; Charles McGrath, "A Lunch Club for Higher-Ups," *NYT,* May 26, 2005; Claudia Roth Pierpont, "The Silver Spire," *The New Yorker,* November 18, 2002; many photos accessed online; the author's periodic encounters with the building, 1984–2006.

98–100   **Bond struggled** (Bond's Cloud Club conversation with Trippe and Morgan, distilled from the following sources): Bixby to Morgan, Letter B-23-37, October 11, 1937, WLB; Bond to John C. Leslie, January 6, 1975, PAA, Box 27, Folder 23; Bond, *Wings for an Embattled China,* pp. 130–31; Marylin Bender and Selig Altschul, *The Chosen Instrument,* pp. 209, 257, 285; Robert Daley, *An American Saga,* pp. 283–84; Willam Leary, *The Dragon's Wings,* pp. 114–15; author's interviews with Langhorne Bond, January 27 and September 14, 2005.

Chapter 9: The Cavalry

102   **At Hayes Manor:** Bond interview, October 23, 1972, PAA, Box 19, Folder 3.

102   **eighteen-hour flight:** William Leary, *The Dragon's Wings,* p. 115.

102   **boarded the *Philippine Clipper*:** "China Aviation Personnel Safe," *The Manila Bulletin,* August 26, 1937.

102   **Sikorsky S-42:** http://www.sikorskyarchives.com/s42.html, accessed October 9, 2006.

103   **eight days:** William Langhorne Bond, *Wings for an Embattled China,* p. 132.

103   **Allison met Bond:** Bond to Kitsi, Saturday, August 28, 1937, WLB; Bond, *Wings for an Embattled China,* pp. 133–34; Leary, *The Dragon's Wings,* pp. 114–16. Bond described a major confrontation between him and Allison in *Wings* and in a letter he wrote to William Leary in 1969, but no such argument is mentioned in the long letter he wrote to his wife on August 28, 1937, a letter that meticulously describes the CNAC situation and everything that had occurred since his Hong Kong arrival. Ernie Allison swore no such argument occurred (Nancy Allison Wright's many conversations with the author, and a letter Allison wrote to William Leary in 1970). If it actually happened, it seems odd that Bond didn't mention it to his wife—Kitsi and Florence Allison were close friends. Nor is there any mention or allusion to a major falling-out between him and Allison in any of Bond's other 1937 or 1938 correspondence. They saw each other regularly and seemingly maintained an ongoing friendship, as is documented in Bond's correspondence, Ernie and Florence Allison's letters, and Florence Allison's diary. Bond and Allison often shared a room in Chungking in 1937–38, and several times Bond "made face" for Allison with his superiors at Pan Am, lobbying to get Allie a job piloting "the big equipment" on a transoceanic run. In 1940, Bond hired Allison to inspect and oversee the overhaul and shipping of aircraft in and from the United States, and Bond rehired Allison as CNAC's operations manager in 1948, all of which lends credence to Allison's contention that no major falling-out ever occurred. I have opted to treat the "fight" like the contemporary correspondence—as if it never occurred.

103   most of the: Frank Havelick interview conducted by Nancy Allison Wright, April 17, 1991, NAW; Bixby to Morgan, August 25, 1937; Havelick to Andre Priester, December 9, 1937; both in WLB.

104–7   "Four years of" (Bond's conversation with Bixby, distilled): Bond to Kitsi, Saturday, August 28, 1937; Bixby to Mr. Peng Sho-pei, September 13, 1937; Bond to Kitsi, November 22, 1937; all in WLB; Bond, *Wings for an Embattled China*, pp. 139–40.

105   Bond chewed at: Bond to John C. Leslie, January 6, 1975, PAA, Box 27, Folder 23.

105   "Bondy, if you fail": Bond, *Wings for an Embattled China*, p. 139.

106–7   Bixby outlined Bond's (Bixby and Bond's phone conversation with Trippe, distilled): Bond, *Wings for an Embattled China*, pp. 139–40; Bond to Leslie, January 6, 1975, PAA, Box 27, Folder 23; Bond to Kitsi, November 23, 1937, WLB, summarizes the conversation and says Trippe agreed to Bixby's conditions "without any discussion." Confirmation that Trippe agreed to continue Bond's insurance and allow him to participate in "any new Pan American Airways Executive Association Stock Purchase Plan": Morgan to Assistant Comptroller, New York, December 31, 1937, cc President [Trippe] and Bond, WLB. Bond and Bixby may have traveled to Manila to call Trippe—I haven't been able to confirm whether it was possible to make telephone calls from Hong Kong to the United States in 1937.

107   After dark: Phillip Snow, *The Fall of Hong Kong*, pp. 1, 4; many period photos of Hong Kong; the author's trip to Hong Kong, 2005.

107   aviation traffic beginning: *SCMP*, November 4, 1937.

107   "Things here are": Bond to Kitsi, August 28, 1937, WLB.

108   Ernie Allison was: Bond to Florence Allison, July 18, 1976, NAW; Bond, *Wings for an Embattled China*, pp. 133–34.

108   Bixby, a made man: Bond, *Wings for an Embattled China*, p. 140; author's interviews with Langhorne Bond, December 2, 2004, and January 27, 2005.

108   only Hal Sweet: Morgan to Bixby, Personal & Confidential, October 15, 1937, WLB; Bond, *Wings for an Embattled China*, p. 135; "R.W. 'Potty' Pottschmidt in Conversation with R. Farrar," *C.N.A.C. Cannonball*, January 3, 1979.

109   "CNAC owes us": Bond, *Wings for an Embattled China*, pp. 140–41.

109   inseparable pilot duo: Bixby to Morgan, October 13, 1937, WLB; Bond, *Wings for an Embattled China*, p. 135.

109   Bond bought three: Bond says he bought a Smith & Wesson pistol in *Wings for an Embattled China*, p. 163, but Bond to Kitsi, October 15, 1937, WLB, reports that he paid $26.00 for a Colt automatic and shells among a meticulous list of expenses. Unless he bought two pistols, I judge it most likely that he was carrying a Colt.

109   Hankow's dirt airfield: author's interview with Moon Chin, April 19, 2006.

109   trying to get: Bond's pistol: Bond to Kitsi, October 15, 1937, WLB.

109   **in the Astoria:** letterhead that reads: "CHINA NATIONAL AVIATION CORPORATION, Astoria Building, the French Bund, Hankow": Lam Whi-shing to Bond, September 16, 1937, WLB.

110   **Colonel Lam received:** author's interview with Moon Chin, April 19, 2006.

110–11   **"I've only just":** Bond to Leslie, January 6, 1975, PAA, Box 20, Folder 2; Bond, *Wings for an Embattled China*, pp. 141–44, 163.

111   **Bond had hoped:** Bond to Vice Minister Peng Sho-pei, September 7, 1937, WLB.

112   **Donald Wong:** Florence Allison diary, September 13, 1937, NAW.

112   **"a position where":** Bixby to Morgan, August 25, 1937, WLB.

112   **extraordinarily complicated situation:** Bond to Kitsi, September 25, 1937, WLB; Bond, *Wings for an Embattled China*, pp. 144–45.

112   **"Mr. Bond, I":** Bond, *Wings for an Embattled China*, p. 146; Florence Allison diary, September 13, 1937, NAW; author's conversations and emails with Dona Lee Wong, Ph.D., Donald Wong's daughter, January 25–30, 2006; author's conversations with Donald Wong's sister, Frieda Chen; author's interview with Moon Chin, April 19, 2006.

112   **DC-2 couldn't leave:** Colonel Lam to Bond, September 16, 1937; Bond to Kitsi, September 25, 1937; Colonel Lam to Bond, September 26, 1937; Colonel Lam to Bond, September 28, 1937; Bond to Colonel W. S. Lam, September 29, 1937; Bixby to Morgan, Letter No. B-23-37, October 11, 1937; all in WLB; "Attachment Relieved," *SCMP*, November 4, 1937; Bond, *Wings for an Embattled China*, pp. 145–47; author's interview with Moon Chin, April 19, 2006. Moon Chin described it as "certainly possible" the attachment of the Hong Kong DC-2 was a Bixby machination.

112   **"astonished to learn":** Colonel Lam to Bond, September 16, 1937.

113   **"hat in hand":** Bond to Kitsi, September 25, 1937.

113   **substantial business:** "Attachment Relieved," *SCMP*, November 4, 1937.

113   **That was an:** Bixby to Morgan, Letter No. B-23-37, October 11, 1937, WLB.

113–14   **cemented the company's:** Bond, *Wings for an Embattled China*, p. 147.

114   **"[President Trippe] was quite":** Morgan to Bixby, October 16, 1937, WLB.

114   **Both partners' hopes:** author's interview with Moon Chin, April 19, 2006.

Chapter 10: Shanghai November

115   **Bond spent most:** Bond to Kitsi, October 10, 1937, and Bond to Kitsi, October 15, 1937; both in WLB.

115   **the Shanghai confrontation:** *NYT*, September 5 to October 25, 1937.

116   **Bond and Bixby set:** Bixby to Dear Family, October 25 and 26, 1937, WLB; numerous *SCMP* articles confirm the cholera epidemic.

116   Not that it: author's interview with Moon Chin, April 19, 2006; Bixby to Morgan, Letter No. B-23-37, October 11, 1937, WLB; William Langhorne Bond, *Wings for an Embattled China*, p. 148.

116–18   They landed in: Bond to Kitsi, Nanking, November 3, 1937; Bond to Kitsi, November 23, 1937; both in WLB; Bond to John C. Leslie, January 6, 1975, PAA, Box 20, Folder 2; Bond, *Wings for an Embattled China*, p. 148; Theodore H. White and Annalee Jacoby, *Thunder out of China*, p. 111; Rhodes Farmer, *Shanghai Harvest*, p. 106; Sterling Seagrave, *The Soong Dynasty*, pp. 97, 130–36; Jonathan Fenby, *Generalissimo: Chiang Kai-shek and the China He Lost*, pp. 163, 237–39; Barbara Tuchman, *Stilwell and the American Experience in China, 1911–1945*, pp. 146, 411–12; photograph of H. H. Kung, managing director Dai Enkai, and Edward P. Howard about to board a CNAC DC-2 in Shanghai, probably taken in 1935, the private collection of Edward P. Howard III.

117   "China didn't start" (Bond's conversation with Kung): Bond to Kitsi, Nanking, November 3, 1937; Bond to Kitsi, November 23, 1937; both in WLB; Bond to Leslie, January 6, 1975, PAA, Box 20, Folder 2; Bond, *Wings for an Embattled China*, p. 148.

118   British river steamer: Bixby to Dear Family, October 26, 1937; Bond to Kitsi, November 3, 1937; both in WLB; Bond says he flew in *Wings*, but his contemporary correspondence says otherwise. Moon Chin confirmed that a steamer could make the downriver run from Hankow to Nanking in one overnight: author's interview with Moon Chin, April 19, 2006.

118   The city center: *See China by Plane*, CNAC travel brochure, 1934 or 1935, the private collection of Lisa and Robert Mitchell; Edith Roberts, *Sketches of Nanking, Revised and Enlarged under the Auspices of the Literary Section of the Nanking Women's Club*, p. 17; Harold M. Bixby, "Top Side Ricksha," chap. 10, p. 64; Iris Chang, *The Rape of Nanking*, p. 63.

118   drafting and redrafting: Bond to Kitsi, November 3, 1937; Bond to Kitsi, undated, but certainly written in November 1937; Bond to Kitsi, November 20, 1937; all in WLB.

118   Chang Kia-ngau: Bond to Leslie, January 6, 1975, PAA, Box 20, Folder 2; Bond, *Wings for an Embattled China*, pp. 148–49.

118   "Felt like old": Bond to Kitsi, November 3, 1937, WLB; Bond to Leslie, January 6, 1975, PAA, Box 20, Folder 2; Bond, *Wings for an Embattled China*, pp. 148–49.

119   a quiet backer: Bond to Kitsi, November 6, 1937, WLB.

119–21   An hour before: Bond to Kitsi, November 6, 1937, WLB; *SCMP*, November 5, 1937.

120   "Listen, if this": Bond to Kitsi, November 6, 1937, WLB; *SCMP*, November 5, 1937.

121   "I hope all": Bond to Kitsi, November 6, 1937, WLB; *SCMP*, November 5, 1937.

121–22   None of Bond's and **"Look, Bondy, we're":** Bond to Kitsi, November 7, 1937, WLB; Bond to Leslie, January 6, 1975, PAA, Box 20, Folder 2; text of a Bond letter, July 18, 1976, NAW; Bond, *Wings for an Embattled China*, p. 153.

122   three Japanese divisions: *SCMP*, November 7 and November 8, 1937; Hsu Long-hsuen and Chang Ming-kai, *History of the Sino-Japanese War, 1937–1945*, p. 210; Edwin P. Hoyt, *Japan's War*, p. 165; Frank Dorn, *The Sino-Japanese War, 1937–1941: From Marco Polo Bridge to Pearl Harbor*, pp. 76–77.

122–23 The landings cut: Bond to Kitsi, November 7, 1937; Bond to Kitsi, "On Board the S.S. *Changsha*, I think it is Nov. 14th"; both in WLB; *CWR*, November 13, 1937, and November 20, 1937, which confirm Gauss's dinner for General Beaumont.

123 In the morning: Bond to Leslie, January 6, 1975, PAA, Box 20, Folder 2; Bond, *Wings for an Embattled China*, pp. 153–54.

124 Tong hadn't given: Bond to Leslie, January 6, 1975, PAA, Box 20, Folder 2; Bond, *Wings for an Embattled China*, pp. 153–54.

124 "I'm not sure": Bond to Leslie, January 6, 1975, PAA, Box 20, Folder 2; Bond, *Wings for an Embattled China*, pp. 153–54.

124 richly carved dark: undated descriptions written on the back of photographs in WLB, presumably by Kitsi Bond.

124 Sounds of combat: *SCMP*, November 8, 1937.

125 "As I sit": Bond to Kitsi, November 7, 1937, WLB.

125–26 At 8:50 A.M. (details of the fighting, November 9, 1937): *SCMP*, November 9, 10, 11, and 12, 1937; Marcia R. Ristaino, *The Jacquinot Safe Zone: Wartime Refugees in Shanghai*, pp. 1–80; Percy Finch, *Shanghai and Beyond*, pp. 260–76.

126 Bond slept well: Bond, *Wings for an Embattled China*, pp. 154–55.

126 he'd missed the: *SCMP*, November 10, 1937. Bond had nothing to add to the correspondent's notebook.

126–27 A cable from Bixby: Bond to Kitsi, November 11, 1937, WLB.

127–29 He rose early (events of November 10, 1937): Bond to Kitsi, November 11, 1937; Bond to Kitsi, "from Nanking," undated, but certainly written in November 1937; both in WLB; *SCMP*, November 11 and 12, 1937; Farmer, *Shanghai Harvest*, p. 91; Edgar Snow, *The Battle for Asia*, pp. 51–54.

127 "That isn't war": Bond to Kitsi, November 11, 1937, WLB.

128–30 A taxi collected (events of November 11, 1937): Bond to Kitsi, November 11, 1937, WLB; *SCMP*, November 12, 1937; *CWR*, November 13 and November 20, 1937; photograph of one of the cruisers taken by Swiss photographer Karl Kengelbacher on November 11, 1937: photo posted at http://www.japan-guide.com/a/shanghai/image.html?92, among many other images that Kengelbacher took of the Shanghai fighting, accessed April 4, 2006; HMS *Cumberland*: http://www.naval-art.com/hms_cumberland.htm; USS *Augusta*: Kemp Tolley, *Yangtze Patrol: The U.S. Navy in China*, p. 312.

129 Whole sections of: photographs in WLB; photos posted online at www.talesofold china.com, accessed summer of 2005; photographic portfolio by Swiss photographer Karl Kengelbacher between August and November, 1937; Farmer, *Shanghai Harvest*, p. 92; Edgar Snow, *The Battle for Asia*, pp. 72, 84, 90; Jonathan D. Spence, *The Search for Modern China*,

p. 447. The 1937 Battle of Shanghai seems to this author to have been a closer-run affair than most historians credit. All the Chinese needed for victory was a prolonged stalemate, and they achieved that for three brutal months. Only Japan's risky Hangchow Bay landings broke the deadlock and turned the stalemate into a massive Chinese defeat. Chiang Kai-shek would never again seek decisive battle with the Japanese. There is a rich and broad record of the fighting. All of the world's major newspapers had correspondents in the city. My prime sources have been Bond's letters to Kitsi; *SCMP*, *CWR*, and *NYT*; Snow, *The Battle for Asia*; Emily Hahn, *China to Me* and *Nobody Told Me Not to Go*; Harriet Sergeant, *Shanghai*; Stella Dong, *Shanghai: The Rise and Fall of a Decadent City*; Farmer, *Shanghai Harvest*; Percy Finch, *Shanghai and Beyond*.

129   **"God damn the":** Bond to Kitsi, November 11, 1937, WLB; *SCMP*, November 13, 1937, confirms Bond's observations of the IJN fleet in the Woosung Roadstead.

129   **Armistice Day:** *SCMP*, November 12, 1937.

129   **General Iwane Matsui:** *SCMP*, November 12, 1937; *CWR*, November 20, 1937; John B. Powell, *My Twenty-five Years in China, 1926–1941*, p. 270; Iris Chang, *The Rape of Nanking*, p. 38; Snow, *The Battle for Asia*, p. 51.

130   **"I am, at":** *SCMP*, November 12, 1937; *CWR*, November 20, 1937. The *CWR* article has a near-complete transcript of Matsui's comments. The two accounts are in exact accord, with the exception of the last quote. The *SCMP* records the quote given, the *CWR* reported that Matsui said, ". . . but came here to *rescue* the civilian population of China."

Chapter 11: Resurrection

131–32   **At dusk on:** Bond to Kitsi, November 11, 1937, WLB.

131–32   **"Sonny, you may":** Bond to Kitsi, November 11, 1937, WLB.

132–33   **Bond rose at:** Bond to Kitsi, November 14, 1937, WLB.

133   **A thousand wounded:** Bond, *Wings for an Embattled China*, p. 160.

133   **That afternoon, November 14:** Bond to Kitsi, November 14, 1937, WLB; Bond, *Wings for an Embattled China*, p. 156.

133   **"Poor China, what":** Bond to Kitsi, November 14, 1937, WLB.

133   **China was taking:** Rhodes Farmer, *Shanghai Harvest*, p. 97; Frank Dorn, *The Sino-Japanese War, 1937–1941: From Marco Polo Bridge to Pearl Harbor*, pp. 87–88; Iris Chang, *The Rape of Nanking*, pp. 35–38.

133   **Every civilian with:** Bond to Kitsi, November 14, 1937, WLB.

134   **He'd barely shut:** Bond to Kitsi, November 16, 1937; Bond to Kitsi, November 23, 1937; both in WLB; Bond to John C. Leslie, January 6, 1975, PAA, Box 20, Folder 2; Bond, *Wings for an Embattled China*, pp. 41, 156–59.

134   **Mr. W. H. Donald:** Kitsi to Dearest Family, June 14, 1938, WLB; Emily Hahn, *China* *to Me,* p. 124; Hahn, *The Soong Sisters,* pp. 179–84; Jonathan Fenby, *Generalissimo: Chiang Kai-Shek and the China He Lost,* pp. 6–11; Earl Albert Selle, *Donald of China,* which, on p. 311, mentions Donald's support of Pan American; Barbara Tuchman, *Stilwell and the American Experience in China, 1911–1945,* p. 433.

134   **"What's all this":** Bond to Kitsi, November 16, 1937; Bond to Kitsi, November 23, 1937; both in WLB.

134   **The Jardine steamer:** Bond to Kitsi, November 16, 1937, says three miles. Bond to Leslie, January 6, 1975, PAA, Box 20, Folder 2, says five or six miles. Bond, *Wings for an Embattled China,* p. 156, says ten miles. I chose the contemporary figure.

135   **"See that moll?":** Bond to Kitsi, November 16, 1937, WLB; Bond to Leslie, January 6, 1975, PAA, Box 27, Folder 23.

135   **"There are several":** Bond to Kitsi, "Nov. something, just east of Kiukian" (presumably November 18 or 19, 1937), WLB.

136   **No place on:** author's interview with Moon Chin, April 19, 2006.

136   **"Let the Chinese":** Bond to Kitsi, November 20, 1937, WLB; Bond to Leslie, January 6, 1975, PAA, Box 27, Folder 23.

136   **The two Americans:** Bond to Kitsi, November 23, 1937, WLB.

136   **Bond anguished over:** Bond to Kitsi, November 20, 1937, WLB; Ernie Allison to Florence Allison, November 22, 1937, NAW.

136   **Chuck Sharp and Hugh Woods:** Florence Allison to Ernie Allison, December 12, 1937, NAW; Bixby to Stokely Morgan, January 7, 1938, WLB.

136   **Ironically, Bond and:** Bond, *Wings for an Embattled China,* p. 161; also, the tone changed in Bond's contemporaneous correspondence.

136   **Chiang Kai-shek and:** Chang, *The Rape of Nanking,* p. 70; Farmer, *Shanghai Harvest,* p. 96, says the shelling started twenty days after the Hangchow landing, which would be November 28, but *The Rape of Nanking,* p. 73, says the bombardment didn't start until December 9.

136   **Heeding a Japanese:** H. T. Jarrell, "Discussions, Comments, Notes: How the Panay Was Sunk," *U.S. Naval Institute Proceedings* 80, No. 5, May 1954, pp. 573–75; Manny T. Koginos, *The Panay Incident: Prelude to War,* pp. 26–30; Frank Dorn, *The Sino-Japanese War, 1937–1941: From Marco Polo Bridge to Pearl Harbor,* pp. 95–96.

137   **"During the World":** Bond to General Beaumont, December 13, 1937, WLB.

137   **The Japanese Army:** Chang, *Rape of Nanking.* The logistics of the massacre defy description—the killing rate in Nanking outstripped the rate at which people died in Nazi gas chambers.

138   **"Please supply me":** Addison E. Southard, American Consul General, to W. L. Bond, December 28, 1937, WLB; Bond to Leslie, January 6, 1975, PAA, Box 27, Folder 23.

138   Bond submitted his: Bond, *Wings for an Embattled China,* p. 163; Bond to Leslie, January 7, 1975, PAA, Box 27, Folder 23. Many of Bond's letters to Kitsi in the fall of 1937 imply that he was plotting to get P. Y. Wong installed.

138–39   "Mr. Bond, I" (Bond and Lam's conversation, distilled): Bond, *Wings for an Embattled China,* pp. 163–64; Bond to Leslie, January 6, 1975, PAA, Box 27, Folder 23. The minutes of the CNAC board meeting, November 17, 1938, imply P. Y. Wong replaced Colonel Lam on January 1, 1938. Bond's salary as CNAC operations manager was paid starting on January 1, 1938, but it may have taken a few days longer to effect the change. In "Bondy to Dearest Kits," January 9, 1938, Bond states, "The necessary orders removing the present incumbent and appointing the new official are out," and that P. Y. Wong would be officially offered the managing directorship at a directors' meeting on January 11, 1938.

Chapter 12: The Provisional Capital

143   600 U.S. dollars: Bond to Morgan, July 28, 1938; Bond to Woodbridge, August 1, 1938; both in WLB.

143   "The new M.D.": Bondy to Dearest Kits, January 9, 1938, WLB.

143   "If you are": "Bix to Bonda," January 7, 1938, WLB.

144   "I confess": Bondy to Dearest Kits, January 9, 1938, WLB.

144   Wong uprooted the: Bixby to Mr. S. C. Hsu, March 12, 1938, WLB; "Minutes of the 37th Meeting of the Board of Directors of China National Aviation Corporation," November 17, 1938; P. Y. Wong to Bond, January 19, 1939; both in ANY; author's interview with Moon Chin, April 19, 2006; author's conversations with Frieda Chen at the 2005 CNAC reunion; William Leary, *The Dragon's Wings,* p. 118; Bond, *Wings for an Embattled China,* p. 169.

144   Complicating the government's retreat: "Szechwan Chief Dies," *NYT,* January 21, 1938; Frank Dorn, *The Sino-Japanese War, 1937–1941: From Marco Polo Bridge to Pearl Harbor,* pp. 203–4.

144   Given all his: Bond to Bixby, February 17, 1938, WLB; "Minutes of the 37th Meeting of the Board of Directors of China National Aviation Corporation," November 17, 1938, ANY.

144   more starkly political: author's interview with Moon Chin, April 19, 2006.

145   "that pave the": "Bix to Bonda," January 7, 1938, WLB.

145   Heeding Bixby's advice: "Bix to Bonda," January 7, 1938, WCB; Bond, *Wings for an Embattled China,* p. 166.

146   "the China Show" and "break the news": Bixby to Bond, April 1, 1938, WLB; also, Debbie Bixby, "H. M. Bixby Family in China, 1934–1938," provided to the author by Elizabeth "Bo" Bixby, the Bixbys' second-eldest daughter.

146   exactly the opposite: Bixby to Colonel Clarence M. Young, January 28, 1938, WLB;

Bond, *Wings for an Embattled China*, p. 171; Phillip Snow, *The Fall of Hong Kong*, p. 352, note 11.

146 Bungalow Number 1: Bond to the Hong Kong Realty & Trust Company, June 3, 1938, WLB.

146 one last *walla-walla:* Bixby to M. Y. Tong, April 16, 1938, WLB; Bond, *Wings for an Embattled China*, p. 179.

147 in Hankow on April 29: Bond to Bixby, May 1, 1938, WLB; "Chinese Air Force Claims Big Victory," *NYT*, April 30, 1938; John Gunther, "People of Hankow Take War in Stride," *NYT*, May 5, 1938; Peter South, "Will Russia's Aid to China Hasten a Clash with Japan?" *CWR*, May 7, 1938; "Reports on Japan's Air Losses," *CWR*, May 14, 1938; Martha Byrd, *Chennault: Giving Wings to the Tiger*, pp. 89–90; Wanda Cornelius and Thayne Short, *Ding Hao: American's Air War in China, 1937–1945*, pp. 87–88; Paul Frillman and Graham Peck, *China: The Remembered Life*, pp. 16–17; Kemp Tolley, *Yangtze Patrol: The U.S. Navy in China*, pp. 252–53; Arthur N. Young, *China and the Helping Hand, 1937–1945*, pp. 54–55; Young, *Cycle of Cathay*, p. 120.

147 Arthur N. Young: Arthur N. Young to Dr. Reginald Farrar, February 11, 1977, *C.N.A.C. Cannonball;* Arthur N. Young, *Cycle of Cathay: A Historical Perspective*, pp. 4, 68–70. Bond wasn't able to secure Young's commitment to fill Bixby's vacated spot on the board of directors until April 1939: Bond to Peng Sho-pei, April 25, 1939, ANY; Bond, *Wings for an Embattled China*, p. 179.

148 "Bombers!": Bond to Bixby, May 1, 1938, WLB.

149 Taierhchuang: "Japanese Defeat a Major Disaster; Crisis in Cabinet," *NYT*, April 15, 1938; Hallett Abend, "Debacle at Taierhchwang," *NYT*, April 15, 1938; F. Tillman Durdin, "Eight Divisions on Move," *NYT*, April 15, 1938; Dorn, *The Sino-Japanese War, 1937–1941*, pp. 146–58; Jonathan Fenby, *Generalissimo: Chiang Kai-shek and the China He Lost*, p. 320. Fenby claims 8,000 Japanese killed; Dorn claims 16,000; *NYT* reported 42,000 Japanese KIA, citing China's Central News Agency, a dubious source.

149–50 The Yangtze and: Bond to Bixby, May 8, 1938, WLB; photos in WLB; F. Tillman Durdin, "Big Air Raid Kills 600 in Wuhan Area," *NYT*, July 20, 1938; John Gunther, "People of Hankow Take War in Stride," *NYT*, May 5, 1938; *SCMP*, June 10, 1938; W. H. Auden and Christopher Isherwood, *Journey to a War*, p. 49; Rhodes Farmer, *Shanghai Harvest*, p. 141; Frillman and Peck, *China*, pp. 3, 11, 12; William Leary, *The Dragon's Wings*, p. 118.

149 To slow the: Bond to Bixby, July 3, 1938, WLB; Hallett Abend, "Chengchow's Fall Is Expected Soon," *NYT*, June 8, 1938; F. Tillman Durdin, "Floods Protect Chengchow," *NYT*, June 12, 1938; Douglas Robertson, "China Floods Ruin Vast Farm Lands," *NYT*, June 16, 1938; "Flood and War," London *Times*, June 16, 1938, and "The Destruction of China," *Washington Post*, June 16, 1938, articles reproduced in *The Chinese Mercury, Special Number, 1938*, Vol. 2, No. 1; "Chinese Resigned to Flood Sacrifice to Check Invaders," *NYT*, June 17, 1938; "Flood Devastation in China Spreading," *NYT*, June 17, 1938; "Japanese Shifting for New Assaults," *NYT*, June 22, 1938; O. J. Todd, "Yellow River Dragons Stir,"

NYT, June 26, 1938; Douglas Robertson, "North China Floods Seen from the Air," *NYT,* July 4, 1938.

150 Bond considered cutting: Bond to Morgan, July 20, 1938; Bond to Morgan, July 27, 1938; both in WLB; Moon Chin confirmed that the Rape of Nanking was common knowledge in China: author's interview with Moon Chin, January 7, 2005. The *CWR* published photos of Japanese execution pits, samurai-sword beheadings, and bayonet practice on live Chinese prisoners on July 23, August 13, and October 1, 1938. Also Edwin P. Hoyt, *Japan's War,* p. 172, says press reports and photographs of the Rape appeared in newspapers all over the world. Many contemporary books discuss the Nanking massacre as if it were common knowledge: Rhodes Farmer, *Shanghai Harvest;* Hallett Abend, *My Life in China, 1926–1941;* John B. Powell, *My Twenty-five Years in China;* Gerald Samson, *The Far East Ablaze.*

150–51 Òne of his: Bond to Morgan, August 9, 1938; Bond to Bixby, April 24, 1938; Kitsi to Dearest Family, June 14, 1938; Bond to Bixby, July 10, 1938; Bond to Morgan, Letter No. 3-38, July 14, 1938; Bond to Morgan, July 16, 1938; Bond to Morgan, July 30, 1938; Bond to Morgan, Letter No. 20, August 9, 1938; Bond to Morgan, June 26, 1939; all in WLB; Hallett Abend, "China's War Loss Is Huge," *NYT,* July 24, 1938.

150 "considerable cash": Bond to Morgan, August 9, 1938, WLB.

150 Ministry of Finance wouldn't: Bond to Bixby, April 24, 1938, WLB.

151 "Ask Mr. Bixby": Bond to Morgan, August 9, 1938, WLB.

151 "Barefoot and pregnant": Bixby interview, 1957, PAA, Box 20, Folder 1.

151–52 Gasoline was Bond's: Bond to Bixby, February 27, 1938; Bond to Bixby, May 1, 1938; Bond to Morgan, July 16, 1938; Bond to Morgan, July 27, 1938; Morgan to Bond, Letter No. B14-38, July 27, 1938; Bond to Morgan, July 30, 1938; Bond to Morgan, August 8, 1938; all in WLB; Bond, *Wings for an Embattled China,* p. 167. "Smart lad" and "Supersqueeze artist" are phrases Bond used in his correspondence.

153 "I note you": Bixby to Bond, July 22, 1938, WLB.

153–54 Ignoring instructions, Bond: Bond to Morgan, "personal," August 8, 1938, WLB.

153 binoculars: they were the personal property of each CNAC pilot, stored in flight bags behind the pilots' seats: author's interview with Moon Chin, April 19, 2006.

154 "Chuck, back in": Bond to Morgan, "personal," August 8, 1938, WLB.

154 the hottest entertainment: Kemp Tolley, *Yangtze Patrol: The U.S. Navy in China,* p. 252; many comments from CNAC pilots about Sharp's propensity for high-stakes gambling; author's interview with Frieda Chen, September 19, 2006; many anecdotes in *C.N.A.C. Cannonballs.*

154 "I hope I": Bond to Morgan, August 8, 1938, WLB.

Chapter 13: The *Kweilin* Incident

155–59 The DC-2 rumbled: Hugh Woods, "Pilot's Report," August 26, 1938; George H. Clark, "Report of Observations and Investigation at Scene of Accident to CNAC Douglas Transport 'Kweilin,'" August 27, 1938; Mrs. Lieu to Bond, October 31, 1938; all in WLB; *Shanghai Evening Post,* August 25 and August 27, 1938; *SCMP,* August 25 and August 29, 1938; author's interview with Moon Chin, April 19, 2006; Royal Leonard, *I Flew for China,* p. 195; Phillip Snow, *The Fall of Hong Kong,* p. 352, note 2; photos in Trea Wiltshire, *Hong Kong: Pages from the Past;* author's trip to Hong Kong, April 2005. Based on an email exchange with C. W. Lam in December 2005, the aircraft complements of IJN seaplane tenders 1938–1941, and Hugh Woods's pilot's report, I surmise the five attacking Japanese planes were likely either Nakajima Type 95 E8N "Dave" or Kawanishi Type 94 E7K "Alf" float planes, two- or three-seat biplanes armed with two or three 7.7 mm machine guns. Woods wrote: "I could see the attacking planes clearly and positively identified them as Japanese. They were pontoon bi-planes. Although I could see the markings clearly, I did not take time to notice whether they were single-place or two-place."

159–60 Bond was in: Bond to Morgan, September 6, 1938, WLB; Bond, *Wings for an Embattled China,* p. 181. The sequence of events in Bond's letter to Morgan differs from his account in *Wings.* I cleaved to the contemporary source; also: Florence Allison to Ernie Allison, August 9, 1938, NAW; Tolley Kemp, *Yangtze Patrol: The U.S. Navy in China,* p. 243; Manny Koginos, *The Panay Incident: Prelude to War,* p. 28; R&S I, p. 62, note 39 (3), discusses the quality of U.S. Navy communications channels.

160 "Do not worry": Bond, *Wings for an Embattled China,* p. 181.

160 "Your Excellency": Bond to Morgan, September 6, 1938, WLB.

162 "Isn't *Mindanao* still": Bond to Morgan, September 6, 1938, WLB.

162 *Mindanao* raced across: George H. Clark, "Report of Observations and Investigation at Scene of Accident to CNAC Douglas Transport 'Kweilin,'" August 27, 1938, WLB.

162 The gruesome details: Bond to Morgan, September 6, 1938, WLB; Bond, *Wings for an Embattled China,* p. 181.

163 As soon as: Bond to Morgan, September 6, 1938; Bond to Morgan, September 9, 1938; both in WLB; Bond, *Wings for an Embattled China,* pp. 182–83. There is significant disagreement between Bond's account in *Wings* and his contemporary correspondence.

163 he hadn't thought: Bond to Bixby, February 21, 1938; Bond to Bixby, March 1, 1938; both in WLB. "I still believe the Japanese government will notify us before they take any active steps to stop our operation . . . the greatest danger is that we will run into some fool pilot like the ones that bombed the *Panay.*"

163 "Does Pan Am's": Bond to Morgan, September 6, 1938; Bond to Morgan, September 9, 1938; both in WLB; Bond, *Wings for an Embattled China,* pp. 182–83.

163–64 Bond crossed (Bond's meeting with Kung): Bond to Morgan, September 6,

1938; Bond to Morgan, September 9, 1938; both in WLB; Bond, *Wings for an Embattled China*, pp. 182–83.

163 **"Doesn't it mean":** Bond to Morgan, September 6, 1938; Bond to Morgan, September 9, 1938; both in WLB; Bond, *Wings for an Embattled China*, pp. 182–83.

164 **Bond's subsequent audience:** Bond to Morgan, September 6, 1938; Bond to Morgan, September 9, 1938; both in WLB; Bond, *Wings for an Embattled China*, pp. 182–83.

164 **The suspended Hong Kong flights:** Bond, *Wings for an Embattled China*, p. 184.

164 **"more active support":** *SCMP*, August 26, 1938.

164 **A colony newspaper:** Bond, *Wings for an Embattled China*, pp. 179–80.

164 **Many speculated:** "I understand Dr. Sun Fo had intended to take my plane that morning, and it is very probable the Japanese War Office thought they were eliminating him when they shot down my plane": Hugh Woods, "Pilot's Report," August 26, 1938, WLB; *North China Daily News*, August 25, 1938; *Shanghai Evening Post*, August 25, 1938; "Japan Again," *The Manchester Guardian*, August 26, 1938, published in *The Chinese Mercury*, Vol. 2, No. 2, New Year Number, 1939, p. 65; "Attack on C.N.A.C. Plane," *SCMP*, August 26, 1938; H.W.G. Woodhead, "The South China Aeroplane Tragedy: International Repercussions," *Shanghai Evening Post*, August 27, 1938; "War in China: By Mistake," *Time*, September 5, 1938; *CWR*, August 27, September 3, and September 9, 1938, and September 17, 1938; Bond, *Wings for an Embattled China*, pp. 179–80; Royal Leonard, *I Flew for China*, p. 194; author's interview with Moon Chin, July 15, 2005.

165 **"pleasant, capable, ambitious":** Gerald Samson, *The Far East Ablaze*, p. 162.

165 **William Bond's opinion:** Bond interview, October 23, 1972, PAA, Box 19, Folder 3, p. 50; Bond, *Wings for an Embattled China*, p. 180.

165 **Chinese secretaries didn't:** Bond interview, October 23, 1972, PAA, Box 19, Folder 3, p. 50.

165 **Japanese consul general:** Bond, *Wings for an Embattled China*, p. 181.

165 **"The Japanese seemed":** *Shanghai Evening Post*, August 25, 1938.

165 **The gunshot wasn't:** *North China Daily News*, August 25, 1938; *CWR*, August 27, 1938.

165 **dozens of bullet holes:** "Minutes of the 37th Meeting of the Board of Directors of China National Aviation Corporation," November 17, 1938, ANY.

165 **fourteen recovered corpses:** *CWR*, September 17, 1938; author's interview with Moon Chin, September 17, 2004.

166 **"engine trouble":** *Shanghai Evening Post*, August 26, 1938.

166 **"the plane acted":** Hallett Abend, "Japan Bars Pledge on Civilian Planes," *NYT*, August 26, 1938.

166 **Noda denied:** *SCMP*, August 26, 1938, p. 12.

166 **"our wild eagles":** *Shanghai Evening Post*, August 27, 1938.

166   **protest instructions:** Secretary of State Cordell Hull to Ambassador Grew: *FRUS, 1938.* Vol. 4, *The Far East*, p. 451.

166   **"diplomatic circles were":** *North China Daily News,* September 1, 1938.

166   **Bond reached Hong Kong:** *SCMP,* September 1, 1938.

166   **Film producers compiled:** *SCMP,* September 7, 1938. Does this newsreel survive? It would be fascinating to see.

166   **Eurasia resumed daytime:** Bond to Morgan, September 20, 1938, WLB; *CWR,* September 24, 1938.

166   **"exercise ordinary care":** Hull to Grew, September 14, 1938, *FRUS, 1938.* Vol. 4, *The Far East*, p. 474.

167   **tenure at Wesleyan:** http://www.wesleyancollege.edu/firstforwomen/soong/index .html, accessed February 14, 2006.

167   **"Your country supplies"** and **"one of these days":** W. T. Woo, "Attack on C.N.A.C. Plane," *SCMP,* August 26, 1938.

167   **The growing crisis:** "Hitler's Speech to Party Leaders," *NYT,* September 10, 1938; "Suspense Chills the Nazis' Nuremberg Rally," *NYT,* September 11, 1938; Frederick T. Birchall, "German Strength Revealed at Rally," *NYT,* September 14, 1938; *CWR,* September 3, 1938, and September 9, 1938; "British Fleet Put on a War Footing," *NYT,* September 11, 1938; David M. Kennedy, *Freedom from Fear,* p. 418.

168   **Prudent Britons:** One prudent Londoner was the author's paternal grandfather, Reginald Crouch. His wife and three sons—one of whom was the author's then three-year-old father—went on family vacation to Elmer in August 1938, but Grandfather Crouch and his brother, Great War veteran Robert Lucas Crouch, stayed home and built an eight-by-eight-by-eighteen-foot bomb shelter in the back garden of No. 9 Chudleigh Crescent in Illford, an East London suburb. The two Crouch brothers dug a long trench, concreted a floor, joined three radial aircraft engine crates end-to-end-to-end to frame the shelter, and then poured concrete outside the walls and over the rooftop. Granddad Crouch doubled the shelter to thirty-six feet long after war broke out in September 1939. A ship's engineer, he screwed bunks into the walls of the shipping crates fifteen inches apart. The family spent most nights in the shelter from the fall of 1940 to mid-1942, and then again in 1944–45, hiding from V-1 and V-2 attacks. Thirty to thirty-five other children on Chudleigh Crescent joined the Crouch family for the early attacks, until government shelters were built in the area. Granddad Crouch was the only one in his neighborhood who had the foresight to dig a bomb shelter. Author's interview with his oldest uncle, Reginald Crouch II, May 4, 2006.

168   **To CNAC's foreign:** *CWR,* September 3, 1938; September 17, 1938; Florence Allison's diary entries, September 9 to October 2, 1938, NAW.

168   **Central Government pressure:** Bond to Morgan, September 20, 1938; Bond to Morgan, September 21, 1938; Bond to Morgan, "Letter No. 31," September 21, 1938; all in WLB.

168   Eurasia embraced: Southard to Hull, October 18, 1938, *FRUS, 1938.* Vol. 4, *The Far East,* p. 499.

168   Bond's reluctance: Bond to Morgan, September 6, 1938; Bond to Morgan, September 8, 1938; Bond to Morgan, September 20, 1938; Bond to Morgan, September 21, 1938; Bond to Morgan, October 19, 1938; all in WLB. Those letters show Bond taking nearly two months to warm to the idea of night flying, whereas *Wings for an Embattled China,* pp. 181–84, makes him seem instantly enthusiastic. As elsewhere, I have opted to give most weight to the contemporary evidence.

168   Bond remained uneasy: Florence Allison's diary, September 9, 1938, to October 2, 1938, NAW.

168   Allison thought Bond: undated letter from Royal Leonard to Allison, NAW.

169   Eurasia's chief pilot: Bond, *Wings for an Embattled China,* p. 185; author's interview with Moon Chin, April 19, 2006; Peter Goutiere email to author, June 20, 2009.

169   "I'm so scared": Bond, *Wings for an Embattled China,* pp. 188–90. In *Wings,* Bond relates this conversation as happening after the first three nocturnal practice flights to Chungking, and according to contemporary evidence the first of those flights was on October 9, 1938. However, in Bond to Bixby, "Dear Bix," September 18, 1938, WLB, Bond reported he'd made a reservation for Kitsi to return to the United States on the Clipper leaving Hong Kong on September 29, ten days before the first practice flight. It is possible circumstances delayed the Clipper's departure into October; also, author's interview with Langhorne Bond, January 27, 2005.

170   "legendary proportions": Bond to Bixby, "Dear Bix," September 18, 1938, WLB.

170   Czech crisis climaxed: Bond to Morgan, October 19, 1938, WLB, which describes the mood of three weeks before; "Commons Jubilant" and "Hitler Agrees to Parley," *NYT,* September 29, 1938; "France Is Calmer," *NYT,* September 30, 1938; "I believe it is peace for our time" and "Peace with Honor, Says Chamberlain," *NYT,* October 1, 1938; "Peace Aid Pledged; Hitler and Chamberlain Voice Their Nations Will Never Fight," *NYT,* October 1, 1938; *CWR,* October 8, 1938; Winston Churchill, *The Gathering Storm,* pp. 279–339; Robert Dallek, *Franklin D. Roosevelt and American Foreign Policy, 1932–1945,* pp. 161–66; Kennedy, *Freedom from Fear,* pp. 418–20; William L. Shirer, *The Rise and Fall of the Third Reich,* pp. 357–454.

170   its ramifications rippled: "Invasion of South China Direct Result of Munich Accord," *CWR,* October 22, 1938: "After the Munich Conference where Britain and France had exposed their weakness and compromised at the expense of Czechoslovakia, the Japanese felt quite free to take definite action in South China"; also, "Certainly the Japanese showed that they had not overlooked the implications of the Munich Agreement when they followed it so quickly with their invasion of South China": Morgan to Bond, November 16, 1938, WLB; "Outstanding Events in the Sino-Japanese War," *CWR,* October 29, 1938; "Europe Returns to the Pursuits of Peace; But the Tide of War Flows on in China," *NYT,* October 30, 1938;

Paul Frillman and Graham Peck, *China: The Remembered Life*, p. 25; Barbara Tuchman, *Stilwell and the American Experience in China, 1911–1945*, pp. 246–47.

170   **"I have been"**: Bond to Morgan, "Letter No. 36," October 19, 1938, WLB.

170   **William Bond never**: dated photographs in WLB and Bond, *Wings for an Embattled China*; Bond to Bixby, May 3, 1939, WLB.

171   **"they hurt like"**: Bond to Bixby, September 18, 1938, WLB.

171   **Bond received anxious**: Bond to Kitsi, October 26, 1938; Bond to Morgan, "Personal," October 29, 1938; both in WLB.

Chapter 14: The Evacuation of Hankow

172   **airstrip on a sandbar**: author's interviews with Moon Chin, Peter Goutiere, and other CNAC pilots; interview with Zigmund Soldinski, *C.N.A.C. Cannonball*, 1973; Edward Churchill, "The Rise and Fall of China's Airlines," *Flying and Popular Aviation*, July 1941.

172–73   **Leonard had flown**: except where otherwise noted, Bond's actions, thoughts, and observations and the details of airline operations, October 21–26, 1938, are gleaned from two long and detailed letters: Bond to Kitsi, October 26, 1938, WLB, and Bond to Morgan, October 29, 1938, ANY, and the author's many interviews with Moon Chin, most importantly on January 7, 2005, and April 19, 2006. Moon Chin's stories sixty-five-plus years after the events described dovetail *exactly* with the facts in Bond's letters written one and three days after the last flight ex-Hankow and with every other concrete detail the author was able to glean from contemporary newspaper accounts, a singular achievement of precision recall, possibly unique among aviators. Also important are: Bond, *Wings for an Embattled China*, pp. 193–201; Royal Leonard, *I Flew for China*, pp. 193–209.

173   **Thirty-six Japanese**: F. Tillman Durdin, "Troops in Hankow Target of Planes," *NYT*, October 23, 1938. This contradicts most book accounts about Hankow in the summer and fall of 1938, most of which claim the Japanese raided Hankow every day. Durdin is a more reliable witness. He was on-scene, recording events as they happened. How to account for the difference? (Aside from the author's observation that time tends to increase the frequency and intensity of remembered air raids.) What I suspect has happened is that people have confused air-raid alerts with actual attacks. As Durdin's comment shows, on October 23, the tri-cities hadn't been bombed in some weeks, but I'd accept the statement that air-raid *alerts* sounded most days. The alert sounded when the air-warning net warned the whole spectrum of potential targets that they were threatened by Japanese planes aloft (a vast area). But the raiders would only attack one target, or at most a handful. Hankow, Wuchang, and Hanyang are natural transportation hubs. It seems logical that most Japanese airplane movements would threaten them, thus accounting for a plethora of daily *alerts*, if not actual attacks. (Analysis confirmed by the author's interview with Moon Chin, April 19, 2006.)

173   **night landings at Chungking:** the difference between landing at Chungking and landing at Chengtu: author's interview with Moon Chin, April 19, 2006.

173   **The moon wouldn't:** http://tycho.usno.navy.mil/vphase.html, accessed March 5, 2006.

173   **teletype machine:** author's interview with Moon Chin, April 19, 2006.

173   **Scarcely a shot:** "Outstanding Events in the Sino-Japanese War," *CWR*, November 12, 1938.

173   **suspected treasonous generals:** "I think the Cantonese Army must have been assisting the Japanese army in their drive on Canton. The Japanese could not have marched that rapidly by themselves. There is only one way to describe that campaign: it stinks": Bond to Kitsi, October 26, 1938, WLB; "Japanese Enter Canton; Find Big Buildings Razed; Fires Rage through City; No Defense Made," *NYT*, October 22, 1938; "Canton Defender Chooses Captivity," *NYT*, October 23, 1938; "'There were those who declared that [the Chinese commander in Canton] had bolted, or had been bought'": W. H. Donald to Mr. Timperley, December 30, 1938, p. 18, SKH, Box 150.

174   **Leonard, in particular:** Bond's letters; Bond, *Wings for an Embattled China*, pp. 194–95; author's interview with Pete Goutiere, January 22, 2005; author's interview with Moon Chin, April 19, 2006; Bond says Leonard left Chengtu about ninety minutes after Sharp in *Wings*, p. 195. His two contemporary letters state that Leonard was twenty minutes behind.

174   **Bluish fog tendrils:** W. H. Donald to Mr. Timperley, December 30, 1938, p. 17, SKH, Box 150. The letter confirms the daybreak air raid and the basic conditions described in Bond's contemporaneous correspondence.

174–75   **"No alarm":** Leonard, *I Flew for China*, pp. 202–3.

174   **Pouring on power:** Leonard, *I Flew for China*, p. 203; W. H. Donald to Mr. Timperley, December 30, 1938, p. 17, SKH, Box 150: "I was later informed that seven Japanese planes had gone up-river after the first raid."

175   **riverside storage facility:** Kemp Tolley, *Yangtze Patrol: The U.S. Navy in China*, p. 254; author's interview with Moon Chin, April 19, 2006.

175   **"Don't be foolish":** Leonard, *I Flew for China*, p. 200; Bond, *Wings for an Embattled China*, p. 195. There is also a glimmer of the conversation in Bond's contemporary letter to his wife, "He was all in so I sent him to bed and cancelled his flights for that night, over his violent protests," Bond to Kitsi, October 26, 1938, WLB.

175   **Bond decided to:** aside from Bond's two contemporary letters, author's interview with Moon Chin, January 7, 2005, confirmed that it had been an error to fly to Chengtu.

176   **"Frantic":** Bond to Kitsi, October 26, 1938, WLB; Bond to Morgan, October 29, 1938, ANY.

176   **threat of icing:** author's interviews with Joe Rosbert, August 14 and 15, 2004; with Donald McBride, November 4, 2004; with Pete Goutiere, January 22, 2005; with Moon Chin, April 19, 2006; Max Springweiler, *Pioneer Aviator in China*, p. 105.

176 **flattening country:** Harold M. Bixby, "Top Side Ricksha," chap. 4, p. 9; Bond to Bixby, January 31, 1938, WLB; author's interview with Moon Chin, April 19, 2006.

177 **foul smells of:** author's interview with Moon Chin, April 19, 2006.

177 *Luzon* **was holding station:** "U.S. Navy Ignores Warning by Japan of Peril of Bombs," and Hallett Abend, "U.S. Ships Stay at Their Posts," *NYT*, October 23, 1938.

177 **"silent dread and":** Bond to Kitsi, October 26, 1938, WLB; Bond to Morgan, October 29, 1938, ANY.

178 **"feeling very warm":** Bond to Kitsi, October 26, 1938, WLB. In *Wings* (p. 196), Bond drank coffee with Commander McVey. The letter Bond wrote to his wife says they drank whisky sodas.

178 **those awake gawking:** photos in WLB; F. Tillman Durdin, "Troops in Hankow Target of Planes," *NYT*, October 23, 1938; Durdin, "Invaders Close to Hankow," *NYT*, October 25, 1938; Paul Frillman and Graham Peck, *China: The Remembered Life*, p. 25.

178 **"the back alley":** W. H. Donald to Mr. Timperley, December 30, 1938, pp. 17–18, SKH, Box 150.

178 **removed portable scrap:** F. Tillman Durdin, "Troops in Hankow Target of Planes," *NYT*, October 23, 1938; Frillman and Peck, *China*, p. 25.

179 **"Thought you fellows":** Bond to Kitsi, October 26, 1938, WLB; Bond to Morgan, October 29, 1938, ANY.

179 **eleventh-hour refugees:** F. Tillman Durdin, "Break in Defenses," *NYT*, October 21, 1938; Durdin, "Troops in Hankow Target of Planes," *NYT*, October 23, 1938; Durdin, "Invaders Close to Hankow," *NYT*, October 25, 1938; Frank Dorn, *The Sino-Japanese War, 1937–1941: From Marco Polo Bridge to Pearl Harbor*, p. 210. Frillman and Peck, *China*, p. 25; Bond, *Wings for an Embattled China*, p. 197.

180 **Chaos crept into:** Durdin, "Hankow Heavily Bombed," *NYT*, October 24, 1938; W. H Donald to Mr. Timperley, December 30, 1938, p. 17, SKH, Box 150: "A short while after I had left the field Japanese bombers reappeared and dropped further explosives on the place, doing no material damage."

180 **corpses adrift:** Durdin, "Invaders Close to Hankow," *NYT*, October 25, 1938.

180 **The Generalissimo, Madame:** Ernest Allison to Frank Roth, October 1, 1974, NAW; William Leary, *The Dragon's Wings*, p. 123; Earl Albert Selle, *Donald of China*, p. 346; Rhodes Farmer, *Shanghai Harvest*, p. 181.

181 **"CNAC's got":** Ernest Allison to Frank Ruth, October 1, 1974, NAW.

184 **the sun dropped:** According to a worldwide sunrise, sunset, and twilight calculator at http://www.csgnetwork.com/sunriseset.html, apparent sunset occurred at 5:08 P.M. on October 25, 1938, which dovetails exactly with Moon Chin's stories and Bond's letters.

184 **120 air miles:** Reuters Radiogram, October 26, 1938, "reuter shanghai 41905," WLB.

184 **An immense explosion:** Durdin, "Blasts Start Vast Fires," *NYT*, October 26, 1938.

184 "We're getting out": author's interview with Moon Chin, January 7, 2005, and April 19, 2006.

185 Three Japanese destroyers: Durdin, "Blasts Start Vast Fires," *NYT,* October 26, 1938.

185 International relief: Durdin, "Hankow Occupation Is Quiet," *NYT,* October 27, 1938; Farmer, *Shanghai Harvest,* p. 175: "in the main, it must be stated, the Japanese occupation of Hankow was well-disciplined"; however, Paul Frillman reported meeting one rape victim: Frillman and Peck, *China,* p. 29, and Frank Dorn, a U.S. military advisor in China, reported that the occupation was orderly—except for the Japanese summarily executing wounded or straggling Chinese soldiers: Dorn, *The Sino-Japanese War, 1937–1941,* p. 222. It is certain, however, that the Hankow occupation had little of Nanking's systemic barbarism.

186 He cabled her: Reuters Radiogram, October 26, 1938, "reuter shanghai 41905," parts one and two, WLB.

186 "beat all over": Bond to Kitsi, October 26, 1938, WLB.

186 Many expected China: Bond to Morgan, October 29, 1938, ANY; "Memorandum for J. T. Trippe from W. L. Bond, CHINA—GOVERNMENT LOAN," undated, but written after the announcement of the $25 million American loan to China, probably in the last days of December 1938, or the first week of 1939, WLB; Dorn, *The Sino-Japanese War, 1937–1941,* p. 200.

187 That night in: "Japan Celebrates Hankow's Capture; Emperor and Empress, Each Carrying Lanterns, Cheered by Million in Tokyo," *NYT,* October 29, 1938.

Chapter 15: Meeting Madame

189–90 Eurasia's prewar routes: Bond to Morgan, Letter No. 42, November 12, 1938, WLB; "Minutes of the 37th Meeting of the Board of Directors of the China National Aviation Corporation," November 17, 1938, ANY; Bixby's reply to a Bond letter I failed to locate: Bixby to Dear Bonda, October 31, 1938, WLB; Memorandum titled "Eurasia," August 30, 1941, ANY.

190 American missionary advisor: William Langhorne Bond, *Wings for an Embattled China,* pp. 202–3.

190–91 "What's your problem?": Bond, *Wings for an Embattled China,* pp. 202–3.

191–93 After seven years: Madame Chiang Kai-shek's appearance: Rhodes Farmer, *Shanghai Harvest,* p. 112; Emily Hahn, *The Soong Sisters,* pp. 57, 104–5; Hahn, *China to Me,* p. 127; Joseph Stilwell, Theodore H. White (ed.), *The Stilwell Papers,* p. 80; Sterling Seagrave, *The Soong Dynasty,* pp. 99, 110–11, 114, 115, 139–40, 268, 282, 285; Jonathan Fenby, *Generalissimo: Chiang Kai-shek and the China He Lost;* Hannah Pakula, *The Last Empress: Madame Chiang Kai-shek and the Birth of Modern China;* Laura Tyson Li, *Madame Chiang Kai-shek;* many period photographs.

192   "the future will": Bond's conversation with Madame Chiang Kai-shek and the Generalissimo: Bond, *Wings for an Embattled China*, pp. 202–5.

192   Chiang Kai-shek: W. H. Auden and Christopher Isherwood, *Journey to a War*, pp. 65–68; Farmer, *Shanghai Harvest*, p. 169; Fenby, *Generalissimo*; Jay Taylor, *The Generalissimo: Chiang Kai-shek and the Struggle for Modern China*; Arthur N. Young, *Cycle of Cathay*, p. 260; many period photographs.

192   "deep gratitude": "Memorandum for J. T. Trippe from W. L. Bond, CHINA—GOVERNMENT LOAN," undated, WLB; it was an attitude mirrored elsewhere in the correspondence of the inner circle of the Soong clique: "In view of the very valuable service being rendered in China by the C.N.A.C. in collaboration with Pan American Airways": H. H. Kung to Chang Kai-ngau, January 6, 1939, ANY.

193   Leaving chief pilot: Bond to Sharp, December 9, 1938, ANY.

193   Arthur Young covering: Bond to Vice Minister Peng Sho-pei, December 10, 1938; Bond to Arthur N. Young, December 14, 1938; all in ANY.

193   Bond reached Baltimore: Bond, *Wings for an Embattled China*, p. 206.

193   it deserved to: Bond, *Wings for an Embattled China*, p. 169. "1938 was probably the most important year in the history of C.N.A.C."

Chapter 16: Bombing Season

194   Life calmed after: William Langhorne Bond, *Wings for an Embattled China*, pp. 206–7.

194   The contract between: Kung to Minister of Communications, Chang Kia-ngau, January 6, 1939; Wong to Bond, January 19, 1939; Bond to Wong, February 1, 1939; all in ANY; Bond to Morgan, Letter No. 14, April 18, 1939; Morgan to Bond, Letter No. 10-39, May 5, 1939; both in WLB.

195   Pan American finances: Marylin Bender and Selig Altschul, *The Chosen Instrument: The Rise and Fall of an American Entrepreneur*, pp. 296–97; Robert Daley, *An American Saga: Juan Trippe and His Pan Am Empire*, pp. 232, 237.

195   Wang Ching-wei: "China Truce Move Reported in South," *NYT*, December 27, 1938; Douglas Robertson, "Drive Toward Sian by Japanese Seen; Chiang Denies Overtures," *NYT*, December 28, 1938; Hallett Abend, "Ex-Premier Wang Urges Peace with Japan in Message to Chiang; Serious Rift in the Chinese Government Is Revealed—Fugitive from Chungking Can Rally Faction to Embarrass Generalissimo," *NYT*, December 31, 1938; "Japanese Pleased by Peace Proposal," *NYT*, January 1, 1939; "Gen. Chiang Ousts Wang in a Purge of Peace Seekers," *NYT*, January 2, 1939; W. H. Donald to Stanley K. Hornbeck, *Headquarters of the Generalissimo*, January 23, 1939, SKH, Box 150, has a large segment devoted to explaining away Wang's desertion and desire to make peace with Japan as not representing the majority of Chinese opinion. Bond may or may not have seen Donald's letter, but he cer-

tainly spent much time with his close friend Stanley K. Hornbeck while he was in Washington in early 1939; also, W. H. Donald to Mr. H. J. Timperley, December 30, 1938; and "Wang Ching-wei Becomes a Political Outcast," *CWR*, January 7, 1939; "Wang Pursues Peace Aim, Attacks Former Reds," *CWR*, January 14, 1939; "The Collapse of Wang's One Man Revolt," *CWR*, January 28, 1939; Jay Taylor, *The Generalissimo*, p. 153.

195 **Japan invaded Hainan:** "Japan Occupies Hainan Island in Violation of Pledge Given France," *CWR*, February 18, 1939; Frank Dorn, *The Sino-Japanese War, 1937–1941*, pp. 249–50.

196 **Hitler annexed the:** Robert Dallek, *Franklin D. Roosevelt and American Foreign Policy, 1932–1945*, p. 184; William Shirer, *The Rise and Fall of the Third Reich*, pp. 460–75.

196 **Recognizing the likelihood:** H. H. Kung to K. P. Chen, February 11, 1939; Bond to Wong, February 17, 1939; Wong to Bond, January, 19, 1939; Bond to Wong, February 1, 1939; Delany to Wong, February 11, 1939; Arthur N. Young and P. Y. Wong to Delany and Sharp, February 13, 1939; Delany to Wong, February 16, 1939; H. H. Kung to K. P Chen, March 2, 1939; H. H. Kung to Kung Ling-kai, March 3, 1939; memorandum, written by Arthur Young, March 3, 1939; H. H. Kung to K. P. Chen, March 10, 1939; all in ANY; Bixby to Wong, March 21, 1939, WLB.

196 **one used DC-2:** Bond to Morgan, April 10, 1939, WLB; H. H. Kung to Central Bank, Hong Kong, July 18, 1939; "Minutes of the 39th Meeting of the Board of Directors of China National Aviation Corporation," August 17, 1939; both in ANY; Bond to Bixby, "Dear Bix," July 10, 1942, PAA, Box 205, Folder 10.

196 **Much refreshed, Bond:** Bixby to P. Y. Wong, March 21, 1939; Bond to Morgan, Letter No. 7, April 6, 1939; both in WLB.

196 **"comparatively little damage":** Bond to Morgan, Letter No. 7, April 6, 1939; Bond to Bixby, May 30, 1939; both in WLB.

196–97 **Mists and light rain:** Bond to Morgan, May 6, 1939; H. H. Kung to Central Bank, Hong Kong, July 18, 1939; both in WLB. Chennault's presence in Chungking confirmed in Martha Byrd, *Chennault: Giving Wings to the Tiger*, p. 100.

196 **fighting the temptation:** Bond to Bruce G. Leighton, May 30, 1939, WLB.

197 **"Bombers just left":** Bond to Morgan, May 6, 1939, WLB.

198 **Ten minutes after:** F. Tillman Durdin, "Hundreds Killed in Chungking Raid," *NYT*, May 4, 1939; Kemp Tolley, *Yangtze Patrol: The U.S. Navy in China*, pp. 265, 266 (Durdin's and Tolley's accounts are substantially in agreement); "Heavenly Dog," *Time*, May 15, 1939.

198 **"buzzing of a":** Tolley, *Yangtze Patrol*, pp. 265, 266, quoting the eyewitness writing of an officer aboard USS *Tutuila*, the Yangtze Patrol gunboat stationed in Chungking.

198 **Mrs. Wei, wife:** Bond to Morgan, Letter No. 25-39, May 22, 1939, WLB; "Minutes of the 40th Meeting of the Board of Directors of C.N.A.C.," June 22, 1940, ANY.

199 381 miles south: "Distances of C.N.A.C. Air Lines," March 1, 1940, ANY.

199 Forty-seven minutes: http://sunearth.gsfc.nasa.gov/eclipse/LEplot/LEplot1901/LE1939 May03T.GIF, accessed May 27, 2006. (63 minutes, 24 seconds of totality, beginning at 22:39:35 local time.)

199 Twenty-seven Japanese: Durdin, "Chungking Is Fighting Vast Fire Started by the Japanese Bombings," *NYT,* May 6, 1939.

199 The Japanese gave: Durdin, "Chungking Casualties Revised," *NYT,* May 14, 1939.

199 Afterward, Bond returned: Bond to Morgan, Letter No. 25-39, May 22, 1939, WLB.

199–200 six-year-old: Bond to Morgan, Letter No. 25-39, May 22, 1939, WLB; Bond, *Wings for an Embattled China,* pp. 210–11. It isn't certain in which raid the boy was hurt (possibilities are May 3, 4, or 12). May 12 would be the most convenient, but *NYT* correspondent F. Tillman Durdin didn't report major fires in downtown Chungking after that raid. He does after the May 4 attack, circumstantial evidence making it seem most likely to the author the boy was hurt in the first raid, on May 3, and then moved when major fires in downtown Chungking threatened the Methodists on May 4.

199–200 For much of: Bond to Morgan, Letter No. 26-39, May 26, 1939, WLB; Durdin, "Chungking Raided; Casualties Heavy" *NYT,* May 26, 1939; Bond, *Wings for an Embattled China,* pp. 209–10.

200 Teddy White: Emily Hahn, *China to Me,* pp. 122, 148; Theodore H. "Teddy" White, *In Search of History,* p. 106. (It was the beginning of one of the great journalistic careers of the twentieth century.)

201 As always during: Mrs. Jack T. Young to Mr. Young, June 18, 1940, WLB. "The psychology of air raids is peculiar; one would rather die with friends in a bad dugout than be alone in a dugout that is one-hundred percent safe."

201 "No time to": Bond, *Wings for an Embattled China,* pp. 209–10. In *Wings,* Bond says the episode was Pepper Martin and Teddy White, but his letter on May 29, 1939, says he was with "Durdin of the *New York Times* and a foreigner named White." The letter does not describe the falling-bomb episode, but *Wings* does, and adds that "years later, Ted sent me a copy of [*Thunder out of China*] autographed *For Bondy, Who once taught a frightened boy the sound of a falling bomb.*" White arrived in Chungking on April 10, 1939. It wouldn't have taken him long to distinguish the sound. Bond wasn't in Chungking for the first three raids. It seems likely Bond misremembered their third companion writing *Wings* thirty-five years later. White says Bond "taught me to recognize the shrill of a bomb from the air" (*In Search of History,* p. 104), but doesn't make the date explicit; Bond also mentioned that "[White] and I were both living at the same place [the Rappe compound]": Bond to Bixby, October 2, 1942, PAA, Box 205, Folder 10; author's interview with Moon Chin, Frieda Chen, and T. T. Chen, on September 19, 2006, confirmed the swish of falling bombs. Moon Chin: "You hear that, you know you're pretty close."

201 "God damn the": Bond, *Wings for an Embattled China,* pp. 209–10.

202   **no-smoking bet:** Bond to Leighton, May 30, 1939, WLB.

202–5   **It was hard** (the wounding of Joe Shen and efforts to save him): Bond to Morgan, Letter No. 38-39, July 10, 1939, WLB; Ernie Allison to K. I. Nieh, April 30, 1940, NAW; Bond, *Wings for an Embattled China,* pp. 257–60; author's interview with Harold Chinn, October 11, 2004; author's interview with Moon Chin, April 19, 2006; author's interview with Frieda Chen, September 19, 2006. (In *Wings,* Bond misremembered this incident as occurring in 1940. It happened the previous year. Other details of the *Wings* episode correlate exactly with what Bond wrote in 1939); Durdin, "Japanese Again Bomb Chungking; Most Citizens Safely in Dugouts," *NYT,* July 7, 1939; Gerald Samson, *The Far East Ablaze,* pp. 160–66; Theodore H. White and Analee Jacoby, *Thunder out of China,* p. 61; White, *In Search of History,* pp. 98–101.

202   **bright silver and:** lunar phase calculator at http://imagiware.com/astro/moon.cgi, accessed May 19, 2006.

205   **By the summer:** Johnson to Morgan, July 10, 1938, WLB.

205   **"most letters of":** Bixby to "Dear Bonda," August 1, 1939, WLB.

205   **Still, he worried:** Bixby to Dear Bonda, August 1, 1939, WLB.

205   **three other letters:** Julean Arnold to Bixby, July 26, 1939, WLB. Bixby received the others from Max Polin and George Sellett.

205   **"until all things":** Bond to Morgan, Letter No. 40, July 17, 1939, WLB.

205   **Bixby and Morgan:** Bixby to Bond, "Personal & Confidential," July 20, 1939, WLB.

206   **"What you did":** Bixby to Bond, "Personal & Confidential," August 1, 1939, WLB.

206   **The Japanese attacked:** Rappe letters, August 14 and September 15, 1939, NAW; Bond to Bixby, August 8, 1939, WLB.

206   **cholera, a disease:** "Chinese Contest Han Valley Drive; Cholera Spreads in Chungking," *NYT,* May 15, 1939; "Japanese Demand Control at Amoy; American Missions Bombed," *NYT,* May 16, 1939; "China Fights Cholera; American Funds Allocated to Combat Chungking Epidemic," *NYT,* June 20, 1939.

206–8   **Dawn broke bright:** Mr. Rappe to Dear Children, August 20, 1939, NAW; Rappe letter, September 15, 1939, NAW.

206   **Mount Emei:** Anthony Huxley, ed., *Standard Encyclopedia of the World's Mountains,* p. 238.

206   **Kiating, a small:** Durdin, "Raid in West China Is Held Terrorism," *NYT,* August 22, 1939; "Japanese Raid Kiating," *NYT,* August 20, 1939.

207   **Aloft in the:** Bond, in *Wings for an Embattled China,* pp. 186–88, describes Woods's departure as happening shortly after he was forced down in 1938. Bond's contemporary correspondence and the August 22, 1939, *NYT* story make it apparent that Woods didn't leave China until late summer, 1939.

208   **Twelve days after:** William Shirer, *The Rise and Fall of the Third Reich,* pp. 597–622;

David M. Kennedy, *Freedom from Fear,* p. 426; http://www.eyewitnesstohistory.com /london1939.htm, accessed October 31, 2006; "To End Oppression," *NYT,* September 3, 1939; "Raid Alarm Halts Chamberlain Talk," *NYT,* September 4, 1939.

208   Bond flew across: Bond was in Chungking for a board of directors' meeting on August 17, 1939: "Minutes of the 39th Meeting of the Board of Directors of China National Aviation Corporation," August 17, 1939, ANY; Rappe letter, September 15, 1939, NAW.

Chapter 17: Ventricular Tachycardia

209–10   "Kitsi, something's wrong": William Langhorne Bond, *Wings for an Embattled China,* pp. 214–17.

209   ventricular tachycardia: Susan Robinson, MD, emails to the author, June 9, 2006, and June 23, 2006, citing Jonathan J. Langberg, MD, and David B. DeLurgio, MD, who wrote the "Ventricular Arrhythmias" chapter in the *ACP Medicine* textbook.

210   Playing without: www.baseball-almanac.com.

210   Bond reached China: Bond, *Wings for an Embattled China,* p. 260; author's interview with Harold Chinn, October 11, 2004; author's interview with Frieda Chen, October 5, 2005.

211   At the next board: "Minutes of the 40th Meeting of the Board of Directors of C.N.A.C.," June 22, 1940, ANY.

211–12   Sharp was doing: Bond, *Wings for an Embattled China,* pp. 221–22.

211   Reconstructed and reconditioned: "Minutes of the 40th Board of Directors Meeting," June 22, 1940, ANY.

212   Chungking to Rangoon: There is discrepancy about the date this line was inaugurated. Two sources support October 30, 1939: "C.N.A.C. Financial Statement, December, 1939," ANY; and "China-Burma Airline Opens," *NYT,* October 31, 1939. However, "Minutes of the 40th Board of Directors Meeting," June 22, 1940, ANY, says the Chungking–Rangoon line opened on December 30, 1939. I have given credence to the more contemporaneous sources, also thinking financial records are more likely to reflect reality than board meeting minutes.

212   CNAC's first DC-3: a blizzard of telegrams and memos in WLB and ANY; Bond, *Wings for an Embattled China,* p. 228; Arthur Pearcy, *Fifty Glorious Years: A Pictorial Tribute to the Douglas DC-3,* pp. 7–22; Carroll V. Glines and Wendell F. Moseley, *The Legendary DC-3,* pp. 40–60. The United States' neutrality legislation was a tremendous burden to the airline: "We are compelled under the existing U.S. neutrality legislation to certify that all equipment shipped to Hong Kong for China has been paid for in full by the consignee . . . [it applies] to all parts, instruments, motors, and aircraft": Bixby to P. Y. Wong, December 21, 1939.

212   even easier to: author's interview with Moon Chin, April 19, 2006.

212   entered service on: "Minutes of the 40th Board of Directors Meeting," June 22, 1940, ANY.

212   auxiliary fuel tanks: "Minutes of the 40th Board of Directors Meeting," June 22, 1940; Bond to Bixby, Letter No. 35-40, July 22, 1940; Memorandum, "Reorganization of Civil Aviation in China," October 15, 1941; all in ANY. The DC-2's original range was 1,000 miles. CNAC added auxiliary tanks to its DC-2s that boosted their range to 1,248 miles: Memorandum, "Reorganization of Civil Aviation in China," October 15, 1941, ANY.

212   order two more: Bixby to Wong, December 21, 1939, ANY.

212   A strange lull: Bond, *Wings for an Embattled China*, p. 217.

213   looking uncharacteristically grim: Bond to Bixby, "Personal," March 28, 1941; Steele to Mr. W. O. Snyder, cc Bond, April 9, 1940; both in WLB; Bond to H. H. Kung, April 14, 1940, ANY; Bond, *Wings for an Embattled China*, pp. 222–24; Woods was born on March 15, 1906: http://CNAC.org/hughwoods01.htm, accessed November 1, 2006.

213   In writing, Bond: Bixby to Chief Engineering, New York (presumably Andre Priester), April 3, 1940, WLB.

213   no desire to: Bond to Bixby, "Personal," March 28, 1941, WLB.

214   adults were exceedingly glum: Florence Allison to Family, April 29, 1940, NAW.

214   Japan didn't hesitate: "Japanese Kill 200 in Chungking Raid," *NYT*, May 27, 1940; "Chungking Again Bombed," *NYT*, May 28, 1940; "Japanese Renew Chungking Raids," *NYT*, May 29, 1940; "Chungking Raiding to Be a Daily Affair," *NYT*, May 30, 1940; "Japanese Press Chungking Raids," *NYT*, May 31, 1940; "Japanese Menace Ichang from East," *NYT*, June 7, 1940; F. Tillman Durdin, "Chungking Raided Again," *NYT*, June 11, 1940; "Chungking Suffers Heaviest Bombing," *NYT*, June 13, 1940; Durdin, "U.S. Warship Rocked by Japanese Bomb," *NYT*, June 17, 1940; Mrs. Jack T. Young to Mr. Young, cc Bond, June 18, 1940, WLB; Edwin P. Hoyt, *Japan's War*, p. 190; Barbara Tuchman, *Stilwell and the American Experience in China, 1911–1945*, pp. 268–69.

214   the Burma Road: "Recommendations for type of trucks to be used on road from Lashio, Burma, to Kunming, Yunnan," undated, but probably written in 1940; "Log and Notes on Yunnan–Burma Highway, January 12, 1940; D. F. Myers to Arthur N. Young, February 28, 1940; all in ANY; "Memorandum of Recommendations Submitted by the American Commission of Highway Transportation Experts"; and M. E. Sheah to K. P. Chen, Universal Trading Corp., December 12, 1939; both in LBC, Box 2, Burma Road Folder; R&S I, pp. 44–46; Madame Chiang Kai-shek to Lauchlin Currie, July 16, 1941, acknowledges corruption on the road; also, Currie to Madame Chiang Kai-shek, September 18, 1941; both in LBC, Box 1, Madame Chiang Kai-shek Folder.

215   Equally horrendous: Otha C. Spencer, *Flying the Hump*, p. 20.

215   to Kunming from: D. F. Myers to Arthur N. Young, February 28, 1940, ANY.

215   Realizing Free China's: Bond to Bixby, Letter No. 21-40, June 27, 1940, ANY; also,

"Japan May Attack French Indo-China," *NYT,* June 16, 1940; F. Tillman Durdin, "Concern Felt in China," *NYT,* June 19, 1940; "Japanese Massing Near Indo-China," *NYT,* June 21, 1940; "Japan Plans Help to Axis in Orient," *NYT,* June 22, 1940; "Japanese Rush on Near Indo-China," *NYT,* June 23, 1940; "Japan Sends Fleet to Indo-China Port," *NYT,* June 25, 1940.

215 Japanese combat units: Bond to Bixby, Letter No. 21-40, June 27, 1940, ANY; Bond, *Wings for an Embattled China,* pp. 234–36.

216–17 On the day: Winston S. Churchill, *Their Finest Hour,* pp. 497–98. Churchill's realpolitik reason: "We are trying our best to avoid war with Japan, both by conceding on points where the Japanese military clique can perhaps force a rupture and by standing up where the ground is less dangerous": Churchill to the prime ministers of Australia and New Zealand, August 11, 1940, *Their Finest Hour,* p. 435; Durdin, "Tokyo Ultimatum to Hanoi Reported," *NYT,* September 3, 1940; "Indochina Allows Japanese to Enter," *NYT,* September 27, 1940; "Churchill to Open China's Vital Road," *NYT,* October 9, 1940; Hallett Abend, "Value of Burma Road to China Is Cut Down," *NYT,* October 13, 1940; "Bombing Planned for Burma Road," *NYT,* October 15, 1940; Robert Dallek, *Franklin D. Roosevelt and American Foreign Policy, 1932–1945,* pp. 240–42; Edwin Hoyt, *Japan's War,* pp. 188–92; Tuchman, *Stilwell and the American Experience in China, 1911–1945,* pp. 268–74; Arthur N. Young, *China and the Helping Hand,* p. 109.

216 "no designs upon": "Frontier Crossed," *NYT,* September 23, 1940.

217 State Department warned: Hugh Byas, "Japan Is Startled by American Step," *NYT,* October 9, 1940.

217–20 The airline gave (Kent's destruction): Arthur N. Young to T. V. Soong, October 30, 1940; Southard to the secretary of state, November 2, 1940 (a detailed and convincing description of events); both ANY; Hugh Woods, "Foxie Kent," *Wings over Asia: Memories of C.N.A.C.,* Vol. 4, p. 38; author's interview with Moon Chin, September 18, 2006; Bond, *Wings for an Embattled China,* pp. 230–31, 252–53 (*Wings* has the Eurasia shoot-down out of sequence); Max Springweiler, *Pioneer Aviator in China,* p. 116; undated memorandum, "Distances of C.N.A.C. Air Lines," ANY; Bond to Allison, December 1, 1940, NAW; "Japanese Fliers Kill U.S. Aviator," *NYT,* October 30, 1940; *SCMP,* October 31, 1940; two newspaper clippings dated October 31, 1940, posted online at http://cnac.org/lu01.htm, accessed June 20, 2006; *SCMP,* November 4, 1940; "Japanese Evacuate Waichow Garrison; Chinese See More Withdrawals; Kent's Death Described," *NYT,* November 4, 1940; Martha Gellhorn, "Flight into Peril," *Collier's,* May 31, 1941; William Leary, *The Dragon's Wings,* pp. 128–29; Bond, *Wings for an Embattled China,* pp. 252–53; http://cnac.org/kent01.htm, although a photo caption has the date incorrect; also, Wong to Young, April 23, 1940, ANY; Bond to Bixby, Letter No. 61-40, September 24, 1940, ANY.

217 "fifteen minutes before": "C.N.A.C. Story," manuscript prepared for censorship, *Southern Flight,* September 7, 1943, PAA, Box 205, Folder 11.

219   *Landing Changyi. Remaining:* Southland to the secretary of state, November 2, 1940, ANY.

220   William Bond rushed: Bond to Bixby, Letter No. 88-40, November 9, 1940, ANY; Bond, *Wings for an Embattled China,* pp. 252–53; undated eulogy in the 1940 files of WLB.

220   "vitally important": Bond to Bixby, Letter No. 88-40, November 9, 1940, ANY.

220   "I'm too old": Bond to Allison, December 1, 1940, NAW.

220   Thirty-nine months: "China Air Tragedy; Airline Service Operates without Interruption," October 30, 1940, clipping from an unidentified newspaper, probably *SCMP,* posted online at http://cnac.org/kent01.htm, accessed August 9, 2006.

220   Kitsi and Langhorne: Bond, *Wings for an Embattled China,* pp. 240–49.

221   hush-hush travelers: Bixby to Arthur N. Young, November 8, 1940, ANY; Martha Byrd, *Chennault: Giving Wings to the Tiger,* pp. 106–7; Daniel Ford, *Flying Tigers,* pp. 42–45; R&S I, pp. 8–12.

221   Kitsi was relieved: Florence Allison to Family, November 25, 1940, NAW. They came through Los Angeles on Wednesday, November 20, 1940.

Chapter 18: A Wing and a Spare, No Prayers Needed

222   Proving the adage: L. C. Reynolds to Arthur N. Young, November 2, 1940; Young to Bixby, December 11, 1940; Allison to Bixby, December 17, 1940; L. C. Reynolds to Allison, November 19, 1940; Bixby to Young, December 12, 1940; Bixby to Allison, December 24, 1940; all in ANY; Florence Allison to family, November 25, 1940; Florence Allison to family, December 3, 1940; Allison to Chennault, December 7, 1940; all in NAW. (I suspect the official was either Treasury Secretary Henry Morgenthau or Harry Dexter White, both of whom were closely involved with China policy.)

223–24   Fronting the Bay: Bond to Bixby, Letter No. 96-40, November 15, 1940, ANY; Bond to Kitsi, November 23, 1940; Bond to Kitsi, November 24, 1940; Bond to Kitsi, November 28, 1940; Bond to Kitsi, handwritten postscript, November 30, 1940; all in WLB; Bond memorandum, "Air Freight Service into China," May 8, 1941, ANY; Bond to Bixby, April 19, 1944, reprinted in *Wings over Asia: Memories of C.N.A.C.,* Vol. 4, pp. 95–97; Hugh Woods, "First Hump Flight," *Wings over Asia: Memories of C.N.A.C.,* Vol. 4, pp. 93–94; William Langhorne Bond, *Wings for an Embattled China,* pp. 254–56; William Leary, *The Dragon's Wings,* p. 135.

224   Bond raised the: Bond to Bixby, Letter No. B111-44, April 19, 1944, PAA; C.A.B. Docket No. 1706, February 17, 1947, p. 30, PAA, Box 205, Folder 14; Leary, *The Dragon's Wings,* p. 135.

224   The year turned: "Financial Report for the Year 1940," ANY; author's interview with Moon Chin, September 17, 2004, and September 18, 2006; Royal Leonard, *I Flew for China,* p. 221.

224　**Bernard Wong:** author's interview with Moon Chin, September 17, 2004; http://cnac
.org/bwong01.htm.

224　**pilot Joy Thom:** "Specially Chartered Plane Missing," *North China Herald,* February
19, 1941, clipping posted online at http://CNAC.org/joythom01.htm, accessed August 14,
2006; author's interview with Harold Chinn, October 11, 2004: "At that time, people getting
killed was nothing. *Nothing.* Nobody worried. We still flew"; author's interview with Frieda
Chen and T. T. Chen, October 2005; and with Moon Chin, Frieda Chen, and T. T. Chen,
September 18, 2006. (Frieda is Donald Wong's sister, and she was married to Paul Chinn at
the time.)

225　**For more than:** It was Charles H. Babb & Company: Bond to H. H. Kung, May 21,
1940; http://www.godickson.com/Charlie_Babb.htm, accessed June 7, 2006; Bond to His
Excellency Dr. H. H. Kung, May 29, 1940; Young to Wong, March 20, 1940; "Statement of
Account: Ministry of Finance Republic of China (China Airmotive Co. Fed. Inc.—U.S.A.—
Condor A/C)," July 18, 1941; Arthur N. Young to P. Y. Wong, March 20, 1940; L. A. Lewis to
H. H. Kung, April 3, 1940; Arthur N. Young to Mr. Li Tang, Director, Treasury Department,
Ministry of Finance, January 4, 1943; Arthur N. Young, Memorandum for His Excellency
H. H. Kung, "Advance for purchase of five Condor Planes," January 18, 1943 (the 1943
documents attempt to close the outstanding balances on the Condors' account); "Draft
Agreement Between Chinese Government and C.N.A.C.," March 21, 1940; "Estimate of
Capital Outlay for the proposed freight service," April 9, 1940; all in ANY; Bond, *Wings
for an Embattled China,* pp. 213, 217–18; Martha Byrd, *Chennault: Giving Wings to the
Tiger,* pp. 67, 98–100; Daniel Ford, *Flying Tigers,* pp. 36–37; Leary, *The Dragon's Wings,*
pp. 132–35.

225　**The first two:** Bond to Allison, December 10, 1940, NAW; author's interview with
Moon Chin, September 18, 2006; Bond memorandum, "Air Freight Service into China," May
8, 1941, ANY; Bond had been uneasy about the Condors since the summer of 1940—he'd
cooked up a plan to sell all five at China's cost and use the proceeds to buy two DC-2s: Bond
to Kung, August 20, 1940; Bond to Bixby, Letter No. 46-40, August 26, 1940; both in ANY.

225　**schemes to airfreight:** Arthur N. Young to H. H. Kung, February 23, 1940; Arthur N.
Young to P. Y. Wong, February 27, 1940; Kung to Bond, February 27, 1940; "Confidential
recommendations re Air Transport of Freight," March 16, 1940; all in ANY; Bixby to Bond,
"Personal & Confidential," August 2, 1939, WLB.

225　**"Since then, many":** Leary, *The Dragon's Wings,* p. 133, quoting Bond to Bixby, January 3, 1941, ANY, a letter I was unable to locate in the collection.

226　**tungsten:** H. W. Davis, "Tungsten," *Minerals Yearbook, 1941,* F. M. Shore, ed., pp. 643,
651; Jonathon Spence, *The Search for Modern China,* p. 401; Edgar Snow, *The Battle for
Asia,* p. 166; *CWR,* September 23, 1933; "Less Chinese Tungsten," *NYT,* June 13, 1939.

226　**The minister arranged:** Bond to H. H. Kung, January 17, 1941; Bond to Wong
Wen-hao, February 13, 1941; "copy of the paragraphs 3, 4, and 5 of the letter from Mr. P. Y.
Wong to Mr. Peng Sho-pei," July 30, 1941; P. Y. Wong to Arthur N. Young, August 11, 1941;

all in ANY; Bond, *Wings for an Embattled China*, pp. 224–28. Leary, *The Dragon's Wings*, p. 134; author's conversations with Moon Chin, Frieda Chen, T. T. Chen, and Harold Chinn.

226 Axis aggressions had: Robert Dallek, *Franklin D. Roosevelt and American Foreign Policy, 1932–1945*, pp. 272–73; R&S I, pp. 63–64; Barbara Tuchman, *Stilwell and the American Experience in China, 1911–1945*, p. 282; *Strategic Planning, 1941–1942*, p. 63; untitled, undated, unsigned strategic memorandum, presumably written by Claire Chennault, LBC, Box 2, AVG Folders.

226 Lauchlin Currie: Currie memorandum, "Notes on conference with Chang Kia-ngau, Minister of Communications, February 21, 1941," LBC, Box 3, Chang Kia-ngau Folder; Currie to Madame Chiang Kai-shek, September 18, 1941, LBC, Box 1, Madame Chiang Kai-shek Folder: "On this matter [airfreight], the Minister relied on the advice of Mr. Bond"; Bond interview, October 23, 1972, PAA, Box 19, Folder 3; Lauchlin Currie to William M. Leary, September 16, 1970, in Leary, *The Dragon's Wings*, p. 140: "I supported C.N.A.C. whenever and however I could, as I had the highest opinion of the efficiency and worthwhileness of the operation. This I attributed largely to W. L. Bond, the manager"; Madame Chiang Kai-shek to Lauchlin Currie, August 7, 1941, LBC, Box 1, Madame Chiang Kai-shek Folder: "I quite agree with the President that you have the ability to put across a point without getting red in the face."

226 what China needed: R&S I, pp. 14, 25–26, 47; Tuchman, *Stilwell and the American Experience in China, 1911–1945*, pp. 284–85.

227 The actual cable: Bond, *Wings for an Embattled China*, pp. 262–64.

227 Soong tasked him: Bond to Vice Minister of Communications Peng Sho-pei, June 2, 1941, WLB; Bond, *Wings for an Embattled China*, pp. 262–63; Daniel Ford, *Flying Tigers*, pp. 53–54; Sterling Seagrave, *The Soong Dynasty*, pp. 364–68.

227 "so obvious that": Bond memorandum, "Air Freight Service into China," May 8, 1941, ANY.

227 much like the: Arthur N. Young to Bixby, October 17, 1941: "For your confidential information, [Bond's freight service plan] is similar to the plan which I drafted which is in operation to finance the American volunteers under Chennault"; Bond to Sharp, July 22, 1941; both in WLB.

228 As usual, spring: "James Roosevelt Escapes Raid," *NYT*, May 4, 1941; "Chungking Target for a Heavy Raid," *NYT*, May 10, 1941; "Japanese Continue Raiding Chungking," *NYT*, May 11, 1941; "Chungking Battered by Japanese Raiders," *NYT*, May 17, 1941.

228–31 Hugh Woods piloted (DC-2½ story): Hugh L. Woods, "Report of Bombing of Plane 46," May 23, 1941; Sharp to Bixby, May 22, 1941; both in ANY; "Recent Imperiling of American Lives and Damage to American Property through Japanese Air Raids on Chinese Cities," May 23, 1941, SKH, Box 55; "U.S. Flier in China Eludes Air Ambush," *NYT*, May 22, 1941; "Bomb Missionary Plane: Japanese Fliers Wreck Craft on Ground in Szechwan," *NYT*, May 26, 1941; "Fliers Outwit Japanese: Americans Save Damaged Plane,

Patch It for Escape," *NYT,* June 1, 1941; "Keeping 'em Flying in China," *Milwaukee Journal,* August 23, 1941; "Incident of the Month," *New Horizons,* August 1941; "Space Machine Patched," *Time,* September 1, 1941, p. 20; "Topside Airline," *New Horizons,* October 1942; Zygmund Soldinski, "My Story of the DC-2½," *Wings over Asia,* Vol. 2, pp. 47–56 (Soldinksi says CNAC had three DC-3s at the time of the DC-2½ story. Soldinski misremembered. The "Irish DC-3," the airline's third, didn't reach Hong Kong until the last week of July, and it was sent because of the damage to No. 46); author's interview with Harold Chinn, October 11, 2004; author's interview with Moon Chin, September 19, 2006; photographs of the damage to No. 46, PAA; the full moon: moon phase calculator at: http://imagiware.com /astro/moon.cgi, accessed June 3, 2006.

230–31   **"If you say"** and **"load it"** and **"Hell, gimme a":** Zygmund Soldinski, "My Story of the DC-2½," *Wings over Asia,* Vol. 2, pp. 47–56.

231   **William Bond spent:** Bond to Vice Minister of Communications Peng Sho-pei, June 2, 1941; Bond to Bixby, June 8, 1941; Bond to Sharp, July 22, 1941; all in WLB; Bond to Minister of Communications Chang Kia-ngau, July 5, 1941; Young to Bixby, August 28, 1941; both in ANY; also, Bond to Currie, December 5, 1941, LBC, Box 1, Bond Folder; "Notes on Conference in Office of Mr. Currie," December 16, 1941, LBC, Box 2, Burma Folder.

231   **"sympathetic"** and **"anxious to assist":** Bond to Vice Minister of Communications Peng Sho-pei, June 2, 1941, WLB.

231   **intended to begin:** Arthur N. Young to Bixby, October 17, 1941, ANY.

231   **one of its prime:** Bond, *Wings for an Embattled China,* p. 263.

232   **the "old man":** Bond to Sharp, July 22, 1941, WLB.

232   **Japan strong-armed:** "Deal on Far East; Vichy Asserts Threats to Indo-China Call for Tokyo 'Protection,'" *NYT,* July 24, 1941; R&S I, p. 23; Tuchman, *Stilwell and the American Experience in China, 1911–1945,* p. 286; threats: Hallett Abend, "Japan Unable to Turn Back, Forced to Continue Her Costly War, She Is Expected to Move on Indo-China Next," *NYT,* July 20, 1941; F. Tillman Durdin, "New Tokyo Moves Expected by Chinese: Threat to Yunnan Province and Thailand Seen after Japanese Get Indo-China," *NYT,* July 26, 1941; "Japanese Occupy Bases at Saigon," *NYT,* July 27, 1941; "Chinese Mass in Yunnan," *NYT,* August 8, 1941; Madame Chiang Kai-shek to Currie, November 5, 1941, LBC, Box 1, Madame Chiang Kai-shek Folder; Winston Churchill to Chiang Kai-shek, November 17, 1941, LBC, Box 3, Chiang Kai-shek Folder; Winston Churchill, *The Grand Alliance,* pp. 591–92.

232   **five-hundred-plane:** R&S I, p. 23; *Strategic Planning, 1941–1942,* p. 73. This plan closely mirrors the one outlined in an untitled, undated, unsigned strategic memorandum, presumably written by Claire Chennault after the Russo-Japanese Pact was signed, LBC, Box 2, AVG Folders.

232   **froze Japanese assets:** Dallek, *Franklin D. Roosevelt and American Foreign Policy, 1932–1945,* pp. 273–85; *Strategic Planning, 1941–1942,* pp. 63–65; Tuchman, *Stilwell and the*

American Experience in China, 1911–1945, pp. 286–87; Doris Kearns Goodwin, *No Ordinary Time,* p. 283.

232   Chennault's American Volunteer Group: Ford, *Flying Tigers,* pp. 71, 73.

232   "I was checking": Currie to Madame Chiang Kai-shek, September 18, 1941; Madame Chiang Kai-shek to Currie, November 29, 1941; both in LBC, Box 1, Madame Chiang Kai-shek Folder: "The Generalissimo wishes me to thank you for your incessant and untiring efforts to further China's cause."

232   Bond spent six: Bond to Sharp, July 22, 1941, WLB; in *Wings,* Bond says he traveled to China via San Francisco, but Allison to Soong, September 16, 1941, ANY, says, "Bond passed through L.A. last Thursday, on his way back to China."

233   functioned perfectly in: Bond, *Wings for an Embattled China,* p. 266.

233   cigarettes-and-minerals: "copy of the paragraphs 3, 4, and 5 of the letter from Mr. P. Y. Wong to Mr. Peng Sho-pei," July 30, 1941; P. Y. Wong to Arthur N. Young, August 11, 1941; Arthur N. Young memorandum, October 15, 1941; Arthur N. Young to Managing Director, April 23, 1942; all in ANY; the United States received 9,474 short tons of tungsten from China in 1941: H. W. Davis, "Tungsten," *Minerals Yearbook, 1941,* F. M. Shore, ed., p. 651. CNAC flew just over 10 percent of that amount, about 1,000 metric tons, and a similar gross amount of pig tin. CNAC seems to have done its mineral accounting in metric—or long—tons, which are about 10 percent heavier than short tons, which could make the percentage closer to 12. The airline flew 328.5 metric tons of tin between March and July, and 247.5 metric tons of tungsten, with the largest monthly totals in June and July. Projecting the July totals forward through the rest of the year yields approximately 1,000 tons. It could have been higher as efficiency increased; also, it was "with a great deal of regret that we see this operation of ours come to an end" [the Namyung freight service]; the Ministry of Economic Resources owed CNAC U.S. $437,104.42 when the Japanese bombed the freight service out of existence on December 8, 1941: Bond to Minister of Economic Resources Wong Wen-hao, January 2, 1942, ANY.

233   Wong's health: author's interview with Moon Chin, Frieda Chen, and T. T. Chen, September 18, 2006; Bond to Bixby, December 17, 1941, WLB; Bond, *Wings for an Embattled China,* pp. 286–87.

233   M. Y. Tong: Bond to Leslie, June 6, 1975, PAA, Box 20, Folder 2: "This is an account of what happened to M. Y. Tong. It is my second start. I filled four pages giving you many small details that would emphasize the closeness of our friendship. However, since none of this will be relative to your history of Pan Am I am omitting all of that and merely asking you to believe that our friendship was such that what will come later will appear to be natural and creditable."

233   Bond spent two: "Notes of Conference in Office of Mr. Lauchlin Currie," December 16, 1941, LBC, Box 2, Burma Folder; Leary, *The Dragon's Wings,* p. 141; Bond, *Wings for an Embattled China,* pp. 268–72; Young to Bixby, August 28, 1941, ANY; according to Bond to Bixby, Letter No. B111-44, April 19, 1944, PAA, Bond had been pushing the Indian government to construct an airfield at Dinjan since January 1941.

233   reconnaissance flight from: it took place on Sunday, November 23, 1941, and it was the first flight over what would become known as "the Hump": Arthur N. Young, "Confidential: First Flight India–China, via the Tibetan Border," Chungking, November 30, 1941, ANY; the philatelists in the party designed about twenty "first flight" airmail covers and had them canceled by the Lashio postmaster.

234   Disquieting stories of: Zygmund Soldinski, "The Last Days of C.N.A.C. in Hong Kong," *Wings over Asia,* Vol. 2, p. 34; Bond, *Wings for an Embattled China,* pp. 268, 271, 274; Emily Hahn, *China to Me,* p. 268; "30,000 Japanese Troops Move Southward; 70 Transports Believed on the Way to Indo-China," *NYT,* November 29, 1941; although the leadership on both sides conceived of the talks as delaying actions, rearguard fights, and smoke screens to actual intentions, such strategic secrets were not apparent to employees of CNAC: Currie to Madame Chiang Kai-shek, February 10, 1942, LBC, Box 1, Madame Chiang Kai-shek Folders; Tuchman, *Stilwell and the American Experience in China, 1911–1945,* pp. 291–92; Dallek, *Franklin D. Roosevelt and American Foreign Policy, 1932–1945,* pp. 306–11; *Strategic Planning, 1941–1942,* p. 79; newspaper headlines about the state of U.S.-Japanese relations in early December 1941 make obvious the fact that the future was uncertain and war was not generally believed to be inevitable: "May Ask Further Talks," *NYT,* December 1, 1941; "4 Powers Ready, Washington Says," *NYT,* December 1, 1941; "Japan Now Looks to U.S. for Reply; Public Takes New Hope from Cabinet Decision to Go On with Parleys," *NYT,* December 2, 1941; "British Dominions Are Watching U.S.-Japanese Parleys Intently," *NYT,* December 3, 1941; "No Common Ground," *NYT,* December 4, 1941; "Singapore Doubts Japanese Threats," *NYT,* December 4, 1941; "Tokyo Reported Halting Troops," *NYT,* December 4, 1941; "Japan Hesitating," *NYT,* December 5, 1941; "Japan Confident Talks Will Go On," *NYT,* December 6, 1941; "Vichy Says Japan Is Limiting Troops," *NYT,* December 6, 1941; and, what surely must be one of the most egregiously inaccurate pieces of headline prognostication ever published: Edwin I. James, "Japan Rattles Sword but Echo Is Pianissimo," *NYT,* December 6, 1941. The text is more reasonable: "One may argue that Tokyo is seeking to gain time in which to get into better shape for the threatened war. One may also argue, however, that Japan does not wish the war." In fairness to Mr. James, he wrote the reasonable text; an editor penned the headline.

234   Most company pilots: Karl Stoffel, "He Has a Job, but Can't Get to It: Americans in China Fooled by Japan's Attack," clipping in an unidentified newspaper (probably a Cincinnati paper) posted online at http://cnac.org/pottschmidt01.htm, accessed August 18, 2006: "Just before he left for Cincinnati . . . Pottschmidt declared there would be no Pacific War. This isn't mentioned to make a bum prophet out of a sincere and intelligent young fellow. Rather it is an example of how even those people long familiar with things in the Orient were upset. . . . I was completely fooled by the attack," said Captain Robert W. Pottschmidt . . . "although the tensions had been see-sawing since July of 1940, when the Department of

State advised American women and children to evacuate China, I had believed that the Japanese had waited too long, and that nothing would mar the negotiations under way"; also, CNAC hadn't executed any portion of the evacuation plan Bond, Sharp, and Soldinski had prepared in the fall of 1941; Kitsi to Bond, December 19, 1941, SDASM; in Hong Kong, the weekend of December 6–7 featured the normal social whirl: Phillip Snow, *The Fall of Hong Kong*, pp. 51–52; Dallek, *Franklin D. Roosevelt and American Foreign Policy, 1932–1945*, pp. 299–311; Leonard, *I Flew for China*, pp. 253–55; Moon Chin, Frieda Chen, and T. T. Chen confirmed that CNAC was "business as usual" in the days prior to December 8, 1941: author's interviews: October 5 and 6, 2005; September 19, 2006. Moon Chin: "Nobody had any idea"; also: "I must confess that the actual attack took me by surprise, as I had thought the Japs were bluffing and would continue to stall for time until they had greater assurance of Russian defeat": Currie to Madame Chiang Kai-shek, February 20, 1942, LBC, Box 1, Madame Chiang Kai-shek Folder.

234 **"heartbreaking delays"**: Currie to Madame Chiang Kai-shek, February 10, 1942, LBC, Box 1, Madame Chiang Kai-shek Folder.

234 **commitment to provide:** Bixby to Bond, December 3, 1941, WLB; Bond to Currie, December 5, 1941, LBC, Box 1, Bond Folder; "Notes on Conference in Office of Mr. Lauchlin Currie," December 16, 1941, LBC, Box 2, Burma Folder; T. V. Soong memorandum for General Stilwell and President Roosevelt, January 20, 1942.

Chapter 19: "Those Planes Are Japanese!"

235–36 **Monday, December 8, 1941:** Of the sources used to shape the story of Hong Kong evacuation, by far the most important is Bond to Bixby, December 17, 1941, SDASM, a ten-page, single-spaced letter, and the author's interviews with Moon Chin, January 7 and July 15, 2005, September 19, 2006, and with Frieda and T. T. Chen, Harold Chinn, and Dolly Wong, P. Y. Wong's daughter. All details in this chapter were cross-checked with Moon Chin, Frieda Chen, and T. T. Chen in a joint interview at Moon Chin's house on September 19, 2006. There are few discrepancies between their stories and the one Bond wrote on December 17, 1941; also important are Charles L. Schafer, "Activities of District Sales Manager (Acting) Hong Kong, December 8th, 1941–June 30th, 1942," PAA, Box 261, Folder 1, a fascinating source describing Hong Kong conditions during the attack and the first six months of occupation; William Langhorne Bond, *Wings for an Embattled China*, pp. 282–87, 298, 306; William Leary, *The Dragon's Wings*, p. 143; Zygmund Soldinski, "The Last Days of C.N.A.C. in Hong Kong, 1941," and Roger Reynolds, "The Evacuation of Hong Kong," both in *Wings over Asia: A Brief History of the China National Aviation Corporation*, Vol. 2; Hugh Woods, "Pre-War Shanghai and Hong Kong," *Wings over Asia: Memories of C.N.A.C.*, Vol. 4; "Oh, By the Way . . ." uncredited manuscript, but obviously written by William McDonald, PAA, Box 58, Folder 7; also used are: "To Treasury, from Fox," January 1, 1942, *Morgenthau Diary*, Vol. 1, pp. 559–60; Chrystal Angle, *Reflections of Chrystal*, p. 179; Arthur N. Young, *Cycle of Cathay: A Historical Perspective*, p. 160; "Loss & Recovery," *New Horizons*,

January 1942; "Hong Kong Drama," *New Horizons,* February 1942; Hal Sweet, as told to Robert Neville, "Whistling Willie," *Douglas Airview,* April 1943; "C.N.A.C. Story," manuscript prepared for censorship, *Southern Flight,* September 7, 1943; text titled "Bansee," manuscript text of what became "The Burma Banshee," dated May 1943; both in PAA, Box 205, Folder 11; "Clipper Attacked by Swarm of Planes," *NYT,* December 10, 1941; Emily Hahn, *China to Me,* pp. 269, 271, 273; Alice Lan and Betty Hu, *We Flee from Hong Kong,* p. 26; Phillip Snow, *The Fall of Hong Kong,* p. 55; important interviews: Bond interview, October 23, 1972, PAA, Box 19, Folder 3; Moon Chin's Oral History, Louis A. Turpin Aviation Museum.

235 **6:50 A.M.:** http://www.srrb.noaa.gov/highlights/sunrise/sunrise.html.

235 **"I'm in a bind":** Bond to Bixby, December 17, 1941, SDASM; Bond, *Wings for an Embattled China,* p. 282; "Hong Kong Drama," *New Horizons,* February 1942; Bond interview, October 23, 1972, PAA, Box 19, Folder 3.

236 **"There will be":** Angle, *Reflections of Chrystal,* p. 181. I examined old issues of *SCMP* on microfilm at the Hong Kong Public Library in 2005, but its collection did not include the issues published in December 1941.

236 **"The Japs just":** Soldinski, "The Last Days of C.N.A.C. in Hong Kong, 1941," *Wings over Asia,* Vol. 2.

236 **Number 24, the *Nanking*:** There is some difficulty determining the precise locations of the airline's three DC-3s on the morning of December 8, 1941. Soldinski's "Last Days of C.N.A.C. in Hong Kong" account, Hugh Woods's "Pre-War Shanghai and Hong Kong," and Moon Chin in interviews are very clear in placing only one DC-3 in the hangar and two out on routes, whereas Bond's letter, Bond to Bixby, December 17, 1941, SDASM, Arthur N. Young, *Cycle of Cathay: A Historical Perspective,* p. 160, and "Loss and Recovery," *New Horizons,* January 1941, locate two of the three DC-3s at Kai Tak. Despite strong reservations— Moon Chin's recollections have proved precisely accurate in every other instance—I've chosen to cleave to Bond's and Young's accounts. Bond very specifically mentions the times the first two DC-3s left Hong Kong on Monday night in his letter (7:00 and 7:15 P.M.), and that doesn't leave enough available darkness for the second DC-3 to approach Hong Kong and land after dark (sunset was at 5:40 P.M.), be loaded and fueled, and take off again by 7:15. (McDonald, coming in from Burma via Chungking in plane number 47, didn't land until after midnight. On Tuesday night, when all the planes were coming in from Chungking, it wasn't judged safe to let them arrive at Kai Tak earlier than 10 P.M.); "Hong Kong Drama," *New Horizons,* February 1942, mentions "five planes remaining at the field," which supports Bond's account—I make them to be two DC-3s, one DC-2, one Condor, and one Vultee trainer; also Harold Sweet and Robert Neville, "Whistling Willie," *Douglas Airview,* April 1943, says "three planes, all Douglas transports, came out of that holocaust, and they had been rushed across the street from the field and camouflaged . . ." (However, to be fair, "Whistling Willie" is full of much obvious malarkey); "C.N.A.C. Story," manuscript prepared for censorship for *Southern Flight,* September 7, 1943, PAA, Box 205, Folder 11.

238 **"Look!":** author's interview with T. T. Chen, September 19, 2006.

238   Twelve single-engine: "At 0800 an estimated 12 Ki-36s from the 45th Sentai, escorted by 9 Ki-27s from the 10th I. F. Chutai led by Captain Akira Takatsuki attacked Kai Tak": http://surfcity.kund.dalnet.se/sino-japanese-1941.htm, accessed September 12, 2006, guided to the site by Mr. Arvo Vercamer; T. T. Chen, who was at Kai Tak during the attack, confirmed that the attacking planes were of the single-engine variety: author's interview with T. T. Chen, October 5, 2005.

238   three minutes: author's interview with T. T. Chen, September 19, 2006.

238   the mangled remains: planes destroyed on the ground (two CNAC DC-2s and three Condors; two of Eurasia's JU-52s): "Douglas DC-2 No. 24 and 26 and Condors No. F2, F3, and F5 attacked by enemy planes and burnt during air-raid on December 8, 1941": "Minutes of a Special meeting of the Board of Directors in Chungking," January 23, 1942, ANY; "Loss & Recovery," *New Horizons,* January 1942; "Hong Kong Drama," *New Horizons,* February 1942.

239   Moon Chin had: author's interviews with Moon Chin: January 7 and July 15, 2005, and with Moon Chin, Frieda Chen, and T. T. Chen on September 19, 2006.

240   CNAC had an office: author's interview with Frieda Chen, September 19, 2006. She had been working as P. Y. Wong's secretary since her husband, Paul Chinn, was killed in February 1941. Wong's office was one of the three at the top of the stairs, directly adjacent to Bond's.

240   "My duty station": Bond to Bixby, December 17, 1941, SDASM.

241   Bond radioed McDonald: Bond to McDonald, December 8, 1941, 9:35 A.M., ANY.

241   "Get ready to": author's interviews with Moon Chin, January 7, 2005; July 15, 2005; September 19, 2006.

243   "Get your goddamned": Soldinski, "The Last Days of C.N.A.C. in Hong Kong, 1941," *Wings over Asia,* Vol. 2.

243   "Staff and families": Soldinski, "The Last Days of C.N.A.C. in Hong Kong, 1941," *Wings over Asia,* Vol. 2.

244   "Hop in, Bondy!": Bond to Bixby, December 17, 1941, SDASM.

245   5:40 P.M.: http://www.srrb.noaa.gov/highlights/sunrise/sunrise.html, accessed September 14, 2006.

246   "Get it ready": Soldinski, "The Last Days of C.N.A.C. in Hong Kong, 1941," *Wings over Asia,* Vol. 2.

247   "The Japanese just": Bond to Leslie, June 6, 1975, PAA, Box 20, Folder 2; Bond to Leslie, July 1, 1975, PAA, Box 27, Folder 23 (Leslie was doing a corporate history for Pan Am); Bond, *Wings for an Embattled China,* p. 284.

248   "shockproof": Bond, *Wings for an Embattled China,* p. 288.

248   "Sorry, Maj, Ten": Woods, "Pre-War Shanghai and Hong Kong," *Wings over Asia,* Vol. 4, p. 8.

249 **M. Y. Tong's office:** Bond describes conversations with M. Y. Tong on December 9 in *Wings* (p. 285), and in Bond to Leslie, June 6, 1975, but in Bond to Bixby, December 17, 1941, Bond wrote: "In the short time I was in Hong Kong I particularly tried to locate Mr. M. Y. Tong but was unable to do so."

250 **Reams of messages:** Carbon copies of three radiograms Bond received on the afternoon of December 9 survive: Peng and Young to Bond and Sharp; Young to Bond; Peng and Young to Bond, Sharp, Liang, and Soldinski; all in ANY.

250 **"come out tonight":** Peng and Young to Bond, Sharp, Liang, and Soldinski, December 9, 1941, ANY.

250 **the quarter moon:** http://imagiware.com/astro/moon.cgi.

250 **"dark as the":** Bond to Bixby, December 17, 1941, SDASM.

251 **"I want to go now":** Bond, *Wings for an Embattled China*, p. 298; Reynolds, "The Evacuation of Hong Kong"; and Soldinski, "The Last Days of C.N.A.C. in Hong Kong, 1941," *Wings over Asia*, Vol. 2, pp. 40, 44–46.

251 **"No way this":** Soldinski, "The Last Days of C.N.A.C. in Hong Kong, 1941," *Wings over Asia*, Vol. 2, p. 42.

252 **"Three Men on a Flying Trapeze":** http://www.cnac.org/williamson01.htm; http://nationalaviation.blade6.donet.com/components/content_manager_v02/view_nahf/htdocs/menu_ps.asp?NodeID=-153532201&group_ID=1134656385&Parent_ID=-1; http://www.historynet.com/magazines/aviation_history/3029241.html?featured=y&c=y; all accessed November 23, 2006.

252 **"pisses ice water":** William McDonald, "Farewell to Chuck Sharp," *C.N.A.C. Cannonball*, March 15, 1974.

252 **The last plane:** It isn't entirely clear from Bond's letter in what order the last planes flew out of Hong Kong, although it does note that Bond left Hong Kong aboard a DC-2 piloted by Moon Chin (Bond loses the discipline of exact chronology toward the end); Moon Chin says he piloted out the last plane, and Frieda and T. T. Chen concur, in many interviews.

252 **Charles Schafer volunteered:** Charles Louis Schafer, "Biographical Data," *C.N.A.C. Cannonball*, March 1, 1981.

254 **two frightened dachshunds:** Young, *Cycle of Cathay*, p. 161; Reynolds, "The Evacuation of Hong Kong," *Wings over Asia*, Vol. 2, pp. 44–47; the libelous version of the story described: Jonathan Fenby, *Generalissimo: Chiang kai-shek and the China He Lost*, pp. 404–5; Hannah Pakula, *The Last Empress: Madame Chiang Kai-shek and the Birth of Modern China*, pp. 368–70.

254 **"black as a":** Bond to Bixby, December 17, 1941, SDASM.

255 **Kowloon was in:** there are some discrepancies about exactly when the British abandoned Kowloon: Charles L. Schafer, "Activities of District Sales Manager (Acting) Hong Kong, December 8th, 1941–June 30th, 1942," PAA, Box 261, Folder 1, says that Kowloon was completely occupied by the Japanese troops on the morning of Friday, December 12, 1941; Snow, *The Fall of Hong Kong*, p. 57, says the Japanese didn't enter Kowloon until Friday night; Emily Hahn, *China to Me*, says Kowloon fell on Wednesday, but that's certainly not true; also "Kowloon Seized, Japanese Report," *NYT*, December 13, 1941, which doesn't specify the time of occupation.

255   **"I am safely"**: Bond to Kitsi, radiogram, December 13, 1941, WLB.

256   **"for reference in"**: Bond to Bixby, December 17, 1941, SDASM.

257   **"the most perilous"**: "Rescues from Hong Kong: Mme Sun and 275 Others Are Taken Out by Plane," *NYT*, December 15, 1941; also, "Chinese Reported Nearing Hong Kong," *NYT*, December 15, 1941.

258   **"without incident"**: author's interviews with Moon Chin, January 7, 2005; July 15, 2005; September 19, 2006.

Chapter 20: In the Fight

261   **Sharp had orchestrated**: William Langhorne Bond, *Wings for an Embattled China*, pp. 299, 302–3.

261   **Bond delighted to**: Bond's feelings about U.S. neutrality and the lost opportunities of the 1930s are enumerated in many of his contemporary letters; author's interviews with Langhorne Bond, December 2, 2004, January 27, 2005, and September 14, 2005.

262–63   **ten years of**: Bond, *Wings for an Embattled China*, pp. 300, 303, 308, 311, 329–30.

262   **nearly thirteen million**: CNAC Financial Statements, December 1941, ANY.

263   **American Volunteer Group**: telegram, Chennault to Currie, December 4, 1941; "Information from Lt. Estes Swindle," December 6, 1941; Chennault to T. V. Soong, cc Madame Chiang Kai-shek and Lauchlin Currie, January 12, 1942; all in LBC, Box 2, AVG Folders; Daniel Ford, *Flying Tigers*, p. 96.

263   **Fortunately, it enjoyed**: Invoice, CNAC for the AVG, attention Colonel Chennault, April 16, 1942, ANY; W. D. Pawley to T. V. Soong, November 22, 1941, LBC, Box 2, AVG Folders; "Pan American Annual Report, 1942," PAA, Box 19, Folder 2; Currie to SEGAC, for GROCO (Currie to Madame Chiang, for Chennault), February 3, 1942; Currie to Magruder, February 7, 1942; both in LBC, Box 1, Chennault Folder; author's interviews with Harold Chinn, October 11, 2004; Moon Chin, April 19, 2006; Joe Rosbert, August 14 and 15, 2004; Dick Rossi, September 23, 2004; "Much Destruction Reported," *NYT*, December 19, 1941; Charles Bond and Terry Anderson, *A Flying Tiger's Diary*, p. 119; Ford, *Flying Tigers*, pp. 102, 108, 153, 176, 255, 268, 289, 350, 351; Olga Greenlaw, *The Lady and the Tigers*, pp. 65, 79; Gregory Boyington, *Baa Baa Black Sheep*, p. 36.

263   **Thursday, December 18**: Paul Frillman and Graham Peck, *China: The Remembered Life*, p. 91, says "three battered old CNAC cargo planes landed at Toungoo" at dusk on December 18; as does Ford, *Flying Tigers*, p. 108, but Bond and Anderson, *A Flying Tiger's*

Diary, p. 55, says CNAC flew in support of the AVG on December 16; also Joe Rosbert, *Flying Tiger Joe's Adventure Cookbook,* p. 73; Jack Samson, *The Flying Tiger: The True Story of General Claire Chennault and the U.S. 14th Air Force in China,* p. 90.

263   **the airline needed Calcutta:** Bond, *Wings for an Embattled China,* pp. 304–5; "Director of Air Civil of India" is the exact title used by Bond: Bond to Bixby, December 17, 1941, SDASM. The precise details of CNAC operations in the immediate weeks post–Pearl Harbor are difficult to ascertain.

264   **AVG squadrons scored:** "U.S. Fliers in China Down 4 Japanese," *NYT,* December 21, 1941; Chennault to T. V. Soong, cc Madame Chiang Kai-shek and Lauchlin Currie, January 12, 1942, LBC, Box 2, AVG Folders; Ford, *Flying Tigers,* pp. 111–19; Greenlaw, *The Lady and the Tigers,* pp. 69–71; Rosbert, *Flying Tiger Joe's Adventure Cookbook,* pp. 75–77; Bond and Anderson, *A Flying Tiger's Diary,* pp. 60–63; Boyington, *Baa Baa Black Sheep,* p. 38.

264   **Japanese air forces:** Chennault to T. V. Soong, January 12, 1942, LBC, Box 2, AVG Folders; SEGAC (Madame Chiang) and GROCO (Chennault, Group Commander) to Currie, January 16, 1942, LBC, Box 2, AVG Folders; Ford, *Flying Tigers,* pp. 181–217.

264   **toiled through the:** Bond, *Wings for an Embattled China,* pp. 308, 313.

265–67   **The only other airplane:** Harold Sweet, as told to Robert Neville, "Whistling Willie (The Flying Sieve)," *Douglas Airview,* April 1943; Zygmund Soldinski, "The Burma Banshee," *Wings over Asia: A Brief History of the China National Aviation Corporation,* Vol. 2, pp. 85–91; "Banshee," May 1943, text prepared for publication, PAA, Box 205, Folder 11; "Banshee," *New Horizons,* December 1942; John H. Murdoch III, "Burma Banshee," *Flying,* July 1943; Stilwell diary, March 3, 1942: "Sharp working on the DC-3 shot up at Hong Kong. Over 500 shots in it,—2,000 holes. O.K. in a week": This sentence is not included in the version of Stilwell's diary edited by Theodore White and published in book form as *The Stilwell Papers.*

265   **"It looks like":** Soldinski, "The Burma Banshee," *Wings over Asia,* Vol. 2, p. 88.

265   **Six engines of:** paraphrased telegram, Bixby to Bond, January 24, 1942, SKH, Box 58.

265   **"She'll fly":** Murdoch, "Burma Banshee," *Flying,* July 1943.

266   **743 miles** and **375 miles:** K. I. Nieh to Z. M. Wong, "C.N.A.C. Airline Distances," May 25, 1942, ANY.

267   **"How did you":** "Banshee," *New Horizons,* December 1942.

267   **"probably the most":** Bond to Bixby, "Report on Operations during 1942," February 24, 1943, ANY. (The "Noodle Strainer" episode with number 41 gained wide notoriety in the press under such monikers as "the Flying Sieve," "Whistling Dixie," and "the Burma Banshee." Several stories mistakenly placed Hal Sweet at the controls, and they filled column after column with breathless prose: "On and on the transport flew through the black clouds, long tongues of brilliant flame shooting from the exhaust stacks." Six Japanese pursuit planes bore down in that story, scenting an easy kill, but "as the wild cry of the fire-streaming transport reached [the Japanese pilots] above the throb of their engines, they suddenly turned tail and streaked off into the sunset, sons of Nippon frightened off by the

Burma Banshee's eerie howling." Chuck Sharp did P. T. Barnum proud with that tale, which must surely rank among the most righteous cargoes of malarkey a pilot ever gulled a journalist into committing to paper.)

267 **Allied strategy:** R&S I, pp. 63–64; *Strategic Planning, 1943–1944,* pp. 120–21; Robert Dallek, *Franklin D. Roosevelt and American Foreign Policy, 1932–1945,* pp. 317–61.

267 **Currie told President:** Currie to the President, January 24, 1942, LBC, Box 5, FDR Memoranda; R&S I, p. 75, note 86.

267 **"It is necessary":** Soong's January 30 letter to Stilwell and FDR reproduced in its entirety: William Leary, *The Dragon's Wings,* pp. 149–50.

267 **Joseph W. Stilwell:** Stilwell, his career, and his relationship with China are best described in Barbara Tuchman's classic *Stilwell and the American Experience in China, 1911–1945,* a must-read; also the biographical note to the register of the Stilwell Papers: posted online by the Hoover Institute Archive; Eric Sevareid, *Not So Wild a Dream,* p. 321; *The Stilwell Papers,* pp. 30–34, 36; R&S I, p. 74; Stilwell diary, February 9, 1942, unedited transcript published online at http://media.hoover.org/documents/1942Stilwell.pdf. (Based on the actual transcript of Stilwell's diary, Theodore White took substantial liberties with the narration of this scene [and others] in *The Stilwell Papers.*)

268 **White House intimate:** Harriman to President, January 31, 1942, in Tuchman, *Stilwell and the American Experience in China, 1911–1945,* p. 316.

268 **"I can now":** President Roosevelt to Generalissimo Chiang Kai-shek, February 9, 1942, *FRUS, 1942, China,* p. 13; R&S I, p. 78.

268 **British surrendered Singapore:** Christopher Bayly and Tim Harper, *Forgotten Armies: The Fall of British Asia, 1941–1945,* p. 146.

268 **aggressive Japanese infantry:** Louis Allen, *Burma: The Longest War, 1941–1945,* pp. 36–44; R&S I, pp. 83–84; Sir William Slim, *Defeat into Victory,* pp. 13–14.

269 **new managing director:** Bond to Colonel C. F. Wang, February 21, 1942, ANY; Bond, *Wings for an Embattled China,* p. 329.

269 **"upright and efficient":** Arthur N. Young, *Cycle of Cathay: A Historical Perspective,* p. 167.

269 **Soong's desire to:** Bond, *Wings for an Embattled China,* p. 315.

269 **Bond gave face:** Bond to C. F. Wang, February 24, 1942; William L. Bond, *Report on Operations during 1942,* February 24, 1943; both in ANY.

269 **Bond flew west:** Tom Culbert and Andy Dawson, *Pan Africa: Across the Sahara in 1942 with Pan Am,* which carefully maps and describes the Pan Africa route and details its history.

270 **"Sharpe [*sic*] working on":** Stilwell diary, unedited, published online by the Hoover Institute at http://media.hoover.org/documents/1942Stilwell.pdf, entry for March 3, 1942; it is possible that Stilwell knew Chuck Sharp from the years he served as American military attaché to China. He would certainly have had knowledge of CNAC and its operations.

Stilwell's diary doesn't make it clear whether or not he flew CNAC from Calcutta to Lashio, although it is specific about CNAC taking him from Lashio to Kunming, and then on to Chungking on March 4. He spent only one hour and ten minutes in Lashio. It seems reasonable that this was CNAC's scheduled layover. Tuchman, *Stilwell and the American Experience in China, 1911–1945*, p. 333 (which also incorrectly asserts that CNAC had only one qualified Chinese pilot on its rolls on March 3, 1942—CNAC had one qualified *DC-3 pilot* who was Chinese, Moon Chin. It had a number of other Chinese pilots qualified in other machines who would soon check out in the DC-3—among them Hugh Chen, Harold Chinn, M. K. Loh, and Donald Wong, who was on his way to Asia from the United States to rejoin the airline he'd left in 1937).

270   **nimble Japanese infantry:** "Last Defense Line Broken in Burma," *NYT*, March 5, 1942; "Burma's Invaders Push West of Gulf," *NYT*, March 6, 1942; the fall of Rangoon: "Foe Gains in Burma," *NYT*, March 9, 1942; "Rangoon Capture Confirmed in India," *NYT*, March 10, 1942; "Rangoon in Ruins as Defenders Quit," *NYT*, March 11, 1942; Allen, *Burma*, pp. 44–57; R&S I, p. 84; Slim, *Defeat into Victory*, pp. 14–15.

270   **All six of:** Arthur N. Young to Sharp, March 8, 1942; "Minutes of the 42nd Meeting of the Board of Directors," August 8, 1942; both in ANY.

270   **Stilwell flew back:** Stilwell diary, March 11, 1942.

270   **RAF and the AVG defended:** Allen, *Burma*, pp. 61–63; Ford, *Flying Tigers*, pp. 260–69; Slim, *Defeat into Victory*, pp. 37–59; Tuchman, *Stilwell and the American Experience in China, 1911–1945*, p. 351; R&S I, p. 110; R&S I, pp. 106–9.

272   **dismal succession of:** Richard Aldworth to Currie, April 16, 1942, LBC, Box 2, AVG Folders; R&S I, p. 93.

272   **"our Mr. Bond":** Bond, *Wings for an Embattled China*, p. 347.

272–73   **The officer took:** Bond, *Wings for an Embattled China*, pp. 347–48.

273   **the Japanese scourged:** R&S I, pp. 163, 184.

273   **The raid made:** Slim, *Defeat into Victory*, pp. 55, 58–80; Tuchman, *Stilwell and the American Experience in China, 1911–1945*, pp. 366–70; Stilwell diary, April 16–24, 1942.

273   **Hugh Woods had:** "Developments Affecting C.N.A.C. Since April 24th Resulting from in Burma" (*sic*), May 5, 1942; Myitkyina Station Manager Lu Cheng Hwa to Sharp, Nieh, Woods, May 2, 1942; both in ANY; President Roosevelt's Personal Representative In India (Johnson) to the Secretary of State, April 16, 1942, *FRUS 1942, China*, pp. 675–76; "200 Indians Daily Flown out of Burma," *NYT*, April 8, 1942; "Minutes of the 42nd Meeting of the Board of Directors," August 8, 1942; radiogram, Sharp to Arthur N. Young, May 6, 1942; Sharp to Nieh, May 6, 1942; all in ANY; Brigadier General Haynes to Lieutenant Colonel Moore, April 20, 1943, AFHRA.

273–74   **Moon Chin was:** author's interviews with Moon Chin, September 17, 2004, and January 7, 2005; "Life Line," *New Horizons*, April 1943; Mamie Hall Porritt, "China Lifeline," *Air Transport*, March 1944; Leary, *The Dragon's Wings*, pp. 152–53, citing a personal letter from Doolittle to the author.

274   **"Calm down, Major"**: "Life Line," *New Horizons,* April 1943.

275   **one relay too long**: Brigadier General Haynes to Lieutenant Colonel Moore, April 20, 1943, AFHRA; William L. Bond, "Report on Operations during 1942," February 23, 1943, ANY; "History of the India-China Ferry under the Tenth Air Force," June 22, 1943, AFHRA; R&S I, p. 93.

275   **"outmaneuvered, outfought, outgeneraled"**: Slim, *Defeat into Victory,* p. 115.

275   **An emergency meeting**: "Minutes of the Special Meeting of the Board of Directors," May 5, 1942; "Developments Affecting C.N.A.C. Since April 24 Resulting in from Burma" (*sic*), May 5, 1942.

275   **Three Chinese divisions**: R&S I, pp. 140–42.

Chapter 21: "For Us It Started Five Years Ago"

277   **"If such conception"**: R. E. Schuirmann, Memorandum for the State Department from the Office of the Chief of Naval Operations, April 16, 1942; General Magruder of AMMISCA echoed this sentiment: The Military Mission in China to the War Department, February 10, 1942; both in *FRUS, 1942, China,* pp. 13–16, 31 ("It is highly possible that such propaganda could lead to grave defects in American war plans, if our own officials should be influenced by it, even to the slightest extent. . . . Such a misconception as to the part China can accurately be expected to play in this war may harm us greatly if our own war plans are based at all substantially on any such exaggerated expectations."); also, Barbara Tuchman, *Stilwell and the American Experience in China, 1911–1945,* pp. 283–84.

277   **Marshall concurred**: R&S I, p. 85, note 3(2), citing Marshall to Magruder, February 15, 1942.

277   **Gauss, had been**: Gauss to the Secretary of State, February 21, 1942, *FRUS, 1942, China,* p. 24.

277   **"shun offensive action"**: R&S I, p. 53, citing MacMorland Diary, December 16 and 18, 1941; another AMMISCA assessment of Chinese capabilities and lack of offensive spirit: R&S I, pp. 42–43, citing a memo from LTC George W. Sliney to General Magruder; also, R&S I, pp. 71, 80; the Military Mission in China to the War Department, February 10, 1942, *FRUS, 1942, China,* pp. 13–16; memorandum from General Stilwell to Lauchlin Currie, August 1, 1942, points 14 and 15, LBC, Box 5, Stilwell Folder.

277   **so did President**: *Strategic Planning, 1943–1944,* pp. 9–15; Memorandum by the Advisor on Political Relations (Hornbeck), May 7, 1942; the Ambassador in China (Gauss) to the Secretary of State, May 20, 1942; Memorandum by the Advisor on Political Relations (Hornbeck), May 20, 1942; Memorandum by the Chief of the Division of Far Eastern Affairs (Hamilton), May 20, 1942; Memorandum Prepared in the Department of State, June 27, 1942; all in *FRUS, 1942, China,* pp. 40, 41, 48–49, 49–51, 52–53, 53–54, 90–91; rosy State Department assessments of China's war potential and Chiang Kai-shek's leadership: Memorandum by the Chief of the Division of Far Eastern Affairs (Hamilton), re

the telegraphic report, No. 256 AMMISCA, from the Magruder Mission; Memorandum by the Advisor on Political Relations (Hornbeck) to the Under Secretary of State (Welles), February 16, 1942; Memorandum by the Chief of the Division of Far Eastern Affairs (Hamilton), re China's War Potential, June 17, 1942; all in *FRUS, 1942, China,* pp. 18–19, 71.

277 **"gallant people of":** Secretary of State (Hull) to the Chief of Staff (Marshall), April 28, 1942, *FRUS, 1942, China,* pp. 44–45.

278 **Committing to China:** Lauchlin Currie to Madame Chiang Kai-shek, May 26, 1942, LBC, Box 1, Madame Chiang Kai-shek Folder; R&S I, p. 165; Sir William Slim, *Defeat into Victory,* pp. 248–49.

278 **"It is essential":** Hap Arnold, *Global Mission,* p. 332; R&S I, p. 164; Tuchman, *Stilwell and the American Experience in China, 1911–1945,* p. 389.

278 **"The President is":** Thomas M. Coffey, *Hap: The Story of the U.S. Air Force and the Man Who Built It, General Henry H. "Hap" Arnold,* p. 270.

278–80 **Arnold duly summoned:** William Langhorne Bond, *Wings for an Embattled China,* pp. 315–18 (in *Wings,* Bond describes the meeting with Arnold as taking place immediately after he returned to Washington, in early March 1942, but it seems unlikely that he and Soong saw Arnold twice on the same subject. I suspect Bond misremembered the sequence of events); William Bond, "Report on Operations during 1942," February 24, 1943, ANY: "This proposed freight service from Dinjan to Kunming was the subject of several very serious discussions in Washington as to whether it was practicable. General P. H. Wong and General T. S. Shen and I insisted that it could be done and must be attempted"; H. H. Arnold, *Global Mission,* pp. 331–33, 417–19, 425; Coffey, *Hap,* pp. 270–71; C&C I, p. 511; Oliver La Farge, *The Eagle in the Egg,* pp. 121–22; R&S I, pp. 202–4; Slim, *Defeat into Victory,* p. 170; Otha C. Spencer, *Flying the Hump,* p. 47.

279 **"Sir, I've heard":** Bond, *Wings for an Embattled China,* pp. 315–18.

280 **assurances of airplanes:** Bond knew as early as April 13, 1942, that T. V. Soong had a commitment for twenty-two DC-3s to be converted to C-53s and sold to China on China's Lend-Lease account, two per month: T. V. Soong to Minister of Communications Chang, April 13, 1942, quoted in Young to Bond, May 21, 1942, ANY.

280 **failed to impress:** author's interviews with Dick Rossi, September 23, 2004; and Joe Rosbert, August 14 and 15, 2004; author's conversations with CNAC personnel, 2002–2009. The opinion is reflected in much company correspondence, postwar writing, and conversation.

280 **Moon Chin had:** Arthur N. Young to General Magruder, March 8, 1942, ANY.

280 **An Air Corps pilot:** President Roosevelt's Personal Representative in India (Johnson) to the Secretary of State, April 16, 1942, *FRUS, 1942, China,* pp. 675–76.

280 **Chuck Sharp rescued:** Colonel C. F. Wang to Sharp, May 14, 1942; Arthur N. Young to Bond, May 21, 1942; both in ANY; Bond, *Wings for an Embattled China,* pp. 339–40.

280 **eight B-17:** C&C I, pp. 484, 493; "History of the India-China Ferry under the Tenth Air Force," June 22, 1943, AFHRA, p. 5.

281 **AVG ground crews:** Daniel Ford, *Flying Tigers: Claire Chennault and the American Volunteer Group,* p. 255; author's interviews with Joe Rosbert, August 14 and 15, 2004, and Dick Rossi, September 23, 2004.

281 **the Flying Tigers** (Trying to fit them into the war effort): Lauchlin Currie wrote the president the day after Pearl Harbor suggesting that the AVG could form the core of an American air task force on the Asian mainland: "Memorandum for the President, re: Suggestions Relating to the American Volunteer Air Corps Now in Burma," December 8, 1941; Chennault to T. V. Soong, January 12, 1942; Currie to SEGAC and GROCO (Currie to Madame Chaing and Chennault), January 19, 1942; Currie to President Roosevelt, April 2, 1942; all in LBC, Box 2, AVG Folders; SEGAC to Currie, from GROCO, January 26, 1942, LBC, Box 1, Chennault Folder; Stilwell diary, April 1, 1942; author's interviews with Joe Rosbert, August 14 and 15, 2004, and Dick Rossi, September 23, 2004; Charles R. Bond, Jr., and Terry H. Anderson, *A Flying Tiger's Diary,* p. 69; Martha Byrd, *Chennault: Giving Wings to the Tiger,* pp. 140–43; Ford, *Flying Tigers,* pp. 289–99; Olga Greenlaw, *The Lady and the Tigers,* p. 83; R&S I, p. 91.

281 **Clayton L. Bissell:** SEGAC (for GROCO) to Currie (Madame Chiang for Chennault, to Currie), February 6, 1942; Currie to Chennault, February 9, 1942; both in LBC, Box 1, Chennault Folder; Currie to Madame Chiang Kai-shek, February 10, 1942; Currie to Madame Chiang Kai-shek, April 1, 1942; Madame Chiang Kai-shek to Lauchlin Currie, May 18, 1942; all in LBC, Box 1, Madame Chiang Kai-shek Folder; George C. Marshall to Lauchlin Currie, September 10, 1942, LBC, Box 1, George C. Marshall Folder; Arnold, *Global Mission,* p. 419; R&S I, p. 73, note 79 (citing McCloy to Soong, February 3, 1942); Tuchman, *Stilwell and the American Experience in China, 1911–1945,* p. 474; Bissell's combat record: http://www.theaerodrome.com/aces/usa/bissell.php.

282 **grounded Air Corps:** "History of the India-China Ferry under the Tenth Air Force," June 22, 1943, AFHRA.

282 **Young was covering:** Arthur N. Young to Sharp, May 26, 1942, ANY.

282 **Sharp didn't appreciate:** Sharp to Arthur N. Young, May 30, 1942, ANY; "History of the India-China Ferry under the Tenth Air Force," June 22, 1943, AFHRA.

282–83 **batch of B-25s:** Brigadier General Caleb Haynes to LTC Samuel T. Moore, April 20, 1943, AFHRA; Lewis Brereton, *The Brereton Diaries, 3 October 1941–8 May 1945,* pp. 127–28; C&C I, pp. 505–6; Ford, *Flying Tigers,* pp. 347–48.

283–84 **Enraged, General Bissell:** Bond to Bixby, "PERSONAL," July 10, 1942, PAA, Box 205, Folder 10.

283 **He'd come to China:** *American Aviation,* Vol. 33, No. 2, June 23, 1969.

283 **the attitude of their leadership:** Bond, *Wings for an Embattled China,* p. 346, quoting an undated 1942 letter from Bond to Kitsi; author's interviews with Joe Rosbert, Dick

Rossi, Pete Goutiere, Moon Chin, Fletcher "Christie" Hanks, William J. Maher, Donald McBride, and many other CNAC veterans.

284 **"jumped right down":** Bond to Bixby, "PERSONAL," July 10, 1942, PAA, Box 205, Folder 10.

284 **Bond's practical expertise:** Memorandum by the Chief of the Division of Far Eastern Affairs (Hamilton) to the Secretary of State, May 28, 1942, *FRUS, 1942, China,* p. 58: Hamilton reminds the secretary that Mr. W. L. Bond "is firmly of the belief an air supply route can successfully be operated between India and China over Japanese held territory"; Memorandum by the Advisor on Political Relations (Hornbeck) to the Secretary of State, May 29, 1942, *FRUS, 1942, China,* pp. 59–60: "defeatist pronouncements on this subject originate for the most part with people who sit at headquarters and make estimates, in contrast with which we have the opinion of Mr. Bond, who, on the basis of practical experience, firmly believes the thing *can* be done"; in Mr. Lauchlin Currie to President Roosevelt, June 3, 1942, *FRUS, 1942, China,* pp. 62–63, Currie noted his good relationship with "Bond of C.N.A.C."; the sentiment Bond was working against: Memorandum of Conversation, by Mr. Calvin H. Oakes of the Division of Near Eastern Affairs, May 26, 1942, *FRUS, 1942, China,* pp. 56–57; William Bond, "Report on Operations During 1942," February 24, 1943; C. F. Wang to Bond, April 30, 1943, both in ANY: "CNAC, through your personal contact with people in Washington, DC, last year, convinced American authorities that carrying war supplies over the Hump could be done."

284 **Bondy and Kitsi:** Bond, *Wings for an Embattled China,* pp. 320–24, 328–29.

285 **"There was some":** Bond to Bixby, "PERSONAL," July 10, 1942; Bond to Bixby, "Dear Bix," July 10, 1942; both in PAA, Box 205, Folder 10.

285 **106 tons:** R&S I, p. 167.

285 **91 tons:** China National Aviation Corporation Operating Statistics, June 1942, ANY.

285–86 **The two Chinese:** Bond to Bixby, "Dear Bix," July 10, 1942, PAA, Box 205, Folder 10; C.A.B. Docket No. 1706, February 17, 1947, p. 31, PAA, Box 205, Folder 14; 42nd Meeting of the Board of Directors, July 1942, ANY; "History of the India-China Ferry under the Tenth Air Force," June 22, 1943, AFHRA; Clayton L. Bissell to General Stilwell, "Memorandum for General Stilwell," July 26, 1942, LBC, Box 5, Stilwell Folder; Leary, *The Dragon's Wings,* p. 153; Stilwell diary, June 24, June 30, July 2, and July 8, 1942; R&S I, pp. 140–42.

286 **"I can't assume":** Bond to Bixby, "Dear Bix," July 10, 1942, PAA, Box 205, Folder 10.

286 **Aside from the:** author's interview with Joe Rosbert, August 14 and 15, 2004; author's interview with Dick Rossi, September 24, 2004; Vietnam Archive Oral History Project, Joe Rosbert interview conducted by Stephen Maxner, April 13 and 17, 2001; "The following message is from C. J. Chow on the recommendation of General Chennault, made with the consent of General Bissell," May 27, 1942, LBC, Box 2, AVG Folders; Bond to Bixby, "Dear Bix," July 10, 1942, PAA, Box 205, Folder 10; Bond and Anderson, *A Flying Tiger's Diary,* pp. 155, 177–79; Byrd, *Chennault,* p. 149; Ford, *Flying Tigers,* pp. 339–40; R&S I, p. 113; Erik

Shilling, "Destiny: A Flying Tiger's Rendezvous with Destiny," pp. 166–69, 169, 177; Clare Boothe, "The A.V.G. Ends Its Famous Career," *Life*, July 20, 1942; Bixby to CNAC, May 14, 1942, ANY: "No A.V.G. pilot or mechanics are to be employed unless you have the written approval of the US Army authorities."

287   "raised hell on": Clare Boothe, "The A.V.G. Ends Its Famous Career," *Life*, July 20, 1942.

287   **Madame Chiang Kai-shek honored:** Ford, *Flying Tigers*, p. 366.

287   "couldn't resist": Bond to Bixby, "Dear Bix," July 10, 1942, PAA, Box 205, Folder 10.

287–88   **Predictably, the Air Corps:** Bond to Bixby, "Dear Bix," July 10, 1942, PAA, Box 205, Folder 10; author's interviews with Joe Rosbert, August 14 and 15, 2004; author's interview with Dick Rossi, September 23, 2004; Rosbert, *Flying Tiger Joe's Adventure Cookbook*, p. 109; Shilling, "Destiny," pp. 170–71; Bond and Anderson, *A Flying Tiger's Diary*, p. 208; Cliff Groh, "Cliff Groh," *C.N.A.C. Cannonball*, March 15, 1974; R&S I, p. 162; in the end, nineteen AVG pilots would fly for the airline: "C.N.A.C. employed about sixteen of these men": William Bond, "Report on Operations during 1942," February 24, 1942, ANY; and the March 15, 1943, pilot roster lists fifteen former AVG pilots then serving with CNAC, not including John Dean, who'd been lost over the Hump on November 17, 1942, but the AVG roster at the end of *Flying Tigers* indicates that nineteen AVG pilots joined CNAC: Ford, *Flying Tigers*, pp. 389–97, the ones not on the March 15, 1943, list being Frank Adkins, Lester Hall, Fred Hodges, and Bob Prescott—they probably joined the airline after March 15, 1943.

288   "Give me the": author's interviews with Joe Rosbert, August 14 and 15, 2004.

288–89   **The tussle did:** Stilwell diary, July 5 and July 6, 1942; Joseph Stilwell and Theodore H. White (ed.), *The Stilwell Papers*, pp. 112–14; Theodore H. White, *In Search of History*, p. 233; Eric Sevareid, *Not So Wild a Dream*, p. 321; C&C IV, p. 413.

289   **the general's Chungking headquarters:** Judy Bonavia and Richard Hayman, *Yangzi: The Yangtze River and the Three Gorges*, pp. 269–71. The villa is now a museum.

289   "General, I'm going": Bond, *Wings for an Embattled China*, pp. 330–35.

289   **The rains of:** Tenth Air Force Air Ferry Command officially activated on July 15, 1942: R&S I, p. 200.

289   "No attention to": R&S I, p. 167.

290   **Ferry Command had** (35 transports at Dinjan on July 10, of which were grounded): R&S I, p. 165.

290   **73 tons:** R&S I, p. 167.

290   **CNAC flew 136:** "Strictly Confidential Memo: C.N.A.C. Freight operations, India to China, Excluding passenger runs," August 18, 1943, ANY (the airline also flew 175 tons out of China); "China National Aviation Corporation Operating Statistics," July 1942, ANY, says CNAC flew a total of 331 tons of freight in July—20 tons more than the Strictly Confidential Memo stated.

290   **the inflationary pace:** *Morgenthau Diary*, Vol. 1, p. 575 ("They are paying for this war by printing banknotes"); the Ambassador in China (Gauss) to the Secretary of State, May 28, 1942, *FRUS, 1942, China*, p. 59; Stanley Hornbeck, "China's Military Capacity— Recent Relevant Information," July 21, 1942, SKH; Memorandum by the Counselor of Embassy in China (Vincent) to the Ambassador in China (Gauss), July 22, 1942, *FRUS, 1942, China*, pp. 212–26; Stilwell and White (ed.), *The Stilwell Papers*, p. 128; White and Jacoby, *Thunder out of China*, pp. 111–17; White, *In Search of History*, pp. 214–21; Young, *Cycle of Cathay: A Historic Perspective*, pp. 176, 179–81; Young, *China's Wartime Finance and Inflation, 1937–1945*, pp. 261–68, 299–328; R&S I, pp. 197, 249.

290–91 Regardless, black markets (all items listed were reported as smuggled in letters in 1942 and 1943): Sharp to All Flight Personnel, April 18, 1942; Sharp to All Flight Personnel, July 4, 1942; "List of Smuggled Goods," August 21, 1942; Bond to All Operations Personnel, November 18, 1942; Bond to Bissell, May 3, 1943; Acting Chief Pilot McDonald to All Flight Personnel, June 5, 1943; K. C. Lee to Sharp, November 25, 1943; all in ANY; James Houston Maupin, "Maupin," *C.N.A.C. Cannonball*, July 1993.

290 thirty qualified or: Owen F. Johnson, "Report on C.N.A.C.," March 15, 1943, PAA, Box 58, Folder 8.

291 an intrepid airman: Colonel Wang Cheng-fu to H.E. Dr. H. H. Kung, Ministry of Finance, October 2, 1942, ANY.

291 William Bond prohibited: Bond to All Operations Personnel, November 18, 1942, ANY.

291 148,000 U.S. dollars: Arthur N. Young to Bond, September 14, 1942; "Approximate Cash Position of C.N.A.C.," September 20, 1942; both in ANY.

292 In continuation of: H. W. Davis, "Tungsten," in E. W. Pehrson, and C. E. Needham (eds.), *Minerals Yearbook, 1942*, pp. 673–84; Secretary of State to the Ambassador in China (Gauss), August 15, 1942, reporting on information provided by "Yin of Chinese National Resources Commission"; Ambassador in China (Gauss) to the Secretary of State, September 14, 1942; Secretary of State to the Ambassador in China, September 22, 1942; Ambassador in China (Gauss) to the Secretary of State, November 11, 1942; Ambassador in China (Gauss) to the Secretary of State, December 29, 1942; all in *FRUS, 1942, China*, pp. 662–63, 664, 665, 668, 672; E. W. Pehrson and John B. Umhau, "Tin," in *Minerals Yearbook, 1941*, F. M. Shore, ed., pp. 731–54.

292 "There exists what": R&S I, pp. 182–83, 186; "Second Front Man," *Time*, October 5, 1942.

292 Only extreme realists: Joseph Stilwell, "Memorandum for Mr. Currie from General Stilwell," August 1, 1942, LBC, Box 5; R&S I, pp. 182–83, 186–87, citing a radiogram, Stilwell to Marshall, September 4, 1942.

293 The monsoon began: Bond to Bixby, Letter No. 40-42, October 29, 1942; Bixby to Juan Trippe, November 28, 1942; both in PAA, Box 205, Folder 10; "NE Assam Air Raid Dope Told," *C.B.I. Roundup*, November 5, 1942; Colonel Jasper N. Bell, "Memorandum for the Public Relations Officer," May 5, 1943, appended to "History of the India-China Ferry under the Tenth Air Force"; "History of the India-China Ferry under the Tenth Air Force," June 22, 1943, p. 8; both in AFHRA; Bond, *Wings for an Embattled China,* pp. 346–47, quoting a letter, Bond to Kitsi, October 1942; Royal Leonard, "Around the Japs over the Hump," *C.N.A.C. Cannonball,* 1990; Carl Molesworth, *P-40 Warhawk Aces of the CBI,* p. 45–46; R&S I, p. 314.

294 **"Yes, I suppose":** Bond to Bixby, Letter No. 40-42, October 29, 1942.

294 **Army's glacial accounts:** K. C. Lee to Major General Wheeler, August 20, 1943, ANY (as of August 20, 1943, the Army hadn't settled its bills for November and December 1942).

294 **Soviet Union's trade representative:** H. W. Meyer and A. W. Mitchell, "Mercury," in Pehrson and Needham (eds.), *Minerals Yearbook, 1942,* pp. 714, 729; C. F. Wang to Bond, Woods, October 19, 1942; K. I. Nieh to Mr. T. May, November 11, 1942; Young to Bond, November 11, 1942; "Report of the Business Department, Chungking," February 15, 1943; all in ANY; Bond, *Wings for an Embattled China,* pp. 335–36; Hugh Woods, "Cargo out of China," *Wings over Asia: A Brief History of C.N.A.C.,* Vol. 2, p. 66; Woods, "Over the Hump," *Wings over Asia: Memories of C.N.A.C.,* Vol. 4, p. 64.

294 **"Why don't you":** Bond, *Wings for an Embattled China,* pp. 335–36.

295 **to house the:** photos of the bungalow in many collections; author's interview with Donald McBride, November 4, 2004; author's interviews with Peter Goutiere, January 22 and 23, 2005; many other interviews with CNAC pilots.

295–96 **One man who:** author's interviews with Peter Goutiere, January 22 and 23, 2005; Peter Goutiere, *Himalayan Rogue,* pp. 66, 74–75; J. Gen Genovese, *We Flew without Guns,* pp. 155–56; Don Riner to cnac.org, October 1, 2001, posted at http://cnac.org/sharkey01.htm.

295–96 **"I heard you":** author's interviews with Peter Goutiere, January 22 and 23, 2005; Goutiere, *Himalayan Rogue,* pp. 66, 74–75.

296 **airline had lost:** William L. Bond, "Report on Operations during 1942," February 24, 1943, ANY; "Crashes," *C.N.A.C. Cannonball,* March 1, 1981; J. Gen Genovese, *We Flew without Guns,* pp. 160–62; http://cnac.org/accident012.htm, accessed September 1, 2009.

298 **"Okay, Pri, let's":** Goutiere, *Himalayan Rogue,* p. 75; "Overheard at the Reunion," undated, *C.N.A.C. Cannonball,* probably July 1976; Robbie Robertson to Reg Farrar, May 20, 1979, *C.N.A.C. Cannonball,* October 1979.

Chapter 22: Clipping the Edge of Bedrock

299 **Unhappy with results:** "History of the India-China Ferry under the 10th Air Force," June 22, 1943, AFHRA; R&S I, p. 268; C&C VII, pp. 120–21 (on December 1, 1942, the India-China Wing had forty-four aircraft and 866 men, more than twice CNAC's size).

299 **General Stilwell tasked:** R&S I, p. 267.

299 **"Ferry line is":** Stilwell diary, January 18, 1943.

299   In contrast, the: William Bond, "Report on Operations during 1942," February 24, 1943, ANY; it's difficult to determine exact operating statistics: Leary, *The Dragon's Wings*, p. 157, says CNAC flew 873 round-trips, carried 1,804.3 tons to China and 1,833.1 tons to India in 1942, but those numbers only approximately jibe with those arrived at by adding the monthly totals in "China National Aviation Corporation: Operating Statistics, May 1942–May 1943," ANY. The latter document seems to account only for freight carried by the airline's Lend-Lease planes. The numbers aren't far off, however, and definitions vary, and it is difficult to ascertain whether the numbers reflect the achievements of the airline's entire fleet, or only the Lend-Lease planes devoted to the Hump; "History of the India-China Ferry under the 10th Air Force," June 22, 1943, p. 9, AFHRA.

300   tons of tungsten: H. W. Davis, "Tungsten," in E. W. Pehrson and C. E. Needham (eds.), *Minerals Yearbook, 1942*, pp. 673–84; Young to Bond, November 11, 1942, ANY; "Report of the Business Department, Chungking," February 15, 1943, ANY.

300   spare-parts shortages: William Bond, "Report on Operations during 1942," February 24, 1943, ANY.

300   Foul weather plagued: Bond to Bixby, Letter No. 57-43, PAA, Box 258, Folder 6; Stilwell diary, January 31, 1943.

300   Of course, it: Minutes of the Special Meeting of the Stockholders for the Year 1943, undated, but probably late February or early March 1943; "Agenda of the 43rd Meeting of the Board of Directors, China National Aviation Corporation," undated, but probably late February or early March1943; Colonel W. F. Courdray to CNAC, May 31, 1943; all in ANY; Arthur N. Young, *Cycle of Cathay: A Historical Perspective*, p. 165; Peter Goutiere email to the author, January 23, 2007.

300–301   In Dinjan on: Peter Goutiere, *Himalayan Rogue*, pp. 77–81; Roy Farrell, unfinished manuscript, *C.N.A.C. Cannonball*, 1999; author's interviews with Peter Goutiere, January 22 and 23, 2005; author's interviews with Joe Rosbert, August 14 and 15, 2004; Peter Goutiere email to the author, January 23, 2007.

302   "You two go": author's interviews with Peter Goutiere, January 22 and 23, 2005.

302   Two fatal accidents: C. F. Wang to Bond, April 30, 1943; the freight pilot's opinions of William Bond: the author's many interviews with CNAC's Hump pilots; the attitudes of the prewar pilots: author's interview with Moon Chin, April 19, 2006 ("But they didn't know him!").

303   seven and a half inches: C&C VII, p. 116.

303   superb extracurricular money: Arthur Young to Bond, May 7, 1943; Arthur Young to the Central Bank of China, May 7, 1943; Arthur N. Young to Bond, May 19, 1943; Arthur N. Young to Chuck Sharp, May 19, 1943; Albert Shao, Sub-Manager, Bank of China, to Arthur Young, May 15, 1943; all in ANY; "Gold bond" scheme: author's interviews with many CNAC pilots.

304–12   For his current (the Rosbert/Hammell adventure): author's interviews with Joe

Rosbert, August 14 and 15, 2004; all quotes checked, details corroborated, and questions answered in three successive telephone interviews on February 21, 23, and 24, 2005; also: interview with Joe Rosbert conducted by Stephen Maxner, April 13 and 17, 2001, Vietnam Archive Oral History Project, Texas Tech University; Albert Ravenholt, "Pilots Given Up for Dead Return after 46 Days," *C.B.I. Roundup*, June 3, 1943; Flight Captain C. J. Rosbert, as told to William Clemens, "Only God Knew the Way," *Saturday Evening Post*, February 12, 1944; "Return from the Dead," *New Horizons*, May 1944; Joe Rosbert, *Flying Tiger Joe's Adventure Cookbook*, pp. 111–25; Link Laughlin, *C.N.A.C. Cannonball*, 1978; author's interview with Donald McBride, November 4, 2004.

305   pissed on the tail wheel: Roy Farrell, manuscript, *C.N.A.C. Cannonball*, 1999.

Chapter 23: "We'll Be Talking About That for the Rest of Our Lives"

313–15   The losses appalled: William Bond, "Report on Operations During 1942," February 23, 1943; Bond to C. F. Wang, April 15, 1943; both in ANY.

313   "nearly always bad": Bond to C. F. Wang, April 15, 1943, ANY.

314   fifty-nine Army flights: C. F. Wang to Bond, April 30, 1943, ANY.

314   twenty-one airplanes: "Statement of hours flown by lend-lease planes for the freight service during month of April, 1943," ANY. (The India-China Wing had 146 airplanes on April, 19, 1943: R&S I, p. 291.)

315–21   Joe Rosbert and Ridge Hammell: author's interviews with Joe Rosbert, August 14 and 15, 2004; all quotes checked, details corroborated, and questions answered in three successive telephone interviews on February 21, 23, and 24, 2005; also: interviews with Joe Rosbert conducted by Stephen Maxner, April 13 and 17, 2001, Vietnam Archive Oral History Project, Texas Tech University; Albert Ravenholt, "Pilots Given Up for Dead Return after 46 Days," *C.B.I. Roundup*, June 3, 1943; Flight Captain C. J. Rosbert, as told to William Clemens, "Only God Knew the Way," *Saturday Evening Post*, February 12, 1944; "Return from the Dead," *New Horizons*, May 1944; Joe Rosbert, *Flying Tiger Joe's Adventure Cookbook*, pp. 111–25; Link Laughlin, *C.N.A.C. Cannonball*, 1978; author's conversations with Donald McBride, Peter Goutiere, Dick and Lydia Rossi, and Fletcher "Christie" Hanks; Peter Goutiere email to author, February 23, 2008; physical and cultural details of the story confirmed by Clayton Kuhles and Kai Frieze, both of whom led expeditions into the Mishmi Hills and befriended relatives of the natives who rescued Rosbert and Hammell.

Chapter 24: Not the Worst Way to Fight a War

322   Flight operations kept: Donald McBride diary, March 3, 1944; many articles about gambling in *C.N.A.C. Cannonball*; author's conversations at the annual CNAC reunions, 2002–8.

322–24   Downcountry in: Peter Goutiere, *Himalayan Rogue*, pp. 75, 79–80; author's interview with Peter Goutiere, January 22 and 23, 2005; Peter Goutiere emails to the author, February 29 and April 9, 2008; author's conversations and interviews with CNAC personnel, 2002–8; many articles in *C.N.A.C. Cannonball;* Michel Peissel, *Tiger for Breakfast,* pp. 115–41.

324 **"What the hell":** author's interview with Peter Goutiere, January 22 and 23, 2005.

325 **"Who's flying the":** author's interview with Donald McBride, November 4, 2004; author's conversations at the annual CNAC reunions, 2002–8.

325 **CNAC expanded 150:** "Report on the Increase of Company Personnel," April 1944, ANY.

326 **extremely dangerous:** http://cnac.org/allaccidents01.htm; "Pilots' Pay—Month of June, 1943"; "Pay of Pilots Serving as Co-Pilots on Freight Service—Month of June, 1943"; both in ANY.

326–27 **Chief among the:** author's interview with Donald McBride, November 4, 2004; author's conversations and interviews with the CNAC pilots, 2002–8; Donald McBride diary, February 25, 1944; author's interview with Peter Goutiere, January 22, 2005; author's conversations at the annual CNAC reunions, 2002–8 (Jimmy Scoff remains a staple of company conversation); many articles in *C.N.A.C. Cannonball;* J. Gen Genovese, *We Flew without Guns,* pp. 232–47.

327 **"Hell yes, I":** author's interview with Donald McBride, November 4, 2004; Donald McBride diary, March 24, 1944; author's interview with Peter Goutiere, January 22, 2005; *The Valley Morning Star,* March 26, 1944; "Crew Leaps from Plane," *NYT,* March 26, 1944; http://cnac.org/accident042.htm.

327 **The Allies had:** Louis Allen, *Burma: The Longest War, 1941–1945,* pp. 91–116; R&S I, pp. 302–3; Sir William Slim, *Defeat into Victory,* pp. 147–61.

328 **General Chennault argued:** Chennault to Wendell Willke, October 8, 1942, reproduced in Jack Samson, *The Flying Tiger: The True Story of General Claire Chennault and the U.S. 14th Air Force in China,* pp. 175–80; R&S I, p. 322; R&S II, p. 18; Barbara Tuchman, *Stilwell and the American Experience in China, 1911–1945,* p. 469.

328–29 **As everywhere, it:** George C. Marshall, "Memorandum for the President," March 16, 1943; Marshall, "Memorandum for General Stilwell," May 3, 1943; "Memorandum for Admiral Leahy, Admiral King, General Arnold," May 3, 1943: all in *Marshall Papers,* Vol. 3, pp. 675–78; Hap Arnold, *Global Mission,* pp. 398–409, 413–20; Martha Byrd, *Chennault: Giving Wings to the Tiger,* pp. 155–57, 172–92; C&C IV, pp. 435–43; Winston S. Churchill, *The Hinge of Fate,* pp. 782–99; Samson, *The Flying Tiger,* pp. 175–80, 183–86, 189–94; Robert E. Sherwood, *Roosevelt and Hopkins: An Intimate History,* p. 749; R&S I, pp. 251–53, 259–60, 269, 274, 277, 310, 313–54; Henry L. Stimson and McGeorge Bundy, *On Active Service,* pp. 534–36; *Strategic Planning, 1943–1944,* pp. 84–88, 126–45; Robert Dallek, *Franklin D. Roosevelt and American Foreign Policy, 1932–1945,* pp. 383–99; Tuchman, *Stilwell and the American Experience in China, 1911–1945,* pp. 446–78; Stilwell diary, September 9, 1943: "These guys believe 100 planes can make the Japs quit!"

328   **Bond returned to:** William Langhorne Bond, *Wings for an Embattled China*, p. 353. Bond was in the United States from May to September 1943.

329   **Madame Chiang Kai-shek cajoled:** C&C VII, pp. 24–26; William R. Peers and Dean Brelis, *Behind the Burma Road*, pp. 145–46; R&S I, p. 344; Eric Sevareid, *Not So Wild a Dream*, p. 248; Otha C. Spencer, *Flying the Hump: Memories of an Air War*, pp. 66, 100–6; Joseph Stilwell, *The Stilwell Papers*, pp. 217–18; Tuchman, *Stilwell and the American Experience in China, 1911–1945*, pp. 450, 479.

329–31   **Stateside business complete:** Arthur N. Young to His Excellency, H. H. Kung, July 9, 1943; "Minutes of a Special Meeting of the Board of Directors," December 30, 1943; both in ANY; Jonathan Fenby, *Generalissimo: Chiang Kai-shek and the China He Lost*, pp. 401–2; Laura Tyson Li, *Madame Chiang Kai-shek*, pp. 235–37; Arthur N. Young, *Cycle of Cathay: A Historical Perspective*, pp. 165–71.

330   **"Who is your":** Young, *Cycle of Cathay*, p. 167.

331   **"very serious demerit":** Young, *Cycle of Cathay*, p. 167.

331   **General Chennault began:** R&S I, pp. 337–39, 347; C&C IV, pp. 522–29; Byrd, *Chennault*, pp. 202–4; Samson, *The Flying Tiger*, pp. 194–98.

331   **"disappointing" and "unacceptable":** *Strategic Planning, 1943–1944*, p. 197.

332   **woefully inadequate compared:** C&C IV, p. 446; R&S I, p. 268, says ATC moved 5,390 tons in September with 228 aircraft; "Monthly Contract Tonnages Carried between Kunming and Dinjan"; "Freight Service Operation under Contract with U.S. Army," "Monthly Operations Productive Flights"; "Summary of Freight Service Operation Month of June, 1943"; "The Inward and Outward Shipment Carried by C.N.A.C.'s Planes for the Month of June, 1943"; "China National Aviation Corporation: Summary of Freight Service Operations Month of September, 1943"; all in ANY. The CNAC statistics in C&C don't precisely agree with the company's records. I used the figures in airline records—which also don't always exactly agree with themselves, either—a frustrating annoyance, but the variance is small. Memo from William McDonald through Arthur N. Young to William Bond and Harold Bixby, September 2, 1943, SKH, Box 58; Memo from Sharp, August 7, 1943, ANY.

332   **"The overpromoted":** Stilwell, *The Stilwell Papers*, pp. 215–18.

332–33   **As bad a:** author's interview with Donald McBride, November 4, 2004; author's interview with Peter Goutiere, January 22, 2005; Peter Goutiere emails to the author, May 5 and May 6, 2008; Theodore H. White and Annalee Jacoby, *Thunder out of China*, pp. 166–78.

333   **Goutiere had checked:** "Pilot's Pay—Month of July, 1943," ANY; Peter Goutiere emails to the author, May 5 and May 6, 2008.

333–34   **Associated risk accompanied:** Anglin crash: http://cnac.org/accident014.htm; Goutiere, *Himalayan Rogue*, p. 82; author's interview with Peter Goutiere, January 22, 2005; Peter Goutiere emails to the author, May 5 and May 6, 2008.

334–35   **The monsoon that:** Schroeder shut down and offensive against the Hump: Bond to K. C. Lee, October 18, 1943, ANY; Stilwell diary, October 15, 1943; C&C IV, pp. 467–68; Goutiere, *Himalayan Rogue,* p. 85; Bond, *Wings for an Embattled China,* pp. 354–55; author's interview with Peter Goutiere, January 22, 2005; Peter Goutiere emails to the author, May 5, May 6, and May 7, 2008; Marshall Schroeder (nephew of the lost pilot) email to the author, May 19, 2008; http://cnac.org/schroeder01.htm.

336   **thirty-eight major crashes:** General William H. Tunner, *Over the Hump,* p. 63; wartime diary of CNAC pilot Donald McBride, December 18 and 19, 1943; author's interview with Donald McBride, November 11, 2004; Goutiere, *Himalayan Rogue,* p. 85; http://cnac.org/allaccidents01.htm; author's interview with Peter Goutiere, January 22, 2005.

336   **dengue fever:** Bond to Stanley K. Hornbeck, November 16, 1943, SKH.

336   *The Chungking Edition:* "China Plans," *NYT,* November 7, 1943.

Chapter 25: To Lose a Friend

337   **in Cairo, the:** Robert Dallek, *Franklin D. Roosevelt and American Foreign Policy, 1932–1945,* pp. 425–30; Jonathan Fenby, *Generalissimo: Chiang Kai-shek and the China He Lost,* pp. 408–12; Hannah Pakula, *The Last Empress: Madame Chiang Kai-shek and the Birth of Modern China,* pp. 469–75; R&S II, pp. 53–82; Robert E. Sherwood, *Roosevelt and Hopkins: An Intimate History,* pp. 770–75; *Strategic Planning, 1943–1944,* pp. 334–87, 433–37; Jay Taylor, *The Generalissimo,* pp. 242–52; Barbara Tuchman, *Stilwell and the American Experience in China, 1911–1945,* pp. 396–97, 399–406; Laura Tyson Li, *Madame Chiang Kai-shek: China's Eternal First Lady,* pp. 242–46.

337   **Kuomintang propaganda continued:** Eric Sevareid, *Not So Wild a Dream,* p. 317.

338–40   **Just before Cairo:** CBI events from October 1943 to April 1944 constructed from: R&S II; *Strategic Planning, 1943–1944;* Martha Byrd, *Chennault: Giving Wings to the Tiger;* Dallek, *Franklin D. Roosevelt and American Foreign Policy, 1932–1945;* Fenby, *Generalissimo;* Pakula, *The Last Empress,* pp. 469–82; William R. Peers and Bean Brelis, *Behind the Burma Road;* Sir William Slim, *Defeat into Victory;* Taylor, *The Generalissimo,* pp. 245–57; Tuchman, *Stilwell and the American Experience in China, 1911–1945;* Tyson Li, *Madame Chiang Kai-shek;* Donovan Webster, *The Burma Road;* Theodore H. White and Annalee Jacoby, *Thunder out of China;* Theodore White, *In Search of History.*

340   **Stilwell conferred with General Slim:** Stilwell diary, April 3, 1944.

340–42   **Well positioned as:** Bond to Bixby, Letter No. B111-44, April 19, 1944, SDAM.

342–43   **And like the:** Bond to H. H. Kung, November 9, 1943; William Bond, "Confidential Memo: The future position of C.N.A.C.," November 25, 1943; William Bond, "Questions to be considered re Chinese Civil Aviation," January 4, 1944; all in ANY.

343   **"a great period":** Bond to H. H. Kung, November 9, 1943, ANY.

343   **Although T. V. Soong still:** "The Ambassador in China to the Secretary of State,"

December 10, 1943, *FRUS, 1943, China*, pp. 387–88; John S. Service, *Lost Chance in China*, pp. 75–86; Tyson Li, *Madame Chiang Kai-shek*, pp. 239–50; Fenby, *Generalissimo*, pp. 402–7; Sterling Seagrave, *The Soong Dynasty*, pp. 393–416; Taylor, *The Generalissimo*, pp. 239–40; Tuchman, *Stilwell and the American Experience in China, 1911–1945*, pp. 495–506; R&S I, pp. 374–79.

344–48   Bond didn't know: Bond to John Leslie, June 6, 1975, PAA, Box 27, Folder 23; Bixby to Dear Family, June 2, 1944, PAA, Box 205, Folder 12. As crucial as this episode is to the story of Bond and CNAC, it has also been the hardest to pinpoint and confirm. Bond's 1975 letter makes its importance plain, but also claims that it happened in early 1945. Bixby's letter of June 2, 1944, mentions the episode, so Bond misplaced the event in his 1975 letter. Also, as further circumstantial evidence, a careful reading of *Wings* gives the impression that Bond is building toward a significant event pertaining to M. Y. Tong. Sadly, Bond died before he was able to pay off his setup. I've chosen to give credence to Bond's account of the events, but have located them in the spring of 1944, when Bixby's letter indicates it occurred; John Service, "The Fall of T. V. Soong," March 7, 1944, has another clue: "The manager of the important Hong Kong office [of the Bank of Canton], named Teng, was arrested by Tai Li sometime ago and there is considerable mystery over his fate—he was reportedly shot." (Service, *Lost Chance in China*, p. 81). I suspect this is M. Y. Tong with his name misspelled, and that Service wasn't aware of how close M. Y. Tong and T. V. Soong had been before Pearl Harbor; in the spring of 1945, T. V. Soong told *The New York Times* China had received peace overtures "by the bushel": "Soong Says Tokyo Often Asks Peace," *NYT,* May 2, 1945.

344–48   "Tell them to": Bond to John Leslie, June 6, 1975, PAA, Box 27, Folder 23.

349   If M. Y. Tong's: *Time,* August 7, 1944; Fenby, *Generalissimo*, pp. 422–23; Pakula, *The Last Empress*, pp. 501–6; Seagrave, *The Soong Dynasty*, pp. 412–16; Taylor, *The Generalissimo*, pp. 276–77; Tyson-Li, *Madame Chiang Kai-shek*, pp. 253–55, 257–59.

Chapter 26: Getting His

350   Getting His: "got his" and "went in" were airman slang for crashing and dying. Could be first-person conditional, too, as in, "If I get mine, make sure my wife gets this letter," or "If I go in . . .": author's conversations with the CNAC pilots; also Eric Sevareid, *Not So Wild a Dream*, p. 331.

351   "My God, have": author's interview with Donald McBride, November 4, 2004; "Burma Air Service Resumed by China," *NYT,* May 27, 1944; Bond letter, May 21, 1944, ANY; Peter Goutiere email to the author, June 7, 2008.

351   Tonnage deliveries: R&S II, p. 254.

351   twenty thousandth trip: Bixby to Director, Public Relations, June 6, 1944, PAA.

352   Nineteen forty-four was a: Sevareid, *Not So Wild a Dream*, pp. 310–44; Barbara Tuchman, *Stilwell and the American Experience in China, 1911–1945*, pp. 581–84, 587–88;

Theodore H. White and Analee Jacoby, *Thunder out of China*, pp. 179–256; Theodore White, *In Search of History*, pp. 207–71.

352 **picul of rice:** Bixby to Dear Family, June 2, 1944, PAA, Box 205, Folder 12.

353–56 **Since the Cairo:** R&S II; R&S III; Tuchman, *Stilwell and the American Experience in China, 1911–1945*, pp. 584–650; White and Jacoby, *Thunder out of China*, pp. 179–98, 214–25.

353 **General Marshall gave:** R&S II, p. 312.

356 **"categorically":** R&S III, pp. 53–56.

356 **"the political triumph":** Brooks Atkinson, "Long Schism Seen; Stilwell Break Stems from Chiang Refusal to Press War Fully," *NYT,* October 31, 1944; other stories: Preston Grover, "U.S. Forced Pledge by Chiang on War," *NYT,* November 1, 1944; Thoburn Wiant, "China in Dictator's Grip," *NYT,* November 1, 1944.

356 **William Bond wasn't:** William Langhorne Bond, *Wings for an Embattled China*, p. 355.

357 **"In practically all":** Bond, *Wings for an Embattled China*, p. 356.

357 **General Marshall:** R&S II, p. 454.

358 **"The amount of":** Henry L. Stimson and McGeorge Bundy, *On Active Service in Peace and War*, p. 538.

358 **23,675 tons:** C&C VII, p. 138; Oliver La Farge, *The Eagle and the Egg*, p. 126.

358–59 **"Do you know":** Donald McBride diary, October 8, 1944; author's interview with Donald McBride, November 4, 2004; the author's many conversations with the CNAC pilots, 2002–8; http://cnac.org/accident051.htm.

359–60 *Pete, special flight:* author's interview with Peter Goutiere, January 22, 2005; Peter Goutiere, *Himalayan Rogue*, pp. 95–96.

Chapter 27: The Gold Missions

361 **ten times bigger:** "CNAC and Postwar China," undated memorandum written in late 1944, PAA, Box 205, Folder 12.

362 **"Mr. Trippe, maybe":** Bond interview, October 23, 1972, PAA, Box 19, Folder 3; Robert Daley, *An American Saga: Juan Trippe and His Pan Am Empire*, pp. 342–43.

362 **forty-six thousand tons:** C&C VII, p. 143 (46,393 tons in May 1945).

363–64 **Charles Ridgley Hammell:** http://cnac.org/accident061.htm; author's interview with Donald McBride, November 4, 2004; author's interview with Peter Goutiere, January 22, 2005.

364 **"That's a damn":** author's interviews with Joe Rosbert, August 14 and 15, 2004. "I don't know how else to put it to you, Greg, but it was no big deal. It was 1945. It happened all the time."

364   Elmer the bear: one of Pete Goutiere's favorite stories.

365-66   contract negotiations: William Langhorne Bond, *Wings for an Embattled China*, pp. 358-61, quoting from a letter, Bond to Bixby, May 24, 1945; "Brief of Pan American Airways, Inc. Before the Civil Aeronautics Board, Docket No. 1706," February 17, 1947, PAA, Box 205, Folder 14; William Leary, *The Dragon's Wings*, pp. 188-92.

366-67   China's economic malaise (the gold shipments): "China National Aviation Corporation, Brief History," January 31, 1946, PAA, Box 58, Folder 8; Arthur Young, *China and the Helping Hand, 1937-1945*, pp. 317-38; Arthur Young, *China's Wartime Finance and Inflation, 1937-1945*, pp. 281-98; Arthur Young, *Cycle of Cathay: A Historical Perspective*, pp. 178-79; Peter Goutiere, *Himalayan Rogue*, p. 105; author's interview with Peter Goutiere, January 22, 2005; author's interview with Donald McBride, November 4, 2004.

367   "Americans, the rubes": author's interview with Peter Goutiere, January 22, 2005.

367   In August: Goutiere, *Himalayan Rogue*, p. 105; author's interview with Peter Goutiere, January 22, 2005.

367   President Truman said: Howard W. Blakeslee, "Power of Atoms Likened to Sun's," *NYT*, August 7, 1945.

Chapter 28: Endgame

368-70   Nothing in China: Dr. Gary J. Bjorge, *Moving the Enemy: Operational Art in the Chinese PLA's Huai Hai Campaign*, pp. 41-43; Jonathan D. Spence, *The Search for Modern China*, pp. 484-85; John King Fairbank and Merle Goldman, *China: A New History*, pp. 331-34; Jay Taylor, *The Generalissimo: Chiang Kai-shek and the Struggle for Modern China*, pp. 310-35; Jung Chang and Jon Halliday, *Mao: The Unknown Story*, pp. 295-98, 310-11.

370   The Japanese capitulation: "To the Stockholders and Employees of the Pan American World Airways System: The Year 1945"; "Contract between Ministry of Communications, National Government, Republic of China and Pan American Airways Corporation," December 21, 1945; both in PAA, Box 19, Folder 2; Docket No. 1706 Before the Civil Aeronautics Board, February 17, 1947, PAA, Box 205, Folder 14.

370-72   As one of: author's interviews with Moon Chin, January 7, 2005, and April 19, 2006; author's interviews with Frieda and T. T. Chen, September 19, 2006; author's conversations with Renee Robertson in 2005 and 2006. T. V. Soong left Ottawa, Canada, on September 2, 1945, and arrived in Chungking on September 22, which jibes with Moon Chin's recollection that these events happened in the last days of September and October 1945.

371   "Dr. Soong, I": author's interviews with Moon Chin, January 7, 2005, and April 19, 2006.

371   Typhoon weather had: W. H. Lawrence, "Shanghai Happy Casting Off Eight-Year Yoke," *NYT*, August 30, 1945; Bond to Bixby, September 22, 1945, letter reproduced in William Langhorne Bond, *Wings for an Embattled China*, pp. 361–64, and referenced in William Leary, *The Dragon's Wings*, pp. 193–94; Stella Dong, *Shanghai: The Rise and Fall of a Decadent City*, pp. 277–83.

372   **low-performing Lockheed:** Leary, *The Dragon's Wings*, p. 196.

373–75   **"What are you":** author's interviews with Moon Chin, January 7, 2005, and April 19, 2006.

375   **William Bond admired:** Bond interview, October 23, 1972, p. 108, PAA, Box 19, Folder 3. "C.A.T.C.—They were a good outfit."

375–76   **Chuck Sharp had:** Leary, *The Dragon's Wings*, pp. 200–4; http://cnac.org /allaccidents01.htm; Nancy Allison Wright email to the author, October 28, 2008.

376   **To many observers:** Bjorge, *Moving the Enemy*, pp. 42–43.

378–79   **None of it stopped:** Bond to Leslie, July 1, 1975, PAA, Box 19, Folder 5; Bond interview, October 23, 1972, pp. 37–45, PAA, Box 19, Folder 3; Leary, *The Dragon's Wings*, p. 208.

378   **Bond's health:** Bond to Leslie, July 1975, PAA, Box 27, Folder 3; Bond interview, October 23, 1972, pp. 60–64, PAA, Box 19, Folder 3; "Airlines Show Upward Trend," *Aviation World News*, undated clipping in WLB; Bond, *Wings for an Embattled China*, pp. 370–72.

379   **Several emergency airstrips:** Roy Rowan, *Chasing the Dragon*, p. 142.

379   **A major battle:** Bjorge, *Moving the Enemy*, pp. 49–267; Jonathan Fenby, *Generalissimo*, pp. 482–84; Spence, *The Search for Modern China*, pp. 507–8; Fairbank and Goldman, *China*, pp. 335–37; Hannah Pakula, *The Last Empress: Madame Chiang Kai-shek and the Birth of Modern China*, pp. 568–69; Taylor, *The Generalissimo*, pp. 393–94, 396, 399–400; Chang and Halliday, *Mao*, pp. 309–10.

381   **The airline had:** Bond interview, October 23, 1972, pp. 21–36, PAA, Box 19, Folder 3; Judge Henry J. Friendly interview, June 8, 1973, PAA, Box 20, Folder 1; Bond to Leslie, July 7, 1975, PAA, Box 27, Folder 23; F. Tillman Durdin, "Chennault, Aide Buy China Airlines," *NYT*, December 19, 1949; "Airline Seeks Aid in Chennault Deal," *NYT*, December 20, 1949; "Interest of Pan American in Chinese Airline Sold," *NYT*, January 1, 1950; Bond, *Wings for an Embattled China*, pp. 373–81; Nancy Allison Wright, "Claire Chennault and China's 'Airline Affair,'" *American Aviation Historical Society*, Vol. 41, No. 4, Winter 1996; Wright, "Allie's Choice," *Air & Space*, December 1998; Leary, *The Dragon's Wings*, pp. 218–23; Robert Daley, *An American Saga: Juan Trippe and His Pan Am Empire*, pp. 393–95.

382   **"For every year":** Bond interview, October 23, 1972, pp. 21–36, PAA, Box 19, Folder 3.

Epilogue

386   "It is not": Bond to Bixby, Letter No. B111-44, April 19, 1944, SDASM.

387   **Moon Chin served:** author's interview with Moon Chin, May 29, 2011.

388   **Chuck Sharp:** Carol Slade (Chuck Sharp's daughter) email to the author, May 30, 2011.

388   **Hugh and Maj Woods:** http://cnac.org/hughwoods01.htm; Carol Slade (Chuck Sharp's daughter) email to the author, May 30, 2011.

388   **Pete Goutiere:** Peter Goutiere, *Himalayan Rogue,* pp. 122–24; Pete Goutiere email to the author, May 28, 2011.

389   **Joe Rosbert:** C. Joe Rosbert, *Flying Tiger Joe's Adventure Cookbook,* pp. 175–312.

389–90   **Ernie Allison:** Nancy Allison Wright emails to the author, May 4, 2011.

390–92   **William Bond:** author's interviews with Langhorne and Thomas Bond; Enriqueta Bond email to the author, April 28, 2011; Thomas Bond emails to the author May 2, 2011, and May 3, 2011.

391   **"constant and kaleidoscopic":** Bond to Leslie, August 28, 1975, PAA, Box 19, Folder 3.

INDEX

ABOUT THE AUTHOR

GREGORY CROUCH graduated from West Point with a degree in military history. He completed U.S. Army Airborne and Ranger schools and led an infantry platoon in Panama, for which he earned the Combat Infantryman's Badge. He left the Army to pursue other interests, most notably in the realms of climbing and surfing. Along the way he became a writer. He is the author of *Enduring Patagonia,* and he lives in the San Francisco Bay Area.

gregcrouch.com

ABOUT THE TYPE

This book was set in Minion, a 1990 Adobe Originals typeface by Robert Slimbach. Minion is inspired by classical, old-style typefaces of the late Renaissance, a period of elegant, beautiful, and highly readable type designs. Created primarily for text setting, Minion combines the aesthetic and functional qualities that make text type highly readable with the versatility of digital technology.